Lifespan Development

Lifespan Development

LUMEN LEARNING

Published by SUNY OER Services

State University of New York Office of Library and Information Services
10 N Pearl
Albany, NY 12207

Distributed by State University of New York Press

Cover image by Conner Baker at https://unsplash.com/photos/M5Zix_4Jc4k

ISBN: 978-1-64176-074-4

Contents

Learning Outcomes 8

Module 1: Lifespan Development

Why It Matters: Lifespan Development 2
Human Development 4
The Lifespan Perspective 15
Research in Lifespan Development 24
Putting It Together: Lifespan Development 44
Discussion: Life Stages 45

Module 2: Developmental Theories

Why It Matters: Developmental Theories 47
Psychodynamic Theories 49
Behavioral and Cognitive Theories 64
The Humanistic, Contextual, and Evolutionary Perspectives of Development 78
Discussion: Developmental Theories 91
Putting It Together: Developmental Theories 92

Module 3: Prenatal Development

Why It Matters: Prenatal Development 94
Biological Foundations of Human Development 95
Prenatal Development 109
Birth and Delivery 120
Putting It Together: Prenatal Development 127
Discussion: Prenatal Development 128

Module 4: Infancy

Why It Matters: Infancy 130
Physical Growth and Development in Newborns and Toddlers 131
Cognitive Development in Infants and Toddlers 150
Emotional and Social Development During Infancy 166
Putting It Together: Infancy 176
Discussion: Infancy 177

Module 5: Early Childhood

Why It Matters: Early Childhood 179
Physical Development in Early Childhood 180
Cognitive Development in Early Childhood 187
Emotional and Social Development in Early Childhood 197
Putting It Together: Early Childhood 218
Discussion: Parenting Styles 219

Module 6: Middle Childhood

Why It Matters: Middle Childhood 221
Physical Development in Middle Childhood 222
Cognitive Development in Middle Childhood 225
Educational Issues during Middle Childhood 230
Emotional and Social Development in Middle Childhood 241
Putting It Together: Middle Childhood 251
Discussion: Middle Childhood 252

Module 7: Adolescence

Why It Matters: Adolescence 254
Physical Growth and Development in Adolescence 256
Cognitive Development in Adolescence 270
Emotional and Social Development in Adolescence 282
Putting It Together: Adolescence 296
Discussion: Adolescence 297

Module 8: Early Adulthood

Why It Matters: Early Adulthood 299
Physical Development in Early Adulthood 300
Cognitive Development in Early Adulthood 307
Theories of Adult Psychosocial Development 314
Relationships in Early Adulthood 323
Putting It Together: Early Adulthood 340
Discussion: Early Adulthood 341

Module 9: Middle Adulthood

Why It Matters: Middle Adulthood 343
Physical Development in Middle Adulthood 345

Cognitive Development in Middle Adulthood 353
Emotional and Social Development in Middle Adulthood 357
Relationships in Middle Adulthood 366
Putting It Together: Middle Adulthood 376
Discussion: Middle Adulthood 377

Module 10: Late Adulthood

Why It Matters: Late Adulthood 379
Physical Development in Late Adulthood 380
Cognitive Development in Late Adulthood 402
Psychosocial Development in Late Adulthood 409
Putting It Together: Late Adulthood 420
Discussion: Late Adulthood 421

Module 11: Death and Dying

Why It Matters: Death and Dying 423
Understanding Death 425
Emotions Related to Death 435
Facing Death 447
Putting It Together: Death and Dying 453
Discussion: Death and Dying 454
Late Adulthood 455

Learning Outcomes

The content, assignments, and assessments for Lifespan Development are aligned to the following learning outcomes. A full list of course learning outcomes can be viewed here: Lifespan Development Learning Outcomes.

Module 1: Lifespan Development

Explain the primary topics of lifespan development and how research is conducted in the field

- Define human development and identify the stages of human development
- Explain the lifespan perspective
- Examine how to do research in lifespan development

Module 2: Developmental Theories

Describe the major developmental theories in lifespan development

- Use psychodynamic theories (like those from Freud and Erikson) to explain development
- Explain key principles of behaviorism and cognitive psychology
- Describe the humanistic, contextual, and evolutionary perspectives of development

Module 3: Prenatal Development

Describe the prenatal development process, including genetics, from the moment of conception through delivery

- Explain the role of genetics in prenatal development
- Explain the main stages of prenatal development
- Describe approaches to childbirth and the labor and delivery process

Module 4: Infancy

Describe human development during infancy

- Describe physical growth and development in infants and toddlers
- Explain cognitive development in infants and toddlers
- Explain emotional and social development during infancy

Module 5: Early Childhood

Describe development during early childhood

- Describe physical changes in early childhood
- Explain cognitive changes in early childhood
- Describe key emotional and social developments of early childhood

Module 6: Middle Childhood

Describe development during middle childhood

- Describe physical development during middle childhood
- Explain changes and advances in cognitive development during middle childhood
- Examine common learning disabilities and other factors related to education during middle childhood
- Explain emotional, social, and moral development during middle childhood

Module 7: Adolescence

Describe the physical, cognitive, emotional, and social changes that occur during adolescence

- Describe the physical changes that occur during puberty and adolescence
- Describe changes in cognitive development and moral reasoning during adolescence
- Describe adolescent identity development and social influences on development

Module 8: Early Adulthood

Describe developmental changes during early adulthood

- Explain developmental tasks and physical changes during early adulthood
- Explain cognitive development in early adulthood
- Explain theories and perspectives on psychosocial development
- Examine relationships in early adulthood

Module 9: Middle Adulthood

Describe development during middle adulthood

- Explain the physiological changes during middle adulthood and their physical and psychological consequences
- Describe cognitive and neurological changes during middle adulthood

- Analyze emotional and social development in middle adulthood
- Explain how relationships are maintained and changed during middle adulthood

Module 10: Late Adulthood

Explain development and change through late adulthood

- Describe physical changes in late adulthood
- Explain cognitive development in late adulthood
- Describe psychosocial development in in late adulthood

Module 11: Death and Dying

Explain experiences and emotions related to death and dying

- Describe the leading causes and types of deaths
- Examine emotions related to death and dying
- Examine care and practices related to death

MODULE 1: LIFESPAN DEVELOPMENT

Why It Matters: Lifespan Development

Why study lifespan development?

Welcome to the study of lifespan development! This is the scientific study of how and why people change or remain the same over time.

Think about how you were five, ten, or even fifteen years ago. In what ways have you changed? In what ways have you remained the same? You have probably changed physically; perhaps you've grown taller and become heavier. But you may have also experienced changes in the way you think and solve problems. Cognitive change is noticeable when we compare how 6-year olds, 16-year olds, and 46-year olds think and reason, for example. Their thoughts about themselves, others, and the world are probably quite different. Consider friendship—a 6 year old may think that a friend is someone with whom they can play and have fun. A 16-year old may seek friends who can help them gain status or popularity. And the 46-year old may have acquaintances, but rely more on family members to do things with and confide in. You may have also experienced psychosocial change. This refers to emotions and psychological issues as well as social roles and relationships. Psychologist Erik Erikson suggests that we struggle with issues of trust, independence, and intimacy at various points in our lives (we will explore this thoroughly throughout the course.)

This is a very interesting and meaningful course because it is about each of us and those with whom we live and work. One of the best ways to gain perspective on our own lives is to compare our experiences with those of others. In this course, we will strive to learn about each phase of human development and the physical, cognitive, and psychosocial changes, all the while making cross-cultural and historical comparisons and connections to the world around us.

In addition, we will take a lifespan developmental approach to learning about human development. That means that we won't just learn about one particular age period by itself; we will learn about each age period, recognizing how it is related to both previous developments and later developments. For instance, it helps us to understand what's happening with the 16-year old by knowing about development in the infant, toddler, early childhood, and middle childhood years. In turn, learning about all of that development and development during adolescence and early adulthood will help us to more fully understand the person at age 46 (and so on throughout midlife and later adulthood).

Development does not stop at a certain age; development is a lifelong process. We may find individual and group differences in patterns of development, so examining the influences of gender, cohort/generation, race, ethnicity, culture, socioeconomic status, education level, and time in history is also important. With the lifespan developmental perspective, we will gain a more comprehensive view of the individual within the context of their own developmental journey and within social, cultural, and historical contexts. In this way, this course covers and crosses multiple disciplines, such as psychology, biology, sociology, anthropology, education, nutrition, economics, and healthcare.

THINK IT OVER

Wherever you are in your own lifespan developmental journey, imagine yourself as an elderly person about to turn 100 years old (becoming a "centenarian"). If researchers want to understand you and your development, would they get the full picture if they just took a snapshot (so to speak) of you at that point in time? What else would you want them to know about you, your development, and experiences to really understand you?

Human Development

What you'll learn to do: define human development and identify the stages of human development

What aspects of ourselves change and develop as we journey through life? We move through significant physical, cognitive, and psychosocial changes throughout our lives—do these changes happen in a systematic way, and to everyone? How much is due to genetics and how much is due to environmental influences and experiences (both within our personal control and beyond)? Is there just one course of development or are there many different courses of development? In this module, we'll examine these questions and learn about the major stages of development and what kind of developmental tasks and transitions we might expect along the way.

LEARNING OUTCOMES

- Describe human development and its three domains: physical, cognitive, and psychosocial development
- Explain key human development issues about the nature of change: continuous/discontinuous, one course/multiple courses, and nature/nurture
- Describe the basic periods of human development

Defining Human Development

Human development refers to the physical, cognitive, and psychosocial development of humans throughout the lifespan. What types of development are involved in each of these three domains, or areas, of life? Physical development involves growth and changes in the body and brain, the senses, motor skills, and health and wellness. Cognitive development involves learning, attention, memory, language, thinking, reasoning, and creativity. Psychosocial development involves emotions, personality, and social relationships.

Figure 1. Human development encompasses the physical, cognitive, and psychosocial changes that occur throughout a lifetime.

Physical Domain

Many of us are familiar with the height and weight charts that pediatricians consult to estimate if babies, children, and teens are growing within normative ranges of physical development. We may also be aware of changes in children's fine and gross motor skills, as well as their increasing coordination, particularly in terms of playing sports. But we may not realize that physical development also involves brain development, which not only enables childhood motor coordination but also greater coordination between emotions and planning in adulthood, as our brains are not done developing in infancy or childhood. Physical development also includes puberty, sexual health, fertility, menopause, changes in our senses, and primary versus secondary aging. Healthy habits with nutrition and exercise are also important at every age and stage across the lifespan.

Cognitive Domain

If we watch and listen to infants and toddlers, we can't help but wonder how they learn so much so fast, particularly when it comes to language development. Then as we compare young children to those in middle childhood, there appear to be huge differences in their ability to think logically about the concrete world around them. Cognitive development includes mental processes, thinking, learning, and understanding, and it doesn't stop in childhood. Adolescents develop the ability to think logically about the abstract world (and may like to debate matters with adults as they exercise their new cognitive skills!). Moral reasoning develops further, as does practical intelligence—wisdom may develop with experience over time. Memory abilities and different forms of intelligence tend to change with age. Brain development and the brain's ability to change and compensate for losses is significant to cognitive functions across the lifespan, too.

Psychosocial Domain

Development in this domain involves what's going on both psychologically and socially. Early on, the focus is on infants and caregivers, as temperament and attachment are significant. As the social world expands and the child grows psychologically, different types of play and interactions with other children and teachers become important. Psychosocial development involves emotions, personality, self-esteem, and relationships. Peers become more important for adolescents, who are exploring new roles and forming their own identities. Dating, romance, cohabitation, marriage, having children, and finding work or a career are all parts of the transition into adulthood. Psychosocial development continues across adulthood with similar (and some different) developmental issues of family, friends, parenting, romance, divorce, remarriage, blended families, caregiving for elders, becoming grandparents and great grandparents, retirement, new careers, coping with losses, and death and dying.

As you may have already noticed, physical, cognitive, and psychosocial development are often interrelated, as with the example of brain development. We will be examining human development in these three domains in detail throughout the modules in this course, as we learn about infancy/toddlerhood, early childhood, middle childhood, adolescence, young adulthood, middle adulthood, and late adulthood development, as well as death and dying.

Who Studies Human Development and Why?

Many academic disciplines contribute to the study of development and this type of course is offered in some schools as psychology (particularly as developmental psychology); in other schools, it is taught under sociology, human development, or family studies. This multidisciplinary course is made up of contributions from researchers in the areas of health care, anthropology, nutrition, child development, biology, gerontology, psychology, and sociology, among others. Consequently, the stories provided are rich and well-rounded and the theories and findings can be part of a collaborative effort to understand human lives.

The main goals of those involved in studying human development are to describe and explain changes. Throughout this course, we will describe observations during development, then examine how theories provide explanations for why these changes occur. For example, you may observe two-year-old children to be particularly temperamental, and researchers offer theories to explain why that is. We'll learn a lot more about theories, especially developmental theories, in the next module.

Key Issues in Human Development

There are many different theoretical approaches regarding human development. As we evaluate them in this course, recall that human development focuses on how people change, and the approaches address the nature of change in different ways:

- Is the change smooth or uneven (continuous versus discontinuous)?
- Is this pattern of change the same for everyone, or are there different patterns of change (one course of development versus many courses)?
- How do genetics and environment interact to influence development (nature versus nurture)?

Is Development Continuous or Discontinuous?

Continuous development views development as a cumulative process, gradually improving on existing skills (Figure 2). With this type of development, there is a gradual change. Consider, for example, a child's physical growth: adding inches to their height year by year. In contrast, theorists who view development as **discontinuous** believe that development takes place in unique stages and that it occurs at specific times or ages. With this type of development, the change is more sudden, such as an infant's ability to demonstrate awareness of object permanence (which is a cognitive skill that develops toward the end of infancy, according to Piaget's cognitive theory—more on that theory in the next module).

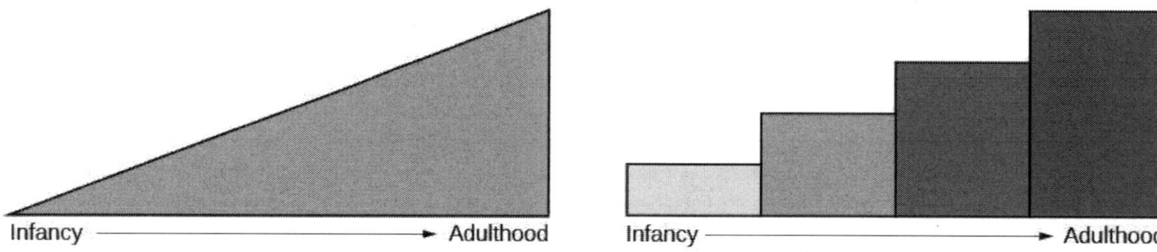

Figure 2. The concept of continuous development can be visualized as a smooth slope of progression, whereas discontinuous development sees growth in more discrete stages.

Is There One Course of Development or Many?

Is development essentially the same, or universal, for all children (i.e., there is one course of development) or does development follow a different course for each child, depending on the child's specific genetics and environment (i.e., there are many courses of development)? Do people across the world share more similarities or more differences in their development? How much do culture and genetics influence a child's behavior?

Stage theories hold that the sequence of development is universal. For example, in cross-cultural studies of language development, children from around the world reach language milestones in a similar sequence (Gleitman & Newport, 1995). Infants in all cultures coo before they babble. They begin babbling at about the same age and utter their first word around 12 months old. Yet we live in diverse contexts that have a unique effect on each of us. For example, researchers once believed that motor development followed one course for all children regardless of culture. However, childcare practices vary by culture, and different practices have been found to accelerate or inhibit the achievement of developmental milestones such as sitting, crawling, and walking (Karasik, Adolph, Tamis-LeMonda, & Bornstein, 2010).

For instance, let's look at the Aché society in Paraguay. They spend a significant amount of time foraging in forests. While foraging, Aché mothers carry their young children, rarely putting them down in order to protect them from getting hurt in the forest. Consequently, their children walk much later: They walk around 23–25 months old, in comparison to infants in Western cultures who begin to walk around 12 months old. However, as Aché children become older, they are allowed more freedom to move about, and by about age 9, their motor skills surpass those of U.S. children of the same age: Aché children are able to climb trees up to 25 feet tall and use machetes to chop their way through the forest (Kaplan & Dove, 1987). As you can see, our development is influenced by multiple contexts, so the timing of basic motor functions may vary across cultures. However, the functions are present in all societies.

(a)

(b)

Figure 3. All children across the world love to play. Whether in (a) Florida or (b) South Africa, children enjoy exploring sand, sunshine, and the sea. (credit a: modification of work by "Visit St. Pete/Clearwater"/Flickr; credit b: modification of work by "stringer_bel"/Flickr)

How Do Nature and Nurture Influence Development?

Are we who we are because of **nature** (biology and genetics), or are we who we are because of **nurture** (our environment and culture)? This longstanding question is known in psychology as the nature versus nurture debate. It seeks to understand how our personalities and traits are the product of our genetic makeup and biological factors, and how they are shaped by our environment, including our parents, peers, and culture. For instance, why do biological children sometimes act like their parents—is it because of genetics or because of early childhood environment and what the child has learned from their parents? What about children who are adopted—are they more like their biological families or more like their adoptive families? And how can siblings from the same family be so different?

We are all born with specific genetic traits inherited from our parents, such as eye color, height, and certain personality traits. Beyond our basic genotype, however, there is a deep interaction between our genes and our environment. Our unique experiences in our environment influence whether and how particular traits are expressed, and at the same time, our genes influence how we interact with our environment (Diamond, 2009; Lobo, 2008). There is a reciprocal interaction between nature and nurture as they both shape who we become, but the debate continues as to the relative contributions of each.

Periods of Human Development

Think about the lifespan and make a list of what you would consider the basic periods of development. How many periods or stages are on your list? Perhaps you have three: childhood, adulthood, and old age. Or maybe four: infancy, childhood, adolescence, and adulthood. Developmentalists often break the lifespan into eight stages:

1. Prenatal Development
2. Infancy and Toddlerhood
3. Early Childhood
4. Middle Childhood
5. Adolescence
6. Early Adulthood
7. Middle Adulthood
8. Late Adulthood

In addition, the topic of "Death and Dying" is usually addressed after late adulthood since overall, the likelihood of dying increases in later life (though individual and group variations exist). Death and dying will be the topic of our last module, though it is not necessarily a stage of development that occurs at a particular age.

The list of the periods of development reflects unique aspects of the various stages of childhood and adulthood that will be explored in this book, including physical, cognitive, and psychosocial changes. So while both an 8-month-old and an 8-year-old are considered children, they have very different motor abilities, cognitive skills, and social relationships. Their nutritional needs are different, and their primary psychological concerns are also distinctive. The same is true of an 18-year-old and an 80-year-old, both considered adults. We will discover the distinctions between being 28 or 48 as well. But first, here is a brief overview of the stages.

Prenatal Development

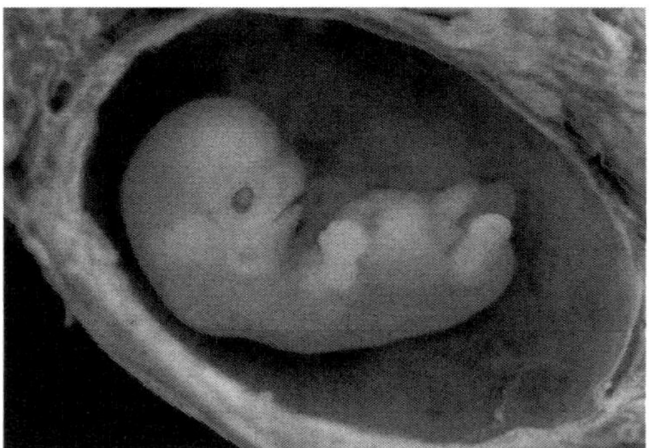

Figure 4. An embryo at 8 weeks of development.

Conception occurs and development begins. There are three stages of prenatal development: germinal, embryonic, and fetal periods. All of the major structures of the body are forming and the health of the mother is of primary concern. There are various approaches to labor, delivery, and childbirth, with potential complications of pregnancy and delivery, as well as risks and complications with newborns, but also advances in tests, technology, and medicine. The influences of nature (e.g., genetics) and nurture (e.g., nutrition and teratogens, which are environmental factors during pregnancy that can lead to birth defects) are evident. Evolutionary psychology, along with studies of twins and adoptions, help us understand the interplay of factors and the relative influences of nature and nurture on human development.

Infancy and Toddlerhood

Figure 5. Major development happens during the first two years of life, as evidenced by this newborn baby and his toddler brother.

The first year and a half to two years of life are ones of dramatic growth and change. A newborn, with many involuntary reflexes and a keen sense of hearing but poor vision, is transformed into a walking, talking toddler within a relatively short period of time. Caregivers similarly transform their roles from those who manage feeding and sleep schedules to constantly moving guides and safety inspectors for mobile, energetic children. Brain development happens at a remarkable rate, as does physical growth and language development. Infants have their own temperaments and approaches to play. Interactions with primary caregivers (and others) undergo changes influenced by possible separation anxiety and the development of attachment styles. Social and cultural issues center around breastfeeding or formula-feeding, sleeping in cribs or in the bed with parents, toilet training, and whether or not to get vaccinations.

Early Childhood

Figure 6. Early childhood, or the preschool years, around ages 2-6, is filled with incredible amounts of growth and change.

Early childhood is also referred to as the preschool years, consisting of the years that follow toddlerhood and precede formal schooling, roughly from around ages 2 to 5 or 6. As a preschooler, the child is busy learning language (with amazing growth in vocabulary), is gaining a sense of self and greater independence, and is beginning to learn the workings of the physical world. This knowledge does not come quickly, however, and preschoolers may initially have interesting conceptions of size, time, space and distance, such as demonstrating how long something will take by holding out their two index fingers several inches apart. A toddler's fierce determination to do something may give way to a four-year-old's sense of guilt for doing something that brings the disapproval of others.

Middle Childhood

Figure 7. Middle childhood spans most of what is traditionally primary school, or the ages between 6-11.

The ages of 6-11 comprise middle childhood and much of what children experience at this age is connected to their involvement in the early grades of school. Now the world becomes one of learning and testing new academic skills and assessing one's abilities and accomplishments by making comparisons between self and others. Schools participate in this process by comparing students and making these comparisons public through team sports, test scores, and other forms of recognition. The brain reaches its adult size around age seven, but it continues to develop. Growth rates slow down and children are able to refine their motor skills at this point in life. Children also begin to learn about social relationships beyond the family through interaction with friends and fellow students; same-sex friendships are particularly salient during this period.

Adolescence

Figure 8. Adolescence, or the age roughly between 12-18, is marked by puberty and sexual maturation, accompanied by major socioemotional changes.

Adolescence is a period of dramatic physical change marked by an overall physical growth spurt and sexual maturation, known as puberty; timing may vary by gender, cohort, and culture. It is also a time of cognitive change as the adolescent begins to think of new possibilities and to consider abstract concepts such as love, fear, and freedom. Ironically, adolescents have a sense of invincibility that puts them at greater risk of dying from accidents or contracting sexually transmitted infections that can have lifelong consequences. Research on brain development helps us understand teen risk-taking and impulsive behavior. A major developmental task during adolescence involves establishing one's own identity. Teens typically struggle to become more independent from their parents. Peers become more important, as teens strive for a sense of belonging and acceptance; mixed-sex peer groups become more common. New roles and responsibilities are explored, which may involve dating, driving, taking on a part-time job, and planning for future academics.

Early Adulthood

Figure 9. Early adulthood, roughly ages 20-40, may be split into yet another category of "emerging adulthood," as there are often profound differences between younger adults and those in their late 30s.

Late teens, twenties, and thirties are often thought of as early adulthood (students who are in their mid to late 30s may love to hear that they are young adults!). It is a time when we are at our physiological peak but are most at risk for involvement in violent crimes and substance abuse. It is a time of focusing on the future and putting a lot of energy into making choices that will help one earn the status of a full adult in the eyes of others. Love and work are the primary concerns at this stage of life. In recent decades, it has been noted (in the U.S. and other developed countries) that young adults are taking longer to "grow up." They are waiting longer to move out of their parents' homes, finish their formal education, take on work/careers, get married, and have children. One psychologist, Jeffrey Arnett, has proposed that there is a new stage of development after adolescence and before early adulthood, called "emerging adulthood," from 18 to 25 (or even 29) when individuals are still exploring their identities and don't quite feel like adults yet. Cohort, culture, time in history, the economy, and socioeconomic status may be key factors in when youth take on adult roles.

Middle Adulthood

Figure 10. Middle adulthood spans the years between ages 40-65.

The late thirties (or age 40) through the mid-60s are referred to as middle adulthood. This is a period in which physiological aging that began earlier becomes more noticeable and a period at which many people are at their peak of productivity in love and work. It may be a period of gaining expertise in certain fields and being able to understand problems and find solutions with greater efficiency than before. It can also be a time of becoming more realistic about possibilities in life; of recognizing the difference between what is possible and what is likely. Referred to as the sandwich generation, middle-aged adults may be in the middle of taking care of their children and also taking care of their aging parents. While caring about others and the future, middle-aged adults may also be questioning their own mortality, goals, and commitments, though not necessarily experiencing a "mid-life crisis."

WATCH IT: THE UP SERIES

In 1964, researchers and filmmakers began a fascinating and landmark documentary series known as the UP Series. The UK-based Granada's World in Action team, inspired by the Jesuit maxim, "Give me the child until he is seven and I will give you the man," interviewed a diverse group of seven-year-old children from all over England. In the first film, called "Seven Up!," they asked seven-year-old children about their lives, dreams, and fears for the future. Michael Apted, a researcher for the original film, has returned to interview these individuals every seven years since then, at ages 14, 21, 28, 35, 42, 49, 56 and now at age 63.

This video gives a nice overview of the series (through the lens of a film analysis of what makes it so successful and engaging). You can watch the Up Series on YouTube.

- https://youtu.be/VVQ96wfbf_0

Late Adulthood

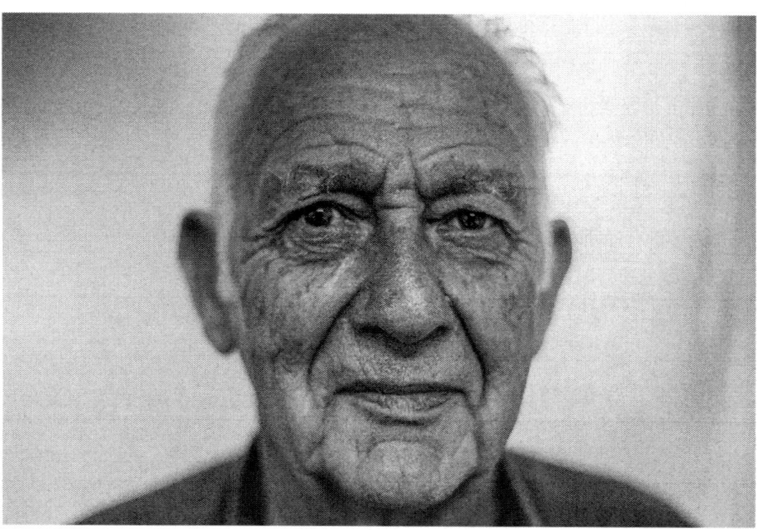

Figure 11. Late adulthood is generally viewed as age 65 and older, but there are incredible variations in health and lifestyle between the "young old" and the "oldest old," who may be well into their 100s.

This period of the lifespan, late adulthood, has increased in the last 100 years, particularly in industrialized countries, as average life expectancy has increased. Late adulthood covers a wide age range with a lot of variation, so it is helpful to divide it into categories such as the "young old" (65-74 years old), "old old" (75-84 years old), and "oldest old" (85+ years old). The young old are similar to middle-aged adults; possibly still working, married, relatively healthy, and active. The old old have some health problems and challenges with daily living activities; the oldest old are often frail and in need of long term care. However, many factors are involved and a better way to appreciate the diversity of older adults is to go beyond chronological age and examine whether a person is experiencing optimal aging (like the gentleman pictured in Figure 8 who is in very good health for his age and continues to have an active, stimulating life), normal aging (in which the changes are similar to most of those of the same age), or impaired aging (referring to someone who has more physical challenge and disease than others of the same age).

Death and Dying

Figure 12. How people think about death, approach death, and cope with death vary depending on many factors. Photo Courtesy Robert Paul Young

The study of death and dying is seldom given the amount of coverage it deserves. Of course, there is a certain discomfort in thinking about death, but there is also a certain confidence and acceptance that can come from studying death and dying. Factors such as age, religion, and culture play important roles in attitudes and approaches to death and dying. There are different types of death: physiological, psychological, and social. The most common causes of death vary with age, gender, race, culture, and time in history. Dying and grieving are processes and may share certain stages of reactions to loss. There are interesting examples of cultural variations in death rituals, mourning, and grief. The concept of a "good death" is described as including personal choices and the involvement of loved ones throughout the process. Palliative care is an approach to maintain dying individuals' comfort level, and hospice is a movement and practice that involves professional and volunteer care and loved ones. Controversy surrounds euthanasia (helping a person fulfill their wish to die)—active and passive types, as well as physician-assisted suicide, and legality varies within the United States.

THINK IT OVER

Think about your own development. Which period or stage of development are you in right now? Are you dealing with similar issues and experiencing comparable physical, cognitive, and psychosocial development as described above? If not, why not? Are important aspects of development missing and if so, are they common for most of your cohort or unique to you?

GLOSSARY

continuous development:
the idea that development is a progressive and cumulative process, gradually improving on existing skills

discontinuous development:
idea that development takes place in unique stages and occurs at specific times or ages

nature:
the influences of biology and genetics on behavior

nurture:
environmental, social, and cultural influences of behavior

The Lifespan Perspective

What you'll learn to do: explain the lifespan perspective

As we have learned, human development refers to the physical, cognitive, and psychosocial changes and constancies in humans over time. There are various theories pertaining to each domain of development, and often theorists and researchers focus their attention on specific periods of development (with most traditionally focusing on infancy and childhood; some on adolescence). But isn't it possible that development during one period affects development in other periods and that humans can grow and change across adulthood too? In this section, we'll learn about development through the lifespan perspective, which emphasizes the multidimensional, interconnected, and ever-changing influences on development.

LEARNING OUTCOMES

- Describe Baltes' lifespan perspective with its key principles about development
- Explain what is meant by development being lifelong, multidimensional, and multidirectional
- Explain contextual influences on development

The Lifespan Perspective

Lifespan development involves the exploration of biological, cognitive, and psychosocial changes and constancies that occur throughout the entire course of life. It has been presented as a theoretical perspective, proposing several fundamental, theoretical, and methodological principles about the nature of human development. An attempt by researchers has been made to examine whether research on the nature of development suggests a specific metatheoretical worldview. Several beliefs, taken together, form the "family of perspectives" that contribute to this particular view.

Figure 1. Baltes' lifespan perspective emphasizes that development is lifelong, multidimensional, multidirectional, plastic, contextual, and multidisciplinary. Think of ways your own development fits in with each of these concepts as you read about the terms in more detail.

German psychologist Paul Baltes, a leading expert on lifespan development and aging, developed one of the approaches to studying development called the **lifespan perspective**. This approach is based on several key principles:

- Development occurs across one's entire life, or is *lifelong*.
- Development is *multidimensional,* meaning it involves the dynamic interaction of factors like physical, emotional, and psychosocial development
- Development is *multidirectional* and results in gains and losses throughout life
- Development is *plastic*, meaning that characteristics are malleable or changeable.
- Development is influenced by *contextual* and socio-cultural influences.
- Development is *multidisciplinary.*

Development is lifelong

Lifelong development means that development is not completed in infancy or childhood or at any specific age; it encompasses the entire lifespan, from conception to death. The study of development traditionally focused almost exclusively on the changes occurring from conception to adolescence and the gradual decline in old age; it was believed that the five or six decades after adolescence yielded little to no developmental change at all. The current view reflects the possibility that specific changes in development can occur later in life, without having been established at birth. The early events of one's childhood can be transformed by later events in one's life. This belief clearly emphasizes that all stages of the lifespan contribute to the regulation of the nature of human development.

Many diverse patterns of change, such as direction, timing, and order, can vary among individuals and affect the ways in which they develop. For example, the developmental timing of events can affect individuals in different ways because of their current level of maturity and understanding. As individuals move through life, they are faced with many challenges, opportunities, and situations that impact their development. Remembering that development is a lifelong process helps us gain a wider perspective on the meaning and impact of each event.

Development is multidimensional

By multidimensionality, Baltes is referring to the fact that a complex interplay of factors influence development across the lifespan, including biological, cognitive, and socioemotional changes. Baltes argues that a dynamic interaction of these factors is what influences an individual's development.

For example, in adolescence, puberty consists of physiological and physical changes with changes in hormone levels, the development of primary and secondary sex characteristics, alterations in height and weight, and several other bodily changes. But these are not the only types of changes taking place; there are also cognitive changes, including the development of advanced cognitive faculties such as the ability to think abstractly. There are also emotional and social changes involving regulating emotions, interacting with peers, and possibly dating. The fact that the term puberty encompasses such a broad range of domains illustrates the multidimensionality component of development (think back to the physical, cognitive, and psychosocial domains of human development we discussed earlier in this module).

Development is multidirectional

Baltes states that the development of a particular domain does not occur in a strictly linear fashion but that development of certain traits can be characterized as having the capacity for both an increase and decrease in efficacy over the course of an individual's life.

If we use the example of puberty again, we can see that certain domains may improve or decline in effectiveness during this time. For example, self-regulation is one domain of puberty which undergoes profound multidirectional changes during the adolescent period. During childhood, individuals have difficulty effectively regulating their actions and impulsive behaviors. Scholars have noted that this lack of effective regulation often results in children engaging in behaviors without fully considering the consequences of their actions. Over the course of puberty, neuronal changes modify this unregulated behavior by increasing the ability to regulate emotions and impulses. Inversely, the ability for adolescents to engage in spontaneous activity and creativity, both domains commonly associated with impulse behavior, decrease over the adolescent period in response to changes in cognition. Neuronal changes to the limbic system and prefrontal cortex of the brain, which begin in puberty lead to the development of self-regulation, and the ability to consider the consequences of one's actions (though recent brain research reveals that this connection will continue to develop into early adulthood).

Extending on the premise of multidirectionality, Baltes also argued that development is influenced by the "joint expression of features of growth (gain) and decline (loss)"[1] This relation between developmental gains and losses occurs in a direction to selectively optimize particular capacities. This requires the sacrificing of other functions, a process known as selective optimization with compensation. According to the process of selective optimization, individuals prioritize particular functions above others, reducing the adaptive capacity of particulars for specialization and improved efficacy of other modalities.

The acquisition of effective self-regulation in adolescents illustrates this gain/loss concept. As adolescents gain the ability to effectively regulate their actions, they may be forced to sacrifice other features to selectively optimize their reactions. For example, individuals may sacrifice their capacity to be spontaneous or creative if they are constantly required to make thoughtful decisions and regulate their emotions. Adolescents may also be forced to sacrifice their fast reaction times toward processing stimuli in favor of being able to fully consider the consequences of their actions.

APPLICATIONS OF THE LIFESPAN PERSPECTIVE

Baltes' ideas about development as a lifelong process is beneficial to society because it may help in the identification of qualities or problems that are distinctive in a particular age period. If these qualities or problems could be identified, specific programs could be established such as after-school interventions that enhance positive youth development (PYD).

1. Baltes, P. (1987). Theoretical propositions of life-span developmental psychology: On the dynamics between growth and decline. Developmental Psychology, 23(5), 611-626.

Positive Youth Development holds the belief that all youths have the potential to become productive, contributing members of society. PYD emphasizes the strengths of youth, promoting their development physically, personally, socially, emotionally, intellectually, and spiritually. Interventions must be conducted with the needs and preferences of the participants kept in mind, however the individuals' choice, values, and culture must always be considered.

Big Brothers/Big Sisters is a positive youth development program targeted in the community domain that demonstrates substantial behavioral outcomes for youth. This program sought to promote positive identity and competence by creating a strong bond with a healthy adult. These healthy adults, or mentors, committed a minimum of several hours, two to four times a month for a year, with a youth who was carefully assigned to them based on their background, preference, and geographic proximity. Youths in this program improved in "school attendance, parental relations, academic performance, and peer emotional support"[2] Substance use and problem behaviors were also reported as either prevented or reduced. Watch this video from Big Brothers Big Sisters of America to learn more about the power of mentoring.

Development is plastic

Plasticity denotes intrapersonal variability and focuses heavily on the potentials and limits of the nature of human development. The notion of plasticity emphasizes that there are many possible developmental outcomes and that the nature of human development is much more open and pluralistic than originally implied by traditional views; there is no single pathway that must be taken in an individual's development across the lifespan. Plasticity is imperative to current research because the potential for intervention is derived from the notion of plasticity in development. Undesired development or behaviors could potentially be prevented or changed.

As an example, recently researchers have been analyzing how other senses compensate for the loss of vision in blind individuals. Without visual input, blind humans have demonstrated that tactile and auditory functions still fully develop and they can use tactile and auditory cues to perceive the world around them. One experiment designed by Röder and colleagues (1999) compared the auditory localization skills of people who are blind with people who are sighted by having participants locate sounds presented either centrally or peripherally (lateral) to them. Both congenitally blind adults and sighted adults could locate a sound presented in front of them with precision but people who are blind were clearly superior in locating sounds presented laterally. Currently, brain-imaging studies have revealed that the sensory cortices in the brain are reorganized after visual deprivation. These findings suggest that when vision is absent in development, the auditory cortices in the brain recruit areas that are normally devoted to vision, thus becoming further refined.

LINK TO LEARNING

Watch Seeing Behind the Visual Cortex, a video about research on blindsight conducted by Dr. Tony Ro to learn more about brain plasticity in blind individuals.

2. Catalano, R., Berglund, L., Ryan, J., Lonczak, H., & Hawkins, D. (2002). Positive youth development in the united states: Research findings on evaluations of positive youth development programs. Prevention & Treatment, 5(15), 27-28.

A significant aspect of the aging process is cognitive decline. The dimensions of cognitive decline are partially reversible, however, because the brain retains the lifelong capacity for plasticity and reorganization of cortical tissue. Mahncke and colleagues developed a brain plasticity-based training program that induced learning in mature adults experiencing age-related decline. This training program focused intensively on aural language reception accuracy and cognitively demanding exercises that have been proven to partially reverse the age-related losses in memory. It included highly rewarding novel tasks that required attention control and became progressively more difficult to perform. In comparison to the control group, who received no training and showed no significant change in memory function, the experimental training group displayed a marked enhancement in memory that was sustained at the 3-month follow-up period. These findings suggest that cognitive function, particularly memory, can be significantly improved in mature adults with age-related cognitive decline by using brain plasticity-based training methods.

Development is contextual

In Baltes' theory, the paradigm of contextualism refers to the idea that three systems of biological and environmental influences work together to influence development. Development occurs in context and varies from person to person, depending on factors such as a person's biology, family, school, church, profession, nationality, and ethnicity. Baltes identified three types of influences that operate throughout the life course: normative age-graded influences, normative history-graded influences, and nonnormative influences. Baltes wrote that these three influences operate throughout the life course, their effects accumulate with time, and, as a dynamic package, they are responsible for how lives develop.

Normative age-graded influences are those biological and environmental factors that have a strong correlation with chronological age, such as puberty or menopause, or age-based social practices such as beginning school or entering retirement. **Normative history-graded influences** are associated with a specific time period that defines the broader environmental and cultural context in which an individual develops. For example, development and identity are influenced by historical events of the people who experience them, such as the Great Depression, WWII, Vietnam, the Cold War, the War on Terror, or advances in technology.

This has been exemplified in numerous studies, including Nesselroade and Baltes', showing that the level and direction of change in adolescent personality development was influenced as strongly by the socio-cultural settings at the time (in this case, the Vietnam War) as age-related factors. The study involved individuals of four different adolescent age groups who all showed significant personality development in the same direction (a tendency to occupy themselves with ethical, moral, and political issues rather than cognitive achievement). Similarly, Elder showed that the Great Depression was a setting that significantly affected the development of adolescents and their corresponding adult personalities, by showing a similar common personality development across age groups. Baltes' theory also states that the historical socio-cultural setting had an effect on the development of an individual's intelligence. The areas of influence that Baltes thought most important to the development of intelligence were health, education, and work. The first two areas, health and education, significantly affect adolescent development because healthy children who are educated effectively will tend to develop a higher level of intelligence. The environmental factors, health and education, have been suggested by Neiss and Rowe to have as much effect on intelligence as inherited intelligence.

Nonnormative influences are unpredictable and not tied to a certain developmental time in a person's development or to a historical period. They are the unique experiences of an individual, whether biological or environmental, that shape the development process. These could include milestones like earning a master's degree or getting a certain job offer or other events like going through a divorce or coping with the death of a child.

The most important aspect of contextualism as a paradigm is that the three systems of influence work together to affect development. Concerning adolescent development, the age-graded influences would help to explain the similarities within a cohort, the history-graded influences would help to explain the differences between cohorts, and the nonnormative influences would explain the idiosyncrasies of each adolescent's individual development. When all influences are considered together, it provides a broader explanation of an adolescent's development.

Other Contextual Influences on Development: Cohort, Socioeconomic Status, and Culture

What is meant by the word "context"? It means that we are influenced by when and where we live. Our actions, beliefs, and values are a response to the circumstances surrounding us. Sternberg describes contextual intelligence as the ability to understand what is called for in a situation (Sternberg, 1996). The key here is to understand that behaviors, motivations, emotions, and choices are all part of a bigger picture. Our concerns are such because of who we are socially, where we live, and when we live; they are part of a social climate and set of realities that surround us. Important social factors include cohort, social class, gender, race, ethnicity, and age. Let's begin by exploring two of these: cohort and social class.

A **cohort** is a group of people who are born at roughly the same time period in a particular society. Cohorts share histories and contexts for living. Members of a cohort have experienced the same historical events and cultural climates which have an impact on the values, priorities, and goals that may guide their lives.

COHORTS

Consider a young boy's concerns if he grew up in the United States during World War II—let's call him Henry. What Henry's family buys is limited by their small budget and by a governmental program set up to ration food and other materials that are in short supply because of the war. He is eager rather than resentful about being thrifty and sees his actions as meaningful contributions to the good of others.

Figure 2. Boys collecting old tires for rubber during WWII.

As Henry grows up and has a family of his own, he is motivated by images of success tied to his past experience: he views a successful man as one who can provide for his family financially, who has a wife who stays at home and cares for the children, and children who are respectful but enjoy the luxury of days filled with school and play without having to consider the burdens of society's struggles. He marries soon after completing high school, has four children, works hard to support his family and is able to do so during the prosperous postwar economics of the 1950s in America. But economic conditions change in the mid-1960s and through the 1970s. Henry's wife, Patricia, begins to work to help the family financially and to overcome her boredom with being a stay-at-home mother. The children are teenagers in a very different social climate: one of social unrest, liberation, and challenging the status quo. They are not sheltered from the concerns of society; they see television broadcasts in their own living room of the war in Vietnam and they fear the draft—they are part of a middle-class youth culture that is very visible and vocal. Henry's employment as an engineer eventually becomes difficult as a result of downsizing in the defense industry. His marriage of 25 years ends in divorce.

This is not a unique personal history, rather it is a story shared by many members of Henry's cohort. Historic contexts shape our life choices and motivations as well as our eventual assessments of success or failure during the course of our existence. Henry shares many normative age-graded influences with his peers, such as entering the workforce at the same time, or having kids around the same age, but also normative history-graded experiences such as living through the Vietnam War and the Cold War. Henry's unique life experiences such as having four kids, getting a divorce, or losing his job, are the non-normative influences that also affect his development.

WATCH IT

This video describes the normative history-graded influences that shaped the development of seven generations over the past 125 years of United States history. Can you identify your generation? Does the description seem accurate?

- https://youtu.be/lfYjGxl6AJ8

Another context that influences our lives is our social standing, socioeconomic status, or social class. Socioeconomic status is a way to identify families and households based on their shared levels of education, income, and occupation. While there is certainly individual variation, members of a social class tend to share similar lifestyles, patterns of consumption, parenting styles, stressors, religious preferences, and other aspects of daily life.

HOW DOES SOCIOECONOMIC STATUS AFFECT LANGUAGE DEVELOPMENT?

The achievement gap refers to the persistent difference in grades, test scores, and graduation rates that exist among students of different ethnicities, races, and—in certain subjects—sexes (Winerman, 2011). Research suggests that these achievement gaps are strongly influenced by differences in socioeconomic factors that exist among the families of these children. While the researchers acknowledge that programs aimed at reducing such socioeconomic discrepancies would likely aid in equalizing the aptitude and performance of children from different backgrounds, they recognize that such large-scale interventions would be difficult to achieve. Therefore, it is recommended that programs aimed at fostering aptitude and achievement among disadvantaged children may be the best option for dealing with issues related to academic achievement gaps (Duncan & Magnuson, 2005).

Low-income children perform significantly more poorly than their middle- and high-income peers on a number of educational variables: They have significantly lower standardized test scores, graduation rates, and college entrance rates, and they have much higher school dropout rates. There have been attempts to correct the achievement gap through state and federal legislation, but what if the problems start before the children even enter school?

Psychologists Betty Hart and Todd Risley (2006) spent their careers looking at early language ability and progression of children in various income levels. In one longitudinal study, they found that although all the parents in the study engaged and interacted with their children, middle- and high-income parents interacted with their children differently than low-income parents. After analyzing 1,300 hours of parent-child interactions, the researchers found that middle- and high-income parents talk to their children significantly more, starting when the children are infants. By 3 years old, high-income children knew almost double the number of words known by their low-income counterparts, and they had heard an estimated total of 30 million more words than the low-income counterparts (Hart & Risley, 2003). And the gaps only become more pronounced. Before entering kindergarten, high-income children score 60% higher on achievement tests than their low-income peers (Lee & Burkam, 2002).

There are solutions to this problem. At the University of Chicago, experts are working with low-income families, visiting them at their homes, and encouraging them to speak more to their children on a daily and hourly basis. Other experts are designing preschools in which students from diverse economic backgrounds are placed in the same classroom. In this research, low-income children made significant gains in their language development, likely as a result of attending the specialized preschool (Schechter & Byeb, 2007). What other methods or interventions could be used to decrease the achievement gap? What types of activities could be implemented to help the children of your community or a neighboring community?

Culture is often referred to as a blueprint or guideline shared by a group of people that specifies how to live. It includes ideas about what is right and wrong, what to strive for, what to eat, how to speak, what is valued, as well as what kinds of emotions are called for in certain situations. Culture teaches us how to live in a society and allows us to advance because each new generation can benefit from the solutions found and passed down from previous generations.

Culture is learned from parents, schools, churches, media, friends, and others throughout a lifetime. The kinds of traditions and values that evolve in a particular culture serve to help members function in their own society and to value their own society. We tend to believe that our own culture's practices and expectations are the right ones. This belief that our own culture is superior is called ethnocentrism and is a normal by-product of growing up in a culture. It becomes a roadblock, however, when it inhibits understanding of cultural practices from other societies. Cultural relativity is an appreciation for cultural differences and the understanding that cultural practices are best understood from the standpoint of that particular culture.

Culture is an extremely important context for human development and understanding development requires being able to identify which features of development are culturally based. This understanding is somewhat new and still being explored. So much of what developmental theorists have described in the past has been culturally bound and difficult to apply to various cultural contexts. For example, Erikson's theory that teenagers struggle with identity assumes that all teenagers live in a society in which they have many options and must make an individual choice about their future. In many parts of the world, one's identity is determined by family status or society's dictates. In other words, there is no choice to make.

Even the most biological events can be viewed in cultural contexts that are extremely varied. Consider two very different cultural responses to menstruation in young girls. In the United States, girls in public school often receive information on menstruation around 5th grade, get a kit containing feminine hygiene products, and receive some sort of education about sexual health. Contrast this with some developing countries where menstruation is not publicly addressed, or where girls on their period are forced to miss school due to limited access to feminine products or unjust attitudes about menstruation.

Development is Multidisciplinary

Any single discipline's account of development across the lifespan would not be able to express all aspects of this theoretical framework. That is why it is suggested explicitly by lifespan researchers that a combination of disciplines is necessary to understand development. Psychologists, sociologists, neuroscientists, anthropologists, educators, economists, historians, medical researchers, and others may all be interested and involved in research related to the normative age-graded, normative history-graded, and nonnormative influences that help shape development. Many disciplines are able to contribute important concepts that integrate knowledge, which may ultimately result in the formation of a new and enriched understanding of development across the lifespan.

THINK IT OVER

- Consider your cohort. Can you identify it? Does it have a name and if so, what does the name imply? To what extent does your cohort shape your values, thoughts, and aspirations? (Some cohort labels popularized in the media for generations in the United States include Baby Boomers, Generation X, Millennials, and Generation Z.)
- Think of other ways culture may have affected your development. How might cultural differences influence interactions between teachers and students, nurses and patients, or other relationships?

GLOSSARY

cohort:
a group of people who are born at roughly the same period in a particular society. Cohorts share histories and contexts for living

culture:
blueprint or guideline shared by a group of people that specifies how to live; passed down from generation to generation; learned from parents and others

lifespan perspective:
an approach to studying development which emphasizes that development is lifelong, multidimensional, multidirectional, plastic, contextual, and multidisciplinary

nonnormative influences:
unpredictable influences not tied to a certain developmental time, personally or historical period

normative age-graded influences:
biological and environmental factors that have a strong correlation with chronological age

normative history-graded influences:
influences associated with a specific time period that define the broader bio-cultural context in which an individual develops

Research in Lifespan Development

What you'll learn to do: examine how to do research in lifespan development

How do we know what changes and stays the same (and when and why) in lifespan development? We rely on research that utilizes the scientific method so that we can have confidence in the findings. How data are collected may vary by age group and by the type of information sought. The developmental design (for example, following individuals as they age over time or comparing individuals of different ages at one point in time) will affect the data and the conclusions that can be drawn from them about actual age changes. What do you think are the particular challenges or issues in conducting developmental research, such as with infants and children? Read on to learn more.

LEARNING OUTCOMES

- Explain how the scientific method is used in researching development
- Compare various types and objectives of developmental research
- Describe methods for collecting research data (including observation, survey, case study, content analysis, and secondary content analysis)
- Explain correlational research
- Describe the value of experimental research
- Compare advantages and disadvantages of developmental research designs (cross-sectional, longitudinal, and sequential)
- Describe challenges associated with conducting research in lifespan development

Research in Lifespan Development

How do we know what we know?

An important part of learning any science is having a basic knowledge of the techniques used in gathering information. The hallmark of scientific investigation is that of following a set of procedures designed to keep questioning or skepticism alive while describing, explaining, or testing any phenomenon. Not long ago a friend said to me that he did not trust academicians or researchers because they always seem to change their story. That, however, is exactly what science is all about; it involves continuously renewing our understanding of the subjects in question and an ongoing investigation of how and why events occur. Science is a vehicle for going on a never-ending journey. In the area of development, we have seen changes in recommendations for nutrition, in explanations of psychological states as people age, and in parenting advice. So think of learning about human development as a lifelong endeavor.

Figure 1. Scientific inquiry and questioning is critical in drawing conclusions about human development.

Personal Knowledge

How do we know what we know? Take a moment to write down two things that you know about childhood. Okay. Now, how do you know? Chances are you know these things based on your own history (experiential reality), what others have told you, or cultural ideas (agreement reality) (Seccombe and Warner, 2004). There are several problems with personal inquiry, or drawing conclusions based on our personal experiences. Read the following sentence aloud:

Paris in the
the spring

Are you sure that is what it said? Read it again:

Paris in the
the spring

If you read it differently the second time (adding the second "the") you just experienced one of the problems with relying on personal inquiry; that is, the tendency to see what we believe. Our assumptions very often guide our perceptions, consequently, when we believe something, we tend to see it even if it is not there. Have you heard the saying, "seeing is believing"? Well, the truth is just the opposite: believing is seeing. This problem may just be a result of cognitive 'blinders' or it may be part of a more conscious attempt to support our own views. Confirmation bias is the tendency to look for evidence that we are right and in so doing, we ignore contradictory evidence.

Philosopher Karl Popper suggested that the distinction between that which is scientific and that which is unscientific is that science is falsifiable; scientific inquiry involves attempts to reject or refute a theory or set of assumptions (Thornton, 2005). A theory that cannot be falsified is not scientific. And much of what we do in personal inquiry involves drawing conclusions based on what we have personally experienced or validating our own experience by discussing what we think is true with others who share the same views.

Science offers a more systematic way to make comparisons and guard against bias. One technique used to avoid sampling bias is to select participants for a study in a random way. This means using a technique to ensure that all members have an equal chance of being selected. Simple random sampling may involve using a set of random numbers as a guide in determining who is to be selected. For example, if we have a list of 400 people and wish to randomly select a smaller group or sample to be studied, we use a list of random numbers and select the case that corresponds with that number (Case 39, 3, 217, etc.). This is preferable to asking only those individuals with whom we are familiar to participate in a study; if we conveniently chose only people we know, we know nothing about those who had no opportunity to be selected. There are many more elaborate techniques that can be used to obtain samples that represent the composition of the population we are studying. But even though a randomly selected representative sample is preferable, it is not always used because of costs and other limitations. As a consumer of research, however, you should know how the sample was obtained and keep this in mind when interpreting results. It is possible that what was found was limited to that sample or similar individuals and not generalizable to everyone else.

Scientific Methods

The particular method used to conduct research may vary by discipline and since lifespan development is multidisciplinary, more than one method may be used to study human development. One method of scientific investigation involves the following steps:

- Determining a research question
- Reviewing previous studies addressing the topic in question (known as a literature review)
- Determining a method of gathering information
- Conducting the study
- Interpreting the results
- Drawing conclusions; stating limitations of the study and suggestions for future research
- Making the findings available to others (both to share information and to have the work scrutinized by others)

The findings of these scientific studies can then be used by others as they explore the area of interest. Through this process, a literature or knowledge base is established. This model of scientific investigation presents research as a linear process guided by a specific research question. And it typically involves **quantitative research**, which relies on numerical data or using statistics to understand and report what has been studied.

Another model of research, referred to as **qualitative research,** may involve steps such as these:

- Begin with a broad area of interest and a research question
- Gain entrance into a group to be researched
- Gather field notes about the setting, the people, the structure, the activities or other areas of interest
- Ask open-ended, broad "grand tour" types of questions when interviewing subjects
- Modify research questions as the study continues
- Note patterns or consistencies
- Explore new areas deemed important by the people being observed
- Report findings

In this type of research, theoretical ideas are "grounded" in the experiences of the participants. The researcher is the student and the people in the setting are the teachers as they inform the researcher of their world (Glazer & Strauss, 1967). Researchers should be aware of their own biases and assumptions, acknowledge them and bracket them in efforts to keep them from limiting accuracy in reporting. Sometimes qualitative studies are used initially to explore a topic and more quantitative studies are used to test or explain what was first described.

A good way to become more familiar with these scientific research methods, both quantitative and qualitative, is to look at journal articles, which are written in sections that follow these steps in the scientific process. Most psychological articles and many papers in the social sciences follow the writing guidelines and format dictated by the American Psychological Association (APA). In general, the structure follows: abstract (summary of the article), introduction or literature review, methods explaining how the study was conducted, results of the study, discussion and interpretation of findings, and references.

LINK TO LEARNING

Brené Brown is a bestselling author and social work professor at the University of Houston. She conducts grounded theory research by collecting *qualitative* data from large numbers of participants. In Brené Brown's TED Talk The Power of Vulnerability, Brown refers to herself as a storyteller-researcher as she explains her research process and summarizes her results.

Research Methods and Objectives

The main categories of psychological research are descriptive, correlational, and experimental research. Research studies that do not test specific relationships between variables are called **descriptive, or qualitative, studies**. These studies are used to describe general or specific behaviors and attributes that are observed and measured. In the early stages of research it might be difficult to form a hypothesis, especially when there is not any existing literature in the area. In these situations designing an experiment would be premature, as the question of interest is not yet clearly defined as a hypothesis. Often a researcher will begin with a non-experimental approach, such as a descriptive study, to gather more information about the topic before designing an experiment or correlational study to address a specific hypothesis. Some examples of descriptive questions include:

- "How much time do parents spend with children?"
- "How many times per week do couples have intercourse?"
- "When is marital satisfaction greatest?"

The main types of descriptive studies include observation, case studies, surveys, and content analysis (which we'll examine further in the module). Descriptive research is distinct from **correlational research**, in which psychologists formally test whether a relationship exists between two or more variables. **Experimental research** goes a step further beyond descriptive and correlational research and randomly assigns people to different conditions, using hypothesis testing to make inferences about how these conditions affect behavior. Some experimental research includes **explanatory** studies, which are efforts to answer the question "why" such as:

- "Why have rates of divorce leveled off?"
- "Why are teen pregnancy rates down?"
- "Why has the average life expectancy increased?"

Evaluation research is designed to assess the effectiveness of policies or programs. For instance, research might be designed to study the effectiveness of safety programs implemented in schools for installing car seats or fitting bicycle helmets. Do children who have been exposed to the safety programs wear their helmets? Do parents use car seats properly? If not, why not?

WATCH IT

This Crash Course video provides a brief overview of psychological research, which we'll cover in more detail on the coming pages.

- https://youtu.be/hFV71QPvX2I

Research Methods

We have just learned about some of the various models and objectives of research in lifespan development. Now we'll dig deeper to understand the methods and techniques used to describe, explain, or evaluate behavior.

All types of research methods have unique strengths and weaknesses, and each method may only be appropriate for certain types of research questions. For example, studies that rely primarily on observation produce incredible amounts of information, but the ability to apply this information to the larger population is somewhat limited because of small sample sizes. Survey research, on the other hand, allows researchers to easily collect data from relatively large samples. While this allows for results to be generalized to the larger population more easily, the information that can be collected on any given survey is somewhat limited and subject to problems associated with any type of self-reported data. Some researchers conduct archival research by using existing records. While this can be a fairly inexpensive way to collect data that can provide insight into a number of research questions, researchers using this approach have no control on how or what kind of data was collected.

Types of Descriptive Research

Observation

Observational studies, also called naturalistic observation, involve watching and recording the actions of participants. This may take place in the natural setting, such as observing children at play in a park, or behind a one-way glass while children are at play in a laboratory playroom. The researcher may follow a checklist and record the frequency and duration of events (perhaps how many conflicts occur among 2-year-olds) or may observe and record as much as possible about an event as a participant (such as attending an Alcoholics Anonymous meeting and recording the slogans on the walls, the structure of the meeting, the expressions commonly used, etc.). The researcher may be a participant or a non-participant. What would be the strengths of being a participant? What would be the weaknesses?

In general, observational studies have the strength of allowing the researcher to see how people behave rather than relying on self-report. One weakness of self-report studies is that what people do and what they say they do are often very different. A major weakness of observational studies is that they do not allow the researcher to explain causal relationships. Yet, observational studies are useful and widely used when studying children. It is important to remember that most people tend to change their behavior when they know they are being watched (known as the **Hawthorne effect**) and children may not survey well.

Case Studies

Case studies involve exploring a single case or situation in great detail. Information may be gathered with the use of observation, interviews, testing, or other methods to uncover as much as possible about a person or situation. Case studies are helpful when investigating unusual situations such as brain trauma or children reared in isolation. And they are often used by clinicians who conduct case studies as part of their normal practice when gathering information about a client or patient coming in for treatment. Case studies can be used to explore areas about which little is known and can provide rich detail about situations or conditions. However, the findings from case studies cannot be generalized or applied to larger populations; this is because cases are not randomly selected and no control group is used for comparison. (Read *The Man Who Mistook His Wife for a Hat* by Dr. Oliver Sacks as a good example of the case study approach.)

Surveys

Surveys are familiar to most people because they are so widely used. Surveys enhance accessibility to subjects because they can be conducted in person, over the phone, through the mail, or online. A survey involves asking a standard set of questions to a group of subjects. In a highly structured survey, subjects are forced to choose from a response set such as "strongly disagree, disagree, undecided, agree, strongly agree"; or "0, 1-5, 6-10, etc." Surveys are commonly used by sociologists, marketing researchers, political scientists, therapists, and others to gather information on many variables in a relatively short period of time. Surveys typically yield surface information on a wide variety of factors, but may not allow for an in-depth understanding of human behavior.

Figure 2. A survey is a common tool for collecting research data.

Of course, surveys can be designed in a number of ways. They may include forced-choice questions and semi-structured questions in which the researcher allows the respondent to describe or give details about certain events. One of the most difficult aspects of designing a good survey is wording questions in an unbiased way and asking the right questions so that respondents can give a clear response rather than choosing "undecided" each time. Knowing that 30% of respondents are undecided is of little use! So a lot of time and effort should be placed on the construction of survey items. One of the benefits of having forced-choice items is that each response is coded so that the results can be quickly entered and analyzed using statistical software. The analysis takes much longer when respondents give lengthy responses that must be analyzed in a different way. Surveys are useful in examining stated values, attitudes, opinions, and reporting on practices. However, they are based on self-report, or what people say they do rather than on observation, and this can limit accuracy. **Validity** refers to accuracy and **reliability** refers to consistency in responses to tests and other measures; great care is taken to ensure the validity and reliability of surveys.

WATCH IT

In this video, Harvard psychologist Dan Gilbert explains survey research that was conducted to explore the way our preferences change over time.

- https://youtu.be/XNbaR54Gpj4

Content Analysis

Content analysis involves looking at media such as old texts, pictures, commercials, lyrics or other materials to explore patterns or themes in culture. An example of content analysis is the classic history of childhood by Aries (1962) called "Centuries of Childhood" or the analysis of television commercials for sexual or violent content or for ageism. Passages in text or television programs can be randomly selected for analysis as well. Again, one advantage of analyzing work such as this is that the researcher does not have to go through the time and expense of finding respondents, but the researcher cannot know how accurately the media reflects the actions and sentiments of the population.

Secondary content analysis, or archival research, involves analyzing information that has already been collected or examining documents or media to uncover attitudes, practices or preferences. There are a number of data sets available to those who wish to conduct this type of research. The researcher conducting secondary analysis does not have to recruit subjects but does need to know the quality of the information collected in the original study. And unfortunately, the researcher is limited to the questions asked and data collected originally.

LINK TO LEARNING

U.S. Census Data is available and widely used to look at trends and changes taking place in the United States (visit the United States Census website and check it out). There are also a number of other agencies that collect data on family life, sexuality, and on many other areas of interest in human development (go to the NORC at the University of Chicago website or the Henry J Kaiser Family Foundation website and see what you find.).

Correlational and Experimental Research

Correlational Research

When scientists passively observe and measure phenomena it is called **correlational research**. Here, researchers do not intervene and change behavior, as they do in experiments. In correlational research, the goal is to identify patterns of relationships, but not cause and effect. Importantly, with correlational research, you can examine only two variables at a time, no more and no less.

So, what if you wanted to test whether spending money on others is related to happiness, but you don't have $20 to give to each participant in order to have them spend it for your experiment? You could use a correlational design—which is exactly what Professor Elizabeth Dunn (2008) at the University of British Columbia did when she conducted research on spending and happiness. She asked people how much of their income they spent on others or donated to charity, and later she asked them how happy they were. Do you think these two variables were related? Yes, they were! The more money people reported spending on others, the happier they were.

Understanding Correlation

To find out how well two variables correlate, you can plot the relationship between the two scores on what is known as a **scatterplot**. In the scatterplot, each dot represents a data point. (In this case it's individuals, but it could be some other unit.) Importantly, each dot provides us with two pieces of information—in this case, information about how good the person rated the past month (x-axis) and how happy the person felt in the past month (y-axis). Which variable is plotted on which axis does not matter.

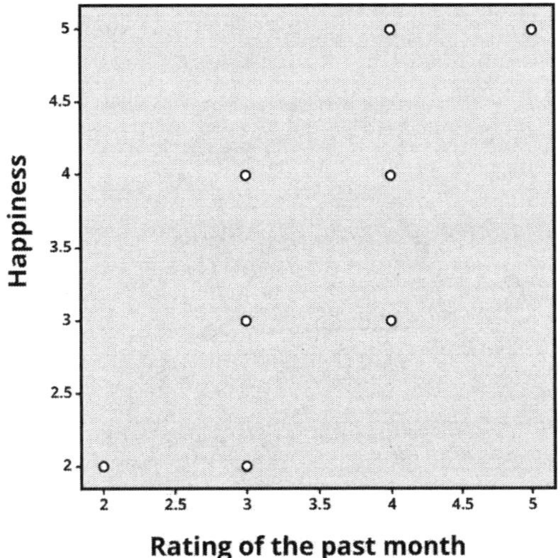

Figure 3. Scatterplot of the association between happiness and ratings of the past month, a positive correlation (r = .81). Each dot represents an individual.

The association between two variables can be summarized statistically using the **correlation coefficient** (abbreviated as r). A correlation coefficient provides information about the direction and strength of the association between two variables. For the example above, the direction of the association is positive. This means that people who perceived the past month as being good reported feeling more happy, whereas people who perceived the month as being bad reported feeling less happy.

With a **positive correlation**, the two variables go up or down together. In a scatterplot, the dots form a pattern that extends from the bottom left to the upper right (just as they do in Figure 1). The r value for a positive correlation is indicated by a positive number (although, the positive sign is usually omitted). Here, the r value is .81.

A **negative correlation** is one in which the two variables move in opposite directions. That is, as one variable goes up, the other goes down. Figure 2 shows the association between the average height of males in a country (y-axis) and the pathogen prevalence (or commonness of disease; x-axis) of that country. In this scatterplot, each dot represents a country. Notice how the dots extend from the top left to the bottom right. What does this mean in real-world terms? It means that people are shorter in parts of the world where there is more disease. The r value for a negative correlation is indicated by a negative number—that is, it has a minus (–) sign in front of it. Here, it is –.83.

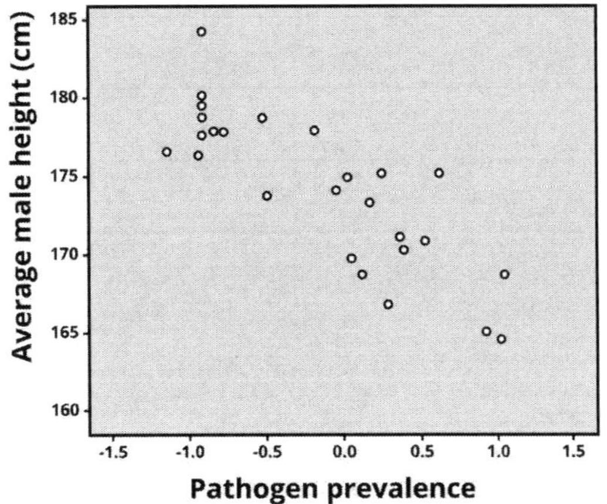

Figure 4. Scatterplot showing the association between average male height and pathogen prevalence, a negative correlation (r = –.83). Each dot represents a country (Chiao, 2009).

The strength of a correlation has to do with how well the two variables align. Recall that in Professor Dunn's correlational study, spending on others positively correlated with happiness; the more money people reported spending on others, the happier they reported to be. At this point you may be thinking to yourself, I know a very generous person who gave away lots of money to other people but is miserable! Or maybe you know of a very stingy person who is happy as can be. Yes, there might be exceptions. If an association has many exceptions, it is considered a weak correlation. If an association has few or no exceptions, it is considered a strong correlation. A strong correlation is one in which the two variables always, or almost always, go together. In the example of happiness and how good the month has been, the association is strong. The stronger a correlation is, the tighter the dots in the scatterplot will be arranged along a sloped line.

The r value of a strong correlation will have a high absolute value (a perfect correlation has an absolute value of the whole number one, or 1.00). In other words, you disregard whether there is a negative sign in front of the r value, and just consider the size of the numerical value itself. If the absolute value is large, it is a strong correlation. A weak correlation is one in which the two variables correspond some of the time, but not most of the time. Figure 3 shows the relation between valuing happiness and grade point average (GPA). People who valued happiness more tended to earn slightly lower grades, but there were lots of exceptions to this. The r value for a weak correlation will have a low absolute value. If two variables are so weakly related as to be unrelated, we say they are uncorrelated, and the r value will be zero or very close to zero. In the previous example, is the correlation between height and pathogen prevalence strong? Compared to Figure 3, the dots in Figure 2 are tighter and less dispersed. The absolute value of –.83 is large (closer to one than to zero). Therefore, it is a strong negative correlation.

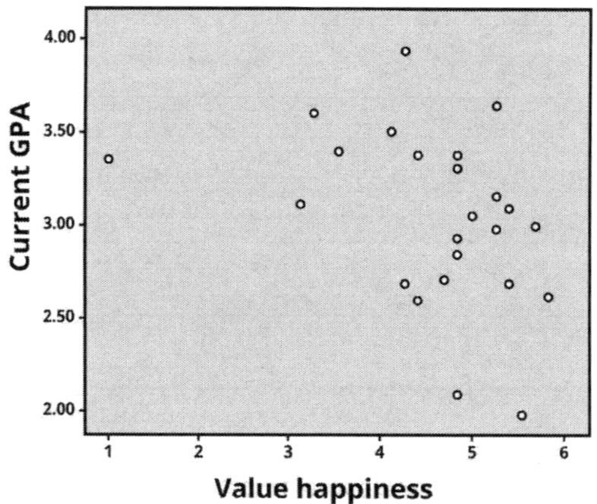

Figure 5. Scatterplot showing the association between valuing happiness and GPA, a weak negative correlation (r = –.32). Each dot represents an individual.

Problems with correlation

If generosity and happiness are positively correlated, should we conclude that being generous causes happiness? Similarly, if height and pathogen prevalence are negatively correlated, should we conclude that disease causes shortness? From a correlation alone, we can't be certain. For example, in the first case, it may be that happiness causes generosity, or that generosity causes happiness. Or, a third variable might cause both happiness and generosity, creating the illusion of a direct link between the two. For example, wealth could be the third variable that causes both greater happiness and greater generosity. This is why correlation does not mean causation—an often repeated phrase among psychologists.

WATCH IT

In this video, University of Pennsylvania psychologist and bestselling author, Angela Duckworth describes the correlational research that informed her understanding of grit.

- https://www.ted.com/talks/angela_lee_duckworth_grit_the_power_of_passion_and_perseverance/transcript

Experimental Research

Experiments are designed to test **hypotheses** (or specific statements about the relationship between **variables**) in a controlled setting in efforts to explain how certain factors or events produce outcomes. A variable is anything that changes in value. Concepts are **operationalized** or transformed into variables in research which means that the researcher must specify exactly what is going to be measured in the study. For example, if we are interested in studying marital satisfaction, we have to specify what marital satisfaction really means or what we are going to use as an indicator of marital satisfaction. What is something measurable that would indicate some level of marital satisfaction? Would it be the amount of time couples spend together each day? Or eye contact during a discussion about money? Or maybe a subject's score on a marital satisfaction scale? Each of these is measurable but these may not be equally valid or accurate indicators of marital satisfaction. What do you think? These are the kinds of considerations researchers must make when working through the design.

The experimental method is the only research method that can measure cause and effect relationships between variables. Three conditions must be met in order to establish cause and effect. Experimental designs are useful in meeting these conditions:

- *The independent and dependent variables must be related.* In other words, when one is altered, the other changes in response. The **independent variable** is something altered or introduced by the researcher; sometimes thought of as the treatment or intervention. The **dependent variable** is the outcome or the factor affected by the introduction of the independent variable; the dependent variable *depends* on the independent variable. For example, if we are looking at the impact of exercise on stress levels, the independent variable would be exercise; the dependent variable would be stress.
- *The cause must come before the effect.* Experiments measure subjects on the dependent variable before exposing them to the independent variable (establishing a baseline). So we would measure the subjects' level of stress before introducing exercise and then again after the exercise to see if there has been a change in stress levels. (Observational and survey research does not always allow us to look at the timing of these events which makes understanding causality problematic with these methods.)
- *The cause must be isolated.* The researcher must ensure that no outside, perhaps unknown variables, are actually causing the effect we see. The experimental design helps make this possible. In an experiment, we would make sure that our subjects' diets were held constant throughout the exercise program. Otherwise, the diet might really be creating a change in stress level rather than exercise.

A basic experimental design involves beginning with a sample (or subset of a population) and randomly assigning subjects to one of two groups: the **experimental group** or the **control group**. Ideally, to prevent bias, the participants would be blind to their condition (not aware of which group they are in) and the researchers would also be blind to each participant's condition (referred to as "**double blind**"). The experimental group is the group that is going to be exposed to an independent variable or condition the researcher is introducing as a potential cause of an event. The control group is going to be used for comparison and is going to have the same experience as the experimental group but will not be exposed to the independent variable. This helps address the placebo effect, which is that a group may expect changes to happen just by participating. After exposing the experimental group to the independent variable, the two groups are measured again to see if a change has occurred. If so, we are in a better position to suggest that the **independent variable** caused the change in the **dependent variable**. The basic experimental model looks like this:

Table 1. Variables and Experimental and Control Groups

Sample is randomly assigned to one of the groups below:	Measure DV	Introduce IV	Measure DV

Experimental Group	X	X	X
Control Group	X	–	X

The major advantage of the experimental design is that of helping to establish cause and effect relationships. A disadvantage of this design is the difficulty of translating much of what concerns us about human behavior into a laboratory setting.

LINK TO LEARNING

Have you ever wondered why people make decisions that seem to be in opposition to their longterm best interest? In Eldar Shafir's TED Talk Living Under Scarcity, Shafir describes a series of experiments that shed light on how scarcity (real or perceived) affects our decisions.

Developmental Research Designs

Now you know about some tools used to conduct research about human development. Remember, *research methods* are tools that are used to collect information. But it is easy to confuse research methods and research design. **Research design** is the strategy or blueprint for deciding how to collect and analyze information. Research design dictates which methods are used and how. Developmental research designs are techniques used particularly in lifespan development research. When we are trying to describe development and change, the research designs become especially important because we are interested in what changes and what stays the same with age. These techniques try to examine how age, cohort, gender, and social class impact development.

Cross-sectional designs

The majority of developmental studies use cross-sectional designs because they are less time-consuming and less expensive than other developmental designs. **Cross-sectional research** designs are used to examine behavior in participants of different ages who are tested at the same point in time. Let's suppose that researchers are interested in the relationship between intelligence and aging. They might have a hypothesis (an educated guess, based on theory or observations) that intelligence declines as people get older. The researchers might choose to give a certain intelligence test to individuals who are 20 years old, individuals who are 50 years old, and individuals who are 80 years old at the same time and compare the data from each age group. This research is cross-sectional in design because the researchers plan to examine the intelligence scores of individuals of different ages within the same study at the same time; they are taking a "cross-section" of people at one point in time. Let's say that the comparisons find that the 80-year-old adults score lower on the intelligence test than the 50-year-old adults, and the 50-year-old adults score lower on the intelligence test than the 20-year-old adults. Based on these data, the researchers might conclude that individuals become less intelligent as they get older. Would that be a valid (accurate) interpretation of the results?

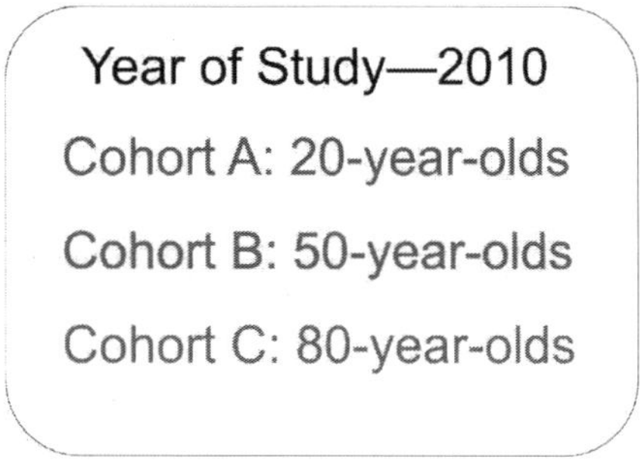

Year of Study—2010

Cohort A: 20-year-olds

Cohort B: 50-year-olds

Cohort C: 80-year-olds

Figure 6. Example of cross-sectional research design

No, that would not be a valid conclusion because the researchers did not follow individuals as they aged from 20 to 50 to 80 years old. One of the primary limitations of cross-sectional research is that the results yield information about age *differences* not necessarily *changes* with age or over time. That is, although the study described above can show that in 2010, the 80-year-olds scored lower on the intelligence test than the 50-year-olds, and the 50-year-olds scored lower on the intelligence test than the 20-year-olds, the data used to come up with this conclusion were collected from different individuals (or groups of individuals). It could be, for instance, that when these 20-year-olds get older (50 and eventually 80), they will still score just as high on the intelligence test as they did at age 20. In a similar way, maybe the 80-year-olds would have scored relatively low on the intelligence test even at ages 50 and 20; the researchers don't know for certain because they did not follow the same individuals as they got older.

It is also possible that the differences found between the age groups are not due to age, per se, but due to cohort effects. The 80-year-olds in this 2010 research grew up during a particular time and experienced certain events as a group. They were born in 1930 and are part of the Traditional or Silent Generation. The 50-year-olds were born in 1960 and are members of the Baby Boomer cohort. The 20-year-olds were born in 1990 and are part of the Millennial or Gen Y Generation. What kinds of things did each of these cohorts experience that the others did not experience or at least not in the same ways?

You may have come up with many differences between these cohorts' experiences, such as living through certain wars, political and social movements, economic conditions, advances in technology, changes in health and nutrition standards, etc. There may be particular cohort differences that could especially influence their performance on intelligence tests, such as education level and use of computers. That is, many of those born in 1930 probably did not complete high school; those born in 1960 may have high school degrees, on average, but the majority did not attain college degrees; the young adults are probably current college students. And this is not even considering additional factors such as gender, race, or socioeconomic status. The young adults are used to taking tests on computers, but the members of the other two cohorts did not grow up with computers and may not be as comfortable if the intelligence test is administered on computers. These factors could have been a factor in the research results.

Another disadvantage of cross-sectional research is that it is limited to one time of measurement. Data are collected at one point in time and it's possible that something could have happened in that year in history that affected all of the participants, although possibly each cohort may have been affected differently. Just think about the mindsets of participants in research that was conducted in the United States right after the terrorist attacks on September 11, 2001.

Longitudinal research designs

Longitudinal research involves beginning with a group of people who may be of the same age and background (cohort) and measuring them repeatedly over a long period of time. One of the benefits of this type of research is that people can be followed through time and be compared with themselves when they were younger; therefore changes with age over time are measured. What would be the advantages and disadvantages of longitudinal research? Problems with this type of research include being expensive, taking a long time, and subjects dropping out over time. Think about the film, *63 Up*, part of the Up Series mentioned earlier, which is an example of following individuals over time. In the videos, filmed every seven years, you see how people change physically, emotionally, and socially through time; and some remain the same in certain ways, too. But many of the participants really disliked being part of the project and repeatedly threatened to quit; one disappeared for several years; another died before her 63rd year. Would you want to be interviewed every seven years? Would you want to have it made public for all to watch?

Figure 7. Longitudinal research studies the same person or group of people over an extended period of time.

Longitudinal research designs are used to examine behavior in the same individuals over time. For instance, with our example of studying intelligence and aging, a researcher might conduct a longitudinal study to examine whether 20-year-olds become less intelligent with age over time. To this end, a researcher might give an intelligence test to individuals when they are 20 years old, again when they are 50 years old, and then again when they are 80 years old. This study is longitudinal in nature because the researcher plans to study the same individuals as they age. Based on these data, the pattern of intelligence and age might look different than from the cross-sectional research; it might be found that participants' intelligence scores are higher at age 50 than at age 20 and then remain stable or decline a little by age 80. How can that be when cross-sectional research revealed declines in intelligence with age?

Person A: 20 years old in 2010	Person A: 50 years old in 2040	Person A: 80 years old in 2070

Figure 8. Example of a longitudinal research design

Since longitudinal research happens over a period of time (which could be short term, as in months, but is often longer, as in years), there is a risk of attrition. **Attrition** occurs when participants fail to complete all portions of a study. Participants may move, change their phone numbers, die, or simply become disinterested in participating over time. Researchers should account for the possibility of attrition by enrolling a larger sample into their study initially, as some participants will likely drop out over time. There is also something known as **selective attrition**—this means that certain groups of individuals may tend to drop out. It is often the least healthy, least educated, and lower socioeconomic participants who tend to drop out over time. That means that the remaining participants may no longer be representative of the whole population, as they are, in general, healthier, better educated, and have more money. This could be a factor in why our hypothetical research found a more optimistic picture of intelligence and aging as the years went by. What can researchers do about selective attrition? At each time of testing, they could randomly recruit more participants from the same cohort as the original members, to replace those who have dropped out.

The results from longitudinal studies may also be impacted by repeated assessments. Consider how well you would do on a math test if you were given the exact same exam every day for a week. Your performance would likely improve over time, not necessarily because you developed better math abilities, but because you were continuously practicing the same math problems. This phenomenon is known as a practice effect. Practice effects occur when participants become better at a task over time because they have done it again and again (not due to natural psychological development). So our participants may have become familiar with the intelligence test each time (and with the computerized testing administration).

Another limitation of longitudinal research is that the data are limited to only one cohort. As an example, think about how comfortable the participants in the 2010 cohort of 20-year-olds are with computers. Since only one cohort is being studied, there is no way to know if findings would be different from other cohorts. In addition, changes that are found as individuals age over time could be due to age or to time of measurement effects. That is, the participants are tested at different periods in history, so the variables of age and time of measurement could be confounded (mixed up). For example, what if there is a major shift in workplace training and education between 2020 and 2040 and many of the participants experience a lot more formal education in adulthood, which positively impacts their intelligence scores in 2040? Researchers wouldn't know if the intelligence scores increased due to growing older or due to a more educated workforce over time between measurements.

Sequential research designs

Sequential research designs include elements of both longitudinal and cross-sectional research designs. Similar to longitudinal designs, sequential research features participants who are followed over time; similar to cross-sectional designs, sequential research includes participants of different ages. This research design is also distinct from those that have been discussed previously in that individuals of different ages are enrolled into a study at various points in time to examine age-related changes, development within the same individuals as they age, and to account for the possibility of cohort and/or time of measurement effects. In 1965, K. Warner Schaie[1] (a leading theorist and researcher on intelligence and aging),

1. Schaie, K.W. (1965). A general model for the study of developmental problems. Psychological Bulletin, 64(2), 92-107.

described particular sequential designs: cross-sequential, cohort sequential, and time-sequential. The differences between them depended on which variables were focused on for analyses of the data (data could be viewed in terms of multiple cross-sectional designs or multiple longitudinal designs or multiple cohort designs). Ideally, by comparing results from the different types of analyses, the effects of age, cohort, and time in history could be separated out.

Consider, once again, our example of intelligence and aging. In a study with a sequential design, a researcher might recruit three separate groups of participants (Groups A, B, and C). Group A would be recruited when they are 20 years old in 2010 and would be tested again when they are 50 and 80 years old in 2040 and 2070, respectively (similar in design to the longitudinal study described previously). Group B would be recruited when they are 20 years old in 2040 and would be tested again when they are 50 years old in 2070. Group C would be recruited when they are 20 years old in 2070 and so on.

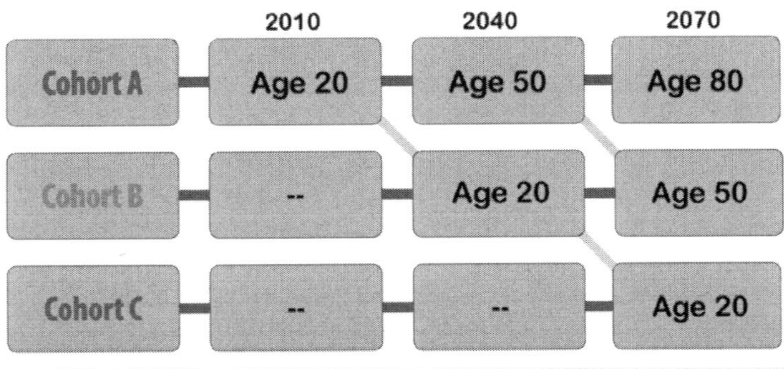

Figure 9. Example of sequential research design

Studies with sequential designs are powerful because they allow for both longitudinal and cross-sectional comparisons—changes and/or stability with age over time can be measured and compared with differences between age and cohort groups. This research design also allows for the examination of cohort and time of measurement effects. For example, the researcher could examine the intelligence scores of 20-year-olds in different times in history and different cohorts (follow the yellow diagonal lines in figure 3). This might be examined by researchers who are interested in sociocultural and historical changes (because we know that lifespan development is multidisciplinary). One way of looking at the usefulness of the various developmental research designs was described by Schaie and Baltes (1975)[2]: cross-sectional and longitudinal designs might reveal change patterns while sequential designs might identify developmental origins for the observed change patterns.

Since they include elements of longitudinal and cross-sectional designs, sequential research has many of the same strengths and limitations as these other approaches. For example, sequential work may require less time and effort than longitudinal research (if data are collected more frequently than over the 30-year spans in our example) but more time and effort than cross-sectional research. Although practice effects may be an issue if participants are asked to complete the same tasks or assessments over time, attrition may be less problematic than what is commonly experienced in longitudinal research since participants may not have to remain involved in the study for such a long period of time.

When considering the best research design to use in their research, scientists think about their main research question and the best way to come up with an answer. A table of advantages and disadvantages for each of the described research designs is provided here to help you as you consider what sorts of studies would be best conducted using each of these different approaches.

Table 2. Advantages and disadvantages of different research designs

	Advantages	Disadvantages

2. Schaie, K.W. & Baltes, B.P. (1975). On sequential strategies in developmental research: Description or Explanation. Human Development, 18: 384-390.

Cross-Sectional	• Examines changes between participants of different ages at the same point in time • Provides information on age differences	• Cannot examine change over time • Limited to one time in history • Cohort differences confounded with age differences
Longitudinal	• Examines changes within individuals over time • Provides a developmental analysis	• Expensive • Takes a long time • Participant attrition • Possibility of practice effects • Limited to one cohort • Time in history effects confounded with age changes
Sequential	• Examines changes within individuals over time • Examines changes between participants of different ages at the same point in time • Can be used to examine cohort effects • Can be used to examine time in history effects	• May be expensive • May take a long time • Possibility of practice effects • Some participant attrition

Challenges Conducting Developmental Research

Challenges Associated with Conducting Developmental Research

The previous sections describe research tools to assess development across the lifespan, as well as the ways that research designs can be used to track age-related changes and development over time. Before you begin conducting developmental research, however, you must also be aware that testing individuals of certain ages (such as infants and children) or making comparisons across ages (such as children compared to teens) comes with its own unique set of challenges. In the final section of this module, let's look at some of the main issues that are encountered when conducting developmental research, namely ethical concerns, recruitment issues, and participant attrition.

Ethical Concerns

As a student of the social sciences, you may already know that **Institutional Review Boards (IRBs)** must review and approve all research projects that are conducted at universities, hospitals, and other institutions (each broad discipline or field, such as psychology or social work, often has its own code of ethics that must also be followed, regardless of institutional affiliation). An IRB is typically a panel of experts who read and evaluate proposals for research. IRB members want to ensure that the proposed research will be carried out ethically and that the potential benefits of the research outweigh the risks and potential harm (psychological as well as physical harm) for participants.

What you may not know though, is that the IRB considers some groups of participants to be more vulnerable or at-risk than others. Whereas university students are generally not viewed as vulnerable or at-risk, infants and young children commonly fall into this category. What makes infants and young children more vulnerable during research than young adults? One reason infants and young children are perceived as being at increased risk is due to their limited cognitive capabilities, which makes them unable to state their willingness to participate in research or tell researchers when they would like to drop out of a study. For these reasons, infants and young children require special accommodations as they participate in the research process. Similar issues and accommodations would apply to adults who are deemed to be of limited cognitive capabilities.

When thinking about special accommodations in developmental research, consider the **informed consent** process. If you have ever participated in scientific research, you may know through your own experience that adults commonly sign an informed consent statement (a contract stating that they agree to participate in research) after learning about a study. As part of this process, participants are informed of the procedures to be used in the research, along with any expected risks or benefits. Infants and young children cannot verbally indicate their willingness to participate, much less understand the balance of potential risks and benefits. As such, researchers are oftentimes required to obtain written informed consent from the parent or legal guardian of the child participant, an adult who is almost always present as the study is conducted. In fact, children are not asked to indicate whether they would like to be involved in a study at all (a process known as assent) until they are approximately seven years old. Because infants and young children cannot easily indicate if they would like to discontinue their participation in a study, researchers must be sensitive to changes in the state of the participant (determining whether a child is too tired or upset to continue) as well as to parent desires (in some cases, parents might want to discontinue their involvement in the research). As in adult studies, researchers must always strive to protect the rights and well-being of the minor participants and their parents when conducting developmental research.

WATCH IT

This video from the US Department of Health and Human Services provides an overview of the Institutional Review Board process.

- https://youtu.be/U8fme1boEbE

Recruitment

An additional challenge in developmental science is participant recruitment. Recruiting university students to participate in adult studies is typically easy. Many colleges and universities offer extra credit for participation in research and have locations such as bulletin boards and school newspapers where research can be advertised. Unfortunately, young children cannot be recruited by making announcements in Introduction to Psychology courses, by posting ads on campuses, or through online platforms such as Amazon Mechanical Turk. Given these limitations, how do researchers go about finding infants and young children to be in their studies?

The answer to this question varies along multiple dimensions. Researchers must consider the number of participants they need and the financial resources available to them, among other things. Location may also be an important consideration. Researchers who need large numbers of infants and children may attempt to recruit them by obtaining infant birth records from the state, county, or province in which they reside. Some areas make this information publicly available for free, whereas birth records must be purchased in other areas (and in some locations birth records may be entirely unavailable as a recruitment tool). If birth records are available, researchers can use the obtained information to call families by phone or mail them letters describing possible research opportunities. All is not lost if this recruitment strategy is unavailable, however. Researchers can choose to pay a recruitment agency to contact and recruit families for them. Although these methods tend to be quick and effective, they can also be quite expensive. More economical recruitment options include posting advertisements and fliers in locations frequented by families, such as mommy-and-me classes, local malls, and preschools or daycare centers. Researchers can also utilize online social media outlets like Facebook, which allows users to post recruitment advertisements for a small fee. Of course, each of these different recruitment techniques requires IRB approval. And if children are recruited and/or tested in school settings, permission would need to be obtained ahead of time from teachers, schools, and school districts (as well as informed consent from parents or guardians).

And what about the recruitment of adults? While it is easy to recruit young college students to participate in research, some would argue that it is too easy and that college students are samples of convenience. They are not randomly selected from the wider population, and they may not represent all young adults in our society (this was particularly true in the past with certain cohorts, as college students tended to be mainly white males of high socioeconomic status). In fact, in the early research on aging, this type of convenience sample was compared with another type of convenience sample—young college students tended to be compared with residents of nursing homes! Fortunately, it didn't take long for researchers to realize that older adults in nursing homes are not representative of the older population; they tend to be the oldest and sickest (physically and/or psychologically). Those initial studies probably painted an overly negative view of aging, as young adults in college were being compared to older adults who were not healthy, had not been in school nor taken tests in many decades, and probably did not graduate high school, let alone college. As we can see, recruitment and random sampling can be significant issues in research with adults, as well as infants and children. For instance, how and where would you recruit middle-aged adults to participate in your research?

Attrition

Another important consideration when conducting research with infants and young children is **attrition**. Although attrition is quite common in longitudinal research in particular (see the previous section on longitudinal designs for an example of high attrition rates and selective attrition in lifespan developmental research), it is also problematic in developmental science more generally, as studies with infants and young children tend to have higher attrition rates than studies with adults. For example, high attrition rates in ERP (event-related potential, which is a technique to understand brain function) studies oftentimes result from the demands of the task: infants are required to sit still and have a tight, wet cap placed on their heads before watching still photographs on a computer screen in a dark, quiet room. In other cases, attrition may be due to motivation (or a lack thereof). Whereas adults may be motivated to participate in research in order to receive money or extra course credit, infants and young children are not as easily enticed. In addition, infants and young children are more likely to tire easily, become fussy, and lose interest in the study procedures than are adults. For these reasons, research studies should be designed to be as short as possible – it is likely better to break up a large study into multiple short sessions rather than cram all of the tasks into one long visit to the lab. Researchers should also allow time for breaks in their study protocols so that infants can rest or have snacks as needed. Happy, comfortable participants provide the best data.

Figure 10. Participating in developmental research can sometimes be difficult for both children and their parents. This can contribute to a higher attrition rate than is typical in other types of research. [Image: Tina Franklin, https://goo.gl/bN19Gm, CC BY 2.0, https://goo.gl/5YbMw6]

Conclusions

Lifespan development is a fascinating field of study – but care must be taken to ensure that researchers use appropriate methods to examine human behavior, use the correct experimental design to answer their questions, and be aware of the special challenges that are part-and-parcel of developmental research. After reading this module, you should have a solid understanding of these various issues and be ready to think more critically about research questions that interest you. For example, what types of questions do you have about lifespan development? What types of research would you like to conduct? Many interesting questions remain to be examined by future generations of developmental scientists – maybe you will make one of the next big discoveries!

GLOSSARY

attrition:
reduction in the number of research participants as some drop out over time

case study:
exploring a single case or situation in great detail. Information may be gathered with the use of observation, interviews, testing, or other methods to uncover as much as possible about a person or situation

content analysis:
involves looking at media such as old texts, pictures, commercials, lyrics or other materials to explore patterns or themes in culture

control group:
a comparison group that is equivalent to the experimental group, but is not given the independent variable

correlation:
the relationship between two or more variables; when two variables are correlated, one variable changes as the other does

correlational research:
research design with the goal of identifying patterns of relationships, but not cause and effect

correlation coefficient:
number from -1 to +1, indicating the strength and direction of the relationship between variables, and usually represented by r

cross-sectional research:
used to examine behavior in participants of different ages who are tested at the same point in time; may confound age and cohort differences

dependent variable:
the outcome or variable that is supposedly affected by the independent variable

descriptive studies:
research focused on describing an occurrence

double-blind:
a research design in which neither the participants nor the researchers know whether an individual is assigned to the experimental group or the control group

evaluation research:
research designed to assess the effectiveness of policies or programs

experimental group:
the group of participants in an experiment who receive the independent variable

experiments:
designed to test hypotheses in a controlled setting in efforts to explain how certain factors or events produce outcomes; the only research method that measures cause and effect relationships between variables

experimental research:
research that involves randomly assigning people to different conditions and using hypothesis testing to make inferences about how these conditions affect behavior; the only method that measures cause and effect between variables

explanatory studies:
research that tries to answer the question "why"

Hawthorne effect:
individuals tend to change their behavior when they know they are being watched

hypotheses:
specific statements or predictions about the relationship between variables

independent variable:
something that is manipulated or introduced by the researcher to the experimental group; treatment or intervention

informed consent:
a process of informing a research participant what to expect during a study, any risks involved, and the implications of the research, and then obtaining the person's agreement to participate

Institutional Review Boards (IRBs):
a panel of experts who review research proposals for any research to be conducted in association with the institution (for example, a university)

longitudinal research:
studying a group of people who may be of the same age and background (cohort), and measuring them repeatedly over a long period of time; may confound age and time of measurement effects

negative correlation:
two variables change in different directions, with one becoming larger as the other becomes smaller; a negative correlation is not the same thing as no correlation

observational studies:
also called naturalistic observation, involves watching and recording the actions of participants

operationalized:
concepts transformed into variables that can be measured in research

positive correlation:
two variables change in the same direction, both becoming either larger or smaller

qualitative research:
theoretical ideas are "grounded" in the experiences of the participants, who answer open-ended questions

quantitative research:
involves numerical data that are quantified using statistics to understand and report what has been studied

reliability:
when something yields consistent results

research design:
the strategy or blueprint for deciding how to collect and analyze information; dictates which methods are used and how

scatterplot:
a plot or mathematical diagram consisting of data points that represent two variables

secondary content analysis:
archival research, involves analyzing information that has already been collected or examining documents or media to uncover attitudes, practices or preferences

selective attrition:
certain groups of individuals may tend to drop out more frequently resulting in the remaining participants longer being representative of the whole population

sequential research design:
combines aspects of cross-sectional and longitudinal designs, but also adding new cohorts at different times of measurement; allows for analyses to consider effects of age, cohort, time of measurement, and socio-historical change

survey:
asking a standard set of questions to a group of subjects

validity:
when something yields accurate results

variables:
factors that change in value

Putting It Together: Lifespan Development

Lifespan development is the scientific study of how and why people change or remain the same over time. As we are beginning to see, lifespan development involves multiple domains and many ages and stages that are important in and of themselves, but that are also interdependent and dynamic and need to be viewed holistically. There are many influences on lifespan development at individual and societal levels (including genetics); cultural, generational, economic, and historical contexts are often significant. And how developmental research is designed and data are collected, analyzed, and interpreted can affect what is discovered about human development across the lifespan.

In this module, we mentioned the "Up" Series several times, which followed individuals beginning from age 7 on through, in the most recent program, age 63. What can we learn about lifespan development from the interviews conducted every seven years and depicted in the series? One analyst summarized the life lessons from the series as the following:

1. Life goes on.
2. Count your blessings.
3. Relationships matter—*a lot*.
4. Money also matters—but only up to a point.
5. Don't compare yourself to others.[1]

Would you agree or disagree with these conclusions? Why or why not? Keep in mind what you've learned about variables of culture, social class, time in history, cohort, and gender. Do you see examples of normative age-graded, normative history-graded, and nonnormative influences on the development in the "Up" Series? How much have the individuals changed and how much have they stayed the same? Has social class defined them and the trajectories of their lives? If you were to conduct your own longitudinal research, what would you aim to discover? Keep these questions in mind as we continue to dig deeper into the study of the lifespan.

1. Smith, J.A. (2013, March 9). Five life lessons from "56 Up." Greater Good Magazine.

Discussion: Life Stages

DISCUSSION: In this discussion, reflect upon and discuss ALL THREE of the following questions:

- Q1: What prompted you to take this class? Please introduce yourself to your classmates.
- Q2: What stage of human development are you currently in and what are your main challenges/activities? What would you consider the best time of life? Why?
- Q2: If you were to choose an age group to work with, which one would it be and why? Are there any age groups you would not want to work with? Why not?

STEP 1: First, write a response with at least EIGHT substantial sentences, integrating concepts you learned from the reading and other materials (include links with necessary). Show that you can think critically on the topic by integrating your own thoughts, analysis, or experiences.

STEP 2: Return to the discussion forum to comment on at least TWO classmates' posts (in at least FIVE sentences). Expand on a classmate's comments in a value-adding, topic-related way. Promote a collaborative, supportive community, and advance the dialogue through follow-up questions. Reply posts cannot be one-liners, off-topic posts, vague statements, unsupported opinions, inadequate explanations or simply say, "I agree" or "good job."

MODULE 2: DEVELOPMENTAL THEORIES

Why It Matters: Developmental Theories

Why describe the major developmental theories in lifespan development?

Figure 1. Child labor in Indiana glassworks. (Hine, 1908) Society's view of childhood has changed through the ages. Many children in the early 1900's worked full time in mines.

Childhood as a concept first emerged around the 17th century. In 1960, Philippe Ariès wrote a book called *L'Enfant et la Vie Familiale sous l'Ancien Régime* (1960), which was translated into English as *Centuries of Childhood* (1962). The book was significant both in that it recognized childhood as a social construction rather than as a biological given and in so doing, it founded the history of childhood as a serious field of study.

Ariès argued that childhood was not understood as a separate stage of life until the 15th century, and children were seen as little adults who shared the same traditions, games, and clothes. He said that parenting during the Middle Ages was largely detached, and there were not nuclear family bonds of love and concern. His account of childhood has since been widely criticized, but even today, Ariès remains the standard reference to the topic. He is most famous for his statement that "in medieval society, the idea of childhood did not exist".

Attitudes towards children have evolved over time along with economic change and social advancement. Before the 17th century, children were generally considered weaker, more insignificant versions of adults. They were were assumed to be subject to the same needs and desires as adults, and to have the same vices and virtues as adults. Therefore they dressed the same, were not warranted more privileges, and they worked the same hours and received the same punishments for misdeeds. If they stole, they were hanged. If they worked hard and did well, they could achieve prosperity. Children were considered adults as soon as they could live alone.

At the time, this was society's view of lifespan development. The only difference between children and adults was size. We now reject this medieval view, but how do we go about formulating contemporary theories? Our own personal theories about development are based on experiences, folklore, stories in the media, or built haphazardly on unverified observation. However, theories presented in this course are more formal. They are based on prior findings and observations by psychologists and other researchers, and provide a framework through which we can draw conclusions and make predictions about human behavior. These theories are subject to rigorous testing though research. In this module, we'll discuss the major theoretical perspectives and theories that pertain to lifespan development. Each perspective emphasizes a different aspect of development and is just one means of studying the ever-evolving discipline of lifespan development. First we'll examine the major characteristics of the psychodynamic, behavioral, and cognitive perspectives and then turn to the humanistic, contextual, and evolutionary approaches.[1]

1. Thomas, R. M. (2001). Recent theories of human development Thousand Oaks, CA: SAGE Publications, Inc. doi: 10.4135/9781452233673

Psychodynamic Theories

What you'll learn to do: use psychodynamic theories (like those from Freud and Erikson) to explain development

Many people sometimes feel intimidated by theory; even the phrase, "Now we are going to look at some theories..." may elicit some blank stares or yawns. But, don't tune out quite yet! Theories are valuable tools for understanding human behavior; they are proposed explanations for the "how" and "whys" of development. In this first section, we'll examine some of the most persistent theories, developed by Sigmund Freud over a hundred years ago. While some of Freud's ideas have since been debunked, others have lasted and continue to shape the way we think about development.

LEARNING OUTCOMES

- Describe theories as they relate to lifespan development
- Describe the historical foundations leading to the development of theories about lifespan development
- Describe Freud's theory of psychosexual development
- Describe Erikson's eight stages of psychosocial development

Understanding Theories

A theory guides and helps us interpret research findings as well. It provides the researcher with a blueprint or model to be used to help piece together various studies. Think of theories are guidelines much like directions that come with an appliance or other object that required assembly. The instructions can help one piece together smaller parts more easily than if trial and error are used.

Theories can be developed using induction in which a number of single cases are observed and after patterns or similarities are noted, the theorist develops ideas based on these examples. Established theories are then tested through research; however, not all theories are equally suited to scientific investigation. Some theories are difficult to test but are still useful in stimulating debate or providing concepts that have practical application. Keep in mind that theories are not facts; they are guidelines for investigation and practice, and they gain credibility through research that fails to disprove them.

What is a theory?

In lifespan development, we need to relying on a systematic approach to understanding behavior, based on observable events and the scientific method. There are so many different observations about childhood, adulthood, and development in general that we use theories to help organize all of the different observable events or variables. A theory is a simplified explanation of the world that attempts to explain how variables interact with each other. It can take complex, interconnected issues and narrow it down to the essentials. This enables developmental theorists and researchers to analyze the problem in greater depth.

Two key concepts in the scientific approach are theory and hypothesis. A **theory** is a well-developed set of ideas that propose an explanation for observed phenomena that can be used to make predictions about future observations. A **hypothesis** is a testable prediction that is arrived at logically from a theory. It is often worded as an if-then statement (e.g., if I study all night, I will get a passing grade on the test). The hypothesis is extremely important because it bridges the gap between the realm of ideas and the real world. As specific hypotheses are tested, theories are modified and refined to reflect and incorporate the result of these tests. In essence, lifespan theories explain observable events in a meaningful way. They are not as specific as hypotheses, which are so specific that we use them to make predictions in research. Theories offer more general explanations about behavior and events.

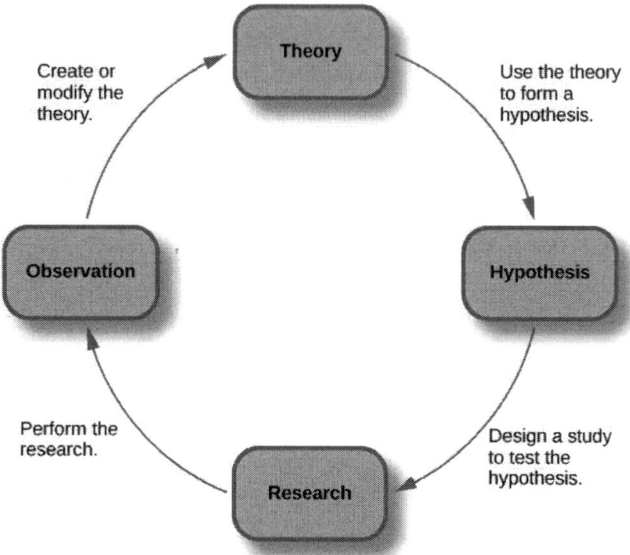

Figure 1. Theories are often revisited and tested through experiments and research.

Think of theories are guidelines much like directions that come with an appliance or other object that required assembly. The instructions can help one piece together smaller parts more easily than if trial and error are used.

Theories can be developed using induction, in which a number of single cases are observed and after patterns or similarities are noted, the theorist develops ideas based on these examples. Established theories are then tested through research; however, not all theories are equally suited to scientific investigation. Some theories are difficult to test but are still useful in stimulating debate or providing concepts that have practical application. Keep in mind that theories are not facts; they are guidelines for investigation and practice, and they gain credibility through research that fails to disprove them.

People who study lifespan development approach the it from different perspectives. Each perspective encompasses one or more theories—the broad, organized explanations and predictions concerning phenomena of interest. Theories of development provide a framework for thinking about human growth, development, and learning. If you have ever wondered about what motivates human thought and behavior, understanding these theories can provide useful insight into individuals and society.

Throughout psychological history and still in present day, three key issues remain among which developmental theorists often disagree. Particularly oft-disputed is the role of early experiences on later development in opposition to current behavior reflecting present experiences–namely the *passive verses active issue*. Likewise, whether or not development is best viewed as occurring in stages or rather as a gradual and cumulative process of change has traditionally been up for debate – a question of *continuity versus discontinuity.* Further, the role of heredity and the environment in shaping human development is a much contested topic of discussion – also referred to as *nature/nurture debate*. We'll examine each of these issues in more detail throughout the course.

History of Developmental Psychology

Figure 2. Some major players in the early development of psychology. Front row: Sigmund Freud, G. Stanley Hall, Carl Jung. Back row: Abraham A. Brill, Ernest Jones, Sándor Ferenczi, at: Clark University in Worcester, Massachusetts. Date: September 1909.

The scientific study of children began in the late nineteenth century, and blossomed in the early twentieth century as pioneering psychologists sought to uncover the secrets of human behavior by studying its development. Developmental psychology made an early appearance in a more literary form, however. William Shakespeare had his melancholy character, "Jacques" (in As You Like It), articulate the "seven ages of man," which included three stages of childhood and four of adulthood.

Three early scholars, John Locke, Jean-Jacques Rousseau, and Charles Darwin proposed theories of human behavior that are the "direct ancestors of the three major theoretical traditions" of developmental psychology today(Vasta et al, 1998, p. 10). Locke, a British empiricist, adhered to a strict environmentalist position, that the mind of the newborn as a tabula rasa ("blank slate") on which knowledge is written through experience and learning. Rousseau, a Swiss philosopher who spent much of his life in France, proposed a nativistic model in his famous novel *Emile*, in which development occurs according to innate processes progressing through three stages: Infans (infancy), puer (childhood), and adolescence. Rousseau detailed some of the necessary progression through these stages in order to develop into an ideal citizen. Although some aspects of his text were controversial, Rousseau's ideas were strongly influential on educators at the time. Finally, the work of Darwin, the British biologist famous for his theory of evolution, led others to suggest that development proceeds through evolutionary recapitulation, with many human behaviors having their origins in successful adaptations in the past as "ontogeny recapitulates phylogeny."

G. Stanley Hall

Darwin's theories greatly influenced G. Stanley Hall, who believed that children developed over their lifetime much in the same way that a species evolved throughout time. His interests focused on childhood development, adolescence, and evolutionary theory. His major contributions to the field are that he taught the first courses in child development, several of his students becoming leading researchers in the field, and he established scientific journals for the publication of child development research. He was also the first president of the American Psychological Association.

James Mark Baldwin

Another early contributor to the study of development was James Mark Baldwin (1861-1934), a Princeton educated American philosopher and psychologist who did quantitative and experimental research on infant development. He made important contributions to early psychology, psychiatry, and to the theory of evolution. Baldwin wrote essays such as "Mental Development in the Child and the Race: Methods and Processes", which made a vivid impression on Jean Piaget (who later developed the most popular theory of cognitive development) and Lawrence Kohlberg (who developed a theory about moral judgment and development).

John B. Watson

The 20th century marked the formation of qualitative distinctions between children and adults. When John Watson wrote the book *Psychological Care of Infant and Child* in 1928, he sought to add clarification surrounding behaviorists views on child care and development. Watson was the founder of the field of behaviorism, which emphasized the role of nurture, or the environment, in human development. He believed, based on Locke's environmentalist position, that human behavior can be understood in terms of experiences and learning. He believed that all behaviors are learned, or conditioned, as evidenced by his famous "Little Albert" study, in which he conditioned an infant to fear a white rat. In Watson's book on care of the infant and child, Watson explained that children should be treated as a young adult—with respect, but also without emotional attachment.

In the book, he warned against the inevitable dangers of a mother providing too much love and affection. Watson explained that love, along with everything else as the behaviorist saw the world, is conditioned. Watson supported his warnings by mentioning invalidism, saying that society does not overly comfort children as they become young adults in the real world, so parents should not set up these unrealistic expectations. His book (obviously) became highly criticized, but was still influential in promoting more research into early childhood behavior and development.

Sigmund Freud

Another name you are probably familiar with who was influential in the study human development is Sigmund Freud. Sigmund Freud's model of "psychosexual development" grew out of his psychoanalytic approach to human personality and psychopathology. In sharp contrast to the objective approach espoused by Watson, Freud based his model of child development on his own and his patients' recollections of their childhood. He developed a stage model of development in which the libido, or sexual energy, of the child focuses on different "zones" or areas of the body as the child grows to adulthood. Freud's model is an "interactionist" one, since he believed that although the sequence and timing of these stages is biologically determined, successful personality development depends on the experiences the child has during each stage. Although the details of Freud's developmental theory have been widely criticized, his emphasis on the importance of early childhood experiences, prior to five years of age, has had a lasting impact.

Arnold Gesell

Arnold Gesell, a student of G. Stanley Hall, carried out the first large-scale detailed study of children's behavior, authoring several books on the topic in the 1920s, 30s, and 40s. His research revealed consistent patterns of development, supporting his view that human development depends on biological "maturation," with the environment providing only minor variations in the age at which a skill might emerge but never affecting the sequence or pattern. Gesell's research produced norms, such as the order and the normal age range in which a variety of early behaviors such as sitting, crawling, and walking emerge. In conducting his studies, Gesell developed sophisticated observational techniques, including one-way viewing screens and recording methods that did not disturb the child.

Jean Piaget

Jean Piaget (1896-1980) is considered one of the most influential psychologists of the twentieth century, and his stage theory of cognitive development revolutionized our view of children's thinking and learning. His work inspired more research than any other theorist, and many of his concepts are still foundational to developmental psychology. His interest lay in children's knowledge, their thinking, and the qualitative differences in their thinking as it develops. Although he called his field "genetic epistemology," stressing the role of biological determinism, he also assigned great importance to experience. In his view, children "construct" their knowledge through processes of "assimilation," in which they evaluate and try to understand new information, based on their existing knowledge of the world, and "accommodation," in which they expand and modify their cognitive structures based on new experiences.

Modern developmental psychology generally focuses on how and why certain modifications throughout an individual's life-cycle (cognitive, social, intellectual, personality) and human growth change over time. There are many theorists that have made, and continue to make, a profound contribution to this area of psychology, amongst whom is Erik Erikson who developed a model of eight stages of psychological development. He believed that humans developed in stages throughout their lifetimes and this would affect their behaviors. In this module, we'll examine some of these major theories and contributions made my prominent psychologists.

Psychodynamic Theory

The Psychodynamic Perspective: A Focus on the Inner Person

Freud and Psychoanalysis

Figure 3. Sigmund Freud.

We begin with Sigmund Freud, one of the most well-known pioneers and early founders of psychology who has been a very influential figure in the area of development. His **psychodynamic perspective** of development and psychopathology dominated the field of psychiatry until the growth of behaviorism in the 1930s and beyond. His assumptions that personality forms during the first few years of life and that the ways in which parents or other caregivers interact with children have a long-lasting impact on children's emotional states have guided parents, educators, clinicians, and policy-makers for many years. We have only recently begun to recognize that early childhood experiences do not always result in certain personality traits or emotional states. There is a growing body of literature addressing resiliency in children who come from harsh backgrounds and yet develop without damaging emotional scars (O'Grady and Metz, 1987). Freud stimulated an enormous amount of research and generated many ideas. Agreeing with Freud's theory in its entirety is hardly necessary for appreciating the contribution he has made to the field of development.

Background

Sigmund Freud (1856-1939) was a Viennese doctor who was trained in neurology and asked to work with patients suffering from hysteria, a conditioned marked my uncontrollable emotional outbursts, fears, and anxiety that had puzzled physicians for centuries. He was also asked to work with women who suffered from physical symptoms and forms of paralysis which had no organic causes. During that time, many people believed that certain individuals were genetically inferior and thus more susceptible to mental illness. Women were thought to be genetically inferior and thus prone to illnesses such as hysteria, which had previously been attributed to a detached womb traveling around in the body (the word "hyster" means "uterus" in Greek).

However, after World War I, many soldiers came home with problems similar to hysteria. This called into questions the idea of genetic inferiority as a cause of mental illness. Freud began working with hysterical patients and discovered that when they began to talk about some of their life experiences, particularly those that took place in early childhood, their symptoms disappeared. This led him to suggest the first purely psychological explanation for physical problems and mental illness. What he proposed was that unconscious motives, desires, fears, and anxieties drive our actions. When upsetting memories or thoughts begin to find their way into our consciousness, we develop defenses to shield us from these painful realities, called defense mechanisms. Freud believed that many mental illnesses are a result of a person's inability to accept reality.

Freud emphasized the importance of early childhood experiences in shaping our personality and behavior. In our natural state, we are biological beings. We are driven primarily by instincts. During childhood, however, we begin to become social beings as we learn how to manage our instincts and transform them into socially acceptable behaviors. The type of parenting the child receives has a very powerful impact on the child's personality development. We will explore this idea further in our discussion of psychosexual development, but first, we must identify the parts of the "self" in Freud's model, or in other words, what constitutes a person's personality and makes us who we are.

Theory of Personality/Self

As adults, our personality or self consists of three main parts: the **id**, the **ego,** and the **superego**. The id, the basic, primal part of the personality, is the part of the self with which we are born. It consists of the biologically-driven self and includes our instincts and drives. It is the part of us that wants immediate gratification. Later in life, it comes to house our deepest, often unacceptable desires, such as sex and aggression. It operates under the pleasure principle which means that the criteria for determining whether something is good or bad is whether it feels good or bad. An infant is all id.

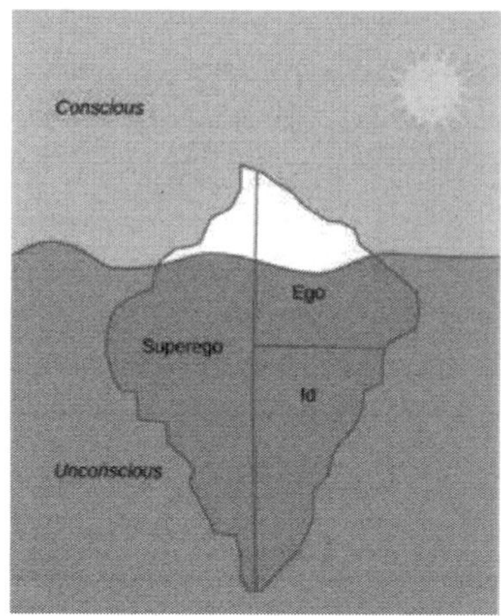

Figure 4. According to Freud's model of the psyche, the id is the primitive and instinctual part of the mind that contains sexual and aggressive drives and hidden memories, the superego operates as a moral conscience, and the ego is the realistic part that mediates between the desires of the id and the superego.

Next, the ego begins to develop during the first three years of a child's life. Finally, the superego. The superego**,** the last component of personality to develop, starts to emerge around the age of five when a child interacts more and more with others, learning the social rules for right and wrong. The superego acts as our conscience; it is our moral compass that tells us how we should behave. It strives for perfection and judges our behavior, leading to feelings of pride or—when we fall short of the ideal—feelings of guilt.

In contrast to the instinctual id and the rule-based superego, the ego is the rational part of our personality. It's what Freud considered to be the self, and it is the part of our personality that is seen by others. Its job is to balance the demands of the id and superego in the context of reality; thus, it operates on what Freud called the "reality principle." The ego helps the id satisfy its desires in a realistic way.

The id and superego are in constant conflict because the id wants instant gratification regardless of the consequences, but the superego tells us that we must behave in socially acceptable ways. Thus, the ego's job is to find the middle ground. It helps satisfy the id's desires in a rational way that will not lead us to feelings of guilt. According to Freud, a person who has a strong ego, which can balance the demands of the id and the superego, has a healthy personality. Freud maintained that imbalances in the system can lead to **neurosis** (a tendency to experience negative emotions), anxiety disorders, or unhealthy behaviors. For example, a person who is dominated by their id might be narcissistic and impulsive. A person with a dominant superego might be controlled by feelings of guilt and deny themselves even socially acceptable pleasures; conversely, if the superego is weak or absent, a person might become a psychopath. An overly dominant superego might be seen in an over-controlled individual whose rational grasp on reality is so strong that they are unaware of their emotional needs, or, in a neurotic who is overly defensive (overusing ego defense mechanisms).

Theory of Psychosexual Development

Freud believed that personality develops during early childhood and that childhood experiences shape our personalities as well as our behavior as adults. He asserted that we develop via a series of stages during childhood. Each of us must pass through these childhood stages, and if we do not have the proper nurturing and parenting during a stage, we will be stuck, or fixated, in that stage even as adults.

In each **psychosexual stage** of development, the child's pleasure-seeking urges, coming from the id, are focused on a different area of the body, called an erogenous zone. The stages are oral, anal, phallic, latency, and genital (Table 1).

Table 1. Freud's Stages of Psychosexual Development

Stage	Age (years)	Erogenous Zone	Major Conflict	Adult Fixation Example
Oral	0–1	Mouth	Weaning off breast or bottle	Smoking, overeating
Anal	1–3	Anus	Toilet training	Neatness, messiness
Phallic	3–6	Genitals	Oedipus/Electra complex	Vanity, overambition

Stage	Age (years)	Erogenous Zone	Major Conflict	Adult Fixation Example
Latency	6–12	None	None	None
Genital	12+	Genitals	None	None

For about the first year of life, the infant is in the **oral stage** of psychosexual development. The infant meets needs primarily through oral gratification. A baby wishes to suck or chew on any object that comes close to the mouth. Babies explore the world through the mouth and find comfort and stimulation as well. Psychologically, the infant is all id. The infant seeks immediate gratification of needs such as comfort, warmth, food, and stimulation. If the caregiver meets oral needs consistently, the child will move away from this stage and progress further. However, if the caregiver is inconsistent or neglectful, the person may stay stuck in the oral stage. As an adult, the person might not feel good unless involved in some oral activity such as eating, drinking, smoking, nail-biting, or compulsive talking. These actions bring comfort and security when the person feels insecure, afraid, or bored.

During the **anal stage**, which coincides with toddlerhood and potty-training, the child is taught that some urges must be contained and some actions postponed. There are rules about certain functions and when and where they are to be carried out. The child is learning a sense of self-control. The ego is being developed. If the caregiver is extremely controlling about potty training (stands over the child waiting for the smallest indication that the child might need to go to the potty and immediately scoops the child up and places him on the potty chair, for example), the child may grow up fearing losing control. He may become fixated in this stage or "anally retentive"—fearful of letting go. Such a person might be extremely neat and clean, organized, reliable, and controlling of others. If the caregiver neglects to teach the child to control urges, he may grow up to be "anal expulsive" or an adult who is messy, irresponsible, and disorganized.

The **phallic stage** occurs during the preschool years (ages 3-5) when the child has a new biological challenge to face. The child will experience the Oedipus complex which refers to a child's unconscious sexual desire for the opposite-sex parent and hatred for the same-sex parent. For example, boys experiencing the Oedipus complex will unconsciously want to replace their father as a companion to their mother but then realize that the father is much more powerful. For a while, the boy fears that if he pursues his mother, his father may castrate him (castration anxiety). So rather than risk losing his penis, he gives up his affections for his mother and instead learns to become more like his father, imitating his actions and mannerisms, thereby learning the role of males in his society. From this experience, the boy learns a sense of masculinity. He also learns what society thinks he should do and experiences guilt if he does not comply. In this way, the superego develops. If he does not resolve this successfully, he may become a "phallic male" or a man who constantly tries to prove his masculinity (about which he is insecure), by seducing women and beating up men.

Girls experience a comparable conflict in the phallic stage—the Electra complex. The Electra complex, while often attributed to Freud, was actually proposed by Freud's contemporary, Carl Jung (Jung & Kerenyi, 1963). A little girl experiences the Electra complex in which she develops an attraction for her father but realizes that she cannot compete with her mother and so gives up that affection and learns to become more like her mother. This is not without some regret, however. Freud believed that the girl feels inferior because she does not have a penis (experiences "penis envy"). But she must resign herself to the fact that she is female and will just have to learn her inferior role in society as a female. However, if she does not resolve this conflict successfully, she may have a weak sense of femininity and grow up to be a "castrating female" who tries to compete with men in the workplace or in other areas of life. The formation of the superego takes place during the dissolution of the Oedipus and Electra complex.

During middle childhood (6-11), the child enters the **latency stage,** focusing their attention outside the family and toward friendships. The biological drives are temporarily quieted (latent) and the child can direct attention to a larger world of friends. If the child is able to make friends, they will gain a sense of confidence. If not, the child may continue to be a loner or shy away from others, even as an adult.

The final stage of psychosexual development is referred to as the **genital stage**. From adolescence throughout adulthood, a person is preoccupied with sex and reproduction. The adolescent experiences rising hormone levels and the sex drive and hunger drives become very strong. Ideally, the adolescent will rely on the ego to help think logically through these urges without taking actions that might be damaging. An adolescent might learn to redirect their sexual urges into a safer activity such as running, for example. Quieting the id with the superego can lead to feeling overly self-conscious and guilty about these urges. Hopefully, it is the ego that is strengthened during this stage and the adolescent uses reason to manage urges.

Freud's psychosexual development theory is quite controversial. To understand the origins of the theory, it is helpful to be familiar with the political, social, and cultural influences of Freud's day in Vienna at the turn of the 20th century. During this era, a climate of sexual repression, combined with limited understanding and education surrounding human sexuality heavily influenced Freud's perspective. Given that sex was a taboo topic, Freud assumed that negative emotional states (neuroses) stemmed from the suppression of unconscious sexual and aggressive urges. For Freud, his own recollections and interpretations of patients' experiences and dreams were sufficient proof that psychosexual stages were universal events in early childhood.

WATCH IT

Watch this video to better understand Freud's theory of psychosexual development.

- https://youtu.be/hsie2EuNCNI

Defense mechanisms

Freud believed that feelings of anxiety result from the ego's inability to mediate the conflict between the id and superego. When this happens, Freud believed that the ego seeks to restore balance through various protective measures known as **defense mechanisms**. When certain events, feelings, or yearnings cause anxiety, the individual wishes to reduce that anxiety. To do that, the individual's unconscious mind uses ego defense mechanisms, unconscious protective behaviors that aim to reduce anxiety. The ego, usually conscious, resorts to unconscious strivings to protect the ego from being overwhelmed by anxiety. When we use defense mechanisms, we are unaware that we are using them. Further, they operate in various ways that distort reality. According to Freud, we all use ego defense mechanisms.

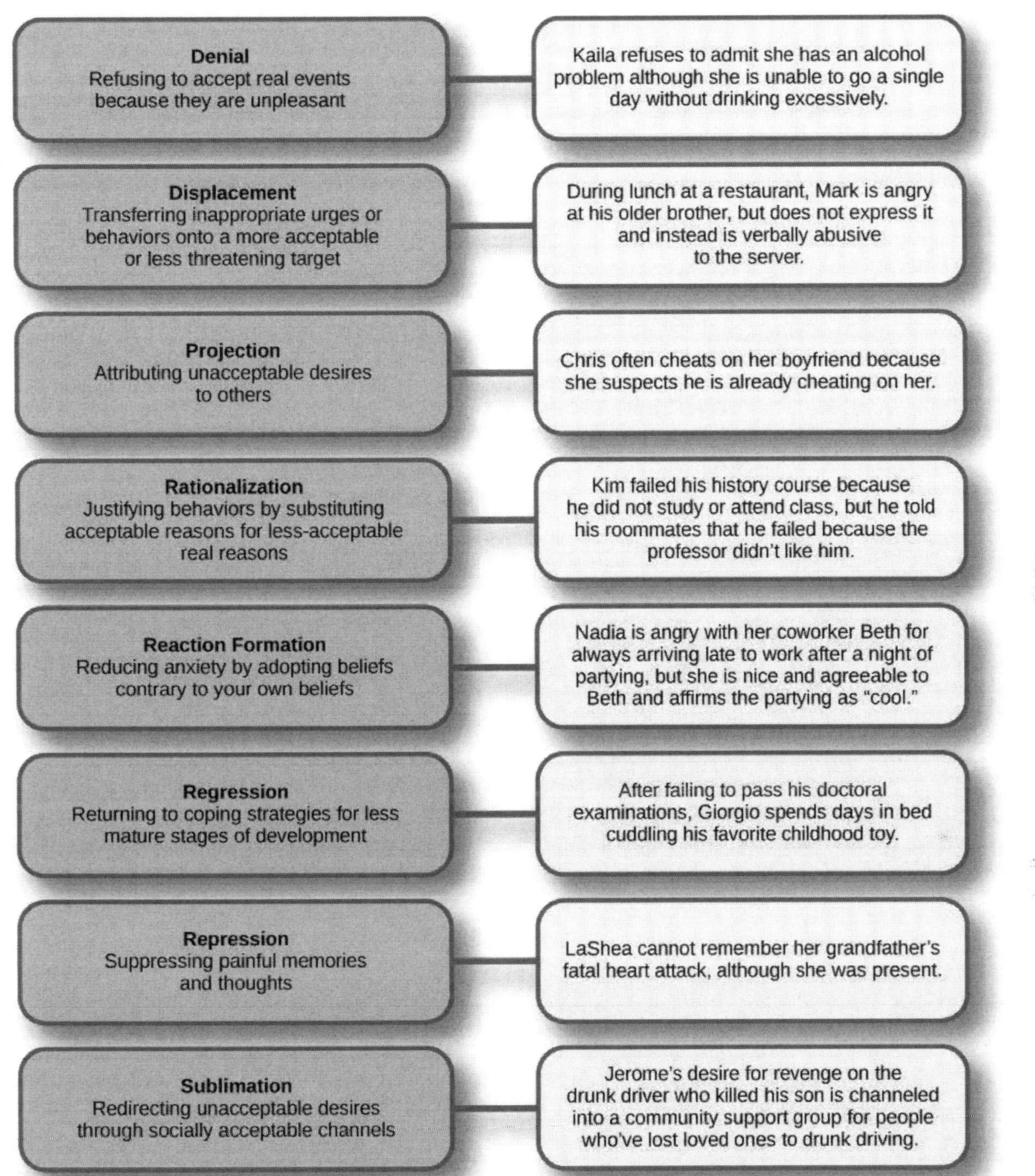

Figure 5. Defense mechanisms are unconscious protective behaviors that work to reduce anxiety.

Defense mechanisms emerge to help a person distort reality so that the truth is less painful. Defense mechanisms include:

- **Denial—**not accepting the truth or lying to oneself. Thoughts such as "it won't happen to me" or "you're not leaving" or "I don't have a problem with alcohol" are examples.
- **Displacement—**taking out frustrations on a safer target. A person who is angry at a boss may take out their frustration at others when driving home or at a spouse upon arrival.
- **Projection—**a defense mechanism in which a person attributes their unacceptable thoughts onto others. If someone is frightened, for example, they accuse someone else of being afraid.

- **Rationalization—**a defense mechanism proposed by Anna Freud (Freud's daughter who continued in her father's path of psychoanalysis). Rationalization involves a cognitive distortion of "the facts" to make an event or an impulse less threatening. We often do it on a fairly conscious level when we provide ourselves with excuses.
- **Reaction formation—**a defense mechanism in which a person outwardly opposes something they inwardly desire, but that they find unacceptable. An example of this might be someone who dislikes or fears people of another race acting overly nice to people of that race.
- **Regression—**going back to a time when the world felt like a safer place, perhaps reverting to one's childhood behaviors.
- **Repression—**to push the painful thoughts out of consciousness (in other words, think about something else).
- **Sublimation—**transforming unacceptable urges into more socially acceptable behaviors. For example, a teenager who experiences strong sexual urges uses exercise to redirect those urges into more socially acceptable behavior.

WATCH IT

This video explains more about each of the defense mechanisms.

- https://youtu.be/v80Nd8w1uts

Assessing the Psychodynamic Perspective

Originating in the work of Sigmund Freud, the psychodynamic perspective emphasizes unconscious psychological processes (for example, wishes and fears of which we're not fully aware), and contends that childhood experiences are crucial in shaping adult personality. When reading Freud's theories, it is important to remember that he was a medical doctor, not a psychologist. There was no such thing as a degree in psychology at the time that he received his education, which can help us understand some of the controversies over his theories today. However, Freud was the first to systematically study and theorize the workings of the unconscious mind in the manner that we associate with modern psychology. The psychodynamic perspective has evolved considerably since Freud's time, encompassing all the theories in psychology that see human functioning based upon the interaction of conscious and unconscious drives and forces within the person, and between the different structures of the personality (id, ego, superego).

Freud's theory has been heavily criticized for several reasons. One is that it is very difficult to test scientifically. How can parenting in infancy be traced to personality in adulthood? Are there other variables that might better explain development? Because psychodynamic theories are difficult to prove wrong, evaluating those theories, in general, is difficult in that we cannot make definite predictions about a given individual's behavior using the theories. The theory is also considered to be sexist in suggesting that women who do not accept an inferior position in society are somehow psychologically flawed. Freud focused on the darker side of human nature and suggested that much of what determines our actions is unknown to us. Others make the criticism that the psychodynamic approach is too deterministic, relating to the idea that all events, including human action, are ultimately determined by causes regarded as external to the will, thereby leaving little room for the idea of free will.[1]

Freud's work has been extremely influential, and its impact extends far beyond psychology (several years ago *Time* magazine selected Freud as one of the most important thinkers of the 20th century). Freud's work has been not only influential but quite controversial as well. As you might imagine, when Freud suggested in 1900 that much of our behavior is determined by psychological forces of which we're largely unaware—that we literally don't know what's going on in our own minds—people

1. The Generative Society: Caring for Future Generations – January 1, 2004 by Ed De St Aubin (Author), Ed St Aubin (Editor), Henry Wade Rogers Professor of Psychology and Chair of the Psychology Department Dan P McAdams PhD (Editor), Tae-Chang Kim (Editor)

were (to put it mildly) displeased (Freud, 1900/1953a). When he suggested in 1905 that we humans have strong sexual feelings from a very early age and that some of these sexual feelings are directed toward our parents, people were more than displeased—they were outraged (Freud, 1905/1953b). Few theories in psychology have evoked such strong reactions from other professionals and members of the public.

So why do we study Freud? As mentioned above, despite the criticisms, Freud's assumptions about the importance of early childhood experiences in shaping our psychological selves have found their way into child development, education, and parenting practices. Freud's theory has heuristic value in providing a framework from which to elaborate and modify subsequent theories of development. Many later theories, particularly behaviorism and humanism, were challenges to Freud's views. Controversy notwithstanding, no competent psychologist, or student of psychology, can ignore psychodynamic theory. It is simply too important for psychological science and practice and continues to play an important role in a wide variety of disciplines within and outside psychology (for example, developmental psychology, social psychology, sociology, and neuroscience; see Bornstein, 2005, 2006; Solms & Turnbull, 2011).

Psychosocial Theory

Erikson's Psychosocial Theory

Now, let's turn to a less controversial psychodynamic theorist, the father of developmental psychology, Erik Erikson (1902-1994). Erikson was a student of Freud's and expanded on his theory of psychosexual development by emphasizing the importance of culture in parenting practices and motivations and adding three stages of adult development (Erikson, 1950; 1968).

Figure 6. Erik Erikson.

Background

As an art school dropout with an uncertain future, young Erik Erikson met Freud's daughter, Anna Freud, while he was tutoring the children of an American couple undergoing psychoanalysis in Vienna. It was Anna Freud who encouraged Erikson to study psychoanalysis. Erikson received his diploma from the Vienna Psychoanalytic Institute in 1933, and as Nazism spread across Europe, he fled the country and immigrated to the United States that same year. Erikson later proposed a psychosocial theory of development, suggesting that an individual's personality develops throughout the lifespan—a departure from Freud's view that personality is fixed in early life. In his theory, Erikson emphasized the social relationships that are important at each stage of personality development, in contrast to Freud's emphasis on erogenous zones. Erikson identified eight stages, each of which includes a conflict or developmental task. The development of a healthy personality and a sense of competence depend on the successful completion of each task.

Psychosocial Stages of Development

Erikson believed that we are aware of what motivates us throughout life and that the ego has greater importance in guiding our actions than does the id. We make conscious choices in life, and these choices focus on meeting certain social and cultural needs rather than purely biological ones. Humans are motivated, for instance, by the need to feel that the world is a trustworthy place, that we are capable individuals, that we can make a contribution to society, and that we have lived a meaningful life. These are all psychosocial problems.

Erikson's theory is based on what he calls the *epigenetic principle*, encompassing the notion that we develop through an unfolding of our personality in predetermined stages, and that our environment and surrounding culture influence how we progress through these stages. This biological unfolding in relation to our socio-cultural settings is done in stages of psychosocial development, where "progress through each stage is in part determined by our success, or lack of success, in all the previous stages."[2]

Erikson described eight stages, each with a major psychosocial task to accomplish or crisis to overcome. Erikson believed that our personality continues to take shape throughout our life span as we face these challenges. We will discuss each of these stages in greater detail when we discuss each of these life stages throughout the course. Here is an overview of each stage:

1. **Trust vs. Mistrust (Hope)**—From birth to 12 months of age, infants must learn that adults can be trusted. This occurs when adults meet a child's basic needs for survival. Infants are dependent upon their caregivers, so caregivers who are responsive and sensitive to their infant's needs help their baby to develop a sense of trust; their baby will see the world as a safe, predictable place. Unresponsive caregivers who do not meet their baby's needs can engender feelings of anxiety, fear, and mistrust; their baby may see the world as unpredictable. If infants are treated cruelly or their needs are not met appropriately, they will likely grow up with a sense of mistrust for people in the world.
2. **Autonomy vs. Shame (Will)**—As toddlers (ages 1–3 years) begin to explore their world, they learn that they can control their actions and act on their environment to get results. They begin to show clear preferences for certain elements of the environment, such as food, toys, and clothing. A toddler's main task is to resolve the issue of autonomy vs. shame and doubt by working to establish independence. This is the "me do it" stage. For example, we might observe a budding sense of autonomy in a 2-year-old child who wants to choose her clothes and dress herself. Although her outfits might not be appropriate for the situation, her input in such basic decisions has an effect on her sense of independence. If denied the opportunity to act on her environment, she may begin to doubt her abilities, which could lead to low self-esteem and feelings of shame.
3. **Initiative vs. Guilt (Purpose)**—Once children reach the preschool stage (ages 3–6 years), they are capable of initiating activities and asserting control over their world through social interactions and play. According to Erikson, preschool children must resolve the task of initiative vs. guilt. By learning to plan and achieve goals while interacting with others, preschool children can master this task. Initiative, a sense of ambition and responsibility, occurs when parents allow a child to explore within limits and then support the child's choice. These children will develop self-confidence and feel a sense of purpose. Those who are unsuccessful at this stage—with their initiative misfiring or stifled by over-controlling parents—may develop feelings of guilt.
4. **Industry vs. Inferiority (Competence)**—During the elementary school stage (ages 7–12), children face the task of industry vs. inferiority. Children begin to compare themselves with their peers to see how they measure up. They either develop a sense of pride and accomplishment in their schoolwork, sports, social activities, and family life, or they feel inferior and inadequate because they feel that they don't measure up. If children do not learn to get along with others or have negative experiences at home or with peers, an inferiority complex might develop into adolescence and adulthood.
5. **Identity vs. Role Confusion (Fidelity)**—In adolescence (ages 12–18), children face the task of *identity vs. role confusion.* According to Erikson, an adolescent's main task is developing a sense of self. Adolescents struggle with questions such as "Who am I?" and "What do I want to do with my life?" Along the way, most adolescents try on many different selves to see which ones fit; they explore various roles and ideas, set goals, and attempt to discover their adult selves. Adolescents who are successful at this stage have a strong sense of identity and are able to remain true to their beliefs and values in the face of problems and other people's perspectives. When adolescents are apathetic, do not make a conscious search for identity, or are pressured to conform to their parents' ideas for the future, they may develop a weak sense of self and experience role confusion. They will be unsure of their identity and confused about the future. Teenagers who struggle to adopt a positive role will likely struggle to find themselves as adults.
6. **Intimacy vs. Isolation (Love)**—People in early adulthood (20s through early 40s) are concerned with intimacy vs. isolation. After we have developed a sense of self in adolescence, we are ready to share our life with others. However, if other stages have not been successfully resolved, young adults may have trouble developing and maintaining successful

2. Erikson, Erik (1968). Identity: Youth and Crisis. Chapter 3: W.W. Norton and Company. p. 92.

relationships with others. Erikson said that we must have a strong sense of self before we can develop successful intimate relationships. Adults who do not develop a positive self-concept in adolescence may experience feelings of loneliness and emotional isolation.

7. **Generativity vs. Stagnation (Care)**—When people reach their 40s, they enter the time known as middle adulthood, which extends to the mid-60s. The social task of middle adulthood is generativity vs. stagnation. Generativity involves finding your life's work and contributing to the development of others through activities such as volunteering, mentoring, and raising children. During this stage, middle-aged adults begin contributing to the next generation, often through caring for others; they also engage in meaningful and productive work which contributes positively to society. Those who do not master this task may experience stagnation and feel as though they are not leaving a mark on the world in a meaningful way; they may have little connection with others and little interest in productivity and self-improvement.
8. **Integrity vs. Despair (Wisdom)**—From the mid-60s to the end of life, we are in the period of development known as late adulthood. Erikson's task at this stage is called integrity vs. despair. He said that people in late adulthood reflect on their lives and feel either a sense of satisfaction or a sense of failure. People who feel proud of their accomplishments feel a sense of integrity, and they can look back on their lives with few regrets. However, people who are not successful at this stage may feel as if their life has been wasted. They focus on what "would have," "should have," and "could have" been. They may face the end of their lives with feelings of bitterness, depression, and despair.

Erikson's Psychosocial Stages of Development

Stage	Approximate Age (years)	Virtue: Developmental Task	Description
1	0–1	**Hope: Trust vs. Mistrust**	Trust (or mistrust) that basic needs, such as nourishment and affection, will be met
2	1–3	**Will: Autonomy vs. Shame**	Sense of independence in many tasks develops
3	3–6	**Purpose: Initiative vs. Guilt**	Take initiative on some activities, may develop guilt when success not met or boundaries overstepped
4	7–11	**Competence: Industry vs. Inferiority**	Develop self-confidence in abilities when competent or sense of inferiority when not
5	12–18	**Fidelity: Identity vs. Role Confusion**	Experiment with and develop identity and roles
6	19–39	**Love: Intimacy vs. Isolation**	Establish intimacy and relationships with others
7	40–64	**Care: Generativity vs. Stagnation**	Contribute to society and be part of a family
8	65+	**Wisdom: Integrity vs. Despair**	Assess and make sense of life and meaning of contributions

Strengths and weaknesses of Erikson's theory

Erikson's eight stages form a foundation for discussions on emotional and social development during the lifespan. Keep in mind, however, that these stages or crises can occur more than once or at different times of life. For instance, a person may struggle with a lack of trust beyond infancy. Erikson's theory has been criticized for focusing so heavily on stages and assuming that the completion of one stage is prerequisite for the next crisis of development. His theory also focuses on the social expectations that are found in certain cultures, but not in all. For instance, the idea that adolescence is a time of searching for identity might translate well in the middle-class culture of the United States, but not as well in cultures where the transition into adulthood coincides with puberty through rites of passage and where adult roles offer fewer choices.

By and large, Erikson's view that development continues throughout the lifespan is very significant and has received great recognition. However, like Freud's theory, it has been criticized for focusing on more men than women and also for its vagueness, making it difficult to test rigorously.

WATCH IT

Watch this video to learn more about each of Erikson's stages.

- https://youtu.be/SIoKwUcmivk

GLOSSARY

anal stage:
the stage of development when children are learning to control impulses; coincides with toddlerhood and toileting

defense mechanisms:
psychological strategies that are unconsciously used to protect a person from anxiety arising from unacceptable thoughts or feelings

ego:
the part of the self that helps balance the id and superego by satisfying the id's desires in a rational way

eight stages of psychosocial development:
Erikson's stages of trust vs. mistrust, autonomy vs. shame/doubt, initiative vs. guilt, industry vs. inferiority, identity vs. role confusion, intimacy vs. isolation, generativity vs. stagnation, and integrity vs. despair

genital stage:
the final stage of psychosexual development when individuals develop sexual interests; begins in adolescence and lasts throughout adulthood

hypothesis:
a testable prediction

id:
the part of the self that is biologically-driven, includes our instincts and drives, and wants immediate gratification

latency stage:
the fourth stage of psychosexual development, spanning middle childhood, during which sexual development and sexual impulses are dormant

neurosis:
a tendency to experience negative emotions

oral stage:
the first stage of psychosexual development when infants needs are met primarily through oral gratification

phallic stage:
the third stage of psychosexual development, spanning the ages of 3 to 6 years, when the young child's libido (desire) centers upon their genitalia as the erogenous zone

psychodynamic perspective:
the perspective that behavior is motivated by inner forces, memories, and conflicts that are generally beyond people's awareness and control

psychosexual stages:
Freud's oral, anal, phallic, latency, and genital stages

psychosocial theory:
the theory that emphasizes the social relationships that are important at each stage of personality development

superego:
the part of the self that acts as our conscience, telling us how we should behave

theory:
a well-developed set of ideas that propose an explanation for observed phenomena that can be used to make predictions about future observations

Behavioral and Cognitive Theories

What you'll learn to do: explain key principles of behaviorism and cognitive psychology

Is all behavior learned from the environment? Should psychology, as science, focus on observable behavior—the result of stimulus-response, as opposed to internal events like thinking and emotion? Is there little difference between the learning that takes place in humans and that in other animals? These are types of questions considered by behaviorists, which we'll learn more about in this section. We'll also consider cognitive theories, which examine the construction of thought processes, including remembering, problem-solving, and decision-making, from childhood through adolescence to adulthood.

LEARNING OUTCOMES

- Describe the principles of classical conditioning
- Describe the principles of operant conditioning
- Describe social learning theory
- Describe Piaget's theory of cognitive development
- Describe information processing approaches to cognitive development

Exploring Behavior

The Behavioral Perspective: A Focus on Observable Behavior

The **behavioral perspective** is the psychological approach that suggests that the keys to understanding development are observable behavior and external stimuli in the environment. Behaviorism is a theory of learning, and learning theories focus on how we respond to events or stimuli rather than emphasizing internal factors that motivate our actions. These theories provide an explanation of how experience can change what we do.

Behaviorism emerged early in the 20th century and became a major force in American psychology. Championed by psychologists such as John B. Watson (1878–1958) and B. F. Skinner (1904–1990), behaviorism rejected any reference to mind and viewed overt and observable behavior as the proper subject matter of psychology. Through the scientific study of behavior, it was hoped that laws of learning could be derived that would promote the prediction and control of behavior. Russian physiologist Ivan Pavlov (1849–1936) influenced early behaviorism in America. His work on conditioned learning, popularly referred to as classical conditioning, provided support for the notion that learning and behavior were controlled by events in the environment and could be explained with no reference to mind or consciousness (Fancher, 1987).

Classical Conditioning and Emotional Responses

Classical conditioning theory helps us to understand how our responses to one situation become attached to new situations. For example, a smell might remind us of a time when we were a kid. If you went to a new cafe with the same smell as your elementary cafeteria, it might evoke the feelings you had when you were in school. Or a song on the radio might remind you of a memorable evening you spent with your first true love. Or, if you hear your entire name (Isaiah Wilmington Brewer, for instance) called as you walk across the stage to get your diploma and it makes you tense because it reminds you of how your father used to use your full name when he was mad at you, then you've been classically conditioned.

Classical conditioning explains how we develop many of our emotional responses to people or events or our "gut level" reactions to situations. New situations may bring about an old response because the two have become connected. Attachments form in this way. Addictions are affected by classical conditioning, as anyone who's tried to quit smoking can tell you. When you try to quit, everything that was associated with smoking makes you crave a cigarette.

Figure 1. Ivan Pavlov

Pavlov and Classical Conditioning

Ivan Pavlov (1849–1936) was a Russian physiologist interested in studying digestion. As he recorded the amount of salivation his laboratory dogs produced as they ate, he noticed that they actually began to salivate before the food arrived as the researcher walked down the hall and toward the cage. "This," he thought, "is not natural!" One would expect a dog to automatically salivate when the food hit their palate, but *before* the food comes? Of course, what happened is that the dogs knew that the food was coming because they had learned to associate the footsteps with the food. The keyword here is "learned."

A learned response is called a "conditioned" response. Pavlov began to experiment with this "psychic" reflex. He began to ring a bell, for instance, prior to introducing the food. Sure enough, after making this connection several times, the dogs could be made to salivate to the sound of a bell. Once the bell had become an event to which the dogs had learned to salivate, it was called a conditioned stimulus. The act of salivating to a bell was a response that had also been learned, now termed in Pavlov's jargon, a conditioned response. Notice that the response, salivation, is the same whether it is conditioned or unconditioned (unlearned or natural). What changed is the stimulus to which the dog salivates. One is natural (unconditioned) and one is learned (conditioned).

Before Conditioning

During Conditioning

After Conditioning

Figure 2. Before conditioning, an unconditioned stimulus (food) produces an unconditioned response (salivation), and a neutral stimulus (bell) does not produce a response. During conditioning, the unconditioned stimulus (food) is presented repeatedly just after the presentation of the neutral stimulus (bell). After conditioning, the neutral stimulus alone produces a conditioned response (salivation), thus becoming a conditioned stimulus.

WATCH IT

View the following video to learn more about Pavlov and his dogs:

- https://youtu.be/hhqumfpxuzI

Watson and Behaviorism

Let's think about how classical conditioning is used on people, and not just with dogs. One of the most widespread applications of classical conditioning principles was brought to us by the psychologist, John B. Watson. Watson proposed that the process of classical conditioning (based on Pavlov's observations) was able to explain all aspects of human psychology. He established the psychological school of behaviorism, after doing research on animal behavior. This school was extremely influential in the middle of the 20th century when B.F. Skinner developed it further.

Watson believed that most of our fears and other emotional responses are classically conditioned. He gained a good deal of popularity in the 1920s with his expert advice on parenting offered to the public. He believed that parents could be taught to help shape their children's behavior and tried to demonstrate the power of classical conditioning with his famous experiment with an 18-month-old boy named "Little Albert." Watson sat Albert down and introduced a variety of seemingly scary objects to him: a burning piece of newspaper, a white rat, etc. But Albert remained curious and reached for all of these things. Watson knew that one of our only inborn fears is the fear of loud noises so he proceeded to make a loud noise each time he introduced one of Albert's favorites, a white rat. After hearing the loud noise several times paired with the rat, Albert soon came to fear the rat and began to cry when it was introduced.

Watson filmed this experiment for posterity and used it to demonstrate that he could help parents achieve any outcomes they desired if they would only follow his advice. Watson wrote columns in newspapers and in magazines and gained a lot of popularity among parents eager to apply science to household order. Parenting advice was not the legacy Watson left us, however; where he really made his impact was in advertising. After Watson left academia, he went into the world of business and showed companies how to tie something that brings about a natural positive feeling to their products to enhance sales. Thus the union of sex and advertising!

LINK TO LEARNING: LITTLE ALBERT

View scenes from John Watson's experiment in which Little Albert was conditioned to respond in fear to furry objects. As you watch the video, look closely at Little Albert's reactions and the manner in which Watson and Rayner present the stimuli before and after conditioning. In the experiment with Little Albert, check to see if you can identify the conditioned and unconditioned stimuli and responses: identify the unconditioned stimulus, the unconditioned response, and, after conditioning, the conditioned stimulus and the conditioned response.

- https://youtu.be/FMnhyGozLyE

Operant Conditioning

Now we turn to the second type of associative learning, operant conditioning. In **operant conditioning**, organisms learn to associate a behavior and its consequence (Table 1). A pleasant consequence makes that behavior more likely to be repeated in the future. For example, Spirit, a dolphin at the National Aquarium in Baltimore, does a flip in the air when her trainer blows a whistle. The consequence is that she gets a fish.

Psychologist B. F. Skinner saw that classical conditioning is limited to existing behaviors that are reflexively elicited, and it doesn't account for new behaviors such as riding a bike. He proposed a theory about how such behaviors come about. Skinner believed that behavior is motivated by the consequences we receive for the behavior: the reinforcements and punishments. His idea that learning is the result of consequences is based on the **law of effect**, which was first proposed by psychologist Edward Thorndike. According to the law of effect, behaviors that are followed by consequences that are satisfying to the organism are more likely to be repeated, and behaviors that are followed by unpleasant consequences are less likely to be repeated (Thorndike, 1911). Essentially, if an organism does something that brings about a desired result, the organism is more likely to do it again. If an organism does something that does not bring about a desired result, the organism is less likely to do it again. An example of the law of effect is in employment. One of the reasons (and often the main reason) we show up for work is because we get paid to do so. If we stop getting paid, we will likely stop showing up—even if we love our job.

Working with Thorndike's law of effect as his foundation, Skinner began conducting scientific experiments on animals (mainly rats and pigeons) to determine how organisms learn through operant conditioning (Skinner, 1938). He placed these animals inside an operant conditioning chamber, which has come to be known as a "Skinner box" (Figure 1). A Skinner box contains a lever (for rats) or disk (for pigeons) that the animal can press or peck for a food reward via the dispenser. Speakers and lights can be associated with certain behaviors. A recorder counts the number of responses made by the animal.

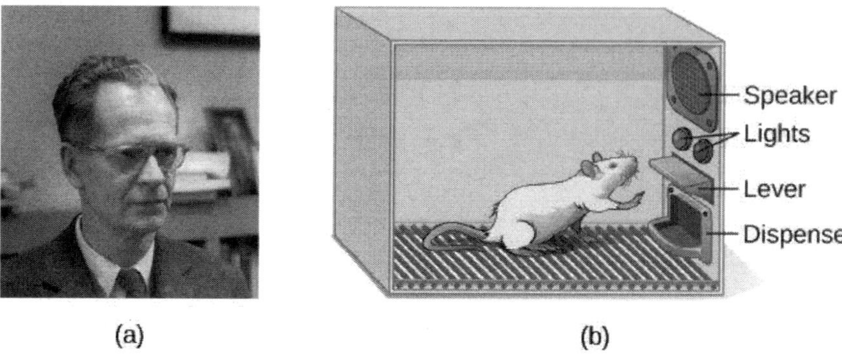

(a) (b)

Figure 3. (a) B. F. Skinner developed operant conditioning for the systematic study of how behaviors are strengthened or weakened according to their consequences. (b) In a Skinner box, a rat presses a lever in an operant conditioning chamber to receive a food reward. (credit a: modification of work by "Silly rabbit"/Wikimedia Commons)

Skinner believed that we learn best when our actions are reinforced. For example, a child who cleans his room and is reinforced (rewarded) with a big hug and words of praise is more likely to clean it again than a child whose deed goes unnoticed. Skinner believed that almost anything could be reinforcing. A reinforcer is anything following a behavior that makes it more likely to occur again. It can be something intrinsically rewarding (called intrinsic or primary reinforcers), such as food or praise, or it can be something that is rewarding because it can be exchanged for what one really wants (such as receiving money and using it buy a cookie). Such reinforcers are referred to as secondary reinforcers.

LINK TO LEARNING

Watch the following clip to learn more about operant conditioning and to watch an interview with Skinner as he talks about conditioning pigeons.

- https://youtu.be/I_ctJqjlrHA

Comparing Classical and Operant Conditioning

Table 1. Classical and Operant Conditioning Compared

	Classical Conditioning	Operant Conditioning
Conditioning approach	An unconditioned stimulus (such as food) is paired with a neutral stimulus (such as a bell). The neutral stimulus eventually becomes the conditioned stimulus, which brings about the conditioned response (salivation).	The target behavior is followed by reinforcement or punishment to either strengthen or weaken it so that the learner is more likely to exhibit the desired behavior in the future.
Stimulus timing	The stimulus occurs immediately before the response.	The stimulus (either reinforcement or punishment) occurs soon after the response.

Social Cognitive (Learning) Theory: Observational Learning

Social Cognitive Theory (SCT), originally known as the Social Learning Theory (SLT), began in the 1960s through research done by Albert Bandura. The theory proposes that learning occurs in a social context. It takes into consideration the dynamic and reciprocal interaction of the person, environment, and their own behavior.[1]

Not all forms of learning are accounted for entirely by classical and operant conditioning. Imagine a child walking up to a group of children playing a game on the playground. The game looks fun, but it is new and unfamiliar. Rather than joining the game immediately, the child opts to sit back and watch the other children play a round or two. Observing the others, the child takes note of the ways in which they behave while playing the game. By watching the behavior of the other kids, the child can figure out the rules of the game and even some strategies for doing well at the game. This is called observational learning.

Figure 4. Children observing a social model (an experienced chess player) to learn the rules and strategies of the game of chess. [Image: David R. Tribble, https://goo.gl/nWsgxl, CC BY-SA 3.0, https://goo.gl/uhHola]

Observational learning is a component of Albert Bandura's Social Learning Theory (Bandura, 1977), which posits that individuals can learn novel responses via observation of key others' behaviors. Observational learning does not necessarily require reinforcement, but instead hinges on the presence of others, referred to as social models. Social models are normally of higher status or authority compared to the observer, examples of which include parents, teachers, and police officers. In the example above, the children who already know how to play the game could be thought of as being authorities—and are therefore social models—even though they are the same age as the observer. By observing how the social models behave, an individual is able to learn how to act in a certain situation. Other examples of observational learning might include a child learning to place her napkin in her lap by watching her parents at the dinner table, or a customer learning where to find the ketchup and mustard after observing other customers at a hot dog stand.

Bandura theorizes that the observational learning process consists of four parts. The first is *attention*—one must pay attention to what they are observing in order to learn. The second part is *retention*: to learn one must be able to retain the behavior they are observing in memory. The third part of observational learning, *initiation*, acknowledges that the learner must be able to execute (or initiate) the learned behavior. Lastly, the observer must possess the *motivation* to engage in observational learning. In our vignette, the child must want to learn how to play the game in order to properly engage in observational learning.

In this experiment, Bandura (Bandura, Ross, & Ross, 1961) had children individually observe an adult social model interact with a clown doll (Bobo). For one group of children, the adult interacted aggressively with Bobo: punching it, kicking it, throwing it, and even hitting it in the face with a toy mallet. Another group of children watched the adult interact with other toys, displaying no aggression toward Bobo. In both instances, the adult left and the children were allowed to interact with Bobo on their own. Bandura found that children exposed to the aggressive social model were significantly more likely to behave aggressively toward Bobo, hitting and kicking him, compared to those exposed to the non-aggressive model. The researchers concluded that the children in the aggressive group used their observations of the adult social model's behavior to determine that aggressive behavior toward Bobo was acceptable.

While reinforcement was not required to elicit the children's behavior in Bandura's first experiment, it is important to acknowledge that consequences do play a role within observational learning. A future adaptation of this study (Bandura, Ross,

1. Behavioral Change Models. The Social Cognitive Theory. Retrieved from http://sphweb.bumc.bu.edu/otlt/MPH-Modules/SB/BehavioralChangeTheories/BehavioralChangeTheories5.html.

& Ross, 1963) demonstrated that children in the aggression group showed less aggressive behavior if they witnessed the adult model receive punishment for aggressing against Bobo. Bandura referred to this process as vicarious reinforcement because the children did not experience the reinforcement or punishment directly yet were still influenced by observing it.

Do parents socialize children or do children socialize parents?

Bandura's (1986) findings suggest that there is interplay between the environment and the individual. We are not just the product of our surroundings, rather we influence our surroundings. There is interplay between our personality and the way we interpret events and how they influence us. This concept is called **reciprocal determinism**. An example of this might be the interplay between parents and children. Parents not only influence their child's environment, perhaps intentionally through the use of reinforcement, etc., but children influence parents as well. Parents may respond differently to their first child than with their fourth. Perhaps they try to be the perfect parents with their firstborn, but by the time their last child comes along, they have very different expectations of themselves and their child. Our environment creates us and we create our environment. Today there are numerous other social influences, from TV, games, the Internet, i-pads, phones, social media, influencers, advertisements, etc.

WATCH

Watch this clip to better understand Bandura's research on social learning.

- https://youtu.be/Eqxjc4lUDyY

Exploring Cognition

The Cognitive Perspective: The Roots of Understanding

Cognitive theories focus on how our mental processes or cognitions change over time. The **theory of cognitive development** is a comprehensive theory about the nature and development of human intelligence first developed by Jean Piaget. It is primarily known as a developmental stage theory, but in fact, it deals with the nature of knowledge itself and how humans come gradually to acquire it, construct it, and use it. Moreover, Piaget claims that cognitive development is at the center of the human organism and language is contingent on cognitive development. Let's learn more about Piaget's views about the nature of intelligence and then dive deeper into the stages that he identified as critical in the developmental process.

Piaget: Changes in thought with maturation

Jean Piaget (1896-1980) is one of the most influential cognitive theorists in development, inspired to explore children's ability to think and reason by watching his own children's development. He was one of the first to recognize and map out the ways in which children's intelligence differs from that of adults. He became interested in this area when he was asked to test the IQ of children and began to notice that there was a pattern in their wrong answers. He believed that children's intellectual skills change over time that that maturation rather than training brings about that change. Children of differing ages interpret the world differently.

Figure 5. Jean Piaget.

Making sense of the world

Piaget believed that we are continuously trying to maintain cognitive equilibrium or a balance or cohesiveness in what we see and what we know. Children have much more of a challenge in maintaining this balance because they are constantly being confronted with new situations, new words, new objects, etc. When faced with something new, a child may either fit it into an existing framework (**schema**) and match it with something known (**assimilation**) such as calling all animals with four legs "doggies" because he or she knows the word doggie, or expand the framework of knowledge to accommodate the new situation (**accommodation**) by learning a new word to more accurately name the animal. This is the underlying dynamic in our own cognition. Even as adults we continue to try and make sense of new situations by determining whether they fit into our old way of thinking or whether we need to modify our thoughts.

Stages of Cognitive Development

Like Freud and Erikson, Piaget thought development unfolded in a series of stages approximately associated with age ranges. He proposed a theory of cognitive development that unfolds in four stages: sensorimotor, preoperational, concrete operational, and formal operational.

Table 1. Piaget's Stages of Cognitive Development

Age (years)	Stage	Description	Developmental issues
0–2	Sensorimotor	World experienced through senses and actions	Object permanence Stranger anxiety
2–7	Preoperational	Use words and images to represent things but lack logical reasoning	Pretend play Egocentrism Language development
7–11	Concrete operational	Understand concrete events and logical analogies; perform arithmetical operations	Conservation Mathematical transformations
11–	Formal operational	Utilize abstract reasoning and hypothetical thinking	Abstract logic Moral reasoning

The first stage is the **sensorimotor** stage, which lasts from birth to about 2 years old. During this stage, children learn about the world through their senses and motor behavior. Young children put objects in their mouths to see if the items are edible, and once they can grasp objects, they may shake or bang them to see if they make sounds. Between 5 and 8 months old, the child develops **object permanence**, which is the understanding that even if something is out of sight, it still exists (Bogartz, Shinskey, & Schilling, 2000). According to Piaget, young infants do not remember an object after it has been removed from sight. Piaget studied infants' reactions when a toy was first shown to an infant and then hidden under a blanket. Infants who had already developed object permanence would reach for the hidden toy, indicating that they knew it still existed, whereas infants who had not developed object permanence would appear confused.

In Piaget's view, around the same time children develop object permanence, they also begin to exhibit stranger anxiety, which is a fear of unfamiliar people. Babies may demonstrate this by crying and turning away from a stranger, by clinging to a caregiver, or by attempting to reach their arms toward familiar faces such as parents. Stranger anxiety results when a child is unable to assimilate the stranger into an existing schema; therefore, she can't predict what her experience with that stranger will be like, which results in a fear response.

Piaget's second stage is the **preoperational stage**, which is from approximately 2 to 7 years old. In this stage, children can use symbols to represent words, images, and ideas, which is why children in this stage engage in pretend play. A child's arms might become airplane wings as he zooms around the room, or a child with a stick might become a brave knight with a sword. Children also begin to use language in the preoperational stage, but they cannot understand adult logic or mentally manipulate information (the term *operational* refers to logical manipulation of information, so children at this stage are considered to be *pre*-operational). Children's logic is based on their own personal knowledge of the world so far, rather than on conventional knowledge. For example, dad gave a slice of pizza to 10-year-old Keiko and another slice to her 3-year-old brother, Kenny. Kenny's pizza slice was cut into five pieces, so Kenny told his sister that he got more pizza than she did. Children in this stage cannot perform mental operations because they have not developed an understanding of **conservation**, which is the idea that even if you change the appearance of something, it is still equal in size as long as nothing has been removed or added.

During this stage, we also expect children to display **egocentrism**, which means that the child is not able to take the perspective of others. A child at this stage thinks that everyone sees, thinks, and feels just as they do. Let's look at Kenny and Keiko again. Keiko's birthday is coming up, so their mom takes Kenny to the toy store to choose a present for his sister. He selects an Iron Man action figure for her, thinking that if he likes the toy, his sister will too. An egocentric child is not able to infer the perspective of other people and instead attributes his own perspective. At some point during this stage and typically between 3 and 5 years old, children come to understand that people have thoughts, feelings, and beliefs that are different from their own. This is known as **theory-of-mind** (TOM).

Piaget's third stage is the **concrete operational stage**, which occurs from about 7 to 11 years old. In this stage, children can think logically about real (concrete) events; they have a firm grasp on the use of numbers and start to employ memory strategies. They can perform mathematical operations and understand transformations, such as addition is the opposite of subtraction, and multiplication is the opposite of division. In this stage, children also master the concept of conservation: Even if something changes shape, its mass, volume, and number stay the same. For example, if you pour water from a tall, thin glass to a short, fat glass, you still have the same amount of water. Remember Keiko and Kenny and the pizza? How did Keiko know that Kenny was wrong when he said that he had more pizza?

Children in the concrete operational stage also understand the principle of **reversibility**, which means that objects can be changed and then returned back to their original form or condition. Take, for example, water that you poured into the short, fat glass: You can pour water from the fat glass back to the thin glass and still have the same amount (minus a couple of drops).

The fourth, and last, stage in Piaget's theory is the **formal operational stage**, which is from about age 11 to adulthood. Whereas children in the concrete operational stage are able to think logically only about concrete events, children in the formal operational stage can also deal with abstract ideas and hypothetical situations. Children in this stage can use abstract thinking to problem solve, look at alternative solutions, and test these solutions. In adolescence, a renewed egocentrism occurs. For example, a 15-year-old with a very small pimple on her face might think it is huge and incredibly visible, under the mistaken impression that others must share her perceptions.

WATCH IT

- https://youtu.be/Jt3-PIC2nCs

Criticisms of Piaget's Theory

As with other major contributors of theories of development, several of Piaget's ideas have come under criticism based on the results of further research. For example, several contemporary studies support a model of development that is more continuous than Piaget's discrete stages (Courage & Howe, 2002; Siegler, 2005, 2006). Many others suggest that children reach cognitive milestones earlier than Piaget describes (Baillargeon, 2004; de Hevia & Spelke, 2010). Looking across cultures reveals considerable variation in what children are able to do at various ages, and Piaget may have underestimated what children are capable of given the right circumstances.

According to Piaget, the highest level of cognitive development is formal operational thought, which develops between 11 and 20 years old. However, many developmental psychologists disagree with Piaget, suggesting a fifth stage of cognitive development, known as the postformal stage (Basseches, 1984; Commons & Bresette, 2006; Sinnott, 1998). In postformal thinking, decisions are made based on situations and circumstances, and logic is integrated with emotion as adults develop principles that depend on contexts. One way that we can see the difference between an adult in postformal thought and an adolescent (or adult) in formal operations is in terms of how they handle emotionally charged issues or integrate systems of thought.

It seems that once we reach adulthood our problem solving abilities change: As we attempt to solve problems, we tend to think more deeply about many areas of our lives, such as relationships, work, and politics (Labouvie-Vief & Diehl, 1999). Because of this, postformal thinkers are able to draw on past experiences to help them solve new problems. Problem-solving strategies using postformal thought vary, depending on the situation. What does this mean? Adults can recognize, for example, that what seems to be an ideal solution to a problem at work involving a disagreement with a colleague may not be the best solution to a disagreement with a significant other.

WATCH IT

Robert Kegan explains the constructive developmental theory, which is based on, and an extension of, Piaget's theory of cognitive development. According to Kegan, development continues into adulthood as we are able to more deeply understand ourselves and the world.

- https://youtu.be/BoasM4cCHBc

Information-Processing Approaches to Development

Information-processing approaches have become an important alternative to Piagetian approaches. The theory is based on the idea that humans process the information they receive, rather than merely responding to stimuli. As a model, it assumes that even complex behavior such as learning, remembering, categorizing, and thinking can be broken down into a series of individual, specific steps, and as a person develops strategies for processing information, they can learn more complex information. This perspective equates the mind to a computer, which is responsible for analyzing information from the environment.

The most common information-processing model is applied to an understanding of memory and the way that information is encoded, stored, and then retrieved from the brain (Atkinson & Shiffrin, 1968), but information processing approaches also apply to cognitive processing in general. In one study, Stephanie Thornton assessed how children solved the problem of building a small bridge out of playing blocks to cross a small "river." A single block was not wide enough to reach across the river, so the bridge could only be built by having two of the blocks meet in the middle, then by using extra blocks on the top of the sides of the bridge to serve as counterweights to hold the bridge upright. This task was relatively easy for older children (7 and 9 years old), but significantly harder for 5-year-olds (in the study, only one 5-year-old eventually completed the task by using trial and error).[2] This supports the idea that cognitive development is specific to the individual.

Psychologists who use information processing approaches examine how children tackle tasks such as the ones described above, whether it be through trial and error, building upon previous life experiences, or generalizing insights from external sources.[3]

According to the standard information-processing model for mental development, the mind's machinery includes attention mechanisms for bringing information in, working memory for actively manipulating information, and long-term memory for passively holding information so that it can be used in the future. This theory addresses how as children grow, their brains likewise mature, leading to advances in their ability to process and respond to the information they received through their senses. The theory emphasizes a continuous pattern of development, in contrast with cognitive-developmental theorists such as Piaget who thought development occurred in stages. Developmental psychologists who adopt the information-processing perspective account for mental development in terms of maturational changes in basic components of a child's mind. At the same time, they do not offer a complete explanation of behavior. For example, they have paid little attention to behavior such as creativity, in which the most profound ideas often are developed in a seemingly not logical, nonlinear manner. Moreover, they do not take into account the social context in which development takes place.

Neo-Piagetian Theories

Some of the information processing approaches that build upon Piaget's research are known as neo-Piagetian theories. In contrast to Piaget's original work, which identified cognition as a single system of increasingly sophisticated general cognitive abilities, neo-Piagetian theories view cognition as a made up of different types of individual skills. Using the same terminology as information processing approaches, neo-Piagetian theories advance the idea that cognitive development proceeds quickly in certain areas and more slowly in others. Consider for example, our reading abilities and all the skills that are needed to recall stories. These abilities and skills may progress sooner than the abstract computational abilities used in algebra or trigonometry. Also, neo-Piagetian theorists believe that experience plays a greater role in furthering cognitive development than traditional Piagetian approaches claim. Neo-Piagetians also adopted principles from other theories, such as the social-cognitive theory that allowed them to consider how culture and interactions with others influenced cognitive development.[4][5]

2. Thorton, S. (1999). Creating conditions for cognitive change: The interaction between task structures and specific strategies. *Child Development*, 70, 588-603.
3. Chen, Zhe and Robert Siegler (2013). Young children's analogical problem solving: Gaining insights from video displays. *Journal of Experimental Child Psychology*. Retrieved from http://siegler.tc.columbia.edu/wp-content/uploads/2019/02/Chen-Sieg13.pdf.
4. Yan, Z., & Fischer, K. W. (2002). Always under construction: Dynamic variations in adult cognitive development. Human Development, 45, 141–160. LeFevre, J.-A. (2016). Numerical cognition: Adding it up. Canadian Journal of Experimental Psychology/Revue canadienne de psychologie expérimentale, 70(1), 3-11. Loewen, Susan. (2006). Exceptional intellectual performance: A neo-Piagetian perspective. High Ability Studies - HIGH ABIL STUD. 17.
5. Feldman, Robert (2018) Discovering the Life Span, 4th Edition. Pearson

Cognitive Neuroscience Approaches

The scientific interface between cognitive neuroscience and human development has evoked considerable interest in recent years, as technological advances make it possible to map in detail the changes in brain structure that take place during development. These approaches look at cognitive development at the level of brain processes. **Cognitive neuroscience** is the scientific field that is concerned with the study of the biological processes and aspects that underlie cognition, with a specific focus on the neural connections in the brain which are involved in mental processes.

Like other cognitive perspectives, cognitive neuroscience approaches consider internal, mental processes, but they focus specifically on the neurological activity that underlies thinking, problem-solving, and other cognitive behavior. Cognitive neuroscientists seek to identify actual locations and functions within the brain that are related to different types of cognitive activities. For example, using sophisticated brain scanning techniques, cognitive neuroscientists have demonstrated that thinking about the meaning of a word activates different areas of the brain than thinking about how the word sounds when spoken.

Also, cognitive abilities based on brain development are studied and examined under the subfield of developmental cognitive neuroscience. It examines how the mind changes as children grow up, interrelations between that and how the brain is changing, and environmental and biological influences on the developing mind and brain. This shows brain development over time, analyzing differences and concocting possible reasons for those differences.[6]

GLOSSARY

accommodation:
a term developed by psychologist Jean Piaget to describe what occurs when new information or experiences cause you to modify your existing schemas

assimilation:
a cognitive process that manages how we take in new information and incorporate that new information into our existing knowledge

behavioral perspective:
the approach that suggests that the keys to understanding development are observable behavior and outside stimuli in the environment

classical conditioning:
a type of learning in which an organism responds in a particular way to a neutral stimulus that normally does not bring about that type of response

cognitive neuroscience:
the scientific field that is concerned with the study of the biological processes and aspects that underlie cognition, with a specific focus on the neural connections in the brain which are involved in mental processes

cognitive perspective:
an approach that focuses on the process that allows people to know, understand, and think about the world

6. Feldman, Robert (2018) Discovering the Life Span, 4th Edition. Pearson

concrete operational stage:
the stage in which children can think logically about real (concrete) events, have a firm grasp on the use of numbers and start to employ memory strategies, lasts from about 7 to 11 years old

conservation:
the idea that even if you change the appearance of something, it is still equal in size as long as nothing has been removed or added, usually develops during the concrete operational stage

egocentrism:
the child is not able to take the perspective of others, typically observed during the preoperational stage

formal operational stage:
the fourth, and last, stage in Piaget's theory and lasts from about age 11 to adulthood. Children in the formal operational stage can deal with abstract ideas and hypothetical situations

information-processing approach:
an alternative to Piagetian approaches, a model that seeks to identify the ways individual take in, use, and store information

law of effect:
behavior that is followed by consequences satisfying to the organism will be repeated and behaviors that are followed by unpleasant consequences will be discouraged

object permanence:
the understanding that even if something is out of sight it still exists, develops between 5 and 8 months old

operant conditioning:
a form of learning in which a voluntary response is strengthened or weakened by its association with positive or negative consequences

Piaget's theory of cognitive development:
a description of cognitive development as four distinct stages in children: sensorimotor, preoperational, concrete, and formal

preoperational stage:
the stage in which children can use symbols to represent words, images, and ideas, which is why children in this stage engage in pretend play, lasts approximately 2 to 7 years old

reciprocal determinism:
the interplay between our personality and the way we interpret events and how they influence us

reversibility:
objects can be changed and then returned back to their original form or condition, typically observed during the concrete operational stage

schemas:
an existing framework for an object or concept

sensorimotor stage:
the stage in which children learn about the world through their senses and motor behavior, lasts from birth to about 2 years old

social-cognitive learning theory:
learning by observing the behavior of another person, called a model

theory-of-mind (TOM):
explains how children come to understand that people have thoughts, feelings, and beliefs that are different from their own, develops during the preoperational stage

The Humanistic, Contextual, and Evolutionary Perspectives of Development

What you'll learn to do: describe the humanistic, contextual, and evolutionary perspectives of development

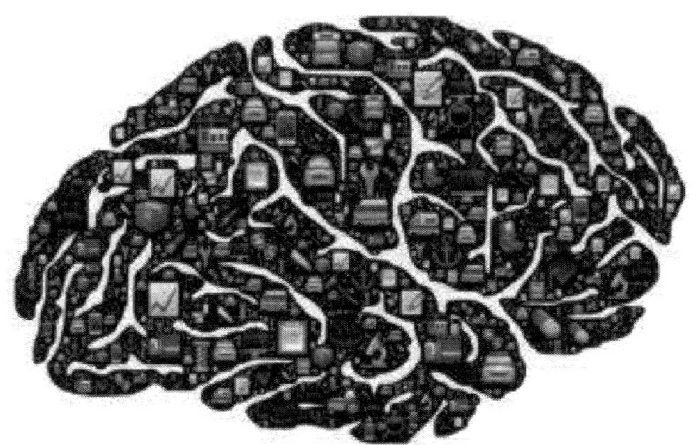

Each perspective that we have seen so far emphasizes different aspects of development. We first looked at the psychodynamic approach and how it emphasizes unconscious determinants of behavior. We then turned to the behavioral perspective which emphasizes overt behavior. Now, we'll turn our attention to the humanistic perspective, which emphasizes empathy and stresses the good in human behavior; it is similar to the cognitive perspective in that it looks more at what people think than at what they do. In this section, we will also look at the contextual perspective, which considers the relationship between individuals and their physical world, cognitive processes, personality, and social worlds. It also examines social and cultural influences on development. And finally, we will briefly examine the evolutionary perspective which focuses on how inherited biological factors underlie development.

LEARNING OUTCOMES

- Describe the major concepts of humanistic theory (unconditional positive regard, the good life), as developed by Carl Rogers
- Explain Maslow's hierarchy of needs
- Describe Vygotsky's sociocultural theory of cognitive development
- Explain Bronfenbrenner's bioecological model
- Describe the evolutionary perspective
- Contrast the main psychological theories that apply to human development

The Humanistic Perspective: A focus on Uniquely Human Qualities

The humanistic perspective rose to prominence in the mid-20th century in response to psychoanalytic theory and behaviorism; this perspective focuses on how healthy people develop and emphasizes an individual's inherent drive towards self-actualization and creativity. **Humanism** emphasizes human potential and an individual's ability to change, and rejects the idea of biological determinism. Humanistic work and research are sometimes criticized for being qualitative (not measurement-based), but there exist a number of quantitative research strains within humanistic psychology, including research on happiness, self-concept, meditation, and the outcomes of humanistic psychotherapy (Friedman, 2008).

Carl Rogers and Humanism

One pioneering humanistic theorist was Carl Rogers. He was an influential humanistic psychologist who developed a personality theory that emphasized the importance of the self-actualizing tendency in shaping human personalities. He also believed that humans are constantly reacting to stimuli with their subjective reality (**phenomenal field**), which changes continuously. Over time, a person develops a self-concept based on the feedback from this field of reality.

One of Rogers's main ideas about personality regards self-concept, our thoughts and feelings about ourselves. How would you respond to the question, "Who am I?" Your answer can show how you see yourself. If your response is primarily positive, then you tend to feel good about who you are, and you probably see the world as a safe and positive place. If your response is mainly negative, then you may feel unhappy with who you are. Rogers further divided the self into two categories: the ideal self and the real self. The ideal self is the person that you would like to be; the real self is the person you actually are. Rogers focused on the idea that we need to achieve consistency between these two selves.

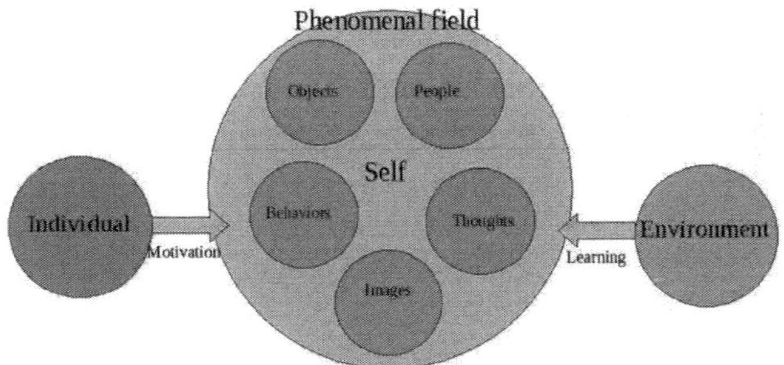

Figure 1. The phenomenal field refers to a person's subjective reality, which includes external objects and people as well as internal thoughts and emotions. The person's motivations and environments both act on their phenomenal field.

Unconditional Positive Regard

Human beings develop an ideal self and a real self, based on the conditional status of positive regard. How closely one's real self matches up with their ideal self is called congruence. We experience congruence when our thoughts about our real self and ideal self are very similar—in other words when our self-concept is accurate. High congruence leads to a greater sense of self-worth and a healthy, productive life. Conversely, when there is a great discrepancy between our ideal and actual selves, we experience a state Rogers called incongruence, which can lead to maladjustment.

According to Rogers, parents can help their children achieve their ideal self by giving them unconditional positive regard, or unconditional love. In the development of self-concept, positive regard is key. Unconditional positive regard is an environment that is free of preconceived notions of value. Conditional positive regard is full of conditions of worth that must be achieved to be considered successful. Rogers (1980) explained it this way: "As persons are accepted and prized, they tend to develop a more caring attitude towards themselves" (p. 116).

The Good Life

Rogers described life in terms of principles rather than stages of development. These principles exist in fluid processes rather than static states. He claimed that a fully functioning person would continually aim to fulfill his or her potential in each of these processes, achieving what he called "the good life." These people would allow personality and self-concept to emanate from experience. He found that fully functioning individuals had several traits or tendencies in common:

1. A growing openness to experience–they move away from defensiveness.

2. An increasingly existential lifestyle–living each moment fully, rather than distorting the moment to fit personality or self-concept.
3. Increasing organismic trust–they trust their own judgment and their ability to choose behavior that is appropriate for each moment.
4. Freedom of choice–they are not restricted by incongruence and are able to make a wide range of choices more fluently. They believe that they play a role in determining their own behavior and so feel responsible for their own behavior.
5. Higher levels of creativity–they will be more creative in the way they adapt to their own circumstances without feeling a need to conform.
6. Reliability and constructiveness–they can be trusted to act constructively. Even aggressive needs will be matched and balanced by intrinsic goodness in congruent individuals.
7. A rich full life–they will experience joy and pain, love and heartbreak, fear and courage more intensely.

Abraham Maslow's Hierarchy of Needs

Abraham Maslow (1908–1970) was an American psychologist who is best known for proposing a **hierarchy of human needs** in motivating behavior. Maslow described a pattern through which human motivations generally move, meaning that in order for motivation to occur at the next level, each level must be satisfied within the individual themselves. These stages include:

- physiological needs: the main physical requirements for human survival, including homeostasis, food, water, sleep, shelter, and sex.
- safety needs: the need for personal, emotional, financial, and physical security. Once a person's physiological needs are relatively satisfied, their safety needs take precedence and dominate behavior. In the absence of physical safety – due to war, natural disaster, family violence, childhood abuse, institutional racism, etc. – people may (re-)experience post-traumatic stress disorder or transgenerational trauma. In the absence of economic safety – due to an economic crisis and lack of work opportunities – these safety needs manifest themselves in ways such as a preference for job security, grievance procedures for protecting the individual from unilateral authority, savings accounts, insurance policies, disability accommodations, etc. This level is more likely to predominate in children as they generally have a greater need to feel safe.
- love and belonging: the need for friendships, intimacy, and belonging. This need is especially strong in childhood and it can override the need for safety as witnessed in children who cling to abusive parents. Deficiencies within this level of Maslow's hierarchy – due to hospitalism, neglect, shunning, ostracism, etc. – can adversely affect the individual's ability to form and maintain emotionally significant relationships in general.
- esteem: the typical human desire to be accepted and valued by others. People often engage in a profession or hobby to gain recognition. Esteem needs are ego needs or status needs. People develop a concern with getting recognition, status, importance, and respect from others. Most humans have a need to feel respected; this includes the need to have self-esteem and self-respect.
- self-actualization: Maslow describes this level as the desire to accomplish everything that one can, to become the most that one can be. Individuals may perceive or focus on this need very specifically. For example, one individual may have a strong desire to become an ideal parent. In another, the desire may be expressed athletically. For others, it may be expressed in paintings, pictures, or inventions. Some examples of this include utilizing abilities and talents, pursuing goals, and seeking happiness.

Furthermore, this theory is a key foundation in understanding how drive and motivation are correlated when discussing human behavior. Each of these individual levels contains a certain amount of internal sensation that must be met in order for an individual to complete their hierarchy. The goal in Maslow's theory is to attain the fifth level or stage of **self-actualization.**

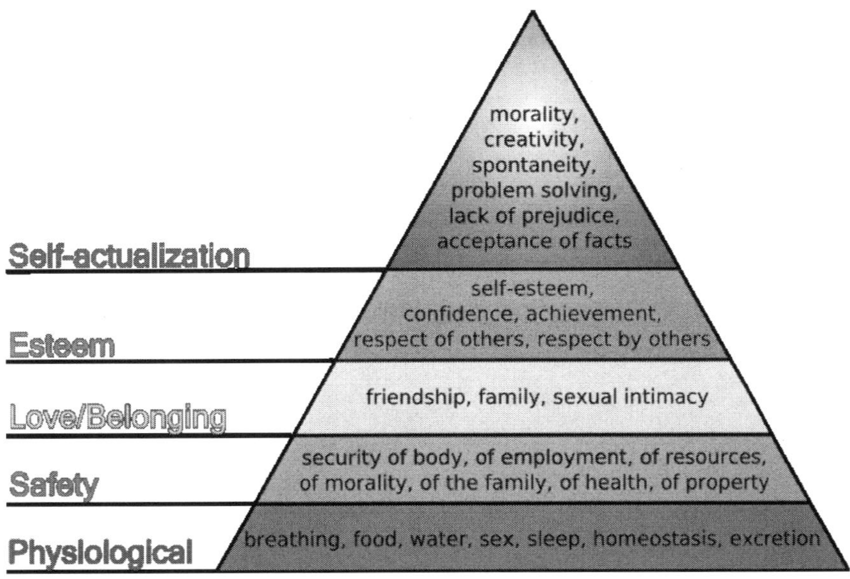

Figure 2. Diagram of Maslow's hierarchy of needs. Maslow's hierarchy of needs is often portrayed in the shape of a pyramid with the largest, most fundamental needs at the bottom and the need for self-actualization and transcendence at the top. In other words, the crux of the theory is that individuals' most basic needs must be met before they become motivated to achieve higher-level needs.

WATCH IT

Watch as Maslow's hierarchy of needs comes to life in this quick video.

- https://youtu.be/O-4ithG_07Q

Contextual Perspectives: A Broad Approach to Development

The **contextual perspective** considers the relationship between individuals and their physical, cognitive, and social worlds. It also examines socio-cultural and environmental influences on development. We will focus on two major theorists who pioneered this perspective: Lev Vygotsky and Urie Bronfenbrenner. Lev Vygotsky was a Russian psychologist who is best known for his sociocultural theory. He believed that social interaction plays a critical role in children's learning; through such social interactions, children go through a continuous process of scaffolded learning. Urie Bronfenbrenner developed the ecological systems theory to explain how everything in a child and the child's environment affects how a child grows and develops. He labeled different aspects or levels of the environment that influence children's development.

Vygotsky's Sociocultural Theory: Changes in thought with guidance

Figure 3. Lev Vygotsky, founder of the sociocultural theory, which emphasizes contextual factors in cognitive development.

Modern social learning theories stem from the work of Russian psychologist Lev Vygotsky, who produced his ideas as a reaction to existing conflicting approaches in psychology (Kozulin, 1990). Vygotsky's ideas are most recognized for identifying the role of social interactions and culture in the development of higher-order thinking skills. His theory is especially valuable for the insights it provides about the dynamic "interdependence between individual and social processes in the construction of knowledge" (John-Steiner & Mahn, 1996, p. 192). Vygotsky's views are often considered primarily as developmental theories, focusing on qualitative changes in behavior over time as attempts to explain unseen processes of development of thought, language, and higher-order thinking skills. Although Vygotsky's intent was mainly to understand higher psychological processes in children, his ideas have many implications and practical applications for learners of all ages.

Three themes are often identified with Vygotsky's ideas of sociocultural learning: (1) human development and learning originate in social, historical, and cultural interactions, (2) use of psychological tools, particularly language, mediate development of higher mental functions, and (3) learning occurs within the Zone of Proximal Development. While we discuss these ideas separately, they are closely interrelated, non-hierarchical, and connected.

Vygotsky's **sociocultural theory** emphasizes the importance of culture and interaction in the development of cognitive abilities. Vygotsky contended that thinking has social origins, social interactions play a critical role especially in the development of higher-order thinking skills, and cognitive development cannot be fully understood without considering the social and historical context within which it is embedded. He explained, "Every function in the child's cultural development appears twice: first, on the social level, and later, on the individual level; first between people (interpsychological) and then inside the child (intrapsychological)" (Vygotsky, 1978, p. 57). It is through working with others on a variety of tasks that a learner adopts socially shared experiences and associated effects and acquires useful strategies and knowledge (Scott & Palincsar, 2013).

Rogoff (1990) refers to this process as guided participation, where a learner actively acquires new culturally valuable skills and capabilities through a meaningful, collaborative activity with an assisting, more experienced other. It is critical to notice that these culturally mediated functions are viewed as being embedded in sociocultural activities rather than being self-contained. Development is a "transformation of participation in a sociocultural activity" not a transmission of discrete cultural knowledge or skills (Matusov, 2015, p. 315).

Scaffolding and the Zone of Proximal Development

Figure 4. According to Vygotsky, children can develop cognitively in their understanding of the world and learn what is important in society through play and cooperation with others.

Vygotsky differed with Piaget in that he believed that a person not only has a set of abilities, but also a set of potential abilities that can be realized if given the proper guidance from others. He believed that through guided participation known as **scaffolding**, with a teacher or capable peer, a child can learn cognitive skills within a certain range known as the **zone of proximal development**. While Piaget's ideas of cognitive development assume that development through certain stages is biologically determined, originates in the individual, and precedes cognitive complexity, Vygotsky presents a different view in which learning drives development. The idea of learning driving development, rather than being determined by the developmental level of the learner, fundamentally changes our understanding of the learning process and has significant instructional and educational implications (Miller, 2011).

Have you ever taught a child to perform a task? Maybe it was brushing their teeth or preparing food. Chances are you spoke to them and described what you were doing while you demonstrated the skill and let them work along with you throughout the process. You gave them assistance when they seemed to need it, but once they knew what to do-you stood back and let them go. This is scaffolding. This approach to teaching has also been adopted by educators. Rather than assessing students on what they are doing, they should be understood in terms of what they are capable of doing with the proper guidance.

This difference in assumptions has significant implications for the design and development of learning experiences. If we believe as Piaget did that development precedes learning, then we will make sure that new concepts and problems are not introduced until learners have developed innate capabilities to understand them. On the other hand, if we believe as Vygotsky did that learning drives development and that development occurs as we learn a variety of concepts and principles, recognizing their applicability to new tasks and new situations, then our instructional design will look very different.

WATCH IT

Watch this video to learn more about Vygotsky's theory of sociocultural development.

- https://youtu.be/-p_-On2f35o

Bronfenbrenner's Ecological Systems Theory

Another psychologist who recognized the importance of the environment on development was American psychologist, Urie Bronfenbrenner (1917-2005), who formulated the **ecological systems theory** to explain how the inherent qualities of a child and their environment interact to influence how they will grow and develop. The term "ecological" refers to a natural environment; human development is understood through this model as a long-lasting transformation in the way one perceives and deals with the environment. Bronfenbrenner's ecological theory stresses the importance of studying children in the context of multiple environments because children typically find themselves enmeshed simultaneously in different ecosystems. Each of these systems inevitably interact with and influence each other in every aspect of the child's life, from the most intimate level to the broadest. Furthermore, he eventually renamed his theory the **bioecological model** in order to recognize the importance of biological processes in development. However, he only recognized biology as producing a person's potential, with this potential being realized or not via environmental and social forces.

An individual is impacted by **microsystems** such as parents or siblings; those who have direct, significant contact with the person. The input of those people is modified by the cognitive and biological state of the individual as well. These influence the person's actions, which in turn influence systems operating on them. The **mesosystem** includes larger organizational structures such as school, the family, or religion. These institutions impact the microsystems just described. For example, the religious teachings and traditions of a family may create a climate that makes the family feel stigmatized and this indirectly impacts the child's view of their self and others. The philosophy of the school system, daily routine, assessment methods, and other characteristics can affect the child's self-image, growth, sense of accomplishment, and schedule, thereby impacting the child physically, cognitively, and emotionally. These mesosystems both influence and are influenced by the larger contexts of the community, referred to as the **exosystem**. A community's values, history, and economy can impact the organizational structures it houses. And the community is influenced by **macrosystems**, which are cultural elements such as global economic conditions, war, technological trends, values, philosophies, and a society's responses to the global community. In sum, a child's experiences are shaped by larger forces such as the family, school, religion, and culture. All of this occurs within the relevant historical context and timeframe, or **chronosystem**. The chronosystem is made up of the environmental events and transitions that occur throughout a child's life, including any socio-historical events. This system consists of all the experiences that a person has had during their lifetime.

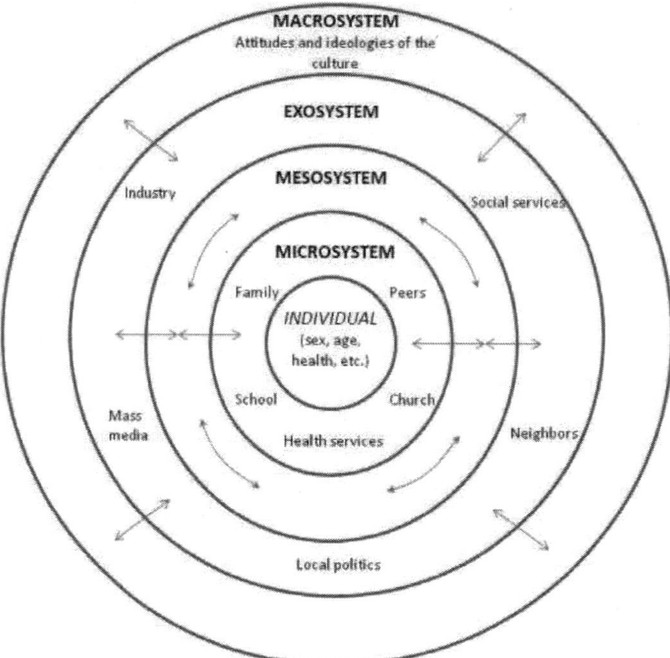

Figure 5. Brofenbrenner's ecological theory emphasizes the influence of microsystems, mesosystems, exosystems, and the macrosystems on an individual. Not pictured is the chronosystem, or the historical context and timeframe which provides the context for all the other systems. The chronosystem includes environmental events, major life transitions, and historical events.

WATCH IT

This short video from Professor Rachelle Tannenbaum of Anne Arundel Community College explains and gives examples of Brofenbrenner's theory.

- https://youtu.be/HV4E05Bnol8

The Evolutionary Perspective: Genetic Inheritance from our Ancestors

The fundamentals of the evolutionary perspective

One very influential approach in understanding human development is the evolutionary perspective, the final developmental perspective that we will consider. This perspective seeks to identify behavior that is the result of our genetic inheritance from our ancestors. **Evolutionary psychology** is a theoretical approach in the social and natural sciences that examines psychological structure from a modern evolutionary perspective. It seeks to identify which human psychological traits are evolved adaptations – that is, the functional products of natural selection or sexual selection in human evolution. David M. Buss is an evolutionary psychologist at the University of Texas at Austin, theorizing and researching human sex differences in mate selection. The primary topics of his research include male mating strategies, conflict between the sexes, social status, social reputation, prestige, the emotion of jealousy, homicide, anti-homicide defenses, and—most recently—stalking. All of these are approached from an evolutionary perspective.

Figure 6. A portrait of Charles Robert Darwin. *In the distant future I see open fields for far more important researches. Psychology will be based on a new foundation, that of the necessary acquirement of each mental power and capacity by gradation.* — DARWIN, CHARLES (1859). *THE ORIGIN OF SPECIES* . P. 488 – VIA WIKISOURCE

Evolutionary psychology has its historical roots in Charles Darwin's theory of natural selection. In *The Origin of Species*, Darwin predicted that psychology would develop an evolutionary basis, and that a process of natural selection creates traits in a species that are adaptive to its environment.

Using Darwin's arguments, evolutionary approaches claim that one's genetic inheritance not only determine such physical traits as skin and eye color, but also certain personality traits and social behaviors. For example, some evolutionary developmental psychologists suggest that behavior such as shyness and jealousy may be produced in part by genetic causes, presumably because they helped increase the survival rates of human's ancient relatives.[1][2][3]

Lorenz and Imprinting

Figure 7. Through a process known as imprinting, birds who leave the nest early attach to the first moving object they see.

The evolutionary perspective draws heavily on the field of **ethology**, which examines the ways in which our biological makeup influences our behavior. The primary proponent of ethology was Konrad Lorenz, who discovered that newborn geese are genetically pre-programmed to become attached to the first moving object they see after birth. Lorenz's work led developmentalists to consider the ways in which human behavior might reflect inborn genetic patterns. Working with geese, he investigated the principle of imprinting**,** the process by which some nidifugous birds (i.e. birds that leave their nest early) bond instinctively with the first moving object that they see within the first hours of hatching. Although Lorenz did not discover the topic, he became widely known for his descriptions of imprinting as an instinctive bond.

1. David M. Buss The Evolution of Desire: Strategies of Human Mating BasicBooks, Jun 25, 2003
2. Buss, A.H 2012 Pathways to individuality: evolution and development of personality traits. Washington, DC: American psychological Association
3. Easton, JM., Schipper, L., And Shackleford, T. 2007 morbid jealousy from an evolutionary psychological perspective. Evolution and human behavior, 28, 399 –402

In psychology and ethology, **imprinting** is any kind of phase-sensitive learning (learning occurring at a particular age or a particular life stage) that is rapid and apparently independent of the consequences of behavior. It was first used to describe situations in which an animal or person learns the characteristics of some stimulus, which is therefore said to be "imprinted" onto the subject. Imprinting is hypothesized to have a critical period.

Behavioral Genetics

The evolutionary perspective encompasses one of the fastest-growing areas within the field of lifespan development: behavioral genetics. **Behavioral genetics** is a field of scientific research that uses genetic methods to investigate the nature and origins of individual differences in behavior and studies the effects of heredity on behavior. Behavioral geneticists strive to understand how we might inherit certain behavioral traits and how the environment influences whether we actually displayed those traits. It also considers how genetic factors may influence psychological disorders such as schizophrenia, depression and substance abuse.[4][5][6]

LINK TO LEARNING

In Stanford professor and author of *Why Zebras Don't Get Ulcers*, Robert Sapolsky's Ted Talk, Sapolsky describes how our history and biology influence our behavior. This tour of our individual and collective history provides an enlightening overview of behavioral genetics.

Criticisms of the Evolutionary Perspective

There is a general acceptance that Darwin's evolutionary theory provides an accurate description of basic genetic processes and that the evolutionary perspective is increasingly visible in the field of lifespan development. However, applications of the evolutionary perspective have been subjected to considerable criticism. Some developmental psychologists are concerned over too much emphasis on genetic and biological aspects of behavior and suggest that the evolutionary perspective places insufficient attention on environmental and social factors involved in producing children's and adults behavior. Other critics argue that there is no good way to experimentally test theories derived from this approach because humans evolved so long ago. For example, we may admit that jealousy helps individuals to survive more effectively, but how do we prove it. All things considered however, the evolutionary approach is continually stimulating research on how our biological inheritance at least partially influences our traits and behaviors.[7][8][9]

4. Origins of the Social Mind: Evolutionary Psychology and Child Development, Bruce J. Ellis, David F. Bjorklund pp 3-18 New York Guilford Press, Jan 1, 2005
5. Rembis , M. 2009(re)defining disability in the "genetic age": behavioral genetics, "new" eugenics and the future of impairment. Disability and society, 24, 585 - 597
6. PLOMIN, R., DEFRIES, J. C. , KnOPIK, V. S., & NEIDERHISER, J. M. 2016. Top 10 replicated findings from behavioral genetics. Perspectives on psychological science, 11, 3–23.
7. Bjorklund, D. 2006 mother knows best, epigenetic inheritance, maternal effects, and the evolution of human intelligence. Developmental review, 26, 213 –242.
8. Baptista, T., Aldana, E., Angeles , F., And Beaulieu , S. 2008. Evolution theory: an overview of its applications in psychiatry. Psychopathology, 41, 17 –27.
9. Del Giudice, M. 2015. Self-regulation in an evolutionary perspective. In G. E. Gendolla, M. Tops, S. L. Koole, G. E. Gendolla, M. Tops, & S. L. Koole (Eds), Handbook of behavioral approaches to self-regulation. New York, New York: Springer science + business media

Comparing and Evaluating Lifespan Theories

Developmental theories provide a set of guiding principles and concepts that describe and explain human development. Some developmental theories focus on the formation of a particular quality, such as Piaget's theory of cognitive development. Other developmental theories focus on growth that happens throughout the lifespan, such as Erikson's theory of psychosocial development. It would be natural to wonder which of the perspectives provides the most accurate account of human development, but clearly, each perspective is based on its own premises and focuses on different aspects of development. Many lifespan developmentalists use an eclectic approach, drawing on several perspectives at the same time because the same developmental phenomenon can be looked at from a number of perspectives.

In the table below, we'll review some of the major theories that you learned about in this module. Recall that three key issues considered in human development examine if development is continuous or discontinuous, if it is the same for everyone or distinct for individuals (one course of development or many), and if development is more influenced by nature or by nurture. The table below reviews how each of these major theories approaches each of these issues.

Table 1. Major Theories in Human Development[10]

Theory	Major ideas	Continuous or discontinuous development?	One course of development or many?	More influenced by nature or nurture?	Major Theorist(s)
Psychosexual theory	Behavior is motivated by inner forces, memories, and conflicts that are generally beyond people's awareness and control. Emphasizes the unconscious, defense mechanisms, and influences of the id, ego, and superego.	Discontinuous; there are distinct stages of development	One course; stages are universal for everyone	Both; natural impulses combined with early childhood experiences impact development	Sigmund Freud
Psychosocial theory	A person negotiates biological and sociocultural influences as they move through eight stages, each characterized by a psychosocial crisis: trust vs. mistrust, autonomy vs. shame/doubt, initiative vs. guilt, industry vs. inferiority, identity vs. role confusion, intimacy vs. isolation, generativity vs. stagnation, ego integrity vs. despair.	Discontinuous; there are distinct stages of development	One course; stages are universal for everyone	Both; natural impulses combined with sociocultural experiences impact development	Erik Erikson
Classical conditioning	Learning by the association of a response with a stimulus; a person comes to respond in a particular way to a neutral stimulus that normally does not bring about that type of response.	Continuous; learning is ongoing without distinct stages	Many courses; learned behaviors vary by person	Mostly nurture; behavior is conditioned	Ivan Pavlov, John Watson
Operant conditioning	Learning that occurs when a voluntary response is strengthened or weakened by its association with positive or negative consequences. Rewards and punishments can strengthen or discourage behaviors.	Continuous; learning is ongoing without distinct stages	Many courses; learned behaviors vary by person	Mostly nurture; behavior is conditioned	B.F. Skinner
Social cognitive	Learning occurs in a social context; considering the	Continuous; learning is gradual and ongoing	Many courses; learned	Mostly nurture; behavior is observed	Albert Bandura

10. Berk, L. E. (1998). "Stances of Major Theories on Basic Issues in Human Development."Development through the lifespan. Boston: Allyn and Bacon. p. 26.

theory (social learning theory)	relationship between the environment and a person's behavior. Learning can occur through observation.	without distinct stages	behaviors vary by person	and learned	
Piaget's theory of cognitive development	A theory about how people come to gradually acquire, construct, and use knowledge and information. It describes cognitive development through four distinct stages: sensorimotor, preoperational, concrete, and formal.	Discontinuous; there are distinct stages of development	One course; stages are universal for everyone	Both; natural impulses combined with experiences that challenge the existing schemas	Jean Piaget
Information processing	A theory that seeks to identify the ways individuals take in, use, and store information (sometimes compared to a computer). It is based on the idea that humans process the information they receive, rather than merely respond to stimuli.	Continuous; cognitive development is gradual and ongoing without distinct stages	One course; the model applies to everyone	Both; natural cognitive development combined with experiences of processing information in new and different ways	Richard Atkinson, Richard Shiffrin
Humanistic theories	Theories that emphasizes an individual's inherent drive towards self-actualization and contend that people have a natural capacity to make decisions about their lives and control their own behavior. Key terms and concepts include unconditional positive regard, striving for "the good life," and the hierarchy of needs.	Continuous; development is ongoing without distinct stages and can be multidirectional depending on environmental circumstances	Mostly one course; Maslow's hierarchy of needs is universally applied, but there is an individual course for self-actualization	Mostly nurture; development is influenced by environmental circumstances and social interactions	Carl Rogers, Abraham Maslow
Sociocultural theory	Vygotsky's theory that emphasizes how cognitive development proceeds as a result of social interactions between members of a culture. Key terms and concepts include the zone of proximal development and scaffolding.	Both, but mostly continuous as an individual learns and progresses	Many courses; there are variations between individuals and cultures	Both; development is influenced by biological preparation and social experiences	Lev Vygotsky
Bioecological systems model	Urie Bronfenbrenner's theory stressing the importance of studying a child in the context of multiple environments, or ecological systems. It is organized into five levels of external influence: microsystem, mesosystem, exosystem, macrosystem, and chronosystem.	Both; the influence of each system can be continuous or discontinuous depending on the system in question	Many courses; the interaction of people and the environment varies	Both; a person's biological potential and the environment interact to impact development	Urie Bronfenbrenner, Stephen Ceci
Evolutionary psychology theory	A theory that seeks to identify behavior that is a result of our genetic inheritance from our ancestors.	Continuous; current behaviors have been shaped over multiple generations based on successful survival and reproduction	Both; behavioral genetics show similarities across the species, but our unique family history also plays a role in development	Both; our genetic history and biological impulses interact with life experiences to produce individual development and development across the history and future of the species	Charles Darwin, David Buss, Konrad Lorenz, Robert Sapolsky

GLOSSARY

behavioral genetics:
one of the fastest-growing areas within the field of lifespan development and studies the effects of heredity on behavior

bioecological model:
the perspective suggesting that multiple levels of the environment interact with biological potential to influence development

chronosystem:
the environmental events and transitions that occur throughout a child's life, including any socio-historical events

congruence:
an instance or point of agreement or correspondence between the ideal self and the real self in Rogers' humanistic personality theory

contextual perspective:
a theory that considers the relationship between individuals and their physical, cognitive, and social worlds

ecological systems theory:
Urie Bronfenbrenner's theory stressing the importance of studying a child in the context of multiple environments, organized into five levels of external influence: microsystem, mesosystem, exosystem, macrosystem, and chronosystem

exosystem:
the larger contexts of the community, including the values, history, and economy

ethology:
the study of behavior through a biological lens

evolutionary psychology:
a field of study that seeks to identify behavior that is a result of our genetic inheritance from our ancestors

humanism:
a psychological theory that emphasizes an individual's inherent drive towards self-actualization and contends that people have a natural capacity to make decisions about their lives and control their own behavior

imprinting:
in psychology and ethology, imprinting is any kind of phase-sensitive learning (learning occurring at a particular age or a particular life stage) that is rapid and apparently independent of the consequences of behavior

macrosystem:
cultural elements such as global economic conditions, war, technological trends, values, philosophies, and a society's responses to the global community which impact a community

Maslow's hierarchy of needs:
a motivational theory in psychology comprising a five-tier model of human needs, often depicted as hierarchical levels within a pyramid. Needs lower down in the hierarchy must be satisfied before individuals are motivated to attend to needs higher up

mesosystem:
larger organizational structures such as school, the family, or religion

microsystem:
immediate surrounds including those who have direct, significant contact with the person, such as parents or siblings

phenomenal field:
our subjective reality, all that we are aware of, including objects and people as well as our behaviors, thoughts, images, and ideas

scaffolding:
a process in which adults or capable peers model or demonstrate how to solve a problem, and then step back, offering support as needed

self-actualization:
according to humanistic theory, the realizing of one's full potential can include creative expression, a quest for spiritual enlightenment, the pursuit of knowledge, or the desire to contribute to society. For Maslow, it is a state of self-fulfillment in which people achieve their highest potential in their own unique way

sociocultural theory:
Vygotsky's theory that emphasizes how cognitive development proceeds as a result of social interactions between members of a culture

zone of proximal development (ZPD):
the difference between what a learner can do without help, and what they can do with help

Discussion: Developmental Theories

DISCUSSION: In this discussion, reflect upon and discuss ALL of the following questions:

- Q1: Is human development best characterized as a slow, gradual process, or is it best viewed as one of more abrupt change?
- Q2: Which developmental theory makes the most sense to you and why? Give examples from your own life or other personal observations on development. What evidences do you see that support this theory?

STEP 1: First, write a response with at least EIGHT substantial sentences, integrating concepts you learned from the reading and other materials (include links with necessary). Show that you can think critically on the topic by integrating your own thoughts, analysis, or experiences.

STEP 2: Then return to the discussion to comment on at least TWO classmates' posts (in at least FIVE sentences). Expand on a classmate's comments in a value-adding, topic-related way. Promote a collaborative, supportive community, and advance the dialogue through follow-up questions. Reply posts cannot be one-liners, off-topic posts, vague statements, unsupported opinions, inadequate explanations or simply say, "I agree" or "good job."

Putting It Together: Developmental Theories

We have considered six major perspectives on development—psychodynamic, behavioral, cognitive, humanistic, contextual, and evolutionary. If you were wondering which approach is considered most important, that would be the wrong question for several reasons. Each perspective focuses on different aspects of development.

The psychodynamic perspective suggests that behavior is motivated by inner forces, memories, and conflicts that are generally beyond people's awareness and control. It focuses on the unconscious determinants of behavior. Freud, in his psychoanalytical theory, proposed that personality has three aspects: id, ego, and superego. Contrary to Freud, Eric Erickson proposed a psychosocial approach and suggested that our social interaction with others, the society, and culture in which we evolve challenge us and shape us. The behavioral perspective focuses on observable behavior and environmental stimuli. Behavioral theories reject the notion that people universally pass through a series of stages. Behaviorists believe that people are affected by the environment to which they happen to be exposed.

The cognitive and humanistic perspectives look more at what people think than what they do. Piaget proposed that all people pass through a fixed sequence of universal stages of cognitive development. His focus was on the change in cognition that occurs as children move from one stage to the next. The humanistic perspective points to other concepts, such as congruence and self-actualization, and has helped describe important aspects of human behavior.

The contextual perspective examines social and cultural influences on development. It considers the relationship between individuals and their physical, cognitive, and social world. This perspective suggests that a person's unique development cannot be properly viewed without seeing how that person is deeply influenced by a rich social and cultural context. Two major theories that fall under this category are Brofenbrenner's bioecological approach and Vygotsky's social-cultural theory.

And finally, the evolutionary perspective focuses on how inherited biological factors underlie development. You may think of several examples of human behavior that you have seen that seem to have been inherited from our ancestors because they helped individuals survive and reproduce.

Each perspective that we have seen bases its premises and focuses on different aspects of development. Furthermore, the same developmental phenomenon can be looked at simultaneously from a number of perspectives. Considering them simultaneously paints a fuller portrait of the countless ways human beings change and grow over the course of their lives.

MODULE 3: PRENATAL DEVELOPMENT

Why It Matters: Prenatal Development

Why learn about prenatal development and genetics?

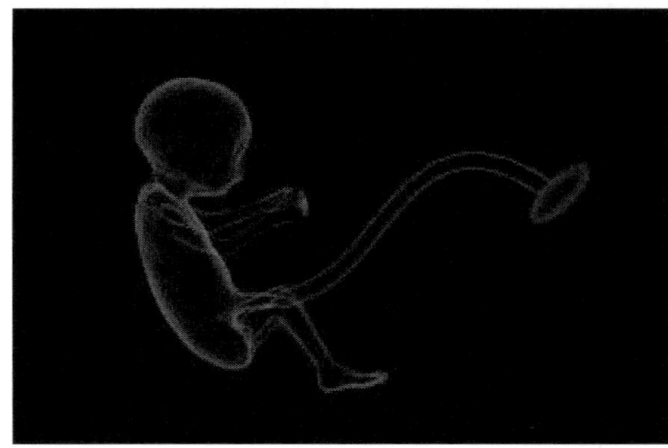

People endure quite an incredible journey before they are born. Think about it—when the timing and conditions are just right, a tiny egg releases from ovulation and a single sperm out of hundreds of millions unite to begin the process of fertilization. Genetic material from the mother and father join together to form a completely new organism. This new organism has to continue to travel and implant in the uterine wall in order to continue to grow and thrive. It is not an easy feat. It still must grow and develop for approximately 268 days before it begins life outside of the womb.

Today we have more knowledge and technology than ever before that has an impact on this process. We are privy to tests that can give us a wealth of information even before we conceive. We have the ability to know the genetic make-up of an embryo before it is implanted in the womb. If you could choose all of the features of your future baby, would you? What would be the pros and cons of this? New parents also have the choice of the prenatal care that they receive and how they want to prepare for labor and delivery. As you can see, the choices that are made along the way and the unforeseen surprises make for a unique pregnancy and birth story.

This module explores this journey and the development process from the moment of conception to delivery.

WATCH IT

Watch the selected clip from this video to see the fascinating animation of a fetus growing and developing inside of the womb.

- https://youtu.be/fKyljukBE70

Biological Foundations of Human Development

What you'll learn to do: explain the role of genetics in prenatal development

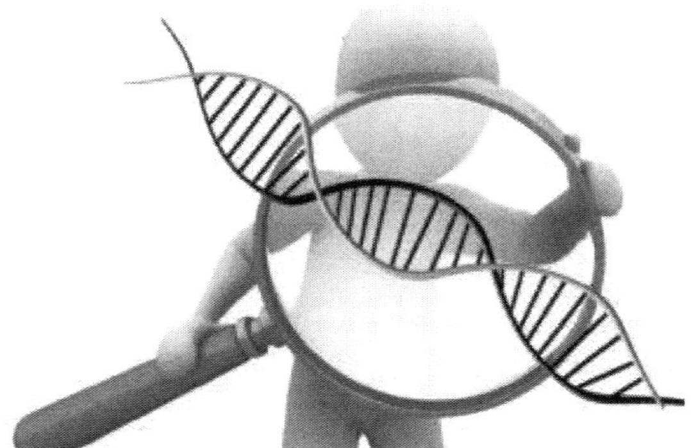

In this section, we will look at some of the ways in which heredity helps to shape the way we are. Heredity involves more than genetic information from our parents. According to evolutionary psychology, our genetic inheritance comes from the most adaptive genes of our ancestors. We will look at what happens genetically during conception and take a brief look at some genetic abnormalities. Before going into these topics, however, it is important to emphasize the interplay between heredity and the environment. Why are you the way you are? As you consider some of your features (height, weight, personality, health, etc.), ask yourself whether these features are a result of heredity, or environmental factors, or both. Chances are, you can see the ways in which both heredity and environmental factors (such as lifestyle, diet, and so on) have contributed to these features.

LEARNING OUTCOMES

- Explain the evolutionary psychology perspective of lifespan development
- Describe genetic components of conception
- Describe genes and their importance in genetic inheritance
- Describe chromosomal abnormalities
- Explain the value of prenatal testing
- Describe the interaction between genetics and the environment
- Compare monozygotic and dizygotic twins

Evolutionary Psychology

Evolutionary Psychology

Evolutionary psychology focuses on how universal patterns of behavior and cognitive processes have evolved over time. Variations in cognition and behavior would make individuals more or less successful in reproducing and passing those genes to their offspring. Evolutionary psychologists study a variety of psychological phenomena that may have evolved as adaptations, including the fear response, food preferences, mate selection, and cooperative behaviors (Confer et al., 2010).

Figure 1. Evolutionary psychology examines the connection between biological adaptation and preferences in mate selection.

Many think of evolution as the development of traits and behaviors that allow us to survive this "dog-eat-dog" world, like strong leg muscles to run fast, or fists to punch and defend ourselves. However, physical survival is only important if it eventually contributes to successful reproduction. That is, even if you live to be 100 years old, if you fail to mate and produce children, your genes will die with your body. Thus, *reproductive* success, not *survival* success, is the engine of evolution by natural selection.

Charles Darwin describes this process in the **theory of evolution by natural selection**. In simple terms, the theory states that organisms that are better suited for their environment will survive and reproduce, while those that are poorly suited for their environment will die off. There is a growing interest in applying the principles of evolutionary psychology to better understand lifespan development in humans.

Lifespan Development and Evolutionary Psychology

As we consider development from conception through the lifespan, there will be many opportunities to understand how evolutionary psychology enhances our understanding of development. For instance, women and men do differ in their preferences for a few key qualities in long-term mating, because of somewhat distinct adaptive concerns. Modern women have inherited the evolutionary trait to desire mates who possess resources, have qualities linked with acquiring resources (e.g., ambition, wealth, industriousness), and are willing to share those resources with them. On the other hand, men more strongly desire youth and health in women, as both are cues to fertility. These male and female differences have historically been universal in humans.

Just because a psychological adaptation was advantageous in our history, doesn't mean it's still useful today. For example, even though women may have preferred men with resources in previous generations, our modern society has advanced such that these preferences are no longer necessary. Nonetheless, it's important to consider how our evolutionary history has shaped our automatic or "instinctual" desires and reflexes of today so that we can better shape them for the future ahead.

As we follow the journey of life, from conception to death, think about how the theory of natural selection and the concepts of evolutionary psychology can enlighten our understanding of why some automatic reflexes or instinctual desires are more common than others. Remember that the end product of the theory of evolution by natural selection is successful survival and reproduction. Can you think of some ways that the ultimate goal of reproductive success affects our selection of a mate, how we parent young children, why we are motivated to achieve certain goals, or what differentiates families with traditionally longer lifespans? In order to achieve reproductive success, the theory of evolution by natural selection states that organisms should be suited to their environment. Think about how different environments or cultures require different traits for successful survival and reproduction. Can you think of some ways that we may be changing to be better suited to our changing culture?

LINK TO LEARNING

David Buss is one of the leading researchers in evolutionary psychology. In David Buss' Ted Talk, he explains several theories related to the selection of sexual partners, mating preferences, and infidelity.

Heredity and Chromosomes

Gametes

There are two types of sex cells or **gametes** involved in reproduction: the male gametes, or sperm, and female gametes, or ova. The male gametes are produced in the testes through a process called spermatogenesis, which begins at about 12 years of age. The female gametes, which are stored in the ovaries, are present at birth but are immature. Each ovary contains about 250,000 ova but only about 400 of these will become mature eggs (Mackon & Fauser, 2000; Rome, 1998). Beginning at puberty, one ovum ripens and is released about every 28 days, a process called oogenesis.

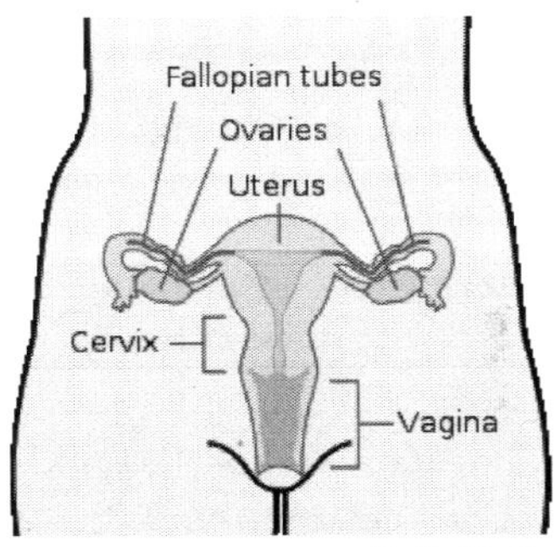

Figure 2. The Female Reproductive System.

After the ovum or egg ripens and is released from the ovary, it is drawn into the fallopian tube and in 3 to 4 days, reaches the uterus. It is typically fertilized in the fallopian tube and continues its journey to the uterus. At ejaculation, millions of sperm are released into the vagina, but only a few reach the egg and typically, only one fertilizes the egg. Once a single sperm has entered the wall of the egg, the wall becomes hard and prevents other sperm from entering. After the sperm has entered the egg, the tail of the sperm breaks off and the head of the sperm, containing the genetic information from the father, unites with the nucleus of the egg. As a result, a new cell is formed. This cell, containing the combined genetic information from both parents, is referred to as a zygote.

WATCH IT

Watch as one single sperm survives the long and treacherous journey to fertilize the mother's egg.

- https://youtu.be/_5OvgQW6FG4

Chromosomes

While other normal human cells have 46 chromosomes (or 23 pair), gametes contain 23 chromosomes. **Chromosomes** are long threadlike structures found in a cell nucleus that contain genetic material known as **deoxyribonucleic acid (DNA)**. DNA is a helix-shaped molecule made up of nucleotide base pairs [adenine (A), guanine (G), cytosine (C), and thymine (T)]. In each chromosome, sequences of DNA make up **genes** that control or partially control a number of visible characteristics, known as traits, such as eye color, hair color, and so on. A single gene may have multiple possible variations or alleles. An **allele** is a specific version of a gene. So, a given gene may code for the trait of hair color, and the different alleles of that gene affect which hair color an individual has.

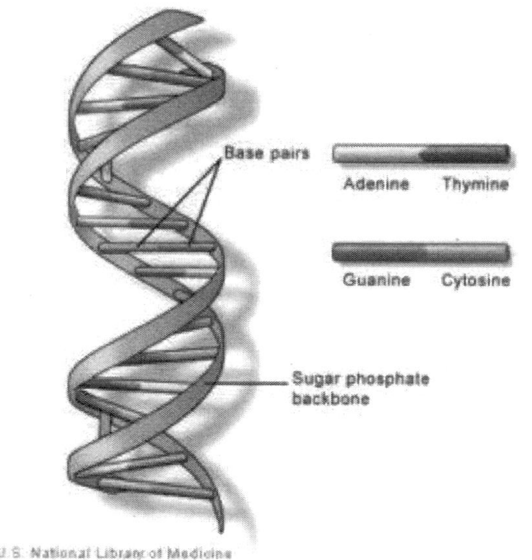

Figure 3. Deoxyribonucleic acid (DNA) is a helix-shaped molecule made up of nucleotide base pairs. Sequences of DNA make up genes.

In a process called meiosis, segments of the chromosomes from each parent form pairs and genetic segments are exchanged as determined by chance. Because of the unpredictability of this exchange, the likelihood of having offspring that are genetically identical (and not twins) is one in trillions (Gould & Keeton, 1997). Genetic variation is important because it allows a species to adapt so that those who are better suited to the environment will survive and reproduce, which is an important factor in natural selection.

Genotypes and Phenotypes

When a sperm and egg fuse, their 23 chromosomes pair up and create a zygote with 23 pairs of chromosomes. Therefore, each parent contributes half the genetic information carried by the offspring; the resulting physical characteristics of the offspring (called the phenotype) are determined by the interaction of genetic material supplied by the parents (called the genotype). A person's **genotype** is the genetic makeup of that individual. **Phenotype,** on the other hand, refers to the individual's inherited physical characteristics.

Look in the mirror. What do you see, your genotype or your phenotype? What determines whether or not genes are expressed? Actually, this is quite complicated. Some features follow the additive pattern which means that many different genes contribute to a final outcome. Height and skin tone are examples. In other cases, a gene might either be turned on or off depending on several factors, including the gene with which it is paired or the inherited epigenetic tags.

WATCH IT

Watch the following clip that explains meiosis.

- https://youtu.be/nMEyeKQClql

LINK TO LEARNING

Visit the webpage "What are DNA and Genes?" from the University of Utah to better understand DNA and genes, then watch the video "What is Inheritance?" to learn how the genes from parents pass on genetic information to their children.

Determining the Sex of the Child

Twenty-two of those chromosomes from each parent are similar in length to a corresponding chromosome from the other parent. However, the remaining chromosome looks like an X or a Y. Half of the male's sperm contain a Y chromosome and half contain an X. All of the ova contain X chromosomes. If the child receives the combination of XY, the child will be genetically male. If it receives the XX combination, the child will be genetically female.

Many potential parents have a clear preference for having a boy or a girl and would like to determine the sex of the child. Through the years, a number of tips have been offered for the potential parents to maximize their chances for having either a son or daughter as they prefer. For example, it has been suggested that sperm which carry a Y chromosome are more fragile than those carrying an X. So, if a couple desires a male child, they can take measures to maximize the chance that the Y sperm reaches the egg. This involves having intercourse 48 hours after ovulation, which helps the Y sperm have a shorter journey to reach the egg, douching to create a more alkaline environment in the vagina, and having the female reach orgasm first so that sperm are not pushed out of the vagina during orgasm. Today, however, there is new technology available that makes it possible to isolate sperm containing either an X or a Y, depending on the preference, and use that sperm to fertilize a mother's egg.

Genetic Variation and Inheritance

Genetic variation, the genetic difference between individuals, is what contributes to a species' adaptation to its environment. In humans, genetic variation begins with an egg, several million sperm, and fertilization. The egg and the sperm each contain 23 chromosomes, which make up our genes. A single gene may have multiple possible variations or alleles (a specific version of a gene), resulting in a variety of combinations of inherited traits.

Genetic inheritance of traits for humans is based upon Gregor Mendel's model of inheritance. For genes on an autosome (any chromosome other than a sex chromosome), the alleles and their associated traits are autosomal dominant or autosomal recessive. In this model, some genes are considered dominant because they will be expressed. Others, termed recessive, are only expressed in the absence of a dominant gene. Some characteristics which were once thought of as dominant-recessive, such as eye color, are now believed to be a result of the interaction between several genes (McKusick, 1998). Dominant traits include curly hair, facial dimples, normal vision, and dark hair. Recessive characteristics include red hair, pattern baldness, and nearsightedness.

Sickle cell anemia is an autosomal recessive disease; Huntington disease is an autosomal dominant disease. Other traits are a result of partial dominance or co-dominance in which both genes are influential. For example, if a person inherits both recessive genes for cystic fibrosis, the disease will occur. But if a person has only one recessive gene for the disease, the person would be a carrier of the disease.

In this example, we will call the normal gene "N," and the gene for cystic fibrosis "c." The normal gene is dominant, which means that having the dominant allele either from one parent (Nc) or both parents (NN) will always result in the phenotype associated with the dominant allele. When someone has two copies of the same allele, they are said to be **homozygous** for that allele. When someone has a combination of alleles for a given gene, they are said to be **heterozygous**. For example, cystic fibrosis is a recessive disease which means that an individual will only have the disease if they are homozygous for that recessive allele (cc).

Imagine that a woman who is a carrier of the cystic fibrosis gene has a child with a man who also is a carrier of the same disease. What are the odds that their child would inherit the disease? Both the woman and the man are heterozygous for this gene (Nc). We can expect the offspring to have a 25% chance of having cystic fibrosis (cc), a 50% chance of being a carrier of the disease (Nc), and a 25% chance of receiving two normal copies of the gene (NN).

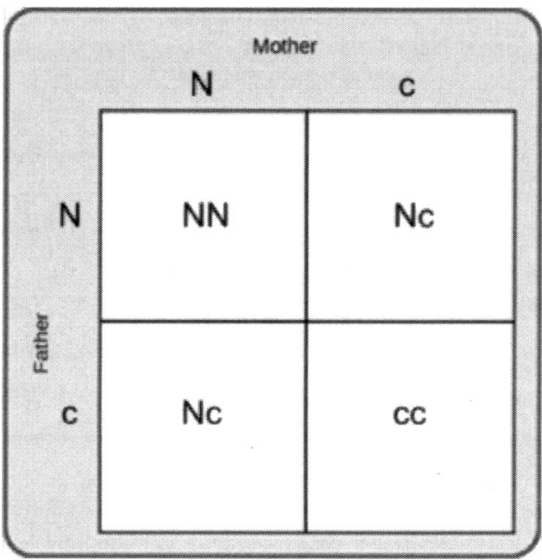

Figure 4. A Punnett square is a tool used to predict how genes will interact in the production of offspring. The capital N represents the dominant allele, and the lowercase c represents the recessive allele. In the example of the cystic fibrosis, where N is the normal gene (dominant allele), wherever a pair contains the dominant allele, N, you can expect a phenotype that does not express the disease. You can expect a cystic fibrosis phenotype only when there are two copies of the c (recessive allele) which contains the gene mutation that causes the disease.

Where do harmful genes that contribute to diseases like cystic fibrosis come from? Gene mutations provide one source of harmful genes. A **mutation** is a sudden, permanent change in a gene. While many mutations can be harmful or lethal, once in a while a mutation benefits an individual by giving that person an advantage over those who do not have the mutation. Recall that the theory of evolution asserts that individuals best adapted to their particular environments are more likely to reproduce and pass on their genes to future generations. In order for this process to occur, there must be competition—more technically, there must be variability in genes (and resultant traits) that allow for variation in adaptability to the environment. If a population consisted of identical individuals, then any dramatic changes in the environment would affect everyone in the same way, and there would be no variation in selection. In contrast, diversity in genes and associated traits allows some individuals to perform slightly better than others when faced with environmental change. This creates a distinct advantage for individuals best suited for their environments in terms of successful reproduction and genetic transmission.

WATCH IT

This video demonstrates another example of the interaction of alleles using the Punnett square.

- https://youtu.be/NR3779ef9yQ

LINK TO LEARNING

Visit the Cystic Fibrosis Foundation to learn more about cystic fibrosis and learn how a mutation in DNA leads to the disease.

Chromosomal Abnormalities and Genetic Testing

Chromosomal Abnormalities

A chromosomal abnormality occurs when a child inherits too many or too few chromosomes. The most common cause of chromosomal abnormalities is the age of the mother. A 20-year-old woman has a 1 in 800 chance of having a child with a common chromosomal abnormality. A woman of 44, however, has a one in 16 chance. It is believed that the problem occurs when the ovum is ripening prior to ovulation each month. As the mother ages, the ovum is more likely to suffer abnormalities at this time.

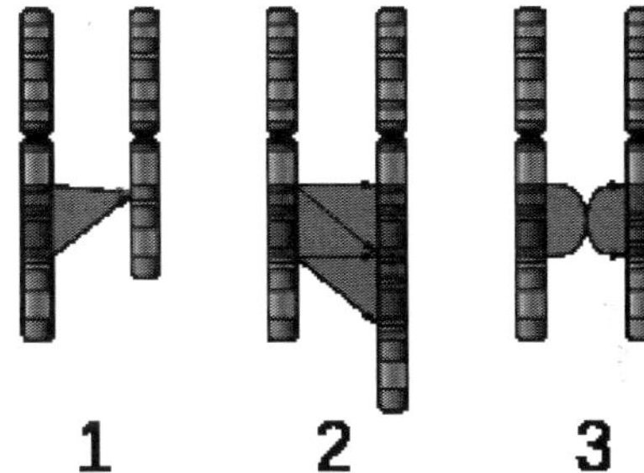

Figure 5. The three major single-chromosome mutations: deletion (1), duplication (2) and inversion (3).

Another common cause of chromosomal abnormalities occurs because the gametes do not divide evenly when they are forming. Therefore, some cells have more than 46 chromosomes. In fact, it is believed that close to half of all zygotes have an odd number of chromosomes. Most of these zygotes fail to develop and are spontaneously aborted by the body. If the abnormal number occurs on pair # 21 or # 23, however, the individual may have certain physical or other abnormalities.

An altered chromosome structure may take several different forms, and result in various disorders or malignancies:

- *Deletions*: A portion of the chromosome is missing or deleted. Known disorders in humans include Wolf-Hirschhorn syndrome, which is caused by partial deletion of the short arm of chromosome 4; and Jacobsen syndrome, also called the terminal 11q deletion disorder.
- *Duplications*: A portion of the chromosome is duplicated, resulting in extra genetic material. Known human disorders include Charcot-Marie-Tooth disease type 1A, which may be caused by duplication of the gene encoding peripheral myelin protein 22 (PMP22) on chromosome 17.

- *Translocations*: A portion of one chromosome is transferred to another chromosome. There are two main types of translocations:
    - *Reciprocal translocation*: Segments from two different chromosomes have been exchanged.
    - *Robertsonian translocation*: An entire chromosome has attached to another at the centromere – in humans, these only occur with chromosomes 13, 14, 15, 21, and 22.
- *Inversions*: A portion of the chromosome has broken off, turned upside down, and reattached, therefore the genetic material is inverted.
- *Insertions*: A portion of one chromosome has been deleted from its normal place and inserted into another chromosome.
- *Rings*: A portion of a chromosome has broken off and formed a circle or ring. This can happen with or without loss of genetic material.
- *Isochromosome*: Formed by the mirror image copy of a chromosome segment including the centromere.

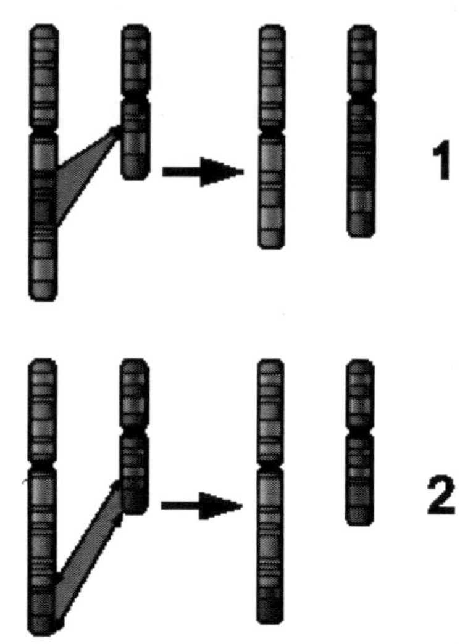

Figure 6. The two major two-chromosome mutations: insertion (1) and Translocation (2).

One of the most common chromosomal abnormalities is on pair # 21. Trisomy 21 occurs when there are three rather than two chromosomes on #21. A person with Down syndrome has distinct facial features, intellectual disability, and oftentimes heart and gastrointestinal disorders. Symptoms vary from person to person and can range from mild to severe. With early intervention, the life expectancy of persons with Down syndrome has increased in recent years. Keep in mind that there is as much variation in people with Down Syndrome as in most populations and those differences need to be recognized and appreciated.

WATCH IT

Watch the following video clip about Down Syndrome from the National Down Syndrome Society:

- https://youtu.be/TIcbFrt4F_c

When the chromosomal abnormality is on pair #23, the result is a sex-linked chromosomal abnormality. A person might have XXY, XYY, XXX, XO, or 45 or 47 chromosomes as a result. Two of the more common sex-linked chromosomal disorders are Turner syndrome and Klinefelter syndrome. Turner's syndrome occurs in 1 of every 2,500 live female births (Carroll, 2007) when an ovum which lacks a chromosome is fertilized by a sperm with an X chromosome. The resulting zygote has an XO composition. Fertilization by a Y sperm is not viable. Turner syndrome affects cognitive functioning and sexual maturation. The external genitalia appear normal, but breasts and ovaries do not develop fully and the woman does not menstruate. Turner's syndrome also results in short stature and other physical characteristics. Klinefelter syndrome (XXY) occurs in 1 out of 700 live male births and results when an ovum containing an extra X chromosome is fertilized by a Y sperm. The Y chromosome stimulates the growth of male genitalia, but the additional X chromosome inhibits this development. An individual with Klinefelter syndrome has some breast development, infertility (this is the most common cause of infertility in males), and has low levels of testosterone.

Prenatal Testing

Prenatal testing consists of prenatal screening and prenatal diagnosis, which are aspects of prenatal care that focus on detecting problems with the pregnancy as early as possible. These may be anatomic and physiologic problems with the health of the zygote, embryo, or fetus, either before gestation even starts or as early in gestation as practical. **Prenatal screening** focuses on finding problems among a large population with affordable and noninvasive methods. The most common screening procedures are routine ultrasounds, blood tests, and blood pressure measurement. **Prenatal diagnosis** focuses on pursuing additional detailed information once a particular problem has been found, and can sometimes be more invasive.

Screening can detect problems such as neural tube defects, anatomical defects, chromosome abnormalities, and gene mutations that would lead to genetic disorders and birth defects, such as spina bifida, cleft palate, Downs Syndrome, Tay–Sachs disease, sickle cell anemia, thalassemia, cystic fibrosis, muscular dystrophy, and fragile X syndrome. Some tests are designed to discover problems which primarily affect the health of the mother, such as PAPP-A to detect pre-eclampsia or glucose tolerance tests to diagnose gestational diabetes. Screening can also detect anatomical defects such as hydrocephalus, anencephaly, heart defects, and amniotic band syndrome.

Common prenatal diagnosis procedures include amniocentesis and chorionic villus sampling. Because of the miscarriage and fetal damage risks associated with amniocentesis and CVS procedures, many women prefer to first undergo screening so they can find out if the fetus' risk of birth defects is high enough to justify the risks of invasive testing. Screening tests yield a risk score which represents the chance that the baby has the birth defect; the most common threshold for high-risk is 1:270. A risk score of 1:300 would, therefore, be considered low-risk by many physicians. However, the trade-off between the risk of birth defects and risk of complications from invasive testing is relative and subjective; some parents may decide that even a 1:1000 risk of birth defects warrants an invasive test while others wouldn't opt for an invasive test even if they had a 1:10 risk score.

There are three main purposes of prenatal diagnosis: (1) to enable timely medical or surgical treatment of a condition before or after birth, (2) to give the parents the chance to abort a fetus with the diagnosed condition, and (3) to give parents the chance to prepare psychologically, socially, financially, and medically for a baby with a health problem or disability, or for the likelihood of a stillbirth. Having this information in advance of birth means that healthcare staff, as well as parents, can better prepare themselves for the delivery of a child with a health problem. For example, Down Syndrome is associated with cardiac defects that may need intervention immediately upon birth.

The American College of Obstetricians and Gynecologists (ACOG) guidelines currently recommend that all pregnant women, regardless of age, be offered invasive testing to obtain a definitive diagnosis of certain birth defects. Therefore, most physicians offer diagnostic testing to all their patients, with or without prior screening and let the patient decide.

WATCH IT

Watch this video to learn more about prenatal testing and screening during pregnancy.

- https://youtu.be/odYHHgzsc_4

Behavioral Genetics

Behavioral geneticists study how individual differences arise, in the present, through the interaction of genes and the environment. When studying human behavior, behavioral geneticists often employ twin and adoption studies to research questions of interest. Twin studies compare the rates that a given behavioral trait is shared among identical and fraternal twins; adoption studies compare those rates among biologically related relatives and adopted relatives. Both approaches provide some insight into the relative importance of genes and environment for the expression of a given trait.

Nature or Nurture?

For decades, scholars have carried on the "nature/nurture" debate. For any particular feature, those on the "nature" side would argue that heredity plays the most important role in bringing about that feature. Those on the "nurture" side would argue that one's environment is most significant in shaping the way we are. This debate continues in questions about what makes us masculine or feminine (Lippa, 2002), concerns about vision (Mutti, Kadnik, & Adams, 1996), and many other developmental issues.

Most scholars agree that there is a constant interplay between the two forces. It is difficult to isolate the root of any single behavior as a result solely of nature or nurture, and most scholars believe that even determining the extent to which nature or nurture impacts a human feature is difficult to answer. In fact, almost all human features are polygenic (a result of many genes) and multifactorial (a result of many factors, both genetic and environmental). It is as if one's genetic make-up sets up a range of possibilities, which may or may not be realized depending upon one's environmental experiences. For instance, a person might be genetically predisposed to develop diabetes, but the person's lifestyle may help bring about the disease.

When you think about your own family history, it is easy to see that there are certain personality traits, behavioral characteristics, and medical conditions that are more common than others. This is the reason that doctors ask you about your family medical history. While genetic predisposition is important to consider, there are some family members who, for a variety of reasons, seemed to defy the odds of developing these conditions. These differences can be explained in part by the effect of **epigenetic** (above the genome) changes.

WATCH IT

This video explains some of the research that gives insights into the complicated relationship between nature and nurture.

- https://youtu.be/k50yMwEOWGU

The Epigenetic Framework

The term "epigenetic" has been used in developmental psychology to describe psychological development as the result of an ongoing, bi-directional interchange between heredity and the environment. Gottlieb (1998; 2000; 2002) suggests an analytic framework for the nature/nurture debate that recognizes the interplay between the environment, behavior, and genetic expression. This bidirectional interplay suggests that the environment can effect the expression of genes just as genetic predispositions can impact a person's potentials. Likewise, environmental circumstances can trigger symptoms of a genetic disorder. For example, a person predisposed genetically for type 2 diabetes may trigger the disease through poor diet and little exercise.

The developmental psychologist Erik Erikson wrote of an *epigenetic principle* in his book *Identity: Youth and Crisis* (1968), encompassing the notion that we develop through an unfolding of our personality in predetermined stages, and that our environment and surrounding culture influence how we progress through these stages. This biological unfolding in relation to our socio-cultural settings is done in stages of psychosocial development, where "progress through each stage is in part determined by our success, or lack of success, in all the previous stages."

In typical human families, children's biological parents raise them, so it is very difficult to know whether children act like their parents due to genetic (nature) or environmental (nurture) reasons. Nevertheless, despite our restrictions on setting up human-based experiments, we do see real-world examples of nature-nurture at work in the human sphere—though they only provide partial answers to our many questions. The science of how genes and environments work together to influence behavior is called **behavioral genetics**. The easiest opportunity we have to observe this is the **adoption study**. When children are put up for adoption, the parents who give birth to them are no longer the parents who raise them. Children aren't assigned to random adoptive parents in order to suit the particular interests of a scientist but adoption still tells us some interesting things, or at least confirms some basic expectations. For instance, if the biological child of tall parents were adopted into a family of short people, do you suppose the child's growth would be affected? What about the biological child of a Spanish-speaking family adopted at birth into an English-speaking family? What language would you expect the child to speak? And what might these outcomes tell you about the difference between height and language in terms of nature-nurture?

Monozygotic and Dizygotic Twins

Another option for observing nature-nurture in humans involves **twin studies**. To analyze nature–nurture using twins, we compare the similarity of monozygotic and dizygotic pairs. **Monozygotic** twins occur when a single zygote or fertilized egg splits apart in the first two weeks of development. The result is the creation of two separate but genetically identical offspring. About one-third of twins are monozygotic twins. Monozygotic twins occur in birthing at a rate of about 3 in every 1000 deliveries worldwide (about 0.3% of the world population). Monozygotic twins are genetically nearly identical and they are always the same sex unless there has been a mutation during development. The children of monozygotic twins test genetically as half-siblings (or full siblings, if a pair of monozygotic twins reproduces with another pair of identical twins or with the same person), rather than first cousins.

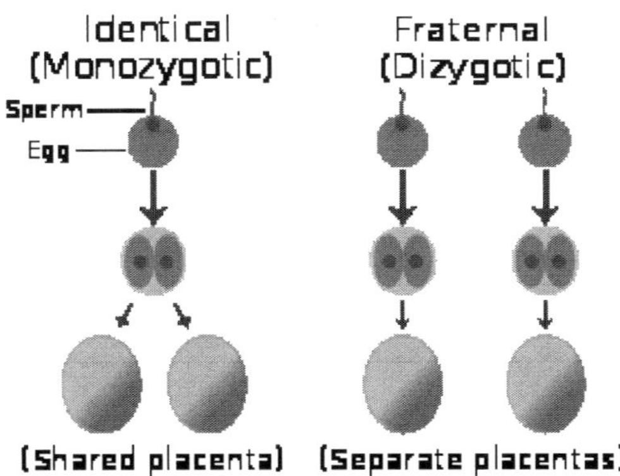

Figure 7. Monozygotic twins come from a single zygote and generally share the same placenta, although some (18-30%) have separate placentas. Dizygotic twins come from two separately fertilized eggs and have their own placentas and amniotic sacs.

Sometimes two eggs or ova are released and fertilized by two separate sperm. The result is **dizygotic** or fraternal twins. About two-thirds of twins are dizygotic. These two individuals share the same amount of genetic material as would any two children from the same mother and father. Older mothers are more likely to have dizygotic twins than are younger mothers and couples who use fertility drugs are also more likely to give birth to dizygotic twins. Consequently, there has been an increase in the number of fraternal twins in recent years (Bortolus et al., 1999). In vitro fertilization (IVF) techniques are more likely to create dizygotic twins. For IVF deliveries, there are nearly 21 pairs of twins for every 1,000.

In the uterus, a majority of monozygotic twins (60–70%) share the same placenta but have separate amniotic sacs. The **placenta** is a temporary organ that connects the developing fetus via the umbilical cord to the uterine wall to allow nutrient uptake, thermo-regulation, waste elimination, and gas exchange via the mother's blood supply. The **amniotic sac** (also called the bag of waters or the membranes), is a thin but tough transparent pair of membranes that hold a developing embryo (and later fetus) until shortly before birth. In 18–30% of monozygotic twins each fetus has a separate placenta and a separate amniotic sac. A small number (1–2%) of monozygotic twins share the same placenta and amniotic sac. Fraternal twins each have their own placenta and own amniotic sac.

Monozygotic (one egg/identical) twins can be categorized into four types depending on the timing of the separation and duplication of cells. Various types of chorionicity and amniosity (how the baby's sac looks) in monozygotic twins are a result of when the fertilized egg divides. This is known as placentation.

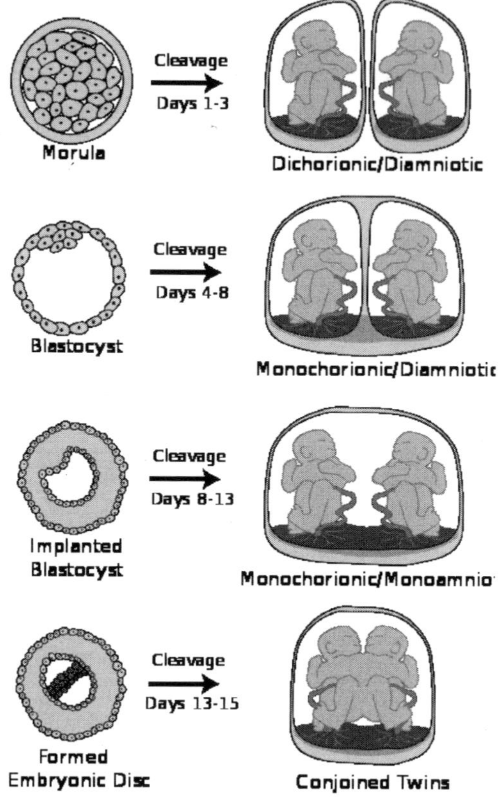

Figure 8. Various types of chorionicity and amniosity (how the baby's sac looks) in monozygotic (one egg/identical) twins as a result of when the fertilized egg divides (Author Kevin Dufenbach)

Conjoined twins

Conjoined twins are monozygotic twins whose bodies are joined together during pregnancy. This occurs when the zygote starts to split after day 12 following fertilization and fails to separate completely. This condition occurs in about 1 in 50,000 human pregnancies. Most conjoined twins are now evaluated for surgery to attempt to separate them into separate functional bodies. The degree of difficulty rises if a vital organ or structure is shared between twins, such as the brain, heart or liver.

Vanishing twins

Researchers suspect that as many as 1 in 8 pregnancies start out as multiples, but only a single fetus is brought to full term because the other fetus has died very early in the pregnancy and has not been detected or recorded. Early obstetric ultrasonography exams sometimes reveal an "extra" fetus, which fails to develop and instead disintegrates and vanishes in the uterus. There are several reasons for the "vanishing" fetus, including it being embodied or absorbed by the other fetus, placenta or the mother. This is known as vanishing twin syndrome. Also, in an unknown proportion of cases, two zygotes may fuse soon after fertilization, resulting in a single chimeric embryo, and, later, fetus.

Twin Studies

Using the features of height and spoken language as examples, let's take a look at how nature and nurture apply: identical twins, unsurprisingly, are almost perfectly similar for height. The heights of fraternal twins, however, are like any other sibling pairs: more similar to each other than to people from other families, but hardly identical. This contrast between twin types gives us a clue about the role genetics plays in determining height.

Now consider spoken language. If one identical twin speaks Spanish at home, the co-twin with whom she is raised almost certainly does too. But the same would be true for a pair of fraternal twins raised together. In terms of spoken language, fraternal twins are just as similar as identical twins, so it appears that the genetic match of identical twins doesn't make much difference.

Figure 9. Identical twins Laurent and Larry Nicolas Bourgeois, also known as the Les Twins, are internationally renowned dancers.

Twin and adoption studies are two instances of a much broader class of methods for observing nature-nurture called **quantitative genetics**, the scientific discipline in which similarities among individuals are analyzed based on how biologically related they are. We can do these studies with siblings and half-siblings, cousins, and twins who have been separated at birth and raised separately (Bouchard, Lykken, McGue, & Segal, 1990). Such twins are very rare and play a smaller role than is commonly believed in the science of nature–nurture, or with entire extended families (Plomin, DeFries, Knopik, & Neiderhiser, 2012).

It would be satisfying to be able to say that nature–nurture studies have given us conclusive and complete evidence about where traits come from, with some traits clearly resulting from genetics and others almost entirely from environmental factors, such as child-rearing practices and personal will; but that is not the case. Instead, *everything* has turned out to have some footing in genetics. The more genetically-related people are, the more similar they are—for *everything*: height, weight, intelligence, personality, mental illness, etc. Sure, it seems like common sense that some traits have a genetic bias. For example, adopted children resemble their biological parents even if they have never met them, and identical twins are more similar to each other than are fraternal twins. And while certain psychological traits, such as personality or mental illness (e.g., schizophrenia), seem reasonably influenced by genetics, it turns out that the same is true for political attitudes, how much television people watch (Plomin, Corley, DeFries, & Fulker, 1990), and whether or not they get divorced (McGue & Lykken, 1992).

GLOSSARY

adoption study:
a behavior genetic research method that involves the comparison of adopted children to their adoptive and biological parents

allele:
a specific version of a gene

amniotic sac:
a fluid-filled sac that protects and contains the fetus in the uterus

behavioral genetics:
the empirical science of how genes and environments combine to generate behavior

chromosome:
a DNA molecule with part or all of the genetic material of an organism

deoxyribonucleic acid (DNA):
a helix-shaped molecule made up of nucleotide base pairs

dizygotic:
derived from two separate ova

epigenetics:
the study of heritable phenotype changes that do not involve alterations in the DNA sequence; the prefix epi- means above

evolutionary psychology:
a field of psychology that focuses on how universal patterns of behavior and cognitive processes have evolved over time

gamete:
a male or female reproductive cell

genes:
sequences of DNA that control or partially control a number of characteristics

genotype:
the genetic makeup of an individual

heterozygous:
a combination of alleles for a given gene

homozygous:
having two copies of the same allele for a given gene

monozygotic:
derived from a single ovum

mutation:
a sudden permanent change in a gene

phenotype:
the individual's inherited physical characteristics

placenta:
an organ that develops in the uterus during pregnancy to provide oxygen and nutrients to the fetus

prenatal diagnosis:
an aspect of prenatal care focused on pursuing additional detailed information once a particular problem has been found

prenatal screening:
an aspect of prenatal care focused on finding problems among a large population with affordable and noninvasive methods

quantitative genetics:
scientific and mathematical methods for inferring genetic and environmental processes based on the degree of genetic and environmental similarity among organisms

theory of evolution by natural selection:
the process by which organisms change over time so that those with genes and behaviors better suited for their environment will survive and reproduce, while those that are poorly suited for their environment will die off

twin studies:
a behavior genetic research method that involves a comparison of the similarity of identical (monozygotic; MZ) and fraternal (dizygotic; DZ) twins

Prenatal Development

What you'll learn to do: explain the main stages of prenatal development

How did you come to be who you are? From beginning as a one-cell structure to your birth, your prenatal development occurred in an orderly and delicate sequence. There are three stages of prenatal development: germinal, embryonic, and fetal. Keep in mind that this is different than the three trimesters of pregnancy. Let's take a look at what happens to the developing baby in each of these stages.

LEARNING OUTCOMES

- Differentiate between development during the germinal, embryonic, and fetal periods
- Examine risks to prenatal development posed by exposure to teratogens
- Explain potential complications of pregnancy and delivery

Prenatal Development

"The body of the unborn baby is more complex than ours. The preborn baby has several extra parts to his body which he needs only so long as he lives inside his mother. He has his own space capsule, the amniotic sac. He has his own lifeline, the umbilical cord, and he has his own root system, the placenta. These all belong to the baby himself, not to his mother. They are all developed from his original cell."[1]

Periods of Prenatal Development

Let's take a look at some of the changes that take place during each of the three periods of prenatal development: the germinal period, the embryonic period, and the fetal period.

The Germinal Period (Weeks 1-2)

Conception occurs when a sperm fertilizes an egg and forms a **zygote,** which begins as a one-cell structure. The mother and father's DNA is passed on to the child at the moment of conception. The genetic makeup and sex of the baby are set at this point. The germinal period (about 14 days in length) lasts from conception to implantation of the zygote (fertilized egg) in the lining of the uterus.

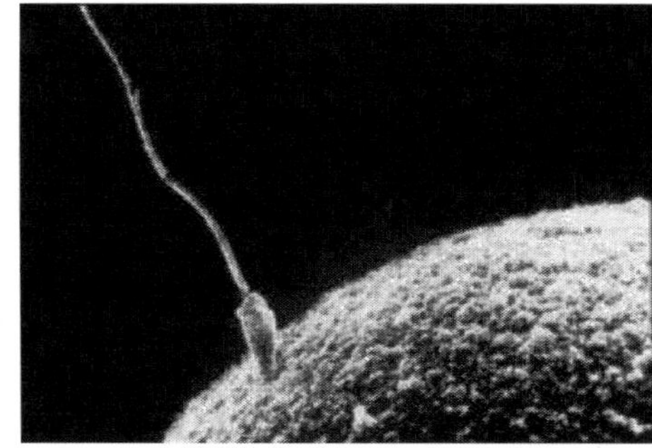

Figure 1. Sperm and Ovum at Conception

During the first week after conception, the zygote divides and multiplies, going from a one-cell structure to two cells, then four cells, then eight cells, and so on. The process of cell division is called **mitosis**. After the fourth division, differentiation of the cells begins to occur as well. Differentiated cells become more specialized, forming different organs and body parts. After 5 days of mitosis, there are 100 cells, and after 9 months there are billions of cells. Mitosis is a fragile process, and fewer than one-half of all zygotes survive beyond the first two weeks (Hall, 2004).

After the zygote divides for about 7–10 days and has 150 cells, it travels down the fallopian tubes and implants itself in the lining of the uterus. It's estimated that about 60 percent of natural conceptions fail to implant in the uterus. The rate is higher for in vitro conceptions. Once the zygote attaches to the uterus, the next stage begins.

1. Day & Liley, The Secret World of a Baby, Random House, 1968, p. 13

The Embryonic Period (Weeks 3-8)

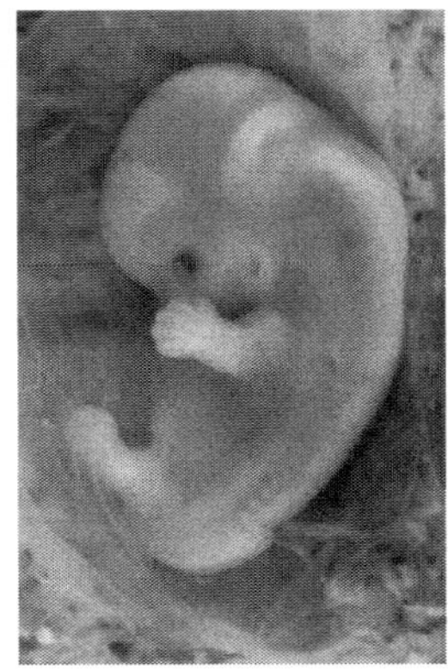

Figure 2. Human Embryo

The embryonic period begins once the zygote is implanted in the uterine wall. It lasts from the third through the eighth week after conception. Upon implantation, this multi-cellular organism is called an **embryo**. Now blood vessels grow, forming the placenta. The **placenta** is a structure connected to the uterus that provides nourishment and oxygen from the mother to the developing embryo via the umbilical cord.

During this period, cells continue to differentiate. Basic structures of the embryo start to develop into areas that will become the head, chest, and abdomen. During the embryonic stage, the heart begins to beat and organs form and begin to function. At 22 days after conception, the neural tube forms along the back of the embryo, developing into the spinal cord and brain.

Growth during prenatal development occurs in two major directions: from head to tail (cephalocaudal development) and from the midline outward (proximodistal development). This means that those structures nearest the head develop before those nearest the feet and those structures nearest the torso develop before those away from the center of the body (such as hands and fingers).

The head develops in the fourth week and the precursor to the heart begins to pulse. In the early stages of the embryonic period, gills and a tail are apparent. But by the end of this stage, they disappear and the organism takes on a more human appearance. The embryo is approximately 1 inch in length and weighs about 4 grams at the end of this period. The embryo can move and respond to touch at this time.

About 20 percent of organisms fail during the embryonic period, usually due to gross chromosomal abnormalities. As in the case of the germinal period, often the mother does not yet know that she is pregnant. It is during this stage that the major structures of the body are taking form making the embryonic period the time when the organism is most vulnerable to the greatest amount of damage if exposed to harmful substances. Potential mothers are not often aware of the risks they introduce to the developing child during this time.

The Fetal Period (Weeks 9-40)

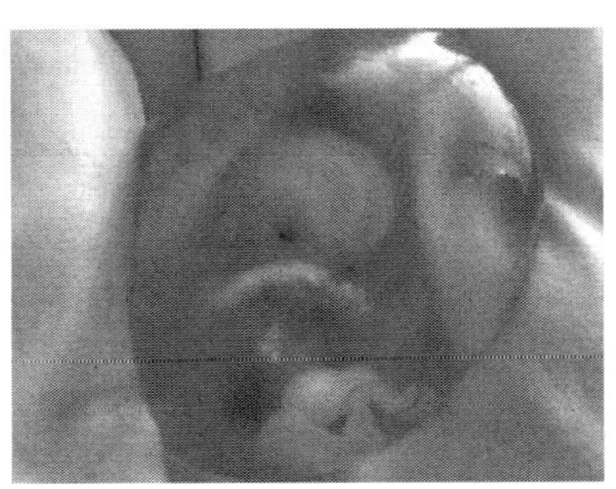

Figure 3. A fetus at 10 weeks of development.

When the organism is about nine weeks old, the embryo is called a **fetus**. At this stage, the fetus is about the size of a kidney bean and begins to take on the recognizable form of a human being as the "tail" begins to disappear.

From 9–12 weeks, the sex organs begin to differentiate. By the 12th week, the fetus has all its body parts including external genitalia. In the following weeks, the fetus will develop hair, nails, teeth and the excretory and digestive systems will continue to develop. At the end of the 12th week, the fetus is about 3 inches long and weighs about 28 grams.

At about 16 weeks, the fetus is approximately 4.5 inches long. Fingers and toes are fully developed, and fingerprints are visible. During the 4-6th months, the eyes become more sensitive to light and hearing develops. The respiratory system continues to develop. Reflexes such as sucking, swallowing and hiccuping develop during the 5th month. Cycles of sleep and wakefulness are present at that time as well. Throughout the fetal stage, the brain continues to grow and develop, nearly doubling in size from weeks 16 to 28. The majority of the neurons in the brain have developed by 24 weeks although they are still rudimentary and the glial or nurse cells that support neurons continue to grow. At 24 weeks the fetus can feel pain (Royal College of Obstetricians and Gynecologists, 1997).

The first chance of survival outside the womb, known as the age of viability is reached at about 22 to 26 weeks (Moore & Persaud, 1998). By the time the fetus reaches the sixth month of development (24 weeks), it weighs up to 1.4 pounds. The hearing has developed, so the fetus can respond to sounds. The internal organs, such as the lungs, heart, stomach, and intestines, have formed enough that a fetus born prematurely at this point has a chance to survive outside of the mother's womb.

Between the 7th and 9th months, the fetus is primarily preparing for birth. It is exercising its muscles, its lungs begin to expand and contract. It is developing fat layers under the skin. The fetus gains about 5 pounds and 7 inches during this last trimester of pregnancy which includes a layer of fat gained during the 8th month. This layer of fat serves as insulation and helps the baby regulate body temperature after birth.

Around 36 weeks, the fetus is almost ready for birth. It weighs about 6 pounds and is about 18.5 inches long, and by week 37 all of the fetus's organ systems are developed enough that it could survive outside the mother's uterus without many of the risks associated with premature birth. The fetus continues to gain weight and grow in length until approximately 40 weeks. By then, the fetus has very little room to move around and birth becomes imminent.

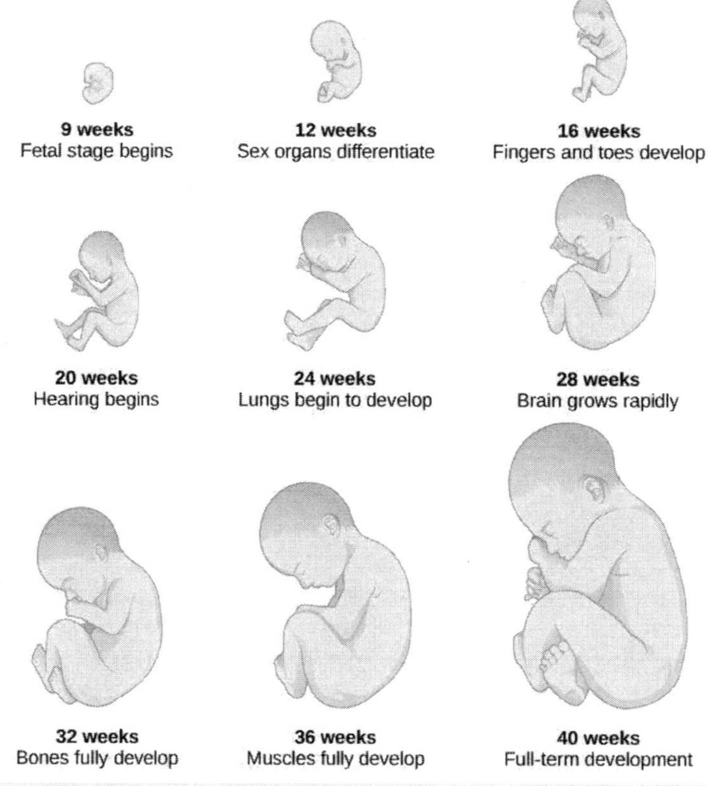

Figure 4. During the fetal stage, the baby's brain develops and the body adds size and weight until the fetus reaches full-term development.

WATCH IT

This video explains many of the developmental milestones and changes that happen during each month of development for the embryo and fetus.

- https://youtu.be/UA-Tk9qlG9A

Environmental Risks

Teratology

Good prenatal care is essential. The developing child is most at risk for some of the most severe problems during the first three months of development. Unfortunately, this is a time at which most mothers are unaware that they are pregnant. It is estimated that 10% of all birth defects are caused by a prenatal exposure or **teratogen**. Teratogens are factors that can contribute to birth defects which include some maternal diseases, drugs, alcohol, and stress. These exposures can also include environmental and occupational exposures. Today, we know many of the factors that can jeopardize the health of the developing child. Teratogen-caused birth defects are potentially preventable.

The study of factors that contribute to birth defects is called teratology. Teratogens are usually discovered after an increased prevalence of a particular birth defect. For example, in the early 1960's, a drug known as thalidomide was used to treat morning sickness. Exposure of the fetus during this early stage of development resulted in cases of phocomelia, a congenital malformation in which the hands and feet are attached to abbreviated arms and legs.

A Look at Some Teratogens

Alcohol

One of the most commonly used teratogens is alcohol. Because half of all pregnancies in the United States are unplanned, it is recommended that women of child-bearing age take great caution against drinking alcohol when not using birth control and when pregnant (Surgeon General's Advisory on Alcohol Use During Pregnancy, 2005). Alcohol consumption, particularly during the second month of prenatal development, but at any point during pregnancy, may lead to neurocognitive and behavioral difficulties that can last a lifetime.

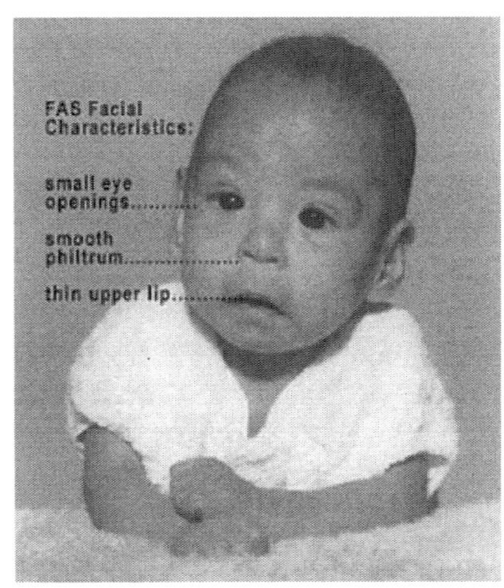

Figure 5. Some distinguishing characteristics of fetal alcohol spectrum disorders include more narrow eye openings, A smooth philtrum, meaning a smooth area between the upper lip and the nose, and a thin upper lip.

There is no acceptable safe limit for alcohol use during pregnancy, but binge drinking (5 or more drinks on a single occasion) or having 7 or more drinks during a single week places a child at particularly high risk. In extreme cases, alcohol consumption can lead to fetal death, but more frequently it can result in **fetal alcohol spectrum disorders (FASD)**. This terminology is now used when looking at the effects of exposure and replaces the term fetal alcohol syndrome. It is preferred because it recognizes that symptoms occur on a spectrum and that all individuals do not have the same characteristics. Children with FASD share certain physical features such as flattened noses, small eye openings, small heads, intellectual developmental delays, and behavioral problems. Those with FASD are more at risk for lifelong problems such as criminal behavior, psychiatric problems, and unemployment (CDC, 2006).

The terms alcohol-related neurological disorder (ARND) and alcohol-related birth defects (ARBD) have replaced the term Fetal Alcohol Effects to refer to those with less extreme symptoms of FASD. ARBD include kidney, bone and heart problems.

WATCH IT

Several medical experts debunk common myths about the safety of drinking alcohol during pregnancy.

- https://youtu.be/pvFqjU43Odo

Tobacco

Smoking is also considered a teratogen because nicotine travels through the placenta to the fetus. When the mother smokes, the developing baby experiences a reduction in blood oxygen levels. Tobacco use during pregnancy has been associated with low birth weight, placenta previa, birth defects, preterm delivery, fetal growth restriction, and sudden infant death syndrome. Smoking in the month before getting pregnant and throughout pregnancy increases the chances of these risks. Quitting smoking *before* getting pregnant is best. However, for women who are already pregnant, quitting as early as possible can still help protect against some health problems for the mother and baby.[2]

Drugs

Prescription, over-the-counter, or recreational drugs can have serious teratogenic effects. In general, if medication is required, the lowest dose possible should be used. Combination drug therapies and first trimester exposures should be avoided. Almost three percent of pregnant women use illicit drugs such as marijuana, cocaine, Ecstasy and other amphetamines, and heroin. These drugs can cause low birth-weight, withdrawal symptoms, birth defects, or learning or behavioral problems. Babies born with a heroin addiction need heroin just like an adult addict. The child will need to be gradually weaned from the heroin under medical supervision; otherwise, the child could have seizures and die.

Environmental Chemicals

Environmental chemicals can include an exposure to a wide array of agents including pollution, organic mercury compounds, herbicides, and industrial solvents. Some environmental pollutants of major concern include lead poisoning, which is connected with low birth weight and slowed neurological development. Children who live in older housing in which lead-based paints have been used have been known to eat peeling paint chips thus being exposed to lead. The chemicals in certain herbicides are also potentially damaging. Radiation is another environmental hazard that a pregnant woman must be aware of. If a mother is exposed to radiation, particularly during the first three months of pregnancy, the child may suffer some congenital deformities. There is also an increased risk of miscarriage and stillbirth. Mercury leads to physical deformities and intellectual disabilities (Dietrich, 1999).

Sexually Transmitted Infections

Sexually transmitted infections (STIs) can complicate pregnancy and may have serious effects on both the mother and the developing baby. Most prenatal care today includes testing for STIs, and early detection is important. STIs, such as chlamydia, gonorrhea, syphilis, trichomoniasis and bacterial vaginosis can all be treated and cured with antibiotics that are safe to take during pregnancy. STIs that are caused by viruses, like genital herpes, hepatitis B, or HIV cannot be cured. However, in some cases these infections can be treated with antiviral medications or other preventive measures can be taken to reduce the risk of passing the infection to the baby.[3]

2. Birth Defects Research and Tracking. Centers for Disease Control and Prevention. Retrieved from https://www.cdc.gov/ncbddd/birthdefects/research.html
3. STDs during Pregnancy - CDC Fact Sheet. Centers for Disease Control and Prevention. Retrieved from https://www.cdc.gov/std/pregnancy/stdfact-pregnancy.htm

Maternal Diseases

Maternal illnesses increase the chance that a baby will be born with a birth defect or have a chronic health problem. Some of the diseases that are known to potentially have an adverse effect on the fetus include: diabetes, cytomegalovirus, toxoplasmosis, Rubella, varicella, hypothyroidism, and Strep B. If the mother contracts Rubella during the first three months of pregnancy, damage can occur in the eyes, ears, heart, or brain of the unborn child. On a positive note, Rubella has been nearly eliminated in the industrial world due to the vaccine created in 1969. Diagnosing these diseases early and receiving appropriate medical care can help improve the outcomes. Routine prenatal care now includes screening for gestational diabetes and Strep B.[4]

Maternal Stress

Stress represents the effects of any factor able to threaten the homeostasis of an organism; these either real or perceived threats are referred to as the "stressors" and comprise a long list of potentially adverse factors, which can be emotional or physical. Because of a link in blood supply between a mother and fetus, it has been found that stress can leave lasting effects on a developing fetus, even before a child is born. The best-studied outcomes of fetal exposure to maternal prenatal stress are preterm birth and low birth weight. Maternal prenatal stress is also considered responsible for a variety of changes of the child's brain, and a risk factor for conditions such as behavioral problems, learning disorders, high levels of anxiety, attention deficit hyperactivity disorder, autism, and schizophrenia. Furthermore, maternal prenatal stress has been associated with a higher risk for a variety of immune and metabolic changes in the child such as asthma, allergic disorders, cardiovascular diseases, hypertension, hyperlipidemia, diabetes, and obesity.[5]

Factors influencing prenatal risks

There are several considerations in determining the type and amount of damage that might result from exposure to a particular teratogen (Berger, 2004). These include:

- **The timing of the exposure**: Structures in the body are vulnerable to the most severe damage when they are forming. If a substance is introduced during a particular structure's critical period (time of development), the damage to that structure may be greater. For example, the ears and arms reach their critical periods at about 6 weeks after conception. If a mother exposes the embryo to certain substances during this period, the arms and ears may be malformed.
- **The amount of exposure:** Some substances are not harmful unless the amounts reach a certain level. The critical level depends in part on the size and metabolism of the mother.
- **Genetics:** Genetic make-up also plays a role on the impact a particular teratogen might have on the child. This is suggested by fraternal twin studies who are exposed to the same prenatal environment, yet do not experience the same teratogenic effects. The genetic make-up of the mother can also have an effect; some mothers may be more resistant to teratogenic effects than others.
- **Being male or female:** Males are more likely to experience damage due to teratogens than are females. It is believed that the Y chromosome, which contains fewer genes than the X, may have an impact.

4. Maternal Illness – Birth Defect Prevention for Expecting Parents. Birth Defect Research for Children. Retrieved from https://www.birthdefects.org/healthy-baby/maternal-illness/
5. Douros Konstantinos, Moustaki Maria, Tsabouri Sophia, Papadopoulou Anna, Papadopoulos Marios, Priftis Kostas N. (2017). Prenatal Maternal Stress and the Risk of Asthma in Children. Frontiers in Pediatrics. Retrieved from https://www.frontiersin.org/article/10.3389/fped.2017.00202

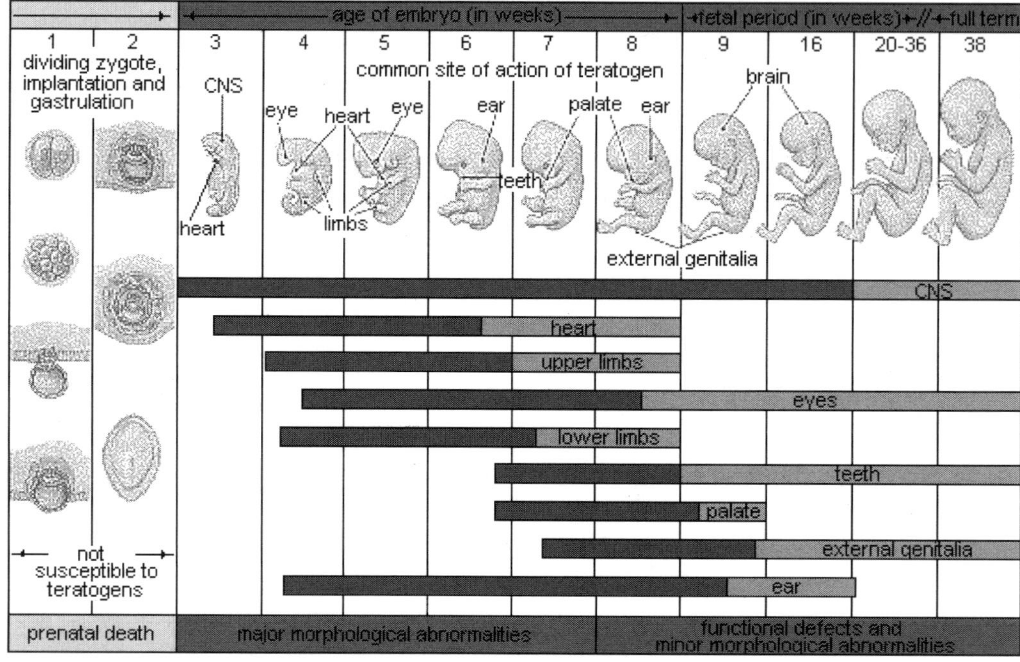

Figure 6. Critical Periods of Prenatal Development. This image summarizes the three developmental periods in prenatal development. The blue images indicate where major development is happening and the aqua indicate where refinement is happening. As shown, the majority of organs are particularly susceptible during the embryonic period. The central nervous system still continues to develop in major ways through the fetal period as well.

Complications of Pregnancy and Delivery

Complications of Pregnancy and Delivery

There are a number of common side effects of pregnancy. Not everyone experiences all of these nor do women experience them to the same degree. And although they are considered "minor" these problems are potentially very uncomfortable. These side effects include nausea (particularly during the first 3-4 months of pregnancy as a result of higher levels of estrogen in the system), heartburn, gas, hemorrhoids, backache, leg cramps, insomnia, constipation, shortness of breath or varicose veins (as a result of carrying a heavy load on the abdomen). What is the cure? Delivery!

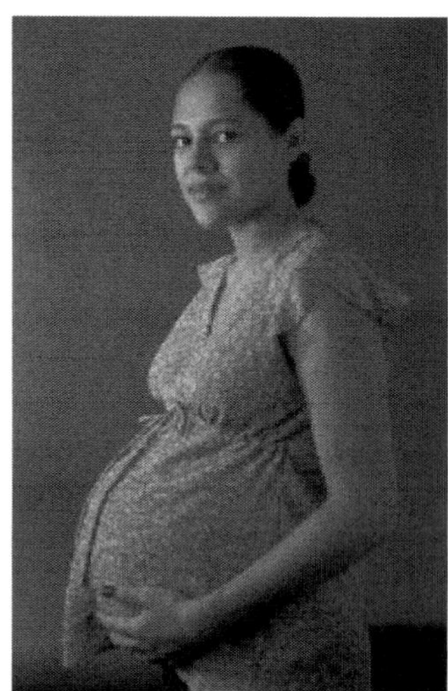

Figure 7. Pregnancy affects women in different ways; some notice few adverse side effects, while others feel high levels of discomfort, or develop more serious complications.

Major Complications

The following are some serious complications of pregnancy which can pose health risks to mother and child and that often require special care.

- Gestational diabetes is when a woman without diabetes develops high blood sugar levels during pregnancy.
- Hyperemesis gravidarum is the presence of severe and persistent vomiting, causing dehydration and weight loss. It is more severe than the more common morning sickness.
- Preeclampsia is gestational hypertension. Severe preeclampsia involves blood pressure over 160/110 with additional signs. Eclampsia is seizures in a pre-eclamptic patient.
- Deep vein thrombosis is the formation of a blood clot in a deep vein, most commonly in the legs.
- A pregnant woman is more susceptible to infections. This increased risk is caused by an increased immune tolerance in pregnancy to prevent an immune reaction against the fetus.
- Peripartum cardiomyopathy is a decrease in heart function which occurs in the last month of pregnancy, or up to six months post-pregnancy.

Maternal Mortality

Maternal mortality is unacceptably high. About 830 women die from pregnancy or childbirth-related complications around the world every day. It was estimated that in 2015, roughly 303,000 women died during and following pregnancy and childbirth. Almost all of these deaths occurred in low-resource settings, and most could have been prevented. The high number of maternal deaths in some areas of the world reflects inequities in access to health services and highlights the gap between rich and poor. Almost all maternal deaths (99%) occur in developing countries. More than half of these deaths occur in sub-Saharan Africa and almost one third occur in South Asia.

Almost all maternal deaths can be prevented, as evidenced by the huge disparities found between the richest and poorest countries. The lifetime risk of maternal death in high-income countries is 1 in 3,300, compared to 1 in 41 in low-income. [6]Maternal mortality (February 2018). World Health Organization. Retrieved from https://www.who.int/news-room/fact-sheets/detail/maternal-mortality

Maternal mortality fell by almost half between 1990 and 2015

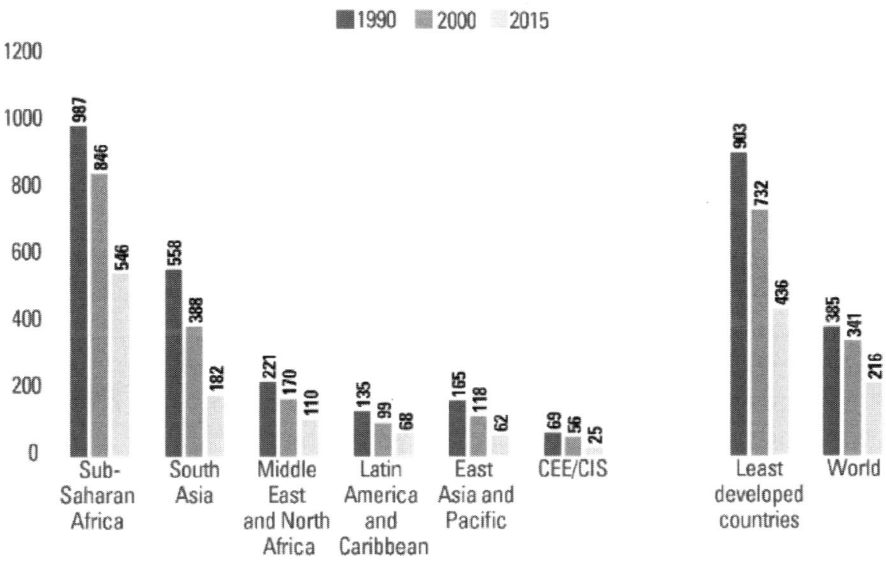

*CEE/CIS: Central and Eastern Europe and the Commonwealth of Independent States

Source: World Health Organization, UNICEF, United Nations Population Fund and The World Bank, *Trends in Maternal Mortality: 1990 to 2015*, WHO, Geneva, 2015.

Figure 8. This graph shows declining maternal mortality rates, as measured as the number of deaths per 100,000 live births. in 1990, 903 out of 100,000 live births resulted in death in the least developed countries, but that number has improved to 436 out of 100,000 births in 2015. Globally, there were 216 deaths for every 100,000 live births in 2015. Source: UNICEF, https://data.unicef.org/topic/maternal-health/maternal-mortality/.

Even though maternal mortality in the United States is relatively rare today because of advanced in medical care, it is still an issue that needs to be addressed. The number of reported pregnancy-related deaths in the United States steadily increased from 7.2 deaths per 100,000 live births in 1987 to 18.0 deaths per 100,000 live births in 2014. The Centers for Disease Control and Prevention define a **pregnancy-related death** as the death of a woman while pregnant or within 1 year of the end of a pregnancy–regardless of the outcome, duration, or site of the pregnancy–from any cause related to or aggravated by the

6.

pregnancy or its management, but not from accidental or incidental causes. The reasons for the overall increase in pregnancy-related mortality are unclear. What do you think are some reasons for this surprising increase in the United States? What can be done to change this statistic?

WATCH IT: MATERNAL MORTALITY IN THE UNITED STATES

In the United States, black women are disproportionately more likely to die from complications related to pregnancy or childbirth than any other race; they are three or four times more likely than white women to die due to pregnancy-related death and are more likely to receive worse maternal care.[7] Black women from higher income groups and with advanced education levels also have heightened risks—even tennis superstar Serena Williams had near-deadly complications during the birth of her daughter, Olympia. Why is this the case in our modern world? Watch this video to learn more:

- https://youtu.be/VYc-Eq-vDuA

The data below shows percentages of the causes of pregnancy-related deaths in the United States during 2011–2014:

- Cardiovascular diseases, 15.2%.
- Non-cardiovascular diseases, 14.7%.
- Infection or sepsis, 12.8%.
- Hemorrhage, 11.5%.
- Cardiomyopathy, 10.3%.
- Thrombotic pulmonary embolism, 9.1%.
- Cerebrovascular accidents, 7.4%.
- Hypertensive disorders of pregnancy, 6.8%.
- Amniotic fluid embolism, 5.5%.
- Anesthesia complications, 0.3%.

The cause of death is unknown for 6.5% of all 2011–2014 pregnancy-related deaths.[8]

Miscarriage

Spontaneous abortion is experienced in an estimated 20-40 percent of undiagnosed pregnancies and in another 10 percent of diagnosed pregnancies. Usually, the body aborts due to chromosomal abnormalities and this typically happens before the 12th week of pregnancy. Cramping and bleeding result and normal periods return after several months. Some women are more likely to have repeated miscarriages due to chromosomal, amniotic, or hormonal problems; but miscarriage can also be a result of defective sperm (Carroll et al., 2003).

7. Black Women's Maternal Health: A Multifaceted Approach to Addressing Persistent and Dire Health Disparities (April 2018). National Partnership for Women and Families. Retrieved from http://www.nationalpartnership.org/our-work/health/reports/black-womens-maternal-health.html.
8. Reproductive Health. Pregnancy Mortality Surveillance System. Centers for Disease Control and Prevention. Retrieved from https://www.cdc.gov/reproductivehealth/maternalinfanthealth/pregnancy-mortality-surveillance-system.htm

GLOSSARY

embryo:
a multi-celled organism between two and eight weeks after fertilization

fetal alcohol spectrum disorders:
a group of abnormalities in babies born to mothers who consume alcohol during pregnancy

fetus:
an unborn human baby from nine weeks after conception until birth

mitosis:
the process of cell division

placenta:
a structure connected to the uterus that provides nourishment and oxygen from the mother to the developing embryo via the umbilical cord

pregnancy-related death:
the death of a woman while pregnant or within 1 year of the end of a pregnancy from any cause related to or aggravated by the pregnancy

teratogen:
any agent which can cause a birth defect

zygote:
a one-cell structure that is created when a sperm and egg merge

Birth and Delivery

What you'll learn to do: describe approaches to childbirth and the labor and delivery process

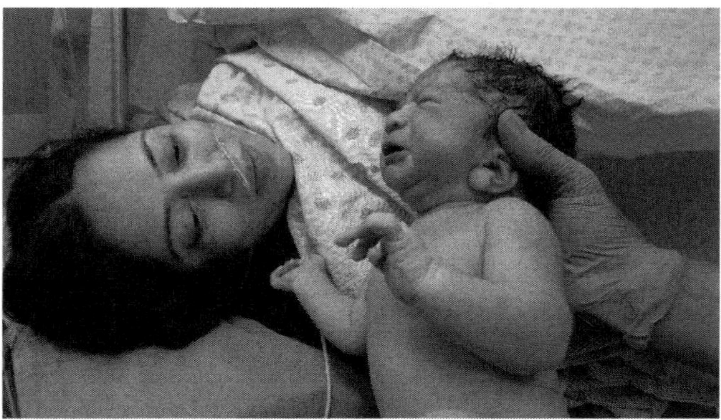

What comes to your mind when you think about a woman giving birth? Some may describe it as beautiful, a miracle, and a rite of passage. Others may think of pain, fear, and discomfort. Labor and delivery is not an easy feat. It is called *labor* after all because it is a lot of work! In this section, you'll learn more about the various approaches to childbirth as well as the actual process.

LEARNING OUTCOMES

- Describe various approaches to childbirth
- Describe a normal delivery, including the stages of childbirth
- Examine risks and complications with newborns

Childbirth

Approaches to Childbirth

Prepared childbirth refers to being not only physically in good condition to help provide a healthy environment for the baby to develop, but also helping a couple to prepare to accept their new roles as parents and to get information and training that will assist them for delivery and life with the baby as much as possible. The more a couple can learn about childbirth and the newborn, the better prepared they will be for the adjustment they must make to a new life. Nothing can prepare a couple for this completely. Once a couple finds that they are to have a child, they begin to conjure up images of what they think the experience will involve. Once the child is born, they must reconcile those images with reality (Galinsky, 1987). Knowing more of what to expect does help them in forming more realistic images thus making the adjustment easier. Let's explore some of the methods of prepared childbirth.

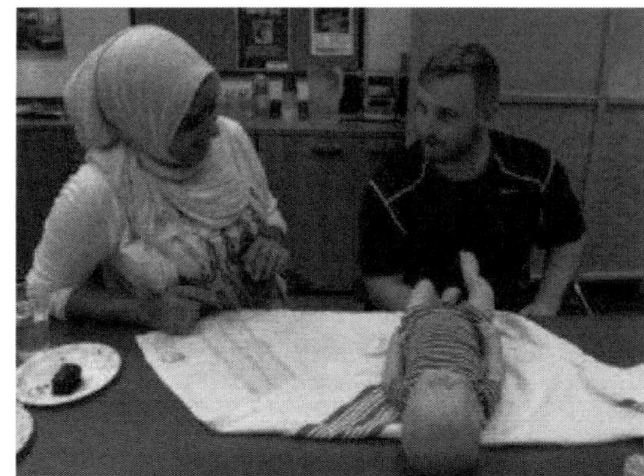

Figure 1. This couple prepares for their baby by attending a class where they learn useful skills related to childbirth and infant care, including swaddling.

HypnoBirthing

Grantley Dick-Read was an English obstetrician and pioneer of prepared childbirth in the 1930s. In his book *Childbirth Without Fear*, he suggests that the fear of childbirth increases tension and makes the process of childbearing more painful. He believed that if mothers were educated, the fear and tension would be reduced and the need for medication could frequently be eliminated. The Dick-Read method emphasized the use of relaxation and proper breathing with contractions as well as family support and education. Today this method is known as the Mongan Method or HypnoBirthing. Women using this method report feeling like they are lost in a daydream, but focused and in control.

The Lamaze Method

This method originated in Russia and was brought to the United States in the 1950s by Fernand Lamaze. The emphasis of this method is on teaching the woman to be in control in the process of delivery. It includes learning muscle relaxation, breathing through contractions, having a focal point (usually a picture to look at) during contractions and having a support person who goes through the training process with the mother and serves as a coach during delivery. The Lamaze Method is still the most commonly taught method in the U.S. today.

The Bradley Method

This method originated in the late 1940's and helps women deliver naturally, with few or no drugs. There are a series of courses that emphasize excellent nutrition and exercise, relaxation techniques to manage pain, and the involvement of the partner as a coach. Parents-to-be are taught to be knowledgeable consumers of birth services and to take responsibility in making informed decisions regarding procedures, attendants and the birthplace. In turn, this will lead to keeping mothers healthy and low-risk in order to avoid complications that may lead to medical intervention.

Nurse Midwives

Historically in the United States, most babies were born under the care of lay midwives. In the 1920s, middle-class women were increasingly using doctors to assist with childbirth but rural women were still being assisted by lay midwives. The nursing profession began educating nurse-midwives to assist these women. Nurse-midwives continued to assist most rural women with delivery until the 1970s and 1980s when their growth is thought to have posed a threat to the medical profession (Weitz, 2007). Women who are at low risk for birth complications can successfully deliver under the care of nurse-midwives. Some hospitals give privileges to nurse-midwives to deliver there. They may also deliver babies at home or in birthing centers.

Home Birth

Because one out of every 20 births involves a complication, most medical professionals recommend that delivery take place in a hospital. However, some couples choose to have their baby at home. About 1 percent of births occur outside of a hospital in the United States. Two-thirds of these are home births and more than half of these are assisted by midwives. In the United States, women who have had previous children, who are over 25 and who are white are most likely to not give birth in a hospital (MacDorman et al., 2010).

Birthing Centers

A birthing center presents a more home-like environment than a hospital labor ward, typically with more options during labor: food/drink, music, and the attendance of family and friends if desired. Other characteristics can also include non-institutional furniture such as queen-sized beds, large enough for both mother and father and perhaps birthing tubs or showers for water births. The decor is meant to emphasize the normality of birth. In a birth center, women are free to act more spontaneously during their birth, such as squatting, walking or performing other postures that assist in labor. Active birth is encouraged. The length of stay after a birth is shorter at a birth center; sometimes just 6 hours after birth the mother and infant can go home. One-third of out-of-hospital births occur in freestanding clinics, birthing centers, or in physicians offices or other locations.

Water Birth

Laboring and/or giving birth in a warm tub of water can help a woman relax. The buoyancy of the water can help alleviate discomfort and pressure for the mother. Many hospitals have birthing tubs that allow women to labor in them. However, only some hospitals allow for the birth to take place in the water. Some believe that water birth gives a more calm and tranquil transition for the baby from the womb. Water births are more common to occur at home or in birthing centers.

WATCH IT

Watch this family's approach to childbirth by having a water birth in their home with a midwife and a doula.

- https://youtu.be/wczscWXk8e4

Not many pregnancies or births go exactly as planned, as seen in the following story of this mother who had to quickly deliver her baby at 30 weeks.

- https://youtu.be/jzBQQXy5XRE

Hospital Birth

Most births in the U.S. occur in hospitals. Mothers have the choice to have a medicated or unmedicated delivery. Some women do fine with "natural methods" of pain relief alone. Many women blend "natural methods" with medications and medical interventions that relieve pain. Building a positive outlook on childbirth and managing fear may also help some women cope with the pain. Labor pain is not like pain due to illness or injury. Instead, it is caused by contractions of the uterus that are pushing the baby down and out of the birth canal. In other words, labor pain has a purpose.

The most common pain relief method used during labor and delivery is an epidural. An epidural is a procedure that involves placing a tube into the lower back, into a small space outside the spinal cord. Small doses of medicine can be given through the tube as needed throughout labor. With an epidural, pain relief starts 10 to 20 minutes after the medicine has been given. The degree of numbness felt can be adjusted. An epidural can prolong the first and second stages of labor. If given late in labor or if too much medicine is used, it might be hard to push when the time comes.

WATCH IT

What are the advantages and disadvantages of receiving an epidural? Watch this video to see how the procedure is done.

- https://youtu.be/2tw-SXI3wKU

Another form of pharmacologic pain relief available for laboring mothers is inhaled nitrous oxide. This is typically a 50/50 mixture of nitrous oxide with air that is an inhaled analgesic and anesthetic. Nitrous oxide has been used for pain management in childbirth since the late 1800's. The use of inhaled analgesia is commonly used in the UK, Finland, Australia, Singapore, and New Zealand, and is gaining in popularity in the United States.[1]

MAKING A BIRTH PLAN

As you can see, women have many choices when it comes to the approach they want to take in preparing for childbirth. What decisions would you make? Learn how to create a birth plan.

1. Giving Birth Naturally: Natural Childbirth Techniques. American Pregnancy Association. Retrieved from http://americanpregnancy.org/labor-and-birth/natural-childbirth-techniques/

The Process of Delivery

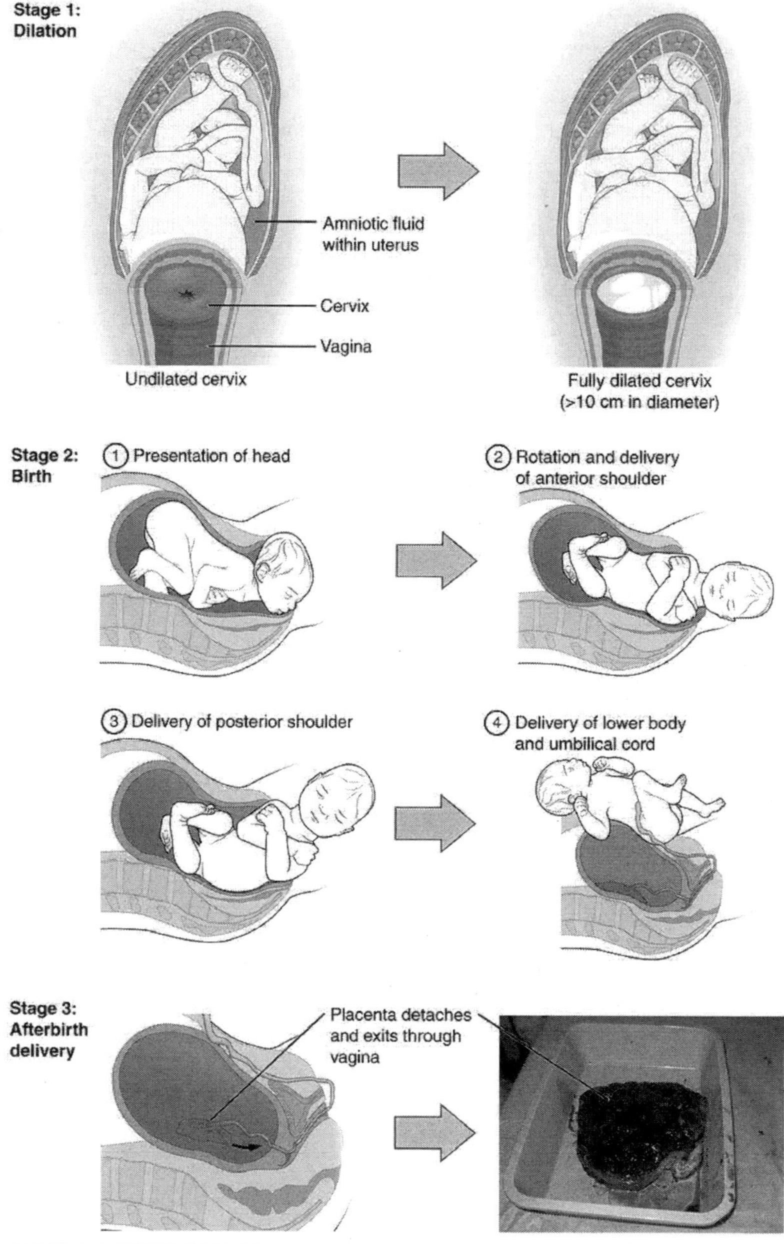

Figure 2. The stages of childbirth.

The first stage of labor is typically the longest. The First Stage of labor begins with uterine contractions that may initially last about 30 seconds and be spaced 15 to 20 minutes apart. These increase in duration and frequency to more than a minute in length and about 3 to 4 minutes apart. Typically, doctors advise that they should be called when contractions are coming about every 5 minutes. Some women experience false labor or Braxton-Hicks contractions, especially with the first child. These may come and go. They tend to diminish when the mother begins walking around. Real labor pains tend to increase with walking.

During this stage, the cervix or opening to the uterus dilates to 10 centimeters or just under 4 inches. This may take around 12-16 hours for first children or about 6-9 hours for women who have previously given birth. It takes one woman in 9 over 24 hours to dilate completely. Labor may also begin with a discharge of blood or amniotic fluid. If the amniotic sack breaks, which happens for one out of eight pregnancies, labor will be induced if necessary to reduce the risk of infection.

The second stage involves the passage of the baby through the birth canal. This stage takes about 10-40 minutes. Contractions usually come about every 2-3 minutes. The mother pushes and relaxes as directed by the medical staff. Normally the head is delivered first. The baby is then rotated so that one shoulder can come through and then the other shoulder. The rest of the baby quickly passes through. The baby's mouth and nose are suctioned out. The umbilical cord is clamped and cut.

The third stage is relatively painless in comparison to the other stages. During this stage, the placenta or afterbirth is delivered. This typically occurs within 20 minutes after delivery of the baby. If tearing of the vagina occurred during birth, the tear may be stitched at this time.

Cesarean Section

Cesarean section, also known as **C-section**, or **cesarean delivery**, is the use of surgery to deliver babies. A cesarean section is often necessary when a vaginal delivery would put the baby or mother at risk. This may include obstructed labor, twin pregnancy, high blood pressure in the mother, breech birth, or problems with the placenta or umbilical cord. Cesarean delivery may be performed based upon the shape of the mother's pelvis or history of a previous C-section. A trial of vaginal birth after C-section may be possible. The World Health Organization recommends that cesarean section be performed only when medically necessary. Some C-sections are performed without a medical reason, upon request by someone, usually the mother.

WATCH IT: VAGINAL AND CESAREAN BIRTH

- Watch an animation of labor and vaginal birth.
- Watch an animation of a cesarean birth.

Newborn Assessment and Risks

Complications of the Newborn

Assessing the Neonate

There are several ways to assess the condition of the newborn. The most widely used tool is the Neonatal Behavioral Assessment Scale (NBAS) developed by T. Berry Brazelton. This tool has been used around the world to help parents get to know their infants and to make comparisons of infants in different cultures (Brazelton & Nugent, 1995). The baby's motor development, muscle tone, and stress response are assessed.

The APGAR is conducted one minute and five minutes after birth. This is a very quick way to assess the newborn's overall condition. Five measures are assessed: the heart rate, respiration, muscle tone (quickly assessed by a skilled nurse when the baby is handed to them or by touching the baby's palm), reflex response (the Babinski reflex is tested), and color. A score of 0 to 2 is given on each feature examined. An APGAR of 5 or less is cause for concern. The second APGAR should indicate improvement with a higher score.

WATCH IT

Watch this video that explains how to calculate the APGAR score for a newborn.

- https://youtu.be/98ikG8a9JKs

Low Birth Weight

We have been discussing a number of teratogens associated with a low birth weight such as cocaine, tobacco, etc. A child is considered to have a low birth weight if they weigh less than 5.8 pounds (2500 grams). About 8.17 percent of babies born in the United States are of low birth weight and 1.4 percent are born very low birth weight.[2] A low birth weight baby has difficulty maintaining adequate body temperature because it lacks the fat that would otherwise provide insulation. Such a baby is also at more risk of infection. And 67 percent of these babies are also preterm which can make them more at risk for a respiratory infection. Very low birth weight babies (2 pounds or less) have an increased risk of developing cerebral palsy. Many causes of low birth weight are preventable with proper prenatal care.

Premature Birth

A child might also have a low birth weight if it is born at less than 37 weeks gestation (which qualifies it as a preterm baby). In 2016, 9.85 percent of babies born in the U.S. were preterm.[3] Early birth can be triggered by anything that disrupts the mother's system. For instance, vaginal infections or gum disease can actually lead to premature birth because such infection causes the mother to release anti-inflammatory chemicals which, in turn, can trigger contractions. Smoking and the use of other teratogens can also lead to preterm birth.

Anoxia and Hypoxia

One of leading causes of infant brain damage is lack of oxygen shortly after birth. Hypoxia occurs when the infant is deprived of the adequate amount of oxygen, leading to mild to moderate brain damage. Apoxia occurs when the infant undergoes a total lack of oxygen, which can lead to severe brain damage. This lack of oxygen is typically caused by umbilical cord problems, birth canal problems, blocked airways, and placenta abruption. Both hypoxia and anoxia can lead to cerebral palsy and a host of other medical disorders.[4]

GLOSSARY

cesarean section:
is the use of surgery to deliver babies through the mother's abdomen and uterus

2. Birthweight and Gestation. Centers for Disease Control and Prevention (2016). Retrieved from https://www.cdc.gov/nchs/fastats/birthweight.htm
3. Birthweight and Gestation. Centers for Disease Control and Prevention (2016). Retrieved from https://www.cdc.gov/nchs/fastats/birthweight.htm
4. Benaron, Harry B.W. et al. (1960). Effect of anoxia during labor and immediately after birth on the subsequent development of the child. American Journal of Obstetrics & Gynecology, Volume 80, Issue 6, 1129 - 1142. Retrieved from https://www.ajog.org/article/0002-9378(60)90080-6/pdf

Putting It Together: Prenatal Development

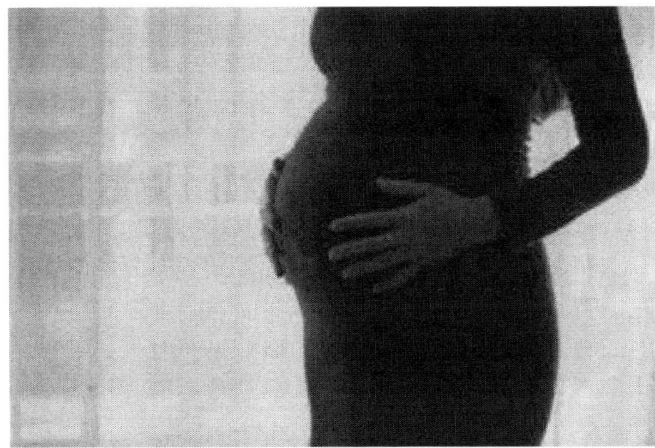

As you can see, what may seem like a simple process is in fact a beautiful and delicate journey. Each pregnancy and birth story is unique and comes with surprises and sometimes challenges. As medical technology has rapidly improved, women are empowered with more information and more choices when it comes to their pregnancy and birth. However, just because interventions are available does not mean that this is the path for all mothers. As we learned in the case with Serena Williams, even in the U.S. sometimes medical care can go awry. Each mother needs to be an active advocate for herself and her baby during her pregnancy and delivery.

Where do you think we are headed with how medical advances are used in pregnancy and delivery? More women are able to get pregnant with reproductive assistance, oftentimes past the age that they would naturally conceive. At the beginning of the module, the topic of "designer babies" was introduced. After completing this module, do you think that we are headed towards this in the near future? What are the ethical ramifications?

LINK TO LEARNING

Read this Scientific American article, "The Need to Regulate Designer Babies" and consider your own thoughts and feelings about the future of reproductive technologies.

Discussion: Prenatal Development

DISCUSSION: In this discussion, reflect upon and discuss ONE of the following questions:

- DQ1: What are the pros and cons of receiving prenatal screening tests? Why might some mothers decide not to have these tests?
- DQ2: As medical technology continues to improve, a person may have the opportunity to "design" their own baby. Do you believe this is ethical? Why or why not?

STEP 1: First, write a response with at least EIGHT substantial sentences, integrating concepts you learned from the reading and other materials (include links with necessary). Show that you can think critically on the topic by integrating your own thoughts, analysis, or experiences.

STEP 2: Then return to the discussion to comment on at least TWO classmates' posts (in at least FIVE sentences). Expand on a classmate's comments in a value-adding, topic-related way. Promote a collaborative, supportive community, and advance the dialogue through follow-up questions. Reply posts cannot be one-liners, off-topic posts, vague statements, unsupported opinions, inadequate explanations or simply say, "I agree" or "good job."

MODULE 4: INFANCY

Why It Matters: Infancy

Why understand human development during infancy?

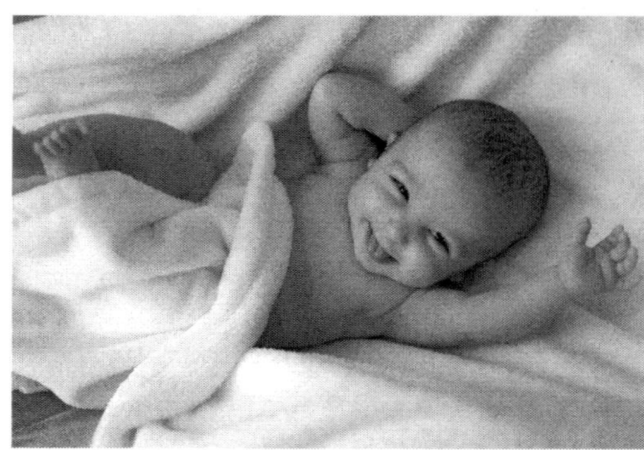

Welcome to the story of development from infancy through toddlerhood; from birth until about two years of age. Did you ever wonder how babies grow from tiny, helpless infants into well-developed and independent adults? It doesn't happen overnight, but the process begins right from day one. Infancy is a time when tremendous growth, coordination, and mental development occur. Most infants learn to walk, manipulate objects and can form basic words by the end of infancy. By 5 months a baby will have doubled its birth weight and tripled its birth weight by the first year. By the age of 2, a baby's weight will have quadrupled!

Researchers have given this part of the life span more attention than any other period, perhaps because changes during this time are so dramatic and so noticeable. We know that much of what happens during these years provides a foundation for one's life to come, however, it has been argued that the significance of development during these years has been overstated (Bruer, 1999). Nevertheless, this is a period of life that contemporary educators, healthcare providers, and parents have focused on quite heavily. It is also a time period that can be tricky to study—how do we learn about infant speech when they cannot articulate their thoughts or feelings? For example, through research we know that infants understand speech much earlier than their bodies have matured enough to physically perform it; thus it is evident that their speech patterns develop before the physical growth of their vocal cords is adequate to facilitate speech.

In this module, we will examine the rapid physical growth and development of infants, look at the influences on physical growth and cognitive development, then turn our attention toward emotional and social development in the early years of life. The early years are a time of rapid physical, cognitive, social, and emotional development, which have a direct effect on a baby's overall development and the adult they will become.

Physical Growth and Development in Newborns and Toddlers

What you'll learn to do: describe physical growth and development in infants and toddlers

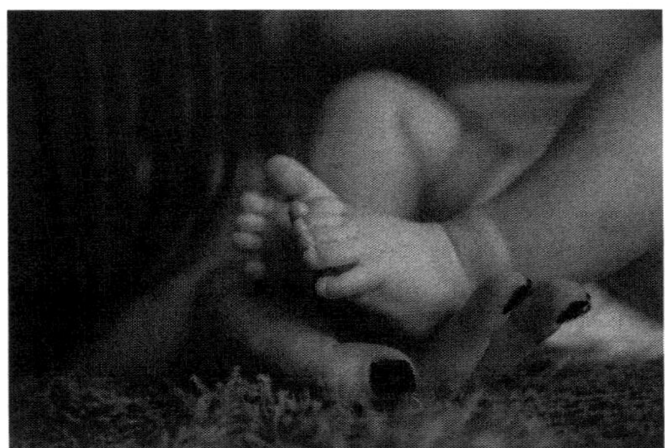

We'll begin this section by reviewing the physical development that occurs during infancy, a period that starts at birth and continues until the second birthday. We'll see how this time involves rapid growth, not only in observable changes like height and weight, but also in brain development.

Next we will explore reflexes. At birth, infants are equipped with a number of reflexes, which are involuntary movements in response to stimulation. We will explore these innate reflexes and then consider how these involuntary reflexes are eventually modified through experiences to become voluntary movements and the basis for motor development as skills emerge that allow an infant to grasp food, roll over, and take the first step.

Third, we will explore the baby's senses. Every sense functions at birth—newborns use all of their senses to attend to everything and every person. We will explore how infants' senses develop and how sensory systems like hearing and vision operate, and how infants take in information through their senses and transform it into meaningful information.

Finally, since growth during infancy is so rapid and the consequence of neglect can be severe, we will consider some of the influences on early physical growth, particularly the importance of nutrition.

LEARNING OUTCOMES

- Summarize overall physical growth patterns during infancy
- Describe the growth of the brain during infancy
- Explain gross and fine motor skills in infants
- Explain newborn perceptual abilities
- Explain the merits of breastfeeding
- Discuss the importance of nutrition to early physical growth, including nutritional concerns for infants and toddlers such as marasmus and kwashiorkor
- Describe sleep concerns for infants
- Explain the vaccination debate and its consequences

Physical Growth and Brain Development in Infancy

Overall Physical Growth

The average newborn weighs approximately 7.5 pounds, although a healthy birth weight for a full-term baby is considered to be between 5 pounds, 8 ounces (2,500 grams) and 8 pounds, 13 ounces (4,000 grams).[1] The average length of a newborn is 19.5 inches, increasing to 29.5 inches by 12 months and 34.4 inches by 2 years old (WHO Multicentre Growth Reference Study Group, 2006).

For the first few days of life, infants typically lose about 5 percent of their body weight as they eliminate waste and get used to feeding. This often goes unnoticed by most parents, but can be cause for concern for those who have a smaller infant. This weight loss is temporary, however, and is followed by a rapid period of growth. By the time an infant is 4 months old, it usually doubles in weight, and by one year has tripled its birth weight. By age 2, the weight has quadrupled. The average length at 12 months (one year old) typically ranges from 28.5-30.5 inches. The average length at 24 months (two years old) is around 33.2-35.4 inches (CDC, 2010).

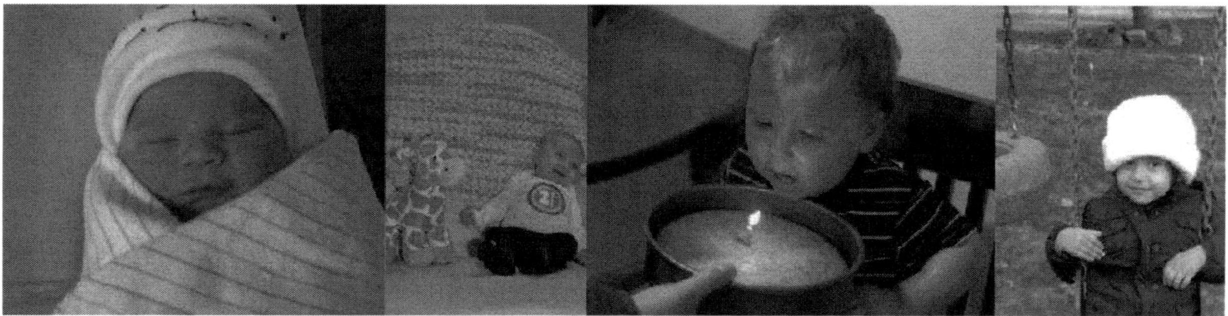

Figure 1. Children experience rapid physical changes through infancy and early childhood. (credit "left": modification of work by Kerry Ceszyk; credit "middle-left": modification of work by Kristi Fausel; credit "middle-right": modification of work by "devinf"/Flickr; credit "right": modification of work by Rose Spielman)

Monitoring Physical Growth

As mentioned earlier, growth is so rapid in infancy that the consequences of neglect can be severe. For this reason, gains are closely monitored. At each well-baby check-up, a baby's growth is compared to that baby's previous numbers. Often, measurements are expressed as a **percentile** from 0 to 100, which compares each baby to other babies the same age. For example, weight at the 40th percentile means that 40 percent of all babies weigh less, and 60 percent weight more. For any baby, pediatricians and parents can be alerted early just by watching percentile changes. If an average baby moves from the 50th percentile to the 20th, this could be a sign of **failure to thrive,** which could be caused by various medical conditions or factors in the child's environment. The earlier the concern is detection, the earlier intervention and support can be provided for the infant and caregiver.

Body Proportions

Another dramatic physical change that takes place in the first several years of life is a change in body proportions. The head initially makes up about 50 percent of a person's entire length when developing in the womb. At birth, the head makes up about

1. Iannelli, V. (2018). What Parents Need to Know About Baby Weight Trends and Newborn Gaining. Retrieved from https://www.verywellfamily.com/baby-birth-weight-statistics-2633630

25 percent of a person's length (just imagine how big your head would be if the proportions remained the same throughout your life!). In adulthood, the head comprises about 15 percent of a person's length.[2] Imagine how difficult it must be to raise one's head during the first year of life!

And indeed, if you have ever seen a 2- to 4-month-old infant lying on their stomach trying to raise the head, you know how much of a challenge this is.

The Brain in the First Two Years

Some of the most dramatic physical change that occurs during this period is in the brain. At birth, the brain is about 25 percent of its adult weight, and this is not true for any other part of the body. By age 2, it is at 75 percent of its adult weight, at 95 percent by age 6, and at 100 percent by age 7 years.

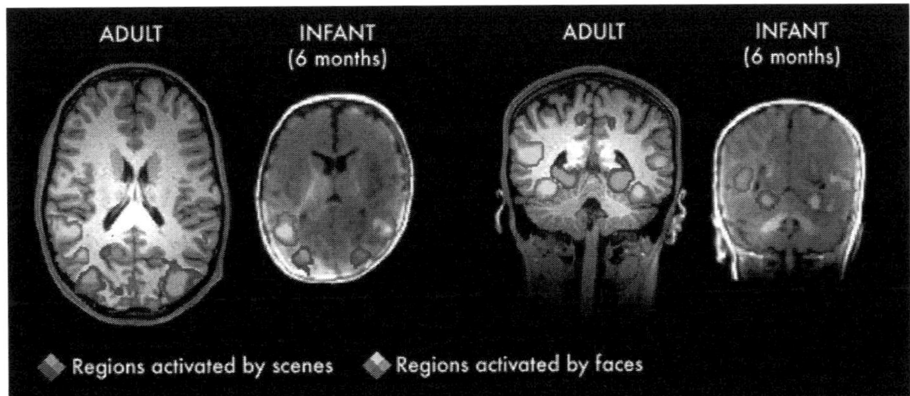

Figure 2. Research shows that as early at 4-6 months, infants utilize similar areas of the brain as adults to process information. Image from research article conducted by Ben Deen, Hilary Richardson, Daniel D. Dilks, Atsushi Takahashi, Boris Keil, Lawrence L. Wald, Nancy Kanwisher & Rebecca Saxe."Article | OPEN | Published: 10 January 2017
Organization of high-level visual cortex in human infants". Image retrieved from https://www.quantamagazine.org/infant-brains-reveal-how-the-mind-gets-built-20170110/.

Communication within the central nervous system (CNS), which consists of the brain and spinal cord, begins with nerve cells called **neurons**. Neurons connect to other neurons via networks of nerve fibers called **axons** and **dendrites**. Each neuron typically has a single axon and numerous dendrites which are spread out like branches of a tree (some will say it looks like a hand with fingers). The axon of each neuron reaches toward the dendrites of other neurons at intersections called **synapses**, which are critical communication links within the brain. Axons and dendrites do not touch, instead, electrical impulses in the axons cause the release of chemicals called **neurotransmitters** which carry information from the axon of the sending neuron to the dendrites of the receiving neuron.

While most of the brain's 100 to 200 billion neurons are present at birth, they are not fully mature. Each neural pathway forms thousands of new connections during infancy and toddlerhood. During the next several years, dendrites**,** or connections between neurons, will undergo a period of **transient exuberance** or temporary dramatic growth (*exuberant* because it is so rapid and *transient* because some of it is temporary). There is a proliferation of these dendrites during the first two years so that by age 2, a single neuron might have thousands of dendrites. After this dramatic increase, the neural pathways that are not used will be eliminated through a process called **pruning**, thereby making those that are used much stronger. It is thought that pruning causes the brain to function more efficiently, allowing for mastery of more complex skills (Hutchinson, 2011). Transient

2. Huelke D. F. (1998). An Overview of Anatomical Considerations of Infants and Children in the Adult World of Automobile Safety Design. Annual Proceedings / Association for the Advancement of Automotive Medicine, 42, 93–113.

exuberance occurs during the first few years of life, and pruning continues through childhood and into adolescence in various areas of the brain. This activity is occurring primarily in the **cortex** or the thin outer covering of the brain involved in voluntary activity and thinking.

WATCH IT

This brief video describes some of the remarkable brain development that takes places in the first few years of life.

- https://youtu.be/R0fiu2SO_3M

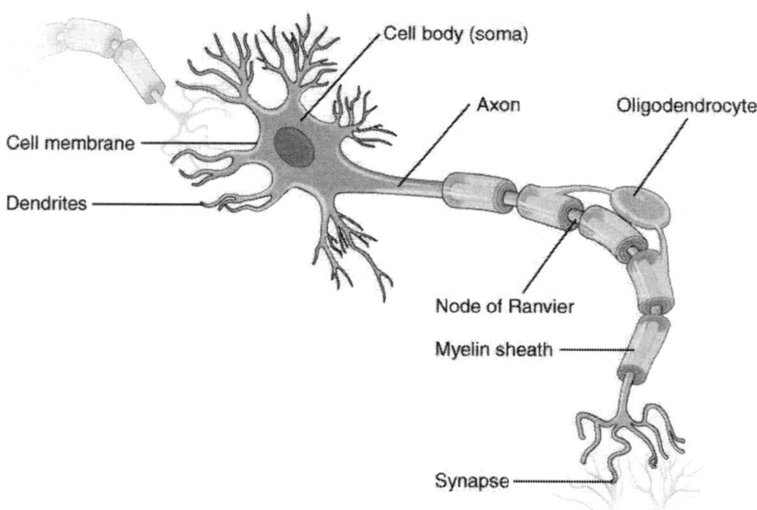

Figure 3. Parts of a neuron.

The **prefrontal cortex,** located behind the forehead, continues to grow and mature throughout childhood and experiences an addition growth spurt during adolescence. It is the last part of the brain to mature and will eventually comprise 85 percent of the brain's weight. Experience will shape which of these connections are maintained and which of these are lost. Ultimately, about 40 percent of these connections will be lost (Webb, Monk, & Nelson, 2001). As the prefrontal cortex matures, the child is increasingly able to regulate or control emotions, to plan activity, to strategize, and have better judgment. Of course, this is not fully accomplished in infancy and toddlerhood but continues throughout childhood and adolescence.

Another major change occurring in the central nervous system is the development of **myelin**, a coating of fatty tissues around the axon of the neuron. Myelin helps insulate the nerve cell and speed the rate of transmission of impulses from one cell to another. This enhances the building of neural pathways and improves coordination and control of movement and thought processes. The development of myelin continues into adolescence but is most dramatic during the first several years of life.

WATCH IT

How does all of this brain growth translate into cognitive abilities? We will discuss this later on in the module, but this video provides a nice overview of new research and some of the impressive abilities of newborns.

- https://youtu.be/nM-GhFzX8yQ

Motor and Sensory Development

From Reflexes to Voluntary Movements

Every basic **motor skill** (any movement ability) develops over the first two years of life. The sequence of motor skills first begins with **reflexes**. Infants are equipped with a number of reflexes, or involuntary movements in response to stimulation, and some are necessary for survival. These include the breathing reflex, or the need to maintain an oxygen supply (this includes hiccups, sneezing, and thrashing reflexes), reflexes that maintain body temperature (crying, shivering, tucking the legs close, and pushing away blankets), the sucking reflex, or automatically sucking on objects that touch their lips, and the rooting reflex, which involves turning toward any object that touches the cheek (which manages feeding, including the search for a nipple). Other reflexes are not necessary for survival, but signify the state of brain and body functions. Some of these include:the babinski reflex (toes fan upward when feet are stroked), the stepping reflex (babies move their legs as if to walk when feet touch a flat surface), the palmar grasp (the infant will tightly grasp any object placed in its palm), and the moro reflex (babies will fling arms out and then bring to chest if they hear a loud noise). These movements occur automatically and are signals that the infant is functioning well neurologically. Within the first several weeks of life, these reflexes are replaced with voluntary movements or motor skills.

WATCH IT

Watch this video to see examples of newborn reflexes.

- https://youtu.be/Sv5SsLH70mY

Motor development

Motor development occurs in an orderly sequence as infants move from reflexive reactions (e.g., sucking and rooting) to more advanced motor functioning. This development proceeds in a **cephalocaudal** (from head-down) and **proximodistal** (from center-out) direction. For instance, babies first learn to hold their heads up, then sit with assistance, then sit unassisted, followed later by crawling, pulling up, cruising, and then walking. As motor skills develop, there are certain developmental milestones that young children should achieve. For each milestone, there is an average age, as well as a range of ages in which the milestone should be reached. An example of a developmental milestone is a baby holding up its head. Babies on average are able to hold up their head at 6 weeks old, and 90% of babies achieve this between 3 weeks and 4 months old. If a baby is not holding up his head by 4 months old, he is showing a delay. On average, most babies sit alone at 7 months old. Sitting involves both coordination and muscle strength, and 90% of babies achieve this milestone between 5 and 9 months old (CDC, 2018). If the child is displaying delays on several milestones, that is a reason for concern, and the parent or caregiver should discuss this with the child's pediatrician. Some developmental delays can be identified and addressed through early intervention.

LINK TO LEARNING

For more information on developmental milestones, please see the CDC's Developmental Milestones.

Gross Motor Skills

Figure 4. This baby is working on his pincer grasp.

Gross motor skills are voluntary movements that involve the use of large muscle groups and are typically large movements of the arms, legs, head, and torso. These skills begin to develop first. Examples include moving to bring the chin up when lying on the stomach, moving the chest up, rocking back and forth on hands and knees. But it also includes exploring an object with one's feet as many babies do, as early as 8 weeks of age, if seated in a carrier or other device that frees the hips. This may be easier than reaching for an object with the hands, which requires much more practice (Berk, 2007). And sometimes an infant will try to move toward an object while crawling and surprisingly move backward because of the greater amount of strength in the arms than in the legs!

Fine Motor Skills

Fine motor skills are more exact movements of the hands and fingers and include the ability to reach and grasp an object. These skills focus on the muscles in the fingers, toes, and eyes, and enable coordination of small actions (e.g., grasping a toy, writing with a pencil, and using a spoon). Newborns cannot grasp objects voluntarily but do wave their arms toward objects of interest. At about 4 months of age, the infant is able to reach for an object, first with both arms and within a few weeks, with only one arm. Grasping an object involves the use of the fingers and palm, but no thumbs. Stop reading for a moment and try to grasp an object using the fingers and the palm. How does that feel? How much control do you have over the object? If it is a pen or pencil, are you able to write with it? Can you draw a picture? The answer is, probably not. Use of the thumb comes at about 9 months of age when the infant is able to grasp an object using the forefinger and thumb (**the pincer grasp**). This ability greatly enhances the ability to control and manipulate an object, and infants take great delight in this newfound ability. They may spend hours picking up small objects from the floor and placing them in containers. By 9 months, an infant can also watch a moving object, reach for it as it approaches, and grab it. This is quite a complicated set of actions if we remember how difficult this would have been just a few months earlier.

Table 1. Timeline of Developmental Milestones.[3] from https://www.webmd.com/parenting/baby/features/is-your-baby-on-track#1.[4]

~2 months	• Can hold head upright on own • Smiles at sound of familiar voices and follows movement with eyes
~3 months	• Can raise head and chest from prone position • Smiles at others • Grasps objects • Rolls from side to back

3. Rauh, Sherry (n.d.). Is Your Baby on Track? WebMD. Retrieved
4. Berk, L. (2007). *Development Through the Lifespan* (4th ed.) (pp 137). Pearson Education.

~4-5 months	• Babbles, laughs, and tries to imitate sounds • Begins to roll from back to side
~6 months	• Moves objects from hand to hand
~7-8 months	• Can sit without support • May begin to crawl • Responds to own name • Finds partially hidden objects
~8-9 months	• Walks while holding on • Babbles "mama" and "dada" • Claps
~11-12 months	• Stands alone • Begins to walk • Says at least one word • Can stack two blocks
~18 months	• Walks independently • Drinks from a cup • Says at least 15 words • Points to body parts
~2 years	• Runs and jumps • Uses two-word sentences • Follows simple instructions • Begins make-believe play
~3 years	• Speaks in multi-word sentences • Sorts objects by shape and color
~4 years	• Draws circles and squares • Rides a tricycle • Gets along with people outside of the family • Gets dressed
~5 years	• Can jump, hop, and skip • Knows name and address • Counts ten or more objects

Sensory Development

As infants and children grow, their senses play a vital role in encouraging and stimulating the mind and in helping them observe their surroundings. Two terms are important to understand when learning about the senses. The first is **sensation**, or the interaction of information with the sensory receptors. The second is **perception**, or the process of interpreting what is sensed. It is possible for someone to sense something without perceiving it. Gradually, infants become more adept at perceiving with their senses, making them more aware of their environment and presenting more affordances or opportunities to interact with objects.

Vision

What can young infants see, hear, and smell? Newborn infants' sensory abilities are significant, but their senses are not yet fully developed. Many of a newborn's innate preferences facilitate interaction with caregivers and other humans. The womb is a dark environment void of visual stimulation. Consequently, vision is the most poorly developed sense at birth. Newborns typically cannot see further than 8 to 16 inches away from their faces, have difficulty keeping a moving object within their gaze, and can detect contrast more than color differences. If you have ever seen a newborn struggle to see, you can appreciate the cognitive efforts being made to take in visual stimulation and build those neural pathways between the eye and the brain.

Although vision is their least developed sense, newborns already show a preference for faces. When you glance at a person, where do you look? Chances are you look into their eyes. If so, why? It is probably because there is more information there than in other parts of the face. Newborns do not scan objects this way; rather, they tend to look at the chin or another less detailed part of the face. However, by 2 or 3 months, they will seek more detail when visually exploring an object and begin showing preferences for unusual images over familiar ones, for patterns over solids, faces over patterns, and three-dimensional objects over flat images. Newborns have difficulty distinguishing between colors, but within a few months are able to discrimination between colors as well as adults. Infants can also sense depth as binocular vision develops at about 2 months of age. By 6 months, the infant can perceive depth perception in pictures as well (Sen, Yonas, & Knill, 2001). Infants who have experience crawling and exploring will pay greater attention to visual cues of depth and modify their actions accordingly (Berk, 2007).

Hearing

The infant's sense of hearing is very keen at birth. If you remember from an earlier module, this ability to hear is evidenced as soon as the 5th month of prenatal development. In fact, an infant can distinguish between very similar sounds as early as one month after birth and can distinguish between a familiar and non-familiar voice even earlier. Babies who are just a few days old prefer human voices, they will listen to voices longer than sounds that do not involve speech (Vouloumanos & Werker, 2004), and they seem to prefer their mother's voice over a stranger's voice (Mills & Melhuish, 1974). In an interesting experiment, 3-week-old babies were given pacifiers that played a recording of the infant's mother's voice and of a stranger's voice. When the infants heard their mother's voice, they sucked more strongly at the pacifier (Mills & Melhuish, 1974). Some of this ability will be lost by 7 or 8 months as a child becomes familiar with the sounds of a particular language and less sensitive to sounds that are part of an unfamiliar language.

Pain and Touch

Immediately after birth, a newborn is sensitive to touch and temperature, and is also sensitive to pain, responding with crying and cardiovascular responses. Newborns who are **circumcised** (the surgical removal of the foreskin of the penis) without anesthesia experience pain, as demonstrated by increased blood pressure, increased heart rate, decreased oxygen in the blood, and a surge of stress hormones (United States National Library of Medicine, 2016). According to the American Academy of Pediatrics (AAP), there are medical benefits and risks to circumcision. They do not recommend routine circumcision, however, they stated that because of the possible benefits (including prevention from urinary tract infections, penile cancer, and some STDs) parents should have the option to circumcise their sons if they want to (AAP, 2012).[5]

The sense of touch is acute in infants and is essential to a baby's growth of physical abilities, language and cognitive skills, and socio-emotional competency. Touch not only impacts short-term development during infancy and early childhood but also has long-term effects, suggesting the power of positive gentle touch from birth. Through touch, infants learn about their world, bond with their caregiver, and communicate their needs and wants. Research emphasizes the great benefits of touch for premature babies, but the presence of such contact has been shown to benefit all children (Stack, D. M. (2010).[6] In an extreme example, some children in Romania were reared in orphanages in which a single care worker may have had as many as 10 infants to care for at one time. These infants were not often helped or given toys with which to play. As a result, many of them were

5. Circumcision Policy Statement. *Pediatrics*. Retrieved from https://pediatrics.aappublications.org/content/130/3/585
6. Stack, D. M. (2010). Touch and Physical Contact during Infancy: Discovering the Richness of the Forgotten Sense. The Wiley-Blackwell Handbook of Infant Development, 532-567

developmentally delayed (Nelson, Fox, & Zeanah, 2014).[7] When we discuss emotional and social development later in this module, you will also see the important role that touch plays in helping infants feel safe and protected, which builds trust and secure attachments between the child and their caregiver.

Taste and Smell

Not only are infants sensitive to touch, but newborns can also distinguish between sour, bitter, sweet, and salty flavors and show a preference for sweet flavors. They can distinguish between their mother's scent and that of others, and prefer the smell of their mothers. A newborn placed on the mother's chest will inch up to the mother's breast, as it is a potent source of the maternal odor. Even on the first day of life, infants orient to their mother's odor and are soothed, when crying, by their mother's odor (Sullivan et al., 2011).[8]

LINK TO LEARNING

The Centers for Disease Control and Prevention (CDC) describes the developmental milestones for children from 2 months through 5 years old. After reviewing the information, take the CDC's Developmental Milestones quiz to see how well you recall what you've learned. If you are a parent with concerns about your child's development, contact your pediatrician.

Nutrition

Good nutrition in a supportive environment is vital for an infant's healthy growth and development. Remember, from birth to 1 year, infants triple their weight and increase their height by half, and this growth requires good nutrition. For the first 6 months, babies are fed breast milk or formula. Starting good nutrition practices early can help children develop healthy dietary patterns. Infants need to receive nutrients to fuel their rapid physical growth. **Malnutrition** during infancy can result in not only physical but also cognitive and social consequences. Without proper nutrition, infants cannot reach their physical potential.

Benefits of Breastfeeding

Breast milk is considered the ideal diet for newborns due to the nutrition makeup of colostrum and subsequent breastmilk production. **Colostrum,** the milk produced during pregnancy and just after birth, has been described as "liquid gold. Colostrum is packed with nutrients and other important substances that help the infant build up his or her immune system. Most babies will get all the nutrition they need through colostrum during the first few days of life (CDC, 2018).[9] Breast milk changes by the third to fifth day after birth, becoming much thinner, but containing just the right amount of fat, sugar, water, and proteins to support overall

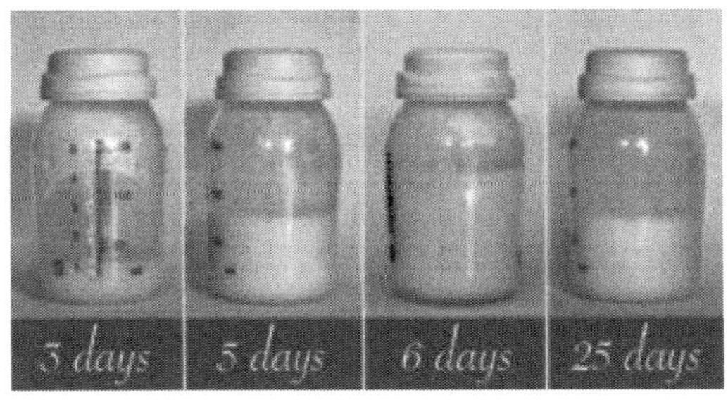

Figure 5. Breastmilk changes in composition with a newborn's development and needs.

7. Nelson, C. A., Fox, N. A., and Zeanah, C. H. (2014). Romania's abandoned children: Deprivation, brain development, and the struggle for recovery. Cambridge, MA, and London, England: Harvard University Press.
8. Sullivan, R., Perry, R., Sloan, A., Kleinhaus, K., & Burtchen, N. (2011). Infant bonding and attachment to the caregiver: insights from basic and clinical science. Clinics in perinatology, 38(4), 643–655. doi:10.1016/j.clp.2011.08.011
9. *What to Expect While Breastfeeding.* CDC. Retrieved from https://www.cdc.gov/nutrition/InfantandToddlerNutrition/breastfeeding/what-to-expect.html.

physical and neurological development. It provides a source of iron more easily absorbed in the body than the iron found in dietary supplements, it provides resistance against many diseases, it is more easily digested by infants than formula, and it helps babies make a transition to solid foods more easily than if bottle-fed.

The reason infants need such a high fat content is the process of myelination which requires fat to insulate the neurons. Therefore, there has been some research, including meta-analyses, to show that breastfeeding is connected to advantages with cognitive development (Anderson, Johnstone, & Remley, 1999)[10]. Low birth weight infants had the greatest benefits from breastfeeding than did normal-weight infants in a meta-analysis that of twenty controlled studies examining the overall impact of breastfeeding (Anderson et al., 1999). This meta-analysis showed that breastfeeding may provide nutrients required for rapid development of the immature brain and be connected to more rapid or better development of neurologic function. The studies also showed that a longer duration of breastfeeding was accompanied by greater differences in cognitive development between breastfed and formula-fed children. Whereas normal-weight infants showed a 2.66-point difference, low-birth-weight infants showed a 5.18-point difference in IQ compared with weight-matched, formula-fed infants (Anderson et al, 1999). These studies suggest that nutrients present in breast milk may have a significant effect on neurologic development in both premature and full-term infants.

For most babies, breast milk is also easier to digest than formula. Formula-fed infants experience more diarrhea and upset stomachs. The absence of antibodies in formula often results in a higher rate of ear infections and respiratory infections. Children who are breastfed have lower rates of childhood leukemia, asthma, obesity, type 1 and 2 diabetes, and a lower risk of SIDS. For all of these reasons, it is recommended that mothers breastfeed their infants until at least 6 months of age and that breast milk be used in the diet throughout the first year (U.S. Department of Health and Human Services, 2004a in Berk, 2007).

Several recent studies have reported that it is not just babies that benefit from breastfeeding. Breastfeeding stimulates contractions in the uterus to help it regain its normal size, and women who breastfeed are more likely to space their pregnancies farther apart. Mothers who breastfeed are at lower risk of developing breast cancer, especially among higher-risk racial and ethnic groups (Islami et al., 2015).[11] Other studies suggest that women who breastfeed have lower rates of ovarian cancer (Titus-Ernstoff, Rees, Terry, & Cramer, 2010)[12], and reduced risk for developing Type 2 diabetes (Gunderson, et al., 2015)[13], and rheumatoid arthritis (Karlson, Mandl, Hankinson, & Grodstein, 2004).[14]

A HISTORIC LOOK AT BREASTFEEDING

The use of wet nurses, or lactating women, hired to nurse others' infants, during the middle ages eventually declined, and mothers increasingly breastfed their own infants in the late 1800s. In the early part of the 20th century, breastfeeding began to go through another decline, and by the 1950s it was practiced less frequently by middle class,

10. Anderson, J.W., Johnstone, B.M., & Remley, D.T. (1999). Breast-feeding and cognitive development: a meta-analysis. The American Journal of Clinical Nutrition, 70, 4, 525–535, https://doi.org/10.1093/ajcn/70.4.525
11. Islami, F., Liu, Y., Jemal, A., Zhou, J., Weiderpass, E., Colditz, G., Boffetta, P., & Weiss, M. (2015). Breastfeeding and breast cancer risks by receptor status- a systematic review and meta-analysis. Annals of Oncology, 26,12. 2398–2407.
12. Titus-Ernstoff, Rees, L. Terry, R.R., & Cramer, D. W. (2010). Breast-feeding the last born child and risk of ovarian cancer. Cancer Causes Control. 21(2), 201–207.
13. Gunderson, E.P., Hurston, S.R., Dewey, K.G., Faith, M.S., Charvat-Aguilar, N., Khoury, V. C., Nguyen, V.T., & Quesenberry, C.P. (2015). The study of women, infant feeding and type 2 diabetes after GDM pregnancy and growth of their offspring (SWIFT Offspring study): prospective design, methodology and baseline characteristics. BMC Pregnancy and Childbirth, 15,150 https://doi.org/10.1186/s12884-015-0587-z
14. Karlson, E.W., Mandl, L.A., Hankinson, S. E., & Grodstein, F. (2004). Do breast-feeding and other reproductive factors influence future risk of rheumatoid arthritis? Results from the Nurses' Health Study. Arthritis Rheum. 50,11, 3458-67.

more affluent mothers as formula began to be viewed as superior to breast milk. In the late 1960s and 1970s, there was again a greater emphasis placed on natural childbirth and breastfeeding and the benefits of breastfeeding were more widely publicized. Gradually, rates of breastfeeding began to climb, particularly among middle-class educated mothers who received the strongest messages to breastfeed.

Today, new mothers receive consultation from lactation specialists before being discharged from the hospital to ensure that they are informed of the benefits of breastfeeding and given support and encouragement to get their infants accustomed to taking the breast. This does not always happen immediately, and first-time mothers, especially, can become upset or discouraged. In this case, lactation specialists and nursing staff can encourage the mother to keep trying until the baby and mother are comfortable with the feeding.

Most mothers who breastfeed in the United States stop breastfeeding at about 6-8 weeks, often in order to return to work outside the home (United States Department of Health and Human Services (USDHHS), 2011[15]). Mothers can certainly continue to provide breast milk to their babies by expressing and freezing the milk to be bottle fed at a later time or by being available to their infants at feeding time, but some mothers find that after the initial encouragement they receive in the hospital to breastfeed, the outside world is less supportive of such efforts. Some workplaces support breastfeeding mothers by providing flexible schedules and welcoming infants, but many do not. And the public support of breastfeeding is sometimes lacking. Women in Canada are more likely to breastfeed than are those in the United States, and the Canadian health recommendation is for breastfeeding to continue until 2 years of age. Facilities in public places in Canada such as malls, ferries, and workplaces provide more support and comfort for the breastfeeding mother and child than found in the United States.

In addition to the nutritional and health benefits of breastfeeding, breast milk is free! Anyone who has priced formula recently can appreciate this added incentive to breastfeeding. Prices for a month's worth of formula can easily range from $130-$200. Prices for a year's worth of formula and feeding supplies can cost well over $1,500 (USDHHS, 2011).

LINKS TO LEARNING

- Watch this video from the Psych SciShow "Bad Science: Breastmilk and Formula" to learn about research related to both breastfeeding and formula-feeding.
- To learn more about breastfeeding, visit this resource from the U.S. Department of Health and Human Resources: Your Guide to Breastfeeding.
- Visit Kids Health on Breastfeeding vs. Formula Feeding to learn more about the benefits and challenges of each. Click on the speaker icon to listen to the narration of the article if you would like.

When Breastfeeding Doesn't Work

There are occasions where mothers may be unable to breastfeed babies, often for a variety of health, social, and emotional reasons. For example, breastfeeding generally does not work:

- when the baby is adopted
- when the biological mother has a transmissible disease such as tuberculosis or HIV

15. United States Department of Health and Human Services, Office of Women's Health (2011). *Your guide to breast feeding*. Washington D.C.

- when the mother is addicted to drugs or taking any medication that may be harmful to the baby (including some types of birth control)
- when the infant was born to (or adopted by) a family with two fathers and the surrogate mother is not available to breastfeed
- when there are attachment issues between mother and baby
- when the mother or the baby is in the Intensive Care Unit (ICU) after the delivery process
- when the baby and mother are attached but the mother does not produce enough breast-milk

One early argument given to promote the practice of breastfeeding (when health issues are not the case) is that it promotes bonding and healthy emotional development for infants. However, this does not seem to be a unique case. Breastfed and bottle-fed infants adjust equally well emotionally (Ferguson & Woodward, 1999). This is good news for mothers who may be unable to breastfeed for a variety of reasons and for fathers who might feel left out as a result.

Introducing Solid Foods

Breast milk or formula is the only food a newborn needs, and the American Academy of Pediatrics recommends exclusive breastfeeding for the first six months after birth. Solid foods can be introduced from around six months onward when babies develop stable sitting and oral feeding skills but should be used only as a supplement to breast milk or formula. By six months, the gastrointestinal tract has matured, solids can be digested more easily, and allergic responses are less likely. The infant is also likely to develop teeth around this time, which aids in chewing solid food. Iron-fortified infant cereal, made of rice, barley, or oatmeal, is typically the first solid introduced due to its high iron content. Cereals can be made of rice, barley, or oatmeal. Generally, salt, sugar, processed meat, juices, and canned foods should be avoided.

Though infants usually start eating solid foods between 4 and 6 months of age, more and more solid foods are consumed by a growing toddler. Pediatricians recommended introducing foods one at a time, and for a few days, in order to identify any potential food allergies. Toddlers may be picky at times, but it remains important to introduce a variety of foods and offer food with essential vitamins and nutrients, including iron, calcium, and vitamin D.

Milk Anemia in the United States

About 9 million children in the United States are malnourished (Children's Welfare, 1998). More still suffer from **milk anemia**, a condition in which milk consumption leads to a lack of iron in the diet. The prevalence of iron deficiency anemia in 1- to 3-year-old children seems to be increasing (Kazal, 2002)[16]. The body gets iron through certain foods. Toddlers who drink too much cow's milk may also become anemic if they are not eating other healthy foods that have iron. This can be due to the practice of giving toddlers milk as a pacifier when resting, riding, walking, and so on. Appetite declines somewhat during toddlerhood and a small amount of milk (especially with added chocolate syrup) can easily satisfy a child's appetite for many hours. The calcium in milk interferes with the absorption of iron in the diet as well. There is also a link between iron deficiency anemia and diminished mental, motor, and behavioral development. In the second year of life, iron deficiency can be prevented by the use of a diversified diet that is rich in sources of iron and vitamin C, limiting cow's milk consumption to less than 24 ounces per day, and providing a daily iron-fortified vitamin.

16. KAZAL, L.A. (2002). Navajo Health Foundation/Sage Memorial Hospital, Ganado, Arizona Am Fam Physician. 66(7): 1217-1225.

Global Considerations and Malnutrition

In the 1960s, formula companies led campaigns in developing countries to encourage mothers to feed their babies on infant formula. Many mothers felt that formula would be superior to breast milk and began using formula. The use of formula can certainly be healthy under conditions in which there is adequate, clean water with which to mix the formula and adequate means to sanitize bottles and nipples. However, in many of these countries, such conditions were not available and babies often were given diluted, contaminated formula which made them become sick with diarrhea and become dehydrated. These conditions continue today and now many hospitals prohibit the distribution of formula samples to new mothers in efforts to get them to rely on breastfeeding. Many of these mothers do not understand the benefits of breastfeeding and have to be encouraged and supported in order to promote this practice.

Figure 6. These children are showing the extended abdomen characteristic of kwashiorkor (Photo Courtesy Centers for Disease Control and Prevention).

The World Health Organization (2018) recommends:

- initiation of breastfeeding within one hour of birth
- exclusive breastfeeding for the first six months of life
- introduction of solid foods at six months together with continued breastfeeding up to two years of age or beyond

LINK TO LEARNING

Breastfeeding could save the lives of millions of infants each year, according to the World Health Organization (WHO), yet fewer than 40 percent of infants are breastfed exclusively for the first 6 months of life. Most women can breastfeed unless they are receiving chemotherapy or radiation therapy, have HIV, are dependent on illicit drugs, or have active untreated tuberculosis. Because of the great benefits of breastfeeding, WHO, UNICEF and other national organizations are working together with the government to step up support for breastfeeding globally.

Find out more statistics and recommendations for breastfeeding at the WHO's 10 facts on breastfeeding. You can also learn more about efforts to promote breastfeeding in Peru: "Protecting Breastfeeding in Peru".

Children in developing countries and countries experiencing the harsh conditions of war are at risk for two major types of malnutrition. **Infantile marasmus** refers to starvation due to a lack of calories and protein. Children who do not receive adequate nutrition lose fat and muscle until their bodies can no longer function. Babies who are breastfed are much less at risk of malnutrition than those who are bottle-fed. After weaning, children who have diets deficient in protein may experience **kwashiorkor,** or the "disease of the displaced child," often occurring after another child has been born and taken over breastfeeding. This results in a loss of appetite and swelling of the abdomen as the body begins to break down the vital organs as a source of protein.

WATCH IT

Watch this video to learn more about the signs and symptoms of kwashiorkor and marasmus.

- https://youtu.be/bqElcMMmj5M

Sleep and Health

Infant Sleep

Infants 0 to 2 years of age sleep an average of 12.8 hours a day, although this changes and develops gradually throughout an infant's life. For the first three months, newborns sleep between 14 and 17 hours a day, then they become increasingly alert for longer periods of time. About one-half of an infant's sleep is rapid eye movement (REM) sleep, and infants often begin their sleep cycle with REM rather than non-REM sleep. They also move through the sleep cycle more quickly than adults. Parents spend a significant amount of time worrying about and losing even more sleep over their infant's sleep schedule when there remains a great deal of variation in sleep patterns and habits for individual children. A 2018 study showed that at 6 months of age, 62% of infants slept at least six hours during the night, 43% of infants slept at least 8 hours through the night, and 38% of infants were *not* sleeping at least six continual hours through the night. At 12 months, 28% of children were still not sleeping at least 6 uninterrupted hours through the night, while 78% were sleeping at least 6 hours, and 56% were sleeping at least 8 hours.[17]

The most common infant sleep-related problem reported by parents is nighttime waking. Studies of new parents and sleep patterns show that parents lose the most sleep during the first three months with a new baby, with mothers losing about an hour of sleep each night, and fathers losing a disproportionate 13 minutes. This decline in sleep quality and quantity for adults persists until the child is about six years old.[18]

While this shows there is no precise science as to when and how an infant will sleep, there are general trends in sleep patterns. Around six months, babies typically sleep between 14-15 hours a day, with 3-4 of those hours happening during daytime naps. As they get older, these naps decrease from several to typically two naps a day between ages 9-18 months. Often, periods of rapid weight gain or changes in developmental abilities such as crawling or walking will cause changes to sleep habits as well. Infants generally move towards one 2-4 hour nap a day by around 18 months, and many children will continue to nap until around four or five years old.[19]

17. Marie-Hélène Pennestri, Christine Laganière, Andrée-Anne Bouvette-Turcot, Irina Pokhvisneva, Meir Steiner, Michael J. Meaney, Hélène Gaudreau, on behalf of the Mavan Research Team (December 2018). *Uninterrupted Infant Sleep, Development, and Maternal Mood.* Pediatrics, Volume 142.
18. David Richter, Michael D Krämer, Nicole K Y Tang, Hawley E Montgomery-Downs, Sakari Lemola, Long-term effects of pregnancy and childbirth on sleep satisfaction and duration of first-time and experienced mothers and fathers, Sleep, Volume 42, Issue 4, April 2019, zsz015, https://doi.org/10.1093/sleep/zsz015
19. Macall Gordon (October 2018). From Safe Sleep to Healthy Sleep: A Systemic Perspective on Sleep In the First Year. Northwest Bulletin: Family and Child Health. University of Washington. retrieved from https://depts.washington.edu/nwbfch/infant-safe-sleep-development.

Sudden Unexpected Infant Deaths (SUID)

Each year in the United States, there are about 3,500 Sudden Unexpected Infant Deaths (SUID). These deaths occur among infants less than one-year-old and have no immediately obvious cause (CDC, 2015). The three commonly reported types of SUID are:

- **Sudden Infant Death Syndrome (SIDS):** SIDS is identified when the death of a healthy infant occurs suddenly and unexpectedly, and medical and forensic investigation findings (including an autopsy) are inconclusive. SIDS is the leading cause of death in infants up to 12 months old, and approximately 1,500 infants died of SIDS in 2013 (CDC, 2015). The risk of SIDS is highest at 4 to 6 weeks of age. Because SIDS is diagnosed when no other cause of death can be determined, possible causes of SIDS are regularly researched. One leading hypothesis suggests that infants who die from SIDS have abnormalities in the area of the brainstem responsible for regulating breathing (Weekes-Shackelford & Shackelford, 2005). Although the exact cause is unknown, doctors have identified the following risk factors for SIDS:
    - low birth weight
    - siblings who have had SIDS
    - sleep apnea
    - of African-American or Eskimo decent
    - low socioeconomic status (SES)
    - smoking in the home
- **Unknown Cause:** The sudden death of an infant less than one year of age that cannot be explained because a thorough investigation was not conducted and the cause of death could not be determined.
- **Accidental Suffocation and Strangulation in Bed:** Reasons for accidental suffocation include the following: Suffocation by soft bedding, another person rolling on top of or against the infant while sleeping, an infant being wedged between two objects such as a mattress and wall, and strangulation such as when an infant's head and neck become caught between crib railings.

The combined SUID rate declined considerably following the release of the American Academy of Pediatrics safe sleep recommendations in 1992, which advocated that infants be placed on their backs for sleep (non-prone position). These recommendations were followed by a major Back to Sleep Campaign in 1994. According to the CDC, the SIDS death rate is now less than one-fourth of what is was (130 per 100,000 live birth in 1990 versus 40 in 2015). However, accidental suffocation and strangulation in bed mortality rates remained unchanged until the late 1990s. Some parents were still putting newborns to sleep on their stomachs partly because of past tradition. Most SIDS victims experience several risks, an interaction of biological and social circumstances. But thanks to research, the major risk, stomach sleeping, has been highly publicized. Other causes of death during infancy include congenital birth defects and homicide.

Co-Sleeping

The location of sleep depends primarily on the baby's age and culture. **Bed-sharing** (in the parents' bed) or **co-sleeping** (in the parents' room) is the norm is some cultures, but not in others (Esposito et al. 2015) [20]. Colvin, Collie-Akers, Schunn and Moon (2014)[21] analyzed a total of 8,207 deaths from 24 states during 2004–2012. The deaths were documented in the National Center for the Review and Prevention of Child Deaths Case Reporting System, a database of death reports from state child death review teams. The results indicated that younger victims (0-3 months) were more likely to die by bed-sharing and sleeping in an adult's bed or on a person. A higher percentage of older victims (4 months to 364 days) rolled into objects in the sleep environment

20. Esposito, G., Setoh, P., & Bornstein, M.H. (2015). Beyond practices and values: Toward a physio-bioecological analysis of sleep arrangements in early infancy. Frontiers in Psychology, 6, 264.
21. Colvin, J.D., Collie-Akers, V., Schunn, C., & Moon, RY (2014). Sleep environment risks for younger and older infants. Pediatrics. 134(2):e406-12. doi: 10.1542/peds.2014-0401.

and changed position from side/back to prone. Carpenter et al. (2013)[22] compared infants who died of SIDS with a matched control and found that infants younger than three months old who slept in bed with a parent were five times more likely to die of SIDS compared to babies who slept separately from the parents, but were still in the same room. They concluded that bed-sharing, even when the parents do not smoke or take alcohol or drugs, increases the risk of SIDS. However, when combined with parental smoking and maternal alcohol consumption and/or drug use, the risks associated with bed-sharing greatly increased.

Despite the risks noted above, the controversy about where babies should sleep has been ongoing. Co-sleeping has been recommended for those who advocate attachment parenting (Sears & Sears, 2001) [23] and other research suggests that bed-sharing and co-sleeping is becoming more popular in the United States (Colson et al., 2013) [24]. So, what are the latest recommendations?

The American Academy of Pediatrics (AAP) actually updated their recommendations for a Safe Infant Sleeping Environment in 2016. The most recent AAP recommendations on creating a safe sleep environment include:

- Back to sleep for every sleep. Always place the baby on his or her back on a firm sleep surface such as a crib or bassinet with a tight-fitting sheet.
- Avoid the use of soft bedding, including crib bumpers, blankets, pillows, and soft toys. The crib should be bare.
- Breastfeeding is recommended.
- Share a bedroom with parents, but not the same sleeping surface, preferably until the baby turns 1 but at least for the first six months. Room-sharing decreases the risk of SIDS by as much as 50 percent.
- Avoid baby's exposure to smoke, alcohol, and illicit drugs.

As you can see, there is a recommendation to now "share a bedroom with parents," but not the same sleeping surface. Breastfeeding is also recommended as adding protection against SIDS, but after feeding, the AAP encourages parents to move the baby to his or her separate sleeping space, preferably a crib or bassinet in the parents' bedroom. Finally, the report included new evidence that supports skin-to-skin care for newborn infants.[25]

LINK TO LEARNING

The website **Zero to Three** has more information on infant sleep patterns and habits. Feel free to explore their multiple topics on the subject.

Immunizations

Preventing communicable diseases from early infancy is one of the major tasks of the Public Health System in the USA. Infants mouth every single object they find as one of their typical developmental tasks. They learn through their senses and tasting objects stimulates their brain and provides a sensory experience as well as learning.

22. https://bmjopen.bmj.com/content/3/5/e002299.long
23. Sears, W. & Sears, M. (2001). The attachment parenting book: A commonsense guide to understanding and nurturing your baby. Boston: MA: Little Brown.
24. Colson, E.R., Willinger, M., Rybin, D., Heeren, T., Smith, L.A., Lister, G. & Corwin, M.J. (2013). Trends and factors associated with infant bed sharing, 1993-2010: The National Sleep Position study. JAMA Pediatrics, 167(11), 1032-1037.
25. SIDS and Other Sleep-Related Infant Deaths: Updated 2016 Recommendations for a Safe Infant Sleeping Environment. Task Force on Sudden Infant Death Syndrome. Pediatrics. Retrieved from https://pediatrics.aappublications.org/content/138/5/e20162938.

Infants have much contact with dirty surfaces. They lay on a carpet that most likely has been contaminated by adults walking on it; they mouth keys, rattles, toys, and books; they crawl on the floor; they hold on to furniture to walk, and much more. How do we prevent infants from getting sick? One possible answer is **immunizations**.

WATCH IT

Watch the selected first ten minutes of this video clip from the Alexander Street Database that illustrates what now has become the vaccine war.

- https://youtu.be/VPOrnU3lmxl

Many decades ago, our society struggled to find vaccines and cures for illnesses such as Polio, whooping cough, and many other medical conditions. A few decades ago parents started changing their minds on the need to vaccinate children. Some children are not vaccinated for valid medical reasons, but some states allow a child to be unvaccinated because of a parent's personal or religious beliefs. At least 1 in 14 children is not vaccinated. What is the outcome of not vaccinating children? Some of the preventable illnesses are returning. Fortunately, each vaccinated child stops the transmission of the disease, a phenomenon called *herd immunity*. Usually, if 90% of the people in a community (a herd) are immunized, no one dies of that disease.

In 2017, Community Care Licensing in California, the agency that regulates childcare centers, changed regulations. Before it was possible for parents to opt-out of vaccinations due to personal beliefs, but this changed after Governor Brown signed a Bill in 2016 to only exclude children from being vaccinated if there were medical reasons. Furthermore, all personnel working with children must be immunized.

LINK TO LEARNING

Read more information about vaccinations at the website **Shots for School.**

GLOSSARY

axons:
fibers that extend from the neurons and transmit electrochemical impulses from that neuron to the dendrites of other neurons

bed-sharing:
when two or more people sleep in the same bed

cephalocaudal:
refers to growth and development that occurs from the head down

circumcision:
the surgical removal of the foreskin of the penis

colostrum:
the first secretion from the mammary glands after giving birth, rich in antibodies

cortex:
the outer layers of the brain in humans and other mammals. Most thinking, feeling, and sensing involves the cortex

co-sleeping:
a custom in which parents and their children (usually infants) sleep together in the same room

dendrites:
fibers that extend from neurons and receive electrochemical impulses transmitted from other neurons via their axons

failure to thrive:
decelerated or arrested physical growth (height and weight measurements fall below the third or fifth percentile or a downward change in growth across two major growth percentiles) and is associated with abnormal growth and development

fine motor skills:
physical abilities involving small body movements, especially of the hands and fingers, such as drawing and picking up a coin. The word "fine" in this context means "small"

gross motor skills:
physical abilities involving large body movements, such as walking and jumping. The word "gross" in this context means "big"

immunization:
a process that stimulates the body's immune system by causing the production of antibodies to defend against attack by a specific contagious disease

infantile marasmus:
starvation due to a lack of calories and protein

kwashiorkor:
also known as the "disease of the displaced child," results in a loss of appetite and swelling of the abdomen as the body begins to break down the vital organs as a source of protein

malnutrition:
a condition that results from eating a diet in which one or more nutrients are deficient

milk anemia:
an iron deficiency in infants who have been maintained on a milk diet for too long

motor skills:
the word "motor" refers to the movement of the muscles. Motor skills refer to our ability to move our bodies and manipulate objects

myelin:
a coating of fatty tissues around the axon of the neuron

neurons:
nerve cells in the central nervous system, especially in the brain

neurotransmitters:
brain chemicals that carry information from the axon of a sending neuron to the dendrites of a receiving neuron

percentile:
a point on a ranking scale of 0 to 100. The 50th percentile is the midpoint; half of the infants in the population being studied rank higher and half rank lower

perception:
the process of interpreting what is sensed

pincer grasp:
a developmental milestone that typically occurs at 9 to 12 months of age; the coordination of the index finger and thumb to hold smaller objects; represents a further development of fine motor skills

prefrontal cortex:
the area of the cortex at the very front of the brain that specializes in anticipation, planning, and impulse control

proximodistal:
development that occurs from the center or core of the body in an outward direction

pruning:
the process by which unused connections in the brain atrophy and die

reflexes:
the inborn, behavioral patterns that develop during uterine life and are fully present at birth. These are involuntary movements (not learned) or actions that are essential for a newborn's survival immediately after birth and include: sucking, swallowing, blinking, urinating, hiccuping, and defecating

sensation:
the interaction of information with the sensory receptors

sudden infant death syndrome (SIDS):
a situation in which a seemingly healthy infant, usually between 2 and 6 months old, suddenly stops breathing and dies unexpectedly while asleep

synapses:
the intersection between the axon of one neuron to the dendrites of another neuron

transient exuberance:
the great, but temporary increase in the number of dendrites that develop in an infant's brain during the first two years of life

Cognitive Development in Infants and Toddlers

What you'll learn to do: explain cognitive development in infants and toddlers

In addition to rapid physical growth, young children also exhibit significant development of their cognitive abilities, particularly in language acquisition and in the ability to think and reason. You already learned a little bit about Piaget's theory of cognitive development, and in this section, we'll apply that model to cognitive tasks during infancy and toddlerhood. Piaget described intelligence in infancy as sensorimotor or based on direct, physical contact where infants use senses and motor skills to taste, feel, pound, push, hear, and move in order to experience the world. These basic motor and sensory abilities provide the foundation for the cognitive skills that will emerge during the subsequent stages of cognitive development.

LEARNING OUTCOMES

- Describe each of Piaget's theories and stages of sensorimotor intelligence
- Explain learning and memory abilities in infants and toddlers
- Describe stages of language development during infancy
- Compare theories of language development in toddlers
- Explain the procedure, results, and implications of Hamlin and Wynn's research on moral reasoning in infants

Cognitive Development

Cognitive Development in Children

In order to adapt to the evolving environment around us, humans rely on cognition, both adapting to the environment and also transforming it. In general, all theorists studying cognitive development address three main issues:

1. The typical course of cognitive development
2. The unique differences between individuals
3. The mechanisms of cognitive development (the way genetics and environment combine to generate patterns of change)

Piaget and Sensorimotor Intelligence

How do infants connect and make sense of what they are learning? Remember that Piaget believed that we are continuously trying to maintain cognitive equilibrium, or balance, between what we see and what we know (Piaget, 1954). Children have much more of a challenge in maintaining this balance because they are constantly being confronted with new situations, new words, new objects, etc. All this new information needs to be organized, and a framework for organizing information is referred to as a **schema**. Children develop schemas through the processes of **assimilation** and **accommodation**.

Figure 1. Toddlers happily explore the world, engaged in purposeful goal-directed behavior.

For example, 2-year-old Deja learned the schema for dogs because her family has a Poodle. When Deja sees other dogs in her picture books, she says, "Look mommy, dog!" Thus, she has assimilated them into her schema for dogs. One day, Deja sees a sheep for the first time and says, "Look mommy, dog!" Having a basic schema that a dog is an animal with four legs and fur, Deja thinks all furry, four-legged creatures are dogs. When Deja's mom tells her that the animal she sees is a sheep, not a dog, Deja must accommodate her schema for dogs to include more information based on her new experiences. Deja's schema for dog was too broad since not all furry, four-legged creatures are dogs. She now modifies her schema for dogs and forms a new one for sheep.

Let's examine the transition that infants make from responding to the external world reflexively as newborns, to solving problems using mental strategies as two-year-olds. Piaget called this first stage of cognitive development **sensorimotor intelligence** (the sensorimotor period) because infants learn through their senses and motor skills. He subdivided this period into six substages:

Table 1. Sensorimotor substages.

Stage	Age
Stage 1 – Reflexes	Birth to 6 weeks
Stage 2 – Primary Circular Reactions	6 weeks to 4 months
Stage 3 – Secondary Circular Reactions	4 months to 8 months
Stage 4 – Coordination of Secondary Circular Reactions	8 months to 12 months
Stage 5 – Tertiary Circular Reactions	12 months to 18 months
Stage 6 – Mental Representation	18 months to 24 months

Substages of Sensorimotor Intelligence

For an overview of the substages of sensorimotor thought, it helps to group the six substages into pairs. The first two substages involve the infant's responses to its own body, call **primary circular reactions**. During the first month first (substage one), the infant's senses, as well motor reflexes are the foundation of thought.

Substage One: Reflexive Action (Birth through 1st month)

This active learning begins with automatic movements or reflexes (sucking, grasping, staring, listening). A ball comes into contact with an infant's cheek and is automatically sucked on and licked. But this is also what happens with a sour lemon, much to the infant's surprise! The baby's first challenge is to learn to adapt the sucking reflex to bottles or breasts, pacifiers or fingers, each acquiring specific types of tongue movements to latch, suck, breath, and repeat. This adaptation demonstrates that infants have begun to make sense of sensations. Eventually, the use of these reflexes becomes more deliberate and purposeful as they move onto substage two.

Substage Two: First Adaptations to the Environment (1st through 4th months)

Fortunately, within a few days or weeks, the infant begins to discriminate between objects and adjust responses accordingly as reflexes are replaced with voluntary movements. An infant may accidentally engage in a behavior and find it interesting, such as making a vocalization. This interest motivates trying to do it again and helps the infant learn a new behavior that originally occurred by chance. The behavior is identified as circular and primary because it centers on the infant's own body. At first, most actions have to do with the body, but in months to come, will be directed more toward objects. For example, the infant may have different sucking motions for hunger and others for comfort (i.e. sucking a pacifier differently from a nipple or attempting to hold a bottle to suck it).

The next two substages (3 and 4), involve the infant's responses to objects and people, called **secondary circular reactions.** Reactions are no longer confined to the infant's body and are now interactions between the baby and something else.

Substage Three: Repetition (4th through 8th months)

During the next few months, the infant becomes more and more actively engaged in the outside world and takes delight in being able to make things happen by responding to people and objects. Babies try to continue any pleasing event. Repeated motion brings particular interest as the infant is able to bang two lids together or shake a rattle and laugh. Another example might be to clap their hands when a caregiver says "patty-cake." Any sight of something delightful will trigger efforts for interaction.

Substage Four: New Adaptations and Goal-Directed Behavior (8th through 12th months)

Now the infant becomes more deliberate and purposeful in responding to people and objects and can engage in behaviors that others perform and anticipate upcoming events. Babies may ask for help by fussing, pointing, or reaching up to accomplish tasks, and work hard to get what they want. Perhaps because of continued maturation of the prefrontal cortex, the infant becomes capable of having a thought and carrying out a planned, goal-directed activity such as seeking a toy that has rolled under the couch or indicating that they are hungry. The infant is coordinating both internal and external activities to achieve a planned goal and begins to get a sense of social understanding. Piaget believed that at about 8 months (during substage 4), babies first understood the concept of **object permanence,** which is the realization that objects or people continue to exist when they are no longer in sight.

The last two stages (5 and 6), called **tertiary circular reactions**, consist of actions (stage 5) and ideas (stage 6) where infants become more creative in their thinking.

Substage Five: Active Experimentation of "Little Scientists" (12th through 18th months)

The toddler is considered a "little scientist" and begins exploring the world in a trial-and-error manner, using motor skills and planning abilities. For example, the child might throw their ball down the stairs to see what happens or delight in squeezing all of the toothpaste out of the tube. The toddler's active engagement in experimentation helps them learn about their world. Gravity is learned by pouring water from a cup or pushing bowls from high chairs. The caregiver tries to help the child by picking it up again and placing it on the tray. And what happens? Another experiment! The child pushes it off the tray again causing it to fall and the caregiver to pick it up again! A closer examination of this stage causes us to really appreciate how much learning is going on at this time and how many things we come to take for granted must actually be learned. This is a wonderful and messy time of experimentation and most learning occurs by trial and error.

WATCH IT

See how even babies think like little scientists in the selected clip from this Ted talk.

- https://youtu.be/y1KIVZw7Jxk

Substage Six: Mental Representations (18th month to 2 years of age)

The child is now able to solve problems using mental strategies, to remember something heard days before and repeat it, to engage in pretend play, and to find objects that have been moved even when out of sight. Take, for instance, the child who is upstairs in a room with the door closed, supposedly taking a nap. The doorknob has a safety device on it that makes it impossible for the child to turn the knob. After trying several times to push the door or turn the doorknob, the child carries out a mental strategy to get the door opened – he knocks on the door! Obviously, this is a technique learned from the past experience of hearing a knock on the door and observing someone opening the door. The child is now better equipped with mental strategies for problem-solving. Part of this stage also involves learning to use language. This initial movement from the "hands-on" approach to knowing about the world to the more mental world of stage six marked the transition to preoperational thinking, which you'll learn more about in a later module.

Development of Object Permanence

A critical milestone during the sensorimotor period is the development of object permanence. Introduced during substage 4 above, **object permanence** is the understanding that even if something is out of sight, it continues to exist. The infant is now capable of making attempts to retrieve the object. Piaget thought that, at about 8 months, babies first understand the concept of objective permanence, but some research has suggested that infants seem to be able to recognize that objects have permanence at much younger ages (even as young as 4 months of age). Other researchers, however, are not convinced (Mareschal & Kaufman, 2012).[1] It may be a matter of "grasping vs. mastering" the concept of objective permanence. Overall, we can expect children to *grasp* the concept that objects continue to exist even when they are not in sight by around 8 months old, but memory may play a factor in their consistency. Because toddlers (i.e., 12–24 months old) have *mastered* object permanence, they enjoy games like hide-and-seek, and they realize that when someone leaves the room they will come back (Loop, 2013). Toddlers also point to pictures in books and look in appropriate places when you ask them to find objects.

WATCH IT

Although the styles and cinematography in this video are dated, the information is valuable in understanding how researchers, like Dr. Rene Baillargeon, study object permanence in young infants.

- https://youtu.be/hwgo2O5Vk_g

1. Mareshcal, D. & Kauffman, J. (2012). Object Permanence in infancy: Revisiting Baillargeon's drawbridge study. In Alan M. Slaster & Paul C. Quinn (Eds.), Developmental Psychology: Revisiting the classic studies. Thousand Oaks, CA: Sage.

Learning and Memory Abilities in Infants

Memory is central to cognitive development. Our memories form the basis for our sense of self, guide our thoughts and decisions, influence our emotional reactions, and allow us to learn (Bauer, 2008)[2].

It is thought that Piaget underestimated memory ability in infants (Schneider, 2015)[3].

As mentioned when discussing the development of infant senses, within the first few weeks of birth, infants recognize their caregivers by face, voice, and smell. Sensory and caregiver memories are apparent in the first month, motor memories by 3 months, and then, at about 9 months, more complex memories including language (Mullally & Maguire, 2014)[4]. There is agreement that memory is fragile in the first months of life, but that improves with age. Repeated sensations and brain maturation are required in order to process and recall events (Bauer, 2008). Infants remember things that happened weeks and months ago (Mullally & Maguire, 2014), although they most likely will not remember it decades later. From the cognitive perspective, this has been explained by the idea that the lack of linguistic skills of babies and toddlers limit their ability to mentally represent events; thereby, reducing their ability to encode memory. Moreover, even if infants do form such early memories, older children and adults may not be able to access them because they may be employing very different, more linguistically based, retrieval cues than infants used when forming the memory.

WATCH IT

Watch this Ted talk from Alison Gopnik to hear about more research done on cognition in babies.

- https://youtu.be/cplaWsiu7Yg

Language Development

Given the remarkable complexity of a language, one might expect that mastering a language would be an especially arduous task; indeed, for those of us trying to learn a second language as adults, this might seem to be true. However, young children master language very quickly with relative ease. B. F. Skinner (1957) proposed that language is learned through reinforcement. Noam Chomsky (1965) criticized this behaviorist approach, asserting instead that the mechanisms underlying language acquisition are biologically determined. The use of language develops in the absence of formal instruction and appears to follow a very similar pattern in children from vastly different cultures and backgrounds. It would seem, therefore, that we are born with a biological predisposition to acquire a language (Chomsky, 1965; Fernández & Cairns, 2011). Moreover, it appears that there is a critical period for language acquisition, such that this proficiency at acquiring language is maximal early in life; generally, as people age, the ease with which they acquire and master new languages diminishes (Johnson & Newport, 1989; Lenneberg, 1967; Singleton, 1995).

2. Bauer PJ, Pathman T. Memory and Early Brain Development. In: Tremblay RE, Boivin M, Peters RDeV, eds. Paus T, topic ed. Encyclopedia on Early Childhood Development [online]. http://www.child-encyclopedia.com/brain/according-experts/memory-and-early-brain-development. Published December 2008. Accessed March 2, 2019.
3. Schneider, Wolfgang. (2015). This belief came in part from findings that adults rarely recall personal events from before the age of 3 years (a phenomenon known as **infantile** or **childhood amnesia**). However, research with infants and young children has made it clear that they can and do form memories of events. Memory development from early childhood through emerging adulthood. Switzerland: Spring International. doi: 10.1007/978-3-319-09611-7.
4. Mullally, Sinead L. & Maguire, Eleanor. A. (2014). Learning to remember: The early ontogeny of episodic memory. Developmental Cognitive Neuroscience, 9(13), 12-29. doi: 10.1016/j.dcn.2013.12.006

Children begin to learn about language from a very early age (Table 1). In fact, it appears that this is occurring even before we are born. Newborns show a preference for their mother's voice and appear to be able to discriminate between the language spoken by their mother and other languages. Babies are also attuned to the languages being used around them and show preferences for videos of faces that are moving in synchrony with the audio of spoken language versus videos that do not synchronize with the audio (Blossom & Morgan, 2006; Pickens, 1994; Spelke & Cortelyou, 1981).

Table 2. Stages of Language and Communication Development

Stage	Age	Developmental Language and Communication
1	0–3 months	Reflexive communication
2	3–8 months	Reflexive communication; interest in others
3	8–12 months	Intentional communication; sociability
4	12–18 months	First words
5	18–24 months	Simple sentences of two words
6	2–3 years	Sentences of three or more words
7	3–5 years	Complex sentences; has conversations

Each language has its own set of **phonemes** that are used to generate **morphemes**, words, and so on. Babies can discriminate among the sounds that make up a language (for example, they can tell the difference between the "s" in vision and the "ss" in fission); early on, they can differentiate between the sounds of all human languages, even those that do not occur in the languages that are used in their environments. However, by the time that they are about 1 year old, they can only discriminate among those phonemes that are used in the language or languages in their environments (Jensen, 2011; Werker & Lalonde, 1988; Werker & Tees, 1984).

WATCH IT

This video explains some of the research surrounding language acquisition in babies, particularly those learning a second language.

- https://youtu.be/Me_v82q0ins

Newborn Communication

Do newborns communicate? Certainly, they do. They do not, however, communicate with the use of language. Instead, they communicate their thoughts and needs with body posture (being relaxed or still), gestures, cries, and facial expressions. A person who spends adequate time with an infant can learn which cries indicate pain and which ones indicate hunger, discomfort, or frustration.

Figure 2. Before they develop language, infants communicate using facial expressions.

Intentional Vocalizations

Infants begin to vocalize and repeat vocalizations within the first couple of months of life. That gurgling, musical vocalization called cooing can serve as a source of entertainment to an infant who has been laid down for a nap or seated in a carrier on a car ride. Cooing serves as practice for vocalization. It also allows the infant to hear the sound of their own voice and try to repeat sounds that are entertaining. Infants also begin to learn the pace and pause of conversation as they alternate their vocalization with that of someone else and then take their turn again when the other person's vocalization has stopped. Cooing initially involves making vowel sounds like "oooo." Later, as the baby moves into babbling (see below), consonants are added to vocalizations such as "nananananana."

Babbling and Gesturing

Between 6 and 9 months, infants begin making even more elaborate vocalizations that include the sounds required for any language. Guttural sounds, clicks, consonants, and vowel sounds stand ready to equip the child with the ability to repeat whatever sounds are characteristic of the language heard. These babies repeat certain syllables (ma-ma-ma, da-da-da, ba-ba-ba), a vocalization called **babbling** because of the way it sounds. Eventually, these sounds will no longer be used as the infant grows more accustomed to a particular language. Deaf babies also use gestures to communicate wants, reactions, and feelings. Because gesturing seems to be easier than vocalization for some toddlers, sign language is sometimes taught to enhance one's ability to communicate by making use of the ease of gesturing. The rhythm and pattern of language are used when deaf babies sign just as when hearing babies babble.

At around ten months of age, infants can understand more than they can say. You may have experienced this phenomenon as well if you have ever tried to learn a second language. You may have been able to follow a conversation more easily than to contribute to it.

Holophrasic Speech

Children begin using their first words at about 12 or 13 months of age and may use partial words to convey thoughts at even younger ages. These one-word expressions are referred to as holophrasic speech (**holophrase**). For example, the child may say "ju" for the word "juice" and use this sound when referring to a bottle. The listener must interpret the meaning of the holophrase. When this is someone who has spent time with the child, interpretation is not too difficult. They know that "ju" means "juice" which means the baby wants some milk! But, someone who has not been around the child will have trouble knowing what is meant. Imagine the parent who exclaims to a friend, "Ezra's talking all the time now!" The friend hears only "ju da ga" which, the parent explains, means "I want some milk when I go with Daddy."

Underextension

A child who learns that a word stands for an object may initially think that the word can be used for only that particular object. Only the family's Irish Setter is a "doggie." This is referred to as underextension. More often, however, a child may think that a label applies to all objects that are similar to the original object. In overextension, all animals become "doggies," for example.

First words and cultural influences

First words for English-speaking children tend to be nouns. The child labels objects such as a cup or a ball. In a verb-friendly language such as Chinese, however, children may learn more verbs. This may also be due to the different emphasis given to objects based on culture. Chinese children may be taught to notice action and relationship between objects while children from the United States may be taught to name an object and its qualities (color, texture, size, etc.). These differences can be seen when comparing interpretations of art by older students from China and the United States.

Vocabulary growth spurt

One-year-olds typically have a vocabulary of about 50 words. But by the time they become toddlers, they have a vocabulary of about 200 words and begin putting those words together in telegraphic speech (short phrases). This language growth spurt is called the **naming explosion** because many early words are nouns (persons, places, or things).

Two-word sentences and telegraphic speech

Words are soon combined and 18-month-old toddlers can express themselves further by using phrases such as "baby bye-bye" or "doggie pretty." Words needed to convey messages are used, but the articles and other parts of speech necessary for grammatical correctness are not yet included. These expressions sound like a telegraph (or perhaps a better analogy today would be that they read like a text message) where unnecessary words are not used. "Give baby ball" is used rather than "Give the baby the ball." Or a text message of "Send money now!" rather than "Dear Mother. I really need some money to take care of my expenses." You get the idea.

Child-directed speech

Why is a horse a "horsie"? Have you ever wondered why adults tend to use "baby talk" or that sing-song type of intonation and exaggeration used when talking to children? This represents a universal tendency and is known as child-directed speech or motherese or parentese. It involves exaggerating the vowel and consonant sounds, using a high-pitched voice, and delivering the phrase with great facial expression. Why is this done? It may be in order to clearly articulate the sounds of a word so that the child can hear the sounds involved. Or it may be because when this type of speech is used, the infant pays more attention to the speaker and this sets up a pattern of interaction in which the speaker and listener are in tune with one another. When I demonstrate this in class, the students certainly pay attention and look my way. Amazing! It also works in the college classroom!

WATCH IT

This video examines new research on infant-directed speech.

- https://www.youtube.com/watch?v=ClGQ-GXS4WQ

Theories of Language Development

How is language learned? Each major theory of language development emphasizes different aspects of language learning: that infants' brains are genetically attuned to language, that infants must be taught, and that infants' social impulses foster language learning. The first two theories of language development represent two extremes in the level of interaction required for language to occur (Berk, 2007).

Chomsky and the language acquisition device

This theory posits that infants teach themselves and that language learning is genetically programmed. The view is known as *nativism* and was advocated by Noam Chomsky, who suggested that infants are equipped with a neurological construct referred to as the **language acquisition device (LAD)**, which makes infants ready for language. The LAD allows children, as their brains develop, to derive the rules of grammar quickly and effectively from the speech they hear every day. Therefore, language develops as long as the infant is exposed to it. No teaching, training, or reinforcement is required for language to develop. Instead, language learning comes from a particular gene, brain maturation, and the overall human impulse to imitate.

Skinner and reinforcement

This theory is the opposite of Chomsky's theory because it suggests that infants need to be taught language. This idea arises from behaviorism. Learning theorist, B. F. Skinner, suggested that language develops through the use of reinforcement. Sounds, words, gestures, and phrases are encouraged by following the behavior with attention, words of praise, treats, or anything that increases the likelihood that the behavior will be repeated. This repetition strengthens associations, so infants learn the language faster as parents speak to them often. For example, when a baby says "ma-ma," the mother smiles and repeats the sound while showing the baby attention. So, "ma-ma" is repeated due to this reinforcement.

Social pragmatics

Another language theory emphasizes the child's active engagement in learning the language out of a need to communicate. Social impulses foster infant language because humans are social beings and we must communicate because we are dependent on each other for survival. The child seeks information, memorizes terms, imitates the speech heard from others, and learns to conceptualize using words as language is acquired. Tomasello & Herrmann (2010) argue that all human infants, as opposed to chimpanzees, seek to master words and grammar in order to join the social world [5] Many would argue that all three of these theories (Chomsky's argument for nativism, conditioning, and social pragmatics) are important for fostering the acquisition of language (Berger, 2004).

Moral Reasoning in Infants

The Foundation of Moral Reasoning in Infants

The work of Lawrence Kohlberg was an important start to modern research on moral development and reasoning. However, Kohlberg relied on a specific method: he presented moral dilemmas and asked children and adults to explain what they would do and—more importantly—why they would act in that particular way. Kohlberg found that children tended to make choices based on avoiding punishment and gaining praise. But children are at a disadvantage compared to adults when they must rely on language to convey their inner thoughts and emotional reactions, so what they say may not adequately capture the complexity of their thinking.

Figure 3. Maybe babies know more than we think they do!

Starting in the 1980s, developmental psychologists created new methods for studying the thought processes of children and infants long before they acquire language. One particularly effective method is to present children with puppet shows to grab their attention and then record nonverbal behaviors, such as looking and choosing, to identify children's preferences or interests.

A research group at Yale University has been using the puppet show technique to study moral thinking of children for much of the past decade. What they have discovered has given us a glimpse of surprisingly complex thought processes that may serve as the foundation of moral reasoning.

EXPERIMENT 1: Do children prefer givers or takers?

In 2011, J. Kiley Hamlin and Karen Wynn put on puppet shows for very young children: 5-month-old infants. The infants watch a puppet bouncing a ball. We'll call this puppet the "bouncer puppet." Two other puppets stand at the back of the stage, one to left and the other to the right. After a few bounces, the ball gets away from the bouncer puppet and rolls to the side of the stage toward one of the other puppets. This puppet grabs the ball. The bouncer puppet turns toward the ball and opens its arms as if asking for the ball back.

5. Tomasello, M. & Hermann, E. (2010). Ape and human cognition. Current Directions in Psychological Science, 19(1), 3-8.

This is where the puppet show gets interesting (for a young infant, anyway!). Sometimes, the puppet with the ball rolls it back to the bouncer puppet. This is the "giver puppet" condition. Other times, the infant sees a different ending. As the bouncer puppet opens its arms to ask for the ball, the puppet with the ball turns and runs away with it. This is the "taker puppet" condition. Although the giver and taker puppets are two copies of the same animal doll, they are easily distinguished because they are wearing different colored shirts, and color is a quality that infants easily distinguish and remember. It looks like this:

> *A video element has been excluded from this version of the text. You can watch it online here: https://milnepublishing.geneseo.edu/lifespananddevelopmentprint/?p=48*

Each infant sees both conditions: the giver condition and the taker condition. Just after the end of the second puppet show (i.e., the second condition), a new researcher, who doesn't know which puppet was the giver and which was the taker, sits in front of the infant with the giver puppet in one hand and the taker puppet in the other. The 5-month-old infants are allowed to reach for a puppet. The one the child reaches out to touch is considered the preferred puppet.

Remember that Lawrence Kohlberg thought that children at this age—and, in fact, through 9 years of age—are primarily motivated to avoid punishment and seek rewards. Neither Kohlberg nor Carol Gilligan nor Jean Piaget was likely to predict that infants would develop preferences based on the type of behavior shown by other individuals.

WORK IT OUT

The puppet show is over and the experimenter is holding the two dolls—the giver puppet and the taker puppet—in front of the infant. The reaching behavior of the infant is being videotaped for later analysis.

What do you think? Make a prediction about the results of this study—which should reflect your own theory of an infant's ability to judge and care about the types of behavior others display. Do you think infants will choose the taker or the giver puppet? Do you expect the results to be significant?

Answer:

Here are the results from Experiment 1:

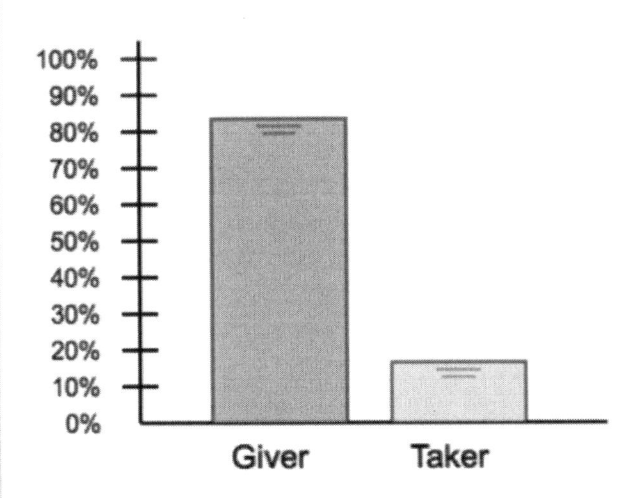

Actual Results:

Giver	Taker	Total
83%	16%	100%

Figure 4. Results from Experiment 1.

Experiment 1 suggests that 5-month-old infants are not just passive observers. They notice what others do and, if we are interpreting the results of experiments like this one correctly, they distinguish helpful behaviors ("prosocial behaviors") from behaviors that hurt others ("antisocial behaviors"). But they do more that that. They are attracted to those who are acting in a prosocial way, and they reject those who act in an antisocial way.

These researchers also tested infants who were only 3-months old. These infants were so immature that they did not yet have good control of their arms, so the experimenter could not use "reaching for one of the puppets" as the dependent variable, as they did with the 5-month-olds. Three-month-old infants can control where they look quite well, and previous research has indicated that very young infants will look longer at objects they want. The researchers showed these very young infants the same puppet shows that were described above and then, during the choice phase, they recorded which puppet (giver or taker) the 3-month-olds looked at longer. The results were very similar to those found with the 5-month-olds. A strong majority of younger infants (92%) looked longer at the giver puppet than the taker puppet.

But this isn't the end of the story...

EXPERIMENT 2: Do infants judge others based on their behavior?

In the research world, the early attempts to study something, when the researchers work to develop a solid and reliable research procedure, is often the most challenging time. Once the researcher works through initial problems and issues and begins to get consistent results, they can gain a deeper understanding by adding new variables or testing different groups of subjects (e.g., older children or children with some interesting psychological characteristics).

The study you just read about is an example of a simple, basic study. The researchers found that infants preferred puppets that help another puppet (the puppet in the giver condition) over puppets that are not nice to another puppet (the puppet in the taker condition). A common sense interpretation of this simple result is that infants like nice behavior and they dislike hurtful behavior. And perhaps that is as complicated as an 8-month-old infant's thoughts can be. But maybe not.

Dr. Hamlin and her colleagues wondered if infants might consider more factors when judging an event. Adults generally prefer situations where good things happen to someone rather than something harmful. However, when adults see someone do something bad, they may find satisfaction in seeing that person punished by having something bad happen to him or her. In a nutshell: good things should happen to good people and bad things should happen to bad people. This is what is called "just world" thinking, where people get what they deserve.

In the study we will call Experiment 2, Hamlin's team tested 8-month-old infants and repeated the procedures from Experiment 1 with a major addition. In Experiment 1 (described above), the puppet bouncing the ball was a neutral character, neither good nor bad. In Experiment 2, the infants saw 2 different shows. First, they saw the bouncer puppet either helping or hindering another puppet. Then, they watched the same ball-bouncing puppet show. Here is what happened:

- Puppet Show #1: A puppet is trying to open a box, but cannot quite succeed. Two puppets stand in the background. For some infants, as the first puppet struggles to open the box, one of the puppets in the back comes forward and helps to open the box. This is the helper puppet. For other children, as the first puppet struggles, a puppet comes from the back and jumps on the box, slamming it shut. This is the hinderer puppet. Each infant sees only a helper or a hinderer—not both. Here is a video showing the helper puppet situation:
    - https://s3-us-west-2.amazonaws.com/oerfiles/Psychology/Boxlidhelper.mp4
- Puppet Show #2: Just after the infants have watched the first show, the second puppet show begins. This is the show that you read about in Experiment 1. The only thing that is new is that the bouncer puppet, the one that loses the ball, is either the helper puppet from Puppet Show #1 or the hinderer puppet from Puppet Show #1. Each infant sees this puppet lose

the ball to a giver, who returns the ball, and to a taker, who runs off with the ball.

This video demonstrates show #2. The elephant in the yellow shirt from the first show is now bouncing a ball. After dropping the ball, the moose in the green shirt gives it back to him, while the moose in the red shirt takes it away.

- https://s3-us-west-2.amazonaws.com/oerfiles/Psychology/sm03.mp4
- https://s3-us-west-2.amazonaws.com/oerfiles/Psychology/sm04.mp4

So far we have concluded that even young babies prefer the "nice" puppet and show a preference for a puppet who helps another puppet. But this only happened when the bouncer puppet was the helper from the first puppet show. What if, instead of the nice elephant in the yellow shirt bouncing the ball, the elephant in the red shirt (the one who jumped on the duck's box, remember?) was the one bouncing the ball? Imagine the same scenario: the mean elephant in the red shirt is bouncing the ball, he drops it, and the moose in the green shirt gives it to him or the moose in the red shirt takes it away.

So now things are getting interesting, right? Do 8-month old infants understand the concepts of revenge or justice? We must always be careful when labeling behaviors of children (or animals) with characteristics we use for human adults. In the description above, we have talked of "nice puppets" and "mean puppets" and used other loaded terms. It is tempting to interpret the choices of the 8-month-olds as a kind of revenge motive: the bad guy gets its just desserts (the hinderer puppet has its ball stolen) and the good guy gets its just reward (the helper puppet is itself helped by the giver). Maybe that is what is going on, but we encourage you to consider these very sophisticated types of thinking as merely one hypothesis. Remember the facts—what did the puppets do and what choices did the infants make?—without committing yourself to the adult-level interpretation.

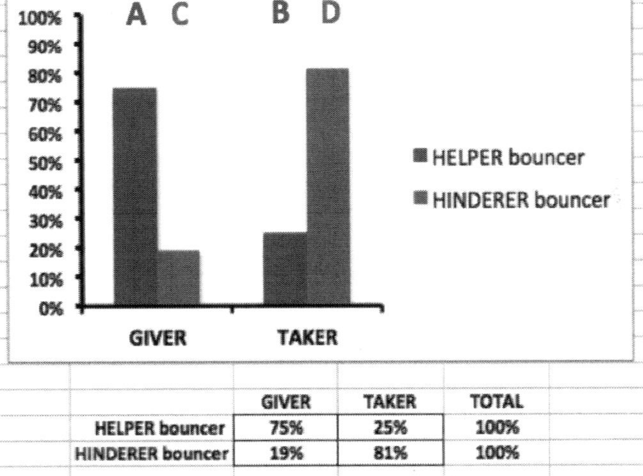

	GIVER	TAKER	TOTAL
HELPER bouncer	75%	25%	100%
HINDERER bouncer	19%	81%	100%

Figure 5. This bar graph shows the results of Experiment 2 for 8-month-old infants. The blue bars show the preferences for the infants who saw the helper from the first show as the bouncer in the second. Bar A is taller than Bar B, showing the greater choice of the giver than the taker puppet. The red bars show the reverse effect. The babies strongly preferred the taker (Bar C) to the giver (Bar D) when the puppet bouncing the ball had been the hinderer, who jumped on the box in the first show.

The researchers believe that this type of thinking, which is remarkably sophisticated, takes some cognitive development. They tested 5-month-olds using the same procedures, and the results with these younger infants were different. The 5-month-olds showed an overwhelming preference for the giver puppets, regardless of who was bouncing the ball. Maybe it is too complex for them to understand that the bouncer puppet in the second show was the same puppet from the first show. Or perhaps their memory processes are too fragile to hold onto information for that length of time. Maybe the revenge motive is too advanced. Or maybe something else is going on. What is clear is that 5-month-olds and 8-month-olds respond differently to the situations tested in the second experiment.

EXPERIMENT 3: Do infants judge others based on their preferences?

Across the first two experiments, infants appear to prefer puppets (and, by extension, maybe people, as well) that are helpful over those that are not helpful. Experiment 2 complicated our story a bit, but it still appears that prosocial behavior is attractive to infants and antisocial behavior is unattractive. But another experiment, again using the bouncing ball show, suggests that infants as young as 8-months of age may have some other motives that are less altruistic than the first two experiments indicate.

In a study by Hamlin, Mahanjan, Liberman, and Wynn from 2013, 9-month-old infants watched the bouncing ball show, but with a new twist.

At the beginning of the experiment—Phase 1—the infants were given a choice between graham crackers and green beans. The experimenters determined which food the infant preferred.

- https://youtu.be/VY005Pia4uA

Then, in Phase 2, the infants watched a puppet make the same choice. For half of the infants, the puppet chose the same food that they preferred, saying "Mmmm, yum! I like ___(graham crackers or green beans)!" and saying "Eww, yuck! I don't like ______ (graham crackers or green beans!" This was called the SIMILAR condition because the puppet was similar to the child in its food preference. For the other half of the infants, the puppet chose the other food, choosing graham crackers if the infant preferred green beans and preferring green beans if the infant liked graham crackers. This was the DISSIMILAR condition.

- https://youtu.be/aT4ljlQw-lo

Why did the experimenters do this? They wanted to know if young children form in-groups and out-groups by perceiving some people as being like them and other people as being unlike them. The experimenters noted in their research introduction that we (adults) are influenced by our perception that others are similar to us or not like us. We tend to project positive qualities—being trustworthy, intelligent, kind—on people we perceive as similar to ourselves, and people we see as unlike us are seen as having negative qualities—being relatively untrustworthy, unintelligent, and unkind.[6]

Of course, there is a big difference between claiming that adults use similarity to make judgments about others and saying that infants less than a year of age do the same thing. However, the researchers note that some recent research has suggested that infants less than a year old are more likely to develop peer friendships with other infants who "share their own food, clothing, or toy preferences" compared to those who don't.

So, back to the experiment. In Phase 3, the infants either saw a similar puppet (one that chose the food the baby preferred) or a dissimilar puppet (one that chose the food the baby did not prefer) bouncing the ball. As in the other experiments, the ball got away from the bouncer and rolled to the back of the stage. In one instance, the giver puppet returned the ball and, in the other instance, the taker puppet ran away with the ball. Finally, in Phase 4, the 9-month-old baby was shown the giver and taker puppet and the experimenters recorded which of the two puppets the baby preferred (reached out to touch). This video shows the dog in the light blue shirt giving the ball back to the red bunny that preferred graham crackers.

- https://youtu.be/ljiru5ggPVQ

Here is a summary of the four phases in Experiment 3:

- Phase 1: The infant chooses graham crackers or green beans.
- Phase 2: The bouncer puppets choose graham crackers or green beans.
    - Similar condition: The bouncer chooses the same food that the infant chose.
    - Dissimilar condition: The bouncer chooses the food that the infant did not choose.
- Phase 3: This is the same bouncing ball experiment that you have been reading about.
    - Remember that each child sees both the Giver and Taker shows.
- Phase 4: This is the same choice—Giver or Taker—that was the final phase in the other two experiments

6. The experimenters support these claims by citing the following studies: (1) DeBruine, L.M. Facial resemblance enhances trust: Proceedings of the Royal Society of London B, 2002, 269: 1307-1312. (2) Brewer, M.B. In-group bias in the minimal intergroup situation: A cognitive-motivational analysis. Psychological Bulletin, 1979, 86: 307-324. (3) Doise, W., Cspely, G., Dann, and others. An experimental investigation into the formation of intergroup representation. European Journal of Social Psychology, 1972, 2: 202-204.

WORK IT OUT

Now make predictions for the results. Here is a matrix picture of the design of the experiment:

		OTHER PUPPET in SHOW	
		GIVER puppet	TAKER puppet
BOUNCER	SIMILAR to child	A	B
food choice	DISSIMILAR from child	C	D

INSTRUCTIONS: Adjust bars A and C to make your predictions. Bar A represents the "nice" puppet who gave the ball to the bouncer puppet that liked the same food as the child, while bar B represents the "mean" puppet who took the ball away from the bouncer puppet who liked the same food as the child. Bar C represents the "nice" puppet who gave the ball back to the puppet who did not like the same food as the child, and bar D represents the puppet who took the ball away from the puppet who did not like the same food.

As before, move the bars on the left to indicate the percentage of infants preferring the giver puppet in the similar condition (purple bars) and in the dissimilar condition (green bars). The bars on the right will adjust to make the total in each of the similarity conditions equal 100%.

Answer:

Here are the results from Experiment 3:

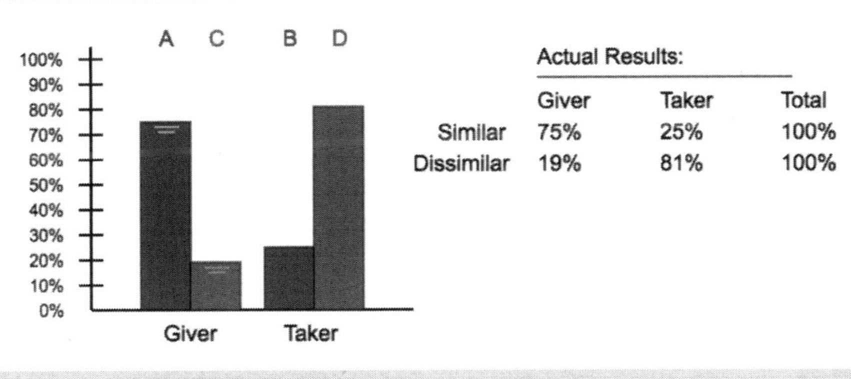

Figure 6. Results from Experiment 3.

These results are similar to those for the 8-month-olds in the previous experiment. But remember that, in this experiment, the variable that distinguishes the two bouncer puppets was a food choice, not the prosocial or antisocial behavior in Experiment 2. If we take the results from Experiments 2 and 3 together, the results here suggest that the similar puppet is being treated as if it is nice or good. Puppets that treat this similar puppet in a nice way are preferred. Conversely, the dissimilar puppets are treated as if they have done something negative and puppets that treat these dissimilar puppets badly are preferred.

The experimenters also tested an older group of babies that were 14-months-old. The results for these older babies were consistent with the 9-month-old and, if anything, the effects were stronger. Their results showed that all infants preferred when the giver puppet was nice to the puppet that was similar to them and all infants preferred when puppets were mean to the puppet that was dissimilar to them.

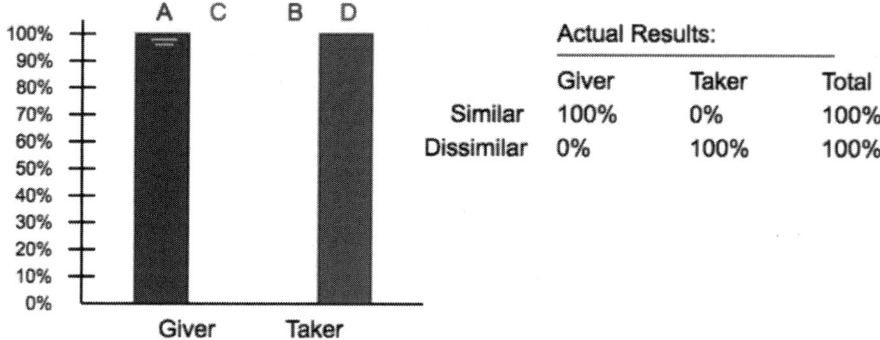

Figure 7. These bar graphs show the results of the experiment when 14-month olds were tested. One hundred percent of the children chose the puppet that gave the ball back to the puppet that was similar to them, and 100% of children chose the puppet that took the ball away from the puppet that had a different preference than they did.

CONCLUSIONS

This exercise started with a reminder that Lawrence Kohlberg found that children went through a long developmental process in their moral reasoning. Based on children's reasoning aloud about moral dilemmas, Kohlberg concluded that children younger than about 8 or 9 years of age make moral decisions based on avoiding punishment and receiving praise. Neither his research nor that of most others in the 1970s and 1980s suggested that young children would use multiple sources of information and judgments about the meaning of behaviors in their thinking about what sorts of behaviors are better or worse.

If Dr. Hamlin and her colleagues are right, then infants are much more sophisticated and complex in their thinking about the world than these earlier researchers thought. In Dr. Hamlin's view, infants like good things to happen to good puppets and people, and bad things to happen to bad puppets and people. Experiment 3 suggests that they make judgments about more than helping and harming behavior. They prefer others who are like them (green beans vs. graham crackers) and they don't mind if others who are not like them have unpleasant experiences.

The research we have been reviewing is just part of an impressive set of research on infant thinking. The ideas that the researchers have developed are intriguing and they are consistent with the modern view of the infant as an active, creative thinker. At the same time, remember that science doesn't rest on an early set of explanations based on a small set of complicated experiments. Science pushes beyond what we currently know and believe. This starts with curiosity on your part. Are the experimenters correct in interpreting reaching behavior as showing a preference or is something else going on? Do infants really prefer prosocial behaviors to antisocial behaviors, or is there some other explanation for their preferences? How else could we test the moral judgments of infants without using puppet shows? The next generation of creative scientists will push beyond what we know now, with new research methods and new ideas about the mind.

We'll give Dr. Hamlin the last word. Here is part of her conclusion section from an article that summarizes some of the research we have been studying: "In sum, recent developmental research supports the claim that at least some aspects of human morality are innate...Indeed, these early tendencies are far from shallow, mechanical predispositions to behave well or knee-jerk reactions to particular states of the world. Infant moral inclinations are sophisticated, flexible, and surprisingly consistent with adults' moral inclinations, incorporating aspects of moral goodness, evaluation, and retaliation." (Hamlin, 2013, p. 191)

GLOSSARY

accommodation:
when we restructure or modify what we already know so that new information can fit in better

assimilation:
when we modify or change new information to fit into our schemas (what we already know)

babbling:
an infant's repetition of certain syllables, such as ba-ba-ba, that begins when babies are between 6 and 9 months old

holophrase:
a single word that is used to express a complete, meaningful thought

infantile or childhood amnesia:
the idea that people forget everything that happened to them before the age of 3

language acquisition device (LAD):
Chomsky's term for the hypothesized mental structure that enables humans to learn the language, including the basic aspects of grammar, vocabulary, and intonation

morpheme:
the smallest unit of language that conveys some type of meaning

naming explosion:
a sudden increase in an infant's vocabulary, especially in the number of nouns, that begins at about 18 months of age

object permanence:
the realization that objects (including people) still exist even if they can no longer be seen, touched, or heard

phoneme:
a basic sound unit of a given language

primary circular reactions:
the first two stages of Piaget's sensorimotor intelligence which involve the infant's responses to its own body

schema:
a set of linked mental representations of the world, which we use both to understand and to respond to situations

secondary circular reactions:
stages 3 and 4 of Piaget's sensorimotor intelligence which involves the infant's responses to objects and people

sensorimotor intelligence:
Piaget's term for the way infants think (by using their senses and motor skills) during the first stage of cognitive development

tertiary circular reactions:
consist of actions (stage 5) and ideas (stage 6) where infants become more creative in their thinking

Emotional and Social Development During Infancy

What you'll learn to do: explain emotional and social development during infancy

Psychosocial development occurs as children form relationships, interact with others, and understand and manage their feelings. In emotional and social development, forming healthy attachments is very important and is the major social milestone of infancy. Attachment is a long-standing connection or bond with others. Developmental psychologists are interested in how infants reach this milestone. They ask such questions as: how do parent and infant attachment bonds form? How does neglect affect these bonds? What accounts for children's attachment differences?

LEARNING OUTCOMES

- Describe emotional development and self-awareness during infancy
- Contrast styles of attachment
- Describe temperament and the goodness-of-fit model
- Use Erikson's theory to characterize psychosocial development during infancy

Emotional Development and Attachment

Emotional Development

At birth, infants exhibit two emotional responses: attraction and withdrawal. They show attraction to pleasant situations that bring comfort, stimulation, and pleasure. And they withdraw from unpleasant stimulation such as bitter flavors or physical discomfort. At around two months, infants exhibit social engagement in the form of **social smiling** as they respond with smiles to those who engage their positive attention. Pleasure is expressed as laughter at 3 to 5 months of age, and displeasure becomes more specific to fear, sadness, or anger (usually triggered by frustration) between ages 6 and 8 months. Where anger is a healthy response to frustration, sadness, which appears in the first months as well, usually indicates withdrawal (Thiam et al., 2017).[1]

1. Thiam, M.A., Flake, E.M. & Dickman, M.M. (2017). Infant and child mental health and perinatal illness. In Melinda A. Thiam (Ed.), Perinatal mental health and the military family: Identifying and treating mood and anxiety disorders. New York, NY: Routledge.

As reviewed above, infants progress from reactive pain and pleasure to complex patterns of socioemotional awareness, which is a transition from basic instincts to learned responses. Fear is not always focused on things and events; it can also involve social responses and relationships. The fear is often associated with the presence of strangers or the departure of significant others known respectively as **stranger wariness** and **separation anxiety**, which appear sometime between 6 and 15 months. And there is even some indication that infants may experience jealousy as young as 6 months of age (Hart & Carrington, 2002).

Stranger wariness actually indicates that brain development and increased cognitive abilities have taken place. As an infant's memory develops, they are able to separate the people that they know from the people that they do not. The same cognitive advances allow infants to respond positively to familiar people and recognize those that are not familiar. **Separation anxiety** also indicates cognitive advances and is universal across cultures. Due to the infant's increased cognitive skills, they are able to ask reasonable questions like "Where is my caregiver going?" "Why are they leaving?" or "Will they come back?" Separation anxiety usually begins around 7-8 months and peaks around 14 months, and then decreases. Both stranger wariness and separation anxiety represent important social progress because they not only reflect cognitive advances but also growing social and emotional bonds between infants and their caregivers.

As we will learn through the rest of this module, caregiving does matter in terms of infant emotional development and emotional regulation. **Emotional regulation** can be defined by two components: emotions as regulating and emotions as regulated. The first, "emotions as regulating," refers to changes that are elicited by activated emotions (e.g., a child's sadness eliciting a change in parent response). The second component is labeled "emotions as regulated," which refers to the process through which the activated emotion is itself changed by deliberate actions taken by the self (e.g., self-soothing, distraction) or others (e.g., comfort).

Throughout infancy, children rely heavily on their caregivers for emotional regulation; this reliance is labeled co-regulation, as parents and children both modify their reactions to the other based on the cues from the other. Caregivers use strategies such as distraction and sensory input (e.g., rocking, stroking) to regulate infants' emotions. Despite their reliance on caregivers to change the intensity, duration, and frequency of emotions, infants are capable of engaging in self-regulation strategies as young as 4 months old. At this age, infants intentionally avert their gaze from overstimulating stimuli. By 12 months, infants use their mobility in walking and crawling to intentionally approach or withdraw from stimuli.

Throughout toddlerhood, caregivers remain important for the emotional development and socialization of their children, through behaviors such as labeling their child's emotions, prompting thought about emotion (e.g., "why is the turtle sad?"), continuing to provide alternative activities/distractions, suggesting coping strategies, and modeling coping strategies. Caregivers who use such strategies and respond sensitively to children's emotions tend to have children who are more effective at emotion regulation, are less fearful and fussy, more likely to express positive emotions, easier to soothe, more engaged in environmental exploration, and have enhanced social skills in the toddler and preschool years.

Self-awareness

During the second year of life, children begin to recognize themselves as they gain a sense of the self as an object. The realization that one's body, mind, and activities are distinct from those of other people is known as **self-awareness** (Kopp, 2011).[2] The most common technique used in research for testing self-awareness in infants is a mirror test known as the "Rouge Test." The rouge test works by applying a dot of rouge (colored makeup) on an infant's face and then placing them in front of the mirror. If the infant investigates the dot on their nose by touching it, they are thought to realize their own existence and have achieved self-awareness. A number of research studies have used this technique and shown self-awareness to develop between 15 and 24 months of age. Some researchers also take language such as "I, me, my, etc." as an indicator of self-awareness.

2. Kopp, C.B. (2011). Development in the early years: Socialization, motor development; and consciousness. Annual Review of Psychology, 62, 165-187.

Cognitive psychologist Philippe Rochat (2003) described a more in-depth developmental path in acquiring self-awareness through various stages. He described self-awareness as occurring in five stages beginning from birth.

Table 1. Stages of acquiring self-awareness

Stage	Description
Stage 1 – Differentiation (from birth)	Right from birth infants are able to differentiate the self from the non-self. A study using the infant rooting reflex found that infants rooted significantly less from self-stimulation, contrary to when the stimulation came from the experimenter.
Stage 2 – Situation (by 2 months)	In addition to differentiation, infants at this stage can also situate themselves in relation to a model. In one experiment infants were able to imitate tongue orientation from an adult model. Additionally, another sign of differentiation is when infants bring themselves into contact with objects by reaching for them.
Stage 3 – Identification (by 2 years)	At this stage, the more common definition of "self-awareness" comes into play, where infants can identify themselves in a mirror through the "rouge test" as well as begin to use language to refer to themselves.
Stage 4 – Permanence	This stage occurs after infancy when children are aware that their sense of self continues to exist across both time and space.
Stage 5 – Self-consciousness or meta-self-awareness	This also occurs after infancy. This is the final stage when children can see themselves in 3rd person, or how they are perceived by others.

Once a child has achieved **self-awareness**, the child is moving toward understanding social emotions such as guilt, shame or embarrassment, and pride, as well as sympathy and empathy. These will require an understanding of the mental state of others which is acquired around age 3 to 5 and will be explored in the next module (Berk, 2007).

WATCH IT

This video shows one study that demonstrates how toddlers become aware of their bodies around 18 months.

- https://youtu.be/k-rWB1jOt9s

Attachment

Psychosocial development occurs as children form relationships, interact with others, and understand and manage their feelings. In social and emotional development, forming healthy attachments is very important and is the major social milestone of infancy. **Attachment** is a long-standing connection or bond with others. Developmental psychologists are interested in how infants reach this milestone. They ask such questions as: How do parent and infant attachment bonds form? How does neglect affect these bonds? What accounts for children's attachment differences?

Researchers Harry Harlow, John Bowlby, and Mary Ainsworth conducted studies designed to answer these questions. In the 1950s, Harlow conducted a series of experiments on monkeys. He separated newborn monkeys from their mothers. Each monkey was presented with two surrogate mothers. One surrogate mother was made out of wire mesh, and she could dispense milk. The other surrogate mother was softer and made from cloth: This monkey did not dispense milk. Research shows that the monkeys preferred the soft, cuddly cloth monkey, even though she did not provide any nourishment. The baby monkeys spent their time clinging to the cloth monkey and only went to the wire monkey when they needed to be feed. Prior to this study, the medical and scientific communities generally thought that babies become attached to the people who provide their nourishment. However, Harlow (1958) concluded that there was more to the mother-child bond than nourishment. Feelings of comfort and security are the critical components of maternal-infant bonding, which leads to healthy psychosocial development.

WATCH IT

Harlow's studies of monkeys were performed before modern ethics guidelines were in place, and today his experiments are widely considered to be unethical and even cruel. Watch this video to see actual footage of Harlow's monkey studies.

- https://youtu.be/OrNBEhzjg8I

Building on the work of Harlow and others, John Bowlby developed the concept of attachment theory. He defined attachment as the affectional bond or tie that an infant forms with the mother (Bowlby, 1969). He believed that an infant must form this bond with a primary caregiver in order to have normal social and emotional development. In addition, Bowlby proposed that this attachment bond is very powerful and continues throughout life. He used the concept of a secure base to define a healthy attachment between parent and child (1988). A **secure base** is a parental presence that gives children a sense of safety as they explore their surroundings. Bowlby said that two things are needed for a healthy attachment: The caregiver must be responsive to the child's physical, social, and emotional needs; and the caregiver and child must engage in mutually enjoyable interactions (Bowlby, 1969).

While Bowlby thought attachment was an all-or-nothing process, Mary Ainsworth's (1970) research showed otherwise. Ainsworth wanted to know if children differ in the ways they bond, and if so, how. To find the answers, she used the **Strange Situation** procedure to study attachment between mothers and their infants (1970). In the Strange Situation, the mother (or primary caregiver) and the infant (age 12-18 months) are placed in a room together. There are toys in the room, and the caregiver and child spend some time alone in the room. After the child has had time to explore their surroundings, a stranger enters the room. The mother then leaves her baby with the stranger. After a few minutes, she returns to comfort her child.

Figure 1. Mutually enjoyable interactions promote the mother-infant bond. (credit: Peter Shanks)

Based on how the toddlers responded to the separation and reunion, Ainsworth identified three types of parent-child attachments: secure, avoidant, and resistant (Ainsworth & Bell, 1970). A fourth style, known as disorganized attachment, was later described (Main & Solomon, 1990).

The most common type of attachment—also considered the healthiest—is called **secure attachment**. In this type of attachment, the toddler prefers their parent over a stranger. The attachment figure is used as a secure base to explore the environment and is sought out in times of stress. Securely attached children were distressed when their caregivers left the room in the Strange Situation experiment, but when their caregivers returned, the securely attached children were happy to see them. Securely attached children have caregivers who are sensitive and responsive to their needs.

Figure 2. In secure attachment, the parent provides a secure base for the toddler, allowing him to securely explore his environment. (credit: Kerry Ceszyk)

With **avoidant attachment**, the child is unresponsive to the parent, does not use the parent as a secure base, and does not care if the parent leaves. The toddler reacts to the parent the same way they react to a stranger. When the parent does return, the child is slow to show a positive reaction. Ainsworth theorized that these children were most likely to have a caregiver who was insensitive and inattentive to their needs (Ainsworth, Blehar, Waters, & Wall, 1978).

In cases of **resistant attachment**, children tend to show clingy behavior, but then they reject the attachment figure's attempts to interact with them (Ainsworth & Bell, 1970). These children do not explore the toys in the room, appearing too fearful. During separation in the Strange Situation, they become extremely disturbed and angry with the parent. When the parent returns, the children are difficult to comfort. Resistant attachment is thought to be the result of the caregivers' inconsistent level of response to their child.

Finally, children with **disorganized attachment** behaved oddly in the Strange Situation. They freeze, run around the room in an erratic manner, or try to run away when the caregiver returns (Main & Solomon, 1990). This type of attachment is seen most often in kids who have been abused or severely neglected. Research has shown that abuse disrupts a child's ability to regulate their emotions.

While Ainsworth's research has found support in subsequent studies, it has also met criticism. Some researchers have pointed out that a child's **temperament** (which we discuss next) may have a strong influence on attachment (Gervai, 2009; Harris, 2009), and others have noted that attachment varies from culture to culture, a factor that was not accounted for in Ainsworth's research (Rothbaum, Weisz, Pott, Miyake, & Morelli, 2000; van Ijzendoorn & Sagi-Schwartz, 2008).

WATCH IT

Watch this video to better understand Mary Ainsworth's research and to see examples of how she conducted the experiment.

- https://youtu.be/m_6rQk7jlrc

Attachment styles vary in the amount of security and closeness felt in the relationship and they can change with new experiences. The type of attachment fostered in parenting styles varies by culture as well. For example, German parents value independence and Japanese mothers are typically by their children's sides. As a result, the rate of insecure-avoidant attachments is higher in Germany and insecure-resistant attachments are higher in Japan. These differences reflect cultural variation rather than true insecurity, however (van Ijzendoorn and Sagi, 1999). Keep in mind that methods for measuring attachment styles have been based on a model that reflects middle-class, US values and interpretation. Newer methods for assessing attachment styles involve using a Q-sort technique in which a large number of behaviors are recorded on cards and the observer sorts the cards in a way that reflects the type of behavior that occurs within the situation.

Attachment is classified into four types: A, B, C, and D. Ainsworth's original schema differentiated only three types of attachment (types A, B, and C), but, as mentioned above, later researchers discovered a fourth category (type D). As we explore styles of attachment below, consider how these may also be evidenced in adult relationships. We'll come back to this idea in later modules.

Types of Attachments

Secure

A **secure attachment** (type B) is one in which the child feels confident that their needs will be met in a timely and consistent way. The caregiver is the base for exploration, providing assurance and enabling discovery. In North America, this interaction may include an emotional connection in addition to adequate care. However, even in cultures where mothers do not talk, cuddle, and play with their infants, secure attachments can develop (LeVine et. al., 1994). Secure attachments can form provided the child has consistent contact and care from one or more caregivers. Consistency of contacts may be jeopardized if the infant is cared for in a daycare with a high turn-over of caregivers or if institutionalized and given little more than basic physical care. And while infants who, perhaps because of being in orphanages with inadequate care, have not had the opportunity to attach in infancy can form initial secure attachments several years later, they may have more emotional problems of depression or anger, or be overly friendly as they make adjustments (O'Connor et. al., 2003).

Insecure Resistant/Ambivalent

Insecure-resistant/ambivalent (type C) attachment style is marked by insecurity and resistance to engaging in activities or play away from the caregiver. It is as if the child fears that the caregiver will abandon them and clings accordingly. (Keep in mind that clingy behavior can also just be part of a child's natural disposition or temperament and does not necessarily reflect some kind of parental neglect.) The child may cry if separated from the caregiver and also cry upon their return. They seek constant reassurance that never seems to satisfy their doubt. This type of insecure attachment might be a result of not having their needs met in a consistent or timely way. Consequently, the infant is never sure that the world is a trustworthy place or that he or she can rely on others without some anxiety. A caregiver who is unavailable, perhaps because of marital tension, substance abuse, or preoccupation with work, may send a message to the infant they cannot rely on having their needs met. A caregiver who attends to a child's frustration can help teach them to be calm and to relax. But an infant who receives only sporadic attention when experiencing discomfort may not learn how to calm down.

Insecure-Avoidant

Insecure-avoidant (type A) is an attachment style marked by insecurity. This style is also characterized by a tendency to avoid contact with the caregiver and with others. This child may have learned that needs typically go unmet and learns that the caregiver does not provide care and cannot be relied upon for comfort, even sporadically. An insecure-avoidant child learns to be more independent and disengaged. Such a child might sit passively in a room filled with toys until it is time to go.

Disorganized

Disorganized attachment (type D) represents the most insecure style of attachment and occurs when the child is given mixed, confused, and inappropriate responses from the caregiver. For example, a mother who suffers from schizophrenia may laugh when a child is hurting or cry when a child exhibits joy. The child does not learn how to interpret emotions or to connect with the unpredictable caregiver.

How common are the attachment styles among children in the United States? It is estimated that about 65 percent of children in the United States are securely attached. Twenty percent exhibit avoidant styles and 10 to 15 percent are resistant. Another 5 to 10 percent may be characterized as disorganized.

Psychosocial Development

Temperament

Figure 3. Babies are born with different temperaments. Some are slow-to-warm-up while others are easy-going.

Perhaps you have spent time with a number of infants. How were they alike? How did they differ? Or compare yourself with your siblings or other children you have known well. You may have noticed that some seemed to be in a better mood than others and that some were more sensitive to noise or more easily distracted than others. These differences may be attributed to temperament. **Temperament** is an inborn quality noticeable soon after birth. Temperament is not the same as personality but may lead to personality differences. Generally, personality traits are learned, whereas temperament is genetic. Of course, for every trait, nature and nurture interact.

According to Chess and Thomas (1996), children vary on nine dimensions of temperament. These include activity level, regularity (or predictability), sensitivity thresholds, mood, persistence or distractibility, among others. These categories include the following:[foodnote]Thomas, A., & Chess, S. (1977). Temperament and development. New York: Brunner/Mazel[/footnote].

1. Activity level. Does the child display mostly active or inactive states?
2. Rhythmicity or Regularity. Is the child predictable or unpredictable regarding sleeping, eating, and elimination patterns?
3. Approach-Withdrawal. Does the child react or respond positively or negatively to a newly encountered situation?
4. Adaptability. Does the child adjust to unfamiliar circumstances easily or with difficulty
5. Responsiveness. Does it take a small or large amount of stimulation to elicit a response (e.g., laughter, fear, pain) from the child?
6. Reaction Intensity. Does the child show low or high energy when reacting to stimuli?
7. Mood Quality. Is the child normally happy and pleasant, or unhappy and unpleasant?
8. Distractibility. Is the child's attention easily diverted from a task by external stimuli?
9. Persistence and Attention Span. Persistence – How long will the child continue at an activity despite difficulty or interruptions? Attention span – For how long a period of time can the child maintain interest in an activity?

The New York Longitudinal Study was a long term study of infants, on these dimensions, which began in the 1950s. Most children do not have their temperament clinically measured, but categories of temperament have been developed and are seen as useful in understanding and working with children. Based on this study, babies can be described according to one of several profiles: easy or flexible (40%), slow to warm up or cautious (15%), difficult or feisty (10%), and undifferentiated, or those who can't easily be categorized (35%).

Easy babies (40% of infants) have a positive disposition. Their body functions operate regularly and they are adaptable. They are generally positive, showing curiosity about new situations and their emotions are moderate or low in intensity. Difficult babies (10% of infants) have more negative moods and are slow to adapt to new situations. When confronted with a new situation, they tend to withdraw. Slow-to-warm babies (15% of infants) are inactive, showing relatively calm reactions to their environment. Their moods are generally negative, and they withdraw from new situations, adapting slowly. The undifferentiated (35%) could not be consistently categorized. These children show a variety of combinations of characteristics. For example, an infant may have an overall positive mood but react negatively to new situations.

No single type of temperament is invariably good or bad, however, infants with difficult temperaments are more likely than other babies to develop emotional problems, especially if their mothers were depressed or anxious caregivers (Garthus-Niegel et al., 2017).[3] Children's long-term adjustment actually depends on the **goodness-of-fit** of their particular temperament to the nature and demands of the environment in which they find themselves. Therefore, what appears to be more important than child temperament is how caregivers respond to it.

Think about how you might approach each type of child in order to improve your interactions with them. An easy or flexible child will not need much extra attention unless you want to find out whether they are having difficulties that have gone unmentioned. A slow to warm up child may need to be given advance warning if new people or situations are going to be introduced. A difficult or feisty child may need to be given extra time to burn off their energy. A caregiver's ability to accurately read and work well with the child will enjoy this **goodness-of-fit,** meaning their styles match and communication and interaction can flow. The temperamentally active children can do well with parents who support their curiosity but could have problems in a more rigid family.

It is this goodness-of-fit between child temperament and parental demands and expectations that can cause struggles. Rather than believing that discipline alone will bring about improvements in children's behavior, our knowledge of temperament may help a parent, teacher or other caregiver gain insight to work more effectively with a child. Viewing temperamental differences as varying styles that can be responded to accordingly, as opposed to 'good' or 'bad' behavior. For example, a persistent child may be difficult to distract from forbidden things such as electrical cords, but this persistence may serve her well in other areas such as problem-solving. Positive traits can be enhanced and negative traits can be subdued. The child's style of reaction, however, is unlikely to change. Temperament doesn't change dramatically as we grow up, but we may learn how to work around and manage our temperamental qualities. Temperament may be one of the things about us that stays the same throughout development.

LINK TO LEARNING

Read the article "Lasting Effects of a Goodness- or Poorness-of-fit" from Psychology Today to learn more about goodness-of-fit and poorness-of-fit.

3. Garthus-Niegel, S., Ayers, S., Martini, J., von Soest, T. & Eberhard-Gran, M. (2017). The impact of postpartum post-traumatic stress disorder symptoms on child development: A population based, 2-year follow-up study. Psychological Medicine, 47(1), 161-170.

Erikson's Stages for Infants and Toddlers

Trust vs. mistrust

Erikson maintained that the first year to year and a half of life involves the establishment of a sense of trust. Infants are dependent and must rely on others to meet their basic physical needs as well as their needs for stimulation and comfort. A caregiver who consistently meets these needs instills a sense of trust or the belief that the world is a safe and trustworthy place. The caregiver should not worry about overindulging a child's need for comfort, contact, or stimulation. This view is in sharp contrast with the Freudian view that a parent who overindulges the infant by allowing them to suck too long or be picked up too frequently will be spoiled or become fixated at the oral stage of development.

Figure 4. Exploring the environment allows the toddler to develop a sense of autonomy and independence.

Consider the implications for establishing trust if a caregiver is unavailable or is upset and ill-prepared to care for a child, or if a child is born prematurely, is unwanted, or has physical problems that could make them less desirable to a parent. However, keep in mind that children can also exhibit strong resiliency to harsh circumstances. Resiliency can be attributed to certain personality factors, such as an easy-going temperament and receiving support from others. A positive and strong support group can help a parent and child build a strong foundation by offering assistance and positive attitudes toward the newborn and parent.

Autonomy vs. shame and doubt

As the child begins to walk and talk, an interest in independence or autonomy replaces their concern for trust. The toddler tests the limits of what can be touched, said, and explored. Erikson believed that toddlers should be allowed to explore their environment as freely as safety allows and, in doing so, will develop a sense of independence that will later grow to self-esteem, initiative, and overall confidence. If a caregiver is overly anxious about the toddler's actions for fear that the child will get hurt or violate others' expectations, the caregiver can give the child the message that they should be ashamed of their behavior and instill a sense of doubt in their abilities. Parenting advice based on these ideas would be to keep your toddler safe, but let them learn by doing. A sense of pride seems to rely on doing rather than being told how capable one is (Berger, 2005).

GLOSSARY

Ainsworth's strange situation:
a sequence of staged episodes that illustrate the type of attachment between a child and (typically) their mother

attachment
the positive emotional bond that develops between a child and a particular individual

autonomy vs. shame and doubt:
Erikson's second crisis of psychosocial development, during which toddlers strive to gain a sense of self-rule over their actions and their bodies

disorganized attachment (type D):
a type of attachment that is marked by an infant's inconsistent reactions to the caregiver's departure and return

emotional regulation:
]the ability to respond to the ongoing demands of experience with the range of emotions in a manner that is socially tolerable and sufficiently flexible to permit spontaneous reactions, as well as the ability to delay spontaneous reactions as needed

goodness-of-fit:
the notion that development is dependent on the degree of match between children's temperament and the nature and demands of the environment in which they are being raised

insecure-avoidant attachment (type A):
a pattern of attachment in which an infant avoids connection with the caregiver, as when the infant seems not to care about the caregiver's presence, departure, or even return

insecure-resistant/ambivalent attachment (type C):
a pattern of attachment in which an infant's anxiety and uncertainty are evident, as when the infant becomes very upset at separation from the caregiver and both resists and seeks contact on reunion

secure attachment (type B):
a relationship in which an infant obtains both comfort and confidence from the presence of their caregiver

secure base:
a parental presence that gives children a sense of safety as they explore their surroundings

self-awareness:
a person's realization that they are a distinct individual whose body, mind, and actions are separate from those of other people

separation anxiety:
fear or distress caused by the departure of familiar significant others; most obvious between 9-14 months

social smile:
a smile evoked by a human face, normally first evident in infants about 6 weeks after birth

stranger wariness:
fear is often associated with the presence of strangers where an infant expresses concern or a look of fear while clinging to a familiar person

temperament:
inborn differences between one person and another in emotions, activity, and self-regulation, typically measured by the person's responses to the environment

trust vs. mistrust
Erikson's first crisis of psychosocial development, during which infants learn basic trust if the world is a secure place where their needs (food, comfort, attention) are met

Putting It Together: Infancy

We have explored the dramatic story of the first two years of life. Rapid physical growth, neurological development, language acquisition, the movement from hands-on to mental learning, an expanding emotional repertoire, and the initial conceptions of self and others make this period of life very exciting. These abilities are shaped into more sophisticated mental processes, self-concepts, and social relationships during the years of early childhood.

Babies begin to learn about the world around them from a very early age. Children's early experiences, meaning the bonds they form with their parents and their first learning experiences, affect their future physical, cognitive, emotional and social development. Various organizations and agencies are dedicated to helping parents (and other caregivers), educators, and health care providers understand the importance of early healthy development. Healthy development means that children of all abilities, including those with special health care needs, are able to grow up where their social, emotional, and educational needs are met. Having a safe and loving home and spending time with family—playing, singing, reading, and talking—are very important. Proper nutrition, exercise, and sleep can also make a big difference; and effective parenting practices are key to supporting healthy development (CDC, 2019). The need to invest in very young children is important to maximize their future well-being.

Discussion: Infancy

DISCUSSION: In this discussion, reflect upon and discuss ONE of the following questions:

- Q1: Should infants share a bed with their parents? Why or why not? At what age is bed sharing appropriate?
- Q2: What advice would you give to a friend whose baby was not meeting the typical developmental milestones?

STEP 1: First, write a response with at least EIGHT substantial sentences, integrating concepts you learned from the reading and other materials (include links with necessary). Show that you can think critically on the topic by integrating your own thoughts, analysis, or experiences.

STEP 2: Return to the discussion to comment on at least TWO classmates' posts (in at least FIVE sentences). Expand on a classmate's comments in a value-adding, topic-related way. Promote a collaborative, supportive community, and advance the dialogue through follow-up questions. Reply posts cannot be one-liners, off-topic posts, vague statements, unsupported opinions, inadequate explanations or simply say, "I agree" or "good job."

MODULE 5: EARLY CHILDHOOD

Why It Matters: Early Childhood

Why learn about development during early childhood?

The time between a child's second and sixth birthday is a time of rich development in many ways. Children are growing rapidly physically, cognitively, and socially. Children are developing language skills that will help them navigate their world as they prepare to enter school. In fact, a child will go from being able to produce approximately 50 words at age 2 to producing over 2000 words at age 6! The number of words these children understand is even greater!

Children in this stage are changing from intuitive problem solvers into more sophisticated logical problem solvers. Their cognitive skills are increasing at a rapid rate, even though their brain is beginning to *lose* neurons through the process of synaptic pruning.

Children are also learning to navigate the social world around them. They are learning about themselves and beginning to develop their own self-concept, while at the same time they are becoming aware that other people have feelings, too. The development that happens in these four years impacts the rest of the child's life in many ways for years to come.

Physical Development in Early Childhood

What you'll learn to do: describe physical changes in early childhood

Children in early childhood are physically growing at a rapid pace. If you want to have fun with a child at the beginning of the period, ask them to take their left hand and use it to go over their head to touch their right ear. They cannot do it. Their body proportions are such that they are still built very much like an infant with a very large head and short appendages. By the time the child is five years old though, their arms will have stretched, and they head is becoming smaller in proportion to the rest of their growing bodies. They can accomplish the task easily because of these physical changes.

LEARNING OUTCOMES

- Summarize overall physical growth and nutrition during early childhood
- Examine nutritional concerns during early childhood
- Describe changes in the brain during early childhood
- Give examples of gross and fine motor skill development in early childhood

Growth and Nutrition in Early Childhood

Growth in early childhood

Children between the ages of 2 and 6 years tend to grow about 3 inches in height each year and gain about 4 to 5 pounds in weight each year. The average 6-year-old weighs about 46 pounds and is about 46 inches in height. The 3-year-old is very similar to a toddler with a large head, large stomach, short arms, and short legs. During early childhood, children start to lose some of their baby fat, making them less like a baby, and more like a child as they progress through this stage. By around age 3, children will have all 20 of their primary teeth, and by around age 4, may have 20/20 vision. Many children take a daytime nap until around age 4 or 5, then sleep between 11 and 13 hours at night.

By the time the child reaches age 6, the torso has lengthened and body proportions have become more like those of adults. It should be noted that these growth patterns are seen where children receive adequate nutrition. Studies from many countries support the assertion that children tend to grow more slowly in low SES areas, and thus they are smaller.[1][2][3]

This growth rate is slower than that of infancy and is accompanied by a reduced appetite between the ages of 2 and 6. This change can sometimes be surprising to parents and lead to the development of poor eating habits.

Nutritional concerns

According to the Centers for Disease Control and Prevention (CDC), 1 in 5 American children between the ages of 2 and 5 are overweight or obese. The American Academy of Pediatrics (AAP) recommends a number of steps to take to help reduce the chances of obesity in young children. Removing high-calorie low-nutrition foods from the diet, offering whole fruits and vegetables instead of just juices, and getting kids active are just some of the recommendations that they make. Muckelbauer and colleagues (2009) found that increasing water consumption in school-aged children by just 220ml (just under 8 oz) per day decreased the risk of obesity by 31%. Finally, the AAP suggests that parents can begin offering milk with a lower fat percentage (2%, 1%, or skim milk) to 2-year-olds. The switch to lower fat milk may help avoid some of the obesity issues discussed above. Parents should avoid giving the child too much milk as calcium interferes with the absorption of iron in the diet as well.

Figure 1. While young children can be picky eaters, it is important to expose them to a variety of healthy foods and avoid too many high-fat or low-nutritional foods, such as corndogs.

Caregivers (whether parents or non-parents) need to keep in mind that they are setting up taste preferences at this age. Young children who grow accustomed to high-fat, very sweet, and salty flavors may have trouble eating foods that have more subtle flavors such as fruits and vegetables. Lack of a healthy diet may lead to obesity during this and future stages. Offering a diet of diverse food options, limiting foods with high calories but low nutritional value, and limiting high-calorie drink options can all contribute greatly to a child's health during this stage of life.

Caregivers who have established a feeding routine with their child can find the normal reduction in appetite a bit frustrating and become concerned that the child is going to starve. However, by providing adequate, sound nutrition, and limiting sugary snacks and drinks, the caregiver can be assured that 1) the child will not starve, and 2) the child will receive adequate nutrition. Preschoolers can experience iron deficiencies if not given well-balanced nutrition.

1. Van Rossem, R., & Pannecoucke, I. (2019). Poverty and a child's height development during early childhood: A double disadvantage? A study of the 2006-2009 birth cohorts in Flanders. PloS one, 14(1), e0209170. doi:10.1371/journal.pone.0209170
2. Neumann, Janice (September 2015). Small height differences among kids may reflect economic disparities. Reuters, Health News. Retried from https://www.reuters.com/article/us-health-children-height-poverty/small-height-differences-among-kids-may-reflect-economic-disparities-idUSKCN0RR11720150927.
3. Kerr GR, Lee ES, Lorimor RJ, Mueller WH, Lam MM (1982) Height distributions of U.S. children: associations with race, poverty status and parental size. Growth 46: 135–149.

TIPS FOR ESTABLISHING HEALTHY EATING PATTERNS

Consider the following advice about establishing eating patterns for years to come (Rice, F.P., 1997). Notice that keeping mealtime pleasant, providing sound nutrition and not engaging in power struggles over food are the main goals.

1. Don't try to force your child to eat or fight over food. Of course, it is impossible to force someone to eat. But the real advice here is to avoid turning food into some kind of ammunition during a fight. Do not teach your child to eat to or refuse to eat in order to gain favor or express anger toward someone else.

2. Recognize that appetite varies. Children may eat well at one meal and have no appetite at another. Rather than seeing this as a problem, it may help to realize that appetites do vary. Continue to provide good nutrition, but do not worry excessively if the child does not eat.

3. Keep it pleasant. This tip is designed to help caregivers create a positive atmosphere during mealtime. Mealtimes should not be the time for arguments or expressing tensions. You do not want the child to have painful memories of mealtimes together or have nervous stomachs and problems eating and digesting food due to stress.

4. No short order chefs. While it is fine to prepare foods that children enjoy, preparing a different meal for each child or family member sets up an unrealistic expectation from others. Children probably do best when they are hungry and a meal is ready. Limiting snacks rather than allowing children to "graze" continuously can help create an appetite for whatever is being served.

5. Limit choices. If you give your preschool-aged child choices, make sure that you give them one or two specific choices rather than asking "What would you like for lunch?" If given an open choice, children may change their minds or choose whatever their sibling does not choose!

6. Serve balanced meals. This tip encourages caregivers to serve balanced meals. A box of macaroni and cheese is not a balanced meal. Meals prepared at home tend to have better nutritional value than fast food or frozen dinners. Prepared foods tend to be higher in fat and sugar content as these ingredients enhance taste and profit margin because fresh food is often more costly and less profitable. However, preparing fresh food at home is not costly. It does, however, require more activity. Preparing meals and including the children in kitchen chores can provide a fun and memorable experience.

7. Don't bribe. Bribing a child to eat vegetable by promising desert is not a good idea. For one reason, the child will likely find a way to get the desert without eating the vegetables (by whining or fidgeting, perhaps, until the caregiver gives in), and for another reason, because it teaches the child that some foods are better than others. Children tend to naturally enjoy a variety of foods until they are taught that some are considered less desirable than others. A child, for example, may learn the broccoli they have enjoyed is seen as yucky by others unless it's smothered in cheese sauce!

To what extent do these tips address cultural practices? How might these tips vary by culture?

Physical Development in Early Childhood

Brain Maturation

If you recall, the brain is about 75 percent of its adult weight by two years of age. By age 6, it is at 95 percent of its adult weight. The development of myelin (**myelination**) and the development of new synapses (through the process of synaptic pruning) continues to occur in the cortex and as it does we see a corresponding change in what the child is capable of doing. Remember that myelin is the coating around the axon that facilitates neural transmission. **Synaptic pruning** refers to the loss of synapses which are unused. As myelination and pruning increase during this stage of development, neural processes become quicker and more complex.

Greater development in the prefrontal cortex, the area of the brain behind the forehead that helps us to think, strategize, and control emotions, makes it increasingly possible to control emotional outbursts and to understand how to play games. Consider 4- or 5-year-old children and how they might approach a game of soccer. Chances are every move would be a response to the commands of a coach standing nearby calling out, "Run this way! Now, stop. Look at the ball. Kick the ball!" And when the child is not being told what to do, he or she is likely to be looking at the clover on the ground or a dog on the other side of the fence! Understanding the game, thinking ahead, and coordinating movement improves with practice and myelination. Demonstrating resilience and recovering from a loss, hopefully, does as well.

Growth in the hemispheres and corpus callosum

Between ages 3 and 6, the left hemisphere of the brain, which tends to lag behind in terms of activity during the first 3 years of life, increases inactivity, which correlates with the burst in language skills during this time period. Activity in the right hemisphere grows steadily throughout early childhood and is especially involved in tasks that require spatial skills such as recognizing shapes and patterns. Both sides of the brain work together, however, and there is no such thing as a person being either left-brained or right-brained. The corpus callosum, which connects the two hemispheres of the brain, undergoes a growth spurt between ages 3 and 6 as well resulting in improved coordination between right and left hemisphere tasks.

I once saw a 5-year-old hopping on one foot, rubbing his stomach and patting his head all at the same time. I asked him what he was doing and he replied, "My teacher said this would help my corpus callosum!" Apparently, his kindergarten teacher had explained the process!

Visual Pathways

Have you ever examined the drawings of young children? If you look closely, you can almost see the development of visual pathways reflected in the way these images change as pathways become more mature. Early scribbles and dots illustrate the use of simple motor skills. No real connection is made between an image being visualized and what is created on paper.

At age 3, the child begins to draw wispy creatures with heads and not much other detail. Gradually pictures begin to have more detail and incorporate more parts of the body. Arm buds become arms and faces take on noses, lips, and eventually eyelashes. Look for drawings that you or your child has created to see this fascinating trend. Here are some examples of pictures drawn by girls from ages 2 to 7 years.

Figure 2. These drawings demonstrate the progression in both drawing skill and visual processing during early childhood. The top left drawing is done by a 2-year old, and the bottom right image is drawn by a 7-year old.

Motor Skill Development

Remember that **gross motor skills** are voluntary movements involving the use of large muscle groups while **fine motor skills** are more exact movements of the hands and fingers and include the ability to reach and grasp an object. Early childhood is a time of development of both gross and fine motor skills.

Early childhood is a time when children are especially attracted to motion and song. Days are filled with moving, jumping, running, swinging and clapping, and every place becomes a playground. Even the booth at a restaurant affords the opportunity to slide around in the seat or disappear underneath and imagine being a sea creature in a cave! Of course, this can be frustrating to a caregiver, but it's the business of early childhood. Children may frequently ask their caregivers to "look at me" while they hop or roll down a hill. Children's songs are often accompanied by arm and leg movements or cues to turn around or move from left to right. Running, jumping, dancing movements, etc. all afford children the ability to improve their gross motor skills.

Fine motor skills are also being refined in activities such as pouring water into a container, drawing, coloring, and using scissors. Some children's songs promote fine motor skills as well (have you ever heard of the song "itsy, bitsy, spider"?). Mastering the fine art of cutting one's own fingernails or tying their shoes will take a lot of practice and maturation. Fine motor skills continue to develop in middle childhood, but for preschoolers, the type of play that deliberately involves these skills is emphasized.

WATCH IT

Watch this video to see examples of gross motor development during early childhood.

- https://youtu.be/W0697717ZdU

Sexual Development in Early Childhood

Historically, children have been thought of as innocent or incapable of sexual arousal (Aries, 1962). A more modern approach to sexuality suggests that the physical dimension of sexual arousal is present from birth. That said, it seems to be the case that the elements of seduction, power, love, or lust that are part of the adult meanings of sexuality are not present in sexual arousal at this stage. In contrast, sexuality begins in childhood as a response to physical states and sensation and cannot be interpreted as similar to that of adults in any way (Carroll, 2007).

Infancy

Boys and girls are capable of erections and vaginal lubrication even before birth (Martinson, 1981). Arousal can signal overall physical contentment and stimulation that accompanies feeding or warmth. Infants begin to explore their bodies and touch their genitals as soon as they have sufficient motor skills. This stimulation is for comfort or to relieve tension rather than to reach orgasm (Carroll, 2007).

Early Childhood

Self-stimulation is common in early childhood for both boys and girls. Curiosity about the body and about others' bodies is a natural part of early childhood as well. Consider this example. A mother is asked by her young daughter: "So it's okay to see a boy's privates as long as it's the boy's mother or a doctor?" The mother hesitates a bit and then responds, "Yes. I think that's alright." "Hmmm," the girl begins, "When I grow up, I want to be a doctor!" Hopefully, this subject is approached in a way that teaches children to be safe and know what is appropriate without frightening them or causing shame.

As children grow, they are more likely to show their genitals to siblings or peers, and to take off their clothes and touch each other (Okami et al., 1997). Masturbation is common for both boys and girls. Boys are often shown by other boys how to masturbate, but girls tend to find out accidentally. Boys masturbate more often and touch themselves more openly than do girls (Schwartz, 1999).

Hopefully, parents respond to this without undue alarm and without making the children feel guilty about their bodies. Instead, messages about what is going on and the appropriate time and place for such activities help the child learn what is appropriate.

Parents should take the time to speak with their children about when it is appropriate for other people to see or touch them. Many experts suggest that this should occur as early as age 3, and of course the discussion should be appropriate for the child's age. One way to help a young child understand inappropriate touching is to discuss "bathing suit areas." Kids First, Inc. suggests discussing the following: "No one should touch you anywhere your bathing suit covers. No one should ask you to touch them somewhere that their bathing suit covers. No one should show you a part of their or someone else's bodies that their bathing suit covers." Further, instead of talking about good or bad touching, talk about safe and unsafe touching. This way children will not feel guilty later on when that sort of touching is appropriate in a relationship.[4]

GLOSSARY

fine motor skills:
precise movements of the wrists, hands, fingers, feet, or toes, such as the ability to reach and grasp an object

4. How to Talk to Young Children About Body Safety. Kids First, Inc. Retrieved from https://www.kidsfirstinc.org/how-to-talk-to-young-children-about-body-safety/.

gross motor skills:
voluntary movements including the use of large muscle groups such as the arms and legs

myelination:
an aspect of brain maturation in which more myelin is formed around the axons of neurons, thereby increasing neural transmission

synaptic pruning:
the selective elimination of non-essential synapses and the strengthening of important neural connections

Cognitive Development in Early Childhood

What you'll learn to do: explain cognitive changes in early childhood

Early childhood is a time of pretending, blending fact and fiction, and learning to think of the world using language. As young children move away from needing to touch, feel, and hear about the world toward learning basic principles about how the world works, they hold some pretty interesting initial ideas. For example, how many of you are afraid that you are going to go down the bathtub drain? Hopefully, none of you! But a child of three might really worry about this as they sit at the front of the bathtub. A child might protest if told that something will happen "tomorrow" but be willing to accept an explanation that an event will occur "today after we sleep." Or the young child may ask, "How long are we staying? From here to here?" while pointing to two points on a table. Concepts such as tomorrow, time, size and distance are not easy to grasp at this young age. Understanding size, time, distance, fact, and fiction are all tasks that are part of cognitive development in the preschool years.

LEARNING OUTCOMES

- Describe Piaget's preoperational stage of development
- Illustrate limitations in early childhood thinking, including animism, egocentrism, and conservation errors
- Explain theory of mind
- Explain language development and the importance of language in early childhood
- Describe Vygotsky's model, including the zone of proximal development

Piaget's Theory of Cognitive Development

Piaget's Second Stage: The Preoperational Stage

Remember that Piaget believed that we are continuously trying to maintain balance in how we understand the world. With rapid increases in motor skill and language development, young children are constantly encountering new experiences, objects, and words. In the module covering main developmental theories, you learned that when faced with something new, a child may either assimilate it into an existing schema by matching it with something they already know or expand their knowledge structure to accommodate the new situation. During the preoperational stage, many of the child's existing schemas will be challenged, expanded, and rearranged. Their whole view of the world may shift.

Figure 1. Young children enjoy pretending to "play school."

Piaget's second stage of cognitive development is called the **preoperational stage** and coincides with ages 2-7 (following the sensorimotor stage). The word *operation* refers to the use of logical rules, so sometimes this stage is misinterpreted as implying that children are illogical. While it is true that children at the beginning of the preoperational stage tend to answer questions intuitively as opposed to logically, children in this stage are learning to use language and how to think about the world symbolically. These skills help children develop the foundations they will need to consistently use operations in the next stage. Let's examine some of Piaget's assertions about children's cognitive abilities at this age.

Pretend Play

Pretending is a favorite activity at this time. For a child in the preoperational stage, a toy has qualities beyond the way it was designed to function and can now be used to stand for a character or object unlike anything originally intended. A teddy bear, for example, can be a baby or the queen of a faraway land!

Piaget believed that children's pretend play and experimentation helped them solidify the new schemas they were developing cognitively. This involves both assimilation and accommodation, which results in changes in their conceptions or thoughts. As children progress through the preoperational stage, they are developing the knowledge they will need to begin to use logical operations in the next stage.

Egocentrism

Egocentrism in early childhood refers to the tendency of young children to think that everyone sees things in the same way as the child. Piaget's classic experiment on egocentrism involved showing children a three-dimensional model of a mountain and asking them to describe what a doll that is looking at the mountain from a different angle might see. Children tend to choose a picture that represents their own, rather than the doll's view. However, when children are speaking to others, they tend to use different sentence structures and vocabulary when addressing a younger child or an older adult. Consider why this difference might be observed. Do you think this indicates some awareness of the views of others? Or do you think they are simply modeling adult speech patterns?

WATCH IT

The boys in this interview display egocentrism by believing that the researcher sees the same thing as they do, even after switching positions.

- https://youtu.be/RDJ0qJTLohM

This video demonstrates that older children are able to look at the mountain from different viewpoints and no longer fall prey to egocentrism.

- https://youtu.be/v4oYOjVDgo0

Precausal Thinking

Similar to preoperational children's egocentric thinking is their structuring of cause-and-effect relationships based on their limited view of the world. Piaget coined the term "precausal thinking" to describe the way in which preoperational children use their own existing ideas or views, like in egocentrism, to explain cause-and-effect relationships. Three main concepts of causality, as displayed by children in the preoperational stage, include animism, artificialism, and transductive reasoning.

Animism is the belief that inanimate objects are capable of actions and have lifelike qualities. An example could be a child believing that the sidewalk was mad and made them fall down, or that the stars twinkle in the sky because they are happy. To an imaginative child, the cup may be alive, the chair that falls down and hits the child's ankle is mean, and the toys need to stay home because they are tired. Young children do seem to think that objects that move may be alive, but after age three, they seldom refer to objects as being alive (Berk, 2007). Many children's stories and movies capitalize on animistic thinking. Do you remember some of the classic stories that make use of the idea of objects being alive and engaging in lifelike actions?

Artificialism refers to the belief that environmental characteristics can be attributed to human actions or interventions. For example, a child might say that it is windy outside because someone is blowing very hard, or the clouds are white because someone painted them that color.

Finally, precausal thinking is categorized by transductive reasoning. **Transductive reasoning** is when a child fails to understand the true relationships between cause and effect. Unlike deductive or inductive reasoning (general to specific, or specific to general), transductive reasoning refers to when a child reasons from specific to specific, drawing a relationship between two separate events that are otherwise unrelated. For example, if a child hears a dog bark and then a balloon pop, the child would conclude that because the dog barked, the balloon popped. Related to this is **syncretism,** which refers to a tendency to think that if two events occur simultaneously, one caused the other. An example of this might be a child asking the question, "if I put on my bathing suit will it turn to summer?"

Cognition Errors

Between about the ages of four and seven, children tend to become very curious and ask many questions, beginning the use of primitive reasoning. There is an increase in curiosity in the interest of reasoning and wanting to know why things are the way they are. Piaget called it the "intuitive substage" because children realize they have a vast amount of knowledge, but they are unaware of how they acquired it.

Centration and conservation are characteristic of preoperative thought. **Centration** is the act of focusing all attention on one characteristic or dimension of a situation while disregarding all others. An example of centration is a child focusing on the *number* of pieces of cake that each person has, regardless of the size of the pieces. Centration is one of the reasons that young children have difficulty understanding the concept of conservation. **Conservation** is the awareness that altering a substance's appearance does not change its basic properties. Children at this stage are unaware of conservation and exhibit centration. Imagine a 2-year-old and 4-year-old eating lunch. The 4-year-old has a whole peanut butter and jelly sandwich. He notices, however, that his younger sister's sandwich is cut in half and protests, "She has more!" He is exhibiting centration by focusing on the number of pieces, which results in a conservation error.

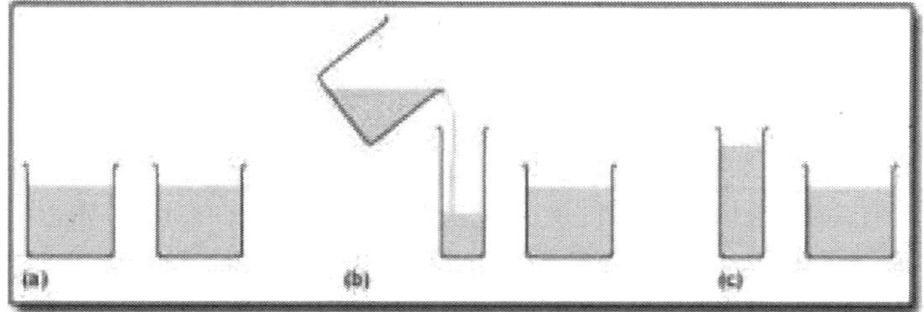

Figure 2. A demonstration of the conservation of liquid. Does pouring liquid in a tall, narrow container make it have more?

In Piaget's famous conservation task, a child is presented with two identical beakers containing the same amount of liquid. The child usually notes that the beakers do contain the same amount of liquid. When one of the beakers is poured into a taller and thinner container, children who are younger than seven or eight years old typically say that the two beakers no longer contain the same amount of liquid, and that the taller container holds the larger quantity (centration), without taking into consideration the fact that both beakers were previously noted to contain the same amount of liquid.

Irreversibility is also demonstrated during this stage and is closely related to the ideas of centration and conservation. **Irreversibility** refers to the young child's difficulty mentally reversing a sequence of events. In the same beaker situation, the child does not realize that, if the sequence of events was reversed and the water from the tall beaker was poured back into its original beaker, then the same amount of water would exist.

Centration, conservation errors, and irreversibility are indications that young children are reliant on visual representations. Another example of children's reliance on visual representations is their misunderstanding of "less than" or "more than". When two rows containing equal amounts of blocks are placed in front of a child with one row spread farther apart than the other, the child will think that the row spread farther contains more blocks.

WATCH IT

This clip shows how younger children struggle with the concept of conservation and demonstrate irreversibility.

- https://youtu.be/GLj0IZFLKvg

Class inclusion refers to a kind of conceptual thinking that children in the preoperational stage cannot yet grasp. Children's inability to focus on two aspects of a situation at once (centration) inhibits them from understanding the principle that one category or class can contain several different subcategories or classes. Preoperational children also have difficulty understanding that an object can be classified in more than one way. For example, a four-year-old girl may be shown a picture of eight dogs and three cats. The girl knows what cats and dogs are, and she is aware that they are both animals. However, when asked, "Are there more dogs or more animals?" she is likely to answer "more dogs." This is due to her difficulty focusing on the two subclasses and the larger class all at the same time. She may have been able to view the dogs as dogs or animals, but struggled when trying to classify them as both, simultaneously. Similar to this is a concept relating to intuitive thought, known as "transitive inference."

Transitive inference is using previous knowledge to determine the missing piece, using basic logic. Children in the preoperational stage lack this logic. An example of transitive inference would be when a child is presented with the information "A" is greater than "B" and "B" is greater than "C." The young child may have difficulty understanding that "A" is also greater than "C."

As the child's vocabulary improves and more schemes are developed, they are more able to think logically, demonstrate an understanding of conservation, and classify objects.

Was Piaget Right?

It certainly seems that children in the preoperational stage make the mistakes in logic that Piaget suggests that they will make. That said, it is important to remember that there is variability in terms of the ages at which children reach and exit each stage. Further, there is some evidence that children can be taught to think in more logical ways far before the end of the preoperational period. For example, as soon as a child can reliably count they may be able to learn conservation of number. For many children, this is around age five. More complex conservation tasks, however, may not be mastered until closer to the end of the stage around age seven.

Theory of Mind

How do we come to understand how our mind works? The **theory of mind** is the understanding that the mind holds people's beliefs, desires, emotions, and intentions. One component of this is understanding that the mind can be tricked or that the mind is not always accurate.

Figure 3. Around age four, most children begin to understand that thoughts and realities do not always match.

A two-year-old child does not understand very much about how their mind works. They can learn by imitating others, they are starting to understand that people do not always agree on things they like, and they have a rudimentary understanding of cause and effect (although they often fall prey to transitive reasoning). By the time a child is four, their theory of the mind allows them to understand that people think differently, have different preferences, and even mask their true feelings by putting on a different face that differs from how they truly feel inside.

To think about what this might look like in the real world, imagine showing a three-year-old child a bandaid box and asking the child what is in the box. Chances are, the child will reply, "bandaids." Now imagine that you open the box and pour out crayons. If you now ask the child what they thought was in the box before it was opened, they may respond, "crayons." If you ask what a friend would have thought was in the box, the response would still be "crayons." Why?

Before about four years of age, a child does not recognize that the mind can hold ideas that are not accurate, so this three-year-old changes their response once shown that the box contains crayons. The child's response can also be explained in terms of egocentrism and irreversibility. The child's response is based on their current view rather than seeing the situation from another person's perspective (egocentrism) or thinking about how they arrived at their conclusion (irreversibility). At around age four, the child would likely reply, "bandaids" when asked after seeing the crayons because by this age a child is beginning to understand that thoughts and realities do not always match.

WATCH IT

Watch as researchers demonstrate several versions of the false belief test to assess the theory of mind in young children.

- https://youtu.be/YGSj2zY2OEM
- https://youtu.be/8hLubgpY2_w

Theory of Mind and Social Intelligence

This awareness of the existence of mind is part of social intelligence and the ability to recognize that others can think differently about situations. It helps us to be self-conscious or aware that others can think of us in different ways, and it helps us to be able to be understanding or empathic toward others. This developing social intelligence helps us to anticipate and predict the actions of others (even though these predictions are sometimes inaccurate). The awareness of the mental states of others is important for communication and social skills. A child who demonstrates this skill is able to anticipate the needs of others.

Impaired Theory of Mind in Individuals with Autism

People with autism or an autism spectrum disorder (ASD) typically show an impaired ability to recognize other people's minds. Under the DSM-5, **autism** is characterized by persistent deficits in social communication and interaction across multiple contexts, as well as restricted, repetitive patterns of behavior, interests, or activities. These deficits are present in early childhood, typically before age three, and lead to clinically significant functional impairment. Symptoms may include lack of social or emotional reciprocity, stereotyped and repetitive use of language or idiosyncratic language, and persistent preoccupation with unusual objects.

About half of parents of children with ASD notice their child's unusual behaviors by age 18 months, and about four-fifths notice by age 24 months, but often a diagnoses comes later, and individual cases vary significantly. Typical early signs of autism include:

- No babbling by 12 months.
- No gesturing (pointing, waving, etc.) by 12 months.
- No single words by 16 months.
- No two-word (spontaneous, not just echolalic) phrases by 24 months.
- Loss of any language or social skills, at any age.

Children with ASD experience difficulties with explaining and predicting other people's behavior, which leads to problems in social communication and interaction. Children who are diagnosed with an autistic spectrum disorder usually develop the theory of mind more slowly than other children and continue to have difficulties with it throughout their lives.

For testing whether someone lacks the theory of mind, the *Sally-Anne* test is performed. The child sees the following story: Sally and Anne are playing. Sally puts her ball into a basket and leaves the room. While Sally is gone, Anne moves the ball from the basket to the box. Now Sally returns. The question is: where will Sally look for her ball? The test is passed if the child correctly assumes that Sally will look in the basket. The test is failed if the child thinks that Sally will look in the box. Children younger than four and older children with autism will generally say that Sally will look in the box.

WATCH IT

Watch this video to see the Sally-Anne test in action.

- https://youtu.be/QjkTQtggLH4

Language Development

A child's vocabulary expands between the ages of two to six from about 200 words to over 10,000 words through a process called **fast-mapping**. Words are easily learned by making connections between new words and concepts already known. The parts of speech that are learned depend on the language and what is emphasized. Children speaking verb-friendly languages such as Chinese and Japanese tend to learn verbs more readily, but those learning less verb-friendly languages such as English seem to need assistance in grammar to master the use of verbs (Imai, et als, 2008). Children are also very creative in creating their own words to use as labels such as a "take-care-of" when referring to John, the character on the cartoon Garfield, who takes care of the cat.

Figure 4. Reading to young children helps them develop language skills by hearing and using new vocabulary words.

Children can repeat words and phrases after having heard them only once or twice, but they do not always understand the meaning of the words or phrases. This is especially true of expressions or figures of speech which are taken literally. For example, two preschool-aged girls began to laugh loudly while listening to a tape-recording of Disney's "Sleeping Beauty" when the narrator reports, "Prince Phillip lost his head!" They imagine his head popping off and rolling down the hill as he runs and searches for it. Or a classroom full of preschoolers hears the teacher say, "Wow! That was a piece of cake!" The children began asking "Cake? Where is my cake? I want cake!"

Overregularization

Children learn the rules of grammar as they learn the language. Some of these rules are not taught explicitly, and others are. Often when learning language intuitively children apply rules inappropriately at first. But even after successfully navigating the rule for a while, at times, explicitly teaching a child a grammar rule may cause them to make mistakes they had previously not been making. For instance, two- to three-year-old children may say "I goed there" or "I doed that" as they understand intuitively that adding "ed" to a word makes it mean "something I did in the past." As the child hears the correct grammar rule applied by the people around them, they correctly begin to say "I went there" and "I did that." It would seem that the child has solidly learned the grammar rule, but it is actually common for the developing child to revert back to their original mistake. This happens as they **overregulate** the rule. This can happen because they intuitively discover the rule and overgeneralize it or because they are explicitly taught to add "ed" to the end of a word to indicate past tense in school. A child who had previously produced correct sentences may start to form incorrect sentences such as, "I goed there. I doed that." These children are able to quickly re-learn the correct exceptions to the -ed rule.

Vygotsky and Language Development

Lev Vygotsky hypothesized that children had a **zone of proximal development (ZPD)**. The ZPD is the range of material that a child is ready to learn if proper support and guidance are given from either a peer who understands the material or by an adult. We can see the benefit of this sort of guidance when we think about the acquisition of language. Children can be assisted in learning language by others who listen attentively, model more accurate pronunciations and encourage elaboration. For example, if the child exclaims, "I'm goed there!" then the adult responds, "You went there?"

Children may be hard-wired for language development, as Noam Chomsky suggested in his theory of universal grammar, but active participation is also important for language development. The process of **scaffolding** is one in which the guide provides needed assistance to the child as a new skill is learned. Repeating what a child has said, but in a grammatically correct way, is scaffolding for a child who is struggling with the rules of language production.

Private Speech

Do you ever talk to yourself? Why? Chances are, this occurs when you are struggling with a problem, trying to remember something or feel very emotional about a situation. Children talk to themselves too. Piaget interpreted this as egocentric speech or a practice engaged in because of a child's inability to see things from other points of view. Vygotsky, however, believed that children talk to themselves in order to solve problems or clarify thoughts. As children learn to think in words, they do so aloud before eventually closing their lips and engaging in **private speech** or inner speech. Thinking out loud eventually becomes thought accompanied by internal speech, and talking to oneself becomes a practice only engaged in when we are trying to learn something or remember something, etc. This inner speech is not as elaborate as the speech we use when communicating with others (Vygotsky, 1962).

VYGOTSKY AND EDUCATION

Vygotsky's theories do not just apply to language development but have been extremely influential for education in general. Although Vygotsky himself never mentioned the term scaffolding, it is often credited to him as a continuation of his ideas pertaining to the way adults or other children can use guidance in order for a child to work within their ZPD. (The term scaffolding was first developed by Jerome Bruner, David Wood, and Gail Ross while applying Vygotsky's concept of ZPD to various educational contexts.)

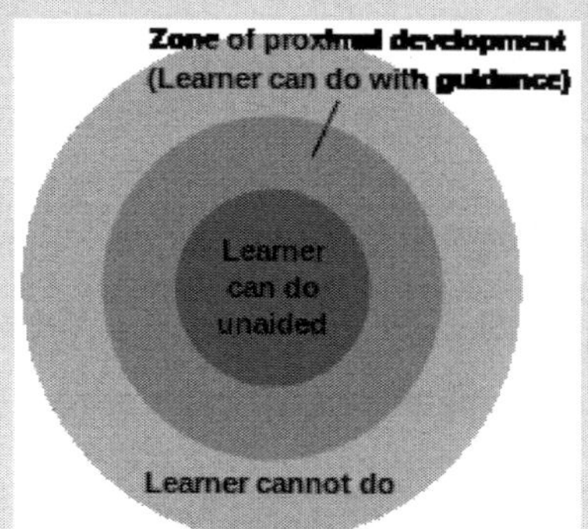

Figure 5. Vygotsky's zone of proximal development represents what a student can learn with the proper support.

Educators often apply these concepts by assigning tasks that students cannot do on their own, but which they can do with assistance; they should provide just enough assistance so that students learn to complete the tasks independently and then provide an environment that enables students to do harder tasks than would otherwise be possible. Teachers can also allow students with more knowledge to assist students who need more guidance. Especially in the context of collaborative learning, group members who have higher levels of understanding can help the less advanced members learn within their zone of proximal development.

The following video shows how Vygotsky's theory applies to learning in early childhood:

- https://youtu.be/InzmZtHuZPY

30 Million Word Gap

To accomplish the tremendous rate of word learning that needs to occur during early childhood, it is important that children are learning new words each day. Research by Betty Hart and Todd Risley in the late 1990s and early 2000s indicated that children from less advantaged backgrounds are exposed to millions of fewer words in their first three years of life than children who come from more privileged socioeconomic backgrounds. In their research, families were classified by socioeconomic status, (SES) into "high" (professional), "middle" (working class), and "low" (welfare) SES. They found that the average child in a professional family hears 2,153 words per waking hour, the average child in a working-class family hears 1,251 words per hour, and an average child in a welfare family only 616 words per hour. Extrapolating, they stated that, "in four years, an average child in a professional family would accumulate experience with almost 45 million words, an average child in a working-class family 26 million words, and an average child in a welfare family 13 million words." The line of thinking following their study is that children from more affluent households would enter school knowing more words, which would give them advantage in school.

Hart and Risley's research has been criticized by scholars. Critics theorize that the language and achievement gaps are not a result of the number of words a child is exposed to, but rather alternative theories suggest it could reflect the disconnect of linguistic practices between home and school. Thus, judging academic success and linguistic capabilities from socioeconomic status may ignore bigger societal issues. A recent replication of Hart and Risley's study with more participants has found that the "word gap" may be closer to 4 million words, not the oft-cited 30 million words previously proposed. The ongoing word gap research is evidence of the importance of language development in early childhood.

WATCH IT

Watch as Dr. John Gabrieli, from the MIT McGovern Institute for Brain Development explains how early language exposure affects language development. His research uses the current technology to correlate home language experiences with brain function. They determined that the number of conversational turns was more important to development in Broca's area (brain region linked to speech production) than the number of words heard or the family's socioeconomic status.

- https://youtu.be/CNJQGbNbl-8

LINK TO LEARNING

Read this article to learn more about common linguistic mistakes that children make and what they mean: 10 Language Mistakes Kids Make That Are Actually Pretty Smart.

GLOSSARY

animism:
the belief that inanimate objects are capable of actions and have lifelike qualities

artificialism:
the belief that environmental characteristics can be attributed to human actions or interventions

autism:
a developmental disorder affecting communication and behavior

centration:
the act of focusing all attention on one characteristic or dimension of a situation, while disregarding all others

egocentricism:
the tendency of young children to think that everyone sees things in the same way as the child

fast-mapping:
a word-learning process in which new words are rapidly learned by making connections between new words and concepts already known

irreversibility:
when a person is unable to mentally reverse a sequence of events

operations
the term used by Piaget to mean the logical rules that children develop with time

overregulation:
a process in learning a language in which children overgeneralize rules to words where the rule is not applicable

preoperational stage:
the second stage in Piaget's theory of cognitive development; describes the development in children ages 2-7

private speech:
speech that a child says aloud, but which is not meant to be part of communication with anyone else

syncretism:
the tendency to think that if two events occur simultaneously, one caused the other

theory of mind:
the understanding that the mind holds people's beliefs, desires, emotions, and intentions. One component of this is understanding that the mind can be tricked or that the mind is not always accurate

transductive reasoning:
a failure in understanding cause and effect relationships which happens when a child reasons from specific to specific; drawing a relationship between two separate events that are otherwise unrelated

zone of proximal development:
the range of material that a child is ready to learn if proper support and guidance are given from either a peer who understands the material or by an adult

Emotional and Social Development in Early Childhood

What you'll learn to do: describe key emotional and social developments of early childhood

The time between a child's second and sixth birthday is full of new social experiences. At the beginning of this stage, a child selfishly engages in the world—the goal is to please the self. As the child gets older, they realize that relationships built on give-and-take. They start to learn to empathize with others. They learn to make friends. Learning to navigate the social sphere is not easy, but children do it readily.

While the child is learning about their place in various relationships, they are also developing an understanding of emotion. A two-year-old does not have a good grasp on their emotions, but by the time a child is six, they understand their emotions better. They also understand how to control their emotions—even to the point that they may put on a different emotion than they are actually feeling. Further, by the time a child is six years old, they understand that other people have emotions and that all of the emotions involved in a situation (theirs and other people's) should be taken into consideration. That said, although the six-year-old understands these things, they are not always good at putting the knowledge into action. We'll examine some of these issues in this section.

LEARNING OUTCOMES

- Describe the development of a self-concept
- Explain Freud's psychodynamic theory as it applies to early childhood
- Explain Erikson's psychosocial theory as it applies to early childhood
- Describe gender identity development in early childhood
- Describe the impact of different parenting styles on children's development
- Apply principles of operant conditioning to parenting and behavior modification
- Examine concerns about childhood stress and trauma

Developing a Concept of Self

Self-Concept

Early childhood is a time of forming an initial sense of self. A **self-concept** or idea of who we are, what we are capable of doing, and how we think and feel is a social process that involves taking into consideration how others view us. It might be said, then, that in order to develop a sense of self, you must have interaction with others. Interactionist theorists, Cooley and Mead offer two interesting explanations of how a sense of self develops.

Cooley's Looking-Glass Self

Charles Horton Cooley (1964) suggested that our self-concept comes from looking at how others respond to us. This process, known as the **looking-glass self** involves looking at how others seem to view us and interpreting this as we make judgments about whether we are good or bad, strong or weak, beautiful or ugly, and so on. Of course, we do not always interpret their responses accurately so our self-concept is not simply a mirror reflection of the views of others. After forming an initial self-concept, we may use our existing self-concept as a mental filter screening out those responses that do not seem to fit our ideas of who we are. So compliments may be negated, for example.

Think of times in your life when you felt more self-conscious. The process of the looking-glass self is pronounced when we are preschoolers. Later in life, we also experience this process when we are in a new school, new job, or are taking on a new role in our personal lives and are trying to gauge our own performance. When we feel more sure of who we are we focus less on how we appear to others.

WATCH IT

Watch this Khan Academy video to learn more about Charles Cooley's looking-glass self.

- https://youtu.be/XCxe9HbfJcM

Mead's I and Me

George Herbert Mead (1967) offered an explanation of how we develop a social sense of self by being able to see ourselves through the eyes of others. There are two parts of the self: the "I" which is the part of the self that is spontaneous, creative, innate, and is not concerned with how others view us and the "me" or the social definition of who we are.

When we are born, we are all "I" and act without concern about how others view us. But the socialized self begins when we are able to consider how one important person views us. This initial stage is called "taking the role of the significant other." For example, a child may pull a cat's tail and be told by his mother, "No! Don't do that, that's bad" while receiving a slight slap on the hand. Later, the child may mimic the same behavior toward the self and say aloud, "No, that's bad" while patting his own hand. What has happened? The child is able to see himself through the eyes of the mother. As the child grows and is exposed to many situations and rules of culture, he begins to view the self in the eyes of many others through these cultural norms or rules. This is referred to as "taking the role of the generalized other" and results in a sense of self with many dimensions. The child comes to have a sense of self as a student, as a friend, as a son, and so on.

WATCH IT

This video explains Mead's understanding of the "I" and the "me," and compares it to other concepts you've already learned about, like egocentrism.

- https://youtu.be/oMNaQjtXSGc

Exaggerated Sense of Self

One of the ways to gain a clearer sense of self is to exaggerate those qualities that are to be incorporated into the self. Preschoolers often like to exaggerate their own qualities or to seek validation as the biggest or smartest or child who can jump the highest. Much of this may be due to the simple fact that the child does not understand their own limits. Young children may really believe that they can beat their parent to the mailbox, or pick up the refrigerator.

This exaggeration tends to be replaced by a more realistic sense of self in middle childhood as children realize that they do have limitations. Part of this process includes having parents who allow children to explore their capabilities and give the child authentic feedback. Another important part of this process involves the child learning that other people have capabilities, too...and that the child's capabilities may differ from those of other people. Children learn to compare themselves to others to understand what they are "good at" and what they are not as good at.

Self-Control

One important aspect of self-concept is how we understand our ability to exhibit self-control and delay gratification. Self-control involves both response inhibition and delayed gratification. Response inhibition involves the ability to recognize a potential behavior before it occurs and stop the initiation of behaviors that could result in undesired consequences. Delayed gratification refers to the process of forgoing immediate or short-term rewards to achieve more valuable goals in the longer term. The ability to delay gratification was traditionally assessed in young children with the "Marshmallow Test." During this experiment, participants were presented with a marshmallow (or another small treat) and were given a choice to eat it or wait for a certain period of time without eating it, so that they could have two marshmallows eventually (Mischel et al., 2011).

While self-control takes many years to develop, we see the beginnings of this skill during early childhood. This ability to delay gratification in young children has been shown to predict many positive outcomes. For instance, preschoolers who were able to delay gratification for a longer period of time had higher levels of resilience, better academic and social competence, and greater planning ability in their adolescence (Mischel et al., 1988). Recent research has linked poor delayed gratification in young children to poor eating self-regulation, specifically regarding eating when not hungry (Hughes et al., 2015) and behavioral problems (Willoughby et al., 2011; Kim et al., 2012).[1]

1. Yu Junhong, Kam Chi-Ming, Lee Tatia M. C. (2016). Better Working Memory and Motor Inhibition in Children Who Delayed Gratification. Frontiers in Psychology. Retrieved from https://www.frontiersin.org/articles/10.3389/fpsyg.2016.01098/full

WATCH IT

Watch as a teacher uses the Marshmallow Test, originally conducted by Walter Mischel, to teach her students about self-control. The Marshmallow Test has demonstrated correlations between self-control in preschool and successful outcomes in later life. According to Mischel, young children can learn strategies to delay gratification and resist engaging in impulsive behaviors. A retest of the study completed in 2018 by Watts, Duncan and Quan found the effects of self-control in the young children and the later life outcomes to be minimal and more closely tied to the education level of the mother, rather than self-control.[2]

- https://youtu.be/BLtQaRrDsC4

Psychodynamic and Psychosocial Theories of Early Childhood

Freud's Theory

Children pass through two stages of Freud's theory during early childhood: stage 2 (anal stage) and stage 3 (phallic stage).

The **anal stage** begins around 18 months of age and lasts until the child is three years old. During the anal stage, Freud believed that the libido source shifted from the mouth (in stage 1) to the anus. The child, then, receives pleasure from defecating. The child, at this point, understands that they have some amount of control over their lives, including control of when and where they defecate. This can set-up difficulties in potty training. What matters, in terms of Freud's theory, is how the parent handles difficulties in potty training. Parental reactions during potty training may set-up their child to react in one of two ways: (1) parents who are harsh or who ridicule the child for mistakes may have children who stubbornly hold on to their feces in an effort to not have an accident – these children may become anal retentive or (2) parents who are too easy going may have a child who reacts by purposefully making a mess – these children may become anal expulsive. Adults who are anal retentive tend to be stubborn, very neat, rigid, and stingy. Adults who are anal expulsive tend to be messy, wasteful, and harsh.

LINK TO LEARNING: TOILET TRAINING

To the relief of most parents, there is very little evidence to suggest that Freud was right about fixations caused during the anal stage, mainly because the theory itself would be very difficult to test. Nevertheless, parents worry about toilet training, and whether they will be able to guide their children through the process unscathed. Kidshealth.org has a good web page on to potty training that may help parents worried about toilet training.

The phallic stage of psychosexual development occurs from ages three to six. According to Freud, during the **phallic stage,** the child develops an attraction to the opposite sex parent, which is called the Oedipus Complex for boys and the Electra Complex for girls. When the child recognizes that the opposite sex parent is unavailable, the child learns to model their own behavior after the same-sex parent. The child develops their own sense of masculinity or femininity from this resolution. According to Freud,

2. Tyler W. Watts, Greg J. Duncan, Haonan Quan (May 25, 2018). *Revisiting the Marshmallow Test: A Conceptual Replication Investigating Links Between Early Delay of Gratification and Later Outcomes.* https://doi.org/10.1177/0956797618761661

a person who does not exhibit gender appropriate behavior, such as a woman who competes with men for jobs or a man who lacks self-assurance and dominance, has not successfully completed this stage of development. Consequently, such a person continues to struggle with his or her own gender identity.

Chodorow, a neo-Freudian, believed that mothering promotes gender stereotypic behavior. Mothers push their sons away too soon and direct their attention toward problem-solving and independence. As a result, sons grow up confident in their own abilities but uncomfortable with intimacy. Girls are kept dependent too long and are given unnecessary and even unwelcome assistance from their mothers. Girls learn to underestimate their abilities and lack assertiveness but feel comfortable with intimacy.

Both of these models assume that early childhood experiences result in lifelong gender self-concepts. However, gender socialization is a process that continues throughout life. Children, teens, and adults refine and can modify their sense of self, based on gender.

Another important part of Freud's phallic stage is that during this time the child is learning right from wrong through the process of **introjection**. Remember that according to Kohlberg, the child during this time is developing a sense of morality. According to Freud, this is occurring through the process of introjection which occurs as children incorporate values from others into their value set. Freud theorized about parental introjection, where children learn that parents seem pleased by certain behaviors (and so want to do those behaviors more to get rewards and love) and displeased by other behaviors (and so want to do those behaviors less to avoid punishment and loss of love). Today, modern psychoanalytic theorists recognize the place of others and society in introjection. Societal introjection is becoming more and more important as more children go to daycare, as we are more surrounded by technology and advertising, and as we travel more.

Social Development: The Importance of Play

The development of play is an important milestone in early childhood. Play holds a crucial role in providing a safe, caring, protective, confidential, and containing space where children can recreate themselves and their experiences through an exploratory process (Winnicott, 1942; Erikson, 1963). During this stage, pretend play is a great way for children to express their thoughts, emotions, fears, and anxieties. Early childhood play can be understood by observing the elements of fantasy, organization, and comfort. Fantasy, the process of make-believe, is an essential behavior the child engages in during pretend play; organization helps the child to structure pretend play into a story and to utilize cause-and-effect thinking; and comfort is used to assess the ease and pleasure in the engagement in play.[3]

As children progress through the stage of early childhood, they also progress through several stages of non-social and social play. Stages of play is a theory and classification of participation in play developed by Mildred Parten Newhall in 1929. Parten observed American children at free play. She recognized six different types of play:

- Unoccupied play – when the child is not playing, just observing. A child may be standing in one spot or performing random movements.
- Solitary (independent) play – when the child is alone and maintains focus on their activity. Such a child is uninterested in or is unaware of what others are doing. More common in young children (age 2–3) as opposed to older ones.
- Onlooker play – when the child watches others at play but does not engage in it. The child may engage in forms of social interaction, such as conversation about the play, without actually joining in the activity. This type of activity is also more common in younger children.
- Parallel play (adjacent play) – when the child plays separately from others but close to them and mimicking their actions. This type of play is seen as a transitory stage from a socially immature solitary and onlooker type of play, to a

3. Salcuni Silvia, Di Riso Daniela, Mabilia Diana, Lis Adriana (2017). "Psychotherapy with a 3-Year-Old Child: The Role of Play in the Unfolding Process". Frontiers in Psychology. Retrieved from https://www.frontiersin.org/articles/10.3389/fpsyg.2016.02021/full

more socially mature associative and cooperative type of play.

- Associative play – when the child is interested in the people playing but not in coordinating their activities with those people, or when there is no organized activity at all. There is a substantial amount of interaction involved, but the activities are not in sync.
- Cooperative play – when a child is interested both in the people playing and in the activity they are doing. In cooperative play, the activity is organized, and participants have assigned roles. There is also increased self-identification with a group, and a group identity may emerge. This is more common toward the end of the early childhood stage. Examples would be dramatic play activities with roles, like playing school, or a game with rules, such as freeze tag.

Erikson: Initiative vs. Guilt

While Erik Erikson was very influenced by Freud, he believed that the relationships that people have, not psychosexual stages, are what influence personality development. At the beginning of early childhood, the child is still in the autonomy versus shame and doubt stage (stage 2).

By age three, the child begins stage 3: initiative versus guilt. The trust and autonomy of previous stages develop into a desire to take initiative or to think of ideas and initiate action. Children are curious at this age and start to ask questions so that they can learn about the world. Parents should try to answer those questions without making the child feel like a burden or implying that the child's question is not worth asking.

These children are also beginning to use their imagination (remember what we learned when we discussed Piaget!). Children may want to build a fort with the cushions from the living room couch, open a lemonade stand in the driveway, or make a zoo with their stuffed animals and issue tickets to those who want to come. Another way that children may express autonomy is in wanting to get themselves ready for bed without any assistance. To reinforce taking initiative, caregivers should offer praise for the child's efforts and avoid being overly critical of messes or mistakes. Soggy washrags and toothpaste left in the sink pale in comparison to the smiling face of a five-year-old emerging from the bathroom with clean teeth and pajamas!

That said, it is important that the parent does their best to kindly guide the child to the right actions. Remember that according to Freud and Kohlberg, children are developing a sense of morality during this time. Erikson agrees. If the child does leave those soggy washrags in the sink, have the child help clean them up. It is possible that the child will not be happy with helping to clean, and the child may even become aggressive or angry, but it is important to remember that the child is still learning how to navigate their world. They are trying to build a sense of autonomy, and they may not react well when they are asked to do something that they had not planned. Parents should be aware of this, and try to be understanding, but also firm. Guilt for a situation where a child did not do their best allows a child to understand their responsibilities and helps the child learn to exercise self-control (remember the marshmallow test). The goal is to find a balance between initiative and guilt, not a free-for-all where the parent allows the child to do anything they want to. The parent must guide the child if they are to have a successful resolution in this stage.

WATCH IT

Movies, television, and media, in general, provide many examples of psychosocial development. The movie clips in this video demonstrate Erikson's third stage of development, initiative versus guilt. What other examples can you think of to demonstrate young children developing a sense of autonomy?

- https://youtu.be/JZJO9KWWkBo

Gender and Early Childhood

Gender Identity, Gender Constancy, and Gender Roles

Another important dimension of the self is the sense of self as male or female. Preschool aged children become increasingly interested in finding out the differences between boys and girls both physically and in terms of what activities are acceptable for each. While two-year-olds can identify some differences and learn whether they are boys or girls, preschoolers become more interested in what it means to be male or female. This self-identification, or gender identity, is followed sometime later with gender constancy, or the understanding that superficial changes do not mean that gender has actually changed. For example, if you are playing with a two-year-old boy and put barrettes in his hair, he may protest saying that he doesn't want to be a girl. By the time a child is four-years-old, they have a solid understanding that putting barrettes in their hair does not change their gender.

Figure 1. Young children are interested in exploring the differences between what activities are acceptable for boys and girls.

Children learn at a young age that there are distinct expectations for boys and girls. Cross-cultural studies reveal that children are aware of gender roles by age two or three. At four or five, most children are firmly entrenched in culturally appropriate gender roles (Kane 1996). Children acquire these roles through socialization, a process in which people learn to behave in a particular way as dictated by societal values, beliefs, and attitudes.

Children may also use gender stereotyping readily. Gender stereotyping involves overgeneralizing about the attitudes, traits, or behavior patterns of women or men. A recent research study examined four- and five-year-old children's predictions concerning the sex of the persons carrying out a variety of common activities and occupations on television. The children's responses revealed strong gender-stereotyped expectations. They also found that children's estimates of their own future competence indicated stereotypical beliefs, with the females more likely to reject masculine activities.

Children who are allowed to explore different toys, who are exposed to non-traditional gender roles, and whose parents and caregivers are open to allowing the child to take part in non-traditional play (allowing a boy to nurture a doll, or allowing a girl to play doctor) tend to have broader definitions of what is gender appropriate, and may do less gender stereotyping.

WATCH IT

This clip from Upworthy shows how some children were surprised to meet women in traditionally male occupations.

- https://youtu.be/G3Aweo-74kY

DIG DEEPER: GENDER IDENTITY DEVELOPMENT

The National Center on Parent, Family, and Community Engagement identified several stages of gender identity development, as outlined below. You can see more of their resources and tips for healthy gender development by reading Healthy Gender Development and Young Children.

- **Infancy**. Children observe messages about gender from adults' appearances, activities, and behaviors. Most parents' interactions with their infants are shaped by the child's gender, and this in turn also shapes the child's understanding of gender (Fagot & Leinbach, 1989; Witt, 1997; Zosuls, Miller, Ruble, Martin, & Fabes, 2011).
- **18–24 months**. Toddlers begin to define gender, using messages from many sources. As they develop a sense of self, toddlers look for patterns in their homes and early care settings. Gender is one way to understand group belonging, which is important for secure development (Kuhn, Nash & Brucken, 1978; Langlois & Downs, 1980; Fagot & Leinbach, 1989; Baldwin & Moses, 1996; Witt, 1997; Antill, Cunningham, & Cotton, 2003; Zoslus, et al., 2009).
- **Ages 3–4**. Gender identity takes on more meaning as children begin to focus on all kinds of differences. Children begin to connect the concept "girl" or "boy" to specific attributes. They form stronger rules or expectations for how each gender behaves and looks (Kuhn, Nash, & Brucken 1978; Martin, Ruble, & Szkrybalo, 2004; Halim & Ruble, 2010).
- **Ages 5–6**. At these ages, children's thinking may be rigid in many ways. For example, 5- and 6-year-olds are very aware of rules and of the pressure to comply with them. They do so rigidly because they are not yet developmentally ready to think more deeply about the beliefs and values that many rules are based on. For example, as early educators and parents know, the use of "white lies" is still hard for them to understand. Researchers call these ages the most "rigid" period of gender identity (Weinraub et al., 1984; Egan, Perry, & Dannemiller, 2001; Miller, Lurye, Zosuls, & Ruble, 2009). A child who wants to do or wear things that are not typical of his gender is probably aware that other children find it strange. The persistence of these choices, despite the negative reactions of others, show that these are strong feelings. Gender rigidity typically declines as children age (Trautner et al., 2005; Halim, Ruble, Tamis-LeMonda, & Shrout, 2013). With this change, children develop stronger moral impulses about what is "fair" for themselves and other children (Killen & Stangor, 2001).

It is important to understand these typical and normal attempts for children to understand the world around them. It is helpful to encourage children and support them as individuals, instead of emphasizing or playing into gender roles and expectations. You can foster self-esteem in children of any gender by giving all children positive feedback about their unique skills and qualities. For example, you might say to a child, "I noticed how kind you were to your friend when she fell down" or "You were very helpful with clean-up today—you are such a great helper" or "You were such a strong runner on the playground today."

Learning Through Reinforcement and Modeling

Learning theorists suggest that gender role socialization is a result of the ways in which parents, teachers, friends, schools, religious institutions, media, and others send messages about what is acceptable or desirable behavior for males or females. This socialization begins early—in fact, it may even begin the moment a parent learns that a child is on the way. Knowing the sex of the child can conjure up images of the child's behavior, appearance, and potential on the part of a parent. And this stereotyping continues to guide perception through life. Consider parents of newborns. Shown a 7-pound, 20-inch baby, wrapped in blue (a color designating males) describe the child as tough, strong, and angry when crying. Shown the same infant in pink (a color used in the United States for baby girls), these parents are likely to describe the baby as pretty, delicate, and frustrated when crying (Maccoby & Jacklin, 1987). Female infants are held more, talked to more frequently and given direct eye contact, while male infants' play is often mediated through a toy or activity.

One way children learn gender roles is through play. Parents typically supply boys with trucks, toy guns, and superhero paraphernalia, which are active toys that promote motor skills, aggression, and solitary play. Daughters are often given dolls and dress-up apparel that foster nurturing, social proximity, and role play. Studies have shown that children will most likely choose to play with "gender appropriate" toys (or same-gender toys) even when cross-gender toys are available because parents give children positive feedback (in the form of praise, involvement, and physical closeness) for gender normative behavior (Caldera, Huston, and O'Brien 1998).

Sons are given tasks that take them outside the house and that have to be performed only on occasion, while girls are more likely to be given chores inside the home, such as cleaning or cooking, that are performed daily. Sons are encouraged to think for themselves when they encounter problems, and daughters are more likely to be given assistance even when they are working on an answer. This impatience is reflected in teachers waiting less time when asking a female student for an answer than when asking for a reply from a male student (Sadker and Sadker, 1994). Girls are given the message from teachers that they must try harder and endure in order to succeed while boys successes are attributed to their intelligence. Of course, the stereotypes of advisors can also influence which kinds of courses or vocational choices girls and boys are encouraged to make.

Figure 2. Little girls are often encouraged to play with toys that support female stereotypes of being nurturing.

Friends discuss what is acceptable for boys and girls, and popularity may be based on modeling what is considered ideal behavior or appearance for the sexes. Girls tend to tell one another secrets to validate others as best friends, while boys compete for position by emphasizing their knowledge, strength or accomplishments. This focus on accomplishments can even give rise to exaggerating accomplishments in boys, but girls are discouraged from showing off and may learn to minimize their accomplishments as a result.

Gender messages abound in our environment. But does this mean that each of us receives and interprets these messages in the same way? Probably not. In addition to being recipients of these cultural expectations, we are individuals who also modify these roles (Kimmel, 2008).

One interesting recent finding is that girls may have an easier time breaking gender norms than boys.[4] Girls who play with masculine toys often do not face the same ridicule from adults or peers that boys face when they want to play with feminine toys. Girls also face less ridicule when playing a masculine role (like doctor) as opposed to a boy who wants to take a feminine role (like caregiver).

WATCH IT

This video provides an overview of common toy commercials and how they can be analyzed based on recent research on gender stereotypes. What gender roles or gender stereotypes have you noticed in toy commercials? How do you think toy commercials have changed over the past few years?

4. Strauss, Elissa (April 2018). "Why girls can be boyish but boys can't be girlish". CNN. Retrieved from https://www.cnn.com/2018/04/12/health/boys-girls-gender-norms-parenting-strauss/index.html.

- https://youtu.be/04loNxkpq5g

The Impact of Gender Discrimination

How much does gender matter? In the United States, gender differences are found in school experiences. Even into college and professional school, girls are less vocal in class and much more at risk for sexual harassment from teachers, coaches, classmates, and professors. These gender differences are also found in social interactions and in media messages. The stereotypes that boys should be strong, forceful, active, dominant, and rational, and that girls should be pretty, subordinate, unintelligent, emotional, and talkative are portrayed in children's toys, books, commercials, video games, movies, television shows, and music. In adulthood, these differences are reflected in income gaps between men and women (women working full-time earn about 74 percent the income of men), in higher rates of women suffering rape and domestic violence, higher rates of eating disorders for females, and in higher rates of violent death for men in young adulthood.

Gender differences in India can be a matter of life and death as preferences for male children have been historically strong and are still held, especially in rural areas (WHO, 2010). Male children are given preference for receiving food, breast milk, medical care, and other resources. In some countries, it is no longer legal to give parents information on the sex of their developing child for fear that they will abort a female fetus. Clearly, gender socialization and discrimination still impact development in a variety of ways across the globe. Gender discrimination generally persists throughout the lifespan in the form of obstacles to education, or lack of access to political, financial, and social power.

Family Life and Parenting Styles

Parenting Styles

Relationships between parents and children continue to play a significant role in children's development during early childhood. We will explore two models of parenting styles. Keep in mind that most parents do not follow any model completely. Real people tend to fall somewhere in between these styles. And sometimes parenting styles change from one child to the next or in times when the parent has more or less time and energy for parenting. Parenting styles can also be affected by concerns the parent has in other areas of their life. For example, parenting styles tend to become more authoritarian when parents are tired and perhaps more authoritative when they are more energetic. Sometimes parents seem to change their parenting approach when others are around, maybe because they become more self-conscious as parents or are concerned with giving others the impression that they are a "tough" parent or an "easy-going" parent. And of course, parenting styles may reflect the type of parenting someone saw modeled while growing up.

Figure 3. Parenting styles may fluctuate or evolve depending on the situation.

Baumrind's Parenting Styles

Baumrind (1971) offers a model of parenting that includes three styles. The first, **authoritarian**, is the traditional model of parenting in which parents make the rules and children are expected to be obedient. Baumrind suggests that authoritarian parents tend to place maturity demands on their children that are unreasonably high and tend to be aloof and distant. Consequently, children reared in this way may fear rather than respect their parents and, because their parents do not allow discussion, may take out their frustrations on safer targets – perhaps as bullies toward peers.

Permissive parenting involves being a friend to a child rather than an authority figure. Children are allowed to make their own rules and determine their own activities. Parents are warm and communicative but provide little structure for their children. Children may fail to learn self-discipline and may feel somewhat insecure because they do not know the limits.

Authoritative parenting involves being appropriately strict, reasonable, and affectionate. Parents allow negotiation where appropriate and discipline matches the severity of the offense. A popular parenting program that is offered in many school districts is called "Love and Logic" and reflects the authoritative or democratic style of parenting just described.

Today we recognize a fourth style within the Baumrind framework: **uninvolved parenting.** These parents are disengaged from their children. They do not make demands on their children and are non-responsive. These children can suffer in school and in their relationships with their peers (Gecas & Self, 1991).

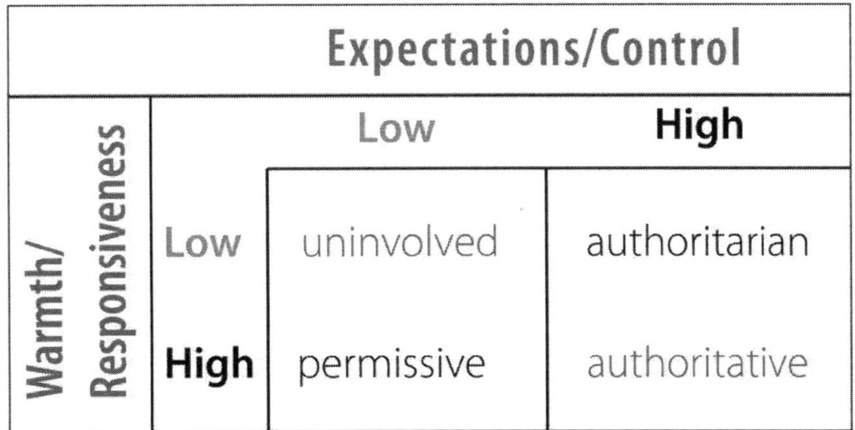

Figure 4. Parents who are both warm and responsive while still maintaining a high level of control are considered authoritative.

Lemasters and Defrain's Parenting Model

Lemasters and Defrain (1989) offered yet another model of parenting. This model is interesting because it looks more closely at the motivations of the parent and suggests that parenting styles are often designed to meet the psychological needs of the parent rather than the developmental needs of the child.

The **martyr** is a parent who will do anything for the child, even tasks that the child should do for himself or herself. All of the good deeds performed for the child, in the name of being a "good parent," may be used later should the parent want to gain compliance from the child. If a child goes against the parent's wishes, the parent can remind the child of all of the times the parent helped the child and evoke a feeling of guilt so that the child will do what the parent wants. The child learns to be dependent and manipulative as a result. (Beware, a parent busy whipping up cookies may really be thinking "control"!)

The **pal** is like the permissive parent described in Baumrind's model above. The pal wants to be the child's friend. Perhaps the parent is lonely, or perhaps the parent is trying to win a popularity contest against an ex-spouse. Pals let children do what they want and focus most on being entertaining and fun. They set few limitations. Consequently, the child may have little self-discipline and may try to test limits with others.

The **police officer/drill sergeant** style of parenting is similar to the authoritarian parent described above. The parent focuses primarily on making sure that the child is obedient and that the parent has full control of the child. Sometimes this can be taken to extremes by giving the child tasks that are really designed to check on their level of obedience. For example, the parent may require that the child fold the clothes and place items back in the drawer in a particular way. If not, the child might be scolded or punished for not doing things "right." This type of parent has a very difficult time allowing the child to grow and learn to make decisions independently. And the child may have a lot of resentment toward the parent that is displaced on others.

The **teacher-counselor** parent is one who pays a lot of attention to expert advice on parenting and who believes that as long as all of the steps are followed, the parent can rear a perfect child. "What's wrong with that?" you might ask. There are two major problems with this approach. First, the parent is taking all of the responsibility for the child's behavior, at least indirectly. If the child has difficulty, the parent feels responsible and thinks that the solution lies in reading more advice and trying more diligently to follow that advice. Parents can certainly influence children, but thinking that the parent is fully responsible for the child's outcome is faulty. A parent can only do so much and can never have full control over the child. Another problem with this approach is that the child may get an unrealistic sense of the world and what can be expected from others. For example, if a teacher-counselor parent decides to help the child build self-esteem and has read that telling the child how special he or she is or how important it is to compliment the child on a job well done, the parent may convey the message that everything the child does is exceptional or extraordinary. A child may come to expect that all of his efforts warrant praise, and in the real world, this is not something one can expect. Perhaps children get more of a sense of pride from assessing their own performance than from having others praise their efforts.

So what is left? Lemasters and Defrain (1989) suggest that the **athletic coach style of parenting** is best. Before you draw conclusions here, set aside any negative experiences you may have had with coaches in the past. The principles of coaching are what are important to Lemasters and Defrain. A coach helps players form strategies, supports their efforts, gives feedback on what went right and what went wrong, and stands at the sideline while the players perform. Coaches and referees make sure that the rules of the game are followed and that all players adhere to those rules. Similarly, the athletic coach as parent helps the child understand what needs to happen in certain situations whether in friendships, school, or home life and encourages and advises the child about how to manage these situations. The parent does not intervene or do things for the child. Rather, the parent's role is to provide guidance while the child learns first hand how to handle these situations. The rules for behavior are consistent and objective and presented in that way. So, a child who is late for dinner might hear the parent respond in this way, "Dinner was at six o'clock." Rather than, "You know good and well that we always eat at six. If you expect me to get up and make something for you now, you have got another thing coming! Just who do you think you are showing up late and looking for food? You're grounded until further notice!"

The most important thing to remember about parenting is that you can be a better, more objective parent when you are directing your actions toward the child's needs while considering what they can reasonably be expected to do at their stage of development. Parenting is more difficult when you are tired and have psychological needs that interfere with the relationship. Some of the best advice for parents is to try not to take the child's actions personally, and be as objective as possible.

Class and Culture

The impact of class and culture cannot be ignored when examining parenting styles. The two models of parenting described above assume that authoritative and athletic coaching styles are best because they are designed to help the parent raise a child who is independent, self-reliant, and responsible. These are qualities favored in "individualistic" cultures such as the United States, particularly by the middle class.

Authoritarian parenting has been used historically and reflects the cultural need for children to do as they are told. African-American, Hispanic, and Asian parents tend to be more authoritarian than non-Hispanic whites. In collectivistic cultures such as China or Korea, being obedient and compliant are favored behaviors. In societies where family members' cooperation is necessary for survival, as in the case of raising crops, rearing children who are independent and who strive to be on their own makes no sense. But in an economy based on being mobile in order to find jobs and where one's earnings are based on education, raising a child to be independent is very important.

Working class parents are more likely than middle-class parents to focus on obedience and honesty when raising their children. In a classic study on social class and parenting styles called *Class and Conformity*, Kohn (1977) explained that parents tend to emphasize qualities that are needed for their own survival when parenting their children. Working class parents are rewarded for being obedient, reliable, and honest in their jobs. They are not paid to be independent or to question the management; rather, they move up and are considered good employees if they show up on time, do their work as they are told, and can be counted on by their employers. Consequently, these parents reward honesty and obedience in their children. Middle-class parents who work as professionals are rewarded for taking initiative, being self-directed, and assertive in their jobs. They are required to get the job done without being told exactly what to do. They are asked to be innovative and to work independently. These parents encourage their children to have those qualities as well by rewarding independence and self-reliance. Parenting styles can reflect many elements of culture.

LINK TO LEARNING

In Scout O'Donnell's TED Talk, she describes the alternative parenting style used by her parents. Can you find elements of authoritative and coaching parenting, along with a little Love and Logic?

Child Care Concerns

About 75.7 percent of mothers of school-aged and 65.1 percent of mothers of preschool aged children in the United States work outside the home[5]. Since more women have been entering the workplace, there has been a concern that families do not spend as much time with their children. This, however, may not be true. Between 1981 and 1997, the amount of time that parents spent with children increased overall (Sandberg and Hofferth, 2001). Modern numbers for this vary widely, as many parents who work outside of the home also devote significant amounts of time to childcare, to 14 hours a week, compared with 10 in 1965.[6] The amount of this time that is undistracted and involved may be close to 34 minutes a day.[7]

Seventy-five percent of children under age 5 are in scheduled child care programs. Others are cared for by family members, friends, or are in Head Start Programs. Older children are often in after school programs, before school programs, or stay at home alone after school once they are older. Quality childcare programs can enhance a child's social skills and can provide rich learning experiences. But long hours in poor quality care can have negative consequences for young children in particular. What determines the quality of child care? One very important consideration is the teacher/child ratio. States specify the maximum number of children that can be supervised by one teacher. In general, the younger the children, the more teachers required for a given number of children. The lower the teacher to child ratio, the more time the teacher has for involvement with the children and the less stressed the teacher may be so that the interactions can be more relaxed, stimulating and positive. The more children there are in a program, the less desirable the program as well. This is because the center may be more rigid in rules and structure to accommodate the large number of children in the facility.

The physical environment should be colorful, stimulating, clean, and safe. The philosophy of the organization and the curriculum available should be child-centered, positive, and stimulating. Providers should be trained in early childhood education as well. A majority of states do not require training for their child care providers. And while formal education is not required for a person to provide a warm, loving relationship to a child, knowledge of a child's development is useful for addressing their social, emotional, and cognitive needs in an effective way. By working toward improving the quality of childcare and increasing family-

5. (April 2018) "Employment Characteristics of Families." Bureau of Labor Statistics. Retrieved from https://www.bls.gov/news.release/pdf/famee.pdf
6. Geiger, A.W., Livingston, Gretchen, and Bialik, Kristen (May 2019). "6 facts about U.S. moms." Pew Research Center. Retrieved from https://www.pewresearch.org/fact-tank/2019/05/08/facts-about-u-s-mothers/
7. Highland Spring Group. "34 minutes: The amount of time the average family gets to spend together each day." Retrieved from http://www.highlandspringgroup.com/press-and-media/group-news/article/34-minutes-the-amount-of-time-the-average-family-gets-to-spend-together-each-day/.

friendly workplace policies, such as more flexible scheduling and perhaps childcare facilities at places of employment, we can accommodate families with smaller children and relieve parents of the stress sometimes associated with managing work and family life.

GLOBAL CONCERNS: THE MARKET WOMEN OF LIBERIA

Work and mothering go hand in hand in many parts of the world. Consider the market women of Liberia. These are women who work as street vendors and are primary providers for their families. They come together in marketplaces along with their children to sell their goods while keeping a watchful eye on their children. Recently, they have been supported by President Sirleaf whose grandmother was a market woman. President Sirleaf has worked to raise funds to improve the marketplaces and conditions for mothers and children. The hope has been to make these marketplaces more safe, to provide childcare, and social services to improve the lives of mothers and children (Nance-Nash, 2009). This video on the Sirleaf Market Women's Fund explains more.

Learning and Behavior Modification

Parenting and Behaviorism

Parenting generally involves many opportunities to apply principles of behaviorism, especially operant conditioning. In discussing operant conditioning, we use several everyday words—positive, negative, reinforcement, and punishment—in a specialized manner. In operant conditioning, positive and negative do not mean good and bad. Instead, *positive* means you are adding something, and *negative* means you are taking something away. *Reinforcement* means you are increasing a behavior, and *punishment* means you are decreasing a behavior. Reinforcement can be positive or negative, and punishment can also be positive or negative. All reinforcers (positive or negative) *increase* the likelihood of a behavioral response. All punishers (positive or negative) *decrease* the likelihood of a behavioral response. Now let's combine these four terms: positive reinforcement, negative reinforcement, positive punishment, and negative punishment. (See table below.)

Table 1. Positive and Negative Reinforcement and Punishment

	Reinforcement	**Punishment**
Positive	Something is *added* to *increase* the likelihood of a behavior.	Something is *added* to *decrease* the likelihood of a behavior.
Negative	Something is *removed* to *increase* the likelihood of a behavior.	Something is *removed* to *decrease* the likelihood of a behavior.

The most effective way to teach a person or animal a new behavior is with positive reinforcement. In **positive reinforcement**, a stimulus is added to the situation to increase a behavior. Parents and teachers use positive reinforcement all the time, from offering dessert after dinner, praising children for cleaning their room or completing some work, offering a toy at the end of a successful piano recital, or earning more time for recess. The goal of providing these forms of positive reinforcement is to increase the likelihood of the same behavior occurring in the future.

Positive reinforcement is an extremely effective learning tool, as evidenced by nearly 80 years worth of research. That said, there are many ways to introduce positive reinforcement into a situation. Many people believe that reinforcers must be tangible, but research shows that verbal praise and hugs are very effective reinforcers for people of all ages. Further, research suggests that constantly providing tangible reinforcers may actually be counterproductive in certain situations. For example, paying children for their grades may undermine their intrinsic motivation to go to school and do well. While children who are paid for their grades may maintain good grades, it is to receive the reinforcing pay, not because they have an intrinsic desire to do well. The impact is especially detrimental to students who initially have a high level of intrinsic motivation to do well in school. Therefore, we must provide appropriate reinforcement, and be careful to ensure that the reinforcement does not undermine intrinsic motivation.

In **negative reinforcement**, an aversive stimulus is removed to increase a behavior. For example, car manufacturers use the principles of negative reinforcement in their seatbelt systems, which go "beep, beep, beep" until you fasten your seatbelt. The annoying sound stops when you exhibit the desired behavior, increasing the likelihood that you will buckle up in the future. Negative reinforcement is also used frequently in horse training. Riders apply pressure—by pulling the reins or squeezing their legs—and then remove the pressure when the horse performs the desired behavior, such as turning or speeding up. The pressure is the negative stimulus that the horse wants to remove.

Sometimes, adding something to the situation is reinforcing as in the cases we described above with cookies, praise, and money. Positive reinforcement involves adding something to the situation in order to encourage a behavior. Other times, taking something away from a situation can be reinforcing. For example, the loud, annoying buzzer on your alarm clock encourages you to get up so that you can turn it off and get rid of the noise. Children whine in order to get their parents to do something and often, parents give in just to stop the whining. In these instances, children have used negative reinforcement to get what they want.

Operant conditioning tends to work best if you focus on trying to encourage a behavior or move a person into the direction you want them to go rather than telling them what not to do. Reinforcers are used to encourage behavior; punishers are used to stop the behavior. A punisher is anything that follows an act and decreases the chance it will reoccur. As with reinforcement, there are also two types of punishment: positive punishment and negative punishment.

Positive punishment involves adding something in order to decrease the likelihood that a behavior will occur again in the future. Spanking is an example of positive punishment. Receiving a speeding ticket is also an example of positive punishment. Both of these punishers, the spanking and the speeding ticket, are intended to decrease the reoccurrence of the related behavior.

Negative punishment involves removing something that is desired in order to decrease the likelihood that a behavior will occur again in the future. Putting a child in time out can serve as a negative punishment if the child enjoys social interaction. Taking away a child's technology privileges can also be a negative punishment. Taking away something that is desired encourages the child to refrain from engaging in that behavior again in order to not lose the desired object or activity.

Often, punished behavior doesn't really go away. It is just suppressed and may reoccur whenever the threat of punishment is removed. For example, a child may not cuss around you because you've washed his mouth out with soap, but he may cuss around his friends. A motorist may only slow down when the trooper is on the side of the freeway. Another problem with punishment is that when a person focuses on punishment, they may find it hard to see what the other does right or well. Punishment is stigmatizing; when punished, some people start to see themselves as bad and give up trying to change.

Reinforcement can occur in a predictable way, such as after every desired action is performed (called continuous reinforcement), or intermittently, after the behavior is performed a number of times or the first time it is performed after a certain amount of time (called partial reinforcement whether based on the number of times or the passage of time). The schedule of reinforcement has an impact on how long a behavior continues after reinforcement is discontinued. So a parent who has rewarded a child's actions each time may find that the child gives up very quickly if a reward is not immediately forthcoming. Children will learn quickest under a continuous schedule of reinforcement. Then the parent should switch to a schedule of partial reinforcement to maintain the behavior.

WATCH IT

This video provides an explanation of the strategies involved with using operant conditioning in parenting. Pay attention to the potential consequences of overusing punishment.

- https://youtu.be/BVbGSVhKGwA

EVERYDAY CONNECTION: BEHAVIOR MODIFICATION IN CHILDREN

Parents and teachers often use behavior modification to change a child's behavior. Behavior modification uses the principles of operant conditioning to accomplish behavior change so that undesirable behaviors are switched for more socially acceptable ones. Some teachers and parents create a sticker chart, in which several behaviors are listed. Sticker charts are a form of token economies. Each time children perform the behavior, they get a sticker, and after a certain number of stickers, they get a prize or reinforcer. The goal is to increase acceptable behaviors and decrease misbehavior. Remember, it is best to reinforce desired behaviors, rather than to use punishment. In the classroom, the teacher can reinforce a wide range of behaviors, from students raising their hands, to walking quietly in the hall, to turning in their homework. At home, parents might create a behavior chart that rewards children for things such as putting away toys, brushing their teeth, and helping with dinner. In order for behavior modification to be effective, the reinforcement needs to be connected with the behavior; the reinforcement must matter to the child and be provided consistently.

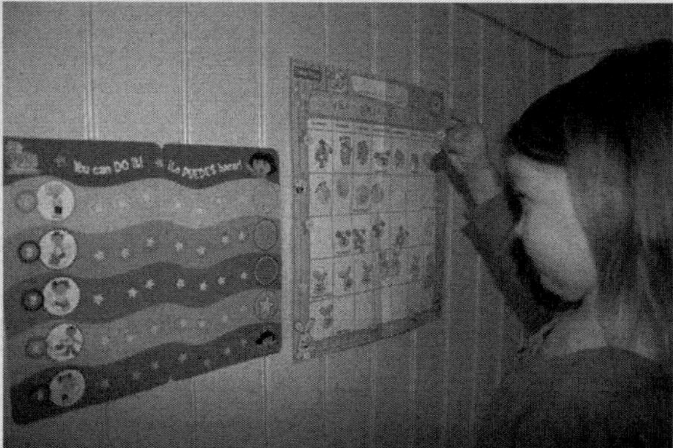

Figure 5. Sticker charts are a form of positive reinforcement and a tool for behavior modification. Once this little girl earns a certain number of stickers for demonstrating a desired behavior, she will be rewarded with a trip to the ice cream parlor. (credit: Abigail Batchelder)

Time-out is another popular technique used in behavior modification with children. It operates on the principle of negative punishment. When a child demonstrates an undesirable behavior, she is removed from the desirable activity at hand. For example, say that Sophia and her brother Mario are playing with building blocks. Sophia throws some blocks at her brother, so you give her a warning that she will go to time-out if she does it again. A few minutes later, she throws more blocks at Mario. You remove Sophia from the room for a few minutes. When she comes back, she doesn't throw blocks.

There are several important points that you should know if you plan to implement time-out as a behavior modification technique. First, make sure the child is being removed from a desirable activity and placed in a less desirable location. If the activity is something undesirable for the child, this technique will backfire because it is more enjoyable for the child to be removed from the activity. Second, the length of the time-out is important. The general rule of thumb is one minute for each year of the child's age. Sophia is five; therefore, she sits in a time-out for five minutes. Setting a timer helps children know how long they have to sit in time-out. Finally, as a caregiver, keep several guidelines in mind over the course of a time-out: remain calm when directing your child to time-out; ignore your child during a time-out (because caregiver attention may reinforce misbehavior), and give the child a hug or a kind word when time-out is over.

(a)

(b)

Figure 6. Time-out is a popular form of negative punishment used by caregivers. When a child misbehaves, he or she is removed from a desirable activity in an effort to decrease unwanted behavior. For example, (a) a child might be playing on the playground with friends and push another child; (b) the child who misbehaved would then be removed from the activity for a short period of time. (credit a: modification of work by Simone Ramella; credit b: modification of work by "JefferyTurner"/Flickr)

Childhood Stress and Development

Stress in Early Childhood

What is the impact of stress on child development? The answer to that question is complex and depends on several factors including the number of stressors, the duration of stress, and the child's ability to cope with stress.

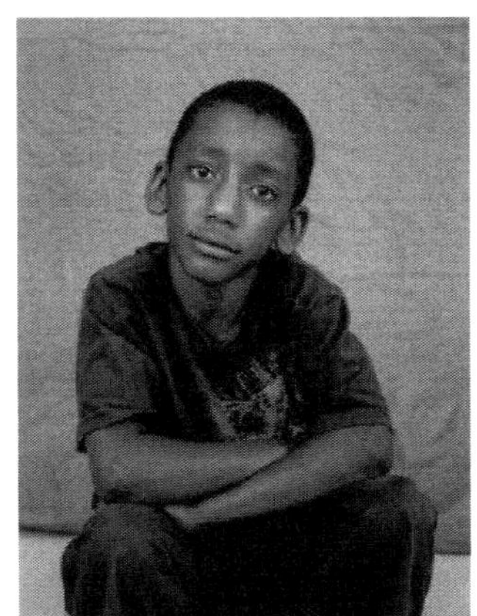

Figure 7. Young children exposed to toxic stress are at risk of developing physical, emotional, and social symptoms.

Children experience different types of stressors that could be manifest in various ways. Normal, everyday stress can provide an opportunity for young children to build coping skills and poses little risk to development. Even long-lasting stressful events, such as changing schools or losing a loved one, can be managed fairly well.

Some experts have theorized that there is a point where prolonged or excessive stress becomes harmful and can lead to serious health effects. When stress builds up in early childhood, neurobiological factors are affected; in turn, levels of the stress hormone cortisol exceed normal ranges. Due in part to the biological consequences of excessive cortisol, children can develop physical, emotional, and social symptoms. Physical conditions include cardiovascular problems, skin conditions, susceptibility to viruses, headaches, or stomach aches in young children. Emotionally, children may become anxious or depressed, violent, or feel overwhelmed. Socially, they may become withdrawn and act out towards others, or develop new behavioral ticks such as biting nails or picking at skin.

Types of Stress

Researchers have proposed three distinct types of responses to stress in young children: positive, tolerable, and toxic. Positive stress (also called eustress) is necessary and promotes resilience, or the ability to function competently under threat. Such stress arises from brief, mild to moderate stressful experiences, buffered by the presence of a caring adult who can help the child cope with the stressor. This type of stress causes minor, temporary physiological and hormonal changes in the young child such as an increase in heart rate and a change in hormone cortisol levels. The first day of school, a family wedding or making new friends are all examples of positive stressors. Tolerable stress comes from adverse experiences that are more intense in nature but short-lived and can usually be overcome. Some examples of tolerable stressors are family disruptions, accidents or the death of a loved one. The body's stress response is more intensely activated due to severe stressors; however, the response is still adaptive and temporary.

Toxic stress is a term coined by pediatrician Jack P. Shonkoff of the Center on the Developing Child at Harvard University to refer to chronic, excessive stress that exceeds a child's ability to cope, especially in the absence of supportive caregiving from adults. Extreme, long-lasting stress in the absence of supportive relationships to buffer the effects of a heightened stress response can produce damage and weakening of bodily and brain systems, which can lead to diminished physical and mental health throughout a person's lifetime. Exposure to such toxic stress can result in the stress response system becoming more highly sensitized to stressful events, producing increased wear and tear on physical systems through over-activation of the body's stress response. This wear and tear increases the later risk of various physical and mental illnesses.

Consequences of Toxic Stress

Children who experience toxic stress or who live in extremely stressful situations of abuse over long periods of time can suffer long-lasting effects. The structures in the midbrain or limbic system, such as the hippocampus and amygdala, can be vulnerable to prolonged stress (Middlebrooks and Audage, 2008). High levels of the stress hormone cortisol can reduce the size of the hippocampus and effect a child's memory abilities. Stress hormones can also reduce immunity to disease. If the brain is exposed to long periods of severe stress, it can develop a low threshold, making a child hypersensitive to stress in the future.

With chronic toxic stress, children undergo long term hyper-arousal of brain stem activity. This includes an increase in heart rate, blood pressure, and arousal states. These children may experience a change in brain chemistry, which leads to hyperactivity and anxiety. Therefore, it is evident that chronic stress in a young child's life can create significant physical, emotional, psychological, social and behavioral changes; however, the effects of stress can be minimized if the child has the support of caring adults.

WATCH IT

This short video explains some of the biological changes that accompany toxic stress.

- https://youtu.be/rVwFkcOZHJw

Coping with Stress

Stress is encountered in four different stages. In the first stage, stress usually causes alarm. Next, in the second or appraisal stage, the child attempts to find meaning from the event. Stage three consists of children seeking out coping strategies. Lastly, in stage four, children execute one or more of the coping strategies. However, children with a lower tolerance for stressors are more susceptible to alarm and find a broader array of events to be stressful. These children often experience chronic or toxic stress.

MANAGING STRESS

Some recommendations to help children manage stressful situations include:

- Preparing children for everyday stressful situations, such as traveling to new places or going to the doctor. For example, talk to children about the experience to help them understand that it is okay to be stressed and scared.
- Keeping communication open. This includes making sure that the child feels comfortable talking to a person. This may include being in a comfortable space, such as their bedroom, where they feel safe. The comfort level of the child is important because if a child is not comfortable, or feels forced to speak, they may not open up at all.
- Spending time together as a family so that no one's feelings go unseen; ensuring that a child knows that their feelings are valued, and should be expressed in healthy ways.
- Modeling healthy and successful coping mechanisms (such as going for a walk).
- Encouraging children to express themselves creatively (as an outlet or to help others to understand what is stressing the child). Some healthy outlets of stress relief include sports or running, writing, reading, art, as well as playing musical instruments.
- Teaching children to act and think positively when they are faced with a situation to manage the stress before it becomes overwhelming.
- Providing a safe and healthy home and environment for children.
- Providing children with proper nutrition and attention.
- Ensuring children are not exposed to substance abuse or violence. When a healthy environment is provided, children are more likely to be emotionally and physically healthy

Trauma in Childhood

Childhood trauma is referred to in academic literature as **adverse childhood experiences** (ACEs). Children may go through a range of experiences that classify as psychological trauma, these might include neglect, abandonment, sexual abuse, physical abuse, parent or sibling treated violently, separation or incarceration of parents, or having a parent with a mental illness. These events have profound psychological, physiological, and sociological impacts and can have negative, lasting effects on health and well-being.

Kaiser Permanente and the Centers for Disease Control and Prevention's 1998 study on adverse childhood experiences determined that traumatic experiences during childhood are a root cause of many social, emotional, and cognitive impairments that lead to increased risk of unhealthy self-destructive behaviors, risk of violence or re-victimization, chronic health conditions, low life potential, and premature mortality. As the number of adverse experiences increases, the risk of problems from childhood through adulthood also rises. Nearly 30 years of study following the initial study has confirmed this. Many states, health providers, and other groups now routinely screen parents and children for ACEs.

Food Insecurity

In 2017 11.8% of households experienced low food security, or **food insecurity**, at some point during that year.[8] Food insecurity happens when a family has limited or uncertain availability of safe, nutritious food. The most recent statistics suggest that households with children are more at risk for food insecurity, with nearly 18% of children under the age of 18 living in households that have experienced food insecurity within the year.[9] Lack of proper nutrition is a stress on the body in general. Children who are undernourished may have physical developmental delays. Further, food insecurity has been correlated with poor school performance in both reading and math.[10]

GLOSSARY

adverse childhood experiences:

abuse, neglect, and violent experiences that contribute to childhood trauma

anal stage:

the second stage in Freud's theory of psychosexual development, lasting from age 18 months to three years, during which time the anus is the primary erogenous zone and pleasure is derived from controlling bladder and bowel movements

athletic coach style of parenting:

the rules for behavior are consistent and objective and presented in that way. The parent's role is to provide guidance while the child learns firsthand how to handle these situations

authoritarian parenting:

the traditional model of parenting in which parents make the rules and children are expected to be obedient

authoritative parenting:

appropriately strict, reasonable, and affectionate. They are willing to negotiate when appropriate

delayed gratification:

the ability to hold out for a larger reward by forgoing a smaller immediate reward

food insecurity:

limited or uncertain availability of safe, nutritious food

gender:

a term that refers to social or cultural distinctions of behaviors that are considered male or female

gender identity:

the way that one thinks about gender and self-identifies, can be female, male, or genderqueer

introjection:

a process Freud described where children incorporate values from others into their value set

8. Coleman-Jensen, Alisha, Matthew Rabbitt, Christian Gregory, and Anita Singh (2018). "Household Food Security in the United States." United States Department of Agriculture
Economic Research Service. Retrieved from https://www.ers.usda.gov/publications/pub-details/?pubid=90022
9. No Kid Hungry. "Facts About Childhood Hunger." Retrieved from https://www.nokidhungry.org/who-we-are/hunger-facts.
10. Diana F. Jyoti, Edward A. Frongillo,4 and Sonya J. Jones (2005)Food Insecurity Affects School Children's Academic Performance,Weight Gain, and Social Skills, American Society for Nutrition.

looking-glass self:
the process by which our sense of self develops as we interact with others through various social relationships and incorporate the way those other people view us into our own sense of self

martyr parent:
parent who will do anything for the child, even tasks that the child should do independently, may later use what they have done for the child to invoke guilt and compliance

negative punishment:
a desirable stimulus is removed to decrease a behavior; for example, losing the privilege of playing a desired game or using a desired item

negative reinforcement:
an undesirable stimulus is removed to increase a behavior; for example, the car beeping goes away when we click into the seatbelt

pal parent:
wants to be the child's friend and focuses on being entertaining and fun

permissive parenting:
involves being a friend to a child rather than an authority figure. Children are allowed to make their own rules and determine their own activities

phallic stage:
the third stage in Freud's theory of psychosexual development, lasting from age three to six years, during which the libido (desire) centers upon the genitalia and children become aware of bodies

police officer/drill sergeant parent:
focuses primarily on making sure that the child is obedient and that the parent has full control of the child

positive punishment:
an undesirable stimulus is added to decrease a behavior; for example, spanking or receiving a speeding ticket

positive reinforcement:
a desirable stimulus is added to increase a behavior; for example, stickers on a behavior chart or words of encouragement

response inhibition:
the ability to recognize a potential behavior and stop the initiation of an undesired behavior

self-concept:
the idea of who we are, what we are capable of doing, and how we think and feel

teacher-counselor parent:
pays a lot of attention to expert advice on parenting and believes that as long as all of the steps are followed, the parent can rear a perfect child

toxic stress:
excessive stress that exceeds a child's ability to cope, especially in the absence of supportive caregiving from adults

uninvolved parenting:
parents who are disengaged from their children, do not make demands on their children, and are non-responsive

Putting It Together: Early Childhood

Usually, sometime at the beginning of early childhood, a parent will suddenly realize that their child is no longer a baby. This may happen because the child has physically grown and no longer has baby-like features, but more often it is because all of a sudden the parent realizes that this child is becoming independent. The child might be choosing their outfit for the day, or trying to learn to tie their shoelaces. It usually happens when the child is around two years old, right as early childhood is beginning. This realization that a baby is no longer a baby, that they are a *child,* is just the beginning.

As you have learned in this module, early childhood is a time of great changes for children. While the child is still obviously a child physically, in the 4-year span of early childhood they make great strides in development—by the end of this period a child's brain is nearly adult-sized! At the same time, that nearly adult-sized brain is not ready to perform many adult tasks—there is much learning still to be done in terms of building relationships, moral decision making, and in other cognitive realms. Children go from knowing around 200 words at age two to being able to communicate in adult-like ways with a vocabulary recognizing over 10,000 words by age five, but think about how many new words you have had to learn just to succeed in this class! Ten thousand words sounds like a lot, but there are over 170,000 words in the English Language, and the average adult knows over 40,000 words.[1]

Parents caring for children in early childhood contribute greatly to development in direct and in indirect ways. Teaching new words, laying-down expectations for behavior in different contexts, choosing daycare centers, helping to build self-confidence, and providing general care for the child all contribute to the child's healthy development through early childhood. Parents and other caretakers should encourage healthy habits in their young children, including making healthy food choices and exercising the body and the brain. They should challenge children to think in new ways and create opportunities for children to learn about themselves so that they can develop a healthy and realistic self-concept.

The learning that happens for children in early childhood is the stepping stone for the next stage, middle childhood. Many of the advances that began in early childhood will continue to be refined in the next stage.

1. de Leon Huld, Nickee. "How Many Words Does the Average Person Know?" Word Counter. Retrieved from https://wordcounter.io/blog/how-many-words-does-the-average-person-know/

Discussion: Parenting Styles

DISCUSSION: In this discussion, reflect upon and discuss the following question:

- DQ: What parenting style did your parents or caregivers use? Did it change over time? Was it different depending on the child? Would you choose to parent in the same style that your parents or caretakers did? Why or why not?

STEP 1: First, write a response with at least EIGHT substantial sentences, integrating concepts you learned from the reading and other materials (include links with necessary). Show that you can think critically on the topic by integrating your own thoughts, analysis, or experiences.

STEP 2: Then return to the discussion to comment on at least TWO classmates' posts (in at least FIVE sentences). Expand on a classmate's comments in a value-adding, topic-related way. Promote a collaborative, supportive community, and advance the dialogue through follow-up questions. Reply posts cannot be one-liners, off-topic posts, vague statements, unsupported opinions, inadequate explanations or simply say, "I agree" or "good job."

MODULE 6: MIDDLE CHILDHOOD

Why It Matters: Middle Childhood

Why learn about development during middle childhood?

When Raekwon first started school, he wasn't sure that he would like it. The thought of going to one place for a long time every day seemed sort of boring. Raekwon found that school was actually really exciting, though. He made friends, he got to learn about new things, he got to play at recess, and the food was good! He found that the days actually went by quickly! Now in fourth grade, Raekwon cannot wait for summer to be over so that he can go to school and meet-up with his friends regularly again.

Middle childhood is the period of life that begins when children enter school and lasts until they reach adolescence. Think for a moment about children at this age that you may know. What are their lives like? What kinds of concerns do they express and with what kinds of activities are their days filled? If it were possible, would you want to return to this period of life? Why or why not?

Early childhood and adolescence seem to get much more attention than middle childhood. Perhaps this is because growth patterns slow at this time, the id becomes hidden during the latent stage, according to Freud, and children spend much more time in schools, with friends, and in structured activities. It may be easy for parents to lose track of their children's development unless they stay directly involved in these worlds. It is important to stop and give full attention to middle childhood to stay in touch with these children and to take notice of the varied influences on their lives in a larger world. After all, they are developing in many incredible ways.

Physical Development in Middle Childhood

What you'll learn to do: describe physical development during middle childhood

Children enter middle childhood still looking very young, and end the stage on the cusp of adolescence. Most children have gone through a growth spurt that makes them look rather grown-up. The obvious physical changes are accompanied by changes in the brain. While we don't see the actual brain changing, we can see the effects of the brain changes in the way that children in middle childhood play sports, write, and play games.

LEARNING OUTCOMES

- Describe physical growth during middle childhood
- Examine health risks in school-aged children

Growth Rates and Motor Skills

Rates of growth generally slow during middle childhood. Typically, a child will gain about 5-7 pounds a year and grow about 2 inches per year. Many girls and boys experience a prepubescent growth spurt, but this growth spurt tends to happen earlier in girls (around age 9-10) than it does in boys (around age 11-12). Because of this, girls are often taller than boys at the end of middle childhood. Children in middle childhood tend to slim down and gain muscle strength and lung capacity making it possible to engage in strenuous physical activity for long periods of time.

The brain reaches its adult size at about age 7. That is not to say, however, that the brain is fully developed by age 7. The brain continues to develop for many years after it has attained its adult size. The school-aged child is better able to plan, coordinate activity using both left and right hemispheres of the brain, and to control emotional outbursts. Paying attention is also improved as the prefrontal cortex matures. As the myelin continues to develop throughout middle childhood, the child's reaction time improves as well.

During middle childhood, physical growth slows down. One result of the slower rate of growth is an improvement in motor skills. Children of this age tend to sharpen their abilities to perform both gross motor skills such as riding a bike and fine motor skills such as cutting their fingernails.

Losing Primary Teeth

Figure 1. A toothless smile is typical of middle childhood.

Deciduous teeth, commonly known as milk teeth, baby teeth, primary teeth, and temporary teeth, are the first set of teeth in the growth development of humans. The primary teeth are important for the development of the mouth, development of the child's speech, for the child's smile, and play a role in chewing of food, Most children lose their first tooth around age 6, then continue to lose teeth for the next 6 years. In general, children lose the teeth in the middle of the mouth first and then lose the teeth next to those in sequence over the 6-year span. By age 12, generally all of the teeth are permanent teeth, however, it is not extremely rare for one or more primary teeth to be retained beyond this age, sometimes well into adulthood, often because the secondary tooth fails to develop.

Health Risks: Childhood Obesity

Nearly 20 percent of school-aged American children are obese.[1] This is defined as being at least 20 percent over their ideal weight.[2] The percentage of obesity in school aged children has increased substantially since the 1960s, and it continues to increase. This is true in part because of the introduction of a steady diet of television and other sedentary activities. In addition, we have come to emphasize high fat, fast foods as a culture. Pizza, hamburgers, chicken nuggets and "lunchables" with soda have replaced more nutritious foods as staples.

SCHOOL LUNCES

School lunches must meet the applicable recommendations of the Dietary Guidelines for Americans. These guidelines state that no more than 30 percent of an individual's calories should come from fat, and less than 10 percent from saturated fat. Regulations also state that school lunches must provide one-third of the recommended dietary allowances of protein, Vitamin A, Vitamin C, iron, calcium, and calories. School lunches must meet federal nutrition requirements over the course of one week's worth of lunches. However, local school food authorities may make decisions about which specific foods to serve and how they are prepared.

Many children in the United States buy their lunches in the school cafeteria, so it might be worthwhile to look at the nutritional content of school lunches. You can obtain this information through your local school district's website. An example of a school menu and nutritional analysis from a school district in north central Texas is a meal consisting of pasta alfredo, bread stick, peach cup, tomato soup, and a brownie, and 2% milk. Students may also purchase chips, cookies, or ice cream along with their meals. Many school districts rely on the sale of desert and other items in the lunchrooms to make additional revenues and many children purchase these additional items so our look at their nutritional intake should also take this into consideration.

1. Centers for Disease Control and Prevention. Childhood Obesity Facts. Retrieved from https://www.cdc.gov/healthyschools/obesity/facts.htm.
2. Harvard School of Public Health. Child Obesity. Retrieved from https://www.hsph.harvard.edu/obesity-prevention-source/obesity-trends/global-obesity-trends-in-children/.

Consider another menu from an elementary school in the state of Washington. This sample meal consists of a chicken burger, tater tots, fruit and veggies and 1% or nonfat milk. This meal is also in compliance with Federal Nutrition Guidelines but has about 300 fewer calories. And, children are not allowed to purchase additional desserts such as cookies or ice cream.

Michelle Obama has been a recent advocate for nutritional school lunches. Since the Healthy, Hunger-Free Act of 2010, she has worked diligently to defend the importance of healthy school lunches but has largely not been successful in her efforts. Schools in the United states are having difficulty enforcing nutrition values in fear of being wasteful because some of the new standards such as whole grains, more vegetables, and reduced sodium levels initially resulted in fewer children eating their lunches. Children are eating 16% more vegetables and 23% more fruit during lunches, and over 90% of schools report that they are meeting the new nutritional guidelines.[3]

One consequence of childhood obesity is that children who are overweight tend to be ridiculed and teased by others. This can certainly be damaging to their self-image and popularity. In addition, obese children run the risk of suffering orthopedic problems such as knee injuries, and an increased risk of heart disease and stroke in adulthood. It may be difficult for a child who is obese to become a non-obese adult. In addition, the number of cases of pediatric diabetes has risen dramatically in recent years.

Dieting is not really the solution to childhood obesity. If you diet, your basal metabolic rate tends to decrease thereby making the body burn even fewer calories in order to maintain the weight. Increased activity is much more effective in lowering the weight and improving the child's health and psychological well-being. Exercise reduces stress and being an overweight child, subjected to the ridicule of others can certainly be stressful. Parents should take caution against emphasizing diet alone to avoid the development of any obsession about dieting that can lead to eating disorders as teens. Again, increasing a child's activity level is most helpful.

ORGANIZED SPORTS: PROS AND CONS

Middle childhood seems to be a great time to introduce children to organized sports. And in fact, many parents do. Nearly 3 million children play soccer in the United States. This activity promises to help children build social skills, improve athletically, and learn a sense of competition. It has been suggested, however, that the emphasis on competition and athletic skill can be counterproductive and lead children to grow tired of the game and want to quit. In many respects, it appears that children's activities are no longer children's activities once adults become involved and approach the games as adults rather than children. The U.S. Soccer Federation recently advised coaches to reduce the amount of drilling engaged in during practice and to allow children to play more freely and to choose their own positions. The hope is that this will build on their love of the game and foster their natural talents.

Figure 2. Organized sports like soccer are especially popular during middle childhood.

3. U.S. Department of Agriculture. FACT SHEET: Healthy, Hunger-Free Kids Act School Meals Implementation. Retrieved from https://www.usda.gov/media/press-releases/2014/05/20/fact-sheet-healthy-hunger-free-kids-act-school-meals-implementation

Cognitive Development in Middle Childhood

What you'll learn to do: explain changes and advances in cognitive development during middle childhood

Children in middle childhood are beginning a new experience—that of formal education. In the United States, formal education begins at a time when children are beginning to think in new and more sophisticated ways. According to Piaget, the child is entering a new stage of cognitive development where they are improving their logical skills. During middle childhood, children also make improvements in short term and long term memory.

LEARNING OUTCOMES

- Describe key characteristics of Piaget's concrete operational intelligence
- Explain the information processing theory of memory
- Describe language development in middle childhood

Concrete Operational Thought

Figure 1. This child is likely in the concrete operational stage of cognitive development.

According to Piaget, children in early childhood are in the preoperational stage of development in which they learn to think symbolically about the world. From ages 7 to 11, the school-aged child continues to develop in what Piaget referred to as the **concrete operational stage of cognitive development**. This involves mastering the use of logic in concrete ways. The child can use logic to solve problems tied to their own direct experience but has trouble solving hypothetical problems or considering more abstract problems. The child uses inductive reasoning, which means thinking that the world reflects one's own personal experience. For example, a child has one friend who is rude, another friend who is also rude, and the same is true for a third friend. Using inductive reasoning, the child may conclude that friends are rude. (We will see that this way of thinking tends to change during adolescence as children begin to use deductive reasoning effectively.)

The word concrete refers to that which is tangible; that which can be seen or touched or experienced directly. The concrete operational child is able to make use of logical principles in solving problems involving the physical world. For example, the child can understand the principles of cause and effect, size, and distance.

As children's experiences and vocabularies grow, they build schema and are able to classify objects in many different ways. **Classification** can include new ways of arranging information, categorizing information, or creating classes of information. Many psychological theorists, including Piaget, believe that classification involves a hierarchical structure, such that information is organized from very broad categories to very specific items.

One feature of concrete operational thought is the understanding that objects have an **identity** or qualities that do not change even if the object is altered in some way. For instance, the mass of an object does not change by rearranging it. A piece of chalk is still chalk even when the piece is broken in two.

During middle childhood, children also understand the concept of **reversibility**, or that some things that have been changed can be returned to their original state. Water can be frozen and then thawed to become liquid again. But eggs cannot be unscrambled. Arithmetic operations are reversible as well: $2 + 3 = 5$ and $5 – 3 = 2$. Many of these cognitive skills are incorporated into the school's curriculum through mathematical problems and in worksheets about which situations are reversible or irreversible. (If you have access to children's school papers, look for examples of these.)

Remember the example from the earlier module of children thinking that a tall beaker filled with 8 ounces of water was "more" than a short, wide bowl filled with 8 ounces of water? Concrete operational children can understand the concept of **reciprocity** which means that changing one quality (in this example, height or water level) can be compensated for by changes in another quality (width). So there is the same amount of water in each container although one is taller and narrower and the other is shorter and wider.

These new cognitive skills increase the child's understanding of the physical world. Operational or logical thought about the abstract world comes later.

Information Processing Theory

Information processing theory is a classic theory of memory that compares the way in which the mind works to computer storing, processing and retrieving information. According to the theory, there are three levels of memory:

1) **Sensory memory:** Information first enters our sensory memory (sometimes called sensory register). Stop reading and look around the room very quickly. (Yes, really. Do it!) Okay. What do you remember? Chances are, not much, even though EVERYTHING you saw and heard entered into your sensory memory. And although you might have heard yourself sigh, caught a glimpse of your dog walking across the room, and smelled the soup on the stove, you may not have registered those sensations. Sensations are continuously coming into our brains, and yet most of these sensations are never really perceived or stored in our minds. They are lost after a few seconds because they were immediately filtered out as irrelevant. If the information is not perceived or stored, it is discarded quickly.

2) **Working memory** (short-term memory): If information is meaningful (either because it reminds us of something else or because we must remember it for something like a history test we will be taking in 5 minutes), it moves from sensory memory into our working memory. The process by which this happens is not entirely clear. Working memory consists of information that we are immediately and consciously aware of. All of the things on your mind at this moment are part of your working memory.

There is a limited amount of information that can be kept in the working memory at any given time. For most people, this is somewhere around 7 + or – 2 pieces or chunks of information. If you are given too much information at a time, you may lose some of it. (Have you ever been writing down notes in a class and the instructor speaks too quickly for you to get it all in your notes? You are trying to get it down and out of your working memory to make room for new information and if you cannot "dump" that information onto your paper and out of your mind quickly enough, you lose what has been said.)

Rehearsal can help you maintain information in your working memory, but the process by which information moves from working memory into long term memory seems to rely on more than simple rehearsal. Information in our working memory must be stored in an effective way in order to be accessible to us for later use. It is stored in our long-term memory or knowledge base.

3) **Long-term memory** (knowledge base): This level of memory has an unlimited capacity and stores information for days, months or years. It consists of things that we know of or can remember if asked. This is where you want the information to ultimately be stored. The important thing to remember about storage is that it must be done in a meaningful or effective way. In other words, if you simply try to repeat something several times in order to remember it, you may only be able to remember the sound of the word rather than the meaning of the concept. So if you are asked to explain the meaning of the word or to apply a concept in some way, you will be lost. Studying involves organizing information in a meaningful way for later retrieval. Passively reading a text is usually inadequate and should be thought of as the first step in learning material. Writing keywords, thinking of examples to illustrate their meaning, and considering ways that concepts are related are all techniques helpful for organizing information for effective storage and later retrieval.

During middle childhood, children are able to learn and remember due to an improvement in the ways they attend to and store information. As children enter school and learn more about the world, they develop more categories for concepts and learn more efficient strategies for storing and retrieving information. One significant reason is that they continue to have more experiences on which to tie new information. New experiences are similar to old ones or remind the child of something else about which they know. This helps them file away new experiences more easily.

Children in middle childhood also have a better understanding of how well they are performing on a task and the level of difficulty of a task. As they become more realistic about their abilities, they can adapt studying strategies to meet those needs. While preschoolers may spend as much time on an unimportant aspect of a problem as they do on the main point, school-aged children start to learn to prioritize and gage what is significant and what is not. They develop metacognition or the ability to understand the best way to figure out a problem. They gain more tools and strategies (such as "i before e except after c" so they know that "receive" is correct but "recieve" is not.)

Language Development

Vocabulary

One of the reasons that children can classify objects in so many ways is that they have acquired a vocabulary to do so. By 5th grade, a child's vocabulary has grown to 40,000 words. It grows at the rate of 20 words per day, a rate that exceeds that of preschoolers. This language explosion, however, differs from that of preschoolers because it is facilitated by being able to associate new words with those already known (fast-mapping) and because it is accompanied by a more sophisticated understanding of the meanings of a word.

A child in middle childhood is also able to think of objects in less literal ways. For example, if asked for the first word that comes to mind when one hears the word "pizza", the preschooler is likely to say "eat" or some word that describes what is done with a pizza. However, the school-aged child is more likely to place pizza in the appropriate category and say "food" or "carbohydrate".

This sophistication of vocabulary is also evidenced in the fact that school-aged children are able to tell jokes and delight in doing do. They may use jokes that involve plays on words such as "knock-knock" jokes or jokes with punch lines. Preschoolers do not understand plays on words and rely on telling "jokes" that are literal or slapstick such as "A man fell down in the mud! Isn't that funny?"

Grammar and Flexibility

School-aged children are also able to learn new rules of grammar with more flexibility. While preschoolers are likely to be reluctant to give up saying "I goed there", school-aged children will learn this rather quickly along with other rules of grammar.

While the preschool years might be a good time to learn a second language (being able to understand and speak the language), the school years may be the best time to be taught a second language (the rules of grammar).

GLOSSARY

classification:
the arrangement of information into categories or classes

concrete operational stage of cognitive development:
Piaget's stage of development during middle childhood that emphasizes the use of logical thought, especially as applied to concrete, or physical objects

fast-mapping:
a word learning process in which children are able to learn words quickly because they associate new words to words that they already know

identity:
the understanding that objects have an identity or qualities that do not change even if the object is altered in some way

long-term memory:
the third component of the memory system where information is stored for long periods of time

reciprocity:
the understanding that changing one quality of an object can be compensated for by changes in another quality of that object

reversibility:
the understanding that some things that have been changed can be returned to their original state

sensory memory:
the first component of the memory system where information comes in through the 5 senses and is processed if the mind believes that the information is important

working memory:
the second component of the memory system where information that has been processed in sensory memory goes. Working memory includes all the information that you are consciously aware of

Educational Issues during Middle Childhood

What you'll learn to do: examine common learning disabilities and other factors related to education during middle childhood

Across the world, by the time a child is entering middle childhood, they are being educated in some form or fashion. In western society, most children are enrolled in a formal education program by the time they are in middle childhood.[1] That said, what children learn within that formal education program varies greatly across cultures. Further, most programs are set-up for typically developing children, but they may not be set-up to handle children who are accelerated learners or children with learning disabilities. In this section, we'll take a look at some of these educational differences and developments, as well as struggles and learning difficulties during middle childhood.

LEARNING OUTCOMES

- Evaluate the impact of labeling on children's self-concept and social relationships
- Describe autism spectrum disorders
- Identify common learning disabilities such as dyslexia and attention deficit hyperactivity disorder
- Compare Gardner's theory of multiple intelligences and Sternberg's triarchic theory of intelligence
- Apply the ecological systems model to explore children's experiences in schools

1. The World Bank. Primary school starting age (years). Retrieved from https://data.worldbank.org/indicator/SE.PRM.AGES.

Developmental Disorders and Learning Disabilities

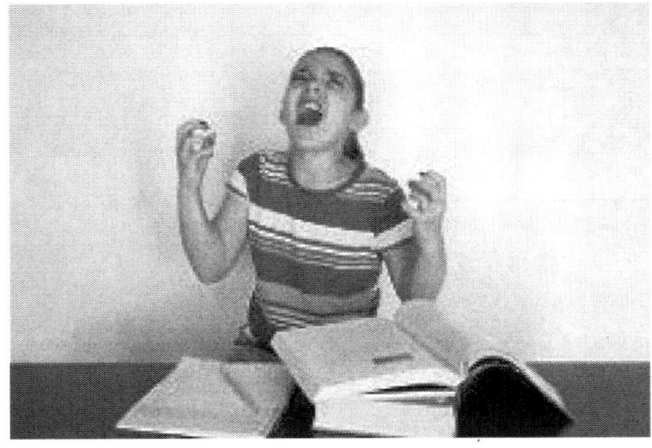

Figure 1. What are the pros and cons of labeling a child with a learning disability?

Children's cognitive and social skills are evaluated as they enter and progress through school. Sometimes this evaluation indicates that a child needs special assistance with language or in learning how to interact with others. Evaluation and diagnosis of a child can be the first step in helping to provide that child with the type of instruction and resources needed. But diagnosis and labeling also have social implications. It is important to consider that children can be misdiagnosed and that once a child has received a diagnostic label, the child, teachers and family members may tend to interpret actions of the child through that label. The label can also influence the child's self-concept. Consider, for example, a child who is misdiagnosed as learning disabled. That child may expect to have difficulties in school, lack confidence, and out of these expectations, have trouble indeed. This **self-fulfilling prophecy**, or tendency to act in such a way as to make what you predict will happen, comes true, calls our attention to the power that labels can have whether or not they are accurately applied.

It is also important to consider that children's difficulties can change over time; a child who has problems in school may improve later or may live under circumstances as an adult where the problem (such as a delay in math skills or reading skills) is no longer relevant. That person, however, will still have a label as learning disabled. It should be recognized that the distinction between abnormal and normal behavior is not always clear; some abnormal behavior in children is fairly common. Misdiagnosis may be more of a concern when evaluating learning difficulties than in cases of autism spectrum disorder where unusual behaviors are clear and consistent.

Keeping these cautionary considerations in mind, let's turn our attention to some developmental and learning difficulties.

Autism Spectrum Disorders

Autism spectrum disorder (ASD) is a developmental disorder that affects communication and behavior. The estimate published by the Center for Disease Control (2018)[is that about 1 out of every 59 children in the United States has been diagnosed with Autism Spectrum Disorder (ASD), which covers a wide variety of ranges in ability, from those with milder forms (formerly known as Asperger's Syndrome) to more severe deficits in communication.[2]

LINK TO LEARNING

Learn more about Autism Spectrum Disorders at Autism Speaks, or the Autistic Self Advocacy Network.

A person with autism has difficulty with and a lack of interest in learning language. An autistic child may respond to a question by repeating the question or might rarely speak. Sometimes autistic children learn more difficult words before simple words or can complete complicated tasks before they are able to complete easier ones. The person often has difficulty reading social cues such as the meanings of non-verbal gestures such as a wave of the hand or the emotion associated with a frown. Intense sensitivity to touch or visual stimulation may also be experienced. Autistic children often have poor social skills and are often

2. Data & Statistics on Autism Spectrum Disorder. Retrieved from https://www.cdc.gov/ncbddd/autism/data.html.

unable to communicate with others or empathize with others emotionally. People with autism often view the world differently and learn differently than people who do not have autism. Autistic children tend to prefer routines and patterns and become upset when routines are altered. For example, moving the furniture or changing the daily schedule can be very upsetting.

Many children with ASD are not identified until they reach school age, although our ability to diagnose children earlier continues to improve. In the 2017-2018 school year, about 710,000 children on the spectrum received special education through the public schools.[3] These disorders are found in all racial and ethnic groups and are more common in boys than in girls. All of these disorders are marked by difficulty in social interactions, problems in various areas of communication, and in difficulty with altering patterns or daily routines. There is no single cause of ASD and the causes of these disorders are to a large extent, unknown. In cases involving identical twins, if one twin has autism, the other is also autistic about 75 percent of the time. Rubella, fragile X syndrome and PKU that has been untreated are some of the medical conditions associated with risks of autism.

Some individuals benefit from medications that alleviate some of the symptoms of ASD, but the most effective treatments involve behavioral intervention and teaching techniques used to promote the development of language and social skills. Children also excel when they are in structured learning environments that accommodate the needs of children on the spectrum.

Learning Disabilities

What is a learning disability? If a child is mentally disabled, that child is typically slow in all areas of learning. However, a child with a learning disability has problems in a specific area or with a specific task or type of activity related to education. A learning difficulty refers to a deficit in a child's ability to perform an expected academic skill (Berger, 2005). These difficulties are identified in school because this is when children's academic abilities are being tested, compared, and measured. Consequently, once academic testing is no longer essential in that person's life (as when they are working rather than going to school) these disabilities may no longer be noticed or relevant, depending on the person's job and the extent of the disability.

Dyslexia is a specific learning disability that is neurobiological in origin. It is characterized by difficulties with accurate and/or fluent word recognition and by poor spelling and decoding abilities (https://dyslexiaida.org/definition-of-dyslexia/). Dyslexia is one of the most commonly diagnosed disabilities and involves having difficulty in the area of reading. This diagnosis is used for a number of reading difficulties. For example, the child may reverse letters, may have difficulty reading from left to right, or may have problems associating letters with sounds. Dyslexia appears to be rooted in some neurological problems involving the parts of the brain active in recognizing letters, verbally responding, or being able to manipulate sounds (National Institute of Neurological Disorders and Stroke, 2006). Treatment typically involves altering teaching methods to accommodate the person's particular problematic area.

WATCH IT

Reading expert Margie Gillis explains dyslexia in the following video:

- https://youtu.be/kE3DqJP-nkI

Attention Deficit Hyperactivity Disorder (ADHD) is considered a neurological and behavioral disorder in which a person has difficulty staying on task, screening out distractions, and inhibiting behavioral outbursts. The most commonly recommended

3. National Center for Education Statistics. Children 3 to 21 years old served under Individuals with Disabilities Education Act (IDEA). Retrieved from https://nces.ed.gov/programs/digest/d18/tables/dt18_204.30.asp.

treatment involves the use of medication, structuring the classroom environment to keep distractions at a minimum, tutoring, and teaching parents how to set limits and encourage age-appropriate behavior (NINDS, 2006). Some people say that the term Attention Deficit is a misnomer because people who suffer from ADHD actually have great difficulty tuning things out. They are bombarded with information... their brains are trying to pay attention to everything. They do not have a deficit of attention- they are trying to pay attention to too many things at once, so everything suffers.

Recent research suggests that several brain structures may be implicated in ADHD. These studies have mainly focused on the frontal lobe and prefrontal cortex.[4] Some studies suggest that the frontal lobe is underdeveloped in children and adults with ADHD.[5][6] The frontal lobe is involved in executive function, attention, planning, impulse control, motivation, and decision making. In some cases the development is delayed, but catches up to expected standards by adulthood; in other cases, the frontal lobe never fully develops.

LINK TO LEARNING

How is ADHD diagnosed? The DSM-V lists the criteria that must be present in order for a diagnosis to be made and an official diagnosis must be made by a qualified mental health professional. It is also important to note that the term ADD is an older term that has been phased out in the newer versions of the DSM. Review the criteria for ADHD. Do you think that making a diagnosis would be difficult? Why or why not?

In general, ADHD is treated with stimulants. While this may seem counter-intuitive (why give a hyperactive child a stimulant?), when you understand the neurological processes involved, it makes a lot of sense. There are two ways that stimulants may work to help people with ADHD focus. Some researchers have found that the stimulants activate the underdeveloped parts of the brain (prefontal cortex and frontal lobe) thereby making these brain areas function more as they should.[7] This allows the child or adult to focus properly. Other researchers suspect that the stimulants affect the way the neurotransmitters function in these brain areas, leading to better function in those areas.[8][9]

There is still a lot of controversy about medicating children with ADHD. While there is clear evidence that medication works to control the negative effects of ADHD, there are also negative side effects that must be dealt with including problems sleeping, changes in appetite, headaches, and more. Further, the long term effects of medicating young children are not well understood. For these reasons, many parents prefer an intervention that does not involve medication. The most common non-pharmaceutical intervention for ADHD is Cognitive Behavioral Therapy (CBT). CBT works by helping children to become aware of their thought processes, and then to learn to change those thought processes to be more beneficial or positive.[10] CBT can

4. Sheridan, M. A., Hinshaw, S., & D'Esposito, M. (2010). Stimulant medication and prefrontal functional connectivity during working memory in ADHD: a preliminary report. Journal of attention disorders, 14(1), 69–78. doi:10.1177/1087054709347444
5. American Academy of Childhood and Adolescent Psychiatry. ADHD & the Brain No. 121 (February 2017). Retrieved from https://www.aacap.org/AACAP/Families_and_Youth/Facts_for_Families/FFF-Guide/ADHD_and_the_Brain.aspx
6. Low, Keath. How Stimulants Work to Reduce ADHD Symptoms. Verywell Mind. Retrieved from https://www.verywellmind.com/how-do-stimulants-for-adhd-work-20895.
7. Sheridan, M. A., Hinshaw, S., & D'Esposito, M. (2010). Stimulant medication and prefrontal functional connectivity during working memory in ADHD: a preliminary report. Journal of attention disorders, 14(1), 69–78. doi:10.1177/1087054709347444
8. Stimulant Medications for ADHD. WebMD. Retrieved from https://www.webmd.com/add-adhd/adhd-stimulant-therapy#1
9. Low, Keath. How Stimulants Work to Reduce ADHD Symptoms. Verywell Mind. Retrieved from https://www.verywellmind.com/how-do-stimulants-for-adhd-work-20895.
10. Understood. Cognitive Behavioral Therapy: What You Need to Know. Retrieved from https://www.understood.org/en/learning-attention-issues/treatments-approaches/therapies/faqs-about-cognitive-behavioral-therapy

also help by educating parents about ways to help their children learn about self-control and discipline. There is very good evidence that CBT is an effective strategy in treating ADHD. Indeed, in some studies, children treated with CBT have better long term outcomes than children treated with medication. Some studies show that a combination of medication and CBT is most beneficial because the medication helps with behavior change more quickly, allowing for the child to learn through CBT more quickly. The CBT then helps with longer-term behavior change so that the child can stop taking medications and deal effectively with their ADHD symptoms based on what they have learned through CBT.

Learning and Intelligence

Schools and Testing

When Should School Begin?

In the United States, children generally begin school around age 5 or 6. In fact, most Western countries follow this model. But WHY do we begin school at 5 or 6? For the most part, this age was chosen as a matter of convenience. In countries where the mother is expected to work, the age at which children begin school tends to be younger. That said, research does not support that children should begin formal education so early. Many research studies suggest age 7 is the most appropriate age to begin formalized school.[11] Before age 7, children learn best through play. By age 7, most children are capable of learning in a more formal academic-forward setting.

Figure 2. An average elementary schooler will spend around 7 hours a day in school.

The Controversy Over Testing In Schools

Children's academic performance is often measured with the use of standardized tests. **Achievement tests** are used to measure what a child has already learned. Achievement tests are often used as measures of teaching effectiveness within a school setting and as a method to make schools that receive tax dollars (such as public schools, charter schools, and private schools that receive vouchers) accountable to the government for their performance. In 2001, President George W. Bush signed into effect the No Child Left Behind Act mandating that schools administer achievement tests to students and publish those results so that parents have an idea of their children's performance and the government has information on the gaps in educational achievement between children from various social class, racial, and ethnic groups. Schools that show significant gaps in these levels of performance are to work toward narrowing these gaps. Educators have criticized the policy for focusing too much on testing as the only indication of performance levels.

Aptitude tests are designed to measure a student's ability to learn or to determine if a person has potential in a particular program. These are often used at the beginning of a course of study or as part of college entrance requirements. The Scholastic Aptitude Test (SAT) and Preliminary Scholastic Aptitude Test (PSAT) are perhaps the most familiar aptitude tests to students in grades 6 and above. Learning test-taking skills and preparing for SATs has become part of the training that some students in

11. Whitebread, David and Sue Bingham (2013). Too much, too young: Should schooling start at age 7? New Scientist. Retrieved from https://www.newscientist.com/article/mg22029435-000-too-much-too-young-should-schooling-start-at-age-7/

these grades receive as part of their pre-college preparation. Other aptitude tests include the MCAT (Medical College Admission Test), the LSAT (Law School Admission Test), and the GRE (Graduate Record Examination). Intelligence tests are also a form of aptitude tests which are designed to measure a person's ability to learn.

Theories of Intelligence

Intelligence tests and psychological definitions of intelligence have been heavily criticized since the 1970s for being biased in favor of Anglo-American, middle-class respondents and for being inadequate tools for measuring non-academic types of intelligence or talent. Intelligence changes with experience and intelligence quotients or scores do not reflect that ability to change. What is considered smart varies culturally as well and most intelligence tests do not take this variation into account. For example, in the West, being smart is associated with being quick. A person who answers a question the fastest is seen as the smartest. But in some cultures, being smart is associated with considering an idea thoroughly before giving an answer. A well-thought-out and contemplative answer is the best answer.

WATCH IT

Watch this video to learn more about the history behind intelligence testing.

- https://youtu.be/7p2a9B35Xn0

Multiple Intelligences

Howard Gardner (1983, 1998, 1999) suggests that there are not one, but nine domains of intelligence. His theory is known as the **theory of multiple intelligences**. The first three are skills that can be measured by IQ tests:

- **Logical-mathematical:** the ability to solve mathematical problems; problems of logic, numerical patterns
- **Linguistic**: vocabulary, reading comprehension, function of language
- **Spatial**: visual accuracy, ability to read maps, understand space and distance

The next six represent skills that are not measured in standard IQ tests but are talents or abilities that can also be important for success in a variety of fields: These are:

- **Musical**: ability to understand patterns in music, hear pitches, recognize rhythms and melodies
- **Bodily-kinesthetic**: motor coordination, grace of movement, agility, strength
- **Naturalistic**: knowledge of plants, animals, minerals, climate, weather
- **Interpersonal**: understand the emotion, mood, motivation of others; able to communicate effectively
- **Intrapersonal**: understanding of the self, mood, motivation, temperament, realistic knowledge of strengths, weaknesses
- **Existential**: concern about and understanding of life's larger questions, meaning of life, or spiritual matters

Gardner contends that these are also forms of intelligence. A high IQ does not always ensure success in life or necessarily indicate that a person has common sense, good interpersonal skills or other abilities important for success.

Triarchic Theory of Intelligence

Another alternative view of intelligence is presented by Sternberg (1997; 1999). Sternberg offers three types of intelligences, known as the **triarchic theory of intelligence**. Sternberg was concerned that there was too much emphasis placed on aptitude test scores and believed that there were other, less easily measured, qualities necessary for success in a higher education and in the world of work. Aptitude test scores indicate the first type of intelligence—academic, or analytical.

- **Analytical** (componential): includes the ability to solve problems of logic, verbal comprehension, vocabulary, and spatial abilities.

Sternberg noted that students who have high academic abilities may still not have what is required to be a successful graduate student or a competent professional. To do well as a graduate student, he noted, the person needs to be creative. The second type of intelligence emphasizes this quality.

- **Creative** (experiential): the ability to apply newly found skills to novel situations.

A potential graduate student might be strong academically and have creative ideas, but still be lacking in the social skills required to work effectively with others or to practice good judgment in a variety of situations. This common sense is the third type of intelligence.

- **Practical** (contextual): the ability to use common sense and to know what is called for in a situation.

This type of intelligence helps a person know when problems need to be solved. Practical intelligence can help a person know how to act and what to wear for job interviews, when to get out of problematic relationships, how to get along with others at work, and when to make changes to reduce stress.

THINK IT OVER

- As an adult, what kind of intellectual skills do you consider to be most important for your success? Consequently, how would you define intelligence?

The World of School

Remember Urie Brofenbrenner's **ecological systems model** we learned about when we first examined theories of development? This model helps us understand an individual by examining the contexts in which the person lives and the direct and indirect influences on that person's life. School becomes a very important component of children's lives during middle childhood and one way to understand children is to look at the world of school. We have discussed educational policies that impact the curriculum in schools above. Now let's focus on the school experience from the standpoint of the student, the teacher and parent relationship, and the cultural messages or hidden curriculum taught in school in the United States.

Parents vary in their level of involvement with their children's schools. Teachers often complain that they have difficulty getting parents to participate in their child's education and devise a variety of techniques to keep parents in touch with daily and overall progress. For example, parents may be required to sign a behavior chart each evening to be returned to school or may be given information about the school's events through websites and newsletters. There are other factors that need to be considered when looking at parental involvement. To explore these, first ask yourself if all parents who enter the school with concerns about their child are received in the same way? If not, what would make a teacher or principal more likely to consider the parent's concerns? What would make this less likely?

Lareau and Horvat (2004) found that teachers seek a particular type of involvement from particular types of parents. While teachers thought they were open and neutral in their responses to parental involvement, in reality teachers were most receptive to support, praise and agreement coming from parents who were most similar in race and social class with the teachers. Parents who criticized the school or its policies were less likely to be given voice. Parents who have higher levels of income, occupational status, and other qualities favored in society have family capital. This is a form of power that can be used to improve a child's education. Parents who do not have these qualities may find it more difficult to be effectively involved. Lareau and Horvat (2004) offer three cases of African-American parents who were each concerned about discrimination in the schools. Despite evidence that such discrimination existed, their children's white, middle-class teachers were reluctant to address the situation directly. Note the variation in approaches and outcomes for these three families:

- The Williams family: This working-class, African-American couple, a minister and a hair stylist, voiced direct complaints about discrimination in the schools. Their claims were thought to undermine the authority of the school and as a result, their daughter was kept in a lower reading class. However, her grade was boosted to "avoid a scene" and the parents were not told of this grade change.
- The Irving family: This middle class, African-American couple was concerned that the school was discriminating against black students. They fought against it without using direct confrontation by staying actively involved in their daughter's schooling and making frequent visits to the school so make sure that discrimination could not occur. They also talked with other African-American teachers and parents about their concerns.
- Ms. Caldron: This poor, single-parent was concerned about discrimination in the school. She was a recovering drug addict receiving welfare. She did not discuss her concerns with other parents because she did not know the other parents and did not monitor her child's progress or get involved with the school. She felt that her concerns would not receive attention. She requested spelling lists from the teacher on several occasions but did not receive them. The teacher complained that Ms. Caldron did not sign forms that were sent home for her signature.

Working within the system without direct confrontation seemed to yield better results for the Irvings, although the issue of discrimination in the school was not completely addressed. Ms. Caldron was the least involved and felt powerless in the school setting. Her lack of family capital and lack of knowledge and confidence keep her from addressing her concerns with the teachers. What do you think would happen if she directly addressed the teachers and complained about discrimination? Chances are, she would be dismissed as undermining the authority of the school, just as the Masons, and might be thought to lack credibility because of her poverty and drug addiction. The authors of this study suggest that teachers closely examine their biases against parents. Schools may also need to examine their ability to dialogue with parents about school policies in more open ways. What happens when parents have concerns over school policy or view student problems as arising from flaws in the educational system? How are parents who are critical of the school treated? And are their children treated fairly even when the school is being criticized? Certainly, any efforts to improve effective parental involvement should address these concerns.

Student Perspectives

Imagine being a 3rd-grader for one day in public school. What would the daily routine involve? To what extent would the institution dictate the activities of the day and how much of the day would you spend on those activities? Would you always be on task? What would you say if someone asked you how your day went? or "What happened in school today?" Chances are, you would be more inclined to talk about whom you sat at lunch with or who brought a puppy to class than to describe how fractions are added.

Ethnographer and Professor of Education Peter McLaren (1999) describes the student's typical day as filled with constrictive and unnecessary ritual that has a damaging effect on the desire to learn. Students move between various states as they negotiate the demands of the school system and their own personal interests. The majority of the day (298 minutes) takes place in the **student state**. This state is one in which the student focuses on a task or tries to stay focused on a task, is passive, compliant, and often frustrated. Long pauses before getting out the next book or finding materials sometimes indicate that frustration. The **street corner state** is one in which the child is playful, energetic, excited, and expresses personal opinions, feelings, and beliefs. About 66 minutes a day take place in this state. Children try to maximize this by going slowly to assemblies or when getting a hall pass-always eager to say 'hello' to a friend or to wave if one of their classmates is in another room. This is the state in which friends talk and play. In fact, teachers sometimes reward students with opportunities to move freely or to talk or to be themselves. But when students initiate the street corner state on their own, they risk losing recess time, getting extra homework, or being ridiculed in front of their peers. The **home state** occurs when parents or siblings visit the school. Children in this state may enjoy special privileges such as going home early or being exempt from certain school rules in the mother's presence, or it can be difficult if the parent is there to discuss trouble at school with a staff member. The **sanctity state** is a time in which the child is contemplative, quiet, or prayerful. Typically the sanctity state is a very brief part of the day.

Since students seem to have so much enthusiasm and energy in street corner states, what would happen if the student and street corner states could be combined? Would it be possible? Many educators feel concern about the level of stress children experience in school. Some stress can be attributed to problems in friendship. And some can be a result of the emphasis on testing and grades, as reflected in a Newsweek article entitled "The New First Grade: Are Kids Getting Pushed Too Fast Too Soon?" (Tyre, 2006). This article reports concerns of a principal who worries that students begin to burn out as early as 3rd grade. In the book, The Homework Myth: Why Our Kids Get Too Much of a Bad Thing, Kohn (2006) argues that neither research nor experience support claims that homework reinforces learning and builds responsibility. Why do schools assign homework so frequently? A look at cultural influences on education my provide some answers.

Cultural Influences

Another way to examine the world of school is to look at the cultural values, concepts, behaviors and roles that are part of the school experience but are not part of the formal curriculum. These are part of the **hidden curriculum** but are nevertheless very powerful messages. The hidden curriculum includes ideas of patriotism, gender roles, the ranking of occupations and classes, competition, and other values. Teachers, counselors, and other students specify and make known what is considered appropriate for girls and boys. The gender curriculum continues into high school, college, and professional school. Students learn a ranking system of occupations and social classes as well. Students in gifted programs or those moving toward college preparation classes may be viewed as superior to those who are receiving tutoring.

Gracy (2004) suggests that cultural training occurs early. Kindergarten is an "academic boot camp" in which students are prepared for their future student role-that of complying with an adult imposed structure and routine designed to produce docile, obedient, children who do not question meaningless tasks that will become so much of their future lives as students. A typical day is filled with structure, ritual, and routine that allows for little creativity or direct, hands-on contact. "Kindergarten, therefore, can be seen as preparing children not only for participation in the bureaucratic organization of large modern school systems, but also for the large-scale occupational bureaucracies of modern society." (Gracy, 2004, p. 148)

Emphasizing math and reading in preschool and kindergarten classes is becoming more common in some school districts. It is not without controversy, however. Some suggest that emphasis is warranted in order to help students learn math and reading skills that will be needed throughout school and in the world of work. This will also help school districts improve their accountability through test performance. Others argue that learning is becoming too structured to be enjoyable or effective and that students are being taught only to focus on performance and test-taking. Students learn student incivility or lack of sincere concern for politeness and consideration of others is taught in kindergarten through 12th grades through the "what is on the test" mentality modeled by teachers. Students are taught to accept routinized, meaningless information in order to perform well on tests. And they are experiencing the stress felt by teachers and school districts focused on test scores and taught that their worth comes from their test scores. Genuine interest, an appreciation of the process of learning, and valuing others are important components of success in the workplace that are not part of the hidden curriculum in today's schools.

THINK IT OVER

- Do an online search for "kindergarten schedule" and look for a typical daily schedule. Do you think it includes a healthy amount of learning and play? Why or why not?
- To what extent do you think that students are being prepared for their future student role? What are the pros

and cons of such preparation? Look at the curriculum for kindergarten and the first few grades in your own school district.

GLOSSARY

achievement tests:
used to measure what a child has already learned

aptitude tests:
used to measure a student's ability to learn or to determine if a person has potential in a particular program

attention deficit hyperactivity disorder:
a neurological and behavioral disorder in which a person has difficulty staying on task, screening out distractions, and inhibiting behavioral outbursts

autism spectrum disorder:
a developmental disorder that affects communication and behavior

dyslexia:
a specific learning disability that is neurobiological in origin. It is characterized by difficulties with accurate and/or fluent word recognition and by poor spelling and decoding abilities

ecological systems model:
Brofenbrenner's theory that we all belong to many communities and are influenced in the context of multiple environments, also known as ecological systems; organized into five levels of external influence: microsystem, mesosystem, exosystem, macrosystem and chronosystem

hidden curriculum:
cultural values, concepts, behaviors and roles that are part of the school experience but are not part of the formal curriculum

home state:
occurs when parents or siblings visit the school. Children in this state may enjoy special privileges such as going home early or being exempt from certain school rules in the mother's presence, or it can be difficult if the parent is there to discuss trouble at school with a staff member

sanctity state:
a time in which the child is contemplative, quiet, or prayerful. It is often only a very brief part of the day

self-fulfilling prophecy:
the tendency to act in a way that makes what you predict will happen come true

street corner state:
state in which the child is playful, energetic, excited, and expresses personal opinions, feelings, and beliefs

student state:
this state is one in which the student focuses on a task or tries to stay focused on a task, is passive, compliant, and often frustrated

theory of multiple intelligences:
Garner's theory that there are many kinds of intelligence. The modern version of the theory recognizes 9 forms of intelligence

triarchic theory of intelligence:
Sternberg's theory that recognizes three forms of intelligence: academic, creative, and practical

Emotional and Social Development in Middle Childhood

What you'll learn to do: explain emotional, social, and moral development during middle childhood

Children in middle childhood are starting to make friends in more sophisticated ways. They are choosing friends for specific characteristics, including shared interests, sense of humor, and being a good person. That is quite a departure from the earlier days of playing with the people in your group just because they are there. Children in middle childhood are starting to realize that there are benefits to friendships, and there are sometimes difficulties as well. In this section, we'll examine some aspects of these relationships.

LEARNING OUTCOMES

- Examine Erikson's stage of industry vs. inferiority as it relates to middle childhood
- Describe the importance of peer relationships to middle childhood
- Understand Kohlberg's theory on preconventional, conventional, and postconventional moral development
- Examine short term-and long term consequences of divorce on children
- Describe issues regarding sexual abuse and children

Psychodynamic and Psychosocial Theories of Middle Childhood

Now let's turn our attention to concerns related to social development, self-concept, the world of friendships, and family life. During middle childhood, children are likely to show more independence from their parents and family, think more about the future, understand more about their place in the world, pay more attention to friendships, and want to be accepted by their peers.

Freud's Psychosexual Development: The Latency Stage

Remember that Freud's theory of psychosexual development suggests that children develop their personality through a series of psychosexual stages. In each stage, the erogenous zone is the source of the libidinal energy. So far we have seen the oral stage (ages birth – 18 months), the anal stage (ages 18 months – 3 years), and the phallic stage (ages 3 years – 6 years).

Freud's fourth stage of psychosexual development is the latency stage. This stage begins around age 6 and lasts until puberty. In the latency stage, children are actually doing very little psychosexual developing according to Freud. Where pleasure and development occurred through erogenous zones in the first 3 stages, in the latency stage all pleasure from erogenous zones is repressed. In other words, it is latent—hence the stage's name. Freud believed that in the latency stage all development and stimulation come from secondary sources since the erogenous forces are repressed. These secondary sources can include education, forming various social relationships, and hobbies.

Erikson's Psychosocial Development: Industry vs. Inferiority

As we have seen in previous modules, Erikson believes that children's greatest source of personality development comes from their social relationships. So far, we have seen 3 psychosocial stages: trust versus mistrust (ages birth – 18 months), autonomy versus shame and doubt (ages 18 months – 3 years), and initiative versus guilt (ages 3 years – around 6 years).

According to Erikson, children in middle childhood are very busy or industrious. They are constantly doing, planning, playing, getting together with friends, and achieving. This is a very active time and a time when they are gaining a sense of how they measure up when compared with friends. Erikson believed that if these industrious children view themselves as successful in their endeavors, they will get a sense of competence for future challenges. If instead, a child feels that they are not measuring up to their peers, feelings of inferiority and self-doubt will develop. These feelings of inferiority can, according to Erikson, lead to an inferiority complex that lasts into adulthood.

To help children have a successful resolution in this stage, they should be encouraged to explore their abilities. They should be given authentic feedback as well. Failure is not necessarily a horrible thing according to Erikson. Indeed, failure is a type of feedback which may help a child form a sense of modesty. A balance of competence and modesty is ideal for creating a sense of competence in the child.

Self-Concept

Children in middle childhood have a more realistic sense of self than do those in early childhood. That exaggerated sense of self as "biggest" or "smartest" or "tallest" gives way to an understanding of one's strengths and weaknesses. This can be attributed to greater experience in comparing one's own performance with that of others and to greater cognitive flexibility. A child's self-concept can be influenced by peers, family, teachers, and the messages they send about a child's worth. Contemporary children also receive messages from the media about how they should look and act. Movies, music videos, the internet, and advertisers can all create cultural images of what is desirable or undesirable and this too can influence a child's self-concept.

TWEENS

The pre-adolescent, or tween, age range of roughly 9-12 is a major force in the marketing world. This group has a spending power of $200 billion,[1] and are primarily targeted as consumers of media, clothing, and products that make them look "cool" and feel independent. This market came under heavy fire a few years ago for being overly sexualized, which led to the creation of a task for by the American Psychological Association to learn more—their findings and recommendations to reduce this problem can be accessed here.

The Society of Children

Friendships during middle childhood take on new importance as judges of one's worth, competence, and attractiveness. Friendships provide the opportunity for learning social skills such as how to communicate with others and how to negotiate differences. Children get ideas from one another about how to perform certain tasks, how to gain popularity, what to wear, what to say, what to listen to, and how to act. This society of children marks a transition from a life focused on the family to a life concerned with peers. In peer relationships, children learn how to initiate and maintain social interactions with other children. They learn skills for managing conflict, such as turn-taking, compromise, and bargaining. Play and communication also involve the mutual, sometimes complex, coordination of goals, actions, and understanding.

Social Comparison and Bullying

However, peer relationships can be challenging as well as supportive (Rubin, Coplan, Chen, Bowker, & McDonald, 2011). Being accepted by other children is an important source of affirmation and self-esteem, but peer rejection can foreshadow later behavior problems (especially when children are rejected due to aggressive behavior). With increasing age, children confront the challenges of bullying, peer victimization, and managing conformity pressures.

Social comparison with peers is an important means by which children evaluate their skills, knowledge, and personal qualities, but it may cause them to feel that they do not measure up well against others. For example, a boy who is not athletic may feel unworthy of his football-playing peers and revert to shy behavior, isolating himself and avoiding conversation. Conversely, an athlete who doesn't "get" Shakespeare may feel embarrassed and avoid reading altogether.

Most children want to be liked and accepted by their friends. Some popular children are nice and have good social skills. These **popular-prosocial** children tend to do well in school and are cooperative and friendly. **Popular-antisocial** children may gain popularity by acting tough or spreading rumors about others (Cillessen & Mayeux, 2004). Rejected children are sometimes excluded because they are shy and withdrawn. The **withdrawn-rejected** children are easy targets for bullies because they are unlikely to retaliate when belittled (Boulton, 1999). Other rejected children are ostracized because they are aggressive, loud, and confrontational. The **aggressive-rejected** children may be acting out of a feeling of insecurity. Unfortunately, their fear of rejection only leads to behavior that brings further rejection from other children. Children who are not accepted are more likely to experience conflict, lack confidence, and have trouble adjusting. Other categories in the most commonly used sociometric system, developed by Coie & Dodge, includes **neglected** children, who tend to go unnoticed but are not especially liked or disliked by their peers; **average** children, who receive an average number of positive and negative votes from their peers, or **controversial** children, who may be strongly liked and disliked by quite a few peers.

1. Pearson, Bryan. My (Kid's) Generation: 5 Ways Today's Tweens Are Changing Retail. Forbes. Retrieved from https://www.forbes.com/sites/bryanpearson/2016/04/14/my-kids-generation-5-ways-todays-tweens-are-changing-retail/#1011b2dd42ef

Also, with the approach of adolescence, peer relationships become focused on psychological intimacy, involving personal disclosure, vulnerability, and loyalty (or its betrayal)—which significantly affects a child's outlook on the world. Each of these aspects of peer relationships requires developing very different social and emotional skills than those that emerge in parent-child relationships. They also illustrate the many ways that peer relationships influence the growth of personality and self-concept.

WATCH IT

The CDC defines bullying as any unwanted aggressive behavior by another youth or group of youths that involves an observed or perceived power imbalance and is repeated multiple times or is highly likely to be repeated. Watch this video to learn how to teach kids how to recognize bullying and how to prevent it.[2]

- https://youtu.be/ynTuA_tlZDE

Moral Development

Lawrence Kohlberg (1963) built on the work of Piaget and was interested in finding out how our moral reasoning changes as we get older. He wanted to find out how people decide what is right and what is wrong. In order to explore this area, he read a story containing a moral dilemma to boys of different age groups (also known as the Heinz dilemma). In the story, a man is trying to obtain an expensive drug that his wife needs in order to treat her cancer. The man has no money and no one will loan him the money he requires. He begs the pharmacist to reduce the price, but the pharmacist refuses. So, the man decides to break into the pharmacy to steal the drug. Then Kohlberg asked the children to decide whether the man was right or wrong in his choice. Kohlberg was not interested in whether they said the man was right or wrong, he was interested in finding out how they arrived at such a decision. He wanted to know what they thought made something right or wrong.

Pre-conventional Moral Development

The youngest subjects seemed to answer based on what would happen to the man as a result of the act. For example, they might say the man should not break into the pharmacy because the pharmacist might find him and beat him, or they might say that the man should break in and steal the drug and his wife will give him a big kiss. Right or wrong, both decisions were based on what would physically happen to the man as a result of the act. This is a self-centered approach to moral decision-making. He called this most superficial understanding of right and wrong pre-conventional moral development.

Pre-conventional development covers stages one and two in Kohlberg's theory. In stage one, the focus is on the direct consequences of their actions. Their main concern is avoiding punishment and being obedient. In stage two, the focus is more "what's in it for me"? A stage two mentality is self-interest driven.

Conventional Moral Development

Middle childhood boys seemed to base their answers on what other people would think of the man as a result of his act. For instance, they might say he should break into the store, and then everyone would think he was a good husband. Or, he shouldn't because it is against the law. In either case, right and wrong is determined by what other people think. Because

2. Centers for Disease Control and Prevention. Stop Bullying. Retrieved from https://www.cdc.gov/violenceprevention/youthviolence/bullyingresearch/fastfact.html.

what other people think is usually a function of socially accepted morality, this view is often thought of as applying society's standards. A good decision is one that gains the approval of others or one that complies with the law. This is conventional moral development.

The conventional moral development covers stages three and four. In stage three, the focus is on what society deems okay or good in order to gain approval from others. In stage four, the focus is on maintaining social order. The person has an understanding that laws and social conventions are created to maintain a properly functioning society.

Post-conventional Moral Development

Older children were the only ones to appreciate the fact that the Heinz dilemma has different levels of right and wrong. Right and wrong are based on social contracts established for the good of everyone or on universal principles of right and wrong that transcend the self and social convention. For example, the man should break into the store because, even if it is against the law, the wife needs the drug and her life is more important than the consequences the man might face for breaking the law. Or, the man should not violate the principle of the right of property because this rule is essential for social order. In either case, the person's judgment goes beyond what happens to the self. It is based on a concern for others, for society as a whole, or for an ethical standard rather than a legal standard. This level is called post-conventional moral development because it goes beyond convention or what other people think to a higher, universal ethical principle of conduct that may or may not be reflected in the law. Notice that such thinking (the kind supreme justices do all day in deliberating whether a law is moral or ethical, etc.) requires being able to think abstractly. Often this is not accomplished until a person reaches adolescence or adulthood.

Post conventional moral development covers stages five and six. In stage five, the person realizes that not everything is black and white. The person realizes that there are many different ways of thinking about what is good and what is right. Further, just because there is a law does not mean that the law is necessarily good for everyone. In stage five, then, the idea is to do the most good for the most people. Kohlberg's sixth stage is interesting in that it does not seem that people make it to this stage and stay. Indeed, many researchers have failed to identify people who operate within a stage six mentality at all, while others have identified a very few people who operate within stage six on occasion. Why might this be the case? Stage six is a way of thinking about the question of morality in a way that is not personal. Instead, a person tries to empathize with other people and to see the world from the other person's perspective before making a decision. While this sounds easy, very few people are capable of doing this well, and even fewer are capable of doing it consistently. Further, the idea of universal justice is involved in stage six. Indeed, a person in stage six is ready to disobey unjust laws. The focus is on doing the right thing, regardless of the personal consequences.

WATCH IT

The Heinz dilemma is a frequently used example used to help us understand Kohlberg's stages of moral development. It is described in the following video:

- https://youtu.be/5czp9S4u26M

From a theoretical point of view, it is not important what the participant thinks that Heinz should do. Kohlberg's theory holds that the justification the participant offers is what is significant, the form of their response. Below are some of many examples of possible arguments that belong to the six stages:

- Stage one (obedience): Heinz should not steal the medicine because he will consequently be put in prison which will mean he is a bad person. OR Heinz should steal the medicine because it is only worth $200 and not how much the druggist wanted for it; Heinz had even offered to pay for it and was not stealing anything else.

- Stage two (self-interest): Heinz should steal the medicine because he will be much happier if he saves his wife, even if he will have to serve a prison sentence. OR Heinz should not steal the medicine because prison is an awful place, and he would more likely languish in a jail cell than over his wife's death.
- Stage three (conformity): Heinz should steal the medicine because his wife expects it; he wants to be a good husband. OR Heinz should not steal the drug because stealing is bad and he is not a criminal; he has tried to do everything he can without breaking the law, you cannot blame him.
- Stage four (law-and-order): Heinz should not steal the medicine because the law prohibits stealing, making it illegal. OR Heinz should steal the drug for his wife but also take the prescribed punishment for the crime as well as paying the druggist what he is owed. Criminals cannot just run around without regard for the law; actions have consequences.
- Stage five (social contract orientation): Heinz should steal the medicine because everyone has a right to choose life, regardless of the law. OR Heinz should not steal the medicine because the scientist has a right to fair compensation. Even if his wife is sick, it does not make his actions right.
- Stage six (universal human ethics): Heinz should steal the medicine, because saving a human life is a more fundamental value than the property rights of another person. OR Heinz should not steal the medicine, because others may need the medicine just as badly, and their lives are equally significant.

Modern Views of Moral Development

Kohlberg continued to explore his theory after the initial theory was researched. He theorized that there could be other stages and that there could be transitions into each stage. One thing that Kohlberg never fully addressed was his use of nearly all male samples. Men and women tend to have very different styles of moral decision making; men tend to be very justice oriented while women tend to be more compassion oriented. In terms of Kohlberg's stages, women tend to be in lower stages than men because of their compassion orientation.

Carol Gilligan was one of Kohlberg's research assistants. She believed that Kohlberg's theory was inherently biased against women. Gilligan suggests that the biggest reason that there is a gender bias in Kohlberg's theory is because males tend to focus on logic and rules while women focus on caring for others and relationships. She suggests, then, that in order to truly measure women's moral development, it was necessary to create a measure specifically for women. Gilligan was clear that she did not believe neither male nor female moral development was better, but rather that they were equally important.

THINK IT OVER

Consider your own decision-making processes. What guides your decisions? Are you primarily concerned with your personal well-being? Do you make choices based on what other people will think about your decision? Or are you guided by other principles? To what extent is this approach guided by your culture?

Stressors in Middle Childhood

Family Life

During middle childhood, children spend less time with parents and more time with peers. Parents may have to modify their approach to parenting to accommodate the child's growing independence. Authoritative parenting which uses reason and joint decision-making whenever possible may be the most effective approach (Berk, 2007). A more harsh form of parenting, authoritarian parenting, uses strict discipline and focuses on obedience. Asian-American, African-American, and Mexican-American parents are more likely than European-Americans to use an authoritarian style of parenting. Children raised in authoritative households tend to be confident, successful, and happy (Chao, 2001; Stewart and Bond, 2002).

Figure 1. Family relationships change as preteens want to spend more time with friends.

Family Tasks

One of the ways to assess the quality of family life is to consider the tasks of families.

Berger (2005) lists five family functions:

1. Providing food, clothing and shelter
2. Encouraging Learning
3. Developing self-esteem
4. Nurturing friendships with peers
5. Providing harmony and stability

Notice that in addition to providing food, shelter, and clothing, families are responsible for helping the child learn, relate to others, and have a confident sense of self. The family provides a harmonious and stable environment for living. A good home environment is one in which the child's physical, cognitive, emotional, and social needs are adequately met. Sometimes families emphasize physical needs, but ignore cognitive or emotional needs. Other times, families pay close attention to physical needs and academic requirements, but may fail to nurture the child's friendships with peers or guide the child toward developing healthy relationships. Parents might want to consider how it feels to live in the household. Is it stressful and conflict-ridden? Is it a place where family members enjoy being?

Family Change: Divorce

A lot of attention has been given to the impact of divorce on the life of children. The assumption has been that divorce has a strong, negative impact on the child and that single-parent families are deficient in some way. Research suggests 75-80 percent of children and adults who experience divorce suffer no long term effects (Hetherington & Kelly, 2002). Children of divorce and children who have not experienced divorce are more similar than different (Hetherington & Kelly, 2002).

Mintz (2004) suggests that the alarmist view of divorce was due in part to the newness of divorce when rates in the United States began to climb in the late 1970s. Adults reacting to the change grew up in the 1950s when rates were low. As divorce has become more common and there is less stigma associated with divorce, this view has changed somewhat. Social scientists have operated from the divorce as deficit model emphasizing the problems of being from a "broken home" (Seccombe &Warner,

2004). More recently, a more objective view of divorce, repartnering, and remarriage indicates that divorce, remarriage, and life in stepfamilies can have a variety of effects. The exaggeration of the negative consequences of divorce has left the majority of those who do well hidden and subjected them to unnecessary stigma and social disapproval (Hetherington & Kelly, 2002).

The tasks of families listed above are functions that can be fulfilled in a variety of family types-not just intact, two-parent households. Harmony and stability can be achieved in many family forms and when it is disrupted, either through divorce, or efforts to blend families, or any other circumstances, the child suffers (Hetherington & Kelly, 2002).

Factors Affecting the Impact of Divorce

As you look at the consequences (both pro and con) of divorce and remarriage on children, keep these family functions in mind. Some negative consequences are a result of financial hardship rather than divorce per se (Drexler, 2005). Some positive consequences reflect improvements in meeting these functions. For instance, we have learned that a positive self-esteem comes in part from a belief in the self and one's abilities rather than merely being complimented by others. In single-parent homes, children may be given more opportunity to discover their own abilities and gain independence that fosters self-esteem. If divorce leads to fighting between the parents and the child is included in these arguments, the self-esteem may suffer.

The impact of divorce on children depends on a number of factors. The degree of conflict prior to the divorce plays a role. If the divorce means a reduction in tensions, the child may feel relief. If the parents have kept their conflicts hidden, the announcement of a divorce can come as a shock and be met with enormous resentment. Another factor that has an great impact on the child concerns financial hardships they may suffer, especially if financial support is inadequate. Another difficult situation for children of divorce is the position they are put into if the parents continue to argue and fight-especially if they bring the children into those arguments.

Short-term consequences: In roughly the first year following divorce, children may exhibit some of these short-term effects:

1. **Grief over losses suffered**. The child will grieve the loss of the parent they no longer see as frequently. The child may also grieve about other family members that are no longer available. Grief sometimes comes in the form of sadness, but it can also be experienced as anger or withdrawal. Preschool-aged boys may act out aggressively while the same aged girls may become more quiet and withdrawn. Older children may feel depressed.
2. **Reduced Standard of Living**. Very often, divorce means a change in the amount of money coming into the household. Children experience in new constraints on spending or entertainment. School-aged children, especially, may notice that they can no longer have toys, clothing, or other items to which they've grown accustomed, or it may mean that there is less eating out or cancelling satellite television, and so on. The custodial parent may experience stress at not being able to rely on child support payments or having the same level of income as before. This can affect decisions regarding healthcare, vacations, rents, mortgages and other expenditures. The stress can result in less happiness and relaxation in the home. The parent who has to take on more work may also be less available to the children.
3. **Adjusting to Transitions**. Children may also have to adjust to other changes accompanying a divorce. The divorce might mean moving to a new home and changing schools or friends. It might mean leaving a neighborhood that has meant a lot to them as well.

Long-Term consequences: The following are some effects found after the first year of a divorce:

1. **Economic/Occupational Status**. One of the most commonly cited long-term effects of divorce is that children of divorce may have lower levels of education or occupational status. This may be a consequence of lower income and resources for funding education rather than to divorce per se. In those households where economic hardship does not occur, there may be no impact on education or occupational status (Drexler, 2005).
2. **Improved Relationships with the Custodial Parent** (usually the mother): The majority of custodial parents are mothers (approximately 80.4 percent) and
19.6 percent of custodial parents are fathers,[3] Shared custody is on the rise, however, and shows promising social, academic, and psychological results for the children.[4] Children from single-parent families talk to their mothers more often

than children of two-parent families (McLanahan and Sandefur, 1994). Most children of divorce lead happy, well-adjusted lives and develop stronger, positive relationships with their custodial parent (Seccombe and Warner, 2004). In a study of college-age respondents, Arditti (1999) found that increasing closeness and a movement toward more democratic parenting styles was experienced. Others have also found that relationships between mothers and children become closer and stronger (Guttman, 1993) and suggest that greater equality and less rigid parenting is beneficial after divorce (Steward, Copeland, Chester, Malley, and Barenbaum, 1997).

3. **Greater emotional independence in sons**. Drexler (2005) notes that sons who are raised by mothers only develop an emotional sensitivity to others that is beneficial in relationships.
4. **Feeling more anxious in their own love relationships.** Children of divorce may feel more anxious about their own relationships as adults. This may reflect a fear of divorce if things go wrong, or it may be a result of setting higher expectations for their own relationships.
5. **Adjustment of the custodial parent**. Furstenberg and Cherlin (1991) believe that the primary factor influencing the way that children adjust to divorce is the way the custodial parent adjusts to the divorce. If that parent is adjusting well, the children will benefit. This may explain a good deal of the variation we find in children of divorce. Adults going though divorce should consider good self-care as beneficial to the children-not as self-indulgent.
6. **Mental health issues**: Some studies suggest that anxiety and depression that are common in children and adults within the first year of divorce may actually not resolve. A 15 year study by Bohman, Låftman, Päären, Jonsson (2017) (https://www.ncbi.nlm.nih.gov/pmc/articles/PMC5370459/) suggests that parental separation significantly increases the risk for depression 15 years later when depression rates were compared to matched controls. In fact, the risk of depression was related more strongly with parental conflict and parental separation than it was with parental depression!

Sexual Abuse in Middle Childhood

Researchers estimate that 1 out of 4 girls and 1 out of 10 boys have been sexually abused (Valente, 2005). The median age for sexual abuse is 8 or 9 years for both boys and girls (Finkelhor et. al. 1990). Most boys and girls are sexually abused by a male. Childhood sexual abuse is defined as any sexual contact between a child and an adult or a much older child. Incest refers to sexual contact between a child and family members. In each of these cases, the child is exploited by an older person without regard for the child's developmental immaturity and inability to understand the sexual behavior (Steele, 1986).

Although rates of sexual abuse are higher for girls than for boys, boys may be less likely to report abuse because of the cultural expectation that boys should be able to take care of themselves and because of the stigma attached to homosexual encounters (Finkelhor et. al. 1990). Girls are more likely to be victims of incest and boys are more likely to be abused by someone outside the family. Sexual abuse can create feelings of self-blame, betrayal, and feelings of shame and guilt (Valente, 2005). Sexual abuse is particularly damaging when the perpetrator is someone the child trusts. Victims of sexual abuse may suffer from depression, anxiety, problems with intimacy, and suicide (Valente, 2005). Sexual abuse has additional impacts as well. Studies suggest that children who have been sexually abused have an increased risk of eating disorders and sleep disturbances Further, sexual abuse can lead to Post Traumatic Stress Disorder.

Being sexually abused as a child can have a powerful impact on self-concept. The concept of **false self-training** (Davis, 1999) refers to holding a child to adult standards while denying the child's developmental needs. Sexual abuse is just one example of false self-training. Children are held to adult standards of desirableness and sexuality while their level of cognitive, psychological, and emotional immaturity is ignored. Consider how confusing it might be for a 9-year-old girl who has physically matured early to be thought of as a potential sex partner. Her cognitive, psychological, and emotional state do not equip her to

3. Wolf, Jennifer. The Single Parent Statistics Based on Census Data. Verywell Family. Retrieved from https://www.verywellfamily.com/single-parent-census-data-2997668.
4. Warshak, Richard (2017). *After divorce, shared parenting is best for children's health and development.* Stat. Retrieved from https://www.statnews.com/2017/05/26/divorce-shared-parenting-children-health/.

make decisions about sexuality or, perhaps, to know that she can say no to sexual advances. She may feel like a 9-year-old in all ways and be embarrassed and ashamed of her physical development. Girls who mature early have problems with low self-esteem because of the failure of others (family members, teachers, ministers, peers, advertisers, and others) to recognize and respect their developmental needs. Overall, youth are more likely to be victimized because they do not have control over their contact with offenders (parents, babysitters, etc.) and have no means of escape (Finkelhor and Dzuiba-Leatherman, in Davis, 1999).

GLOSSARY

aggressive-rejected:
children who are ostracized because they are aggressive, loud, and confrontational

average:
children who receive an average number of positive and negative nominations from their peers

controversial:
children who are either strongly liked or strongly disliked by quite a few peers

conventional moral development:
stages 3 and 4 of moral development where morality is internalized, and the concern is on society norms

false self-training:
holding a child to adult standards while denying the child's developmental needs

neglected:
children who tend to go unnoticed but are not especially liked or disliked by their peers

popular-antisocial:
children who gain popularity by acting tough or spreading rumors about others

popular-prosocial:
children who are popular because they are nice and have good social skills

post-conventional moral development:
stages 5 and 6 of moral development where morality comes from personal understanding of rights and justice, regardless of whether that understanding matches societal norms

pre-conventional moral development:
first 2 stages of moral development where morality comes from outside the person, and the concern is on physical consequences of actions

withdrawn-rejected:
children who are excluded because they are shy and withdrawn

Putting It Together: Middle Childhood

Up until middle childhood, the process of development isn't usually as structured as it becomes during middle childhood, when children enter into the formal education setting. Children in school are taught new ways of thinking about things that they already know—they learn *why* they structure sentences the way they do, they learn new words not through hearing them from others, but from lists provided by teachers or determined by committees. They are even taught how to play sports in specific ways with explicit rules that they get tested on in written form. This is quite a departure from the organic learning of younger years.

Learning in this new way is difficult for some children who have never had to sit down for formal instruction. Structured learning can also shed light on learning difficulties and learning disabilities. Educators today are trained to recognize the signs of many learning disabilities so that children can get help early on in their academic careers.

Developing social relationships in the school environment and keeping up with the changing relationships at home can be difficult tasks for children during middle childhood. Children begin the period relatively dependent on parents and by the end of the period, children should be able to act autonomously in terms of decision making and caring for themselves. This change may feel quick to parents, and it can be difficult for them to let go of control and to allow the child to make more decisions. In order for the child to continue healthy development, though, that gradual letting go is necessary. Parents should pay close attention to their children to recognize signs that the child is capable of taking on new responsibilities.This will help the child continue to develop their skills, their sense of self, their sense of place in the family, and their sense of place in the greater community.

Discussion: Middle Childhood

DISCUSSION: In this discussion, reflect upon and discuss ONE of the following questions:

- Q1: A friend of yours is considering getting a divorce, but is concerned about how this might affect her 10-year-old daughter. What advice would you give to your friend based on the research from the text?
- Q2: Show your understanding of Kohlberg's theory by coming up with an original moral dilemma example. Give examples of how someone in the pre-conventional, conventional, and post-conventional stage would respond.

STEP 1: First, write a response with at least EIGHT substantial sentences, integrating concepts you learned from the reading and other materials (include links with necessary). Show that you can think critically on the topic by integrating your own thoughts, analysis, or experiences.

STEP 2: Return to the discussion to comment on at least TWO classmates' posts (in at least FIVE sentences). Expand on a classmate's comments in a value-adding, topic-related way. Promote a collaborative, supportive community, and advance the dialogue through follow-up questions. Reply posts cannot be one-liners, off-topic posts, vague statements, unsupported opinions, inadequate explanations or simply say, "I agree" or "good job."

MODULE 7: ADOLESCENCE

Why It Matters: Adolescence

Why understand the physical, cognitive, emotional, and social changes that occur during adolescence?

Adolescence is a socially constructed concept. In pre-industrial society, children were considered adults when they reached physical maturity; however, today we have an extended time between childhood and adulthood known as adolescence. Adolescence is the period of development that begins at puberty and ends at early adulthood or emerging adulthood; the typical age range is from 12 to 18 years, and this stage of development has some predictable milestones.

Media portrayals of adolescents often seem to emphasize the problems that can be a part of adolescence. Gang violence, school shootings, alcohol-related accidents, drug abuse, and suicides involving teens are all too frequently reflected in newspaper headlines and movie plots.[1] In the professional literature, too, adolescence is frequently portrayed as a negative stage of life—a period of storm and stress to be survived or endured (Arnett, 1999).[2] Adolescents are often characterized as impulsive, reckless and emotionally unstable. This tends to be attributed to "raging hormones" or what is now known as the "teen brain."

With all of the attention given to negative images of adolescents, the positive aspects of adolescence can be overlooked (APA, 2000). Most adolescents in fact succeed in school, are attached to their families and their communities, and emerge from their teen years without experiencing serious problems such as substance abuse or involvement with violence. Recent research suggests that it may be time to lay the stereotype of the "wild teenage brain" to rest. This research posits that brain deficits do not make teens do risky things; lack of experience and a drive to explore the world are the real factors. Evidence supports that risky behavior during adolescence is a normal part of development and reflects a biologically driven need for exploration

1. American Psychological Association (2002). Developing adolescent: A reference for professionals. Retrieved from https://www.apa.org/pubs/info/brochures/develop
2. Arnett, J. (1999). Adolescent storm and stress, reconsidered. American Psychologist, 54(5), 317-326.

– a process aimed at acquiring experience and preparing teens for the complex decisions they will need to make as adults (Romer, Reyna, & Satterthwaite, 2017).[3] Furthermore, McNeely & Blanchard (2009) described the adolescent years as a "time of opportunity, not turmoil."[4]

Second only to infant development, adolescents experience rapid development in a short period of time. During adolescence, children gain 50% of their adult body weight, experience puberty and become capable of reproducing, and experience an astounding transformation in their brains. All of these changes occur in the context of rapidly expanding social spheres. Adolescents begin to learn about adult responsibilities and adult relationships. The details of growing bodies and the rational and irrational thinking of adolescents are covered in this module. As you will learn, although the physical development of adolescents is often completed by age 18, the brain requires many more years to reach maturity. Understanding these changes developmentally can help both adults and adolescents enjoy this second decade of life.

This module will outline changes that occur during adolescence in three domains: physical, cognitive, and psychosocial. Physical changes associated with puberty are triggered by hormones. Cognitive changes include improvements in complex and abstract thought, as well as development that happens at different rates in distinct parts of the brain and increases adolescents' propensity for risky behavior because increases in sensation-seeking and reward motivation precede increases in cognitive control. Within the psychosocial domain, changes in relationships with parents, peers, and romantic partners will be considered. Adolescents' relationships with parents go through a period of redefinition in which adolescents become more autonomous, and aspects of parenting, such as distal monitoring and psychological control, become more salient. Peer relationships are important sources of support and companionship during adolescence yet can also promote problem behaviors. Same-sex peer groups evolve into mixed-sex peer groups, and adolescents' romantic relationships tend to emerge from these groups. Identity formation occurs as adolescents explore and commit to different roles and ideological positions.

No adolescent can truly be understood in separate parts—an adolescent is a "package deal." Change in one area of development typically leads to, or occurs in conjunction with, changes in other areas. Furthermore, no adolescent can be fully understood outside the context of his or her family, neighborhood, school, workplace, or community or without considering such factors as gender, race, sexual orientation, disability or chronic illness, and religious beliefs (APA, 2002).[5]

3. Romer, D., Reyna, R.F., & Satterthwaite, T.D. (2017). Beyond stereotypes of adolescent risk taking: Placing the adolescent brain in developmental context. Developmental Cognitive Neuroscience, 27, 19-34.
4. McNeely, Clea and Jayne Blanchard. A Guide to Healthy Adolescent Development. Johns Hopkins Bloomberg School of Public Health. Retrieved from https://www.jhsph.edu/research/centers-and-institutes/center-for-adolescent-health/_docs/TTYE-Guide.pdf.
5. American Psychological Association (2002). Developing adolescent: A reference for professionals.

Physical Growth and Development in Adolescence

What you'll learn to do: describe the physical changes that occur during puberty and adolescence

Physical changes of puberty mark the onset of adolescence (Lerner & Steinberg, 2009). For both boys and girls, these changes include a growth spurt in height, growth of pubic and underarm hair, and skin changes (e.g., pimples). Boys also experience growth in facial hair and a deepening of their voice. Girls experience breast development and begin menstruating. These pubertal changes are driven by hormones, particularly an increase in testosterone for boys and estrogen for girls. The physical changes that occur during adolescence are greater than those of any other time of life, with the exception of infancy. In some ways, however, the changes in adolescence are more dramatic than those that occur in infancy—unlike infants, adolescents are aware of the changes that are taking place and of what the changes mean. In this section, you will learn about the pubertal changes in body size, proportions, and sexual maturity, the social and emotional attitudes and reactions toward puberty, and some of the health concerns during adolescence, including eating disorders.

LEARNING OUTCOMES

- Describe pubertal changes in body size, proportions, and sexual maturity
- Explain social and emotional attitudes and reactions toward puberty, including sex differences
- Describe brain development during adolescence
- Describe health and sexual concerns during adolescence
- Discuss concerns associated with eating disorders

Physical Development during Adolescence

Puberty Begins

Puberty is the period of rapid growth and sexual development that begins in adolescence and starts at some point between ages 8 and 14. While the sequence of physical changes in puberty is predictable, the onset and pace of puberty vary widely. Every person's individual timetable for puberty is different and is primarily influenced by heredity; however environmental factors—such as diet and exercise—also exert some influence.

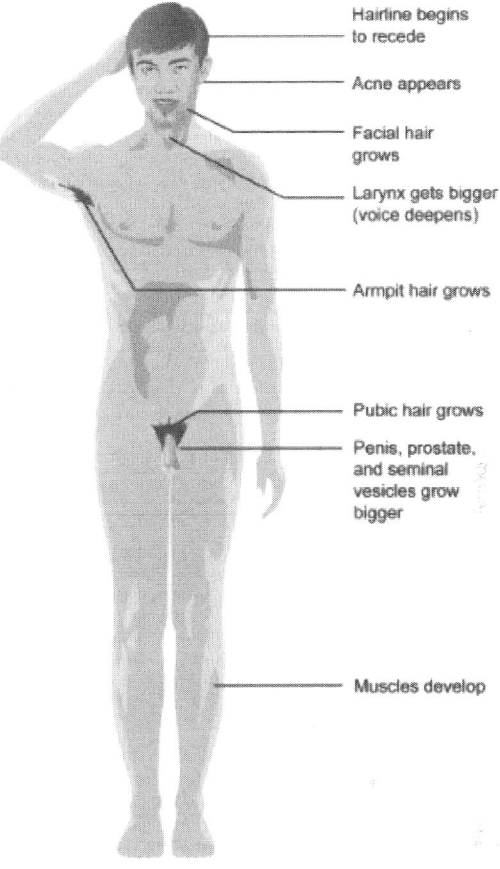

Figure 1. Major physical changes in males during puberty.

Adolescence has evolved historically, with evidence indicating that this stage is lengthening as individuals start puberty earlier and transition to adulthood later than in the past. Puberty today begins, on average, at age 10–11 years for girls and 11–12 years for boys. This average age of onset has decreased gradually over time since the 19th century by 3–4 months per decade, which has been attributed to a range of factors including better nutrition, obesity, increased father absence, and other environmental factors (Steinberg, 2013).[1] Completion of formal education, financial independence from parents, marriage, and parenthood have all been markers of the end of adolescence and beginning of adulthood, and all of these transitions happen, on average, later now than in the past. In fact, the prolonging of adolescence has prompted the introduction of a new developmental period called emerging adulthood that captures these developmental changes out of adolescence and into adulthood, occurring from approximately ages 18 to 29 (Arnett, 2000).[2] We'll learn more about this phase in the next module on early adulthood.

Hormonal Changes

Puberty involves distinctive physiological changes in an individual's height, weight, body composition, and circulatory and respiratory systems, and during this time, both the adrenal glands and sex glands mature. These changes are largely influenced by hormonal activity. Many hormones contribute to the beginning of puberty, but most notably a major rush of **estrogen** for girls and **testosterone** for boys. Hormones play an *organizational role* (priming the body to behave in a certain way once puberty begins) and an *activational role* (triggering certain behavioral and physical changes). During puberty, the adolescent's hormonal balance shifts strongly towards an adult state; the process is triggered by the pituitary gland, which secretes a surge of hormonal agents into the blood stream and initiates a chain reaction.

Puberty occurs over two distinct phases, and the first phase, **adrenarche**, begins at 6 to 8 years of age and involves increased production of adrenal androgens that contribute to a number of pubertal changes—such as skeletal growth. The second phase of puberty, **gonadarche**, begins several years later and involves increased production of hormones governing physical and sexual maturation.

1. Steinberg, L. (2013). Adolescence (10th ed.). New York, NY: McGraw-Hill.
2. Arnett, J. J. (2000). Emerging adulthood: A theory of development from the late teens through the twenties. American Psychologist, 55, 469–480.

Sexual Maturation

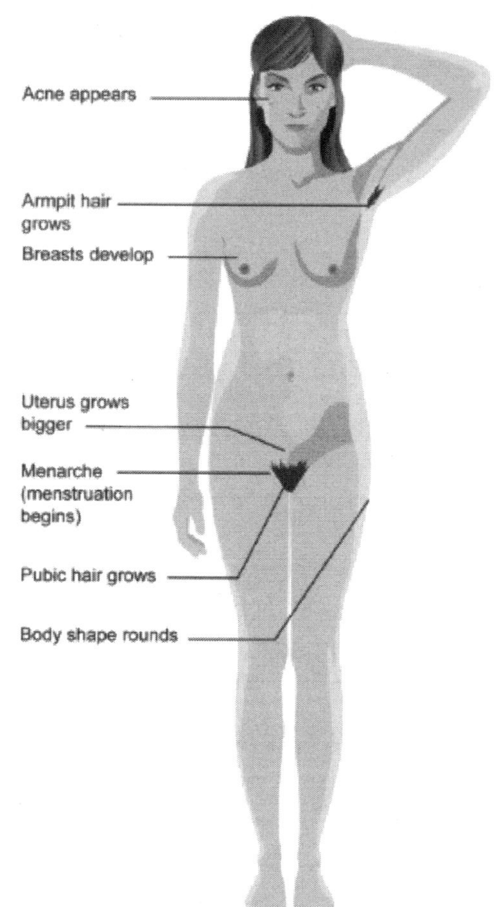

Figure 2. Major physical changes in females during puberty.

During puberty, primary and secondary sex characteristics develop and mature. **Primary sex characteristics** are organs specifically needed for reproduction—the uterus and ovaries in females and testes in males. **Secondary sex characteristics** are physical signs of sexual maturation that do not directly involve sex organs, such as development of breasts and hips in girls, and development of facial hair and a deepened voice in boys. Both sexes experience development of pubic and underarm hair, as well as increased development of sweat glands.

The male and female **gonads** are activated by the surge of the hormones discussed earlier, which puts them into a state of rapid growth and development. The testes primarily release testosterone and the ovaries release estrogen; the production of these hormones increases gradually until sexual maturation is met.

For girls, observable changes begin with nipple growth and pubic hair. Then the body increases in height while fat forms particularly on the breasts and hips. The first menstrual period (**menarche**) is followed by more growth, which is usually completed by four years after the first menstrual period began. Girls experience menarche usually around 12–13 years old. For boys, the usual sequence is growth of the testes, initial pubic-hair growth, growth of the penis, first ejaculation of seminal fluid (**spermarche**), appearance of facial hair, a peak growth spurt, deepening of the voice, and final pubic-hair growth. (Herman-Giddens et al, 2012).[3] Boys experience spermarche, the first ejaculation, around 13–14 years old.

Physical Growth: The Growth Spurt

During puberty, both sexes experience a rapid increase in height and weight (referred to as a **growth spurt**) over about 2-3 years resulting from the simultaneous release of growth hormones, thyroid hormones, and androgens. Males experience their growth spurt about two years later than females. For girls the growth spurt begins between 8 and 13 years old (average 10-11), with adult height reached between 10 and 16 years old. Boys begin their growth spurt slightly later, usually between 10 and 16 years old (average 12-13), and reach their adult height between 13 and 17 years old. Both nature (i.e., genes) and nurture (e.g., nutrition, medications, and medical conditions) can influence both height and weight.

Before puberty, there are nearly no differences between males and females in the distribution of fat and muscle. During puberty, males grow muscle much faster than females, and females experience a higher increase in body fat and bones become harder and more brittle. An adolescent's heart and lungs increase in both size and capacity during puberty; these changes contribute to increased strength and tolerance for exercise.

3. Herman-Giddens, M.E., Steffes, J., Harris, D., Slora, E., Hussey, M., Dowshen, S.A, & Reiter, E.O. (2012). Secondary sexual characteristics in boys: Data from the pediatric research in office settings network. Pediatrics, 130(5), 1058-1068.

WATCH IT

Watch this video to see a summary of the main biological changes that occur during puberty.

- https://youtu.be/DWKWjpVsGng

Reactions Toward Puberty and Physical Development

The accelerated growth in different body parts happens at different times, but for all adolescents it has a fairly regular sequence. The first places to grow are the extremities (head, hands, and feet), followed by the arms and legs, and later the torso and shoulders. This non-uniform growth is one reason why an adolescent body may seem out of proportion. Additionally, because rates of physical development vary widely among teenagers, puberty can be a source of pride or embarrassment.

Most adolescents want nothing more than to fit in and not be distinguished from their peers in any way, shape or form (Mendle, 2015).[4] So when a child develops earlier or later than his or her peers, there can be long-lasting effects on mental health. Simply put, beginning puberty earlier than peers presents great challenges, particularly for girls. The picture for early-developing boys isn't as clear, but evidence suggests that they, too, eventually might suffer ill effects from maturing ahead of their peers. The biggest challenges for boys, however, seem to be more related to late development.

As mentioned in the Khan Academy video about physical development, early maturing boys tend to be stronger, taller, and more athletic than their later maturing peers. They are usually more popular, confident, and independent, but they are also at a greater risk for substance abuse and early sexual activity (Flannery, Rowe, & Gulley, 1993; Kaltiala-Heino, Rimpela, Rissanen, & Rantanen, 2001). Additionally, more recent research found that while early-maturing boys initially had lower levels of depression than later-maturing boys, over time they showed signs of increased anxiety, negative self-image and interpersonal stress. (Rudolph, Troop-Gordon, Lambert, & Natsuaki, 2014).[5]

Early maturing girls may be teased or overtly admired, which can cause them to feel self-conscious about their developing bodies. These girls are at increased risk of a range of psychosocial problems including depression, substance use and early sexual behavior (Graber, 2013).[6] These girls are also at a higher risk for eating disorders, which we will discuss in more detail later in this module (Ge, Conger, & Elder, 2001; Graber, Lewinsohn, Seeley, & Brooks-Gunn, 1997; Striegel-Moore & Cachelin, 1999).

Late blooming boys and girls (i.e., they develop more slowly than their peers) may feel self-conscious about their lack of physical development. Negative feelings are particularly a problem for late maturing boys, who are at a higher risk for depression and conflict with parents (Graber et al., 1997) and more likely to be bullied (Pollack & Shuster, 2000).

4. Mendle, J., Moore, S. R., Briley, D. A., & Harden, K. P. (2015). Puberty, socioeconomic status, and depression in girls: Evidence for gene x environment interactions. Clinical Psychological Science. Advance online publication.
5. Rudolph, K. D., Troop-Gordon, W., Lambert, S. F., & Natsuaki, M. N. (2014). Long-term consequences of pubertal timing for youth depression: Identifying personal and contextual pathways of risk. Development and Psychopathology, 26, 1423–1444.
6. Graber, J. A. (2013). Pubertal timing and the development of psychopathology in adolescence and beyond. Hormones and Behavior, 64, 262–269.

Brain Development During Adolescence

The human brain is not fully developed by the time a person reaches puberty. Between the ages of 10 and 25, the brain undergoes changes that have important implications for behavior. The brain reaches 90% of its adult size by the time a person is six or seven years of age. Thus, the brain does not grow in size much during adolescence. However, the creases in the brain continue to become more complex until the late teens. The biggest changes in the folds of the brain during this time occur in the parts of the cortex that process cognitive and emotional information.

Up until puberty, brain cells continue to bloom in the frontal region. Some of the most developmentally significant changes in the brain occur in the **prefrontal cortex**, which is involved in decision making and cognitive control, as well as other higher cognitive functions. During adolescence, **myelination** and **synaptic pruning** in the prefrontal cortex increases, improving the efficiency of information processing, and neural connections between the prefrontal cortex and other regions of the brain are strengthened. However, this growth takes time and the growth is uneven.

THE TEEN BRAIN: 6 THINGS TO KNOW

As you learn about brain development during adolescence, consider these six facts from the The National Institute of Mental Health:

Your brain does not keep getting bigger as you get older

For girls, the brain reaches its largest physical size around 11 years old and for boys, the brain reaches its largest physical size around age 14. Of course, this difference in age does not mean either boys or girls are smarter than one another!

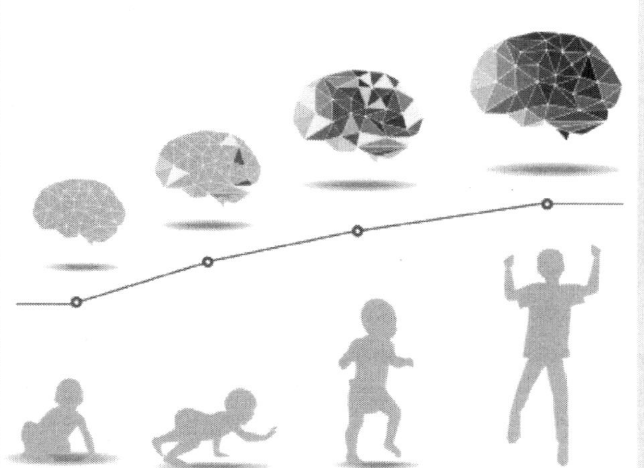

Figure 3. The brain reaches its largest size in the early teen years, but continues to mature well into the 20s.

But that doesn't mean your brain is done maturing

For both boys and girls, although your brain may be as large as it will ever be, your brain doesn't finish developing and maturing until your mid- to late-20s. The front part of the brain, called the prefrontal cortex, is one of the last brain regions to mature. It is the area responsible for planning, prioritizing and controlling impulses.

The teen brain is ready to learn and adapt

In a digital world that is constantly changing, the adolescent brain is well prepared to adapt to new technology—and is shaped in return by experience.

Many mental disorders appear during adolescence

All the big changes the brain is experiencing may explain why adolescence is the time when many mental disorders—such as schizophrenia, anxiety, depression, bipolar disorder, and eating disorders—emerge.

The teen brain is resilient

Although adolescence is a vulnerable time for the brain and for teenagers in general, most teens go on to become healthy adults. Some changes in the brain during this important phase of development actually may help protect against long-term mental disorders.

Teens need more sleep than children and adults

Although it may seem like teens are lazy, science shows that melatonin levels (or the "sleep hormone" levels) in the blood naturally rise later at night and fall later in the morning than in most children and adults. This may explain why many teens stay up late and struggle with getting up in the morning. Teens should get about 9-10 hours of sleep a night, but most teens don't get enough sleep. A lack of sleep makes paying attention hard, increases impulsivity and may also increase irritability and depression.

The **limbic system** develops years ahead of the prefrontal cortex. Development in the limbic system plays an important role in determining rewards and punishments and processing emotional experience and social information. Pubertal hormones target the **amygdala** directly and powerful sensations become compelling (Romeo, 2013).[7] Brain scans confirm that cognitive control, revealed by fMRI studies, is not fully developed until adulthood because the prefrontal cortex is limited in connections and engagement (Hartley & Somerville, 2015).[8] Recall that this area is responsible for judgment, impulse control, and planning, and it is still maturing into early adulthood (Casey, Tottenham, Liston, & Durston, 2005).

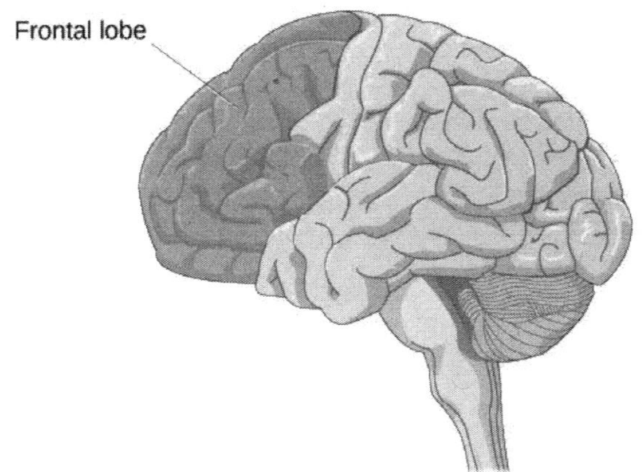

Figure 4. Brain development continues into the early 20s. The development of the frontal lobe, in particular, is important during this stage.

Additionally, changes in both the levels of the neurotransmitters **dopamine** and **serotonin** in the limbic system make adolescents more emotional and more responsive to rewards and stress. Dopamine is a neurotransmitter in the brain associated with pleasure and attuning to the environment during decision-making. During adolescence, dopamine levels in the limbic system increase and input of dopamine to the prefrontal cortex increases. The increased dopamine activity in adolescence may have implications for adolescent risk-taking and vulnerability to boredom. Serotonin is involved in the regulation of mood and behavior. It affects the brain in a different way. Known as the "calming chemical," serotonin eases tension and stress. Serotonin also puts a brake on the excitement and sometimes recklessness that dopamine can produce. If there is a defect in the serotonin processing in the brain, impulsive or violent behavior can result.

When the overall brain chemical system is working well, it seems that these chemicals interact to balance out extreme behaviors. But when stress, arousal or sensations become extreme, the adolescent brain is flooded with impulses that overwhelm the prefrontal cortex, and as a result, adolescents engage in increased risk-taking behaviors and emotional outbursts possibly because the frontal lobes of their brains are still developing.

7. Romeo, R.D. (2013). The teenage brain: The stress response and the adolescent brain. Current Directions in Psychological Science, 22 (2), 140-145.
8. Hartley, C.A. & Somerville, L.H. (2015). The neuroscience of adolescent decision-making. Current Opinion in Behavioral Sciences, 5, 108-115.

Later in adolescence, the brain's cognitive control centers in the prefrontal cortex develop, increasing adolescents' self-regulation and future orientation. The difference in timing of the development of these different regions of the brain contributes to more risk taking during middle adolescence because adolescents are motivated to seek thrills that sometimes come from risky behavior, such as reckless driving, smoking, or drinking, and have not yet developed the cognitive control to resist impulses or focus equally on the potential risks (Steinberg, 2008).[9] One of the world's leading experts on adolescent development, Laurence Steinberg, likens this to engaging a powerful engine before the braking system is in place. The result is that adolescents are more prone to risky behaviors than are children or adults.

WATCH IT

This video further explains and highlights some of the key developments in the brain during adolescence.

- https://youtu.be/5Fa8U6BkhNo

As mentioned in the introduction to adolescence, too many who have read the research on the teenage brain come to quick conclusions about adolescents as irrational loose cannons. However, adolescents are actually making choices influenced by a very different set of chemical influences than their adult counterparts—a hopped up reward system that can drown out warning signals about risk. Adolescent decisions are not always defined by impulsivity because of lack of brakes, but because of planned and enjoyable pressure to the accelerator. It is helpful to put all of these brain processes in developmental context. Young people need to somewhat enjoy the thrill of risk taking in order to complete the incredibly overwhelming task of growing up.

WATCH IT

Watch the selected portion of this video to learn more about research related to brain changes and behavior during adolescence.

- https://youtu.be/hiduiTq1ei8

To learn more, watch this TED talk by Sarah-Jayne Blakemore: The mysterious workings of the adolescent brain about the latest adolescent brain research and more about how these changes in brain development also result in behavioral changes.

9. Steinberg, L. (2013). Adolescence (10th ed.). New York, NY: McGraw-Hill.

KEY TAKEAWAYS

In sum, the adolescent years are a time of intense brain changes. Interestingly, two of the primary brain functions develop at different rates. Brain research indicates that the part of the brain that perceives rewards from risk, the limbic system, kicks into high gear in early adolescence. The part of the brain that controls impulses and engages in longer-term perspective, the frontal lobes, matures later. This may explain why teens in mid-adolescence take more risks than older teens. As the frontal lobes become more developed, two things happen. First, self-control develops as teens are better able to assess cause and effect. Second, more areas of the brain become involved in processing emotions, and teens become better at accurately interpreting others' emotions.[10]

Sleep

Brain development even affects the way teens sleep. Adolescents' normal sleep patterns are different from those of children and adults. Teens are often drowsy upon waking, tired during the day, and wakeful at night. Although it may seem like teens are lazy, science shows that **melatonin** levels (or the "sleep hormone" levels) in the blood naturally rise later at night and fall later in the morning in teens than in most children and adults. This may explain why many teens stay up late and struggle with getting up in the morning. Teens should get about 9-10 hours of sleep a night, but most teens don't get enough sleep. A lack of sleep makes paying attention hard, increases impulsivity, and may also increase irritability and depression.[11]

LINK TO LEARNING: SCHOOL START TIMES

As research reveals the importance of sleep for teenagers, many people advocate for later high school start times. Read about some of the research at the National Sleep Foundation on school start times or watch this TED talk by Wendy Troxel: "Why Schools Should Start Later for Teens".

Health During Adolescence

Health Concerns During Adolescence

Nutrition

Adequate adolescent nutrition is necessary for optimal growth and development. Dietary choices and habits established during adolescence greatly influence future health, yet many studies report that teens consume few fruits and vegetables and are not receiving the calcium, iron, vitamins, or minerals necessary for healthy development.[12]

10. Steinberg, L. (2008) A social neuroscience perspective on adolescent risk-taking. Developmental Review, 28:78-106.
11. National Institute of Mental Health. The Teen Brain: 6 Things to Know. Retrieved from https://www.nimh.nih.gov/health/publications/the-teen-brain-6-things-to-know/index.shtml#pub6.
12. Christian P, Smith E, R: Adolescent Undernutrition: Global Burden, Physiology, and Nutritional Risks. Ann Nutr Metab 2018;72:316-328. doi: 10.1159/000488865

One of the reasons for poor nutrition is anxiety about **body image,** which is a person's idea of how his or her body looks. The way adolescents feel about their bodies can affect the way they feel about themselves as a whole. Few adolescents welcome their sudden weight increase, so they may adjust their eating habits to lose weight. Adding to the rapid physical changes, they are simultaneously bombarded by messages, and sometimes teasing, related to body image, appearance, attractiveness, weight, and eating that they encounter in the media, at home, and from their friends/peers (both in person and via social media).

Much research has been conducted on the psychological ramifications of body image on adolescents. Modern day teenagers are exposed to more media on a daily basis than any generation before them. Recent studies have indicated that the average teenager watches roughly 1500 hours of television per year, and 70% use social media multiple times a day.[13] As such, modern day adolescents are exposed to many representations of ideal, societal beauty. The concept of a person being unhappy with their own image or appearance has been defined as "**body dissatisfaction**." In teenagers, body dissatisfaction is often associated with body mass, low self-esteem, and atypical eating patterns. Scholars continue to debate the effects of media on body dissatisfaction in teens. What we do know is that two-thirds of U.S. high school girls are trying to lose weight and one-third think they are overweight, while only one-sixth are actually overweight (MMWR, June 10, 2016).[14]

Eating Disorders

Dissatisfaction with body image can explain why many teens, mostly girls, eat erratically or ingest diet pills to lose weight and why boys may take steroids to increase their muscle mass. Although eating disorders can occur in children and adults, they frequently appear during the teen years or young adulthood (National Institute of Mental Health (NIMH), 2019). https://www.nimh.nih.gov/health/topics/eating-disorders/index.shtml Eating disorders affect both genders, although rates among women are 2½ times greater than among men. Similar to women who have eating disorders, some men also have a distorted sense of body image, including **muscle dysmorphia** or an extreme concern with becoming more muscular.

Because of the high mortality rate, researchers are looking into the etiology of the disorder and associated risk factors. Researchers are finding that eating disorders are caused by a complex interaction of genetic, biological, behavioral, psychological, and social factors (NIMH, 2019). Eating disorders appear to run in families, and researchers are working to identify DNA variations that are linked to the increased risk of developing eating disorders. Researchers have also found differences in patterns of brain activity in women with eating disorders in comparison with healthy women. The main criteria for the most common eating disorders: **anorexia nervosa**, **bulimia nervosa**, and **binge-eating disorder** are described in the Diagnostic and Statistical Manual of Mental Disorders-Fifth Edition, DSM-5 (American Psychiatric Association, 2013).

Health Consequences of Eating Disorders

For those suffering from anorexia, health consequences include an abnormally slow heart rate and low blood pressure, which increases the risk for heart failure. Additionally, there is a reduction in bone density (osteoporosis), muscle loss and weakness, severe dehydration, fainting, fatigue, and overall weakness. Anorexia nervosa has the highest mortality rate of any psychiatric disorder. Individuals with this disorder may die from complications associated with starvation, while others die of suicide. In women, suicide is much more common in those with anorexia than with most other mental disorders.

The binging and purging cycle of bulimia can affect the digestive system and lead to electrolyte and chemical imbalances that can affect the heart and other major organs. Frequent vomiting can cause inflammation and possible rupture of the esophagus,

13. Markey, Charlotte (2019). "Teens, Body Image, and Social Media." Psychology Today. Retrieved from https://www.psychologytoday.com/us/blog/smart-people-don-t-diet/201902/teens-body-image-and-social-media.
14. MMWR, (206, June 10). Youth risk behavior surveillance- United States, 2015: Morbidity Weekly Report, 65 (6). Altlanta, GA: U.S. Department of Health and Human Services, Centers for Disease Control and Prevention.

as well as tooth decay and staining from stomach acids. Lastly, binge eating disorder results in similar health risks to obesity, including high blood pressure, high cholesterol levels, heart disease, Type II diabetes, and gall bladder disease (National Eating Disorders Association, 2016).

Eating Disorders Treatment

To treat eating disorders, getting adequate nutrition and stopping inappropriate behaviors, such as purging, are the foundations of treatment. Treatment plans are tailored to individual needs and include medical care, nutritional counseling, medications (such as antidepressants), and individual, group, and/or family psychotherapy (NIMH, 2019). For example, the Maudsley Approach has parents of adolescents with anorexia nervosa be actively involved their child's treatment, such as assuming responsibility for feeding their child. To eliminate binge eating and purging behaviors, cognitive behavioral therapy (CBT) assists sufferers by identifying distorted thinking patterns and changing inaccurate beliefs.

LINK TO LEARNING

Visit National Eating Disorders Association to learn more about eating disorders.

Sexual Development

Developing sexually is an expected and natural part of growing into adulthood. Healthy sexual development involves more than sexual behavior. It is the combination of physical sexual maturation (puberty, age-appropriate sexual behaviors), the formation of a positive sexual identity, and a sense of sexual well-being (discussed more in depth later in this module). During adolescence, teens strive to become comfortable with their changing bodies and to make healthy, safe decisions about which sexual activities, if any, they wish to engage in.

Earlier in the physical development section, we discussed **primary and secondary sex characteristics**. During puberty, every primary sex organ (the ovaries, uterus, penis, and testes) increases dramatically in size and matures in function. During puberty, reproduction becomes possible. Simultaneously, secondary sex characteristics develop. These characteristics are not required for reproduction, but they do signify masculinity and femininity. At birth, boys and girls have similar body shapes, but during puberty, males widen at the shoulders and females widen at the hips and develop breasts (examples of secondary sex characteristics). Sexual development is impacted by a dynamic mixture of physical and cognitive change coupled with social expectations. With physical maturation, adolescents may become alternately fascinated with and chagrined by their changing bodies, and often compare themselves to the development they notice in their peers or see in the media. For example, many adolescent girls focus on their breast development, hoping their breasts will conform to an ideal body image.

As the sex hormones cause biological changes, they also affect the brain and trigger sexual thoughts. Culture, however, shapes actual sexual behaviors. Emotions regarding sexual experience, like the rest of puberty, are strongly influenced by cultural norms regarding what is expected at what age, with peers being the most influential. Simply put, the most important influence on adolescents' sexual activity is not their bodies, but their close friends, who have more influence than do sex or ethnic group norms (van de Bongardt et al., 2015).[15]

Sexual interest and interaction are a natural part of adolescence. Sexual fantasy and **masturbation** episodes increase between the ages of 10 and 13. Masturbation is very ordinary—even young children have been known to engage in this behavior. As

15. van de Bongardt, D., Reitz, E., Sandfort, T. & Dekovic, J (2015). A meta-analysis of the relations between three types of peer norms and adolescent sexual behavior. Personality and Social Psychology Review, 19 (3), 203-234.

the bodies of children mature, powerful sexual feelings begin to develop, and masturbation helps release sexual tension. For adolescents, masturbation is a common way to explore their erotic potential, and this behavior can continue throughout adult life.

Sexual Interactions

Many early social interactions tend to be nonsexual—text messaging, phone calls, email—but by the age of 12 or 13, some young people may pair off and begin dating and experimenting with kissing, touching, and other physical contact, such as oral sex. The vast majority of young adolescents are not prepared emotionally or physically for oral sex and sexual intercourse. If adolescents this young do have sex, they are highly vulnerable for sexual and emotional abuse, **sexually transmitted infections (STIs)**, HIV, and early pregnancy (https://pedsinreview.aappublications.org/content/34/1/29). For STI's in particular, adolescents are slower to recognize symptoms, tell partners, and get medical treatment, which puts them at risk of infertility and even death.

LINK TO LEARNING

Visit the CDC website to learn more about sexual behavior in adolescence.

Adolescents ages 14 to 16 understand the consequences of unprotected sex and teen parenthood, if properly taught, but cognitively they may lack the skills to integrate this knowledge into everyday situations or consistently to act responsibly in the heat of the moment. By the age of 17, many adolescents have willingly experienced sexual intercourse. Teens who have early sexual intercourse report strong peer pressure as a reason behind their decision. Some adolescents are just curious about sex and want to experience it.[16]

Becoming a sexually healthy adult is a developmental task of adolescence that requires integrating psychological, physical, cultural, spiritual, societal, and educational factors. It is particularly important to understand the adolescent in terms of his or her physical, emotional, and cognitive stage. Additionally, healthy adult relationships are more likely to develop when adolescent impulses are not shamed or feared. Guidance is certainly needed, but acknowledging that adolescent sexuality development is both normal and positive would allow for more open communication so adolescents can be more receptive to education concerning the risks (Tolman & McClelland, 2011).[17]

Adolescents are receptive to their culture, to the models they see at home, in school, and in the mass media. These observations influence moral reasoning and moral behavior, which we discuss in more detail later in this module. Decisions regarding sexual behavior are influenced by teens' ability to think and reason, their values, and their educational experience. Helping adolescents recognize all aspects of sexual development encourages them to make informed and healthy decisions about sexual matters.

Freud and Sexual Development

According to Sigmund Freud, adolescents are in the genital stage of psychosexual development. This stage begins around the time that puberty starts, and ends at death. According to Freud, the genital stage is similar to the phallic stage, in that its

16. Adolescent Sexuality Trisha Tulloch, Miriam Kaufman Pediatrics in Review Jan 2013, 34 (1) 29-38; DOI: 10.1542/pir.34-1-29
17. Tolman, D.L. & McClelland, S.I. (2011). Normative sexuality development in adolescence; A decade in review, 2000-2009. Journal of Research on Adolescence, 21 (1), 242-255.

main concern is the genitalia; however, this concern is now conscious. The genital stage comes about when the sexual and aggressive drives have returned, but the source of sexual pleasure expands outside of the mother and father (as in the Oedipus or Electra complex).

During the genital stage the ego and superego have become more developed. This allows the individual to have a more realistic way of thinking and to establish an assortment of social relations apart from the family. The genital stage is the last stage and is considered the highest level of maturity. In this stage a person's concern shifts from primary-drive gratification (instinct) to applying secondary process-thinking to gratify desire symbolically and intellectually by means of friendships, intimate relationships, and family and adult responsibilities.

GLOSSARY

adolescent growth spurt:
rapid increase in the individual's height and weight during puberty resulting from simultaneous release of growth hormones, thyroid hormones, and androgens. Males experience their growth spurt about two years later, on average, than females

adrenarche:
an increase in the production of androgens by the adrenal cortex that usually occurs during the eighth or ninth year of life and typically peaks at around 10 to 14 years of age and is eventually involved in the development of pubic hair, body odor, skin oiliness, and acne

amygdala:
part of the limbic system in the brain, which is involved with emotions and emotional responses and is particularly active during puberty

anorexia nervosa:
an eating disorder characterized by self-starvation. Affected individuals voluntarily undereat and often overexercise, depriving their vital organs of nutrition. Anorexia can be fatal

binge-eating disorder:
an eating disorder characterized by recurrent episodes of eating large quantities of food (often very quickly and to the point of discomfort); a feeling of a loss of control during the binge; experiencing shame, distress or guilt afterwards; and not regularly using unhealthy compensatory measures (e.g., purging) to counter the binge eating. It is the most common eating disorder in the United States

body dissatisfaction:
negative subjective evaluation of the weight and shape of one's own body, which may predict the onset, severity, and treatment outcomes of eating disorders

body image:
a person's idea of how his or her body looks

bulimia nervosa:
an eating disorder characterized by binge eating and subsequent purging, usually by induced vomiting and/or use of laxatives

dopamine:
a neurotransmitter in the brain that plays a role in pleasure and the reward system; increases in the limbic system and later in the prefrontal cortex during adolescence

estrogen:
primary female sex hormone that is responsible for the development and regulation of the female reproductive system and secondary sex characteristics

frontal lobes:
the parts of the brain involved in impulse control, planning, and higher order thinking; still developing in adolescence

gonad:
a sex organ that produces gametes; specifically, a testicle or ovary

gonadarche:
refers to the earliest gonadal changes of puberty. In response to pituitary gonadotropins, the ovaries in girls and the testes in boys begin to grow and increase the production of the sex steroids, especially estradiol and testosterone

limbic system:
structures in the brain (including the amygdala) that involve processing emotional experience and social information and determining rewards and punishments; develops years before the prefrontal cortex

masturbation:
sexual self-stimulation, usually achieved by touching, stroking, or massaging the male or female genitals until this triggers an orgasm

melatonin:
sleep hormone whose levels rise later at night and decrease later in the morning for teens, compared to children and adults

menarche:
a girl's first menstrual period, signaling that she has begun ovulation. Pregnancy is biologically possible, but ovulation and menstruation are often irregular for years after menarche

muscle dysmorphia:
sometimes called "reverse anorexia" this is an obsession with being small and underdeveloped; extreme concern with becoming more muscular

myelination:
insulation of neurons' axons with fatty substance (myelin sheath) that helps speed up the processing of information; myelination starts to increase in the prefrontal cortex during adolescence

primary sex characteristics:
the parts of the body that are directly involved in reproduction, including the vagina, uterus, ovaries, testicles, and penis

prefrontal cortex:
part of the frontal lobes, involved with decision making, cognitive control, and other higher order functions; prefrontal cortex develops further during adolescence

puberty:
the period of rapid growth and sexual development that begins in adolescence

secondary sex characteristics:
physical traits that are not directly involved in reproduction but that indicate sexual maturity, such as a man's beard or a woman's breasts

serotonin:
"calming chemical," a neurotransmitter in the brain involved with the regulation of mood and behavior; serotonin levels increase in the limbic system during adolescence

sexually transmitted infections (STIs):
diseases that are spread by sexual contact, including syphilis, gonorrhea, genital herpes, chlamydia, and HIV/AIDS

spermarche:
a boy's first ejaculation of sperm. Erections can occur as early as infancy, but ejaculation signals sperm production. Spermarche may occur during sleep (nocturnal emission or "wet dream") or via direct stimulation

synaptic pruning:
connections in the brain that are not used much are lost so that other connections can be strengthened; this pruning happens with prefrontal cortex connections in adolescence

testosterone:
the primary male sex hormone that plays a key role in the development of male reproductive tissues such as testes and prostate, as well as promoting secondary sexual characteristics such as increased muscle and bone mass, and the growth of body hair. Females also produce testosterone, but at lower level than males

Cognitive Development in Adolescence

What you'll learn to do: describe changes in cognitive development and moral reasoning during adolescence

Teenagers from Travis Air Force Base, Calif., participate in a scenario-based training called "In Their Shoes," Feb 16, 2017. The training to help participants talk about what dating is like for today's teens and to generate thoughtful discussion what happens in unhealthy relationships. (U.S. Air Force photo/Louis Briscese)

Here we learn about adolescent cognitive development. In adolescence, changes in the brain interact with experience, knowledge, and social demands and produce rapid cognitive growth. The changes in how adolescents think, reason, and understand can be even more dramatic than their obvious physical changes. This stage of cognitive development, termed by Piaget as the formal operational stage, marks a movement from the ability to think and reason logically only about concrete, visible events to an ability to also think logically about abstract concepts.

Adolescents are now able to analyze situations logically in terms of cause and effect and to entertain hypothetical situations and entertain what-if possibilities about the world. This higher-level thinking allows them to think about the future, evaluate alternatives, and set personal goals. Although there are marked individual differences in cognitive development among teens, these new capacities allow adolescents to engage in the kind of introspection and mature decision making that was previously beyond their cognitive capacity.

LEARNING OUTCOMES

- Explain Piaget's theory on formal operational thought
- Describe cognitive abilities and changes during adolescence
- Describe the role of secondary education in adolescent development
- Describe moral development during adolescence

Cognitive Development during Adolescence

Adolescence is a time of rapid cognitive development. Biological changes in brain structure and connectivity in the brain interact with increased experience, knowledge, and changing social demands to produce rapid cognitive growth. These changes generally begin at puberty or shortly thereafter, and some skills continue to develop as an adolescent ages. Development of executive functions, or cognitive skills that enable the control and coordination of thoughts and behavior, are generally associated with the prefrontal cortex area of the brain. The thoughts, ideas, and concepts developed at this period of life greatly influence one's future life and play a major role in character and personality formation.

Figure 1. Adolescents practice their developing abstract and hypothetical thinking skills, coming up with alternative interpretations of information.

Perspectives and Advancements in Adolescent Thinking

There are two perspectives on adolescent thinking: constructivist and information-processing. The ***constructivist perspective***, based on the work of Piaget, takes a quantitative, stage-theory approach. This view hypothesizes that adolescents' cognitive improvement is relatively sudden and drastic. The ***information-processing perspective*** derives from the study of artificial intelligence and explains cognitive development in terms of the growth of specific components of the overall process of thinking.

Improvements in basic thinking abilities generally occur in five areas during adolescence:

- *Attention*. Improvements are seen in **selective attention** (the process by which one focuses on one stimulus while tuning out another), as well as **divided attention** (the ability to pay attention to two or more stimuli at the same time).
- *Memory*. Improvements are seen in working memory and long-term memory.
- *Processing Speed*. Adolescents think more quickly than children. Processing speed improves sharply between age five and middle adolescence, levels off around age 15, and does not appear to change between late adolescence and adulthood.
- *Organization*. Adolescents are more aware of their own thought processes and can use **mnemonic devices** and other strategies to think and remember information more efficiently.
- *Metacognition*. Adolescents can think about thinking itself. This often involves monitoring one's own cognitive activity during the thinking process. **Metacognition** provides the ability to plan ahead, see the future consequences of an action, and provide alternative explanations of events.

Formal Operational Thought

In the last of the Piagetian stages, a child becomes able to reason not only about tangible objects and events, but also about hypothetical or abstract ones. Hence it has the name formal operational stage—the period when the individual can "operate" on "forms" or representations. This allows an individual to think and reason with a wider perspective. This stage of cognitive development, termed by Piaget as **formal operational thought**, marks a movement from an ability to think and reason from concrete visible events to an ability to think hypothetically and entertain what-if possibilities about the world. An individual can solve problems through abstract concepts and utilize hypothetical and deductive reasoning. Adolescents use trial and error to solve problems, and the ability to systematically solve a problem in a logical and methodical way emerges.

WATCH IT

This video explains some of the cognitive development consistent with formal operational thought.

- https://youtu.be/hvq7tq2fx1Y

FORMAL OPERATIONAL THINKING IN THE CLASSROOM

School is a main contributor in guiding students towards formal operational thought. With students at this level, the teacher can pose hypothetical (or contrary-to-fact) problems: "What *if* the world had never discovered oil?" or "What *if* the first European explorers had settled first in California instead of on the East Coast of the United States?" To answer such questions, students must use hypothetical reasoning, meaning that they must manipulate ideas that vary in several ways at once, and do so entirely in their minds.

The hypothetical reasoning that concerned Piaget primarily involved scientific problems. His studies of formal operational thinking therefore often look like problems that middle or high school teachers pose in science classes. In one problem, for example, a young person is presented with a simple pendulum, to which different amounts of weight can be hung (Inhelder & Piaget, 1958). The experimenter asks: "What determines how fast the pendulum swings: the length of the string holding it, the weight attached to it, or the distance that it is pulled to the side?" The young person is not allowed to solve this problem by trial-and-error with the materials themselves, but must reason a way to the solution mentally. To do so systematically, he or she must imagine varying each factor separately, while also imagining the other factors that are held constant. This kind of thinking requires facility at manipulating mental representations of the relevant objects and actions—precisely the skill that defines formal operations.

As you might suspect, students with an ability to think hypothetically have an advantage in many kinds of school work: by definition, they require relatively few "props" to solve problems. In this sense they can in principle be more self-directed than students who rely only on concrete operations—certainly a desirable quality in the opinion of most teachers. Note, though, that formal operational thinking is desirable but not *sufficient* for school success, and that it is far from being the only way that students achieve educational success. Formal thinking skills do not insure that a student is motivated or well-behaved, for example, nor does it guarantee other desirable skills. The fourth stage in Piaget's theory is really about a particular kind of formal thinking, the kind needed to solve scientific problems and devise scientific experiments. Since many people do not normally deal with such problems in the normal course of their lives, it should be no surprise that research finds that many people never achieve or use formal thinking fully or consistently, or that they use it only in selected areas with which they are very familiar (Case & Okomato, 1996). For teachers, the limitations of Piaget's ideas suggest a need for additional theories about development—ones that focus more directly on the social and interpersonal issues of childhood and adolescence.

Hypothetical and abstract thinking

One of the major premises of formal operational thought is the capacity to think of possibility, not just reality. Adolescents' thinking is less bound to concrete events than that of children; they can contemplate possibilities outside the realm of what currently exists. One manifestation of the adolescent's increased facility with thinking about possibilities is the improvement of skill in **deductive reasoning (also called top-down reasoning),** which leads to the development of **hypothetical thinking**. This provides the ability to plan ahead, see the future consequences of an action and to provide alternative explanations of events. It also makes adolescents more skilled debaters, as they can reason against a friend's or parent's assumptions. Adolescents also develop a more sophisticated understanding of probability.

This appearance of more systematic, abstract thinking allows adolescents to comprehend the sorts of higher-order abstract logic inherent in puns, proverbs, metaphors, and analogies. Their increased facility permits them to appreciate the ways in which language can be used to convey multiple messages, such as satire, metaphor, and sarcasm. (Children younger than age nine often cannot comprehend sarcasm at all). This also permits the application of advanced reasoning and logical processes to social and ideological matters such as interpersonal relationships, politics, philosophy, religion, morality, friendship, faith, fairness, and honesty.

Metacognition

Metacognition refers to "thinking about thinking." It is relevant in social cognition as it results in increased introspection, self-consciousness, and intellectualization. Adolescents are much better able to understand that people do not have complete control over their mental activity. Being able to introspect may lead to forms of egocentrism, or self-focus, in adolescence. **Adolescent egocentrism** is a term that David Elkind used to describe the phenomenon of adolescents' inability to distinguish between their perception of what others think about them and what people actually think in reality. Elkind's theory on adolescent egocentrism is drawn from Piaget's theory on cognitive developmental stages, which argues that formal operations enable adolescents to construct imaginary situations and abstract thinking.

Accordingly, adolescents are able to conceptualize their own thoughts and conceive of other people's thoughts. However, Elkind pointed out that adolescents tend to focus mostly on their own perceptions, especially on their behaviors and appearance, because of the "physiological metamorphosis" they experience during this period. This leads to adolescents' belief that other people are as attentive to their behaviors and appearance as they are of themselves. According to Elkind, adolescent egocentrism results in two distinct problems in thinking: the imaginary audience and the personal fable**.** These likely peak at age fifteen, along with self-consciousness in general.

Imaginary audience is a term that Elkind used to describe the phenomenon that an adolescent anticipates the reactions of other people to him/herself in actual or impending social situations. Elkind argued that this kind of anticipation could be explained by the adolescent's preoccupation that others are as admiring or as critical of them as they are of themselves. As a result, an audience is created, as the adolescent believes that they will be the focus of attention.

However, more often than not the audience is imaginary because in actual social situations individuals are not usually the sole focus of public attention. Elkind believed that the construction of imaginary audiences would partially account for a wide variety of typical adolescent behaviors and experiences; and imaginary audiences played a role in the self-consciousness that emerges in early adolescence. However, since the audience is usually the adolescent's own construction, it is privy to his or her own knowledge of him/herself. According to Elkind, the notion of imaginary audience helps to explain why adolescents usually seek privacy and feel reluctant to reveal themselves–it is a reaction to the feeling that one is always on stage and constantly under the critical scrutiny of others.

Elkind also addressed that adolescents have a complex set of beliefs that their own feelings are unique and they are special and immortal. **Personal fable** is the term Elkind created to describe this notion, which is the complement of the construction of imaginary audience. Since an adolescent usually fails to differentiate their own perceptions and those of others, they tend to believe that they are of importance to so many people (the imaginary audiences) that they come to regard their feelings as something special and unique. They may feel that only they have experienced strong and diverse emotions, and therefore others could never understand how they feel. This uniqueness in one's emotional experiences reinforces the adolescent's belief of invincibility, especially to death.

This adolescent belief in personal uniqueness and invincibility becomes an illusion that they can be above some of the rules, disciplines and laws that apply to other people; even consequences such as death (called the **invincibility fable).** This belief that one is invincible removes any impulse to control one's behavior (Lin, 2016).[1] Therefore, adolescents will engage in risky behaviors, such as drinking and driving or unprotected sex, and feel they will not suffer any negative consequences.

Intuitive and Analytic Thinking

Piaget emphasized the sequence of thought throughout four stages. Others suggest that thinking does not develop in sequence, but instead, that advanced logic in adolescence may be influenced by intuition. Cognitive psychologists often refer to intuitive and analytic thought as the **dual-process model**; the notion that humans have two distinct networks for processing information (Kuhn, 2013.)[2] **Intuitive thought** is automatic, unconscious, and fast, and it is more experiential and emotional.

In contrast, **analytic thought** is deliberate, conscious, and rational (logical). While these systems interact, they are distinct (Kuhn, 2013). Intuitive thought is easier, quicker, and more commonly used in everyday life. As discussed in the adolescent brain development section earlier in this module, the discrepancy between the maturation of the limbic system and the prefrontal cortex, may make teens more prone to emotional intuitive thinking than adults. As adolescents develop, they gain in logic/analytic thinking ability and sometimes regress, with social context, education, and experiences becoming major influences. Simply put, being "smarter" as measured by an intelligence test does not advance cognition as much as having more experience, in school and in life (Klaczynski & Felmban, 2014).[3]

Risk-taking

Because most injuries sustained by adolescents are related to risky behavior (alcohol consumption and drug use, reckless or distracted driving, and unprotected sex), a great deal of research has been done on the cognitive and emotional processes underlying adolescent risk-taking. In addressing this question, it is important to distinguish whether adolescents are more likely to engage in risky behaviors (prevalence), whether they make risk-related decisions similarly or differently than adults (cognitive processing perspective), or whether they use the same processes but value different things and thus arrive at different conclusions. The **behavioral decision-making theory** proposes that adolescents and adults both weigh the potential rewards and consequences of an action. However, research has shown that adolescents seem to give more weight to rewards, particularly social rewards, than do adults. Adolescents value social warmth and friendship, and their hormones and brains are more attuned to those values than to long-term consequences (Crone & Dahl, 2012).[4]

1. Linn, P. (2016). Risky behaviors: Integrating adolescent egocentrism with the theory of planned behavior. Review of General Psychology, 20 (4), 392-398.
2. Kuhn, D. (2013). Reasoning. In Philip D. Zelazo (Ed.), The Oxford handbook of developmental psychology (Vol. 1, pp. 744-764). New York: NY: Oxford University Press.
3. Klaczynski, P.A. & Felmban, W.S. (2014). Heuristics and biases during adolescence: Developmental reversals and individual differences. In Henry Markovitz (Ed.), The developmental psychology of reasoning and decision making (pp. 84-111). New York, NY: Psychology Press.
4. Crone, E.A., & Dahl, R.E. (2012). Understanding adolescence as a period of social-affective engagement and goal flexibility. Nature Reviews Neuroscience, 13 (9), 636-650.

Some have argued that there may be evolutionary benefits to an increased propensity for risk-taking in adolescence. For example, without a willingness to take risks, teenagers would not have the motivation or confidence necessary to leave their family of origin. In addition, from a population perspective, there is an advantage to having a group of individuals willing to take more risks and try new methods, counterbalancing the more conservative elements more typical of the received knowledge held by older adults.

Figure 2. Teenage thinking is characterized by the ability to reason logically and solve hypothetical problems such as how to design, plan, and build a structure. (credit: U.S. Army RDECOM)

Relativistic Thinking

Adolescents are more likely to engage in **relativistic thinking**—in other words, they are more likely to question others' assertions and less likely to accept information as absolute truth. Through experience outside the family circle, they learn that rules they were taught as absolute are actually relativistic. They begin to differentiate between rules crafted from common sense (don't touch a hot stove) and those that are based on culturally relative standards (codes of etiquette). This can lead to a period of questioning authority in all domains.

As we continue through this module, we will discuss how this influences moral reasoning, as well as psychosocial and emotional development. These more abstract developmental dimensions (cognitive, moral, emotional, and social dimensions) are not only more subtle and difficult to measure, but these developmental areas are also difficult to tease apart from one another due to the inter-relationships among them. For instance, our cognitive maturity will influence the way we understand a particular event or circumstance, which will in turn influence our moral judgments about it, and our emotional responses to it. Similarly, our moral code and emotional maturity influence the quality of our social relationships with others.

School During Adolescence

Secondary Education

Adolescents spend more waking time in school than in any other context (Eccles & Roeser, 2011). **Secondary education** is traditionally grades 7-12 and denotes the school years after elementary school (known as primary education) and before college or university (known as tertiary education). Adolescents who complete primary education (learning to read and write) and continue on through secondary and tertiary education tend to also have better health, wealth, and family life (Rieff, 1998).[5] Because the average age of puberty has declined over the years, **middle schools** were created for grades 5 or 6 through 8 as a way to distinguish between early adolescence and late adolescence, especially because these adolescents different biologically, cognitively and emotionally and definitely have different needs.

Transition to middle school is stressful and the transition is often complex. When students transition from elementary to middle school, many students are undergoing physical, intellectual, social, emotional, and moral changes (Parker, 2013).[6] Research suggests that early adolescence is an especially sensitive developmental period (McGill et al., 2012).[7] Some students mature faster than others. Students who are developmentally behind typically experience more stress than their counterparts (U.S.

5. Rieff, M.I. (1998). Adolescent school failure: Failure to thrive in adolescence. Pediatrics in Review, 19 (6).
6. Parker, A. K. (2013). Understanding and supporting young adolescents during the transition into middle school. In P. G. Andrews (Ed.), Research to guide practice in middle grades education (pp. 495-510). Westerville, OH: Association for Middle Level Education.
7. McGill, R.K., Hughes, D., Alicea, S., & Way, N. (2012). Academic adjustment across middle school: The role of public regard and parenting. Developmental Psychology, 48 (4), 1003-1008.

Department of Education, 2008).[8] Consequently, they may earn lower grades and display decreased academic motivation, which may increase the rate of dropping out of school (U.S. Department of Education, 2008). For many middle school students, academic achievement slows down and behavioral problems can increase.

Specific Middle School Issues

Regardless of a student's gender or ethnicity, middle school is challenging. Although young adolescents seem to desire independence, they also need protection, security, and structure (Brighton, 2007).[9] Baly, Cornell, & Lovegrove (2014) found that bullying increases in middle school, particularly in the first year.[10] Additionally, unlike elementary school, concerns arise regarding procedural changes. Just when egocentrism is at it's height, students are worried about being thrown into an environment of independence and responsibility. They are expected to get to and from classes on their own, manage time wisely, organize and keep up with materials for multiple classes, be responsible for all classwork and homework from multiple teachers, and at the same time develop and maintain a social life (Meece & Eccles, 2010).[11] Students are trying to build new friendships and maintain ones they already have. As noted throughout this module, peer acceptance is particularly important.

Another aspect to consider is technology. Typically, adolescents get their first cell phone at about age 11 and, simultaneously, they are also expected to research items on the Internet. Social media use and texting increase dramatically and the research finds both harm and benefits to this use (Coyne et al., 2018).[12]

TEENS, TECHNOLOGY, AND BULLYING

Bullying is unwanted, aggressive behavior among school aged children that involves a real or perceived power imbalance. The behavior is repeated, or has the potential to be repeated, over time. Both kids who are bullied and who bully others may have serious, lasting problems. It is a prevalent problem during the middle and high school years, exacerbated by access to technology and the means to easily spread damaging information online. These are some key statistics about bullying from StopBullying.gov:

- ***Been Bullied***
  - The 2017 School Crime Supplement (National Center for Education Statistics and Bureau of Justice) indicates that, nationwide, about 20% of students ages 12-18 experienced bullying.
  - The 2017 Youth Risk Behavior Surveillance System (Centers for Disease Control and Prevention) indicates that, nationwide, 19% of students in grades 9–12 report being bullied on school property in the 12 months preceding the survey.

8. U.S. Department of Education Mentoring Resource Center (2008). Making the transition to middle school: How mentoring can help. MRC: Mentoring Resource Center Fact Sheet, No. 24. Retrieved from http://fbmentorcenter.squarespace.com/storage/MiddleSchoolTransition.pdf
9. Brighton, K. L. (2007). Coming of age: The education and development of young adolescents. Westerville, OH: National Middle School Association.
10. Baly, M.W., Cornell, D.G., & Lovegrove, P. (2014). A longitudinal investigation of self and peer reports of bullying victimization across middle school. Psychology in the Schools, 51 (3), 217-240.
11. Meece, J.L. & Eccles, J.S. (Eds.). (2010). Handbook on research on schools, schooling, and human development. New York, NY: Routledge.
12. Coyne, S.M., Padilla-Walker, L.M., & Holmgren, H.G. (2018). A six-year longitudinal study of texting trajectories during adolescence. Child Development, 89 (1), 58-65.

- ***Bullied Others***
    - Approximately 30% of young people admit to bullying others in surveys.
- ***Seen Bullying***
    - 70.6% of young people say they have seen bullying in their schools.
    - 70.4% of school staff have seen bullying. 62% witnessed bullying two or more times in the last month and 41% witness bullying once a week or more.
    - When bystanders intervene, bullying stops within 10 seconds 57% of the time.
- ***Been Cyberbullied***
    - The 2017 School Crime Supplement (National Center for Education Statistics and Bureau of Justice) indicates that, among students ages 12-18 who reported being bullied at school during the school year, 15% were bullied online or by text.
    - The 2017 Youth Risk Behavior Surveillance System (Centers for Disease Control and Prevention) indicates that an estimated 14.9% of high school students were electronically bullied in the 12 months prior to the survey.
    - Pew Center Research reports a much higher number, stating that 59% of teens have experienced cyberbullying.

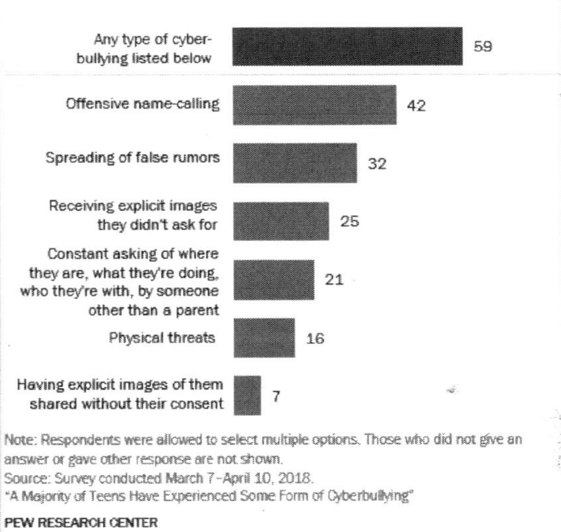

Figure 3. Cyberbullying comes in many forms.

- ***How Often Bullied***
    - In one large study, about 49% of children in
    - grades 4–12 reported being bullied by other students at school at least once during the past month, whereas 30.8% reported bullying others during that time.
    - Defining "frequent" involvement in bullying as occurring two or more times within the past month, 40.6% of students reported some type of frequent involvement in bullying, with 23.2% being the youth frequently bullied, 8.0% being the youth who frequently bullied others, and 9.4% playing both roles frequently.
- ***Types of Bullying***
    - The most common types of bullying are verbal and social. Physical bullying happens less often. Cyberbullying happens the least frequently.
    - According to one large study, the following percentages of middle schools students had experienced these various types of bullying: name calling (44.2 %); teasing (43.3 %); spreading rumors or lies (36.3%); pushing or shoving (32.4%); hitting, slapping, or kicking (29.2%); leaving out (28.5%); threatening (27.4%); stealing belongings (27.3%); sexual comments or gestures (23.7%); e-mail or blogging (9.9%).

- ***Where Bullying Occurs***
    - Most bullying takes place in school, outside on school grounds, and on the school bus. Bullying also happens wherever kids gather in the community. And of course, cyberbullying occurs on cell phones and online.
    - According to one large study, the following percentages of middle schools students had experienced bullying in these various places at school: classroom (29.3%); hallway or lockers (29.0%); cafeteria (23.4%); gym or PE class (19.5%); bathroom (12.2%); playground or recess (6.2%).[3]

Many organizations, schools, teachers, parents, and lawmakers are working to address the issue of bullying. One example is that of ReThink, a technology designed by teenager Trisha Prabhu to recognize bullying online and encourage posters to reconsider their behavior (watch Trisha Prabhu's TED talk)

High School

As adolescents enter into high school, their continued cognitive development allows them to think abstractly, analytically, hypothetically, and logically, which is all formal operational thought. High school emphasizes formal thinking in attempt to prepare graduates for college where analysis is required. Overall, high school graduation rates in the United States have increased steadily over the past decade, reaching 83.2 percent in 2016 after four years in high school (Gewertz, 2017).[13] Additionally, many students in the United States do attend college. Unfortunately, though, about half of those who go to college leave without a degree (Kena et al., 2016).[14] Those that do earn a degree, however, do make more money and have an easier time finding employment. The key here is understanding adolescent development and supporting teens in making decisions about college or alternatives to college after high school.

LINK TO LEARNING

What do you think, is college necessary? Is it worth the investment? Read the article "Is College Necessary?" from Psychology Today geared towards parents who can help their teenager decide if college is right for them.

Academic Achievement

Academic achievement during adolescence is predicted by interpersonal (e.g., parental engagement in adolescents' education), intrapersonal (e.g., intrinsic motivation), and institutional (e.g., school quality) factors. Academic achievement is important in its own right as a marker of positive adjustment during adolescence but also because academic achievement sets the stage for future educational and occupational opportunities. The most serious consequence of school failure, particularly dropping out of school, is the high risk of unemployment or underemployment in adulthood that follows. High achievement can set the stage for college or future vocational training and opportunities.

13. Gewertz, C. (2017, May 3). Is the high school graduation rate inflated? No, study says (Web log post). Education Week.
14. Kena, G., Hussar, W., McFarland, J., de Brey, C., Musu-Gillette, L., Wang, X., & Dunlop Velez, E. (2016). The condition of education 2016, Washington, DC: U.S. Department of Education, National Center for Education Statistics.

Moral Reasoning During Adolescence

Moral Reasoning in Adolescence

As adolescents become increasingly independent, they also develop more nuanced thinking about morality, or what is right or wrong. We all make moral judgments on a daily basis. As adolescents' cognitive, emotional, and social development continue to mature, their understanding of morality expands and their behavior becomes more closely aligned with their values and beliefs. Therefore, moral development describes the evolution of these guiding principles and is demonstrated by the ability to apply these guidelines in daily life. Understanding moral development is important in this stage where individuals make so many important decisions and gain more and more legal responsibility.

Figure 4. Adolescents' moral development gets put to the test in real life situations, often along with peer pressure to behave or not behave in particular ways.

If you recall from the module on Middle Childhood, Lawrence Kohlberg (1984) argued that moral development moves through a series of stages, and reasoning about morality becomes increasingly complex (somewhat in line with increasing cognitive skills, as per Piaget's stages of cognitive development). As children develop intellectually, they pass through three stages of moral thinking: the *preconventional level*, the *conventional level*, and the *postconventional level*. In middle childhood into early adolescence, the child begins to care about how situational outcomes impact others and wants to please and be accepted (conventional morality). At this developmental phase, people are able to value the good that can be derived from holding to social norms in the form of laws or less formalized rules. From adolescence and beyond, adolescents begin to employ abstract reasoning to justify behaviors. Moral behavior is based on self-chosen ethical principles that are generally comprehensive and universal, such as justice, dignity, and equality, which is postconventional morality.

Influences on Moral Development

Adolescents are receptive to their culture, to the models they see at home, in school and in the mass media. These observations influence moral reasoning and moral behavior. When children are younger, their family, culture, and religion greatly influence their moral decision-making. During the early adolescent period, peers have a much greater influence. Peer pressure can exert a powerful influence because friends play a more significant role in teens' lives. Furthermore, the new ability to think abstractly enables youth to recognize that rules are simply created by other people. As a result, teens begin to question the absolute authority of parents, schools, government, and other traditional institutions (Vera-Estay, Dooley, & Beauchamp, 2014)[15] By late adolescence, most teens are less rebellious as they have begun to establish their own identity, their own belief system, and their own place in the world.

Unfortunately, some adolescents have life experiences that may interfere with their moral development. Traumatic experiences may cause them to view the world as unjust and unfair. Additionally, social learning also impacts moral development. Adolescents may have observed the adults in their lives making immoral decisions that disregarded the rights and welfare of others, leading these youth to develop beliefs and values that are contrary to the rest of society. That being said, adults have opportunities to support moral development by modeling the moral character that we want to see in our children. Parents

15. Vera-Estay,E. Dooley, J.J. & Beauchamp, M.H. (2014). Cognitive underpinnings of moral reasoning in adolescence: The contribution of executive functions. Journal of Moral Education, 44 (1), 17-33.

are particularly important because they are generally the original source of moral guidance. Authoritative parenting facilitates children's moral growth better than other parenting styles and one of the most influential things a parent can do is to encourage the right kind of peer relations.[16] While parents may find this process of moral development difficult or challenging, it is important to remember that this developmental step is essential to their children's well-being and ultimate success in life.

LINK TO LEARNING

Parenting has the largest impact on adolescent moral development. Read more here in this article, "Building Character: Moral Development in Adolescence" from the Center for Parent and Teen Communication.

GLOSSARY

adolescent egocentrism:
a characteristic of adolescent thinking that leads young people (ages 10-13) to focus on themselves to the exclusion of others (according to David Elkind)

analytic thought:
thought that results from analysis, such as a systematic ranking of pros and cons, risks and consequences, possibilities and facts. Analytic thought depends on logic and rationality

behavioral decision-making theory:
proposes that adolescents and adults both weigh the potential rewards and consequences of an action. However, research has shown that adolescents seem to give more weight to rewards, particularly social rewards, than do adults

constructivist perspective:
based on the work of Piaget, a quantitative, stage-theory approach. This view hypothesizes that adolescents' cognitive improvement is relatively sudden and drastic, as adolescents learn by acting on their environment and they actively construct knowledge

deductive reasoning:
reasoning from a general statement, premise, or principle, though logical steps to figure out (deduce) specifics. Also called top-down processing

divided attention:
the ability to pay attention to two or more stimuli at the same time; this ability improves during adolescence

dual process model/dual processing:
the notion that two networks exist within the human brain, one for emotional processing of stimuli and one for analytic reasoning

16. McDevitt, T.M. & Ormrod, J.E. (2004). Child development: Educating and working with children and adolescents. Upper Saddle River, NJ: Pearson Prentice Hall.

formal operational thought:
the fourth and final stage of Piaget's theory of cognitive development, characterized by more systematic logical thinking and by the ability to understand and systematically manipulate abstract concepts

hypothetical thought:
reasoning that includes propositions and possibilities that may not reflect reality

imaginary audience:
the other people who, in an adolescent's egocentric belief, are watching and taking note of his or her appearance, ideas, and behavior. This belief makes many adolescents very self-conscious

information-processing perspective:
derives from the study of artificial intelligence and explains cognitive development in terms of the growth of specific components of the overall process of thinking

intuitive thought:
thoughts that arise from an emotion or a hunch, beyond rational explanation, and are influenced by past experiences and cultural assumptions

invincibility fable:
an adolescent's egocentric conviction that he or she cannot be overcome or even harmed by anything that might defeat a normal mortal, such as unprotected sex, drug abuse, or high-speed driving

metacognition:
refers to "thinking about thinking" and it is relevant in social cognition and results in increased introspection, self-consciousness, and intellectualization during adolescence

middle school:
a school for children in the grades between elementary school and high school. Middle school usually begins with grade 6 and ends with grade 8

mnemonic devices:
mental strategies to help learn and remember information more efficiently; improves during adolescence

personal fable:
an aspect of adolescent egocentrism characterized by an adolescent's belief that his or her thoughts, feelings, and experiences are unique, more wonderful, or more awful than anyone else's

relativistic thinking:
thinking that understands the relative or situational nature of circumstances

secondary education:
the period after primary education (elementary or grade school) and before tertiary education (college). It usually occurs from about ages 12 to 18, although there is some variation by school and by nation

selective attention:
the process by which one focuses on one stimulus while tuning out another; this ability improves during adolescence

Emotional and Social Development in Adolescence

What you'll learn to do: describe adolescent identity development and social influences on development

Adolescence is a period of personal and social identity formation, in which different roles, behaviors, and ideologies are explored. In the United States, adolescence is seen as a time to develop independence from parents while remaining connected to them. Some key points related to social development during adolescence include the following:

- Adolescence is the period of life known for the formation of personal and social identity.
- Adolescents must explore, test limits, become autonomous, and commit to an identity, or sense of self.
- Erik Erikson referred to the task of the adolescent as one of identity versus role confusion. Thus, in Erikson's view, an adolescent's main questions are "Who am I?" and "Who do I want to be?"
- Early in adolescence, cognitive developments result in greater self-awareness, the ability to think about abstract, future possibilities, and the ability to consider multiple possibilities and identities at once.
- Changes in the levels of certain neurotransmitters (such as dopamine and serotonin) influence the way in which adolescents experience emotions, typically making them more emotional and more sensitive to stress.
- When adolescents have advanced cognitive development and maturity, they tend to resolve identity issues more easily than peers who are less cognitively developed.
- As adolescents work to form their identities, they pull away from their parents, and the peer group becomes very important; despite this, relationships with parents still play a significant role in identity formation.

LEARNING OUTCOMES

- Describe changes in self-concept and identity development during adolescence
- Explain Marcia's four identity statuses
- Examine changes in family relationships during adolescence
- Describe adolescent friendships and dating relationships as they apply to development
- Explain the role that aggression, anxiety, and depression play in adolescent development

Identity Formation

Psychosocial Development

Identity Development

Identity development is a stage in the adolescent life cycle. For most, the search for identity begins in the adolescent years. During these years, adolescents are more open to 'trying on' different behaviors and appearances to discover who they are. In an attempt to find their identity and discover who they are, adolescents are likely to cycle through a number of identities to find one that suits them best. Developing and maintaining identity (in adolescent years) is a difficult task due to multiple factors such as family life, environment, and social status. Empirical studies suggest that this process might be more accurately described as identity development, rather than formation, but confirms a normative process of change in both content and structure of one's thoughts about the self.

Figure 1. Adolescents simultaneously struggle to fit in with their peers and to form their own unique identities.

Self-Concept

Two main aspects of identity development are self-concept and self-esteem. The idea of **self-concept** is known as the ability of a person to have opinions and beliefs that are defined confidently, consistently and with stability. Early in adolescence, cognitive developments result in greater self-awareness, greater awareness of others and their thoughts and judgments, the ability to think about abstract, future possibilities, and the ability to consider multiple possibilities at once. As a result, adolescents experience a significant shift from the simple, concrete, and global self-descriptions typical of young children; as children they defined themselves by physical traits whereas adolescents define themselves based on their values, thoughts, and opinions.

Adolescents can conceptualize multiple "possible selves" that they could become and long-term possibilities and consequences of their choices. Exploring these possibilities may result in abrupt changes in self-presentation as the adolescent chooses or rejects qualities and behaviors, trying to guide the actual self toward the ideal self (who the adolescent wishes to be) and away from the feared self (who the adolescent does not want to be). For many, these distinctions are uncomfortable, but they also appear to motivate achievement through behavior consistent with the ideal and distinct from the feared possible selves.

Further distinctions in self-concept, called "differentiation," occur as the adolescent recognizes the contextual influences on their own behavior and the perceptions of others, and begin to qualify their traits when asked to describe themselves. Differentiation appears fully developed by mid-adolescence. Peaking in the 7th-9th grades, the personality traits adolescents use to describe themselves refer to specific contexts, and therefore may contradict one another. The recognition of inconsistent content in the self-concept is a common source of distress in these years, but this distress may benefit adolescents by encouraging structural development.

Self-Esteem

Another aspect of identity formation is self-esteem. **Self-esteem** is defined as one's thoughts and feelings about one's self-concept and identity. Most theories on self-esteem state that there is a grand desire, across all genders and ages, to maintain, protect and enhance their self-esteem. Contrary to popular belief, there is no empirical evidence for a significant drop in self-esteem over the course of adolescence. "Barometric self-esteem" fluctuates rapidly and can cause severe distress and anxiety, but baseline self-esteem remains highly stable across adolescence. The validity of global self-esteem scales has been questioned, and many suggest that more specific scales might reveal more about the adolescent experience. Girls are most likely to enjoy high self-esteem when engaged in supportive relationships with friends, the most important function of friendship to them is having someone who can provide social and moral support. When they fail to win friends' approval or can't find someone with whom to share common activities and common interests, in these cases, girls suffer from low self-esteem.

In contrast, boys are more concerned with establishing and asserting their independence and defining their relation to authority. As such, they are more likely to derive high self-esteem from their ability to successfully influence their friends; on the other hand, the lack of romantic competence, for example, failure to win or maintain the affection of the opposite or same-sex (depending on sexual orientation), is the major contributor to low self-esteem in adolescent boys.

Identity Formation: Who am I?

Adolescents continue to refine their sense of self as they relate to others. Erik Erikson referred to life's fifth psychosocial task as one of **identity versus role confusion** when adolescents must work through the complexities of finding one's own identity. Individuals are influenced by how they resolved all of the previous childhood psychosocial crises and this adolescent stage is a bridge between the past and the future, between childhood and adulthood. Thus, in Erikson's view, an adolescent's main questions are "Who am I?" and "Who do I want to be?" Identity formation was highlighted as the primary indicator of successful development during adolescence (in contrast to role confusion, which would be an indicator of not successfully meeting the task of adolescence). This crisis is resolved positively with **identity achievement** and the gain of fidelity (ability to be faithful) as a new virtue, when adolescents have reconsidered the goals and values of their parents and culture. Some adolescents adopt the values and roles that their parents expect for them. Other teens develop identities that are in opposition to their parents but align with a peer group. This is common as peer relationships become a central focus in adolescents' lives.

Expanding on Erikson's theory, Marcia (1966)[1]) described identify formation during adolescence as involving both decision points and commitments with respect to ideologies (e.g., religion, politics) and occupations. **Foreclosure** occurs when an individual commits to an identity without exploring options. **Identity confusion/diffusion** occurs when adolescents neither explore nor commit to any identities. **Moratorium** is a state in which adolescents are actively exploring options but have not yet made commitments. As mentioned earlier, individuals who have explored different options, discovered their purpose, and have made identity commitments are in a state of **identity achievement.**

Developmental psychologists have researched several different areas of identity development and some of the main areas include:

1. Marcia, J. E. (1966). Development and validation of ego identity status. Journal of Personality and Social Psychology, 3, 551–558.

- **Religious identity**: The religious views of teens are often similar to those of their families (Kim-Spoon, Longo, & McCullough, 2012) [2] Most teens may question specific customs, practices, or ideas in the faith of their parents, but few completely reject the religion of their families.
- **Political identity**: An adolescent's political identity is also influenced by their parents' political beliefs. A new trend in the 21st century is a decrease in party affiliation among adults. Many adults do not align themselves with either the democratic or republican party and their teenage children reflect their parents' lack of party affiliation. Although adolescents do tend to be more liberal than their elders, especially on social issues (Taylor, 2014) [3], like other aspects of identity formation, adolescents' interest in politics is predicted by their parents' involvement and by current events (Stattin et al., 2017). [4]
- **Vocational identity:** While adolescents in earlier generations envisioned themselves as working in a particular job, and often worked as an apprentice or part-time in such occupations as teenagers, this is rarely the case today. Vocational identity takes longer to develop, as most of today's occupations require specific skills and knowledge that will require additional education or are acquired on the job itself. In addition, many of the jobs held by teens are not in occupations that most teens will seek as adults.
- **Ethnic identity:** Ethnic identity refers to how people come to terms with who they are based on their ethnic or racial ancestry. According to the U.S. Census (2012) more than 40% of Americans under the age of 18 are from ethnic minorities. For many ethnic minority teens, discovering one's ethnic identity is an important part of identity formation. Phinney (1989)[5] proposed a model of ethnic identity development that included stages of unexplored ethnic identity, ethnic identity search, and achieved ethnic identity.

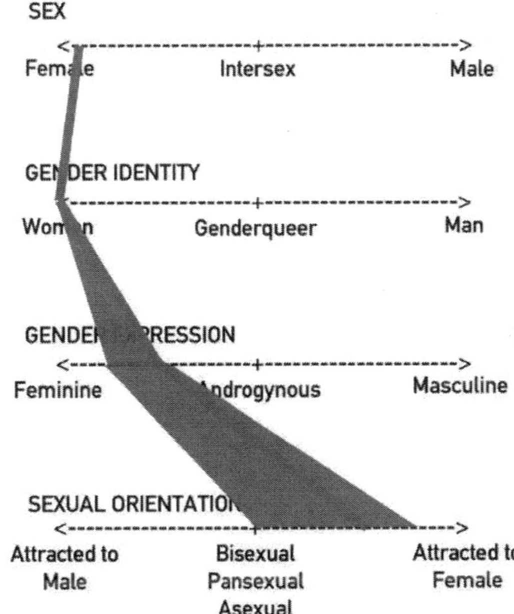

Figure 2. This identity spectrum shows the fluidity between sex, gender identity, gender expression, and sexual orientation.

- **Gender identity:** A person's sex, as determined by his or her biology, does not always correspond with his or her gender. **Sex** refers to the biological differences between males and females, such as the genitalia and genetic differences. **Gender** refers to the socially constructed characteristics of women and men, such as norms, roles, and relationships between groups of women and men. Many adolescents use their analytic, hypothetical thinking to question traditional gender roles and expression. If their genetically assigned sex does not line up with their gender identity, they may refer to themselves as transgender, non-binary, or gender-nonconforming.
    - **Gender identity** refers to a person's self-perception as male, female, both, genderqueer, or neither. **Cisgender** is an umbrella term used to describe people whose sense of personal identity and gender corresponds with their birth sex, while **transgender** is a term used to describe people whose sense of personal identity does not correspond with their

2. Kim-Spoon, J., Longo, G.S., & McCullough, M.E. (2012) Parent-adolescent relationship quality as a moderator for the influence of parents' religiousness on adolescents' religiousness and adjustment. Journal of Youth and Adolescence, 41(12), 1576-1587.
3. Taylor, P. (2014). The next America: Boomers, millennials, and the looming generational showdown. New York, NY: Public Affairs.
4. Stattin, H., Hussein, O., Ozdemir, M., & Russo, S. (2017). Why do some adolescents encounter everyday events that increase their civil interest whereas others do not? Developmental Psychology, 53 (2), 306-318.
5. Phinney, J. (1989). Stages of ethnic identity in minority group adolescents. Journal of Early Adolescence, 9, 34–49.

birth sex. **Gender expression**, or how one demonstrates gender (based on traditional gender role norms related to clothing, behavior, and interactions) can be feminine, masculine, androgynous, or somewhere along a spectrum.

- Fluidity and uncertainty regarding sex and gender are especially common during early adolescence, when hormones increase and fluctuate creating difficulty of self-acceptance and identity achievement (Reisner et al., 2016).[6] Gender identity, like vocational identity, is becoming an increasingly prolonged task as attitudes and norms regarding gender keep changing. The roles appropriate for males and females are evolving and some adolescents may foreclose on a gender identity as a way of dealing with this uncertainty by adopting more stereotypic male or female roles (Sinclair & Carlsson, 2013)[7]. Those that identify as transgender or other face even bigger challenges.

WATCH IT

This video takes a deeper look at Marcia's theory of identity development and relates the four identity statuses to college students figuring out their major.

- https://youtu.be/-JrZwmHU9xE

GENDER IDENTITY AND TRANSGENDER INDIVIDUALS

Individuals who identify with the role that is different from their biological sex are called transgender. Approximately 1.4 million U.S. adults or .6 percent of the population are transgender according to a 2016 report.[8]

Transgender individuals may choose to alter their bodies through medical interventions such as surgery and hormonal therapy so that their physical being is better aligned with gender identity. They may also be known as male-to-female (MTF) or female-to-male (FTM). Not all transgender individuals choose to alter their bodies; many will maintain their original anatomy but may present themselves to society as another gender. This is typically done by adopting the dress, hairstyle, mannerisms, or other characteristic typically assigned to another gender. It is important to note that people who cross-dress, or wear clothing that is traditionally assigned to a different gender is not the same as identifying as trans. Cross-dressing is typically a form of self-expression, entertainment, or personal style, and it is not necessarily an expression against one's assigned gender (APA 2008).

After years of controversy over the treatment of sex and gender in the *American Psychiatric Association Diagnostic and Statistical Manual for Mental Disorders* (Drescher 2010), the most recent edition, DSM-5, responds to allegations that the term "gender identity disorder" is stigmatizing by replacing it with "**gender dysphoria**." Gender identity disorder as a diagnostic category stigmatized the patient by implying there was something "disordered" about them. Gender dysphoria, on the other hand, removes some of that stigma by taking the word "disorder" out while maintaining a

6. Reisner, S.L., Katz-Wise, S.L., Gordon, A.R., Corliss, H.L., & Austin, S.B. (2016). Social epidemiology of depression and anxiety by gender identity. Journal of Adolescent Health, 59 (2), 203-208.
7. Sinclair, S. & Carlsson, R. (2013). What will I be when I grow up? The impact of gender identity threat on adolescents' occupational preferences. Journal of Adolescence, 36(3), 465-474.
8. Flores, A., J. Herman, G. Gates, and T. N.T. Brown. "How many adults identify as transgender." The Williams Institute. http://williamsinstitute.law.ucla.edu/wp-content/uploads/How-Many-Adults-Identify-as-Transgender-in-the-United-States.pdf.

category that will protect patient access to care, including hormone therapy and gender reassignment surgery. In the DSM-5, gender dysphoria is a condition of people whose gender at birth is contrary to the one they identify with. For a person to be diagnosed with gender dysphoria, there must be a marked difference between the individual's expressed/experienced gender and the gender others would assign him or her, and it must continue for at least six months. In children, the desire to be of the other gender must be present and verbalized (APA 2013).

Changing the clinical description may contribute to a larger acceptance of transgender people in society. A 2017 poll showed that 54 percent of Americans believe gender is determined by sex at birth and 32 percent say society has "gone too far" in accepting transgender people; views are sharply divided along political and religions lines.[9]

Studies show that people who identify as transgender are twice as likely to experience assault or discrimination as nontransgender individuals; they are also one and a half times more likely to experience intimidation (National Coalition of Anti-Violence Programs 2010; Giovanniello 2013). Trans women of color are most likely be to victims of abuse. A practice called "deadnaming" by the American Civil Liberties Union, whereby trans people who are murdered are referred to by their birth name and gender, is a discriminatory tool that effectively erases a person's trans identity and also prevents investigations into their deaths and knowledge of their deaths.[10] Organizations such as the National Coalition of Anti-Violence Programs and Global Action for Trans Equality work to prevent, respond to, and end all types of violence against transgender and homosexual individuals. These organizations hope that by educating the public about gender identity and empowering transgender individuals, this violence will end.

Social Development during Adolescence

Parents

It appears that most teens do not experience adolescent "storm and stress" to the degree once famously suggested by G. Stanley Hall, a pioneer in the study of adolescent development. Only small numbers of teens have major conflicts with their parents (Steinberg & Morris, 2001), and most disagreements are minor. For example, in a study of over 1,800 parents of adolescents from various cultural and ethnic groups, Barber (1994) found that conflicts occurred over day-to-day issues such as homework, money, curfews, clothing, chores, and friends. These disputes occur because an adolescent's drive for independence and autonomy conflicts with the parent's supervision and control. These types of arguments tend to decrease as teens develop (Galambos & Almeida, 1992).

As adolescents work to form their identities, they pull away from their parents, and the peer group becomes very important (Shanahan, McHale, Osgood, & Crouter, 2007). Despite spending less time with their parents, most teens report positive feelings toward them (Moore, Guzman, Hair, Lippman, & Garrett, 2004). Warm and healthy parent-child relationships have been associated with positive child outcomes, such as better grades and fewer school behavior problems, in the United States as well as in other countries (Hair et al., 2005).

Although peers take on greater importance during adolescence, family relationships remain important too. One of the key changes during adolescence involves a renegotiation of parent–child relationships. As adolescents strive for more independence and autonomy during this time, different aspects of parenting become more salient. For example, parents' distal supervision and monitoring become more important as adolescents spend more time away from parents and in the

9. Salam, M. "For transgender Americans, the political gets even more personal" (2018). The New York Times. https://www.nytimes.com/2018/10/26/us/transgender-lgbt-rights-trump.html.
10. Strangio, C. 2018. "Deadly violence against transgender people." ACLU. https://www.aclu.org/blog/lgbt-rights/criminal-justice-reform-lgbt-people/deadly-violence-against-transgender-people-rise.

presence of peers. Parental monitoring encompasses a wide range of behaviors such as parents' attempts to set rules and know their adolescents' friends, activities, and whereabouts, in addition to adolescents' willingness to disclose information to their parents. (Stattin & Kerr, 2000)[11] Psychological control, which involves manipulation and intrusion into adolescents' emotional and cognitive world through invalidating adolescents' feelings and pressuring them to think in particular ways is another aspect of parenting that becomes more salient during adolescence and is related to more problematic adolescent adjustment.[12]

Peers

As children become adolescents, they usually begin spending more time with their peers and less time with their families, and these peer interactions are increasingly unsupervised by adults. Children's notions of friendship often focus on shared activities, whereas adolescents' notions of friendship increasingly focus on intimate exchanges of thoughts and feelings.

Figure 3. Crowds refer to different collections of people, like the "theater kids" or the "environmentalists." In a way, they are kind of like clothing brands that label the people associated with that crowd. [Image: Garry Knight]

During adolescence, peer groups evolve from primarily single-sex to mixed-sex. Adolescents within a peer group tend to be similar to one another in behavior and attitudes, which has been explained as being a function of **homophily** (adolescents who are similar to one another choose to spend time together in a "birds of a feather flock together" way) and influence (adolescents who spend time together shape each other's behavior and attitudes). **Peer pressure** is usually depicted as peers pushing a teenager to do something that adults disapprove of, such as breaking laws or using drugs. One of the most widely studied aspects of adolescent peer influence is known as **deviant peer contagion** (Dishion & Tipsord, 2011)[13], which is the process by which peers reinforce problem behavior by laughing or showing other signs of approval that then increase the likelihood of future problem behavior. Although deviant peer contagion is more extreme, regular peer pressure is not always harmful. Peers can serve both positive and negative functions during adolescence. Negative peer pressure can lead adolescents to make riskier decisions or engage in more problematic behavior than they would alone or in the presence of their family. For example, adolescents are much more likely to drink alcohol, use drugs, and commit crimes when they are with their friends than when they are alone or with their family. However, peers also serve as an important source of social support and companionship during adolescence, and adolescents with positive peer relationships are happier and better adjusted than those who are socially isolated or who have conflictual peer relationships.

Crowds are an emerging level of peer relationships in adolescence. In contrast to friendships (which are reciprocal dyadic relationships) and **cliques** (which refer to groups of individuals who interact frequently), crowds are characterized more by shared reputations or images than actual interactions (Brown & Larson, 2009)[14] These crowds reflect different prototypic identities (such as jocks or brains) and are often linked with adolescents' social status and peers' perceptions of their values or behaviors.

11. Stattin, H., & Kerr, M. (2000). Parental monitoring: A reinterpretation. Child Development, 71, 1072–1085.
12. Barber, B. K. (1996). Parental psychological control: Revisiting a neglected construct. Child Development, 67, 3296–3319.
13. Dishion, T. J., & Tipsord, J. M. (2011). Peer contagion in child and adolescent social and emotional development. Annual Review of Psychology, 62, 189–214.
14. Brown, B. B., & Larson, J. (2009). Peer relationships in adolescence. In R. M. Lerner & L. Steinberg (Eds.), Handbook of adolescent psychology (pp. 74–103). New York, NY: Wiley.

LINK TO LEARNING: GENDER ROLES

It is interesting to note that even in today's progressive social climate and with advances in gender equality, there are still considerable differences in the ways teenage boys and girls spend their time, as shown in 2019 research by the Pew Research Center. During the school year, teenage boys spend an average of 24 minutes a day helping around the house and 12 minutes preparing food, while teenage girls spend an average of 38 minutes a day helping around the house and 29 minutes preparing food. Both boys and girls spend more equal amounts of time on maintenance chores and lawn care. Girls also spend an average of 23 more minutes on grooming each day, which is perhaps explained by the fact that 35% of girls say they feel pressure to look good (compared with 23% of boys).[15] Read the article "The Way U.S. Teens Spend Their Time is Changing, but Differences Between Boys and Girls Persist" to learn more.

Romantic relationships

Adolescence is the developmental period during which romantic relationships typically first emerge. Initially, same-sex peer groups that were common during childhood expand into mixed-sex peer groups that are more characteristic of adolescence. Romantic relationships often form in the context of these mixed-sex peer groups (Connolly, Furman, & Konarski, 2000)[16] Although romantic relationships during adolescence are often short-lived rather than long-term committed partnerships, their importance should not be minimized. Adolescents spend a great deal of time focused on romantic relationships, and their positive and negative emotions are more tied to romantic relationships (or lack thereof) than to friendships, family relationships, or school (Furman & Shaffer, 2003)[17] Romantic relationships contribute to adolescents' identity formation, changes in family and peer relationships, and adolescents' emotional and behavioral adjustment.

Furthermore, romantic relationships are centrally connected to adolescents' emerging sexuality. Parents, policymakers, and researchers have devoted a great deal of attention to adolescents' sexuality, in large part because of concerns related to sexual intercourse, contraception, and preventing teen pregnancies. However, sexuality involves more than this narrow focus. **Sexual orientation** refers to whether a person is sexually and romantically attracted to others of the same sex, the opposite sex, or both sexes. For example, adolescence is often when individuals who are lesbian, gay, bisexual, or transgender come to perceive themselves as such (Russell, Clarke, & Clary, 2009)[18] Thus, romantic relationships are a domain in which adolescents experiment with new behaviors and identities.

Many adolescents may choose to come out during this period of their life once an identity has been formed; many others may go through a period of questioning or denial, which can include experimentation with both homosexual and heterosexual experiences. A study of 194 lesbian, gay, and bisexual youths under the age of 21 found that having an awareness of one's sexual orientation occurred, on average, around age 10, but the process of coming out to peers and adults occurred around age 16 and 17, respectively. Coming to terms with and creating a positive LGBT identity can be difficult for some youth for a variety of reasons. Peer pressure is a large factor when youth who are questioning their sexuality or gender identity are

15. Livingston, Gretchen (February 2018). The way U.S. teens spend their time is changing, but differences between boys and girls persist. Pew Research Center.
16. Connolly, J., Furman, W., & Konarski, R. (2000). The role of peers in the emergence of heterosexual romantic relationships in adolescence. Child Development, 71, 1395–1408.
17. Furman, W., & Shaffer, L. (2003). The role of romantic relationships in adolescent development. In P. Florsheim (Ed.), Adolescent romantic relations and sexual behavior: Theory, research, and practical implications (pp. 3–22). Mahwah, NJ: Erlbaum.
18. Russell, S. T., Clarke, T. J., & Clary, J. (2009). Are teens "post-gay"? Contemporary adolescents' sexual identity labels. Journal of Youth and Adolescence, 38, 884–890.

surrounded by heteronormative peers and can cause great distress due to a feeling of being different from everyone else. While coming out can also foster better psychological adjustment, the risks associated are real. Indeed, coming out in the midst of a heteronormative peer environment often comes with the risk of ostracism, hurtful jokes, and even violence. Because of this, statistically the suicide rate amongst LGBT adolescents is up to four times higher than that of their heterosexual peers due to bullying and rejection from peers or family members.

Diversity

Adolescent development does not necessarily follow the same pathway for all individuals. Certain features of adolescence, particularly with respect to biological changes associated with puberty and cognitive changes associated with brain development, are relatively universal. But other features of adolescence depend largely on circumstances that are more environmentally variable. For example, adolescents growing up in one country might have different opportunities for risk taking than adolescents in another country, and supports and sanctions for different behaviors in adolescence depend on laws and values that might be specific to where adolescents live. Likewise, different cultural norms regarding family and peer relationships shape adolescents' experiences in these domains. For example, in some countries, adolescents' parents are expected to retain control over major decisions, whereas in other countries, adolescents are expected to begin sharing in or taking control of decision making.

Even within the same country, adolescents' gender, ethnicity, immigrant status, religion, sexual orientation, socioeconomic status, and personality can shape both how adolescents behave and how others respond to them, creating diverse developmental contexts for different adolescents. For example, early puberty (that occurs before most other peers have experienced puberty) appears to be associated with worse outcomes for girls than boys, likely in part because girls who enter puberty early tend to associate with older boys, which in turn is associated with early sexual behavior and substance use. For adolescents who are ethnic or sexual minorities, discrimination sometimes presents a set of challenges that non-minorities do not face.

Finally, genetic variations contribute an additional source of diversity in adolescence. Current approaches emphasize gene X environment interactions, which often follow a *differential susceptibility* model (Belsky & Pluess, 2009)[19] That is, particular genetic variations are considered riskier than others, but genetic variations also can make adolescents more or less susceptible to environmental factors. For example, the association between the CHRM2 genotype and adolescent externalizing behavior (aggression and delinquency) has been found in adolescents whose parents are low in monitoring behaviors (Dick et al., 2011)[20] Thus, it is important to bear in mind that individual differences play an important role in adolescent development.

19. Belsky, J., & Pluess, M. (2009). Beyond diathesis-stress: Differential susceptibility to environmental influences. Psychological Bulletin, 135, 885–908.
20. Dick, D. M., Meyers, J. L., Latendresse, S. J., Creemers, H. E., Lansford, J. E., ... Huizink, A. C. (2011). CHRM2, parental monitoring, and adolescent externalizing behavior: Evidence for gene-environment interaction. Psychological Science, 22, 481–489.

Behavioral and Psychological Adjustment

Aggression and Antisocial Behavior

Several major theories of the development of antisocial behavior treat adolescence as an important period. Patterson's (1982)[21] *early versus late starter model* of the development of aggressive and antisocial behavior distinguishes youths whose antisocial behavior begins during childhood (early starters) versus adolescence (late starters). According to the theory, early starters are at greater risk for long-term antisocial behavior that extends into adulthood than are late starters. Late starters who become antisocial during adolescence are theorized to experience poor parental monitoring and supervision, aspects of parenting that become more salient during adolescence. Poor monitoring and lack of supervision contribute to increasing involvement with deviant peers, which in turn promotes adolescents' own antisocial behavior. Late starters desist from antisocial behavior when changes in the environment make other options more appealing.

Figure 4. Early antisocial behavior leads to befriending others who also engage in antisocial behavior, which only perpetuates the downward cycle of aggression and wrongful acts. [Image: Philippe Put]

Similarly, Moffitt's (1993)[22] *life-course persistent versus adolescent-limited model* distinguishes between antisocial behavior that begins in childhood versus adolescence. Moffitt regards adolescent-limited antisocial behavior as resulting from a "maturity gap" between adolescents' dependence on and control by adults and their desire to demonstrate their freedom from adult constraint. However, as they continue to develop, and legitimate adult roles and privileges become available to them, there are fewer incentives to engage in antisocial behavior, leading to desistance in these antisocial behaviors.

WATCH IT

Experiencing violence as an adolescent increases the odds of that adolescent later becoming an abusive adult, although it is not a given. Watch this video to learn more about the effects of abuse and perpetuated violence.

- https://youtu.be/3ZeMOsXSc6Q

PSYCHOLOGY AND MASS SHOOTINGS

Virginia Tech, Columbine, Stoneman Douglas High School, Santa Fe High School, Sandy Hook, Aurora, Las Vegas, Orlando—all sites of horrific and tragic mass shootings. Why are they so common? And what led the perpetrators to commit these acts of violence? Several possible factors may work together to create a fertile environment for mass murder in the United States. Most commonly suggested include:

21. Patterson, G. R. (1982). Coercive family process. Eugene, OR: Castalia Press.
22. Moffitt, T. E. (1993). Adolescence-limited and life course persistent antisocial behavior: Developmental taxonomy. Psychological Review, 100, 674–701.

- Higher accessibility and ownership of guns. The U.S. has the highest per-capita gun ownership in the world with 120.5 firearms per 100 people; the second highest is Yemen with 52.8 firearms per 100 people.[23]
- Mental illness[24] and its treatment (or the lack thereof) with psychiatric drugs. This is controversial.[25] Many of the mass shooters in the U.S. suffered from mental illness, but the estimated number of mental illness cases has not increased as significantly as the number of mass shootings.[26] Under 5% of violent behaviors in the U.S. are committed by persons with mental health diagnoses. A 2002 report by the U.S. Secret Service and U.S. Department of Education found evidence that a majority of school shooters displayed evidence of mental health symptoms, often undiagnosed or untreated. Criminologists Fox and DeLateur note that mental illness is only part of the issue, however, and mass shooters tend to externalize their problems, blaming others, and are unlikely to seek psychiatric help, even if available.[27] Other scholars have concluded that mass murderers display a common constellation of chronic mental health symptoms, chronic anger or antisocial traits, and a tendency to blame others for problems.[28] However, they note that attempting to "profile" school shooters with such a constellation of traits will likely result in many false positives as many individuals with such a profile do not engage in violent behaviors.
- The desire to seek revenge for a long history of being bullied at school. In recent years, citizens calling themselves "targeted individual" have cited adult bullying campaigns as a reason for their deadly violence.[29]
- The widespread chronic gap between people's expectations for themselves and their actual achievement, and individualistic culture.
- Desire for fame and notoriety. Also, mass shooters learn from one another through "media contagion," that is, "the mass media coverage of them and the proliferation of social media sites that tend to glorify the shooters and downplay the victims."
- The copycat phenomenon.
- Failure of government background checks due to incomplete databases and/or staff shortages

Read this NPR article on school shooters to learn more about common threads shared by *some* who commit mass violence.

Anxiety and Depression

Developmental models of anxiety and depression also treat adolescence as an important period, especially in terms of the emergence of gender differences in prevalence rates that persist through adulthood (Rudolph, 2009)[30] Starting in early adolescence, compared with males, females have rates of anxiety that are about twice as high and rates of depression that are

23. Healy, Melissa (August 24, 2015). "Why the U.S. is No. 1 – in mass shootings". Los Angeles Times. Retrieved November 6, 2017.
24. Grinberg, Emanuella (January 25, 2016). "The real mental health issue behind gun violence". CNN. Retrieved November 7, 2017.
25. Campbell, Holly (December 2, 2015). "Inside the mind of a mass murderer". WANE-TV. Retrieved November 9, 2017.
26. Christensen, Jen (October 5, 2017). "Why the US has the most mass shootings". CNN. Retrieved November 6, 2017.
27. Peters, Justin (December 19, 2013). "Everything You Think You Know about Mass Murder Is Wrong". Slate.
28. Ferguson, Christopher J.; Coulson, Mark; Barnett, Jane (January 1, 2011). "Psychological Profiles of School Shooters: Positive Directions and One Big Wrong Turn". Journal of Police Crisis Negotiations. 11 (2): 141–158. doi:10.1080/15332586.2011.581523.
29. Burgess, Ann Wolbert; Garbarino, Christina; Carlson, Mary I. (2006). "Pathological teasing and bullying turned deadly: Shooters and suicide". Victims and Offenders. 1 (1): 1–14. doi:10.1080/15564880500498705.
30. Rudolph, K. D. (2009). The interpersonal context of adolescent depression. In S. Nolen-Hoeksema & L. M. Hilt (Eds.), Handbook of depression in adolescents (pp. 377–418). New York, NY: Taylor and Francis.

1.5 to 3 times as high (American Psychiatric Association, 2013) [31] Although the rates vary across specific anxiety and depression diagnoses, rates for some disorders are markedly higher in adolescence than in childhood or adulthood. For example, prevalence rates for specific phobias are about 5% in children and 3%–5% in adults but 16% in adolescents. Additionally, some adolescents sink into **major depression**, a deep sadness and hopelessness that disrupts all normal, regular activities. Causes include many factors such as genetics and early childhood experiences that predate adolescence, but puberty may push vulnerable children, especially girls into despair.

During puberty, the rate of major depression more than doubles to an estimated 15%, affecting about one in five girls and one in ten boys. The gender difference occurs for many reasons, biological and cultural (Uddin et al., 2010) [32] Anxiety and depression are particularly concerning because **suicide** is one of the leading causes of death during adolescence. Some adolescents experience **suicidal ideation** (distressing thoughts about killing oneself) which become most common at about age 15 (Berger, 2019) [33] and can lead to **parasuicide**, also called attempted suicide or failed suicide. Suicidal ideation and parasuicide should be taken seriously and serve as a warning that emotions may be overwhelming.

WATCH IT

This short video emphasizes how suicide is a major health issue and concern for teenagers, and also how it is important for parents, caregivers, teachers, and friends to be open enough to talk about it.

- https://youtu.be/axoTuFd51Pk

Developmental models focus on interpersonal contexts in both childhood and adolescence that foster depression and anxiety (e.g., Rudolph, 2009) [34] Family adversity, such as abuse and parental psychopathology, during childhood sets the stage for social and behavioral problems during adolescence. Adolescents with such problems generate stress in their relationships (e.g., by resolving conflict poorly and excessively seeking reassurance) and select into more maladaptive social contexts (e.g., "misery loves company" scenarios in which depressed youths select other depressed youths as friends and then frequently co-ruminate as they discuss their problems, exacerbating negative affect and stress). These processes are intensified for girls compared with boys because girls have more relationship-oriented goals related to intimacy and social approval, leaving them more vulnerable to disruption in these relationships. Anxiety and depression then exacerbate problems in social relationships, which in turn contribute to the stability of anxiety and depression over time.

31. American Psychiatric Association. (2013). Diagnostic and statistical manual of mental disorders (5th ed.). Arlington, VA: American Psychiatric Publishing.
32. Uddin, M., Koenen, K.C., de los Santos, R., Bakshis, E., Aielle, A.E., & Galea, S. (2010). Gender differences in the genetic and environmental determinants of adolescent depression. Depression and Anxiety, 27(7), 658-666.
33. Berger, K.S. (2019). Invitation to the Lifespan (4th ed). Worth Publishers, NY.
34. Rudolph, K. D. (2009). The interpersonal context of adolescent depression. In S. Nolen-Hoeksema & L. M. Hilt (Eds.), Handbook of depression in adolescents (pp. 377–418). New York, NY: Taylor and Francis.

GLOSSARY

cisgender:
an umbrella term used to describe people whose sense of personal identity and gender corresponds with their birth sex

clique:
used to describe a group of persons who interact with each other more regularly and intensely than others in the same setting. Cliques are distinguished from "crowds" in that their members interact with one another

crowds:
large groups of adolescents defined by their shared image and reputation

deviant peer contagion:
process by which peers reinforce problem behavior by laughing or showing other signs of approval that then increase the likelihood of future problem behavior

foreclosure:
term for premature identity formation, which occurs when an adolescent adopts his or her parents' or society's role and values without questioning or analysis, according to Marcia's theory

gender:
a term that refers to social or cultural distinctions of behaviors that are considered male or female

gender dysphoria:
a condition listed in the DSM-5 in which people whose gender at birth is contrary to the one they identify with. This condition replaces "gender identity disorder"

gender expression:
how one demonstrates gender (based on traditional gender role norms related to clothing, behavior, and interactions); can be feminine, masculine, androgynous, or somewhere along a spectrum

gender identity:
the way that one thinks about gender and self-identifies, can be woman, man, or genderqueer

homophily:
a tendency of individuals to form links disproportionately with others like themselves

identity achievement:
Erikson's term for the attainment of identity, or the point at which a person understands who he or she is as a unique individual, in accord with past experiences and future plans; already questioned and made commitment according to Marcia's theory

identity vs. role confusion:
Erikson's term for the fifth stage of development, in which the person tries to figure out "Who am I?" but is confused as to which of many possible roles to adopt

major depression:
feelings of hopelessness, lethargy, and worthlessness that last two weeks or more

moratorium:
an adolescent's choice of a socially acceptable way to postpone making identity-achievement decisions. Going to college is a common example. Engaged in questioning, but not yet making a commitment, according to Marcia's theory

parasuicide:
any potentially lethal action against the self that does not result in death. (also called attempted suicide or failed suicide)

peer pressure:
encouragement to conform to one's friends or contemporaries in behavior, dress, and attitude; usually considered a negative force, as when adolescent peers encourage one another to defy adult authority

role confusion:
a situation in which an adolescent does not seem to know or care what his or her identity is. (Sometimes called identity diffusion or role diffusion)

self-concept:
our individual perceptions of our behavior, abilities, and unique characteristics. It is essentially a mental picture of who you are as a person. For example, beliefs such as "I am a good friend" or "I am a kind person" are part of an overall self-concept

self-esteem:
considered an important component of emotional health, self-esteem encompasses both self-confidence and self-acceptance. It is the way individuals perceive themselves and their self-value

sex:
a term that denotes the presence of physical or physiological differences between males and females

sexual orientation:
a term that refers to whether a person is sexually and romantically attracted to others of the same sex, the opposite sex, or both sexes

suicide:
the act of intentionally causing one's own death

suicidal ideation:
thinking about suicide, usually with some serious emotional and intellectual or cognitive overtones

transgender:
a term used to describe people whose sense of personal identity does not correspond with their birth sex

Putting It Together: Adolescence

Adolescent development is characterized by significant biological, cognitive, and pyschosocial changes. Physical changes associated with puberty are triggered by hormones and changes in the brain in which reward-processing centers develop more rapidly than cognitive control systems, making adolescents more sensitive to rewards than to possible negative consequences. Cognitive changes include improvements in complex and abstract thought and moral reasoning. Psychosocial changes are particularly notable as adolescents become more autonomous from their parents, spend more time with peers, and begin exploring romantic relationships and sexuality.

Adjustment during adolescence is reflected in identity formation, which often involves a period of exploration followed by commitments to particular identities. Adolescents' relationships with parents go through a period of redefinition in which adolescents become more autonomous, and aspects of parenting, such as monitoring and psychological control, become more salient. Peer relationships are important sources of support and companionship during adolescence, yet can also promote problem behaviors. Same-sex peer groups evolve into mixed-sex peer groups, and adolescents' romantic relationships tend to emerge from these groups. Identity formation occurs as adolescents explore and commit to different roles and ideological positions. Despite these generalizations, factors such as country of residence, gender, ethnicity, and sexual orientation shape development in ways that lead to diversity of experiences across adolescence.

Discussion: Adolescence

DISCUSSION: In this discussion, reflect upon and discuss ONE of the following questions:

- Q1: Which of Marcia's four identity stages do you believe that you are in at this point in your life? Explain your reasoning.
- Q2: Give an example of adolescent egocentrism that you experienced in your own life.

STEP 1: First, write a response with at least EIGHT substantial sentences, integrating concepts you learned from the reading and other materials (include links with necessary). Show that you can think critically on the topic by integrating your own thoughts, analysis, or experiences.

STEP 2: Return to the discussion to comment on at least TWO classmates' posts (in at least FIVE sentences). Expand on a classmate's comments in a value-adding, topic-related way. Promote a collaborative, supportive community, and advance the dialogue through follow-up questions. Reply posts cannot be one-liners, off-topic posts, vague statements, unsupported opinions, inadequate explanations or simply say, "I agree" or "good job."

MODULE 8: EARLY ADULTHOOD

Why It Matters: Early Adulthood

Why learn about development changes during early adulthood?

Figure 1. Age or another key milestone, such as graduation, may signify the transition to adulthood, but becoming an adult is a process that varies widely across cultures and individuals.

When we are children and teens, we eagerly anticipate each and every birthday, waiting for the next big one...when we'll finally be grown up and have all the freedoms and rights enjoyed by those who are older than us. Indeed, there are opportunities to drive, buy a car, vote, go to college, join the military, drink, move out on our own, date, live together, get married, work, have children, buy a house, and more. This can be an awesome time in our lives, as we tend to be physically and cognitively strong and healthy, we dream and make plans for the future, find people to share our experiences, and try out new roles. It can also be challenging, stressful, and scary as we realize that a lot of responsibility comes with such freedom. We have probably all seen the coffee mugs that proclaim, "Adulting is hard," or the t-shirts that announce, "I can't adult today" (typically worn by young adults!).

Development is a process, and we aren't suddenly adults at a certain age. In fact, we may even take longer to grow up these days. In this module, we'll learn about norms, trends, and theories about why certain patterns are forming. It's even been proposed that there is a new stage of development between adolescence and early adulthood, called "emerging adulthood," when young people don't quite feel like they are adults yet and wait longer to join the workforce, move out on their own, get married, and have children. Yet by the end of early adulthood, most of us will have accomplished the important developmental tasks of becoming more autonomous, taking care of ourselves and even others, committing to relationships and jobs/careers, getting married, raising families, and becoming part of our communities. There are, of course, many individual and cultural differences.

Think of your own life. When will you feel like an adult? Or do you already feel like an adult? Why or why not? Did your parents become adults earlier or later in their lives, compared to you?

Physical Development in Early Adulthood

What you'll learn to do: explain developmental tasks and physical changes during early adulthood

In this section, we will see how young adults are often at their peak physically, sexually, and in terms of health and reproduction; yet they are also particularly at risk for injury, violence, substance abuse, sexually transmitted diseases, and more. As you read, consider whether or not you think young adults are in the prime of their lives.

LEARNING OUTCOMES

- Summarize the developmental tasks of early adulthood
- Describe physical development and health in early adulthood
- Summarize risky behaviors and causes of death in early adulthood
- Describe sexuality and fertility issues related to early adulthood

Developmental Tasks of Early Adulthood

Before we dive into the specific physical changes and experiences of early adulthood, let's consider the key developmental tasks during this time—the ages between 18 and 40. The beginning of early adulthood, ages 18-25, is sometimes considered its own phase, emerging adulthood, but the developmental tasks that are the focus during emerging adulthood persist throughout the early adulthood years. Look at the list below and try to think of someone you know between 18 and 40 who fits each of the descriptions.

Figure 1. How old do you think this group of young adults are? What clues can you use to help you estimate their age?

Developmental Tasks of Early Adulthood

Havighurst (1972) describes some of the developmental tasks of young adults. These include:

1. Achieving autonomy: trying to establish oneself as an independent person with a life of one's own
2. Establishing identity: more firmly establishing likes, dislikes, preferences, and philosophies
3. Developing emotional stability: becoming more stable emotionally which is considered a sign of maturing
4. Establishing a career: deciding on and pursuing a career or at least an initial career direction and pursuing an education
5. Finding intimacy: forming first close, long-term relationships
6. Becoming part of a group or community: young adults may, for the first time, become involved with various groups in the community. They may begin voting or volunteering to be part of civic organizations (scouts, church groups, etc.). This is especially true for those who participate in organizations as parents.
7. Establishing a residence and learning how to manage a household: learning how to budget and keep a home maintained.
8. Becoming a parent and rearing children: learning how to manage a household with children.
9. Making marital or relationship adjustments and learning to parent.

THINK IT OVER

To what extent do you think these early adulthood developmental tasks have changed in the last several years? How might these tasks vary by culture?

Physical Development in Early Adulthood

The Physiological Peak

People in their twenties and thirties are considered young adults. If you are in your early twenties, you are probably at the peak of your physiological development. Your body has completed its growth, though your brain is still developing (as explained in the previous module on adolescence). Physically, you are in the "prime of your life" as your reproductive system, motor ability, strength, and lung capacity are operating at their best. However, these systems will start a slow, gradual decline so that by the time you reach your mid to late 30s, you will begin to notice signs of aging. This includes a decline in your immune system, your response time, and in your ability to recover quickly from physical exertion. For example, you may have noticed that it takes you quite some time to stop panting after running to class or taking the stairs. But, remember that both nature and nurture continue to influence development. Getting out of shape is not an inevitable part of aging; it is probably due to the fact that you have become less physically active and have experienced greater stress. The good news is that there are things you can do to combat many of these changes. So keep in mind, as we continue to discuss the lifespan, that some of the changes we associate with aging can be prevented or turned around if we adopt healthier lifestyles.

Figure 2. Early adulthood is generally a time of peak physical health.

In fact, research shows that the habits we establish in our twenties are related to certain health conditions in middle age, particularly the risk of heart disease. What are healthy habits that young adults can establish now that will prove beneficial in later life? Healthy habits include maintaining a lean body mass index, moderate alcohol intake, a smoke-free lifestyle, a healthy diet, and regular physical activity. When experts were asked to name one thing they would recommend young adults do to facilitate good health, their specific responses included: weighing self often, learning to cook, reducing sugar intake, developing an active lifestyle, eating vegetables, practicing portion control, establishing an exercise routine (especially a "post-party" routine, if relevant), and finding a job you love.[1]

Being overweight or obese is a real concern in early adulthood. Medical research shows that American men and women with moderate weight gain from early to middle adulthood have significantly increased risks of major chronic disease and mortality (Zheng, et al, 2017).[2] Given the fact that American men and women tend to gain about one to two pounds per year from early to middle adulthood, developing healthy nutrition and exercise habits across adulthood is important (Nichols, 2017).[3]

WATCH IT

This video explains how the brain continues to develop into adulthood.

- https://youtu.be/_KxRAfXEzIQ

A Healthy, but Risky Time

Early adulthood tends to be a time of relatively good health. For instance, in the United States, adults ages 18-44 have the lowest percentage of physician office visits than any other age group, younger or older. However, early adulthood seems to be a particularly risky time for violent deaths (rates vary by gender, race, and ethnicity). The leading causes of death for both age groups 15-24 and 25-34 in the U.S. are unintentional injury, suicide, and homicide. Cancer and heart disease follow as the fourth and fifth top causes of death among young adults (Centers for Disease Control and Prevention, 2019).

Substance Abuse

Rates of violent death are influenced by substance abuse, which peaks during early adulthood. Some young adults use drugs and alcohol as a way of coping with stress from family, personal relationships, or concerns over being on one's own. Others "use" because they have friends who use and in the early 20s, there is still a good deal of pressure to conform. Youth transitioning into adulthood have some of the highest rates of alcohol and substance abuse. For instance, rates of binge drinking (drinking five or more drinks on a single occasion) in 2014 were: 28.5 percent for people ages 18 to 20 and 43.3 percent for people ages 21-25.[4] Recent data from the Centers for Disease Control and Prevention show increases in drug overdose deaths between 2006 and 2016 (with higher rates among males), but with the steepest increases between 2014 and 2016 occurring among males aged 24-34 and females aged 24-34 and 35-44. Rates vary by other factors including race and geography; increased use and abuse of opioids may also play a role.

1. Parker-Pope, T. (October 17, 2016). The 8 Health Habits Experts Say You Need in Your 20s. *NY Times*. https://www.nytimes.com/interactive/2016/10/16/well/live/health-tips-for-your-20s.html
2. Zheng, Y., Manson, J.E., Yuan, C., Liang, M.H., Grodstein, F., Stampfer, M.J., Willett, W.C., & Hu, F.B. (2017, July 18). Associations of weight gain from early to middle adulthood with major health outcomes later in life. JAMA, 318(3): 255-272. doi:10.1001/jama.2017.7092
3. Nichols, H. (2017, July 18). Weight gain in early adulthood linked to health risks later in life. Medical News Today.
4. Substance Abuse and Mental Health Services Administration (2018). *SAMHSA*. Retrieved from https://www.samhsa.gov/behavioral-health-equity

WATCH IT

To learn more about opioid drugs and the current opioid crisis, please watch the following video:

- https://youtu.be/oHlaz0kQIRE

Drugs impair judgment, reduce inhibitions, and alter mood, all of which can lead to dangerous behavior. Reckless driving, violent altercations, and forced sexual encounters are some examples. College campuses are notorious for binge drinking, which is particularly concerning since alcohol plays a role in over half of all student sexual assaults. Alcohol is involved nearly 90 percent of the time in acquaintance rape (when the perpetrator knows the victim). Over 40 percent of sexual assaults involve alcohol use by the victim and almost 70 percent involve alcohol use by the perpetrator.[5].

LINK TO LEARNING

After she was the victim of an assault in London, college student Ione Wells published a letter to her attacker in a student newspaper that went viral and sparked the #NotGuilty campaign against sexual violence and victim-blaming. Watch Ione Wells' TED talk "How We Talk About Sexual Assault Online" to learn more [Note: this is a sensitive topic.]

Drug and alcohol use increase the risk of sexually transmitted infections because people are more likely to engage in risky sexual behavior when under the influence. This includes having sex with someone who has had multiple partners, having anal sex without the use of a condom, having multiple partners, or having sex with someone whose history is unknown. Such risky sexual behavior puts individuals at increased risk for both sexually transmitted diseases (STDs) and human immunodeficiency virus (HIV). STDs are especially common among young people. There are about 20 million new cases of STDs each year in the United States and about half of those infections are in people between the ages of 15 and 24. Also, young people are the most likely to be unaware of their HIV infection, with half not knowing they have the virus (Centers for Disease Control and Prevention, 2019).

Sex and Fertility in Early Adulthood

Sexual Responsiveness and Reproduction in Early Adulthood

Sexual Responsiveness

Men and women tend to reach their peak of sexual responsiveness at different ages. For men, sexual responsiveness tends to peak in the late teens and early twenties. Sexual arousal can easily occur in response to physical stimulation or fantasizing. Sexual responsiveness begins a slow decline in the late twenties and into the thirties although a man may continue

5. Alcohol.org (2018). *Sexual Assaults on College Campuses Involving Alcohol.* Retrieved from https://www.alcohol.org/effects/sexual-assault-college-campus/

to be sexually active throughout adulthood. Over time, a man may require more intense stimulation in order to become aroused. Women often find that they become more sexually responsive throughout their 20s and 30s and may peak in the late 30s or early 40s. This is likely due to greater self-confidence and reduced inhibitions about sexuality.

There are a wide variety of factors that influence sexual relationships during emerging adulthood; this includes beliefs about certain sexual behaviors and marriage. For example, among emerging adults in the United States, it is common for oral sex to not be considered "real sex". In the 1950s and 1960s, about 75 percent of people between the ages of 20–24 engaged in premarital sex; today, that number is 90 percent. Unintended pregnancy and sexually transmitted infections and diseases (STIs/STDs) are a central issue. As individuals move through emerging adulthood, they are more likely to engage in monogamous sexual relationships and practice safe sex.

Reproduction

For many couples, early adulthood is the time for having children. However, delaying childbearing until the late 20s or early 30s has become more common in the United States. The mean age of first-time mothers in the United States increased 1.4 years, from 24.9 in 2000 to 26.3 in 2014. This shift can primarily be attributed to a larger number of first births to older women along with fewer births to mothers under age 20 (CDC, 2016).[6]

Couples delay childbearing for a number of reasons. Women are now more likely to attend college and begin careers before starting families. And both men and women are delaying marriage until they are in their late 20s and early 30s. In 2018, the average age for a first marriage in the United States was 29.8 for men and 27.8 for women.[7]

Infertility

Infertility affects about 6.7 million women or 11 percent of the reproductive age population (American Society of Reproductive Medicine [ASRM], 2006-2010. Male factors create infertility in about a third of the cases. For men, the most common cause is a lack of sperm production or low sperm production. Female factors cause infertility in another third of cases. For women, one of the most common causes of infertility is ovulation disorder. Other causes of female infertility include blocked fallopian tubes, which can occur when a woman has had **pelvic inflammatory disease (PID)** or **endometriosis**. PID is experienced by 1 out of 7 women in the United States and leads to infertility about 20 percent of the time. One of the major causes of PID is **Chlamydia**, the most commonly diagnosed sexually transmitted infection in young women. Another cause of pelvic inflammatory disease is **gonorrhea**. Both male and female factors contribute to the remainder of cases of infertility and approximately 20 percent are unexplained.

WATCH IT

Watch this video to learn more about the reasons for infertility and the main treatment methods available for conceiving.

- https://youtu.be/QLGrmYgow8I

6. T.J. Mathews, M.S. and Brady E. Hamilton, Ph.D. Mean Age of Mothers is on the Rise: United States, 2000–2014. NCHS Data Brief No. 232, January 2016. Retrieved from https://www.cdc.gov/nchs/products/databriefs/db232.htm.
7. U.S Census Bureau (2018) Historical Marital Status Tables. Retrieved from https://www.census.gov/data/tables/time-series/demo/families/marital.html

Fertility Treatment

The majority of infertility cases (85-90 percent) are treated using fertility drugs to increase ovulation or with surgical procedures to repair the reproductive organs or remove scar tissue from the reproductive tract. **In vitro fertilization (IVF)** is used to treat infertility in less than 5 percent of cases. IVF is used when a woman has blocked or deformed fallopian tubes or sometimes when a man has a very low sperm count. This procedure involves removing eggs from the female and fertilizing the eggs outside the woman's body. The fertilized egg is then reinserted in the woman's uterus. The average cost of an IVF cycle in the U.S. is $10,000-15,000 and the average live delivery rate for IVF in 2005 was 31.6 percent per retrieval. IVF makes up about 99 percent of artificial reproductive procedures. [ASRM, 2006-2010]

Less common procedures include **gamete intrafallopian tube transfer (GIFT)** which involves implanting both sperm and ova into the fallopian tube and fertilization is allowed to occur naturally. **Zygote intrafallopian tube transfer (ZIFT)** is another procedure in which sperm and ova are fertilized outside of the woman's body and the fertilized egg or zygote is then implanted in the fallopian tube. This allows the zygote to travel down the fallopian tube and embed in the lining of the uterus naturally.

Insurance coverage for infertility is required in fourteen states, but the amount and type of coverage available vary greatly (ASRM, 2006-2010). The majority of couples seeking treatment for infertility pay much of the cost. Consequently, infertility treatment is much more accessible to couples with higher incomes. However, grants and funding sources may be available for lower-income couples seeking infertility treatment.

Fertility for Singles and Same-Sex Couples

The journey to parenthood may look different for singles same-sex couples. However, there are several viable options available to them to have their own biological children. Men and women may choose to donate their sperm or eggs to help others reproduce for monetary or humanitarian reasons. Some gay couples may decide to have a surrogate pregnancy. One or both of the men would provide the sperm and choose a carrier. The chosen woman may be the source of the egg and uterus or the woman could be a third party that carries the created embryo.

Reciprocal IVF is used by couples who both possess female reproductive organs. Using in vitro fertilization, eggs are removed from one partner to be used to make embryos that the other partner will hopefully carry in a successful pregnancy.

Artificial insemination (**AI**) is the deliberate introduction of sperm into a female's cervix or uterine cavity for the purpose of achieving a pregnancy through in vivo fertilization by means other than sexual intercourse. AI is most often used by single women who desire to give birth to their own child, women who are in a lesbian relationship, or women who are in a heterosexual relationship but with a male partner who is infertile or who has a physical impairment which prevents intercourse. The sperm used could be anonymous or from a known donor.

GLOSSARY

artificial insemination:
the deliberate introduction of sperm into a female's cervix in order to become pregnant by means other than sexual intercourse

chlamydia:
a sexually transmitted infection caused by the bacterium chlamydia trachomatis

endometriosis:
a condition in which the layer of tissue that normally covers the inside of the uterus, grows outside of it

gamete intrafallopian tube transfer:
involves implanting both sperm and ova into the fallopian tube which allows fertilization to occur naturally

gonorrhea:
a sexually transmitted infection (STI) caused by the bacterium neisseria gonorrhoeae

in vitro fertilization:
this procedure involves removing eggs from the female, fertilizing the eggs outside the woman's body, and then reinserting into the woman's uterus

pelvic inflammatory disease:
an infection of the upper part of the female reproductive system, namely the uterus, fallopian tubes, and ovaries, and inside of the pelvis

zygote intrafallopian tube transfer:
sperm and ova are fertilized outside of the woman's body and the zygote is then implanted in the fallopian tube to allow the zygote to travel and embed in the lining of the uterus naturally

Cognitive Development in Early Adulthood

What you'll learn to do: explain cognitive development in early adulthood

We have learned about cognitive development from infancy through adolescence, ending with Piaget's stage of formal operations. Does that mean that cognitive development stops with adolescence? Couldn't there be different ways of thinking in adulthood that come after (or "post") formal operations?

In this section, we will learn about these types of postformal operational thought and consider research done by William Perry related to types of thought and advanced thinking. We will also look at education in early adulthood, the relationship between education and work, and some tools used by young adults to choose their careers.

LEARNING OUTCOMES

- Distinguish between formal and postformal thought
- Describe cognitive development and dialectical thought during early adulthood
- Describe educational trends in early adulthood
- Explain the relationship between education and work in early adulthood

Cognitive Development in Early Adulthood

Beyond Formal Operational Thought: Postformal Thought

In the adolescence module, we discussed Piaget's formal operational thought. The hallmark of this type of thinking is the ability to think abstractly or to consider possibilities and ideas about circumstances never directly experienced. Thinking abstractly is only one characteristic of adult thought, however. If you compare a 14-year-old with someone in their late 30s, you would probably find that the later considers not only what is possible, but also what is likely. Why the change? The young adult has gained experience and understands why possibilities do not always become realities. This difference in adult and adolescent thought can spark arguments between the generations.

Figure 1. As young adults gain more experience, they think increasingly more in the abstract, and are able to understand different perspectives and complexities.

Here is an example. A student in her late 30s relayed such an argument she was having with her 14-year-old son. The son had saved a considerable amount of money and wanted to buy an old car and store it in the garage until he was old enough to drive. He could sit in it, pretend he was driving, clean it up, and show it to his friends. It sounded like a perfect opportunity. The mother, however, had practical objections. The car would just sit for several years while deteriorating. The son would probably change his mind about the type of car he wanted by the time he was old enough to drive and they would be stuck with a car that would not run. She was also concerned that having a car nearby would be too much temptation and the son might decide to sneak it out for a quick ride before he had a permit or license.

Piaget's theory of cognitive development ended with formal operations, but it is possible that other ways of thinking may develop after (or "post") formal operations in adulthood (even if this thinking does not constitute a separate "stage" of development). **Postformal thought** is practical, realistic and more individualistic, but also characterized by understanding the complexities of various perspectives. As a person approaches the late 30s, chances are they make decisions out of necessity or because of prior experience and are less influenced by what others think. Of course, this is particularly true in individualistic cultures such as the United States. Postformal thought is often described as more flexible, logical, willing to accept moral and intellectual complexities, and dialectical than previous stages in development.

Perry's Scheme

One of the first theories of cognitive development in early adulthood originated with William Perry (1970)[1], who studied undergraduate students at Harvard University. Perry noted that over the course of students' college years, cognition tended to shift from **dualism** (absolute, black and white, right and wrong type of thinking) to **multiplicity** (recognizing that some problems are solvable and some answers are not yet known) to **relativism** (understanding the importance of the specific context of knowledge—it's all relative to other factors). Similar to Piaget's formal operational thinking in adolescence, this change in thinking in early adulthood is affected by educational experiences.

1. Perry, W.G., Jr. (1970). Forms of ethical and intellectual development in the college years: A scheme. New York, NY: Holt, Rinehart, and Winston.

Table 1. Stages of Perry's Scheme

	Summary of Position in Perry's Scheme	Basic Example
Dualism	The authorities know	*"the tutor knows what is right and wrong"*
	The true authorities are right, the others are frauds	*"my tutor doesn't know what is right and wrong but others do"*
Multiplicity	There are some uncertainties and the authorities are working on them to find the truth	*"my tutors don't know, but somebody out there is trying to find out"*
	(a) Everyone has the right to their own opinion (b) The authorities don't want the right answers. They want us to think in a certain way	*"different tutors think different things"* *"there is an answer that the tutors want and we have to find it"*
Relativism	Everything is relative but not equally valid	*"there are no right and wrong answers, it depends on the situation, but some answers might be better than others"*
	You have to make your own decisions	*"what is important is not what the tutor thinks but what I think"*
	First commitment	*"for this particular topic I think that...."*
	Several Commitments	*"for these topics I think that...."*
	Believe own values, respect others, be ready to learn	*"I know what I believe in and what I think is valid, others may think differently and I'm prepared to reconsider my views"*

WATCH IT

Please watch this brief lecture by Dr. Eric Landrum to better understand the way that thinking can shift during college, according to Perry's scheme. Notice the overall shifts in beliefs over time. Do you recognize your own thinking or the thinking of others you know in this clip?

- https://youtu.be/XkEJIXvwROs

Dialectical Thought

In addition to moving toward more practical considerations, thinking in early adulthood may also become more flexible and balanced. Abstract ideas that the adolescent believes in firmly may become standards by which the individual evaluates reality. As Perry's research pointed out, adolescents tend to think in dichotomies or absolute terms; ideas are true or false; good or bad; right or wrong and there is no middle ground. However, with education and experience, the young adult comes to recognize that there is some right and some wrong in each position. Such thinking is more realistic because very few positions, ideas, situations, or people are completely right or wrong.

Some adults may move even beyond the relativistic or contextual thinking described by Perry; they may be able to bring together important aspects of two opposing viewpoints or positions, synthesize them, and come up with new ideas. This is referred to as **dialectical thought** and is considered one of the most advanced aspects of postformal thinking (Basseches, 1984). There isn't just one theory of postformal thought; there are variations, with emphasis on adults' ability to tolerate ambiguity or to accept contradictions or find new problems, rather than solve problems, etc. (as well as relativism and dialecticism that we just learned about). What they all have in common is the proposition that the way we think may change during adulthood with education and experience.

Education and Work

Education in Early Adulthood

According to the U.S. Census Bureau (2017), 90 percent of the American population 25 and older have completed high school or higher level of education—compare this to just 24 percent in 1940! Each generation tends to earn (and perhaps need) increased levels of formal education. As we can see in the graph, approximately one-third of the American adult population has a bachelor's degree or higher, as compared with less than 5 percent in 1940. Educational attainment rates vary by gender and race. All races combined, women are slightly more likely to have graduated from college than men; that gap widens with graduate and professional degrees. However, wide racial disparities still exist. For example, 23 percent of African-Americans have a college degree and only 16.4 percent of Hispanic Americans have a college degree, compared to 37 percent of non-Hispanic white Americans. The college graduation rates of African-Americans and Hispanic Americans have been growing in recent years, however (the rate has doubled since 1991 for African-Americans and it has increased 60 percent in the last two decades for Hispanic-Americans).

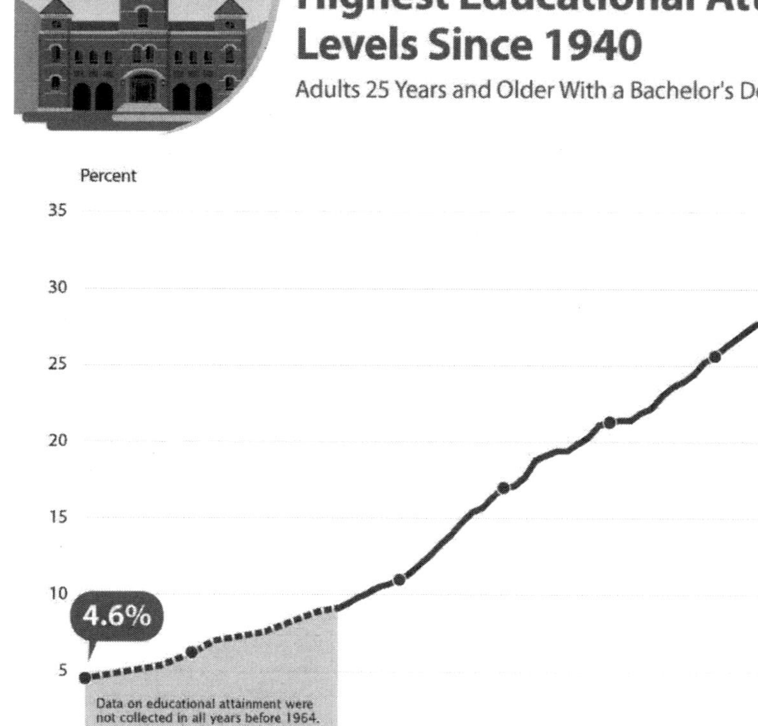

Figure 2. Since 1940, there has been a significant rise in educational attainment for adults over age 25.

What about those young or emerging adults graduating high school today—is the majority of that group going to college? According to the U.S. Bureau of Labor Statistics (2017), 66.7 percent of youth ages 16-24 who graduated high school between January and October 2017 were enrolled in colleges or universities in October 2017. There were gender differences (71.7 percent of females vs. 61.1 percent of males) and racial differences (83 percent of Asians, 67.1 percent of non-Hispanic whites, 61 percent Hispanics, and 59.4 percent Blacks). Not all of these students will persist and earn college degrees, however.[2]

Education and the Workplace

With the rising costs of higher education, various news headlines have asked if a college education is worth the cost. One way to address this question is in terms of the earning potential associated with various levels of educational achievement. In 2016, the average earnings for Americans 25 and older with only a high school education was $35,615, compared with $65,482 for those with a bachelor's degree, compared with $92,525 for those with more advanced degrees. Average earnings vary by gender, race, and geographical location in the United States.[3]

Of concern in recent years is the relationship between higher education and the workplace. In 2005, American educator and then Harvard University President, Derek Bok, called for a closer alignment between the goals of educators and the demands of the economy. Companies outsource much of their work, not only to save costs but to find workers with the skills they need. What is required to do well in today's economy? Colleges and universities, he argued, need to promote global awareness, critical thinking skills, the ability to communicate, moral reasoning, and responsibility in their students. Regional accrediting agencies and state organizations provide similar guidelines for educators. Workers need skills in listening, reading, writing, speaking, global awareness, critical thinking, civility, and computer literacy—all skills that enhance success in the workplace.

More than a decade later, the question remains: does formal education prepare young adults for the workplace? It depends on whom you ask. In an article referring to information from the National Association of Colleges and Employers' 2018 Job Outlook Survey, Bauer-Wolf (2018) explains that employers perceive gaps in students' competencies but many graduating college seniors are overly confident. The biggest difference was in perceived professionalism and work ethic (only 43 percent of employers thought that students are competent in this area compared to 90 percent of the students).[4] Similar differences were also found in terms of oral communication, written communication, and critical thinking skills. Only in terms of digital technology skills were more employers confident about students' competencies than were the students (66 percent compared to 60 percent).

It appears that students need to learn what some call "soft skills," as well as the particular knowledge and skills within their college major. As education researcher Loni Bordoloi Pazich (2018) noted, most American college students today are enrolling in business or other pre-professional programs and to be effective and successful workers and leaders, they would benefit from the communication, teamwork, and critical thinking skills, as well as the content knowledge, gained from liberal arts education.[5] In fact, two-thirds of children starting primary school now will be employed in jobs in the future that currently do not exist. Therefore, students cannot learn every single skill or fact that they may need to know, but they can learn how to learn, think, research, and communicate well so that they are prepared to continually learn new things and adapt effectively in their careers and lives since the economy, technology, and global markets will continue to evolve.[6]

Career Choices in Early Adulthood

Hopefully, we are each becoming lifelong learners, particularly since we are living longer and will most likely change jobs multiple times during our lives. However, for many, our job changes will be within the same general occupational field, so our initial career choice is still significant. We've seen with Erikson that identity largely involves occupation and, as we will learn in the

2. US Census Bureau. (2017, March). Highest Educational Levels Reached by Adults in the U.S. Since 1940. Retrieved from https://www.census.gov/newsroom/press-releases/2017/cb17-51.html
3. US Census Bureau. (2017, March). Highest Educational Levels Reached by Adults in the U.S. Since 1940. Retrieved from https://www.census.gov/newsroom/press-releases/2017/cb17-51.html
4. Bauer-Wolf, J. (2018, February 23). Study: students believe they are prepared for the workplace; employers disagree. Inside Higher Ed. https://www.insidehighered.com/print/news/2018/02/23/study-student
5. Bordoloi Pazich, L. (2018, September 26). The power of academic friendship. Inside Higher Ed. https://www.insidehighered.com/views/2018/09/26/need-combine-business
6. Henseler, C. (2017, September 6). Liberal arts is the foundation for professional success in the 21st century. Huffington Post.

next section, Levinson found that young adults typically form a dream about work (though females may have to choose to focus relatively more on work or family initially with "split" dreams). The American School Counselor Association recommends that school counselors aid students in their career development beginning as early as kindergarten and continue this development throughout their education. [7]

One of the most well-known theories about career choice is from John Holland (1985), who proposed that there are six personality types (realistic, investigative, artistic, social, enterprising, and conventional), as well as varying types of work environments.[8] The better matched one's personality is to the workplace characteristics, the more satisfied and successful one is predicted to be with that career or vocational choice. Research support has been mixed and we should note that there is more to satisfaction and success in a career than one's personality traits or likes and dislikes. For instance, education, training, and abilities need to match the expectations and demands of the job, plus the state of the economy, availability of positions, and salary rates may play practical roles in choices about work.

LINK TO LEARNING: WHAT'S YOUR RIGHT CAREER?

To complete a free online career questionnaire and identify potential careers based on your preferences, go to:

Career One Stop Questionnaire

Did you find out anything interesting? Think of this activity as a starting point to your career exploration. Other great ways for young adults to research careers include informational interviewing, job shadowing, volunteering, practicums, and internships. Once you have a few careers in mind that you want to find out more about, go to the Occupational Outlook Handbook from the U.S. Bureau of Labor Statistics to learn about job tasks, required education, average pay, and projected outlook for the future.

GLOSSARY

dialectical thought:
the ability to reason from multiple perspectives and synthesize various viewpoints in order to come up with new ideas

dualism:
absolute, black and white, right and wrong type of thinking

multiplicity:
recognizing that some problems are solvable and some answers are not yet known

postformal thought:
a more individualistic and realistic type of thinking that occurs after Piaget's last stage of formal operations

7. The School Counselor and Career Development (2017). American School Counselor Association. Retrieved from https://www.schoolcounselor.org/asca/media/asca/PositionStatements/PS_CareerDevelopment.pdf
8. Holland, J.L. (1985). Making vocational choices: A theory of vocational personalities and work environments. Englewood Cliffs, NJ: Prentice-Hall.

relativism:
understanding the importance of the specific context of knowledge—it's all relative to other factors

Theories of Adult Psychosocial Development

What you'll learn to do: explain theories and perspectives on psychosocial development

From a lifespan developmental perspective, growth and development do not stop in childhood or adolescence; they continue throughout adulthood. In this section we will build on Erikson's psychosocial stages, then be introduced to theories about transitions that occur during adulthood. According to Levinson, we alternate between periods of change and periods of stability. More recently, Arnett notes that transitions to adulthood happen at later ages than in the past and he proposes that there is a new stage between adolescence and early adulthood called, "emerging adulthood." Let's see what you think.

LEARNING OUTCOMES

- Describe Erikson's stage of intimacy vs. isolation
- Summarize Levinson's theory of early adulthood transitions
- Explain Arnett's concept of emerging adulthood

Theories of Early Adult Psychosocial Development

Erikson's Theory

Intimacy vs. Isolation

Figure 1. Young adulthood is a time to connect with others in both friendships and romantic relationships.

Erikson (1950) believed that the main task of early adulthood is to establish intimate relationships and not feel isolated from others. Intimacy does not necessarily involve romance; it involves caring about another and sharing one's self without losing one's self. This developmental crisis of "intimacy versus isolation" is affected by how the adolescent crisis of "identity versus role confusion" was resolved (in addition to how the earlier developmental crises in infancy and childhood were resolved). The young adult might be afraid to get too close to someone else and lose her or his sense of self, or the young adult might define her or himself in terms of another person. Intimate relationships are more difficult if one is still struggling with identity. Achieving a sense of identity is a life-long process, but there are periods of identity crisis and stability. And, according to Erikson, having some sense of identity is essential for intimate relationships.[1] Although, consider what that would mean for previous generations of women who may have defined themselves through their husbands and marriages, or for Eastern cultures today that value interdependence rather than independence.

Friendships as a source of intimacy

In our twenties, intimacy needs may be met in friendships rather than with partners. This is especially true in the United States today as many young adults postpone making long-term commitments to partners either in marriage or in cohabitation. The kinds of friendships shared by women tend to differ from those shared by men (Tannen,1990). Friendships between men are more likely to involve sharing information, providing solutions, or focusing on activities rather than discussing problems or emotions. Men tend to discuss opinions or factual information or spend time together in an activity of mutual interest. Friendships between women are more likely to focus on sharing weaknesses, emotions, or problems. Women talk about difficulties they are having in other relationships and express their sadness, frustrations, and joys. These differences in approaches could lead to problems when men and women come together. She may want to vent about a problem she is having; he may want to provide a solution and move on to some activity. But when he offers a solution, she thinks he does not care! Effective communication is the key to good relationships.

1. Erikson, E. (1950). Childhood and society. New York, NY: Norton.

Many argue that other-sex friendships become more difficult for heterosexual men and women because of the unspoken question about whether the friendships will lead to a romantic involvement. Although common during adolescence and early adulthood, these friendships may be considered threatening once a person is in a long-term relationship or marriage. Consequently, friendships may diminish once a person has a partner or single friends may be replaced with couple friends.[2]

Figure 2. Many young adulthoods find intimacy through friendships rather than through committed romantic relationships. The increase of young adults attending college has contributed to this trend.

Gaining Adult Status

Many of the developmental tasks of early adulthood involve becoming part of the adult world and gaining independence. Young adults sometimes complain that they are not treated with respect, especially if they are put in positions of authority over older workers. Consequently, young adults may emphasize their age to gain credibility from those who are even slightly younger. "You're only 23? I'm 27!" a young adult might exclaim. [Note: This kind of statement is much less likely to come from someone in their 40s!]

The focus of early adulthood is often on the future. Many aspects of life are on hold while people go to school, go to work, and prepare for a brighter future. There may be a belief that the hurried life now lived will improve 'as soon as I finish school' or 'as soon as I get promoted' or 'as soon as the children get a little older.' As a result, time may seem to pass rather quickly. The day consists of meeting many demands that these tasks bring. The incentive for working so hard is that it will all result in a better future.

Levinson's Theory

In 1978, Daniel Levinson published a book entitled, *The Seasons of a Man's Life* in which he presented a theory of development in adulthood. Levinson's work was based on in-depth interviews with 40 men between the ages of 35-45. According to Levinson, young adults have an image of the future that motivates them. This image is called "the dream" and for the men interviewed, it was a dream of how their career paths would progress and where they would be at midlife. Dreams are very motivating. Dreams of a home bring excitement to couples as they look, save, and fantasize about how life will be. Dreams of careers motivate students to continue in school as they fantasize about how much their hard work will pay off. Dreams of playgrounds on a summer day inspire would-be parents. A dream is perfect and retains that perfection as long as it remains in the future. But as the realization of it moves closer, it may or may not measure up to its image. If it does, all is well. But if it does not, the image must be replaced or modified. And so, in adulthood, plans are made, efforts follow, and plans are reevaluated. This creating and recreating characterizes Levinson's theory.[footnote]Levinson, D. (1978). *The seasons of a man's life*. New York, NY: Alfred A. Knopf, Inc.[/footnote] (The shift from idealistic dreams to more realistic experiences might remind us of the cognitive development progression from formal to postformal thought in adulthood.)

Levinson's stages (at least up to midlife) are presented below (Levinson, 1978).[3] He suggested that periods of transition last about five years and periods of stability last about seven years. The ages presented below are based on life in the middle-class several decades ago. Think about how these ages and transitions might be different today, or in other cultures, or for women compared to men.

2. Ward, Adrian (2012). Men and Women Can't Be Just Friends. Scientific American. Retrieved from https://www.scientificamerican.com/article/men-and-women-cant-be-just-friends/.
3. Levinson, D. (1978) The seasons of a man's life. New York, NY: Alfred A. Knopf, Inc.

- Early adult transition (17-22): Leaving home, leaving family; making first choices about career and education
- Entering the adult world (22-28): Committing to an occupation, defining goals, finding intimate relationships
- Age 30 transition (28-33): Reevaluating those choices and perhaps making modifications or changing one's attitude toward love and work
- Settling down (33 to 40): Reinvesting in work and family commitments; becoming involved in the community
- Midlife transition (40-45): Reevaluating previous commitments; making dramatic changes if necessary; giving expression to previously ignored talents or aspirations; feeling more of a sense of urgency about life and its meaning
- Entering middle adulthood (45-50): Committing to new choices made and placing one's energies into these commitments

Nearly twenty years after his original research, Levinson interviewed 45 women ages 35-45 and published the book, *The seasons of a woman's life.*[4] He reported similar patterns with women, although women held a "split dream"—an image of the future in both work and family life and a concern with the timing and coordination of the two. Traditionally, by working outside the home, men were seen as taking care of their families. However, for women, working outside the home and taking care of their families were perceived as separate and competing for their time and attention. Hence, one aspect of the women's dreams was focused on one goal for several years and then their time and attention shifted towards the other, often resulting in delays in women's career dreams.

Figure 3. Women are often torn between caring for their families and advancing their careers outside of the home.

Adulthood, then, is a period of building and rebuilding one's life. Many of the decisions that are made in early adulthood are made before a person has had enough experience to really understand the consequences of such decisions. And, perhaps, many of these initial decisions are made with one goal in mind – to be seen as an adult. As a result, early decisions may be driven more by the expectations of others. For example, imagine someone who chose a career path based on other's advice but now finds that the job is not what was expected.

The age 30 transition may involve recommitting to the same job, not because it's stimulating, but because it pays well; or the person may decide to go back to school and change careers. Settling down may involve settling down with a new set of expectations. As the adult gains status, he or she may be freer to make more independent choices. And sometimes these are very different from those previously made. The midlife transition differs from the age 30 transition in that the person is more aware of how much time has gone by and how much time is left. This brings a sense of urgency and impatience about making changes. The future focus of early adulthood gives way to an emphasis on the present in midlife–we will explore this in our next module. Overall, Levinson calls our attention to the dynamic nature of adulthood.

4. Levinson, D. (1996). The seasons of a woman's life. New York, NY: Ballantine Books.

THINK IT OVER

- How well do you think Levinson's theory translates culturally? Do you think that personal desire and a concern with reconciling dreams with the realities of work and family is equally important in all cultures? Do you think these considerations are equally important in all social classes, races and ethnic groups? Why or why not? How might this model be modified in today's economy?

Emerging Adulthood

Arnett's Theory of Emerging Adulthood

Have you noticed that many young adults in our society today are taking longer to accomplish the early adulthood developmental tasks of becoming independent? If so, you're not alone. Jeffrey Arnett (2000) pointed out this prolonged transitional period and described it as "emerging adulthood."[5]

Figure 4. The years of emerging adulthood are often times of identity exploration through work, fashion, music, education, and other venues. [Image: CC0 Public Domain, https://goo.gl/m25gce]

The theory of **emerging adulthood** proposes that a new life stage has arisen between adolescence and young adulthood over the past half-century in industrialized countries. Fifty years ago, most young people in these countries had entered stable adult roles in love and work by their late teens or early twenties. Relatively few people pursued education or training beyond secondary school, and, consequently, most young men were full-time workers by the end of their teens. Relatively few women worked in occupations outside the home, and the median marriage age for women in the United States and in most other industrialized countries in 1960 was around 20 (Arnett & Taber, 1994; Douglass, 2005). The median marriage age for men was around 22, and married couples usually had their first child about one year after their wedding day. All told, for most young people half a century ago, their teenage adolescence led quickly and directly to stable adult roles in love and work by their late teens or early twenties. These roles would form the structure of their adult lives for decades to come.

Now all that has changed. A higher proportion of young people than ever before—about 70% in the United States—pursue education and training beyond secondary school (National Center for Education Statistics, 2012). The early twenties are not a time of entering stable adult work but a time of immense job instability: In the United States, the average number of job changes from ages 20 to 29 is seven. The median age of entering marriage in the United States is now 27 for women and 29 for men (U.S. Bureau of the Census, 2011). Consequently, a new stage of the life span, emerging adulthood, has been created, lasting from the late teens through the mid-twenties, roughly ages 18 to 25.

Five features make emerging adulthood distinctive:

5. Arnett, J.J. (2000). Emerging adulthood: A theory of development from the late teens through the twenties. American Psychologist, 55, 469-480.

- identity exploration,
- instability,
- self-focus,
- feeling in-between adolescence and adulthood,
- a sense of broad possibilities for the future.

If the years 18-25 are classified as "young adulthood," Arnett believes it is then difficult to find an appropriate term for the thirties. Emerging adults are still in the process of obtaining an education, are unmarried, and are childless. By age thirty, most of these individuals do see themselves as adults, based on the belief that they have more fully formed "individualistic qualities of character" such as self-responsibility, financial independence, and independence in decision-making. Arnett suggests that many of the individualistic characteristics associated with adult status correlate to, but are not dependent upon the role responsibilities with a career, marriage, and/or parenthood.

Whether or not "emerging adulthood" is considered to be a distinct developmental stage, it can be a useful concept in discussing developmental patterns in early adulthood in our culture today.

WATCH IT

To hear about emerging adulthood and why it takes longer to reach adulthood today, please view this video clip of Dr. Jeffrey Arnett. In the first 6 1/2 minutes he describes four societal revolutions that may have caused emerging adulthood. In the second half of the clip, Arnett discusses how "30 is the new 20," as twenty-somethings today enjoy unparalleled freedoms when compared with other generations.

- https://youtu.be/fv8KpQY0m6o

Is Emerging Adulthood a Global Phenomenon?

The five features proposed in the theory of emerging adulthood originally were based on research involving about 300 Americans between ages 18 and 29 from various ethnic groups, social classes, and geographical regions (Arnett, 2004). To what extent does the theory of emerging adulthood apply internationally?

The answer to this question depends greatly on what part of the world is considered. Demographers make a useful distinction between the developing countries that comprise the majority of the world's population and the economically developed countries that are part of the Organization for Economic Co-operation and Development (OECD), including the United States, Canada, western Europe, Japan, South Korea, Australia, and New Zealand. The current population of OECD countries (also called developed countries) is 1.2 billion, about 18% of the total world population (UNDP, 2011). The rest of the human population resides in developing countries, which have much lower median incomes; much lower median educational attainment; and much higher incidence of illness, disease, and early death. Let us consider emerging adulthood in OECD countries first, then in developing countries.

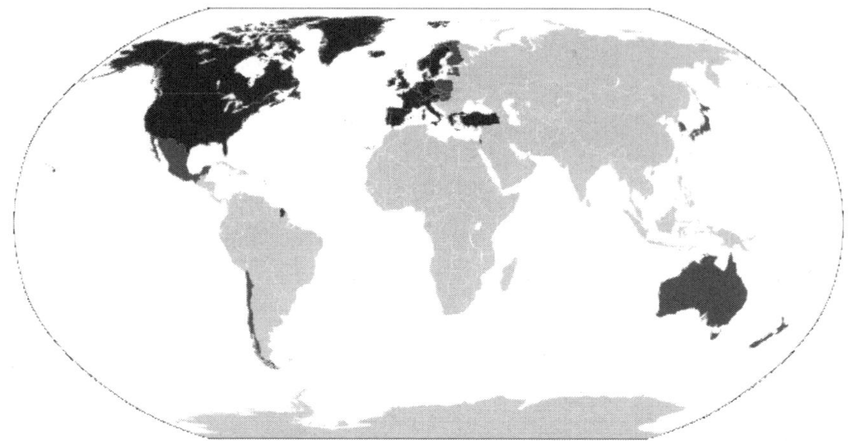

Figure 5. Map of OECD countries. Darker shaded countries are original members. [Image: Parastscilveks, https://goo.gl/MlvmOY, CC BY-SA 2.0, https://goo.gl/eH69he]

The same demographic changes as described above for the United States have taken place in other OECD countries as well. This is true of participation in postsecondary education as well as median ages for entering marriage and parenthood (UNdata, 2010). However, there is also substantial variability in how emerging adulthood is experienced across OECD countries. Europe is the region where emerging adulthood is longest and most leisurely. The median ages for entering marriage and parenthood are near 30 in most European countries (Douglass, 2007). Europe today is the location of the most affluent, generous, and egalitarian societies in the world—in fact, in human history (Arnett, 2007). Governments pay for tertiary education, assist young people in finding jobs, and provide generous unemployment benefits for those who cannot find work. In northern Europe, many governments also provide housing support. Emerging adults in European societies make the most of these advantages, gradually making their way to adulthood during their twenties while enjoying travel and leisure with friends.

The lives of Asian emerging adults in developed countries such as Japan and South Korea are in some ways similar to the lives of emerging adults in Europe and in some ways strikingly different. Like European emerging adults, Asian emerging adults tend to enter marriage and parenthood around age 30 (Arnett, 2011). Like European emerging adults, Asian emerging adults in Japan and South Korea enjoy the benefits of living in affluent societies with generous social welfare systems that provide support for them in making the transition to adulthood—for example, free university education and substantial unemployment benefits.

However, in other ways, the experience of emerging adulthood in Asian OECD countries is markedly different than in Europe. Europe has a long history of individualism, and today's emerging adults carry that legacy with them in their focus on self-development and leisure during emerging adulthood. In contrast, Asian cultures have a shared cultural history emphasizing collectivism and family obligations. Although Asian cultures have become more individualistic in recent decades as a consequence of globalization, the legacy of collectivism persists in the lives of emerging adults. They pursue identity explorations and self-development during emerging adulthood, like their American and European counterparts, but within narrower boundaries set by their sense of obligations to others, especially their parents (Phinney & Baldelomar, 2011). For example, in their views of the most important criteria for becoming an adult, emerging adults in the United States and Europe consistently rank financial independence among the most important markers of adulthood. In contrast, emerging adults with an Asian cultural background especially emphasize becoming capable of supporting parents financially as among the most important criteria (Arnett, 2003; Nelson, Badger, & Wu, 2004). This sense of family obligation may curtail their identity explorations in emerging adulthood to some extent, as they pay more heed to their parents' wishes about what they should study, what job they should take, and where they should live than emerging adults do in the West (Rosenberger, 2007).

Another notable contrast between Western and Asian emerging adults is in their sexuality. In the West, premarital sex is normative by the late teens, more than a decade before most people enter marriage. In the United States and Canada, and in northern and eastern Europe, cohabitation is also normative; most people have at least one cohabiting partnership before marriage. In southern Europe, cohabiting is still taboo, but premarital sex is tolerated in emerging adulthood. In contrast, both premarital sex and cohabitation remain rare and forbidden throughout Asia. Even dating is discouraged until the late twenties, when it would be a prelude to a serious relationship leading to marriage. In cross-cultural comparisons, about three fourths of emerging adults in the United States and Europe report having had premarital sexual relations by age 20, versus less than one fifth in Japan and South Korea (Hatfield and Rapson, 2006).

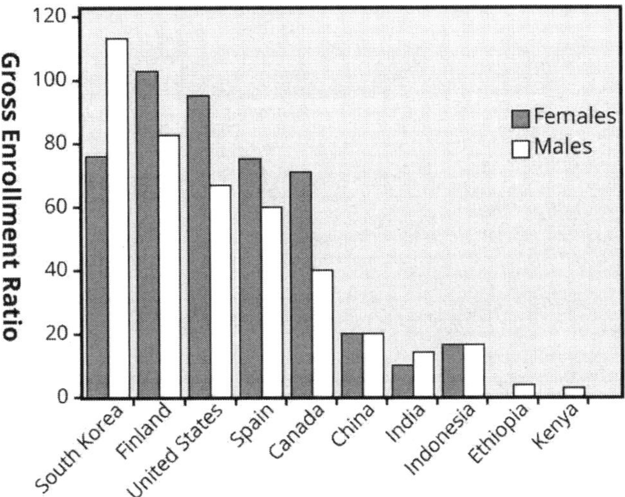

Figure 6. Gross tertiary enrollment, selected countries, 2007. Source: UNdata (2010). Note. Gross enrollment ratio is the total enrollment in a specific level of education, regardless of age, expressed as a percentage of the eligible official school-age population corresponding to the same level of education in a given school year. For the tertiary level, the population used is that of the five-year age group following the end of secondary schooling.

For young people in developing countries, emerging adulthood exists only for the wealthier segment of society, mainly the urban middle class, whereas the rural and urban poor—the majority of the population—have no emerging adulthood and may even have no adolescence because they enter adult-like work at an early age and also begin marriage and parenthood relatively early. What Saraswathi and Larson (2002) observed about adolescence applies to emerging adulthood as well: "In many ways, the lives of middle-class youth in India, South East Asia, and Europe have more in common with each other than they do with those of poor youth in their own countries." However, as globalization proceeds, and economic development along with it, the proportion of young people who experience emerging adulthood will increase as the middle class expands. By the end of the 21st century, emerging adulthood is likely to be normative worldwide.

A COUNTER ARGUMENT: NO EMERGING ADULTHOOD?

While Arnett describes "emerging adulthood" as a time of delayed entry into early adulthood, not everyone agrees. View this clip from Dr. Meg Jay, as she cautions young adults not to procrastinate since what happens during their twenties is important for the rest of adulthood: "Why 30 is not the new 20!"

GLOSSARY

emerging adulthood:

life stage extending from approximately ages 18 to 25, during which the foundation of an adult life is gradually constructed in love and work. Primary features include identity explorations, instability, focus on self-development, feeling incompletely adult, and a broad sense of possibilities

Relationships in Early Adulthood

What you'll learn to do: examine relationships in early adulthood

We have learned from Erikson that the psychosocial developmental task of early adulthood is "intimacy versus isolation" and if resolved relatively positively, it can lead to the virtue of "love." In this section, we will look more closely at relationships in early adulthood, particularly in terms of love, dating, cohabitation, marriage, and parenting.

LEARNING OUTCOMES

- Describe some of the factors related to attraction in relationships
- Apply Sternberg's theory of love to relationships
- Summarize attachment theory in adulthood
- Describe trends and norms in dating, cohabitation, and marriage in the United States
- Describe challenges, transitions, and factors associated with parenthood

Attraction and Love

Attraction

Why do some people hit it off immediately? Or decide that the friend of a friend was not likable? Using scientific methods, psychologists have investigated factors influencing attraction and have identified a number of variables, such as similarity, proximity (physical or functional), familiarity, and reciprocity, that influence with whom we develop relationships.

Figure 1. Great and important relationships can develop by chance and physical proximity helps. For example, seeing someone regularly on your daily bus commute to work or school may be all that's necessary to spark a genuine friendship. [Image: Cheri Lucas Rowlands, https://goo.gl/crCc0Q, CC BY-SA 2.0, https://goo.gl/rxiUsF]

Proximity

Often we "stumble upon" friends or romantic partners; this happens partly due to how close in proximity we are to those people. Specifically, **proximity** or *physical nearness* has been found to be a significant factor in the development of relationships. For example, when college students go away to a new school, they will make friends consisting of classmates, roommates, and teammates (i.e., people close in proximity). Proximity allows people the opportunity to get to know one other and discover their similarities—all of which can result in a friendship or intimate relationship. Proximity is not just about geographic distance, but rather functional distance, or the frequency with which we cross paths with others. For example, college students are more likely to become closer and develop relationships with people on their dorm-room floors because they see them (i.e., cross paths) more often than they see people on a different floor. How does the notion of proximity apply in terms of online relationships? Deb Levine (2000) argues that in terms of developing online relationships and attraction, functional distance refers to being at the same place at the same time in a virtual world (i.e., a chat room or Internet forum)—crossing virtual paths.

Familiarity

One of the reasons why proximity matters to attraction is that it breeds *familiarity*; people are more attracted to that which is familiar. Just being around someone or being repeatedly exposed to them increases the likelihood that we will be attracted to them. We also tend to feel safe with familiar people, as it is likely we know what to expect from them. Dr. Robert Zajonc (1968) labeled this phenomenon the mere-exposure effect. More specifically, he argued that the more often we are exposed to a stimulus (e.g., sound, person) the more likely we are to view that stimulus positively. Moreland and Beach (1992) demonstrated this by exposing a college class to four women (similar in appearance and age) who attended different numbers of classes, revealing that the more classes a woman attended, the more familiar, similar, and attractive she was considered by the other students.

There is a certain comfort in knowing what to expect from others; consequently, research suggests that we like what is familiar. While this is often on a subconscious level, research has found this to be one of the most basic principles of attraction (Zajonc, 1980). For example, a young man growing up with an overbearing mother may be attracted to other overbearing women *not* because he likes being dominated but rather because it is what he considers normal (i.e., familiar).

Similarity

When you hear about celebrity couples such as Kim Kardashian and Kanye West, do you shake your head thinking "this won't last"? It is probably because they seem so different. While many make the argument that opposites attract, research has found that is generally not true; *similarity* is key. Sure, there are times when couples can appear fairly different, but overall we like others who are like us. Ingram and Morris (2007) examined this phenomenon by inviting business executives to a cocktail mixer, 95% of whom reported that they wanted to meet new people. Using electronic name tag tracking, researchers revealed that the executives did not mingle or meet new people; instead, they only spoke with those they already knew well (i.e., people who were similar).

When it comes to marriage, research has found that couples tend to be very similar, particularly when it comes to age, social class, race, education, physical attractiveness, values, and attitudes (McCann Hamilton, 2007; Taylor, Fiore, Mendelsohn, & Cheshire, 2011). This phenomenon is known as the **matching hypothesis** (Feingold, 1988; Mckillip & Redel, 1983). We like others who validate our points of view and who are similar in thoughts, desires, and attitudes.

Reciprocity

Another key component in attraction is **reciprocity**; this principle is based on the notion that we are more likely to like someone if they feel the same way toward us. In other words, it is hard to be friends with someone who is not friendly in return. Another way to think of it is that relationships are built on give and take; if one side is not reciprocating, then the relationship is doomed. Basically, we feel obliged to give what we get and to maintain equity in relationships. Researchers have found that this is true across cultures (Gouldner, 1960).

Love

Figure 2. Romantic relationships are so central to psychological health that most people in the world are or will be in a romantic relationship in their lifetime. [Image: CC0 Public Domain, https://goo.gl/m25gce]

Is all love the same? Are there different types of love? Examining these questions more closely, Robert Sternberg's (2004; 2007) work has focused on the notion that all types of love are comprised of three distinct areas: intimacy, passion, and commitment. Intimacy includes caring, closeness, and emotional support. The passion component of love is comprised of physiological and emotional arousal; these can include physical attraction, emotional responses that promote physiological changes, and sexual arousal. Lastly, commitment refers to the cognitive process and decision to commit to love another person and the willingness to work to keep that love over the course of your life. The elements involved in intimacy (caring, closeness, and emotional support) are generally found in all types of close relationships—for example, a mother's love for a child or the love that friends share. Interestingly, this is not true for passion. Passion is unique to romantic love, differentiating friends from lovers. In sum, depending on the type of love and the stage of the relationship (i.e., newly in love), different combinations of these elements are present.

Taking this theory a step further, anthropologist Helen Fisher explained that she scanned the brains (using fMRI) of people who had just fallen in love and observed that their brain chemistry was "going crazy," similar to the brain of an addict on a drug high (Cohen, 2007). Specifically, serotonin production increased by as much as 40% in newly-in-love individuals. Further, those newly in love tended to show obsessive-compulsive tendencies. Conversely, when a person experiences a breakup, the brain processes it in a similar way to quitting a heroin habit (Fisher, Brown, Aron, Strong, & Mashek, 2009). Thus, those who believe that breakups are physically painful are correct! Another interesting point is that long-term love and sexual desire activate different areas of the brain. More specifically, sexual needs activate the part of the brain that is particularly sensitive to innately pleasurable things such as food, sex, and drugs (i.e., the striatum—a rather simplistic reward system), whereas love requires conditioning—it is more like a habit. When sexual needs are rewarded consistently, then love can develop. In other words, love grows out of positive rewards, expectancies, and habit (Cacioppo, Bianchi-Demicheli, Hatfield & Rapson, 2012).

LINK TO LEARNING

Dive deeper into Helen Fisher's research by watching her TED talk "The Brain in Love."

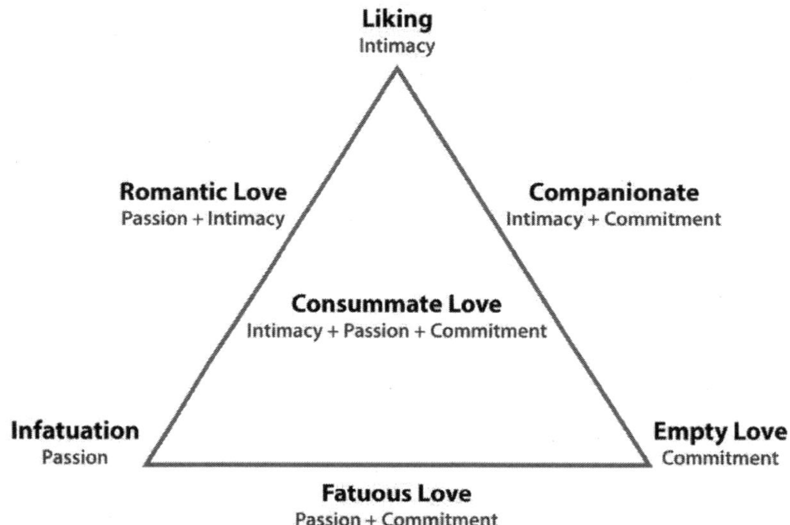

Figure 3. The Triangular Theory of Love. Adapted from Wikipedia Creative Commons, 2013.

ATTACHMENT THEORY IN ADULTHOOD

The need for intimacy, or close relationships with others, is universal and persistent across the lifespan. What our adult intimate relationships look like actually stems from infancy and our relationship with our primary caregiver (historically our mother)—a process of development described by attachment theory, which you learned about in the module on infancy. Recall that according to attachment theory, different styles of caregiving result in different relationship "attachments."

For example, responsive mothers—mothers who soothe their crying infants—produce infants who have secure attachments (Ainsworth, 1973; Bowlby, 1969). About 60% of all children are securely attached. As adults, secure individuals rely on their working models—concepts of how relationships operate—that were created in infancy, as a result of their interactions with their primary caregiver (mother), to foster happy and healthy adult intimate relationships. Securely attached adults feel comfortable being depended on and depending on others.

As you might imagine, inconsistent or dismissive parents also impact the attachment style of their infants (Ainsworth, 1973), but in a different direction. In early studies on attachment style, infants were observed interacting with their caregivers, followed by being separated from them, then finally reunited. About 20% of the observed children were "resistant," meaning they were anxious even before, and especially during, the separation; and 20% were "avoidant," meaning they actively avoided their caregiver after separation (i.e., ignoring the mother when they were reunited). These early attachment patterns can affect the way people relate to one another in adulthood. Anxious-resistant adults worry that others don't love them, and they often become frustrated or angry when their needs go unmet. Anxious-avoidant adults will appear not to care much about their intimate relationships and are uncomfortable being depended on or depending on others themselves.

Table 1. Types of Early Attachment and Adult Intimacy

Secure	"I find it relatively easy to get close to others and am comfortable depending on them and having them depend on me. I don't often worry about being abandoned or about someone getting too close to me,"
Anxious-avoidant	"I am somewhat uncomfortable being close to others; I find it difficult to trust them completely, difficult to allow myself to depend on them. I am nervous when anyone gets too close, and often, love partners want me to be more intimate than I feel comfortable being."
Anxious-resistant	"I find that others are reluctant to get as close as I would like. I often worry that my partner doesn't really love me or won't want to stay with me. I want to merge completely with another person, and this desire sometimes scares people away."

The good news is that our attachment can be changed. It isn't easy, but it is possible for anyone to "recover" a secure attachment. The process often requires the help of a supportive and dependable other, and for the insecure person to achieve coherence—the realization that his or her upbringing is not a permanent reflection of character or a reflection of the world at large, nor does it bar him or her from being worthy of love or others of being trustworthy (Treboux, Crowell, & Waters, 2004).

You can watch this video "What is Your Attachment Style?" from The School of Life to learn more.

Trends in Dating, Cohabitation, and Marriage

Dating

In general, traditional dating among teens and those in their early twenties has been replaced with more varied and flexible ways of getting together (and technology with social media, no doubt, plays a key role). The Friday night date with dinner and a movie that may still be enjoyed by those in their 30s gives way to less formal, more spontaneous meetings that may include several couples or a group of friends. Two people may get to know each other and go somewhere alone. How would you describe a "typical" date? Who calls, texts, or face times? Who pays? Who decides where to go? What is the purpose of the date? In general, greater planning is required for people who have additional family and work responsibilities.

Dating and the Internet

The ways people are finding love has changed with the advent of the Internet. In a poll, 49% of all American adults reported that either themselves or someone they knew had dated a person they met online (Madden & Lenhart, 2006). As Finkel and colleagues (2007) found, social networking sites, and the Internet generally, perform three important tasks. Specifically, sites provide individuals with access to a database of other individuals who are interested in meeting someone. Dating sites generally reduce issues of proximity, as individuals do not have to be close in proximity to meet. Also, they provide a medium in which individuals can communicate with others. Finally, some Internet dating websites advertise special matching strategies, based on factors such as personality, hobbies, and interests, to identify the "perfect match" for people looking for love online. In general, scientific questions about the effectiveness of Internet matching or online dating compared to face-to-face dating remain to be answered.

It is important to note that social networking sites have opened the doors for many to meet people that they might not have ever had the opportunity to meet; unfortunately, it now appears that the social networking sites can be forums for unsuspecting people to be duped. In 2010 a documentary, Catfish, focused on the personal experience of a man who met a woman online and carried on an emotional relationship with this person for months. As he later came to discover, though, the person he thought he was talking and writing with did not exist. As Dr. Aaron Ben-Zeév stated, online relationships leave room for deception; thus, people have to be cautious.

Cohabitation

Cohabitation is an arrangement where two people who are not married live together. They often involve a romantic or sexually intimate relationship on a long-term or permanent basis. Such arrangements have become increasingly common in Western countries during the past few decades, being led by changing social views, especially regarding marriage, gender roles and religion. Today, cohabitation is a common pattern among people in the Western world. In Europe, the Scandinavian countries have been the first to start this leading trend, although many countries have since followed. Mediterranean Europe has traditionally been very conservative, with religion playing a strong role. Until the mid-1990s, cohabitation levels remained low in this region, but have since increased. Cohabitation is common in many countries, with the Scandinavian nations of Iceland, Sweden, and Norway reporting the highest percentages, and more traditional countries like India, China, and Japan reporting low percentages (DeRose, 2011).

In countries where cohabitation is increasingly common, there has been speculation as to whether or not cohabitation is now part of the natural developmental progression of romantic relationships: dating and courtship, then cohabitation, engagement, and finally marriage. Though, while many cohabitating arrangements ultimately lead to marriage, many do not.

How prevalent is cohabitation today in the United States? According to the U.S. Census Bureau (2018), cohabitation has been increasing, while marriage has been decreasing in young adulthood. As seen in the graph below, over the past 50 years, the percentage of 18-24 year olds in the U.S. living with an unmarried partner has gone from 0.1 percent to 9.4 percent, while living with a spouse has gone from 39.2 percent to 7 percent. More 18-24 year olds live with an unmarried partner now than with a married partner.

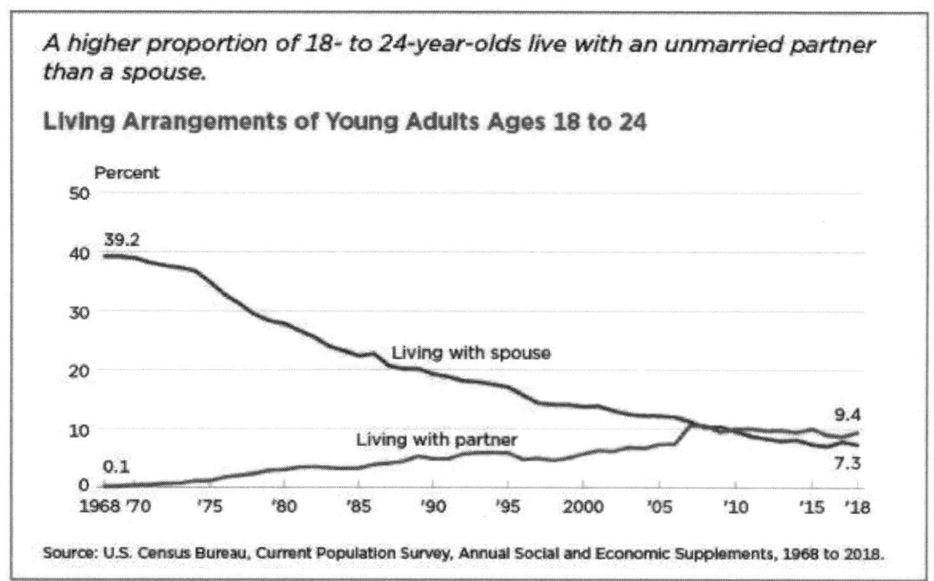

Figure 4. The rates of those between ages 18-24 living with a spouse have gone down dramatically, while rates of those living with a partner are gradually on the rise.

While the percent living with a spouse is still higher than the percent living with an unmarried partner among 25 to 34-year-olds today, the next graph clearly shows a similar pattern of decline in marriage and increase in cohabitation over the last five decades. The percent living with a spouse in this age group today is only half of what it was in 1968 (40.3 percent vs. 81.5

percent), while the percent living with an unmarried partner rose from 0.2 percent to 14.8 percent in this age group. Another way to look at some of the data is that only 30% of today's 18 to 34-year-olds in the U.S. are married, compared with almost double that, 59 percent forty years ago (1978). The marriage rates for less-educated young adults (who tend to have lower income) have fallen at faster rates than those of better educated young adults since the 1970s. Past and present economic climate are key factors; perhaps more couples are waiting until they can afford to get married, financially. Gurrentz (2018) does caution that there are limitations of the measures of cohabitation, particularly in the past.[1]

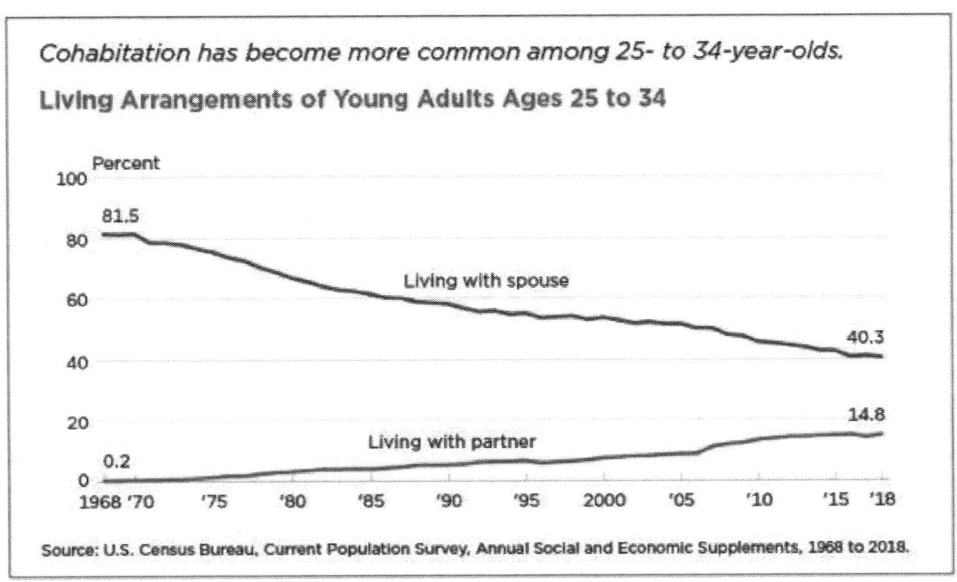

Figure 5. Rates of those living with spouses between the ages of 25 and 34 has been declining, while those cohabitating is on the rise.

How long do cohabiting relationships last?

Cohabitation tends to last longer in European countries than in the United States. Half of cohabiting relationships in the U. S. end within a year; only 10 percent last more than 5 years. These short-term cohabiting relationships are more characteristics of people in their early 20s. Many of these couples eventually marry. Those who cohabit more than five years tend to be older and more committed to the relationship. Cohabitation may be preferable to marriage for a number of reasons. For partners over 65, cohabitation is preferable to marriage for practical reasons. For many of them, marriage would result in a loss of Social Security benefits and consequently is not an option. Others may believe that their relationship is more satisfying because they are not bound by marriage.

LEARNING OUTCOMES

Do you think that you will cohabitate before marriage? Or did you cohabitate? Why or why not? Does your culture play a role in your decision? Does what you learned in this module change your thoughts on this practice?

1. Gurrentz, B. (2018, November 15). Living with an unmarried partner now common for young adults. https://www.census.gov/library/stories/2018/11/cohabitation-is-up-marriage-is-down-for-young-adults.html

Same-Sex Couples

As of 2019, same-sex marriage is legal in 28 countries, and counting. Many other countries either recognize same-sex couples for the purpose of immigration, grant rights for domestic partnerships or grant common law marriage status to same-sex couples.

Same-sex couples struggle with concerns such as the division of household tasks, finances, sex, and friendships as do heterosexual couples. One difference between same-sex and heterosexual couples, however, is that same-sex couples have to live with the added stress that comes from social disapproval and discrimination. And continued contact with an ex-partner may be more likely among homosexuals and bisexuals because of the closeness of the circle of friends and acquaintances.

Figure 6. While marriage is common across cultures, the details such as "How" and "When" are often quite different. Now the "Who" of marriage is experiencing an important change as laws are updated in a growing number of countries and states to give same-sex couples the same rights and benefits through marriage as heterosexual couples. [Image: Bart Vis, http://goo.gl/liSy9P, CC BY 2.0, http://goo.gl/T4qgSp]

The number of adults who remain single has increased dramatically in the last 30 years. We have more people who never marry, more widows and more divorcees driving up the number of singles. Singles represent about 25 percent of American households. Singlehood has become a more acceptable lifestyle than it was in the past and many singles are very happy with their status. Whether or not a single person is happy depends on the circumstances of their remaining single.

Stein's Typology of Singles

Many of the research findings about singles reveal that they are not all alike. Happiness with one's status depends on whether the person is single by choice and whether the situation is permanent. Let's look at Stein's (1981) four categories of singles for a better understanding of this.

- **Voluntary temporary singles**: These are younger people who have never been married and divorced people who are postponing marriage and remarriage. They may be more involved in careers or getting an education or just wanting to have fun without making a commitment to any one person. They are not quite ready for that kind of relationship. These people tend to report being very happy with their single status.
- **Voluntary permanent singles**: These individuals do not want to marry and aren't intending to marry. This might include cohabiting couples who don't want to marry, priests, nuns, or others who are not considering marriage. Again, this group is typically single by choice and understandably more contented with this decision.
- **Involuntary temporary**: These are people who are actively seeking mates. They hope to marry or remarry and may be involved in going on blind dates, seeking a partner on the internet or placing "getting personal" aids in search of a mate. They tend to be more anxious about being single.
- **Involuntary permanent**: These are older divorced, widowed, or never-married people who wanted to marry but have not found a mate and are coming to accept singlehood as a probable permanent situation. Some are bitter about not having married while others are more accepting of how their life has developed.

Engagement and Marriage

Most people will marry in their lifetime. In the majority of countries, 80% of men and women have been married by the age of 49 (United Nations, 2013). Despite how common marriage remains, it has undergone some interesting shifts in recent times. Around the world, people are tending to get married later in life or, increasingly, not at all. People in more developed countries (e.g., Nordic and Western Europe), for instance, marry later in life—at an average age of 30 years. This is very different than, for example, the economically developing country of Afghanistan, which has one of the lowest average-age statistics for marriage—at 20.2 years (United Nations, 2013). Another shift seen around the world is a gender gap in terms of age when people get married. In every country, men marry later than women. Since the 1970's, the average age of marriage has increased for both women and men.

As illustrated, the courtship process can vary greatly around the world. So too can an engagement—a formal agreement to get married. Some of these differences are small, such as on which hand an engagement ring is worn. In many countries, it is worn on the left, but in Russia, Germany, Norway, and India, women wear their ring on their right. There are also more overt differences, such as who makes the proposal. In India and Pakistan, it is not uncommon for the family of the groom to propose to the family of the bride, with little to no involvement from the bride and groom themselves. In most Western industrialized countries, it is traditional for the male to propose to the female. What types of engagement traditions, practices, and rituals are common where you are from? How are they changing?

Contemporary young adults in the United States are waiting longer than before to marry. The median age of entering marriage in the United States is 27 for women and 29 for men (U.S. Bureau of the Census, 2011). This trend in delays of young adults taking on adult roles and responsibilities is discussed in our earlier section about "emerging adulthood" or the transition from adolescence to adulthood identified by Arnett (2000).

A fair exchange

Social exchange theory suggests that people try to maximize rewards and minimize costs in social relationships. Each person entering the marriage market comes equipped with assets and liabilities or a certain amount of social currency with which to attract a prospective mate. For men, assets might include earning potential and status while for women, assets might include physical attractiveness and youth.

Customers in the "marriage market" do not look for a "good deal," however. Rather, most look for a relationship that is mutually beneficial or equitable. One of the reasons for this is because most a relationship in which one partner has far more assets than the other will result if power disparities and a difference in the level of commitment from each partner. According to Waller's principle of least interest, the partner who has the most to lose without the relationship (or is the most dependent on the relationship) will have the least amount of power and is in danger of being exploited. A greater balance of power, then, may add stability to the relationship.

Societies specify through both formal and informal rules who is an appropriate mate. Consequently, mate selection is not completely left to the individual. Rules of endogamy indicate within which groups we should marry. For example, many cultures specify that people marry within their own race, social class, age group, or religion. These rules encourage **homogamy** or marriage between people who share social characteristics (the opposite is known as **heterogamy**). The majority of marriages in the U.S. are homogamous with respect to race, social class, age and to a lesser extent, religion.

In a comparison of educational homogamy in 55 countries, Smits (2003) found strong support for higher-educated people marrying other highly educated people. As such, education appears to be a strong filter people use to help them select a mate. The most common filters we use—or, put another way, the characteristics we focus on most in potential mates—are age, race, social status, and religion (Regan, 2008). Other filters we use include compatibility, physical attractiveness (we tend to pick people who are as attractive as we are), and proximity (for practical reasons, we often pick people close to us) (Klenke-Hamel & Janda, 1980).

According to the **filter theory of mate selection,** the pool of eligible partners becomes narrower as it passes through filters used to eliminate members of the pool (Kerckhoff & Davis, 1962). One such filter is propinquity or geographic proximity. Mate selection in the United States typically involves meeting eligible partners face to face. Those with whom one does not come into contact are simply not contenders (though this has been changing with the Internet). Race and ethnicity is another filter used to eliminate partners. Although interracial dating has increased in recent years and interracial marriage rates are higher than before, interracial marriage still represents only 5.4 percent of all marriages in the United States. Physical appearance is another feature considered when selecting a mate. Age, social class, and religion are also criteria used to narrow the field of eligibles. Thus, the field of eligibles becomes significantly smaller before those things we are most conscious of such as preferences, values, goals, and interests, are even considered.

Figure 7. In some countries, many people are coupled and committed to marriage through arrangements made by parents or professional marriage brokers. [Image: Ananabanana, http://goo.gl/gzCR0x, CC BY-NC-SA 2.0, http://goo.gl/iF4hmM]

Arranged Marriages

In some cultures, however, it is not uncommon for the families of young people to do the work of finding a mate for them. For example, the Shanghai Marriage Market refers to the People's Park in Shanghai, China—a place where parents of unmarried adults meet on weekends to trade information about their children in attempts to find suitable spouses for them (Bolsover, 2011). In India, the marriage market refers to the use of marriage brokers or marriage bureaus to pair eligible singles together (Trivedi, 2013). To many Westerners, the idea of arranged marriage can seem puzzling. It can appear to take the romance out of the equation and violate values about personal freedom. On the other hand, some people in favor of arranged marriage argue that parents are able to make more mature decisions than young people.

While such intrusions may seem inappropriate based on your upbringing, for many people of the world such help is expected, even appreciated. In India for example, "parental arranged marriages are largely preferred to other forms of marital choices" (Ramsheena & Gundemeda, 2015, p. 138). Of course, one's religious and social caste plays a role in determining how involved family may be.

Parenting

Having Children

Do you want children? Do you already have children? Increasingly, families are postponing or not having children. Families that choose to forego having children are known as childfree families, while families that want but are unable to conceive are referred to as childless families. As more young people pursue their education and careers, age at first marriage has increased; similarly, so has the age at which people become parents. With a college degree, the average age for women to have their first child is 30.3, but without a college degree, the average age is 23.8. Marital status is also related, as the average age for married women to have their first child is 28.8, while the average age for unmarried women is 23.1. Overall, the average age of first time mothers has increased to 26, up from 21 in 1972, and the average age of first time fathers has increased to 31, up from 27 in 1972 in the United States.[2] The age of first-time parents in the U.S. increased sharply in the 1970s after abortion was legalized. Since the age of first-time parents varies by geographic region in the U.S. and women's rights to abortion are being challenged in some states, it will be interesting to follow the norms and trends for first-time parents in the future.

2. Bui, Quoctrung & Claire Cain Miller (August 2018). The Age That Women Have Babies: How A Gap Divides America. The New York Times. Retrieved from https://www.nytimes.com/interactive/2018/08/04/upshot/up-birth-age-gap.html>

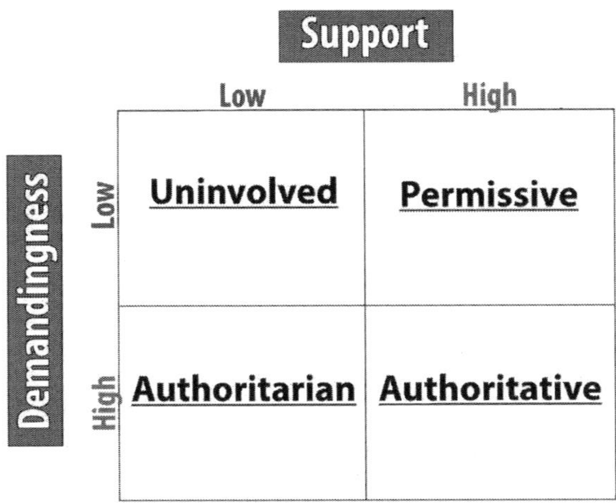

Figure 8. Authoritative parenting, or those parents who give high levels of support but also have high demands and expectations, are associated with the best outcomes for children,

The decision to become a parent should not be taken lightly. There are positives and negatives associated with parenting that should be considered. Many parents report that having children increases their well-being (White & Dolan, 2009). Researchers have also found that parents, compared to their non-parent peers, are more positive about their lives (Nelson, Kushlev, English, Dunn, & Lyubomirsky, 2013). On the other hand, researchers have also found that parents, compared to non-parents, are more likely to be depressed, report lower levels of marital quality, and feel like their relationship with their partner is more businesslike than intimate (Walker, 2011).

If you do become a parent, your parenting style will impact your child's future success in romantic and parenting relationships. Recall from the module on early childhood that there are several different parenting styles. **Authoritative** parenting, arguably the best parenting style, is both demanding and supportive of the child (Maccoby & Martin, 1983). Support refers to the amount of affection, acceptance, and warmth a parent provides. **Demandingness** refers to the degree a parent controls their child's behavior. Children who have authoritative parents are generally happy, capable, and successful (Maccoby, 1992).

Other, less advantageous parenting styles include authoritarian (in contrast to authorit*ative*), permissive, and uninvolved (Tavassolie, Dudding, Madigan, Thorvardarson, & Winsler, 2016). **Authoritarian** parents are low in support and high in demandingness. Arguably, this is the parenting style used by Harry Potter's harsh aunt and uncle, and Cinderella's vindictive stepmother. Children who receive authoritarian parenting are more likely to be obedient and proficient but score lower in happiness, social competence, and self-esteem. **Permissive** parents are high in support and low in demandingness. Their children rank low in happiness and self-regulation and are more likely to have problems with authority. **Uninvolved** parents are low in both support and demandingness. Children of these parents tend to rank lowest across all life domains, lack self-control, have low self-esteem, and are less competent than their peers.

Support for the benefits of authoritative parenting has been found in countries as diverse as the Czech Republic (Dmitrieva, Chen, Greenberger, & Gil-Rivas, 2004), India (Carson, Chowdhurry, Perry, & Pati, 1999), China (Pilgrim, Luo, Urberg, & Fang, 1999), Israel (Mayseless, Scharf, & Sholt, 2003), and Palestine (Punamaki, Qouta, & Sarraj, 1997). In fact, authoritative parenting appears to be superior in Western, individualistic societies—so much so that some people have argued that there is no longer a need to study it (Steinberg, 2001). Other researchers are less certain about the superiority of authoritative parenting and point to differences in cultural values and beliefs. For example, while many European-American children do poorly with too much strictness (authorit*arian* parenting), Chinese children often do well, especially academically. The reason for this likely stems from Chinese culture viewing strictness in parenting as related to training, which is not central to American parenting (Chao, 1994).

The Development of Parents

Think back to an emotional event you experienced as a child. How did your parents react to you? Did your parents get frustrated or criticize you, or did they act patiently and provide support and guidance? Did your parents provide lots of rules for you or let you make decisions on your own? Why do you think your parents behaved the way they did?

Figure 9. Parenthood has a huge impact on a person's identity, emotions, daily behaviors, and many other aspects of their lives. [Image: Kim881231, CC0 Public Domain, https://goo.gl/m25gce]

Psychologists have attempted to answer these questions about the influences on parents and understand why parents behave the way they do. Because parents are critical to a child's development, a great deal of research has been focused on the impact that parents have on children. Less is known, however, about the development of parents themselves and the impact of children on parents. Nonetheless, parenting is a major role in an adult's life. Parenthood is often considered a normative developmental task of adulthood. Cross-cultural studies show that adolescents around the world plan to have children. In fact, most men and women in the United States will become parents by the age of 40 years (Martinez, Daniels, & Chandra, 2012).

People have children for many reasons, including emotional reasons (e.g., the emotional bond with children and the gratification the parent–child relationship brings), economic and utilitarian reasons (e.g., children provide help in the family and support in old age), and social-normative reasons (e.g., adults are expected to have children; children provide status) (Nauck, 2007).

The Changing Face of Parenthood

Parenthood is undergoing changes in the United States and elsewhere in the world. Children are less likely to be living with both parents, and women in the United States have fewer children than they did previously. The average fertility rate of women in the United States was about seven children in the early 1900s and has remained relatively stable at 2.1 since the 1970s (Hamilton, Martin, & Ventura, 2011; Martinez, Daniels, & Chandra, 2012). Not only are parents having fewer children, but the context of parenthood has also changed. Parenting outside of marriage has increased dramatically among most socioeconomic, racial, and ethnic groups, although college-educated women are substantially more likely to be married at the birth of a child than are mothers with less education (Dye, 2010). Parenting is occurring outside of marriage for many reasons, both economic and social. People are having children at older ages, too. Despite the fact that young people are more often delaying childbearing, most 18- to 29-year-olds want to have children and say that being a good parent is one of the most important things in life (Wang & Taylor, 2011).

Table 2. Demographic Changes in Parenthood in the United States

	1960	2012
Average number of children (fertility rate)	3.6	2.1
Percent of births to unmarried women	5%	41%
Median age at first marriage for women	20.8	26.5
Percent of adults ages 18 to 29 married	59%	20%

Galinsky (1987) was one of the first to emphasize the development of parents themselves, how they respond to their children's development, and how they grow as parents. Parenthood is an experience that transforms one's identity as parents take on new roles. Children's growth and development force parents to change their roles. They must develop new skills and abilities in response to children's development. Galinsky identified six stages of parenthood that focus on different tasks and goals (see Table 2).

Table 3. Galinsky's Stages of Parenthood

	Age of Child	Main Tasks and Goals
Stage 1: The Image-Making Stage	Planning for a child; pregnancy	Consider what it means to be a parent and plan for changes to accommodate a child
Stage 2: The Nurturing Stage	Infancy	Develop an attachment relationship with child and adapt to the new baby
Stage 3: The Authority Stage	Toddler and preschool	Parents create rules and figure out how to effectively guide their children's behavior
Stage 4: The Interpretative Stage	Middle childhood	Parents help their children interpret their experiences with the social world beyond the family
Stage 5: The Interdependent Stage	Adolescence	Parents renegotiate their relationship with their adolescent children to allow for shared power in decision-making.
Stage 6: The Departure Stage	Early Adulthood	Parents evaluate their successes and failures as parents

1. The Image-Making Stage

As prospective parents think about and form images about their roles as parents and what parenthood will bring, and prepare for the changes an infant will bring, they enter the image-making stage. Future parents develop their ideas about what it will be like to be a parent and the type of parent they want to be. Individuals may evaluate their relationships with their own parents as a model of their roles as parents.

2. The Nurturing Stage

The second stage, the nurturing stage, occurs at the birth of the baby. A parent's main goal during this stage is to develop an attachment relationship with their baby. Parents must adapt their romantic relationships, their relationships with their other children, and with their own parents to include the new infant. Some parents feel attached to the baby immediately, but for other parents, this occurs more gradually. Parents may have imagined their infant in specific ways, but they now have to reconcile those images with their actual baby. In incorporating their relationship with their child into their other relationships, parents often have to reshape their conceptions of themselves and their identity. Parenting responsibilities are the most demanding during infancy because infants are completely dependent on caregiving.

3. The Authority Stage

The authority stage occurs when children are 2 years old until about 4 or 5 years old. In this stage, parents make decisions about how much authority to exert over their children's behavior. Parents must establish rules to guide their child's behavior and development. They have to decide how strictly they should enforce rules and what to do when rules are broken.

4. The Interpretive Stage

The interpretive stage occurs when children enter school (preschool or kindergarten) to the beginning of adolescence. Parents interpret their children's experiences as children are increasingly exposed to the world outside the family. Parents answer their children's questions, provide explanations, and determine what behaviors and values to teach. They decide what experiences to provide their children, in terms of schooling, neighborhood, and extracurricular activities. By this time, parents have experience in the parenting role and often reflect on their strengths and weaknesses as parents, review their images of parenthood, and determine how realistic they have been. Parents have to negotiate how involved to be with their children, when to step in, and when to encourage children to make choices independently.

5. The Interdependent Stage

Parents of teenagers are in the interdependent stage. They must redefine their authority and renegotiate their relationship with their adolescent as the children increasingly make decisions independent of parental control and authority. On the other hand, parents do not permit their adolescent children to have complete autonomy over their decision-making and behavior, and thus adolescents and parents must adapt their relationship to allow for greater negotiation and discussion about rules and limits.

6. The Departure Stage

During the departure stage of parenting, parents evaluate the entire experience of parenting. They prepare for their child's departure, redefine their identity as the parent of an adult child, and assess their parenting accomplishments and failures. This stage forms a transition to a new era in parents' lives. This stage usually spans a long time period from when the oldest child moves away (and often returns) until the youngest child leaves. The parenting role must be redefined as a less central role in a parent's identity.

Figure 10. When a child achieves a new level of independence and leaves the home it marks another turning point in the identity of a parent. [Image: State Farm, https://goo.gl/Npw2fb, CC BY 2.0, https://goo.gl/BRvSA7]

Despite the interest in the development of parents among laypeople and helping professionals, little research has examined developmental changes in parents' experience and behaviors over time. Thus, it is not clear whether these theoretical stages are generalizable to parents of different races, ages, and religions, nor do we have empirical data on the factors that influence individual differences in these stages. On a practical note, how-to books and websites geared toward parental development should be evaluated with caution, as not all advice provided is supported by research.

Influences on Parenting

Parenting is a complex process in which parents and children influence one another. There are many reasons that parents behave the way they do. The multiple influences on parenting are still being explored. Proposed influences on parental behavior include 1) parent characteristics, 2) child characteristics, and 3) contextual and sociocultural characteristics (Belsky, 1984; Demick, 1999).

Parent Characteristics

Parents bring unique traits and qualities to the parenting relationship that affect their decisions as parents. These characteristics include the age of the parent, gender, beliefs, personality, developmental history, knowledge about parenting and child development, and mental and physical health. Parents' personalities affect parenting behaviors. Mothers and fathers who are more agreeable, conscientious, and outgoing are warmer and provide more structure to their children. Parents who are more agreeable, less anxious, and less negative also support their children's autonomy more than parents who are anxious and less agreeable (Prinzie, Stams, Dekovic, Reijntjes, & Belsky, 2009). Parents who have these personality traits appear to be better able to respond to their children positively and provide a more consistent, structured environment for their children.

Parents' developmental histories, or their experiences as children, also affect their parenting strategies. Parents may learn parenting practices from their own parents. Fathers whose own parents provided monitoring, consistent and age-appropriate discipline, and warmth were more likely to provide this constructive parenting to their own children (Kerr, Capaldi, Pears, & Owen, 2009). Patterns of negative parenting and ineffective discipline also appear from one generation to the next. However, parents who are dissatisfied with their own parents' approach may be more likely to change their parenting methods with their own children.

Child Characteristics

Parenting is bidirectional. Not only do parents affect their children, but children also influence their parents. Child characteristics, such as gender, birth order, temperament, and health status, affect parenting behaviors and roles. For example, an infant with an easy temperament may enable parents to feel more effective, as they are easily able to soothe the child and elicit smiling and cooing. On the other hand, a cranky or fussy infant elicits fewer positive reactions from his or her parents and may result in parents feeling less effective in the parenting role (Eisenberg et al., 2008). Over time, parents of more difficult children may become more punitive and less patient with their children (Clark, Kochanska, & Ready, 2000; Eisenberg et al., 1999; Kiff, Lengua, & Zalewski, 2011). Parents who have a fussy, difficult child are less satisfied with their marriages and have greater challenges in balancing work and family roles (Hyde, Else-Quest, & Goldsmith, 2004). Thus, child temperament is one of the child characteristics that influences how parents behave with their children.

Figure 11. A child with a difficult temperament can have a significant impact on a parent. [Image: Harald Groven, https://goo.gl/cwemLg, CC BY-SA 2.0, https://goo.gl/eH69he]

Another child characteristic is the gender of the child. Parents respond differently to boys and girls. Parents often assign different household chores to their sons and daughters. Girls are more often responsible for caring for younger siblings and household chores, whereas boys are more likely to be asked to perform chores outside the home, such as mowing the lawn (Grusec, Goodnow, & Cohen, 1996). Parents also talk differently with their sons and daughters, providing more scientific explanations to their sons and using more emotion words with their daughters (Crowley, Callanan, Tenenbaum, & Allen, 2001).

Contextual Factors and Sociocultural Characteristics

The parent–child relationship does not occur in isolation. Sociocultural characteristics, including economic hardship, religion, politics, neighborhoods, schools, and social support, also influence parenting. Parents who experience economic hardship are more easily frustrated, depressed, and sad, and these emotional characteristics affect their parenting skills (Conger & Conger, 2002). Culture also influences parenting behaviors in fundamental ways. Although promoting the development of skills necessary to function effectively in one's community is a universal goal of parenting, the specific skills necessary vary widely from culture to culture. Thus, parents have different goals for their children that partially depend on their culture (Tamis-LeMonda et al., 2008). For example, parents vary in how much they emphasize goals for independence and individual achievements, and goals involving maintaining harmonious relationships and being embedded in a strong network of social relationships. These differences in parental goals are influenced by culture and by immigration status. Other important contextual characteristics, such as the neighborhood, school, and social networks, also affect parenting, even though these settings don't always include both the child and the parent (Brofenbrenner, 1989). For example, Latina mothers who perceived their neighborhood as more dangerous showed less warmth with their children, perhaps because of the greater stress associated with living a threatening environment (Gonzales et al., 2011). Many contextual factors influence parenting.

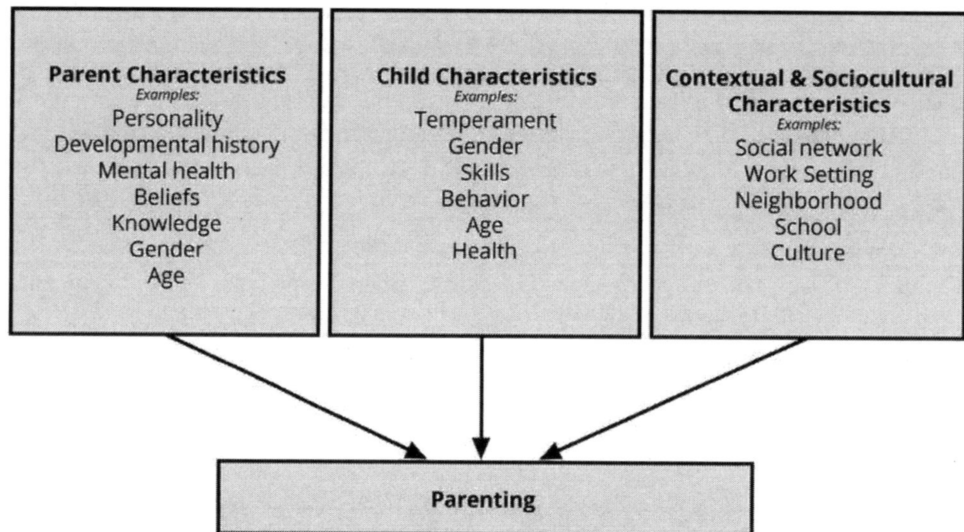

Figure 12. Influences on parenting include characteristics of the parent and child, as well as the context and world around them.

GLOSSARY

authoritative parenting:
parenting that is both demanding and supportive of the child

authoritarian parenting:
parenting style that is high in demandingness and low in support

cohabitation:
an arrangement where two people who have not married live together

demandingness:
the degree a parent controls their child's behavior

filter theory of mate selection:
the pool of eligible partners becomes narrower as it passes through filters used to eliminate members of the pool

heterogamy:
marriage between people who do not share social characteristics

homogamy:
marriage between people who share social characteristics

matching hypothesis:
we tend to be attracted to those who are similar to us in age, social class, race, education, physical attractiveness, values, and attitudes

permissive parenting:
parenting that is low in demandingness and high in support

proximity:
a term for physical nearness which been found to be a significant factor in the development of relationships

reciprocity:
we are more likely to like someone if they feel the same way toward us

social exchange theory:
people try to maximize rewards and minimize costs in social relationships

uninvolved parenting:
parenting that is low in both support and demandingness

Putting It Together: Early Adulthood

As we have learned in this module, young adults are often in the "prime of life," especially physically and sexually. However, young adults may be engaged in risky behaviors and be particularly vulnerable to injuries, accidents, alcohol and drug use/abuse, sexually transmitted diseases, rape, and suicide. Nutrition and exercise habits in this stage are important since they are associated with health and certain illnesses in middle age. Cognitive and brain development continues, with the influences of education and experience. Young adults may move from formal logical thinking to postformal thinking, becoming better at considering multiple perspectives and contexts, appreciating ambiguity and uncertainty, and using practical experience in making decisions.

Higher education plays an important role for more and more young adults—in this module we examined the connections between education and work and learned about how exploring and choosing one's career is key during this stage. We saw that establishing intimacy in friendships, romance, and family relationships is another significant aspect of young adulthood; love, dating, cohabitation, marriage, and becoming parents were all examined.

We were introduced to the major theories of adult development, primarily those of Erikson and Levinson, and we learned about Arnett's "emerging adulthood," a potentially new stage involving the transition from adolescence to young adulthood, with young adults taking on "adult roles" later than expected. By the late thirties, though, most young adults have become independent of their parents/families of origin and are in the throes of adult work, family, and community activities and responsibilities.

Please read the article below for a summary of some of these early adulthood topics, but from a slightly different perspective—that of generations or cohorts. "Millennials" are defined as individuals who were born between 1981 and 1996, and as such, they make up a large part of today's young adults. Read about this group in terms of education, work, finances, living with parents, getting married, and having children, comparing their norms with those of previous generations and potentially future generations of young adults. Consider "emerging adulthood"; how much do you think generation, history, and culture are affecting this observed phenomenon? Will it continue to be part of early adulthood development in the future? Why or why not?

LINK TO LEARNING: MILLENIALS AND OTHER GENERATIONS

Read this article "Millennial life: How young adulthood today compares with prior generations" from the Pew Research Center.

Discussion: Early Adulthood

DISCUSSION: In this discussion, reflect upon and discuss BOTH of the following questions:

- Q1: At what age would you consider a person to be an adult? Explain your reasoning. Are there specific milestones that need to be accomplished?
- Q2: How important do you think the accomplishment of intimacy vs. isolation is? Can a person lead a happy life without finding a significant other? Explain using examples from your life supported by information from the reading.

STEP 1: First, write a response with at least EIGHT substantial sentences, integrating concepts you learned from the reading and other materials (include links with necessary). Show that you can think critically on the topic by integrating your own thoughts, analysis, or experiences.

STEP 2: Then return to the discussion to comment on at least TWO classmates' posts (in at least FIVE sentences). Expand on a classmate's comments in a value-adding, topic-related way. Promote a collaborative, supportive community, and advance the dialogue through follow-up questions. Reply posts cannot be one-liners, off-topic posts, vague statements, unsupported opinions, inadequate explanations or simply say, "I agree" or "good job."

MODULE 9: MIDDLE ADULTHOOD

Why It Matters: Middle Adulthood

Why learn about human development during middle adulthood?

In 1225, St. Marher observed that "time and tide wait for no man." It is perhaps during middle adulthood that this observation begins its journey from the subconscious to its realization in the world of the everyday—too old to dream, but too young to die (we hope). However, this stage of life is truly as multi-faceted as any other. It is a period of negotiation, and renegotiation, across the three main facets of human existence: physical, psychological, and social.

Firstly, we will learn about the maintenance, protection, and promotion of physical health in middle adulthood. Our body may be the basis of our identity, of how we see ourselves; and one of the sources of our sense of self and self-worth. Who do you see when, quite literally, you look in the mirror? Secondly, there is the psychological accompaniment to that change. Does an individual resent, accept, or confront, issues that arise at this time of life? Positive attitudes and mindfulness impact how change is perceived. Thirdly, social engagement and social support are critically important at this stage of life. Social roles may feel limiting, but they can also motivate and energize, and provide impetus to neurological and cognitive acuity. Our concept of self may not be fully ours to shape or control alone. How others see us, and their expectations of us, are age-sensitive as well.

From the developmental perspective, middle adulthood (or midlife) refers to the period of the lifespan between young adulthood and old age. This period lasts from 20 to 40 years depending on how these stages, ages, and tasks are culturally defined. The most common definition by chronological age for middle adulthood is from 40 to 65, but there can be a range of up to 10 years (ages 30-75) on either side of these parameters.

Research on this period of life is relatively sparse, and many aspects of midlife are still relatively unexplored; in fact it may be the least studied period of the lifespan. This is not as surprising as might initially appear. One hundred years ago, life expectancy in the United States was about 47 years. According to the Centers for Disease Control (CDC), in 2017 it stood at 76.1 for males and 81.1 for females. There is variation between groups, and it is generally agreed that this is due to patterns of social and economic inequality which impact health outcomes across the board, not just longevity. There are also variations across cultures. By 2040 it is estimated that the USA will have been reduced to 64th in the world from a position of 43rd in 2016 in mortality rankings (Foreman et al, 2018).[1]. Such projections must be placed in context. Longevity in the USA is still projected to rise, albeit more slowly than other developed countries such as Japan and Spain. Rates of so-called "lifestyle diseases" such as HBP, diabetes Type 2, substance abuse, smoking,are difficult to predict with exactness, as is the level of air pollution and other toxic environmental contaminants. This is not simply a question of people living longer, it is about the quality of life that they will enjoy, and how individuals and society are equipped to deal with these non-communicable diseases.

1. The Lancet, 2018.

In the United States, the large Baby Boom cohort (those born between 1946 and 1964) are now midlife adults, which has led to increased interest in this developmental stage. The U.S. Census (2018) predicts that by 2030, when all boomers will be over 65, they will constitute 21% of the population, up from 15% today. Older adults (those over 65) will outnumber children (those under 18) for the first time in U.S. history by 2035. This will have profound social consequences. This demographic shift is already well advanced in European countries like Germany and Italy. How individuals prepare in middle adulthood for living longer, and being part of an older community, will assume even more critical importance. It may also present a formidable challenge in the areas of health and public policy, as the relative numbers of those who are economically active, or economically inactive, shift.

Developmental Tasks

Margie Lachman (2004) provides a comprehensive overview of the challenges facing midlife adults, outlining the roles and responsibilities of those entering the "afternoon of life" (Jung). These include:

1. Losing parents and experiencing associated grief.
2. Launching children into their own lives.
3. Adjusting to home life without children (often referred to as the empty nest).
4. Dealing with adult children who return to live at home (known as boomerang children in the United States).
5. Becoming grandparents.
6. Preparing for late adulthood.
7. Acting as caregivers for aging parents or spouses.

Taken singly or together, these can represent a fundamental reorientation of outlook, investment, attitudes, and personal relationships which can present formidable obstacles in terms of social and economic challenges. They may also be affected by circumstances outside our control, at a time that we may have envisaged as planned and under control.

Physical Development in Middle Adulthood

What you'll learn to do: explain the physiological changes during middle adulthood and their physical and psychological consequences

Hippocrates (author of the famous "Hippocratic oath") was of the opinion that "walking is the best medicine." This was his learned opinion in 400 BCE and there is now considerable, and increasing, evidence that he may have been correct.

As we will see, there are simple physiological changes that accompany middle adulthood. These are somewhat inevitable, but the importance of physical activity at this age range would be difficult to overstate looking at the evidence. Exercise does not necessarily mean running marathons, it may simply mean a commitment to using your legs in a brisk fashion for thirty minutes. "Use it or lose it" is a good mantra for this stage of development—the technical term for the the loss of muscle tissue and function as we age is sarcopenia. From age 30, the body loses 3-8% of its muscle mass per decade, and this accelerates after the age of 60 (Volpi et al, 2010). Diet and exercise can ameliorate both the extent and lifestyle consequences of these kinds of processes. In this section, we will examine some of the changes associated with middle adulthood and consider how they impact human life.[1]

LEARNING OUTCOMES

- Detail the most important physiological changes occurring in men and and women during middle adulthood
- Describe how physiological changes during middle adulthood can impact life experience, health, and sexuality

1. Volpi, E., Nazemi, R., & Fujita, S. (2004). Muscle tissue changes with aging. *Current opinion in clinical nutrition and metabolic care*, *7*(4), 405-10.

Physical Mobility in Middle Adulthood

The importance of not succumbing to the temptations of a sedentary lifestyle was as obvious to Hippocrates in 400 BCE as it is now. Piasecki et al (2018) are of the opinion that **sarcopenia** (loss of muscle tissue and function as we age) in legs might be the result of leg muscles becoming detached from the nervous system. Further, Piasescki et al (2018) believe that exercise encourages new nerve growth slowing the progression of sarcopenia. Persons aged 75 may have up to 30-60% fewer nerve endings in their leg muscles than they did in their early 20s.[2]

Figure 1. Exercise during middle adulthood is important not only for the body, but for the brain.

Sarcopenia has only recently been recognized an independent disease entity since 2016 (ICD-10). In 2018 the U.S. Center for Disease Control and prevention assigned sarcopenia its own discrete medical code. Disease entities that affect mobility will become an increasingly costly phenomenon, and will affect the quality of life of millions of people as the population ages. In many ways it is a natural phenomenon, and many doctors and researchers have been reticent to overly pathologize natural changes associated with age. However, mobility is now becoming a central concern, and some researchers are now identifying some conditions like **osteosarcopenia,** which describes the decline of both muscle tissue (sarcopenia) and bone tissue (osteoporosis). Diagnoses and pharmaceuticals which deal with the central question of mobility will become ever more important, even more so as the burgeoning costs associated with caring for those with mobility issues becomes apparent.

The years between 30 and 60 can see the onset of **rheumatoid arthritis** (RA). This is the third most common form of arthritis and its specific etiology is unknown at this time. RA occurs when antibodies attack normal synovial fluid in the joints mistaking them for an alien threat. **It affects women more than men by a factor of around 3 to 1**. Peak onset for women is reckoned to be sometime in the early 40s. This has led to the conclusion, albeit a preliminary one, that RA is caused by hormonal changes. Women who are pregnant, and have RA, often experience a temporary remission, again leading to the identification of hormonal changes in the body as the most likely culprit. Women also experience symptoms at an earlier age. This condition is often associated with people in their 60s, but only about a third first experience symptoms at this age, though they become more acute with the passage of time.

Human beings reach peak bone mass around 35-40. **Osteoporosis** is a “silent disease” which progresses until a fracture occurs. The sheer scale and cost of this illness is radically underestimated. It is often associated with women due to the fact that bone mass can deteriorate in women much more quickly in middle age due to menopause. After menopause women can lose 5-10% bone mass per year, rendering it advisable to monitor intakes of calcium and Vitamin D, and evaluate individual risk factors. Beginning in their 60s, though, men and women lose bone mass at roughly the same rate. The number of American men diagnosed with osteoporosis is currently around the 2 million mark, with a further 12 million reckoned to be at risk. The National Osteoporosis Foundation (NOF) estimates that 50% of women and 25% of men over the age of 50 will suffer a bone fracture due to osteoporosis. Attention at this stage of the life may bring pronounced health benefits now and later for both women and men. Fixing the damage takes a considerable amount of the Medicare budget.

The health benefits that walking and other physical activity have on the nervous system are becoming increasingly obvious to those who study aging. Adami et al (2018) found pronounced links between weight bearing exercise and neuron production.

2. Piasecki, M., Piasecki, J., Stashuk, D. W., Swiecicka, A., Rutter, M. K., Jones, D. A., & McPhee, J. S. (2018, March 23). Failure to expand the motor unit size to compensate for declining motor unit numbers distinguishes sarcopenic from non-sarcopenic older men. Retrieved from https://physoc.onlinelibrary.wiley.com/doi/full/10.1113/JP275520

We tend to think of the brain as a central processing unit giving instructions to the body via the conduit of of the central nervous system, but contemporary science is now coalescing around the idea that muscles and nerves also communicate with the brain—it is a two-way informational and sustaining process. Many studies suggest that voluntary physical activity (VPA) extends and improves quality of life. Such studies show that even moderate physical activity can bring large gains.[3].

In addition, there is often an increase in **chronic inflammation** at this time of life with no discernible discrete cause (as opposed to acute inflammation associated with something like an infection). Inflammation is the body's natural way of responding to injury or harmful pathogens in the body. The function of inflammation is to eliminate the initial cause of injury and initiate tissue repair, but when this happens consistently and for longer periods of time, the body's stress response systems become overworked. This can have serious effects on health, such as fatigue, fever, chest or abdominal pain, rashes, or greater susceptibility to diseases such as cancer, rheumatoid arthritis, and heart disease. Untreated acute inflammation, autoimmune disorders, or long-term exposure to irritants are some contributing factors,[4] as is social isolation (Nersessian et al, 2018).

Chronic inflammation has been implicated as part of the cause of the muscle loss that occurs with aging.[5] Chronic inflammatory disorder is now implicated in a whole series of chronic diseases such as dementia, and the biomedical evidence for its centrality is now emerging in the medical research literature.

Because of the aging population, health issues associated with autoimmune disease, chronic inflammation, and bone mass density will become central concerns in health and social policy in the coming decades.

Normal Physiological Changes in Middle Adulthood

There are a few primary biological physical changes in midlife. There are changes in vision, hearing, more joint pain, and weight gain (Lachman, 2004). Vision is affected by age. As we age, the lens of the eye gets larger but the eye loses some of the flexibility required to adjust to visual stimuli. This is known as **presbyopia**. Middle aged adults often have trouble seeing up close as a result. Night vision is also affected as the pupil loses some of its ability to open and close to accommodate drastic changes in light.

Presbycusis is the most common cause of hearing loss, afflicting one out of four persons between ages 65 and 74, and one out of two by age 75. This loss accumulates after years of being exposed to intense noise levels, and is generally due to the loss or damage of nerve hair cells inside the cochlea. It is more common in men, but men are also more likely to work in noisy occupations, which may explain their nearly doubled rates of hearing loss levels.[6] Hearing loss is also exacerbated by cigarette smoking, high blood pressure, and stroke. High frequency sounds are the first affected by such hearing loss. Hearing loss could be prevented by guarding against being exposed to extremely noisy environments.

There is new concern over hearing loss as early as childhood with the widespread use of headphones, as loud and/or prolonged listening can cause damage to the cilia, or the tiny sensory hairs, within the cochlea. Another cause of hearing loss in middle age is **otosclerosis**, a physiological condition affecting the middle ear and its bone structure. This occurs when one of the bones in the middle ear, the stapes, acquires a rigidity via abnormal bone growth which it should not have. Unable to vibrate, it induces hearing impairment. Otosclerosis is often described as a rare condition, but it afflicts a good number of Americans, with

3. Raffaella, Pagano, Jessica, Michela, Platonova, Natalia, . . . Daniele. (2018, April 30). Reduction of Movement in Neurological Diseases: Effects on Neural Stem Cells Characteristics. Retrieved from https://www.frontiersin.org/articles/10.3389/fnins.2018.00336/full?utm_source=G-BLO&utm_medium=WEXT&utm_campaign=ECO_FNINS_20180607_leg-exercise
4. Santos-Longhurst, Adrienne. Understanding and Managing Chronic Inflammation. *Healthline*. Retrieved from https://www.healthline.com/health/chronic-inflammation#symptoms.
5. oth, M. J.; Matthews, DE; Tracy, RP; Previs, MJ (29 December 2004). "Age-related differences in skeletal muscle protein synthesis: relation to markers of immune activation". AJP: Endocrinology and Metabolism. 288 (5): E883–E891. doi:10.1152/ajpendo.00353.2004. PMID 15613683
6. National Institute on Deafness and Other Communication Disorders. Quick Statistics on Hearing. Retrieved from https://www.nidcd.nih.gov/health/statistics/quick-statistics-hearing.

white women being more prone, though there has been some speculation that this was the origin of deafness in the composer Beethoven. Its cause is unknown, but chronic inflammation may be a risk factor. We tend to associate hearing loss with older adults, but peak onset is in the middle adulthood age bracket.

Weight gain, sometimes referred to as the middle-aged spread, or the accumulation of fat in the abdomen is one of the common complaints of midlife adults. Men tend to gain fat on their upper abdomen and back while women tend to gain more fat on their waist and upper arms. Many adults are surprised at this weight gain because their diets have not changed. However, the metabolism slows by about one-third during midlife (Berger, 2005). Consequently, midlife adults have to increase their level of exercise, eat less, and watch their nutrition to maintain their earlier physique.

Many of the changes that occur in midlife can be easily compensated for (by buying glasses, exercising, and watching what one eats, for example.) Most midlife adults experience generally good health. However, the percentage of adults who have a disability increases through midlife; while 7 percent of people in their early 40s have a disability, the rate jumps to 30 percent by the early 60s. This increase is highest among those of lower socioeconomic status (Bumpass and Aquilino, 1995).

What can we conclude from this information? Again, lifestyle has a strong impact on the health status of midlife adults. Smoking tobacco, drinking alcohol, poor diet, stress, physical inactivity, and chronic disease such as diabetes or arthritis reduce overall health. It becomes important for midlife adults to take preventative measures to enhance physical well-being. Those midlife adults who have a strong sense of mastery and control over their lives, who engage in challenging physical and mental activity, who engage in weight bearing exercise, monitor their nutrition, and make use of social resources are most likely to enjoy a plateau of good health through these years. Not only that, but those who begin an exercise regimen in their 40s may enjoy comparable benefits to those who began in their 20s according to Saint-Maurice et al (2019), who also found that while it is never too late to begin, continuing to do as much as possible, is just as important.[7]

The Climacteric

One biologically based change that occurs during midlife is the **climacteric**. During midlife, men may experience a reduction in their ability to reproduce. Women, however, lose their ability to reproduce once they reach menopause.

7. P.Saint-Maurice et al (2019) Association of leisure Time Physical Activity Across the Adult Life Course with all cause and cause specific mortality JAMA Netw Open. 2019;2(3):e190355. doi:10.1001/jamanetworkopen.2019.0355

Menopause

Menopause refers to a period of transition in which a woman's ovaries stop releasing eggs and the level of estrogen and progesterone production decreases. After menopause, a woman's menstruation ceases (U. S. National Library of Medicine and National Institute of Health [NLM/NIH], 2007).

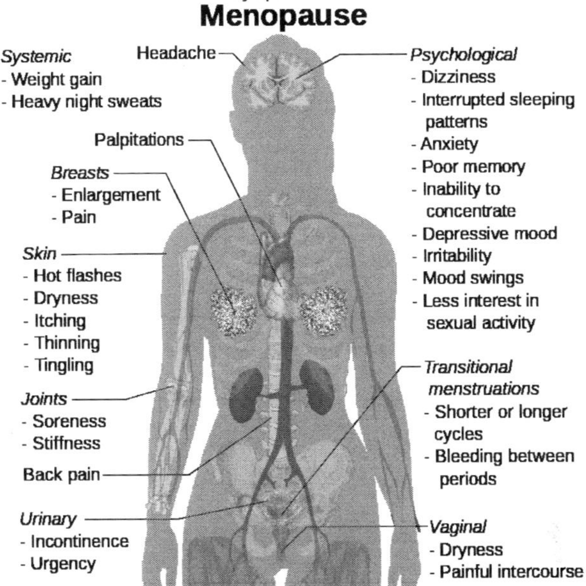

Figure 2. Most women experience some of these common symptoms of menopause, but the severity and experience of these symptoms is also influenced by cultural expectations.

Changes typically occur between the mid 40s and mid 50s. The median age range for a women to have her last menstrual period is 50-52, but ages vary. A woman may first begin to notice that her periods are more or less frequent than before. These changes in menstruation may last from 1 to 3 years. After a year without menstruation, a woman is considered menopausal and no longer capable of reproduction. (Keep in mind that some women, however, may experience another period even after going for a year without one.) The loss of estrogen also affects vaginal lubrication which diminishes and becomes more watery. The vaginal wall also becomes thinner, and less elastic.

Menopause is not seen as universally distressing (Lachman, 2004). Changes in hormone levels are associated with hot flashes and sweats in some women, but women vary in the extent to which these are experienced. Depression, irritability, and weight gain are not necessarily due to menopause (Avis, 1999; Rossi, 2004). Depression and mood swings are more common during menopause in women who have prior histories of these conditions rather than those who have not. The incidence of depression and mood swings is not greater among menopausal women than non-menopausal women.

Cultural influences seem to also play a role in the way menopause is experienced. For example, once after listing the symptoms of menopause in a psychology course, a woman from Kenya responded, "We do not have this in my country or if we do, it is not a big deal," to which some U.S. students replied, "I want to go there!" Indeed, there are cultural variations in the experience of menopausal symptoms. Hot flashes are experienced by 75 percent of women in Western cultures, but by less than 20 percent of women in Japan (Obermeyer in Berk, 2007).

Women in the United States respond differently to menopause depending upon the expectations they have for themselves and their lives. White, career-oriented women, African-American, and Mexican-American women overall tend to think of menopause as a liberating experience. Nevertheless, there has been a popular tendency to erroneously attribute frustrations and irritations expressed by women of menopausal age to menopause and thereby not take her concerns seriously. Fortunately, many practitioners in the United States today are normalizing rather than pathologizing menopause.

Concerns about the effects of hormone replacement have changed the frequency with which estrogen replacement and hormone replacement therapies have been prescribed for menopausal women. Estrogen replacement therapy was once commonly used to treat menopausal symptoms. But more recently, hormone replacement therapy has been associated with breast cancer, stroke, and the development of blood clots (NLM/NIH, 2007). Most women do not have symptoms severe enough to warrant estrogen or hormone replacement therapy (HRT). Women who do require HRT can be treated with lower doses of estrogen and monitored with more frequent breast and pelvic exams. There are also some other ways to reduce symptoms. These include avoiding caffeine and alcohol, eating soy, remaining sexually active, practicing relaxation techniques, and using water-based lubricants during intercourse.

Fifty million women in the USA aged 50-55 are post-menopausal. During and after menopause a majority of women will experience weight gain. Changes in estrogen levels lead to a redistribution of body fat from hips and back to stomachs. This is more dangerous to general health and wellbeing because abdominal fat is largely visceral, meaning it is contained within the abdominal cavity and may not look like typical weight gain. That is, it accumulates in the space between the liver, intestines and other vital organs. This is far more harmful to health than subcutaneous fat which is the kind of fat located under the skin. It is possible to be relatively thin and retain a high level of visceral fat, yet this type of fat is deemed especially harmful by medical research.

Andropause

Do males experience a climacteric? Yes. While they do not lose their ability to reproduce as they age, they do tend to produce lower levels of testosterone and fewer sperm. However, men are capable of reproduction throughout life after puberty. It is natural for sex drive to diminish slightly as men age, but a lack of sex drive may be a result of extremely low levels of testosterone. About 5 million men experience low levels of testosterone that results in symptoms such as a loss of interest in sex, loss of body hair, difficulty achieving or maintaining erection, loss of muscle mass, and breast enlargement. This decrease in libido and lower testosterone (androgen) levels is known as **andropause**, although this term is somewhat controversial as this experience is not clearly delineated, as menopause is for women. Low testosterone levels may be due to glandular disease such as testicular cancer. Testosterone levels can be tested and if they are low, men can be treated with testosterone replacement therapy. This can increase sex drive, muscle mass, and beard growth. However, long term HRT for men can increase the risk of prostate cancer (The Patient Education Institute, 2005).

The debate around declining testosterone levels in men may hide a fundamental fact. The issue is not about individual males experiencing individual hormonal change at all. We have all seen the adverts on the media promoting substances to boost testosterone: "Is it low-T?" The answer is probably in the affirmative, if somewhat relative. That is, in all likelihood they will have lower testosterone levels than their fathers. However, it is equally likely that the issue does not lie solely in their individual physiological make up, but is rather a generational transformation (Travison et al, 2007). Why this has occurred in such a dramatic fashion is still unknown. There is evidence that low testosterone may have negative health effects on men. In addition, there are studies which show evidence of rapidly decreasing sperm count and grip strength. Exactly why these changes are happening is unknown and will likely involve more than one cause.[8]

The Climacteric and Sexuality

Sexuality is an important part of people's lives at any age. Midlife adults tend to have sex lives that are very similar to that of younger adulthood. And many women feel freer and less inhibited sexually as they age. However, a woman may notice less vaginal lubrication during arousal and men may experience changes in their erections from time to time. This is particularly true for men after age 65. Men who experience consistent problems are likely to have other medical conditions (such as diabetes or heart disease) that impact sexual functioning (National Institute on Aging, 2005).

Couples continue to enjoy physical intimacy and may engage in more foreplay, oral sex, and other forms of sexual expression rather than focusing as much on sexual intercourse. Risk of pregnancy continues until a woman has been without menstruation for at least 12 months, however, and couples should continue to use contraception. People continue to be at risk of contracting sexually transmitted infections such as genital herpes, chlamydia, and genital warts. Seventeen percent of new cases of AIDS in the United States are in people 50 and older (https://www.cdc.gov/hiv/group/age/olderamericans/index.html). Of all people living with HIV, 47% are aged 50 or over (https://aidsinfo.nih.gov/understanding-hiv-aids/fact-sheets/25/80/hiv-and-older-adults). Practicing safe sex is important at any age- safe sex is not just about avoiding an unwanted pregnancy... it is about protecting

8. Travison et al (2007) Testosterone levels

yourself from STDs as well. Hopefully, when partners understand how aging affects sexual expression, they will be less likely to misinterpret these changes as a lack of sexual interest or displeasure in the partner and be more able to continue to have satisfying and safe sexual relationships.

Exercise, Nutrition, and Health

The impact of exercise

Figure 3. Exercise has both physical and psychological benefits.

Exercise is a powerful way to combat the changes we associate with aging. Exercise builds muscle, increases metabolism, helps control blood sugar, increases bone density, and relieves stress. Unfortunately, fewer than half of midlife adults exercise and only about 20 percent exercise frequently and strenuously enough to achieve health benefits. Many stop exercising soon after they begin an exercise program-particularly those who are very overweight. The best exercise programs are those that are engaged in regularly—regardless of the activity, but a well-rounded program that is easy to follow includes walking and weight training. Having a safe, enjoyable place to walk can make the difference in whether or not someone walks regularly. Weight lifting and stretching exercises at home can also be part of an effective program. Exercise is particularly helpful in reducing stress in midlife. Walking, jogging, cycling, or swimming can release the tension caused by stressors, and learning relaxation techniques can have healthful benefits. Exercise can be thought of as preventative health care; promoting exercise for the 78 million "baby boomers" may be one of the best ways to reduce health care costs and improve quality of life (Shure & Cahan, 1998).

Nutrition

Aging brings about a reduction in the number of calories a person requires. Many Americans respond to weight gain by dieting. However, eating less does not necessarily mean eating right and people often suffer vitamin and mineral deficiencies as a result. Very often, physicians will recommend vitamin supplements to their middle aged patients. As stated above, chronic inflammation is now identified as one of the so called "pillars of aging". The link between diet and inflammation is yet unclear, but there is now some information available on the Diet Inflammation Index (Shivappa et, 2014).[9], which in popular parlance, supports a diet rich in plant-based foods, healthy fats, nuts, fish in moderation, and sparing use of red meat— often referred to as "the Mediterranean Diet."

The ideal diet is one low in fat, low in sugar, high in fiber, low in sodium, and low in cholesterol. In 2005, the Food Pyramid, a set of nutritional guidelines established by the U. S. Government was updated to accommodate new information on nutrition and to provide people with guidelines based on age, sex, and activity levels. The ideal diet is low in sodium (less than 2300 mg per day). Sodium causes fluid retention which may in turn exacerbate high blood pressure. The ideal diet is also low in cholesterol (less than 300 mg per day) and high in fiber. Fiber is thought to reduce the risk of certain cancers and heart disease. Finally, an ideal diet is low in sugar. Sugar is not only a problem for diabetics; it is also a problem for most people. Sugar satisfies the appetite but provides no protein, vitamins or minerals. It provides empty calories. High starch diets are also a problem because

9. Shivappa et al (2014). Diet Inflammation Index

starch is converted to sugar in the body. A 1-2 ounce serving of red wine (or grape juice) may have beneficial effects on health, as red wine can increase "good cholesterol" or HDLs (high density lipoproteins) in the blood and provide antioxidants important for combating aging.[10]

GLOSSARY

andropause:
age-related hormone changes in men due to lower testosterone levels

chronic inflammation:
when the body's immune system is working to fight off infections and toxins for prolonged periods of time, having a negative impact on tissues and organs

climacteric:
term used to describe the menopausal period and hormonal changes associated with the gradual change in ovarian production

menopause:
period of transition in which a woman's ovaries stop releasing eggs and the level of estrogen and progesterone production decreases

osteoporosis:
the decline and loss of bone density and the increasing fragile and brittle condition of bones from a loss of tissue

osteosarcopenia:
when someone has both sarcopenia and osteoporosis, or both muscle and bone tissue loss

presbycusis:
hearing loss as a result of aging

presbyopia:
farsightedness caused by loss of flexibility of the lens of the eye as a result of aging

sarcopenia:
the technical term for the loss of muscle tissue and function as we age

10. P.Nersessian et al (2018*) Loneliness in middle age and biomarkers of systemic inflammation.* Findings from midlife in the US Social Science and Medicine 209 174-81

Cognitive Development in Middle Adulthood

What you'll learn to do: describe cognitive and neurological changes during middle adulthood

While we sometimes associate aging with cognitive decline (often due to the the way it is portrayed in the media), aging does not necessarily mean a decrease in cognitive function. In fact, tacit knowledge, verbal memory, vocabulary, inductive reasoning, and other types of practical thought skills *increase* with age. We'll learn about these advances as well as some neurological changes that happen in middle adulthood in the section that follows.

LEARNING OUTCOMES

- Outline cognitive gains/deficits typically associated with middle adulthood
- Explain changes in fluid and crystallized intelligence during adulthood

Cognition in Middle Adulthood

Figure 1. Remaining cognitively active can reduce cognitive decline.

One of the most influential perspectives on cognition during middle adulthood has been that of the Seattle Longitudinal Study (SLS) of adult cognition, which began in 1956. Schaie & Willis (2010) summarized the general findings from this series of studies as follows: "We have generally shown that reliably replicable average age decrements in psychometric abilities do not occur prior to age 60, but that such reliable decrement can be found for all abilities by 74 years of age." In short, decreases in cognitive abilities begin in the sixth decade and gain increasing significance from that point on. However, Singh-Maoux et al (2012) argue for small but significant cognitive declines beginning as early as age 45. There is some evidence that adults should be as aggressive in maintaining their cognitive health as they are their physical health during this time as the two are intimately related.

A second source of longitudinal research data on this part of the lifespan has been the The Midlife in the United States Studies (MIDUS), which began in 1994. The MIDUS data supports the view that this period of life is something of a trade-off, with some cognitive and physical decreases of varying degrees. The cognitive mechanics of processing speed, often referred to as fluid intelligence, physiological lung capacity, and muscle mass, are in relative decline. However, knowledge, experience and the increased ability to regulate our emotions can compensate for these loses. Continuing cognitive focus and exercise can also reduce the extent and effects of cognitive decline.

Control Beliefs

Central to all of this are personal **control beliefs**, which have a long history in psychology. Beginning with the work of Julian Rotter (1954), a fundamental distinction is drawn between those who believe that they are the fundamental agent of what happens in their life, and those who believe that they are largely at the mercy of external circumstances. Those who believe that life outcomes are dependent on what they say and do are said to have a strong internal locus of control. Those who believe that they have little control over their life outcomes are said to have an external locus of control.

Empirical research has shown that those with an internal locus of control enjoy better results in psychological tests across the board; behavioral, motivational, and cognitive. It is reported that this belief in control declines with age, but again, there is a great deal of individual variation. This raises another issue: directional causality. Does my belief in my ability to retain my intellectual skills and abilities at this time of life ensure better performance on a cognitive test compared to those who believe in their inexorable decline? Or, does the fact that I enjoy that intellectual competence or facility instill or reinforce that belief in control and controllable outcomes? It is not clear which factor is influencing the other. The exact nature of the connection between control beliefs and cognitive performance remains unclear.[1].

Brain science is developing exponentially and will unquestionably deliver new insights on a whole range of issues related to cognition in midlife. One of them will surely be on the brain's capacity to renew, or at least replenish itself, at this time of life. The capacity to renew is called neuorgenesis; the capacity to replenish what is there is called neuroplasticity. At this stage it is impossible to ascertain exactly what effect future pharmacological interventions may have on possible cognitive decline at this, and later, stages of life.

Cognitive Aging

Researchers have identified areas of loss and gain in cognition in older age. Cognitive ability and intelligence are often measured using standardized tests and validated measures. The psychometric approach has identified two categories of intelligence that show different rates of change across the life span (Schaie & Willis, 1996). Fluid and crystallized intelligence were first identified by Cattell in 1971. **Fluid intelligence** refers to information processing abilities, such as logical reasoning, remembering lists, spatial ability, and reaction time. **Crystallized intelligence** encompasses abilities that draw upon experience and knowledge. Measures of crystallized intelligence include vocabulary tests, solving number problems, and understanding texts. There is a general acceptance that fluid intelligence decreases continually from the 20s, but that crystallized intelligence continues to accumulate. One might expect to complete the NY Times crossword more quickly at 48 than 22, but the capacity to deal with novel information declines.

1. Lachman, M. E., Teshale, S., & Agrigoroaei, S. (2014). Midlife as a Pivotal Period in the Life Course: Balancing Growth and Decline at the Crossroads of Youth and Old Age. International journal of behavioral development, 39(1), 20-31.

With age, systematic declines are observed on cognitive tasks requiring self-initiated, effortful processing, without the aid of supportive memory cues (Park, 2000). Older adults tend to perform poorer than young adults on memory tasks that involve recall of information, where individuals must retrieve information they learned previously without the help of a list of possible choices. For example, older adults may have more difficulty recalling facts such as names or contextual details about where or when something happened (Craik, 2000). What might explain these deficits as we age?

Figure 2. While typing speed and reaction time slow with age, older typists can compensate in other ways, by looking farther ahead at printed text.

As we age, working memory, or our ability to simultaneously store and use information, becomes less efficient (Craik & Bialystok, 2006). The ability to process information quickly also decreases with age. This slowing of processing speed may explain age differences on many different cognitive tasks (Salthouse, 2004). Some researchers have argued that inhibitory functioning, or the ability to focus on certain information while suppressing attention to less pertinent information, declines with age and may explain age differences in performance on cognitive tasks (Hasher & Zacks, 1988).

Fewer age differences are observed when memory cues are available, such as for recognition memory tasks, or when individuals can draw upon acquired knowledge or experience. For example, older adults often perform as well if not better than young adults on tests of word knowledge or vocabulary. With age often comes expertise, and research has pointed to areas where aging experts perform as well or better than younger individuals. For example, older typists were found to compensate for age-related declines in speed by looking farther ahead at printed text (Salthouse, 1984). Compared to younger players, older chess experts are able to focus on a smaller set of possible moves, leading to greater cognitive efficiency (Charness, 1981). Accrued knowledge of everyday tasks, such as grocery prices, can help older adults to make better decisions than young adults (Tentori, Osheron, Hasher, & May, 2001).

We began with Schaie and Willis (2010) observing that no discernible general cognitive decline could be observed before 60, but other studies contradict this notion. How do we explain this contradiction? In a thought-provoking article, Ramscar et al (2014) argued that an emphasis on information processing speed ignored the effect of the process of learning/experience itself; that is, that such tests ignore the fact that more information to process leads to slower processing in both computers and humans. We are more complex cognitive systems at 55 than 25.

WATCH IT

This video highlights some of the cognitive changes during adulthood as well as the characteristics that either decline, improve, or remain stable.

- https://youtu.be/45qlm6cfHgg

Performance in Middle Adulthood

Research on interpersonal problem solving suggests that older adults use more effective strategies than younger adults to navigate through social and emotional problems (Blanchard-Fields, 2007). In the context of work, researchers rarely find that older individuals perform less well on the job (Park & Gutchess, 2000). Similar to everyday problem solving, older workers may develop more efficient strategies and rely on expertise to compensate for cognitive decline.

Empirical studies of cognitive aging are often difficult, and quite technical, given their nature. Similarly, experiments focused on one kind of task may tell you very little in terms of general capacities. Memory and attention as psychological constructs are now divided into very specific subsets which can be confusing and difficult to compare.

However, one study does show with relative clarity the issues involved. In the USA, The Federal Aviation Authority insists that all air traffic controllers retire at 56 and that they cannot begin until age 31 unless they have previous military experience. However, in Canada controllers are allowed to work until aged 65 and are allowed to train at a much earlier age. Nunes and Kramer (2009) studied four groups: a younger group of controllers (20-27), an older group of controllers aged 53 to 64, and two other groups of the same age who were not air traffic controllers. On simple cognitive tasks, not related to their occupational lives as controllers, older controllers were slower than their younger peers. However, when it came to job-related tasks their results were largely identical. This was not true of the older group of non-controllers who had significant deficits in comparison. Specific knowledge or expertise in a domain acquired over time (crystallized intelligence), can offset a decline in fluid intelligence.[2]

Tacit Knowlege

The idea of **tacit knowledge** was first introduced by Michael Polanyi (1954). He argued that each individual had a huge store of knowledge based on life experience, but that it was often difficult to describe, codify, and thus transfer, as stated in his famous formulation, "we always know more than we can tell." Organizational theorists have spent a great deal of time thinking about the problem of tacit knowledge in this setting. Think of someone you have encountered who is extremely good at what they do. They may have no more (or less) education, formal training, and even experience, than others who are supposedly at an equivalent level. What is the "something" that they have? Tacit knowledge is highly prized and older workers often have the greatest amount, even if they are not conscious of that fact.

GLOSSARY

control beliefs:
he belief that an individual can influence life outcomes, encompassing estimations of relevant external constraints and our own capabilities

crystallized intelligence:
knowledge, skills, and experience acquired over a lifetime, accessible via memory and expressible in word/number form

fluid intelligence:
the ability to recognize patterns and solve problems, irrespective of any past experience of the context in which these patterns or problems arise

tacit knowledge:
pragmatic or practical and learned through experience rather than explicitly taught

2. A. Nunes & A. Kramer, Experience-Based Mitigation of Age-Related Performance Declines: Evidence From Air Traffic Control. Journal of Experimental Psychology: Applied, Vol. 15, No. 1

Emotional and Social Development in Middle Adulthood

What you'll learn to do: analyze emotional and social development in middle adulthood

Traditionally, middle adulthood has been regarded as a period of reflection and change. In the popular imagination (and academic press) there has been reference to a "mid-life crisis." There is an emerging view that this may have been an overstatement—certainly, the evidence on which it is based has been seriously questioned. However, there is some support for the view that people do undertake a sort of emotional audit, reevaluate their priorities, and emerge with a slightly different orientation to emotional regulation and personal interaction in this time period. Why, and the mechanisms through which this change is affected, are a matter of some debate. We will examine the ideas of Erikson, Baltes, and Carstensen, and how they might inform a more nuanced understanding of this vital part of the lifespan.

LEARNING OUTCOMES

- Describe Erikson's stage of generativity vs. stagnation
- Evaluate Levinson's notion of the midlife crisis
- Examine key theories on aging, including socio-emotional selectivity theory (SSC) and selection, optimization, and compensation (SOC)
- Describe personality and work related issues in midlife

Psychosocial Development in Midlife

What do you think is the happiest stage of life? What about the saddest stages? Perhaps surprisingly, Blanchflower & Oswald (2008) found that reported levels of unhappiness and depressive symptoms peak in the early 50s for men in the U.S., and interestingly, the late 30s for women. In Western Europe, minimum happiness is reported around the mid 40s for both men and women, albeit with some significant national differences. Stone, Schneider and Bradoch (2017), reported a precipitous drop in perceived stress in men in the U.S. from their early 50s. There is now a view that "older people" (50+) may be "happier" than younger people, despite some cognitive and functional losses. This is often referred to as "the paradox of aging." Positive attitudes to the continuance of cognitive and behavioral activities, interpersonal engagement, and their vitalizing effect on human neural plasticity, may lead not only to more life, but to an extended period of both self-satisfaction and continued communal engagement.[1]

Erikson's Theory

As you know by now, Erikson's theory is based on an idea called epigenesis, meaning that development is progressive and that each individual must pass through the eight different stages of life—all while being influenced by context and environment. Each stage forms the basis for the following stage, and each transition to the next is marked by a crisis which must be resolved. The sense of self, each "season", was wrested, from and by, that conflict. The ages 40-65 are no different. The individual is still driven to engage productively, but the nurturing of children and income generation assume lesser functional importance. From where will the individual derive their sense of self and self-worth?

Generativity versus Stagnation is Erikson's characterization of the fundamental conflict of adulthood. It is the seventh conflict of his famous "8 seasons of man" (1950) and negotiating this conflict results in the virtue of care. **Generativity** is "primarily the concern in establishing and guiding the next generation" (Erikson, 1950 p.267). Generativity is a concern for a generalized other (as well as those close to an individual) and occurs when a person can shift their energy to care for and mentor the next generation. One obvious motive for this generative thinking might be parenthood, but others have suggested intimations of mortality by the self. John Kotre (1984) theorized that generativity is a selfish act, stating that its fundamental task was to outlive the self. He viewed generativity as a form of investment. However, a commitment to a "belief in the species" can be taken in numerous directions, and it is probably correct to say that most modern treatments of generativity treat it as collection of facets or aspects—encompassing creativity, productivity, commitment, interpersonal care, and so on.

On the other side of generativity is **stagnation**. It is the feeling of lethargy and a lack of enthusiasm and involvement in both individual and communal affairs. It may also denote an underdeveloped sense of self, or some form of overblown narcissism. Erikson sometimes used the word "rejectivity" when referring to severe stagnation

The Stage-Crisis View and the Midlife Crisis

In 1977, Daniel Levinson published an extremely influential article that would be seminal in establishing the idea of a profound crisis which lies at the heart of middle adulthood. The concept of a midlife crisis is so pervasive that over 90% of Americans are familiar with the term, although those who actually report experiencing such a crisis is significantly lower (Wethington, 2000).

Levinson based his findings about a midlife crisis on biographical interviews with a limited sample of 40 men (no women!), and an entirely American sample at that. Despite these severe methodological limitations, his findings proved immensely influential. Levinson (1986) identified five main stages or "seasons" of a man's life as follows:

1. Preadulthood: Ages 0-22 (with 17 – 22 being the Early Adult Transition years)
2. Early Adulthood: Ages 17-45 (with 40 – 45 being the Midlife Transition years)
3. Middle Adulthood: Ages 40-65 (with 60-65 being the Late Adult Transition years)
4. Late Adulthood: Ages 60-85
5. Late Late Adulthood: Ages 85+

1. Blanchflower, D. G., & Oswald, A. J. (2008, April).Is well-being U-shaped over the life cycle? Retrieved from https://www.ncbi.nlm.nih.gov/pubmed/18316146

Levinson's theory is known as the stage-crisis view. He argued that each stage overlaps, consisting of two distinct phases—a stable phase, and a transitional phase into the following period. The latter phase can involve questioning and change, and Levinson believed that 40-45 was a period of profound change, which could only culminate in a reappraisal, or perhaps reaffirmation, of goals, commitments and previous choices—a time for taking stock and recalibrating what was important in life. Crucially, Levinson would argue that a much wider range of factors, involving, primarily, work and family, would affect this taking stock – what he had achieved, what he had not; what he thought important, but had brought only a limited satisfaction.

Figure 1. According to Levinson, we go through a midlife crisis. While most people have heard of the midlife crisis, and often associate with sports cars, joining a band, or exploring new relationships, there is very little support for the theory as it was proposed by Levinson.

In 1996, two years after his death, the study he was conducting with his co-author and wife Judy Levinson, was published on "the seasons of life" as experienced by women. Again, it was a small scale study, with 45 women who were professionals / businesswomen, academics, and homemakers, in equal proportion. The changing place of women in society was reckoned by Levinson to be a profound moment in the social evolution of the human species, however, it had led to a fundamental polarity in the way that women formed and understood their social identity. Levinson referred to this as the "dream." For men, the "dream" was formed in the age period of 22-28, and largely centered on the occupational role and professional ambitions. Levinson understood the female "dream" as fundamentally split between this work-centered orientation, and the desire/imperative of marriage/family; a polarity which heralded both new opportunities, and fundamental angst.

Levinson found that the men and women he interviewed sometimes had difficulty reconciling the "dream" they held about the future with the reality they currently experienced. "What do I really get from and give to my wife, children, friends, work, community-and self?" a man might ask (Levinson, 1978, p. 192). Tasks of the midlife transition include:

1. ending early adulthood;
2. reassessing life in the present and making modifications if needed; and
3. reconciling "polarities" or contradictions in ones sense of self.

Perhaps early adulthood ends when a person no longer seeks adult status but feels like a full adult in the eyes of others. This "permission" may lead to different choices in life—choices that are made for self-fulfillment instead of social acceptance. While people in their 20s may emphasize how old they are (to gain respect, to be viewed as experienced), by the time people reach their 40s, they tend to emphasize how young they are (few 40 year olds cut each other down for being so young: "You're only 43? I'm 48!!").

This new perspective on time brings about a new sense of urgency to life. The person becomes focused more on the present than the future or the past. The person grows impatient at being in the "waiting room of life," postponing doing the things they have always wanted to do. "If it's ever going to happen, it better happen now." A previous focus on the future gives way to an emphasis on the present. Neugarten (1968) notes that in midlife, people no longer think of their lives in terms of how long they have lived. Rather, life is thought of in terms of how many years are left. If an adult is not satisfied at midlife, there is a new sense of urgency to start to make changes now.

Changes may involve ending a relationship or modifying one's expectations of a partner. These modifications are easier than changing the self (Levinson, 1978). Midlife is a period of transition in which one holds earlier images of the self while forming new ideas about the self of the future. A greater awareness of aging accompanies feelings of youth, and harm that may have been done previously in relationships haunts new dreams of contributing to the well-being of others. These polarities are the quieter struggles that continue after outward signs of "crisis" have gone away.

Levinson characterized midlife as a time of developmental crisis. However, like any body of work, it has been subject to criticism. Firstly, the sample size of the populations on which he based his primary findings is too small. By what right do we generalize findings from interviews with 40 men, and 45 women, however thoughtful and well conducted? Secondly, Chiriboga (1989) could not find any substantial evidence of a midlife crisis, and it might be argued that this, and further failed attempts at replication, indicate a cohort effect. The findings from Levinson's population indicated a shared historical and cultural situatedness, rather than a cross-cultural universal experienced by all or even most individuals. Midlife is a time of revaluation and change, that may escape precise determination in both time and geographical space, but people do emerge from it, and seem to enjoy a period of contentment, reconciliation and acceptance of self.

WATCH IT

This video explains research and controversy surrounding the concept of a midlife crisis.

- https://youtu.be/Kis4Ziz0TPk

Socio-Emotional Selectivity Theory (SST)

It is the inescapable fate of human beings to know that their lives are limited. As people move through life, goals and values tend to shift. What we consider priorities, goals, and aspirations are subject to renegotiation. Attachments to others, current and future, are no different. Time is not the unlimited good as perceived by a child under normal social circumstances; it is very much a valuable commodity, requiring careful consideration in terms of the investment of resources. This has become known in the academic literature as mortality salience.

Mortality salience posits that reminders about death or finitude (at either a conscious or subconscious level), fills us with dread. We seek to deny its reality, but awareness of the increasing nearness of death can have a potent effect on human judgement and behavior. This has become a very important concept in contemporary social science. It is with this understanding that Laura Carstensen developed the theory of **socioemotional selectivity theory**, or SST. The theory maintains that as time horizons shrink, as they typically do with age, people become increasingly selective, investing greater resources in emotionally meaningful goals and activities. According to the theory, motivational shifts also influence cognitive processing. Aging is associated with a relative preference for positive over negative information. This selective narrowing of social interaction maximizes positive emotional experiences and minimizes emotional risks as individuals become older. They systematically hone their social networks so that available social partners satisfy their emotional needs. The French philosopher Sartre observed that "hell is other people".An adaptive way of maintaining a positive affect might be to reduce contact with those we know may negatively affect us, and avoid those who might.

SST is a theory which emphasizes a time perspective rather than chronological age. When people perceive their future as open ended, they tend to focus on future-oriented development or knowledge-related goals. When they feel that time is running out, and the opportunity to reap rewards from future-oriented goals' realization is dwindling, their focus tends to shift towards present-oriented and emotion or pleasure-related goals. Research on this theory often compares age groups (*e.g.*, young adulthood vs. old adulthood), but the shift in goal priorities is a gradual process that begins in early adulthood. Importantly, the theory contends that the cause of these goal shifts is not age itself, *i.e.*, not the passage of time itself, but rather an age-associated shift in time perspective. The theory also focuses on the types of goals that individuals are motivated to achieve. Knowledge-related goals aim at knowledge acquisition, career planning, the development of new social relationships and other endeavors that will pay off in the future. Emotion-related goals are aimed at emotion regulation, the pursuit of emotionally gratifying interactions with social partners, and other pursuits whose benefits which can be realized in the present.

This shift in emphasis, from long term goals to short term emotional satisfaction, may help explain the previously noted "paradox of aging." That is, that despite noticeable physiological declines, and some notable self-reports of reduced life-satisfaction around this time, post- 50 there seems to be a significant increase in reported subjective well-being. SST does not champion social isolation, which is harmful to human health, but shows that increased selectivity in human relationships, rather than abstinence, leads to more positive affect. Perhaps "midlife crisis and recovery" may be a more apt description of the 40-65 period of the lifespan.

WATCH IT

Watch Laura Carstensen in this TED talk explain how happiness actually increases with age.

- https://youtu.be/CAdJcnrSgR8

Selection, Optimization, Compensation (SOC)

Another perspective on aging was identified by German developmental psychologists Paul and Margret Baltes. Their text *Successful Aging* (1990) marked a seismic shift in moving social science research on aging from largely a deficits-based perspective to a newer understanding based on a holistic view of the life-course itself. The former had tended to focus exclusively on what was lost during the aging process, rather than seeing it as a balance between those losses and gains in areas like the regulation of emotion, experience and wisdom.

Figure 2. Italian soccer player Paulo Maldini in 2008, just one year before he retired at age 41. He appeared in an incredible 8 champions league finals during his 25-year career. Defensive players like Maldini tend to have a longer career due to their experience compensating for a decline in pace, while offensive players are generally sought after for their agility and speed.

The Baltes' model for successful aging argues that across the lifespan, people face various opportunities or challenges such as, jobs, educational opportunities, and illnesses. According to the SOC model, a person may select particular goals or experiences, or circumstances might impose themselves on them. Either way, the selection process includes shifting or modifying goals based on choice or circumstance in response to those circumstances. The change in direction may occur at the subconscious level. This model emphasizes that setting goals and directing efforts towards a specific purpose is beneficial to healthy aging. Optimization is about making the best use of the resources we have in pursuing goals. Compensation, as its name suggests, is about using alternative strategies in attaining those goals.[2]

The processes of selection, optimization, and compensation can be found throughout the lifespan. As we progress in years, we select areas in which we place resources, hoping that this selection will optimize the resources that we have, and compensate for any defects accruing from physiological or cognitive changes. Previous accounts of aging had understated the degree to which possibilities from which we choose had been eliminated, rather than reduced, or even just changed. As we select areas in which to invest, there is always an opportunity cost. We are masters of our own destiny, and our own individual orientation to the SOC processes will dictate "successful aging." Rather than seeing aging as a process of progressive disengagement from social and communal roles undertaken by a group, Baltes argued that "successful aging" was a matter of sustained individual engagement, accompanied by a belief in individual self-efficacy and mastery.

2. Stephanie, R., Margie, L., & Elizabeth, R. (2015). Self-Regulatory Strategies in Daily Life: Selection, Optimization, and Compensation and Everyday Memory Problems. International journal of behavioral development, 40(2), 126-136.

The SOC model covers a number of functional domains—motivation, emotion, and cognition. We might become more adept at playing the SOC game as time moves on, as we work to compensate and adjust for changing abilities across the lifespan. For example, a soccer a player at 35 may no longer have the vascular and muscular fitness that they had at 20 but her "reading" of the game might compensate for this decline. She may well be a better player than she was at 20, even with fewer physical resources in a game which ostensibly prioritizes them. The work of Paul and Margaret Baltes was very influential in the formation of a very broad developmental perspective which would coalesce around the central idea of resiliency.[3]

Personality and Work Satisfaction

Personality in Midlife

Research on adult personality examines normative age-related increases and decreases in the expression of the so-called "Big Five" traits—extroversion, neuroticism, conscientiousness, agreeableness, and openness to experience. These are assumed to be based largely on biological heredity. These five traits are sometimes summarized via the OCEAN acronym. Individuals are assessed by the measurement of these traits along a continuum (e.g. high extroversion to low extroversion). They now dominate the field of empirical personality research. Does personality change throughout adulthood? Previously the answer was thought to be no. It was William James who stated in his foundational text, *The Principles of Psychology* (1890), that "[i]n most of us, by the age of thirty, the character is set like plaster, and will never soften again". Not surprisingly, this became known as the **plaster hypothesis.**

Figure 3. Personalities in midlife are not as set as researchers once thought, and may still mature as we get older.

Contemporary research shows that, although some people's personalities are relatively stable over time, others' are not (Lucas & Donnellan, 2011; Roberts & Mroczek, 2008). Longitudinal studies reveal average changes during adulthood, and individual differences in these patterns over the lifespan may be due to idiosyncratic life events (e.g., divorce, illness). Roberts, Wood & Caspi (2008) report evidence of increases in agreeableness and conscientiousness as persons age, mixed results in regard to openness, reduction in neuroticism but only in women, and no change with regard to extroversion. Whether this "maturation" is the cause or effect of some of the changes noted in the section devoted to psycho social development is still unresolved. Longitudinal research also suggests that adult personality traits, such as conscientiousness, predict important life outcomes including job success, health, and longevity (Friedman, Tucker, Tomlinson-Keasey, Schwartz, Wingard, & Criqui, 1993; Roberts, Kuncel, Shiner, Caspi, & Goldberg, 2007). How important these changes are remains somewhat unresolved. Thus, we have the hard plaster hypothesis, emphasizing fixity in personality over the age of thirty with some very minor variation, and the soft plaster version which views these changes as possible and important.[4]

Carl Jung believed that our personality actually matures as we get older. A healthy personality is one that is balanced. People suffer tension and anxiety when they fail to express all of their inherent qualities. Jung believed that each of us possess a "shadow side." For example, those who are typically introverted also have an extroverted side that rarely finds expression unless we are relaxed and uninhibited. Each of us has both a masculine and feminine side, but in younger years, we feel societal

3. Weiss, L. A., Westerhof, G. J., & Bohlmeijer, E. T. (2016). Can We Increase Psychological Well-Being? The Effects of Interventions on Psychological Well-Being: A Meta-Analysis of Randomized Controlled Trials. PloS one, 11(6), e0158092. doi:10.1371/journal.pone.0158092
4. Roberts, B. W., Wood, D., & Caspi, A. (2008). The development of personality traits in adulthood. In O. P. John, R. W. Robins, & L.A. Pervin (Eds.),Handbook of personality: Theory and research(Vol.3, pp. 375–398). New York: Guilford.

pressure to give expression only to one. As we get older, we may become freer to express all of our traits as the situation arises. We find gender convergence in older adults. Men become more interested in intimacy and family ties. Women may become more assertive. This gender convergence is also affected by changes in society's expectations for males and females. With each new generation we find that the roles of men and women are less stereotypical, and this allows for change as well.

Subjective Aging

One aspect of the self that particularly interests life span and life course psychologists is the individual's perception and evaluation of their own aging and identification with an age group. Subjective age is a multidimensional construct that indicates how old (or young) a person feels, and into which age group a person categorizes themself. After early adulthood, most people say that they feel younger than their chronological age, and the gap between subjective age and actual age generally increases. On average, after age 40 people report feeling 20% younger than their actual age (e.g., Rubin & Berntsen, 2006). Asking people how satisfied they are with their own aging assesses an evaluative component of age identity. Whereas some aspects of age identity are positively valued (e.g., acquiring seniority in a profession or becoming a grandparent), others may be less valued, depending on societal context. Perceived physical age (i.e., the age one looks in a mirror) is one aspect that requires considerable self-related adaptation in social and cultural contexts that value young bodies. Feeling younger and being satisfied with one's own aging are expressions of positive self-perceptions of aging. They reflect the operation of self-related processes that enhance well-being. Levy (2009) found that older individuals who are able to adapt to and accept changes in their appearance and physical capacity in a positive way report higher well-being, have better health, and live longer.

There is now an increasing acceptance of the view within developmental psychology that an uncritical reliance on chronological age may be inappropriate. People have certain expectations about getting older, their own idiosyncratic views, and internalized societal beliefs. Taken together they constitute a tacit knowledge of the aging process. A negative perception of how we are aging can have real results in terms of life expectancy and poor health. Levy et al (2002) estimated that those with positive feelings about aging lived 7.5 years longer than those who did not. Subjective aging encompasses a wide range of psychological perspectives and empirical research. However, there is now a growing body of work centered around a construct referred to as Awareness of Age Related Change (AARC) (Diehl et al, 2015), which examines the effects of our subjective perceptions of age and their consequential, and very real, effects. Neuport & Bellingtier (2017) report that this subjective awareness can change on a daily basis, and that negative events or comments can disproportionately affect those with the most positive outlook on aging.

Work Satisfaction

Middle adulthood is characterized by a time of transition, change, and renewal. Accordingly, attitudes about work and satisfaction from work tend to undergo a transformation or reorientation during this time. Age is positively related to job satisfaction—the older we get the more we derive satisfaction from work(Ng & Feldman, 2010).[5] However, that is far from the entire story and repeats, once more, the paradoxical nature of the research findings from this period of the life course. Dobrow, Gazach & Liu (2018) found that job satisfaction in those aged 43-51 was correlated with advancing age, but that there was increased dissatisfaction the longer one stayed in the same job. Again, as socio-emotional selectivity theory would predict, there is a marked reluctance to tolerate a work situation deemed unsuitable or unsatisfying. Years left, as opposed to years spent, necessitates a sense of purpose in all daily activities and interactions, including work.[6]

The workplace today is one in which many people from various walks of life come together. Work schedules are more flexible and varied, and more work independently from home or anywhere there is an internet connection. The midlife worker must be flexible, stay current with technology, and be capable of working within a global community.

5. (Ng & Feldman (2010) The relationship of age with job attitudes: a meta analysis Personnel Psychology 63 677-715
6. Riza, S., Ganzach, Y & Liu Y (2018) Time and job satisfaction: a longitudinal study of the differential roles of age and tenure Journal of Management 44,7 2258-2579

WATCH IT

Seeking job enjoyment may account for the fact that many people over 50 sometimes seek changes in employment known as "encore careers." Some midlife adults anticipate retirement, while others may be postponing it for financial reasons, or others may simple feel a desire to continue working.

- https://youtu.be/UMIFOSrzmNM

Relationships at Work

Figure 4. Healthy work relationships have a big impact on job satisfaction.

Working adults spend a large part of their waking hours in relationships with coworkers and supervisors. Because these relationships are forced upon us by work, researchers focus less on their presence or absence and instead focus on their quality. High quality work relationships can make jobs enjoyable and less stressful. This is because workers experience mutual trust and support in the workplace to overcome work challenges. Liking the people we work with can also translate to more humor and fun on the job. Research has shown that supervisors who are more supportive have employees who are more likely to thrive at work (Paterson, Luthans, & Jeung, 2014; Monnot & Beehr, 2014; Winkler, Busch, Clasen, & Vowinkel, 2015). On the other hand, poor quality work relationships can make a job feel like drudgery. Everyone knows that horrible bosses can make the workday unpleasant. Supervisors that are sources of stress have a negative impact on the subjective well-being of their employees (Monnot & Beehr, 2014). Specifically, research has shown that employees who rate their supervisors high on the so-called "dark triad"—psychopathy, narcissism, and Machiavellianism—reported greater psychological distress at work, as well as less job satisfaction (Mathieu, Neumann, Hare, & Babiak, 2014).

In addition to the direct benefits or costs of work relationships on our well-being, we should also consider how these relationships can impact our job performance. Research has shown that feeling engaged in our work and having a high job performance predicts better health and greater life satisfaction (Shimazu, Schaufeli, Kamiyama, & Kawakami, 2015). Given that so many of our waking hours are spent on the job—about 90,000 hours across a lifetime—it makes sense that we should seek out and invest in positive relationships at work.

One of the most influential researchers in this field, Dorien Kooij (2013) identified four key motivations in older adults continuing to work. First, growth or development motivation- looking for new challenges in the work environment. The second are feelings of recognition and power. Third, feelings of power and security afforded by income and possible health benefits. Interestingly enough, the fourth area of motivation was Erikson's generativity. The latter has been criticized for a lack of support in terms of empirical research findings, but two studies (Zacher et al, 2012; Ghislieri & Gatti, 2012) found that a primary motivation in continuing to work was the desire to pass on skills and experience, a process they describe as **leader generativity**. Perhaps a more straightforward term might be mentoring. In any case, the concept of generative leadership is now firmly established in the business and organizational management literature.

Organizations, public and private, are going to have to deal with an older workforce. The proportion of people in Europe over 60 will increase from 24% to 34% by 2050 (United Nations 2015), the US Bureau of Labor Statistics predicts that 1 in 4 of the US workforce will be 55 or over. Workers may have good reason to avoid retirement, although it is often viewed as a time of relaxation and well-earned rest, statistics may indicate that a continued focus on the future may be preferable to stasis, or inactivity. In fact, Fitzpatrick & Moore (2018) report that death rates for American males jump 2% immediately after they turn 62, most likely a result of changes induced by retirement. Interestingly, this small spike in death rates is not seen in women, which may be the result of women having stronger social determinants of health (SDOH), which keep them active and interacting with others out of retirement.

GLOSSARY

generativity:
the ability to look beyond self-interest and motivate oneself to care for, and contribute to, the welfare of the next generation

leader generativity:
mentoring and passing on of skills and experience that older adults can provide at work to feel motivated

plaster hypothesis:
the belief that personality is set like plaster by around the age of thirty

selection, optimization, compensation (SOC) theory:
theory which argues that the declines experienced at this time are not simple or absolute losses. Or, rather, they need not be. Baltes argues that life is a series of adaptations and that the selection of fewer goals, optimizing our personal and social resources to attain them, and then compensating for any loss with the experience of a lifetime, should ameliorate those losses. They do not completely negate them but a positive attitude of engagement can, and does, lead to successful ageing

socioemotional selectivity theory:
theory associated with the developmentalist Laura Carestensen which posits a shift at this time in the life course, caused by a shift in time horizons. Time left in our lives is now shorter than time previously spent. Consciously, or subconsciously, this influences a greater unwillingness to "suffer fools gladly" or endure unsatisfactory situations at work or elsewhere. Emotional regulation, and the satisfactions that affords, becomes more important, and demands fulfillment in the present

stage-crisis view:
theory associated with Levinson (and Erikson before) that each life stage is characterized by a fundamental conflict(s) which must be resolved before moving on to the next. Each stage has its challenges which are resolved, instigating a period of transition which sets the stage for the next

stagnation:
a feeling of a disconnect from wider society experience by those 40-65 who fail to develop the attitude of care associated with generativity

Relationships in Middle Adulthood

What you'll learn to do: explain how relationships are maintained and changed during middle adulthood

The importance of establishing and maintaining relationships in middle adulthood is now well established in academic literature—there are now thousands of published articles purporting to demonstrate that social relationships are integral to any and all aspects of subjective well being and physiological functioning, and these help to inform actual healthcare practices. Studies show an increased risk of dementia, cognitive decline, susceptibility to vascular disease, and increased mortality in those who feel isolated and alone. However, loneliness is not confined to people living a solitary existence. It can also refer to those who endure a perceived discrepancy in the socio-emotional benefits of interactions with others, either in number or nature. One may have an expansive social network and still feel a dearth of emotional satisfaction in one's own life.

Socioemotional selectivity theory (SST) predicts a quantitative decrease in the number of social interactions in favor of those bringing greater emotional fulfillment. Over the past thirty years, or more, there have been significant social changes which have in turn, had a large effect on human bonding. These have affected the way we manage our emotional interactions, and the manner in which society views, shapes and supports that emotional regulation. Government policy has also changed, and had a profound influence on how families are shaped, reshaped, and operate as social and economic agents.

LEARNING OUTCOMES

- Describe the link between intimacy and subjective well-being
- Discuss issues related to family life in middle adulthood
- Discuss divorce and recoupling during middle adulthood

Relationships and Family Life in Middle Adulthood

Types of Relationships

Intimate Relationships

It makes sense to consider the various types of relationships in our lives when trying to determine just how relationships impact our well-being. For example, would you expect a person to derive the same happiness from an ex-spouse as from a child or coworker? Among the most important relationships for most people is their long-time romantic partner. Most researchers begin their investigation of this topic by focusing on intimate relationships because they are the closest form of social bond. Intimacy is more than just physical in nature; it also entails psychological closeness. Research findings suggest that having a single confidante—a person with whom you can be authentic and trust not to exploit your secrets and vulnerabilities—is more important to happiness than having a large social network (Taylor, 2010).

Another important aspect of relationships is the distinction between formal and informal. Formal relationships are those that are bound by the rules of politeness. In most cultures, for instance, young people treat older people with formal respect, avoiding profanity and slang when interacting with them. Similarly, workplace relationships tend to be more formal, as do relationships with new acquaintances. Formal connections are generally less relaxed because they require a bit more work, demanding that we exert more self-control. Contrast these connections with informal relationships—friends, lovers, siblings, or others with whom you can relax. We can express our true feelings and opinions in these informal relationships, using the language that comes most naturally to us, and generally be more authentic. Because of this, it makes sense that more intimate relationships—those that are more comfortable and in which you can be more vulnerable—might be the most likely to translate to happiness.

Marriage and Happiness

One of the most common ways that researchers often begin to investigate intimacy is by looking at marital status. The well-being of married people is compared to that of people who are single or have never been married. In other research, married people are compared to people who are divorced or widowed (Lucas & Dyrenforth, 2005). Researchers have found that the transition from singlehood to marriage brings about an increase in subjective well-being (Haring-Hidore, Stock, Okun, & Witter, 1985; Lucas, 2005; Williams, 2003). In fact, this finding is one of the strongest in social science research on personal relationships over the past quarter of a century.

Figure 1. Relationships that allow us to be our authentic self bring the most happiness.

As is usually the case, the situation is more complex than might initially appear. As a marriage progresses, there is some evidence for a regression to a **hedonic set-point**—that is, most individuals have a set happiness point or level, and that both good and bad life events – marriage, bereavement, unemployment, births and so on – have some effect for a period of time, but over many months, they will return to that set-point. One of the best studies in this area is that of Luhmann et al (2012), who report a gradual decline in subjective well-being after a few years, especially in the component of affective well-being. Adverse events obviously have an effect on subjective well-being and happiness, and these effects can be stronger than the positive effects of being married in some cases (Lucas, 2005).

Although research frequently points to marriage being associated with higher rates of happiness, this does not guarantee that getting married will make you happy! The quality of one's marriage matters greatly. When a person remains in a problematic marriage, it takes an emotional toll. Indeed, a large body of research shows that people's overall life satisfaction is affected by their satisfaction with their marriage (Carr, Freedman, Cornman, Schwarz, 2014; Dush, Taylor, & Kroeger, 2008; Karney, 2001; Luhmann, Hofmann, Eid, & Lucas, 2012; Proulx, Helms, & Buehler, 2007). The lower a person's self-reported level of marital quality, the more likely he or she is to report depression (Bookwala, 2012). In fact, longitudinal studies—those that follow the same people over a period of time—show that as marital quality declines, depressive symptoms increase (Fincham, Beach, Harold, & Osborne, 1997; Karney, 2001). Proulx and colleagues (2007) arrived at this same conclusion after a systematic review of 66 cross-sectional and 27 longitudinal studies.

Marital satisfaction has peaks and valleys during the course of the life cycle. Rates of happiness are highest in the years prior to the birth of the first child. It hits a low point with the coming of children. Relationships typically become more traditional and there are more financial hardships and stress in living. Children bring new expectations to the marital relationship. Two people who are comfortable with their roles as partners may find the added parental duties and expectations more challenging to meet. Some couples elect not to have children in order to have more time and resources for the marriage. These child-free couples are happy keeping their time and attention on their partners, careers, and interests.

What is it about bad marriages, or bad relationships in general, that takes such a toll on well-being? Research has pointed to conflict between partners as a major factor leading to lower subjective well-being (Gere & Schimmack, 2011). This makes sense. Negative relationships are linked to ineffective social support (Reblin, Uchino, & Smith, 2010) and are a source of stress (Holt-Lunstad, Uchino, Smith, & Hicks, 2007). In more extreme cases, physical and psychological abuse can be detrimental to well-being (Follingstad, Rutledge, Berg, Hause, & Polek, 1990). Victims of abuse sometimes feel shame, lose their sense of self, and become less happy and prone to depression and anxiety (Arias & Pape, 1999). However, the unhappiness and dissatisfaction that occur in abusive relationships tend to dissipate once the relationships end. (Arriaga, Capezza, Goodfriend, Rayl & Sands, 2013).

TYPOLOGY OF MARRIAGE

One way marriages vary is with regard to the reason the partners are married. Some marriages have intrinsic value: the partners are together because they enjoy, love and value one another. Marriage is not thought of as a means to another end, instead it is regarded as an end in itself. These partners look for someone they are drawn to, and with whom they feel a close and intense relationship. Other marriages called utilitarian marriages are unions entered into primarily for practical reasons. For example, the marriage brings financial security, children, social approval, housekeeping, political favor, a good car, a great house, and so on.

There have been a few attempts to establish a typological framework for marriages. The best-known is that of Olson (1993), who referred to five typical kinds of marriage. Using a sample of 6,267 couples, Olson & Fowers (1993) identified eleven relationship domains which covered both areas related to relationship satisfaction, and the more functional areas related to marriage. So, five of the eleven included areas such as marital satisfaction, communication, and, things like financial management, parenting and egalitarian roles. Using these eleven areas they came up with five kinds of marriage. One aspect of this early study is **the link between marital satisfaction and income/college education**. The link between these factors is now commonplace in the literature. Olson & Fowers (1993) were one of the first studies to point to this link. The less well off are more prone to divorce, as are those with less college-level education. Income and college education are of course linked, and there is now increasing concern that marital dissolution and broader patterns of social inequality are now inextricably linked. [1]

- vitalized: Very high relationship quality. Tend to belong in a higher income bracket. Happy with their spouse

1. D.Olson & B.Fowers (1993) Five Types of Marriage The Family Journal, 1993 Vol. 1, No. 3, 196-207. Retrieved from https://www.prepare-enrich.com/pe/pdf/research/study6.pdf.

across all areas: personality, communication, roles and expectations.

- harmonious relationships: These marriages have some areas of tension and disagreement but there is still broad agreement on major issues. Lack of agreement on parenting was the primary feature of this group, although the couples still scored highly on relationship quality.
- traditional marriages: Much less emphasis on emotional closeness, but still slightly above average. High levels of compatibility in relation to parenting.
- conflicted: These marriages accomplish functional goals such as parenting but are marked by a great deal of interpersonal disagreement. Communication and conflict resolution scores are extremely low.
- devitalized: low scores across all eleven areas – Little interpersonal closeness and little agreement on family roles.

Marital Communication

Advice on how to improve one's marriage is centuries old. One of today's experts on marital communication is John Gottman. Gottman differs from many marriage counselors in his belief that having a good marriage does not depend on compatibility, rather, the way that partners communicate with one another is crucial. At the University of Washington in Seattle, Gottman has measured the physiological responses of thousands of couples as they discuss issues which have led to disagreements. Fidgeting in one's chair, leaning closer to or further away from the partner while speaking, and increases in respiration and heart rate are all recorded and analyzed, along with videotaped recordings of the partners' exchanges.

Gottman believes he can accurately predict whether or not a couple will stay together by analyzing their communication. In marriages destined to fail, partners engage in the "marriage killers" such as contempt, criticism, defensiveness, and stonewalling. Each of these undermines the politeness and respect that healthy marriages require. According to Gottman, stonewalling, or shutting someone out, is the strongest sign that a relationship is destined to fail. Perhaps the most interesting aspect of Gottman's work is the emphasis on the fact that marriage is about constant negotiation rather than conflict resolution.

What Gottman terms perpetual problems, are responsible for 69% of conflicts within marriage. For example, if someone in a couple has said, "I am so sick of arguing over this," then that may be a sign of perpetual problem. While this may seem problematic, Gottman argues that couples can still be connected despite these perpetual problems if they can laugh about it, treat it as a "third thing" (not reducible to the perspective of either party), and recognize that these are part of relationships that need to be aired and dealt with as best you can. It is somewhat refreshing to hear that differences lie at the heart of marriage, rather than a rationale for its dissolution!

LINK TO LEARNING

Listen to NPR's *Act One: What Really Happens in Marriage* to hear John Gottman talk about his work.

Parenting in Later Life

Just because children grow up does not mean their family stops being a family, rather the specific roles and expectations of its members change over time. One major change comes when a child reaches adulthood and moves away. When exactly children leave home varies greatly depending on societal norms and expectations, as well as on economic conditions such as employment opportunities and affordable housing options. Some parents may experience sadness when their adult children leave the home—a situation called an **empty nest**.

Many parents are also finding that their grown children are struggling to launch into independence. It's an increasingly common story: a child goes off to college and, upon graduation, is unable to find steady employment. In such instances, a frequent outcome is for the child to return home, becoming a "boomerang kid." The boomerang generation, as the phenomenon has come to be known, refers to young adults, mostly between the ages of 25 and 34, who return home to live with their parents while they strive for stability in their lives—often in terms of finances, living arrangements, and sometimes romantic relationships. These boomerang kids can be both good and bad for families. Within American families, 48% of boomerang kids report having paid rent to their parents, and 89% say they help out with household expenses—a win for everyone (Parker, 2012). On the other hand, 24% of boomerang kids report that returning home hurts their relationship with their parents (Parker, 2012). For better or for worse, the number of children returning home has been increasing around the world. The Pew Research Center (2016) reported that the most common living arrangement for people aged 18-34 was living with their parents (32.1%).[2]

Adult children typically maintain frequent contact with their parents, if for no other reason, money and advice. Attitudes toward one's parents may become more accepting and forgiving, as parents are seen in a more objective way, as people with good points and bad. As adults children can continue to be subjected to criticism, ridicule, and abuse at the hand of parents. How long are we "adult children"? For as long as our parents are living, we continue in the role of son or daughter. (I had a neighbor in her nineties who would tell me her "boys" were coming to see her this weekend. Her boys were in their 70s-but they were still her boys!) But after one's parents are gone, the adult is no longer a child; as one 40 year old man explained after the death of his father, "I'll never be a kid again."

Family Issues and Considerations

In addition to middle-aged parents spending more time, money, and energy taking care of their adult children, they are also increasingly taking care of their own aging and ailing parents. Middle-aged people in this set of circumstances are commonly referred to as the **sandwich generation** (Dukhovnov & Zagheni, 2015). Of course, cultural norms and practices again come into play. In some Asian and Hispanic cultures, the expectation is that adult children are supposed to take care of aging parents and parents-in-law. In other Western cultures—cultures that emphasize individuality and self-sustainability—the expectation has historically been that elders either age in place, modifying their home and receiving services to allow them to continue to live independently, or enter long-term care facilities. However, given financial constraints, many families find themselves taking in and caring for their aging parents, increasing the number of multigenerational homes around the world.

Being a midlife child often involves **kinkeeping**; organizing events and communication in order to maintain family ties. This role was first defined by Carolyn Rosenthal (1985). Kinkeepers are often midlife daughters (they are the person who tells you what food to bring to a gathering, or makes arrangement for a family reunion). They can often function as "managers" who maintain family ties and lines of communication. This is true for both large nuclear families, reconstituted, and multi-generational families. Rosenthal found that over half of the families she sampled were capable of identifying the individual who performed this role. Often adults at this stage of their lives are pressed into caregiving roles. Often referred to as the "sandwich generation", they are still looking out for their own children while simultaneously caring for elderly parents. Given shifts in longevity and increasing costs for professional care of the elderly, this role will likely expand, placing ever greater pressure on careers.

2. Fry, Richard. For First Time in Modern Era (2016). Living With Parents Edges Out Other Living Arrangements for 18- to 34-Year-Olds. Pew Research Center. Retrieved from https://www.pewsocialtrends.org/2016/05/24/for-first-time-in-modern-era-living-with-parents-edges-out-other-living-arrangements-for-18-to-34-year-olds/.

Abuse in Family Life

Abuse can occur in multiple forms and across all family relationships. Breiding, Basile, Smith, Black, & Mahendra (2015) define the forms of abuse as:

- **Physical abuse:** the use of intentional physical force to cause harm. Scratching, pushing, shoving, throwing, grabbing, biting, choking, shaking, slapping, punching, and hitting are common forms of physical abuse
- **Sexual abuse:** the act of forcing someone to participate in a sex act against his or her will. Such abuse is often referred to as sexual assault or rape. A marital relationship does not grant anyone the right to demand sex or sexual activity from anyone, even a spouse
- **Psychological abuse:** aggressive behavior that is intended to control someone else. Such abuse can include threats of physical or sexual abuse, manipulation, bullying, and stalking.

Abuse between partners is referred to as intimate partner violence; however, such abuse can also occur between a parent and child (child abuse), adult children and their aging parents (elder abuse), and even between siblings.

The most common form of abuse between parents and children is that of neglect. Neglect refers to a family's failure to provide for a child's basic physical, emotional, medical, or educational needs (DePanfilis, 2006). Harry Potter's aunt and uncle, as well as Cinderella's stepmother, could all be prosecuted for neglect in the real world.

Abuse is a complex issue, especially within families. There are many reasons people become abusers: poverty, stress, and substance abuse are common characteristics shared by abusers, although abuse can happen in any family. There are also many reasons adults stay in abusive relationships: (a) learned helplessness (the abused person believing he or she has no control over the situation); (b) the belief that the abuser can/will change; (c) shame, guilt, self-blame, and/or fear; and (d) economic dependence. All of these factors can play a role.

Children who experience abuse may "act out" or otherwise respond in a variety of unhealthy ways. These include acts of self-destruction, withdrawal, and aggression, as well as struggles with depression, anxiety, and academic performance. Researchers have found that abused children's brains may produce higher levels of stress hormones. These hormones can lead to decreased brain development, lower stress thresholds, suppressed immune responses, and lifelong difficulties with learning and memory (Middlebrooks & Audage, 2008).

Happy Healthy Families

Our families play a crucial role in our overall development and happiness. They can support and validate us, but they can also criticize and burden us. For better or worse, we all have a family. In closing, here are strategies you can use to increase the happiness of your family:

- Teach morality—fostering a sense of moral development in children can promote well-being (Damon, 2004).
- Savor the good—celebrate each other's successes (Gable, Gonzaga & Strachman, 2006).
- Use the extended family network—family members of all ages, including older siblings and grandparents, who can act as caregivers can promote family well-being (Armstrong, Birnie-Lefcovitch & Ungar, 2005).
- Create family identity—share inside jokes, fond memories, and frame the story of the family (McAdams, 1993).
- Forgive—Don't hold grudges against one another (McCullough, Worthington & Rachal, 1997).

Divorce and Remarriage

Divorce

Divorce refers to the legal dissolution of a marriage. Depending on societal factors, divorce may be more or less of an option for married couples. Despite popular belief, divorce rates in the United States actually declined for many years during the 1980s and 1990s, and only just recently started to climb back up—landing at just below 50% of marriages ending in divorce today (Marriage & Divorce, 2016); however, it should be noted that divorce rates increase for each subsequent marriage, and there is considerable debate about the exact divorce rate. Are there specific factors that can predict divorce? Are certain types of people or certain types of relationships more or less at risk for breaking up? Indeed, there are several factors that appear to be either risk factors or protective factors.

Pursuing education decreases the risk of divorce. So too does waiting until we are older to marry. Likewise, if our parents are still married we are less likely to divorce. Factors that increase our risk of divorce include having a child before marriage and living with multiple partners before marriage, known as serial cohabitation (cohabitation with one's expected marital partner does not appear to have the same effect). Of course, societal and religious attitudes must also be taken into account. In societies that are more accepting of divorce, divorce rates tend to be higher. Likewise, in religions that are less accepting of divorce, divorce rates tend to be lower. See Lyngstad & Jalovaara (2010) for a more thorough discussion of divorce risk.

Divorce Factors

Protective Factors	Risk Factors
• Higher-levels of education	• Children before marriage
• Marrying at older age	• Co-habitation
• Parents remain married	• Live in a society accepting of divorce
• Member of religious group less accepting of divorce	

Figure 2. Factors of divorce.

If a couple does divorce, there are specific considerations they should take into account to help their children cope. Parents should reassure their children that both parents will continue to love them and that the divorce is in no way the children's fault. Parents should also encourage open communication with their children and be careful not to bias them against their "ex" or use them as a means of hurting their "ex" (Denham, 2013; Harvey & Fine, 2004; Pescosoido, 2013).

A "Gray Divorce Revolution"?

In 2013 Brown and Lin referred to a "gray divorce revolution". The figures certainly seem to support their contention. The rate of divorce had doubled for those aged 50-64 in the twenty years between 1990 and 2010. One in 10 persons who divorced in 1990 was over age 50, by 2010 it was over 1 in 4, accounting for some 25% of all divorces in the USA. Various explanations have been offered for this phenomenon. The "baby boomers" had divorced in large numbers in early adulthood, and a large number of remarriages within this group also ended in divorce. Remarriages are about 2.5 times more likely to end in divorce than first marriages. People are living longer and are no longer satisfied with relationships deemed insufficient to meet their emotional needs. The shift to companionate marriage in the later half of the 20th century had followed this segment of the population into midlife, with divorce rates diminishing or stabilizing for other segments of the population.

Socio-emotional selectivity theory would predict that the shift of perspective from time spent to time remaining would predict people valuing experiences and relationships in the present, rather than holding onto memories of the past, or an idealized vision of what might yet come to be. Nevertheless, Cohen (2018) predicts a substantial decline in divorce rates for those who are not part of the "baby boom" generation, and that marriage rates will stabilize once more in subsequent generational cohorts.[3]

3. Philip Cohen (2018) The Coming Divorce Decline. Retrieved from https://osf.io/preprints/socarxiv/h2sk6/.

There has been a marked decline in divorce rates for those under 45 and the link between college education and marriage is now quite pronounced. People are now waiting until later in life to marry for the first time. The average age is now 27 for women and 29 for men, and it is even higher in urban centers like NYC. However, Reeves et al (2016) show that just over half of women with high school diplomas in their 40s are married, with the figures rising to 75% of those women with Bachelors degrees.[4] Increasing economic insecurity may have played a part in ensuring that marriage may increasingly be correlated with educational attainment and socioeconomic status rather than cohorts based solely on age.

U.S. households are now increasingly single person households. The number is reckoned to be in excess of 28% of all households, and may become the most common form in the near future, if trends in Europe are anything to go by. There, the number of one-person households in countries and Denmark and Germany exceeds 40%, with other major European countries like France not far from reaching that proportion. The number of Americans who are unmarried continues to increases. About 45% of all Americans over the age of 18 are unmarried, in 1960 that number was 28% (US Census, 2017). Around 1 in 4 young adults in the USA today will never marry (Pew, 2014). The diversity of households will continue to increase. Currently, the number of one person households in Japan and Germany is double that of households with children under 18.

Remarriage and Repartnering

Middle adulthood seems to be the prime time for remarriage, as the Pew Research Center reported in 2014 that of those aged between 55-64 who had previously been divorced, 67% had remarried. In 1960, it was 55%.[5] Every other age category reported declines in the number of remarriages. Notably, remarriage is more popular with men than women, a gender gap that not only persists, but grows substantially in middle and later adulthood. Cohabitation is the main way couples prepare for remarriage, but even when living together, many important issues are still not discussed. Issues concerning money, ex-spouses, children, visitation, future plans, previous difficulties in marriage, etc. can all pose problems later in the relationship. Few couples engage in premarital counseling or other structured efforts to cover this ground before entering into marriage again.

The divorce rate for second marriages is reckoned to be in excess of 60%, and for third marriages even higher. There is little research in the area of repartnering and remarriage, and the choices and decisions made during the process. A notable exception is that of Brown et al (2019) who offer an overview of the little that there is, and their own conclusions. One important constraint which they note is that men prefer younger women, at least as far as remarriage is concerned. Indeed, the gap in age is often more pronounced in second marriages than in the first, according to Pew (2014).[6] Allied to the fact that women live, on average, five years longer in the USA, then the pool of available partners shrinks for women. Brown et al (2019), also argue that this is further reinforced by the fact that women have a preference for retaining their autonomy and not playing the role of caregiver again. Perhaps the most interesting aspect of their research is the fact that those who repartner tend to do so quickly, and that longer term singles are more likely to remain so.

Reviews are mixed as to how happy remarriages are. Some say that they have found the right partner and have learned from mistakes. But the divorce rates for remarriages are higher than for first marriages. This is especially true in stepfamilies for reasons which we have already discussed. People who have remarried tend to divorce more quickly than those first marriages. This may be due to the fact that they have fewer constraints on staying married (are more financially or psychologically independent).

4. Richard Reeves et al (2016). Retrieved from https://www.brookings.edu/blog/social-mobility-memos/2016/08/19/the-most-educated-women-are-the-most-likely-to-be-married/.
5. Livingston, Gretchen (2014). *Chapter 2: The Demographics of Remarriage.* Pew Research Center. Retrieved from https://www.pewsocialtrends.org/2014/11/14/chapter-2-the-demographics-of-remarriage/.
6. Pew (2014) Tying the Knot Again? https://www.pewresearch.org/fact-tank/2014/12/04/tying-the-knot-again-chances-are-theres-a-bigger-age-gap-than-the-first-time-around/

Factors Affecting Remarriage

The chances of remarrying depend on a number of things. First, it depends on the availability of partners. As time goes by, there are more available women than men in the marriage pool as noted above. Consequently, men are more likely than women to remarry. This lack of available partners is experienced by all women, but especially by African-American women where the ratio of women to men is quite high. Women are more likely to have children living with them, and this diminishes the chance of remarriage as well. And marriage is more attractive for males than females (Seccombe & Warner, 2004). Men tend to remarry sooner (3 years after divorce on average vs. 5 years on average for women).

Many women do not remarry because they do not want to remarry. Traditionally, marriage has provided more benefits to men than to women. Women typically have to make more adjustments in work (accommodating work life to meet family demands or the approval of the husband) and at home (taking more responsibility for household duties). Education increases men's likelihood of remarrying but may reduce the likelihood for women. Part of this is due to the expectation (almost an unspoken rule) referred to as the "marriage gradient." This rule suggests among couples, the man is supposed to have more education than the woman. Today, there are more women with higher levels of education than before and women with higher levels are less likely to find partners matching this expectation. Being happily single requires being economically self-sufficient and being psychologically independent. Women in this situation may find remarriage much less attractive.

One key factor in understanding some of these issues is the level of continuing parental investment in adult children, and possibly their children. The number of grandparents raising children in the USA is reckoned to be in the vicinity of 2.7 million. In addition, there is the continued support of adult children themselves which can be substantial. The Pew Research document "Helping Adult Children" (2015) gives some indication of the nature and extent of this support, which tends to be even greater in Europe than the USA, with 60% of Italian parents reporting an adult child residing with them most of the year.

Blended Families

Most academic research on reconstituted or blended families focuses on younger adults and the kind of difficulties which ensue when trying to blend children raised by a different spouse/partner and one or more adults with perhaps different views or experience on how this might be accomplished. All sorts of issues can arise: conflicted loyalties, different attitudes to discipline, role-ambiguity, and the simple fact of a far-reaching change easily perceived as a disruption on the part of a child. Given the rise of the gray divorce, it is increasingly the case that this age group will encounter later age, or adult children (sometimes called the "boomerang generation"), in the house of their new partners. Such encounters are even more likely given the rise of the so-called "silver surfer" utilizing online dating sites, and the fact that an increasing number of adult children continue to live at home given the increased cost of housing.

There has not been substantial research on recoupling and blended families in later life, but Papernow (2018) notes that all of the factors normally in play with younger children can be just as present, and even exacerbated, by the fact that previous relationships have had an even longer time to grow and solidify. In addition, stepfamilies formed in later life may have very difficult and complicated decisions to make about estate planning and elder care, as well as navigating daily life together, as an increasing number of young adults live at home ("grown but not gone"). Papernow lists five challenges for later-life stepfamilies:

- Stepparents are stuck as outsiders, while parents are the insiders in their relationships with their families.
- Stepchildren struggle with the change, even as adults, as they navigate new dynamics in family gatherings, status, and loyalty issues
- Parenting and discipline issues polarize the parents and stepparents. In general, stepparents want more discipline and are viewed as more harsh, while parents want more understanding and are viewed more as the pushover. There are often disagreements about how much support (financial, physical, and emotional) to give older children.
- Stepfamilies must build a new family culture, even after there are already at least two established family cultures coming together.
- Ex-spouses are still part of a stepfamily, and children, even adult children, are worse off when they are involved in the

conflict between their parents ex-spouses.[7]

GLOSSARY

kinkeeping:
"emotion work", often undertaken by women, to foster and maintain family relationships

physical abuse:
the use of intentional physical force to cause harm

psychological abuse:
aggressive behavior that is intended to control someone else

sandwich generation:
a cohort of people charged with the dual responsibility of looking after elderly parents while raising their own children

sexual abuse:
the act of forcing someone to participate in a sex act against his or her will

7. P.Papernow (2018) Recoupling in midlife and beyond. Family Process 57,1 52-69

Putting It Together: Middle Adulthood

At the beginning of this section we referred to the physical, psychological, and social/spiritual Can we take out the spiritual? I don't see it here... aspects of middle adulthood. These have ranged from minor physiological changes to the way that knowledge of our own mortality may influence how we behave and feel during this part of the lifespan. The central theme might be identified as that of connection—the way that the body and mind are connected, how one can effect the other, exemplified by the way that physical mobility can impact cerebral acuity. In addition, we have learned that we are more selective in regard to interpersonal connection as we age. The positive aspects of relationships, work, and family assume ever greater importance. Hope is ever present, but these sorts of positive and fulfilling connections cannot be postponed indefinitely. Freud believed that civilization was only possible if humans could be induced, or trained, to defer immediate gratification. That was what the process of primary childhood socialization was about. Perhaps middle adulthood demands that we unlearn this, if only partially. At this stage of the life course, it is now or never. Time is finite and there is none left for indefinite postponement. This is what modern developmental theory has come to understand as mortality salience.

Developmental perspectives have tended to view intimacy and familial relationships as a universal need and function. It has largely left their transformation by divorce, cohabitation and so forth to the sociologists. However, there is now a clearer understanding of the way that structural economic and social change have impacted family structures, often in those least able to resist the disruptive effects of social inequality (Cherlin, 2014). Income and education levels play as large a part in all of this as lifestyle choices, and selectivity. We can only hope that advances in medical science can lead to greater quality of life at this stage of the life course, and that they are made widely available.

Discussion: Middle Adulthood

DISCUSSION: In this discussion, reflect upon and discuss ONE of the following questions:

- Q1: How do you plan to achieve generativity in your own life? If a person does not have their own children do you think it is important to find other ways to accomplish this goal? Why or why not?
- Q2: What are ways to protect against divorce? Do you see marriage trends to continue to change in the future? Why or why not?

STEP 1: First, write a response with at least EIGHT substantial sentences, integrating concepts you learned from the reading and other materials (include links with necessary). Show that you can think critically on the topic by integrating your own thoughts, analysis, or experiences.

STEP 2: Then return to the discussion to comment on at least TWO classmates' posts (in at least FIVE sentences). Expand on a classmate's comments in a value-adding, topic-related way. Promote a collaborative, supportive community, and advance the dialogue through follow-up questions. Reply posts cannot be one-liners, off-topic posts, vague statements, unsupported opinions, inadequate explanations or simply say, "I agree" or "good job."

MODULE 10: LATE ADULTHOOD

Why It Matters: Late Adulthood

Why explain development and change through late adulthood?

Figure 1. Calment celebrating her 121st birthday in 1996. She died in 1997 at age 122.

Jeanne Calment was a typical woman of her time. Born in Arles, France, in 1875, she lived a rather unremarkable life by most accounts—except for one thing: when she died in 1997 at the age of 122, she was on record as the oldest person to have ever lived. "I just kept getting older and couldn't help it," she once said.

So what does the extraordinary life of this ordinary woman have to do with us today? More than you might think. In her day, living to 100 was extremely rare. But today in the United States, people 100 and over represent the second-fastest-growing age group in the country. The fastest? People over 85. Many 65-year-olds today will live well into their 90s.

Furthermore, because of increases in average life expectancy, each new generation can expect to live longer than their parents' generation and certainly longer than their grandparents' generation. Think of it another way: a 10-year-old child todayhas a 50 percent chance of living to the age of 104. Some demographers have even speculated that the first person ever to live to be 150 is alive today.

As a consequence, it is time for individuals of all ages to rethink their personal life plans and consider prospects for a long life. We need to ask ourselves questions such as:

- What do we know about longevity?
- How does our brain and body change during this part of our lifespan?
- How can I age successfully and enjoy life to the fullest?

In this module we will discuss several different domains of physical, cognitive, psychological and social development, as well as research on aging that will help answer these important questions.

Physical Development in Late Adulthood

What you'll learn to do: describe physical changes in late adulthood

In this section, you'll learn more about physical changes in late adulthood. While late adulthood is generally a time of physical decline, there are no set rules as to when and how it happens. We are continually learning more about how to promote greater health during the aging process.

WATCH IT

Watch this clip from Marco Pahor, a professor in the University of Florida department of aging and geriatric research, as he discusses his research about ways physical activity affects the mobility of older adults and how it may result in longer life, lower medical costs, and increased long-term independence.

- https://youtu.be/b6Q_KvvM_o4

LEARNING OUTCOMES

- Describe age categories of late adulthood
- Explain trends in life expectancies, including factors that contribute to longer life
- Describe primary aging, including vision and hearing loss
- Explain secondary aging concerns that are common in late adulthood, including illnesses and diseases
- Describe and compare theories of aging

Defining Late Adulthood

Defining Late Adulthood: Age or Quality of Life?

Figure 1. 82-year old body builder Ernestine Shepard is quoted with saying, "You're not getting old; you're getting ready."

We are considered in late adulthood from the time we reach our mid-sixties until death. Because we are living longer, late adulthood is getting longer. Whether we start counting at 65, as demographers may suggest, or later, there is a greater proportion of people alive in late adulthood than anytime in world history. A 10-year-old child today has a 50 percent chance of living to age 104. Some demographers have even speculated that the first person ever to live to be 150 is alive today.

About 15.2 percent of the U.S. population or 49.2 million Americans are 65 and older.[1] This number is expected to grow to 98.2 million by the year 2060, at which time people in this age group will comprise nearly one in four U.S. residents. Of this number, 19.7 million will be age 85 or older. Developmental changes vary considerably among this population, so it is further divided into categories of 65 plus, 85 plus, and centenarians for comparison by the census.[2]

Demographers use chronological age categories to classify individuals in late adulthood. Developmentalists, however, divide this population in to categories based on physical and psychosocial well-being, in order to describe one's functional age. The "young old" are healthy and active. The "old old" experience some health problems and difficulty with daily living activities. The "oldest old" are frail and often in need of care. A 98 year old woman who still lives independently, has no major illnesses, and is able to take a daily walk would be considered as having a functional age of "young old". Therefore, *optimal aging* refers to those who enjoy better health and social well-being than average.

Normal aging refers to those who seem to have the same health and social concerns as most of those in the population. However, there is still much being done to understand exactly what *normal aging* means. *Impaired aging* refers to those who experience poor health and dependence to a greater extent than would be considered normal. Aging successfully involves making adjustments as needed in order to continue living as independently and actively as possible. This is referred to as selective optimization with compensation. **Selective Optimization With Compensation** is a strategy for improving health and well being in older adults and a model for successful aging. It is recommended that seniors select and optimize their best abilities and most intact functions while compensating for declines and losses. This means, for example, that a person who can no longer drive, is able to find alternative transportation, or a person who is compensating for having less energy, learns how to reorganize the daily routine to avoid over-exertion. Perhaps nurses and other allied health professionals working with this population will begin to focus more on helping patients remain independent by optimizing their best functions and abilities rather than on simply treating illnesses. Promoting health and independence are essential for successful aging.

1. US Census Bureau. (2018, April 10). The Nation's Older Population Is Still Growing, Census Bureau Reports. Retrieved from https://www.census.gov/newsroom/press-releases/2017/cb17-100.html
2. US Census Bureau. (2018, August 03). Newsroom. Retrieved from https://www.census.gov/newsroom/facts-for-features/2017/cb17-ff08.html

WATCH IT: AGING SUCCESSFULLY

Systematic examination of old age is a new field inspired by the unprecedented number of people living long enough to become elderly. Developmental psychologists Paul and Margret Baltes have proposed a model of adaptive competence for the entire life span, but the emphasis here is on old age. Their model SOC (Selection, Optimization, and Compensation) is illustrated with engaging vignettes of people leading fulfilling lives, including writers Betty Friedan and Joan Erikson, and dancer Bud Mercer. Segments of the cognitive tests used by the Baltes in assessing the mental abilities of older people are shown. Although the video clip show below is old and dated, it remains an intellectually appealing video in which the Baltes discuss personality components that generally lead to positive aging experiences.

- https://youtu.be/g2JXyl-gek4

Age Categories

Senescence, or **biological aging,** is the gradual deterioration of functional characteristics.[3]

The Young Old—65 to 74

These 18.3 million Americans tend to report greater health and social well-being than older adults. Having good or excellent health is reported by 41 percent of this age group (Center for Disease Control, 2004). Their lives are more similar to those of midlife adults than those who are 85 and older. This group is less likely to require long-term care, to be dependent or to be poor, and more likely to be married, working for pleasure rather than income, and living independently. About 65 percent of men and 50 percent of women between the ages of 65-69 continue to work full-time (He et al., 2005).

Figure 2. The word senescence, can be traced back to Latin senex, meaning "old." Lots of other English words come from senex—senile, senior, senate, etc. The word senate to describe a legislative assembly dates back to ancient Rome, where the Senatus was originally a council of elders composed of the heads of patrician families. There's also the much rarer senectitude, which, like senescence, refers to the state of being old (specifically, to the final stage of the normal life span).

Physical activity tends to decrease with age, despite the dramatic health benefits enjoyed by those who exercise. People with more education and income are more likely to continue being physically active. And males are more likely to engage in physical activity than are females. The majority of the young-old continue to live independently. Only about 3 percent of those 65-74 need help with daily living skills as compared with about 22.9 percent of people over 85. (Another way to consider think of this is that 97 percent of people between 65-74 and 77 percent of people over 85 do not require assistance!) This age group is less likely to experience heart disease, cancer, or stroke than the old, but nearly as likely to experience depression (U.S. Census, 2005).

3. Senescence. (n.d.). Retrieved from https://www.merriam-webster.com/dictionary/senescence

The Old Old—75 to 84

This age group is more likely to experience limitations on physical activity due to chronic disease such as arthritis, heart conditions, hypertension (especially for women), and hearing or visual impairments. Rates of death due to heart disease, cancer, and cerebral vascular disease are double that experienced by people 65-74. Poverty rates are 3 percent higher (12 percent) than for those between 65 and 74. However, the majority of these 12.9 million Americans live independently or with relatives. Widowhood is more common in this group-especially among women.

The Oldest Old—85 plus

The number of people 85 and older is 34 times greater than in 1900 and now includes 5.7 million Americans. This group is more likely to require long-term care and to be in nursing homes. However, of the 38.9 million American over 65, only 1.6 million require nursing home care. Sixty-eight percent live with relatives and 27 percent live alone (He et al., 2005; U. S. Census Bureau, 2011).

Figure 3. Kirk Douglas, actor and filmmaker, is a centenarian.

The Centenarians

Centenarians, or people aged 100 or older, are both rare and distinct from the rest of the older population. Although uncommon, the number of people living past age 100 is on the rise; between the year 2000 and 2014, then number of centarians increased by over 43.6%, from 50,281 in 2000 to 72,197 in 2014.[4] In 2010, over half (62.5 percent) of the 53,364 centenarians were age 100 or 101.[5]

This number is expected to increase to 601,000 by the year 2050 (U. S. Census Bureau, 2011). The majority is between ages 100 and 104 and eighty percent are women. Out of almost 7 billion people on the planet, about 25 are over 110. Most live in Japan, a few live the in United States and three live in France (National Institutes of Health, 2006). These "super-Centenarians" have led varied lives and probably do not give us any single answers about living longer. Jeanne Clement smoked until she was 117. She lived to be 122. She also ate a diet rich in olive oil and rode a bicycle until she was 100. Her family had a history of longevity. Pitskhelauri (in Berger, 2005) suggests that moderate diet, continued work and activity, inclusion in family and community life, and exercise and relaxation are important ingredients for long life.

BLUE ZONES

Recent research on longevity reveals that people in some regions of the world live significantly longer than people elsewhere. Efforts to study the common factors between these areas and the people who live there is known as **blue zone research**. Blue zones are regions of the world where Dan Buettner claims people live much longer than average. The term first appeared in his November 2005 National Geographic magazine cover story, "The Secrets of a Long Life."

4. Xu, Giaquan, M.C. (2016). Centers for Disease Control and Prevention.Mortality Among Centenarians in the United States, 2000–2014. https://www.cdc.gov/nchs/data/databriefs/db233.pdf.
5. US Census Bureau. (2018, August 03). Newsroom. Retrieved from https://www.census.gov/newsroom/facts-for-features/2017/cb17-ff08.html

Buettner identified five regions as "Blue Zones": Okinawa (Japan); Sardinia (Italy); Nicoya (Costa Rica); Icaria (Greece); and the Seventh-day Adventists in Loma Linda, California. He offers an explanation, based on data and first hand observations, for why these populations live healthier and longer lives than others.

The people inhabiting blue zones share common lifestyle characteristics that contribute to their longevity. The Venn diagram below highlights the following six shared characteristics among the people of Okinawa, Sardinia, and Loma Linda blue zones. Though not a lifestyle choice, they also live as isolated populations with a related gene pool.

- Family – put ahead of other concerns
- Less smoking
- Semi-vegetarianism – the majority of food consumed is derived from plants
- Constant moderate physical activity – an inseparable part of life
- Social engagement – people of all ages are socially active and integrated into their communities
- Legumes – commonly consumed

In his book, Buettner provides a list of nine lessons, covering the lifestyle of blue zones people:

- Moderate, regular physical activity.
- Life purpose.
- Stress reduction.
- Moderate caloric intake.
- Plant-based diet.
- Moderate alcohol intake, especially wine.
- Engagement in spirituality or religion.
- Engagement in family life.
- Engagement in social life.

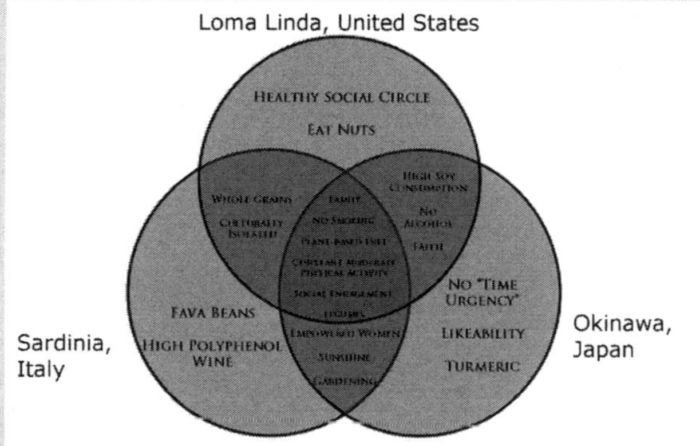

Figure 4. Blue zones share many common healthy habits contributing to longer lifespans.

The "Graying" Population and Life Expectancy

The "Graying" of America

The term "graying of America" refers to the fact that the American population is steadily becoming more dominated by older people. In other words, the median age of Americans is going up.

According to the U.S. Census Bureau's 2017 National Population Projections, the year 2030 marks an important demographic turning point in U.S. history. By 2030, all baby boomers will be older than age 65. This will expand the size of the older population so that 1 in every 5 residents will be retirement age. And by 2035, it's projected that there will be 76.7 million people under the age of 18 but 78 million people above the age of 65.[6]

6. US Census Bureau. (2018, October 05). Population Projections. Retrieved from https://www.census.gov/programs-surveys/popproj.html

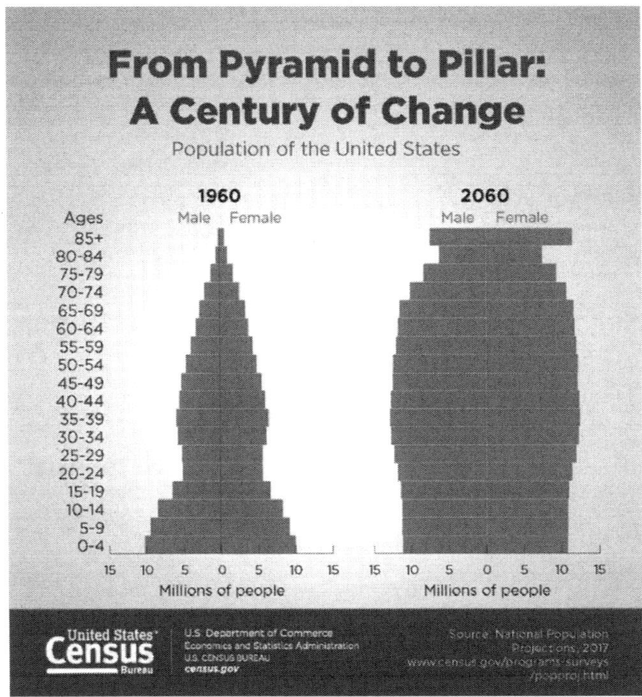

Figure 5. 2030 marks an important demographic change as international migration is expected to overtake natural increase in the United States.

The 2030s are projected to be a transformative decade for the U.S. population. The population is expected to grow at a slower pace, age considerably and become more racially and ethnically diverse. Net international migration is projected to overtake natural increase in 2030 as the primary driver of population growth in the United States, another demographic first for the United States.

Although births are projected to be nearly four times larger than the level of net international migration in coming decades, a rising number of deaths will increasingly offset how much births are able to contribute to population growth. Between 2020 and 2050, the number of deaths is projected to rise substantially as the population ages and a significant share of the population, the baby boomers, age into older adulthood. As a result, the population will naturally grow very slowly, leaving net international migration to overtake natural increase as the leading cause of population growth, even as projected levels of migration remain relatively constant.[7]

"Graying" Around the World

While the world's oldest countries are mostly in Europe today, some Asian and Latin American countries are quickly catching up. The percentage of the population aged 65 and over in 2015 ranged from a high of 26.6 percent for Japan to a low of around 1 percent for Qatar and United Arab Emirates. Of the world's 25 oldest countries, 22 are in Europe, with Germany and Italy leading the ranks of European countries for many years (He, Goodkind, and Kowal, 2015).

By 2050, Slovenia and Bulgaria are projected to be the oldest European countries. Japan, however, is currently the oldest nation in the world and is projected to retain this position through at least 2050. With the rapid aging taking place in Asia, the countries of South Korea, Hong Kong, and Taiwan are projected to join Japan at the top of the list of oldest countries and areas by 2050, when more than one-third of these Asian countries' total populations are projected to be aged 65 and over.[8]

Life Expectancy

Life expectancy is a statistical measure of the average time an organism is expected to live, based on the year of birth, current age and other demographic factors including gender. The most commonly used measure of life expectancy is at birth (LEB). There are great variations in life expectancy in different parts of the world, mostly due to differences in public health, medical care, and diet, but also affected by education, economic circumstances, violence, mental health, and sex.

7. US Census Bureau. (2018, December 03). Older People Projected to Outnumber Children. Retrieved from https://www.census.gov/newsroom/press-releases/2018/cb18-41-population-projections.html
8. He, Wan, Daniel Goodking, and Paul Kowal. An Aging World: 2015. United States Census Bureau. Retrieved from https://www.census.gov/content/dam/Census/library/publications/2016/demo/p95-16-1.pdf.

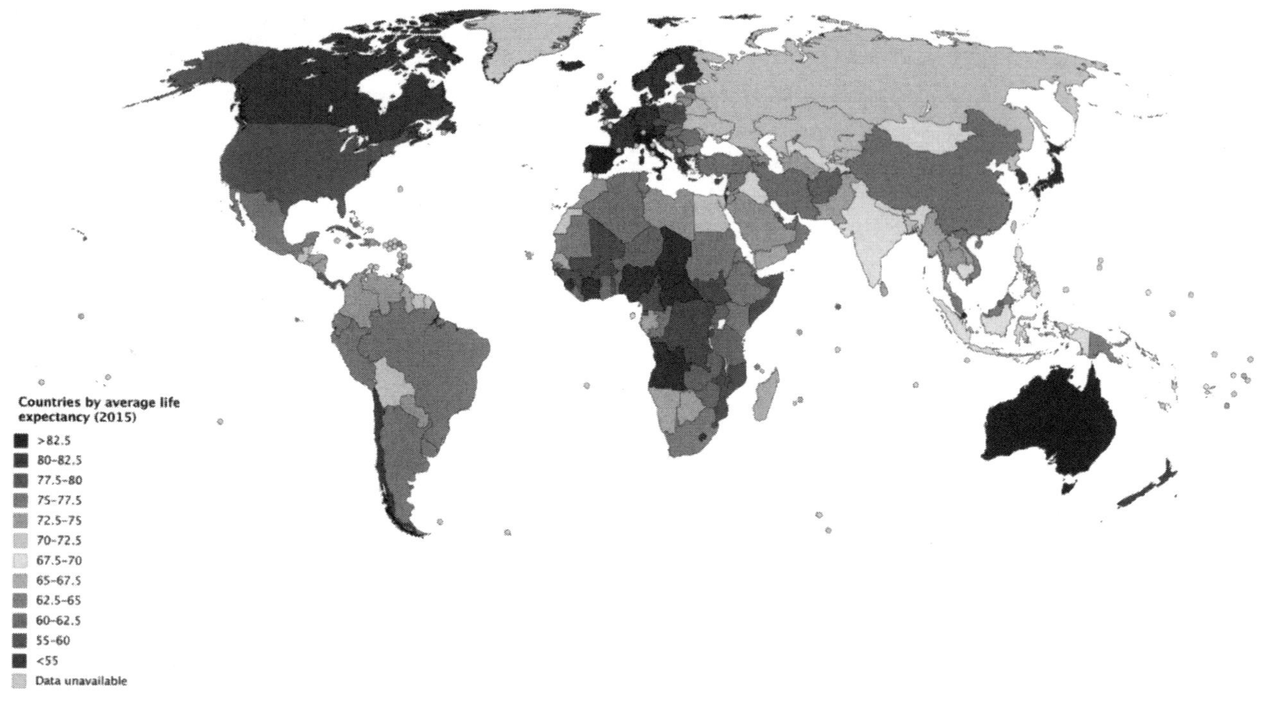

Figure 6. Life expectancies around the world in 2015.

Life Expectancy in the United States

According to the CDC (Centers for Disease Control and Prevention), life expectancy in the U.S. now stands at 78.7 years. Women continue to outlive men, with life expectancy being 76.3 years for males, and 81.1 years for females. Life expectancy varies according to race and ethnicity. It is highest for Hispanics, for both males and females, and lower for blacks than for whites or Hispanics.

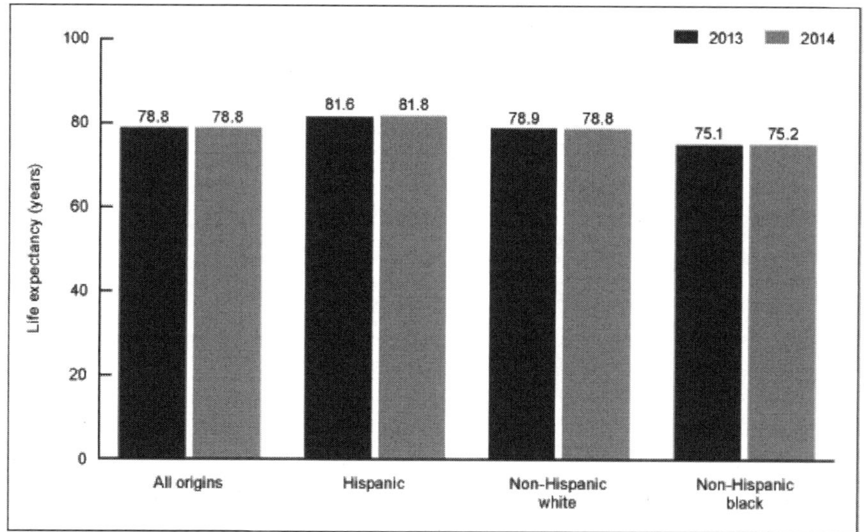

Figure 7. Life expectancy at birth, by race and Hispanic origin: United States, 2013 and 2014. From CDC/ NCHS, National Vital Statistics System, Mortality.

Statistics from the U.S. Census Bureau reveal that the 85-and over age group is the fastest-growing age group in America. According to the Census Bureau and AgingStats.gov, the over-65 population grew from 3 million in 1900 to 40 million in 2010, an increase of more than 1200%. But during this same time, the over-85 population grew from just over 100,000 in 1900 to 5.5 million in 2010–an increase of 5400%!

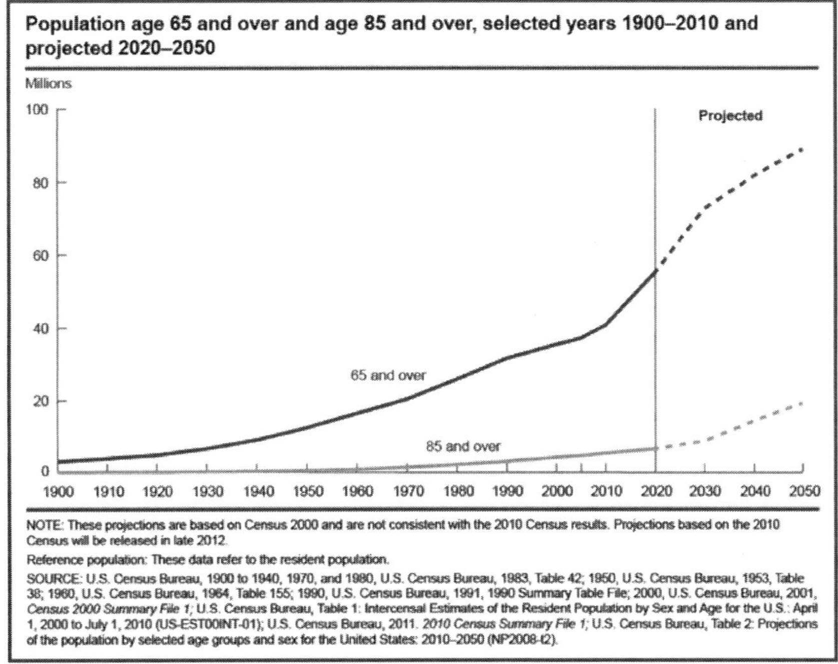

Figure 8. The elderly population is projected to grow significantly in the coming decades. Retrieved from https://partners4prosperity.com//wp-content/uploads/2014/09/aging-85-and-over.gif.

When calculating life expectancy, we consider all of the elements of heredity, health history, current health habits, and current life experiences which contribute to a longer life or subtract from a person's life expectancy. Recent studies concluded that cutting calorie intake by 15 percent over two years can slow aging and protect against diseases such as cancer, diabetes, and Alzheimer's.[9]

Some life factors are beyond a person's control, and some are controllable. The rising cost of health care is a source of financial vulnerability to older adults. Vaccines are especially important for older adults. As you get older you're more likely to get diseases like the flu, pneumonia, and shingles, and to have complications that can lead to long-term illness, hospitalization, and even death.

Things that contribute to longer life expectancies include eating a healthy diet that is rich in plants and nuts. Staying physically active, not smoking, and consuming moderate amounts of alcohol, tea, or coffee are also reported to be beneficial to leading a long life. Other recommendations include being conscientious, prioritizing your happiness, avoiding stress and anxiety, and having a strong social support network. Establishing a consistent sleep schedule and maintaining between 7-8 hours of sleep per night is also beneficial.[10]

9. Leanne M. Redman,Steven R. Smith,Jeffrey H. Burton,Corby K. Martin,Dora Il'yasova,Eric Ravussin (April 2018).Metabolic Slowing and Reduced Oxidative Damage with Sustained Caloric Restriction Support the Rate of Living and Oxidative Damage Theories of Aging.Cell Metabolism. Retrieved from https://www.cell.com/cell-metabolism/fulltext/S1550-4131(18)30130-X?_returnURL=https%3A%2F%2Flinkinghub.elsevier.com%2Fretrieve%2Fpii%2FS155041311830130X%3Fshowall%3Dtrue
10. Petre, Alina (April 2019). 13 Habits Linked to a Long Life (Backed by Science. *Healthline*. Retrieved from https://www.healthline.com/nutrition/13-habits-linked-to-a-long-life.

A major reason a person will statistically live longer once they reach an older age is simply that they have made it this far without anything killing them. Also, there appears to be several factors which may explain changes in life expectancy in the United States and around the world—health conditions are better, many diseases have been eliminated or better controlled through medicine, working conditions are better and better lifestyles choices are being made. Such factors significantly contribute to longer life expectancies.

LIFE EXPECTANCY TABLES

Sometimes referred to mortality tables, death charts or actuarial life tables, these life expectancy tables are strictly statistical, and do not take into consideration any personal health information or lifestyle information. Take a look at life expectancy tables on the Life Expectancy Calculators website.

Understanding Life Expectancy

Life expectancy is also used in describing the physical quality of life. **Quality of life** is the general well-being of individuals and societies, outlining negative and positive features of life. Quality of life considers life satisfaction, including everything from physical health, family, education, employment, wealth, safety, security, freedom, religious beliefs, and the environment.

Increased life expectancy brings concern over the health and independence of those living longer. Greater attention is now being given to the number of years a person can expect to live without disability, which is called **active life expectancy**. When this distinction is made, we see that although women live longer than men, they are more at risk of living with disability (Weitz, 2007).

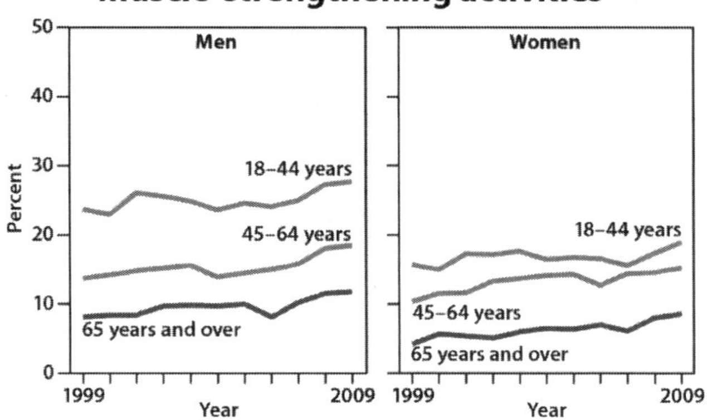

Figure 9. Physical activity remains low for those above age 65, although exercise can have tremendous health benefits and result in longer life expectancy.

What factors contribute to poor health in women? Marriage has been linked to longevity, but spending years in a stressful marriage can increase the risk of illness. This negative effect is experienced more by women than men and seems to accumulate through the years. The impact of a stressful marriage on health may not occur until a woman reaches 70 or older (Umberson, Williams, et. al., 2006). Sexism can also create chronic stress. The stress experienced by women as they work outside the home as well as care for family members can also ultimately have a negative impact on health (He et als, 2005).

The shorter life expectancy for men in general, is attributed to greater stress, poorer attention to health, more involvement in dangerous occupations, and higher rates of death due to accidents, homicide, and suicide. Social support can increase longevity. For men, life expectancy and health seems to improve with marriage. Spouses are less likely to engage in risky health practices and wives are more likely to monitor their husband's diet and health regimes. But men who live in stressful marriages can also experience poorer health as a result.

Health and Sexuality

It has been suggested that an active sex life can increase longevity among the elderly.[11] Dr. Maggie Syme found in her research on sexuality in old age that, "Having a sexual partnership, with frequent sexual expression, having a good quality sex life, and being interested in sex have been found to be positively associated with health among middle-aged and older adults."[12] Positive sexual health in older age is gradually becoming more of a common topic and less taboo. Population percentage increase among older Americans has resulted in placing more attention on the needs of this age group, including their ideas on sexual health, desires, and attitudes. This shift in attitudes and behaviors, combined with medical advances to prolong a sexually active life, has changed the landscape of aging sexuality.

There are a number of associated health benefits with practicing positive sexual health. Positive sexual health often acts as a de-stressor promoting increased relaxation. Researchers also report health benefits such as decreased pain sensitivity, improved cardiovascular health, lower levels of depression, increased self-esteem, and better relationship satisfaction. This could also imply that there are negative consequences of poor sexual health or lack of sexual activity, including depression, low self-esteem, increased frustration, and loneliness.

Key players in improving the quality of life among older adults are the adults themselves. By exercising, reducing stress, not smoking, limiting use of alcohol, consuming more fruits and vegetables, and eating less meat and dairy, older adults can expect to live longer and more active lives (He et. als, 2005). Regular exercise is also associated with a lower risk of developing neurodegenerative disorders, especially Alzheimer's disease and Parkinson's disease. Stress reduction both in late adulthood and earlier in life is also crucial. The reduction of societal stressors can promote active life expectancy. In the last 40 years, smoking rates have decreased, but obesity has increased, and physical activity has only modestly increased.

Health in Late Adulthood: Primary Aging

Normal Aging

The Baltimore Longitudinal Study on Aging (BLSA, 2011) began in 1958 and has traced the aging process in 1,400 people from age 20 to 90. Researchers from the BLSA have found that the aging process varies significantly from individual to individual and from one organ system to another. Kidney function may deteriorate earlier in some individuals. Bone strength declines more rapidly in others. Much of this is determined by genetics, lifestyle, and disease. However, some generalizations about the aging process have been found:

- Heart muscles thicken with age
- Arteries become less flexible
- Lung capacity diminishes
- Brain cells lose some functioning but new neurons can also be produced
- Kidneys become less efficient in removing waste from the blood
- The bladder loses its ability to store urine
- Body fat stabilizes and then declines
- Muscle mass is lost without exercise
- Bone mineral is lost. Weight bearing exercise slows this down.

11. Castleman, Michael. The Prescription for a Longer Life? More Sex. Psychology Today. Retrieved from https://www.psychologytoday.com/us/blog/all-about-sex/201705/the-prescription-longer-life-more-sex.
12. Syme, Maggie. (2014). The evolving concept of older adult sexual behavior and its benefits. *Generations*. 38. 35-41.

LINK TO LEARNING

Watch this video clip from the National Institute of Health as it explains the research involved in the Baltimore Longitudinal Study on Aging. You'll see some of the tests done on individuals, including measurements on energy expenditure, strength, proprioception, and brain imaging and scans. Watch the The Baltimore Longitudinal Study of Aging (BLSA) here.

Primary and Secondary Aging

Healthcare providers need to be aware of which aspects of aging are reversible and which ones are inevitable. By keeping this distinction in mind, caregivers may be more objective and accurate when diagnosing and treating older patients. And a positive attitude can go a long way toward motivating patients to stick with a health regime. Unfortunately, stereotypes can lead to misdiagnosis. For example, it is estimated that about 10 percent of older patients diagnosed with dementia are actually depressed or suffering from some other psychological illness (Berger, 2005). The failure to recognize and treat psychological problems in older patients may be one consequence of such stereotypes.

Figure 10. Primary aging includes inevitable changes such as skin that becomes more wrinkled and less elastic.

Primary Aging

Senescence is the biological aging is the gradual deterioration of functional characteristics**.** It is the process by which cells irreversibly stop dividing and enter a state of permanent growth arrest without undergoing cell death. This process is also referred to as **primary aging** and thus, refers to the inevitable changes associated with aging (Busse, 1969). These changes include changes in the skin and hair, height and weight, hearing loss, and eye disease. However, some of these changes can be reduced by limiting exposure to the sun, eating a nutritious diet, and exercising.

Skin and hair change with age. The skin becomes drier, thinner, and less elastic during the aging process. Scars and imperfections become more noticeable as fewer cells grow underneath the surface of the skin. Exposure to the sun, or photoaging, accelerates these changes. Graying hair is inevitable, and hair loss all over the body becomes more prevalent.

Height and weight vary with age. Older people are more than an inch shorter than they were during early adulthood (Masoro in Berger, 2005). This is thought to be due to a settling of the vertebrae and a lack of muscle strength in the back. Older people weigh less than they did in mid-life. Bones lose density and can become brittle. This is especially prevalent in women. However, weight training can help increase bone density after just a few weeks of training.

Muscle loss occurs in late adulthood and is most noticeable in men as they lose muscle mass. Maintaining strong leg and heart muscles is important for independence. Weight-lifting, walking, swimming, or engaging in other cardiovascular and weight bearing exercises can help strengthen the muscles and prevent atrophy.

Vision

Some typical vision issues that arise along with aging include:

- Lens becomes less transparent and the pupils shrink.
- The optic nerve becomes less efficient.
- Distant objects become less acute.
- Loss of peripheral vision (the size of the visual field decreases by approximately one to three degrees per decade of life.)[13]
- More light is needed to see and it takes longer to adjust to a change from light to darkness and vice versa.
- Driving at night becomes more challenging.
- Reading becomes more of a strain and eye strain occurs more easily.

The majority of people over 65 have some difficulty with vision, but most is easily corrected with prescriptive lenses. Three percent of those 65 to 74 and 8 percent of those 75 and older have hearing or vision limitations that hinder activity. The most common causes of vision loss or impairment are glaucoma, cataracts, age-related macular degeneration, and diabetic retinopathy (He et al., 2005).

- **Glaucoma** occurs when pressure in the fluid of the eye increases, either because the fluid cannot drain properly or because too much fluid is produced. Glaucoma can be corrected with drugs or surgery. It must be detected early enough.
- **Cataracts** are cloudy or opaque areas of the lens of the eye that interfere with passing light, frequently develop. Cataracts can be surgically removed or intraocular lens implants can replace old lenses.
- **Macular degeneration** is the most common cause of blindness in people over the age of 60. Age-related macular degeneration (AMD) affects the macula, a yellowish area of the eye located near the retina at which visual perception is most acute. A diet rich in antioxidant vitamins (C, E, and A) can reduce the risk of this disease.
- **Diabetic retinopathy**, also known as diabetic eye disease, is a medical condition in which damage occurs to the retina due to diabetes mellitus. It is a leading cause of blindness. There are three major treatments for diabetic retinopathy, which are very effective in reducing vision loss from this disease: laser photocoagulation, medications, surgery.

Hearing

Hearing Loss, is experienced by 25% of people between ages 65 and 74, then by 50% of people above age 75.[14] Among those who are in nursing homes, rates are even higher. Older adults are more likely to seek help with vision impairment than with hearing loss, perhaps due to the stereotype that older people who have difficulty hearing are also less mentally alert.

Conductive hearing loss may occur because of age, genetic predisposition, or environmental effects, including persistent exposure to extreme noise over the course of our lifetime, certain illnesses, or damage due to toxins. Conductive hearing loss involves structural damage to the ear such as failure in the vibration of the eardrum and/or movement of the ossicles (the three bones in our middle ear). Given the mechanical nature by which the sound wave stimulus is transmitted from the eardrum through the ossicles to the oval window of the cochlea, some degree of hearing loss is inevitable. These problems are often dealt with through devices like hearing aids that amplify incoming sound waves to make vibration of the eardrum and movement of the ossicles more likely to occur.

When the hearing problem is associated with a failure to transmit neural signals from the cochlea to the brain, it is called **sensorineural hearing loss**. This type of loss accelerates with age and can be caused by prolonged exposure to loud noises, which causes damage to the hair cells within the cochlea. **Presbycusis** is age-related sensorineural hearing loss resulting from degeneration of the cochlea or associated structures of the inner ear or auditory nerves. The hearing loss is most marked at higher frequencies. Presbycusis is the second most common illness next to arthritis in aged people.

13. Heiting, Gary. How vision changes as you age. All About Vision. Retrieved from https://www.allaboutvision.com/over60/vision-changes.htm.
14. National Institute on Deafness and Other Communication Disorders. Quick Statistics on Hearing. Retrieved from https://www.nidcd.nih.gov/health/statistics/quick-statistics-hearing.

One disease that results in sensorineural hearing loss is **Ménière's disease**. Although not well understood, Ménière's disease results in a degeneration of inner ear structures that can lead to hearing loss, tinnitus (constant ringing or buzzing), **vertigo** (a sense of spinning), and an increase in pressure within the inner ear (Semaan & Megerian, 2011). This kind of loss cannot be treated with hearing aids, but some individuals might be candidates for a cochlear implant as a treatment option. **Cochlear implants** are electronic devices consisting of a microphone, a speech processor, and an electrode array. The device receives incoming sound information and directly stimulates the auditory nerve to transmit information to the brain.

Being unable to hear causes people to withdraw from conversation and others to ignore them or shout. Unfortunately, shouting is usually high pitched and can be harder to hear than lower tones. The speaker may also begin to use a patronizing form of 'baby talk' known as **elderspeak** (See et al., 1999). This language reflects the stereotypes of older adults as being dependent, demented, and childlike. Hearing loss is more prevalent in men than women. And it is experienced by more white, non-Hispanics than by Black men and women. Smoking, middle ear infections, and exposure to loud noises increase hearing loss.

NUTRITION AND AGING RESEARCH

The Jean Mayer Human Nutrition Research Center on Aging (HNRCA), located in Boston, Massachusetts, is one of six human nutrition research centers in the United States supported by the United States Department of Agriculture and Agricultural Research Service. The goal of the HNRCA, which is managed by Tufts University, is to explore the relationship between nutrition, physical activity, and healthy and active aging.

The HNRCA has made significant contributions to U.S. and international nutritional and physical activity recommendations, public policy, and clinical healthcare. These contributions include advancements in the knowledge of the role of dietary calcium and vitamin D in promoting nutrition and bone health, the role of nutrients in maintaining the optimal immune response, the prevention of infectious diseases, the role of diet in prevention of cancer, obesity research, modifications to the Food Guide Pyramid, contribution to USDA nutrient data bank, advancements in the study of sarcopenia, heart disease, vision, brain and cognitive function, front of packaging food labeling initiatives, and research of how genetic factors impact predisposition to weight gain and various health indicators. Research clusters within the HNRCA address four specific strategic areas: 1) cancer, 2) cardiovascular disease, 3) inflammation, immunity, and infectious disease and 4) obesity.

WATCH IT

Research done by T. Colin Campbell M.D., Michael Greger M.D., Neal Bernard M.D. and others have demonstrated the impact of diet upon longevity and quality of life. As discussed in the video below, consumption of less animal based protein has been linked with the slowing of degradation of function which was traditionally seen as part of the normal aging process.

- https://youtu.be/dwJASNFy9XQ

Primary aging can be compensated for through exercise, corrective lenses, nutrition, and hearing aids. Just as important, by reducing stereotypes about aging, people of age can maintain self-respect, recognize their own strengths, and count on receiving the respect and social inclusion they deserve.

Health in Late Adulthood: Secondary Aging

Secondary Aging

Secondary aging refers to changes that are caused by illness or disease. These illnesses reduce independence, impact quality of life, affect family members and other caregivers, and bring financial burden. The major difference between primary aging and secondary aging is that primary aging is irreversible and is due to genetic predisposition; secondary aging is potentially reversible and is a result of illness, health habits, and other individual differences.

Chronic Illnesses

Figure 11. Secondary aging refers to the aspects of aging that are not universally shared by everyone, but are brought about by disease or chronic illness.

In the United States, nearly one in two Americans (133 million) has at least one chronic medical condition, with most subjects (58%) between the ages of 18 and 64. The number is projected to increase by more than one percent per year by 2030, resulting in an estimated chronically ill population of 171 million. The most common chronic conditions are high blood pressure, arthritis, respiratory diseases like emphysema, and high cholesterol.

According to research by the Centers for Disease Control and Prevention, chronic disease is also especially a concern in the elderly population in America. Chronic diseases like stroke, heart disease, and cancer are among the leading causes of death among Americans aged 65 or older. While the majority of chronic conditions are found in individuals between the ages of 18 and 64, it is estimated that at least 80% of older Americans are currently living with some form of a chronic condition, with 50% of this population having two or more chronic conditions. The two most common chronic conditions in the elderly are high blood pressure and arthritis, with diabetes, coronary heart disease, and cancer also being reported at high rates among the elderly population. The presence of type 2 diabetes, high blood pressure, and obesity, is termed "metabolic syndrome" and impacts 50% of individuals over the age of 60.[15]

Heart disease is the leading cause of death from chronic disease for adults older than 65, followed by cancer, stroke, diabetes, chronic lower respiratory diseases, influenza and pneumonia, and, finally, Alzheimer's disease (which we'll examine further when we talk about cognitive decline). Though the rates of chronic disease differ by race for those living with chronic illness, the statistics for leading causes of death among elderly are nearly identical across racial/ethnic groups.

Heart Disease

As stated above, heart disease is the leading cause of death from chronic disease for adults older than 65. Cardiovascular disease (CVD) is a class of diseases that involve the heart or blood vessels. CVD includes coronary artery diseases (CAD) such as angina and myocardial infarction (commonly known as a heart attack). Other CVDs include stroke, heart failure, hypertensive heart disease, rheumatic heart disease, cardiomyopathy, heart arrhythmia, congenital heart disease, valvular heart disease, carditis, aortic aneurysms, peripheral artery disease, thromboembolic disease, and venous thrombosis.

15. Aguilar M, Bhuket T, Torres S, Liu B, Wong RJ. Prevalence of the Metabolic Syndrome in the United States, 2003-2012. JAMA. 2015;313(19):1973–1974. doi:10.1001/jama.2015.4260

The underlying mechanisms vary depending on the disease. Coronary artery disease, stroke, and peripheral artery disease involve atherosclerosis. This may be caused by high blood pressure, smoking, diabetes mellitus, lack of exercise, obesity, high blood cholesterol, poor diet, and excessive alcohol consumption, among others. High blood pressure is estimated to account for approximately 13% of CVD deaths, while tobacco accounts for 9%, diabetes 6%, lack of exercise 6% and obesity 5%.

It is estimated that up to 90% of CVD may be preventable. Prevention of CVD involves improving risk factors through: healthy eating, exercise, avoidance of tobacco smoke and limiting alcohol intake. Treating risk factors, such as high blood pressure, blood lipids and diabetes is also beneficial. The use of aspirin in people, who are otherwise healthy, is of unclear benefit.

Cancer

Age in itself is one of the most important risk factors for developing cancer. Currently, 60% of newly diagnosed malignant tumors and 70% of cancer deaths occur in people aged 65 years or older. Many cancers are linked to aging; these include breast, colorectal, prostate, pancreatic, lung, bladder and stomach cancers. Men over 75 have the highest rates of cancer at 28 percent. Women 65 and older have rates of 17 percent. Rates for older non-Hispanic Whites are twice as high as for Hispanics and non-Hispanic Blacks. The most common types of cancer found in men are prostate and lung cancer. Breast and lung cancer are the most common forms in women.

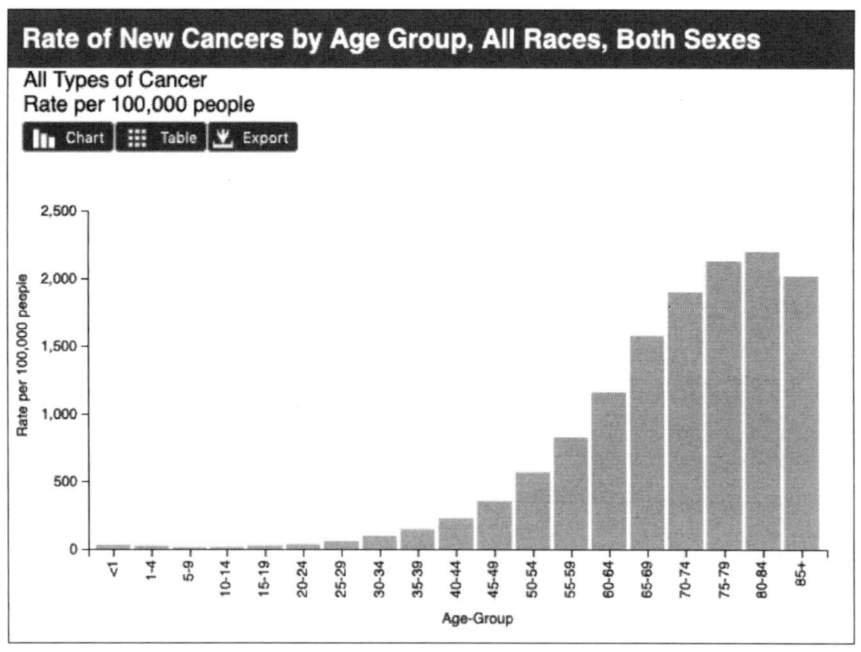

Figure 12. Age is a risk factor for cancer development. Source: https://gis.cdc.gov/Cancer/USCS/DataViz.html.

For many reasons, older adults with cancer have different needs than younger adults with the disease. For example, older adults:

- May be less able to tolerate certain cancer treatments.
- Have a decreased reserve (the capacity to respond to disease and treatment).
- May have other medical problems in addition to cancer.
- May have functional problems, such as the ability to do basic activities (dressing, bathing, eating) or more advanced activities (such as using transportation, going shopping or handling finances), and have less available family support to assist them as they go through treatment.
- May not always have access to transportation, social support or financial resources.
- May have different views of quality versus quantity of life

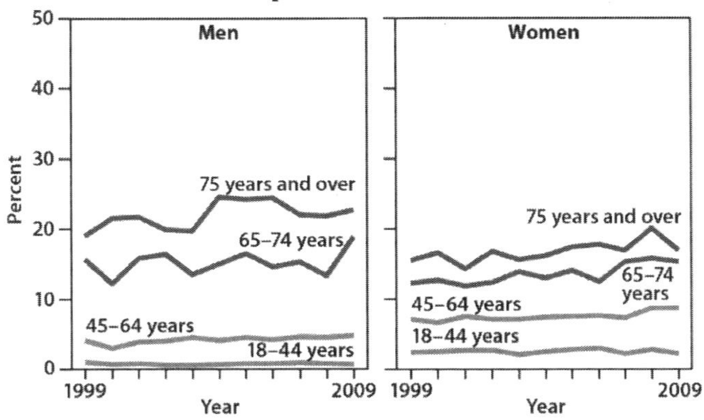

Figure 13. Cancer rates are significantly higher for those above age 65, and is more common in men than in women.

Hypertension and Stroke

Hypertension or high blood pressure and associated heart disease and circulatory conditions increase with age. Stroke is a leading cause of death and severe, long-term disability. Most people who've had a first stroke also had high blood pressure (HBP or hypertension).High blood pressure damages arteries throughout the body, creating conditions where they can burst or clog more easily. Weakened arteries in the brain, resulting from high blood pressure, increase the risk for stroke—which is why managing high blood pressure is critical to reduce the chance of having a stroke. Hypertension disables 11.1 percent of 65 to 74 year olds and 17.1 percent of people over 75. Rates are higher among women and blacks. Rates are highest for women over 75. Coronary disease and stroke are higher among older men than women. The incidence of stroke is lower than that of coronary disease, but it is the No. 5 cause of death and a leading cause of disability in the United States.[16][17]

Arthritis

While **arthritis** can affect children, it is predominantly a disease of the elderly. Arthritis is more common in women than men at all ages and affects all races, ethnic groups and cultures. In the United States a CDC survey based on data from 2007–2009 showed 22.2% (49.9 million) of adults aged ≥18 years had self-reported doctor-diagnosed arthritis, and 9.4% (21.1 million or 42.4% of those with arthritis) had arthritis-attributable activity limitation (AAAL). With an aging population, this number is expected to increase.

Arthritis is a term often used to mean any disorder that affects joints. Symptoms generally include joint pain and stiffness. Other symptoms may include redness, warmth, swelling, and decreased range of motion of the affected joints. In some types of arthritis, other organs are also affected. Onset can be gradual or sudden.

There are over 100 types of arthritis. The most common forms are osteoarthritis (degenerative joint disease) and rheumatoid arthritis. Osteoarthritis usually increases in frequency with age and affects the fingers, knees, and hips. Rheumatoid arthritis is an autoimmune disorder that often affects the hands and feet. Other types include gout, lupus, fibromyalgia, and septic arthritis. They are all types of rheumatic disease

16. How High Blood Pressure Can Lead to Stroke. Retrieved from https://www.heart.org/en/health-topics/high-blood-pressure/health-threats-from-high-blood-pressure/how-high-blood-pressure-can-lead-to-stroke.
17. About Stroke. American Stroke Association. Retrieved from https://www.strokeassociation.org/en/about-stroke.

Treatment may include resting the joint and alternating between applying ice and heat. Weight loss and exercise may also be useful. Pain medications such as ibuprofen and paracetamol (acetaminophen) may be used. In some a joint replacement may be useful.

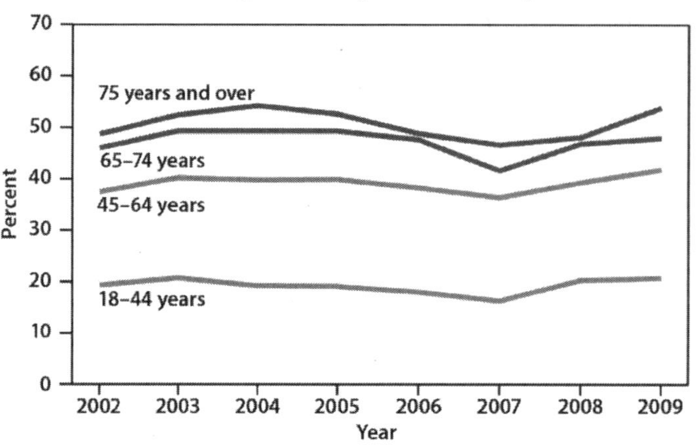

SOURCE: CDC/NCHS, *Health, United States, 2010*, Figure 7. Data from the National Health Interview Survey.

Figure 14. Joint pain increases with age.

OLDER AMERICANS & CARDIOVASCULAR DISEASES

Visit this statistical fact sheet from the American Heart Association to learn more about some facts and figures related to heart disease.

Diabetes

Type 2 diabetes (T2D), formerly known as adult-onset diabetes, is a form of diabetes characterized by high blood sugar, insulin resistance, and relative lack of insulin. Common symptoms include increased thirst, frequent urination, and unexplained weight loss. Symptoms may also include increased hunger, feeling tired, and sores that do not heal. Often symptoms come on slowly. Long-term complications from high blood sugar include heart disease, strokes, diabetic retinopathy which can result in blindness, kidney failure, and poor blood flow in the limbs which may lead to amputations.

Type 2 diabetes primarily occurs as a result of obesity and lack of exercise. Some people are more genetically at risk than others. Type 2 diabetes makes up about 90% of cases of diabetes, with the other 10% due primarily to type 1 diabetes and gestational diabetes. In type 1 diabetes there is a lower total level of insulin to control blood glucose, due to an autoimmune induced loss of insulin-producing beta cells in the pancreas. Diagnosis of diabetes is by blood tests such as fasting plasma glucose, oral glucose tolerance test, or glycated hemoglobin (A1C).

Type 2 diabetes is partly preventable by staying a normal weight, exercising regularly, and eating properly. Treatment involves exercise and dietary changes. If blood sugar levels are not adequately lowered, the medication metformin is typically recommended. Many people may eventually also require insulin injections. In those on insulin, routinely checking blood sugar levels is advised; however, this may not be needed in those taking pills. Bariatric surgery often improves diabetes in those who are obese.

Rates of type 2 diabetes have increased markedly since 1960 in parallel with obesity. As of 2015 there were approximately 392 million people diagnosed with the disease compared to around 30 million in 1985. Typically it begins in middle or older age, although rates of type 2 diabetes are increasing in young people. Type 2 diabetes is associated with a ten-year-shorter life expectancy.

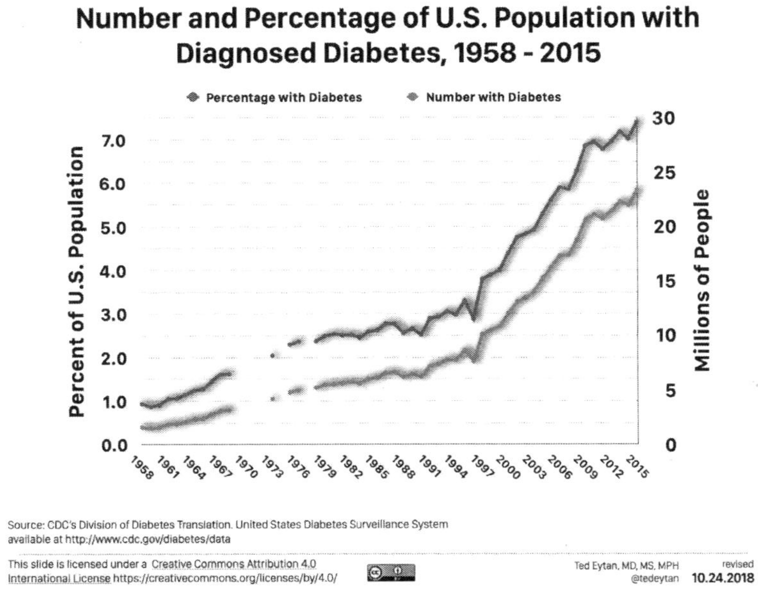

Number and Percentage of U.S. Population with Diagnosed Diabetes, 1958 - 2015

Percentage with Diabetes
Number with Diabetes

Percent of U.S. Population
Millions of People

Source: CDC's Division of Diabetes Translation. United States Diabetes Surveillance System available at http://www.cdc.gov/diabetes/data

Ted Eytan, MD, MS, MPH @tedeytan revised 10.24.2018

Figure 15. In 1990, 2.52% of the total population had diabetes. It's now 9% of total, 12% of adults. It's estimated that 25% of adults will have diabetes in the US by 2030, 33% by 2050.

Osteoporosis

Osteoporosis comes from the Greek word for "porous bones" and is a disease in which bone weakening increases the risk of a broken bone. It is defined as having a bone density of 2.5 standard deviations below that of a healthy young adult. Osteoporosis increases with age as bones become brittle and lose minerals. It is the most common reason for a broken bone among the elderly.

Osteoporosis becomes more common with age. About 15% of white people in their 50s and 70% of those over 80 are affected. It is four times more likely to affect women than men—in the developed world, depending on the method of diagnosis, 2% to 8% of males and 9% to 38% of females are affected. In the United States in 2010, about eight million women and one to two million men had osteoporosis. White and Asian people are at greater risk are more likely to have osteoporosis than non-Hispanic blacks.

Parkinson's Disease

Parkinson's disease (PD) is a long-term degenerative disorder of the central nervous system which mainly affects the motor system, although as the disease worsens, non-motor symptoms become increasingly common. Early in the disease, the most obvious symptoms are shaking, rigidity, slowness of movement, and difficulty with walking, but thinking and behavioral problems may also occur. Dementia becomes common in the advanced stages of the disease, and depression and anxiety also occur in more than a third of people with PD.

The cause of Parkinson's disease is generally unknown, but believed to involve both genetic and environmental factors. Those with a family member affected are more likely to get the disease themselves. There is also an increased risk in people exposed to certain pesticides and among those who have had prior head injuries, while there is a reduced risk in tobacco smokers (though smokers are at a substantially greater risk of stroke) and those who drink coffee or tea. The motor symptoms of the disease result from the death of cells in the substantia nigra, a region of the midbrain, which results in not enough dopamine in these areas. The reason for this cell death is poorly understood, but involves the build-up of proteins into Lewy bodies in the neurons.

In 2015, PD affected 6.2 million people and resulted in about 117,400 deaths globally. Parkinson's disease typically occurs in people over the age of 60, of which about one percent are affected. Males are more often affected than females at a ratio of around 3:2. The average life expectancy following diagnosis is between 7 and 14 years. People with Parkinson's who have increased the public's awareness of the condition include actor Michael J. Fox, Olympic cyclist Davis Phinney, and professional boxer Muhammad Ali.

Theories on Aging

Why do we age?

There are a number of attempts to explain why we age and many factors that contribute to aging. The **peripheral slowing hypothesis** suggests that overall processing speed declines in the peripheral nervous system, affecting the brain's ability to communicate with muscles and organs. Some of the peripheral nervous system (PNS) is under a person's voluntary control, such as the nerves carrying instructions from the brain to the limbs. As well as controlling muscles and joints, the PNS sends all the information from the senses back to the brain.

Figure 16. There are several plausible theories as to why aging happens

The **generalized slowing hypothesis** theory suggests that processing in all parts of the nervous system, including the brain, are less efficient with age. This may be why older people have more accidents. Genetics, diet, lifestyle, activity, and exposure to pollutants all play a role in the aging process.[18][19][20]

Cell Life

Cells divide a limited number of times and then stop. This phenomenon, known as the **Hayflick limit**, is evidenced in cells studied in test tubes which divide about 50 times before becoming senescent. In 1961, Dr. Hayflick theorized that the human cell's ability to divide is limited to approximately 50-times, after which they simply stop dividing (the Hayflick limit theory of aging). According to telomere theory, telomeres have experimentally been shown to shorten with each successive cell division.[21]

Senescent cells do not die. They simply stop replicating. Senescent cells can help limit the growth of other cells which may reduce risk of developing tumors when younger, but can alter genes later in life and result in promoting the growth of tumors as we age (Dollemore, 2006). Limited cell growth is attributed to telomeres which are the tips of the protective coating around chromosomes. Each time cells replicate, the telomere is shortened. Eventually, loss of telomere length is thought to create damage to chromosomes and produce cell senescence.

18. Plude, D. J., & Doussard-Roosevelt, J. A. (1989). *Aging, selective attention, and feature integration. Psychology and Aging, 4(1), 98-105.*
19. NCBI Bookshelf. A service of the National Library of Medicine, National Institutes of Health. Murray MM, Wallace MT, editors
20. The Neural Bases of Multisensory Processes. Boca Raton (FL): CRC Press/Taylor & Francis; 2012. Chapter 20Multisensory Integration and Aging Authors Jennifer L. Mozolic, Christina E. Hugenschmidt, Ann M. Peiffer, and Paul J. Laurienti.
21. Jin K. (2010). Modern Biological Theories of Aging. Aging and disease, 1(2), 72–74.

LINK TO LEARNING

Watch this Ted talk by molecular biologist Elizabeth Blackburn on "The Science of Cells That Never Get Old." Blackburn won a Nobel Prize for her pioneering work on telomeres and telomerase, which may play central roles in how we age.

Biochemistry and Aging

Free Radical Theory of Aging

The **free radical theory of aging** (**FRTA**) states that organisms age because cells accumulate free radical damage over time. A free radical is any atom or moleculewhich has a single unpaired electron in an outer shell. This means that as oxygen is metabolized, mitochondria in the cells convert the oxygen to adenosine triphosphate (ATP) which provides energy to the cell. Unpaired electrons are a byproduct of this process and these unstable electrons cause cellular damage as they find other electrons with which to bond. These free radicals have some benefits and are used by the immune system to destroy bacteria. However, cellular damage accumulates and eventually reduces functioning of organs and systems. Many food products and vitamin supplements are promoted as age-reducing. Antioxidant drugs have been shown to increase the longevity in nematodes (small worms), but the ability to slow the aging process by introducing antioxidants in the diet is still controversial.

Protein Crosslinking

This theory focuses on the role blood sugar, or glucose, plays in the aging of cells. Glucose molecules attach themselves to proteins and form chains or crosslinks. These crosslinks reduce the flexibility of tissue and thus it becomes stiff and loses functioning. The circulatory system becomes less efficient as the tissue of the heart, arteries and lungs lose flexibility. Joints grow stiff as glucose combines with collegen.

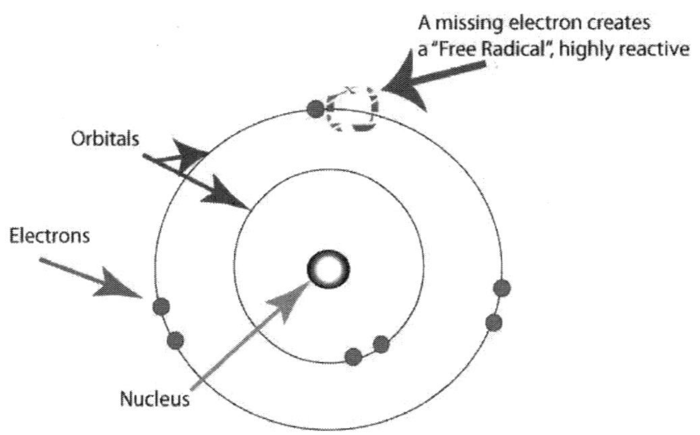

Figure 17. In chemistry, a free radical is any atom, molecule, or ion with an unpaired valence electron

DNA Damage

Through the normal growth and aging process, DNA is damaged by environmental factors such as toxic agents, pollutants, and sun exposure (Dollemore, 2006). This results in deletions of genetic material, and mutations in the DNA duplicated in new cells. The accumulation of these errors results in reduced functioning in cells and tissues. Theories that suggest that the body's DNA genetic code contains a built-in time limit for the reproduction of human cells are called the genetic programming theories of aging. These theories promote the view that the cells of the body can only duplicate a certain number of times and that the genetic instructions for running the body can be read only a certain number of times before they become illegible. Such theories also promote the existence of a "death gene" which is programmed to direct the body to deteriorate and die, and the idea that a long life after the reproductive years is unnecessary for the survival of the species.[22]

22. Kunlin, Jin. (2010). Modern Biological Theories Of Aging. Aging Dis. 2010 Oct; 1(2): 72–74. Published online 2010 Aug 1. PMCID: PMC2995895 NIHMSID: NIHMS248183 PMID: 21132086.

Decline in the Immune System

As we age, B-lymphocytes and T-lymphocytes become less active. These cells are crucial to the immune system as they secrete antibodies and directly attack infected cells. The thymus, where T-cells are manufactured, shrinks as aging progresses. This reduces our body's ability to fight infection (Berger, 2005).

GLOSSARY

active life expectancy:
the number of years a person can expect to live without disability

arthritis:
arthritis is inflammation of one or more of the joints, characterized by joint pain and stiffness, which typically worsen with age

blue zones:
regions of the world where Dan Buettner claims people live much longer than average

centenarians:
people aged 100 or older

cochlear implant:
electronic device that consists of a microphone, a speech processor, and an electrode array to directly stimulate the auditory nerve to transmit information to the brain

conductive hearing loss:
failure in the vibration of the eardrum and/or movement of the ossicles

free radical theory of aging (FRTA):
theory that organisms age because cells accumulate free radical damage over time

generalized slowing hypothesis:
the theory that processing in all parts of the nervous system, including the brain, is less efficient

Hayflick limit:
the number of times a normal human cell population will divide before cell division stops

hypertension:
high blood pressure that can lead to severe complications and increases the risk of heart disease, stroke, and death

life expectancy:
a statistical measure of the average time an organism is expected to live, based on the year of its birth, its current age and other demographic factors including gender

Ménière's disease:
results in a degeneration of inner ear structures that can lead to hearing loss, tinnitus, vertigo, and an increase in pressure within the inner ear

osteoporosis:
a condition in which the bones become brittle, fragile, and thin, often brought about by a lack of calcium in the diet

Parkinson's disease:
long-term degenerative disorder of the central nervous system which mainly affects the motor system, first characterized by shaking, rigidity, slowness of movement, and difficulty with walking, but thinking and behavioral problems may also occur

peripheral slowing hypothesis:
the theory that overall processing speed declines with age in the peripheral nervous system

presbycusis:
age-related sensorineural hearing loss resulting from degeneration of the cochlea or associated structures of the inner ear or auditory nerves

primary aging:
aging that is irreversible and is due to genetic predisposition

secondary aging:
refers to changes that are caused by illness or disease

Selective Optimization with Compensation (SOC):
a strategy for improving health and well being in older adults and a model for successful aging

senescence:
biological aging and the gradual deterioration of functional abilities

sensorineural hearing loss:
failure to transmit neural signals from the cochlea to the brain

quality of life:
the general well-being of individuals and societies, including life satisfaction, physical health, family, education, employment, wealth, safety, security, freedom, religious beliefs, and the environment

temporal theory of pitch perception:
sound's frequency is coded by the activity level of a sensory neuron

type 2 diabetes (T2D):
diabetes characterized by high blood sugar, insulin resistance, and relative lack of insulin primarily from obesity or lack of exercise

vertigo:
spinning sensation

Cognitive Development in Late Adulthood

What you'll learn to do: explain cognitive development in late adulthood

There are numerous stereotypes regarding older adults as being forgetful and confused, but what does the research on memory and cognition in late adulthood actually reveal? In this section, we will focus upon the impact of aging on memory, how age impacts cognitive functioning, and abnormal memory loss due to Alzheimer's disease, delirium, and dementia.

LEARNING OUTCOMES

- Discuss the impact of aging on memory
- Explain how age impacts cognitive functioning
- Describe abnormal memory loss due to Alzheimer's disease, delirium, and dementia

Cognitive Development and Memory in Late Adulthood

How does aging affect memory?

The Sensory Register

Aging may create small decrements in the sensitivity of the senses. And, to the extent that a person has a more difficult time hearing or seeing, that information will not be stored in memory. This is an important point, because many older people assume that if they cannot remember something, it is because their memory is poor. In fact, it may be that the information was never seen or heard.

Figure 1. During late adulthood, memory and attention decline, but continued efforts to learn and engage in cognitive activities can minimize aging effects on cognitive development.

The Working Memory

Older people have more difficulty using memory strategies to recall details (Berk, 2007). **Working memory** is a cognitive system with a limited capacity responsible for temporarily holding information available for processing. As we age, the working memory loses some of its capacity. This makes it more difficult to concentrate on more than one thing at a time or to remember details of an event. However, people often compensate for this by writing down information and avoiding situations where there is too much going on at once to focus on a particular cognitive task.

When an elderly person demonstrates difficulty with multi-step verbal information presented quickly, the person is exhibiting problems with working memory. Working memory is among the cognitive functions most sensitive to decline in old age. Several explanations have been offered for this decline in memory functioning; one is the processing speed theory of cognitive aging by Tim Salthouse. Drawing on the findings of general slowing of cognitive processes as people grow older, Salthouse argues that slower processing causes working-memory contents to decay, thus reducing effective capacity.[1] For example, if an elderly person is watching a complicated action movie, they may not process the events quickly enough before the scene changes, or they may processing the events of the second scene, which causes them to forget the first scene. The decline of working-memory capacity cannot be entirely attributed to cognitive slowing, however, because capacity declines more in old age than speed.

Another proposal is the inhibition hypothesis advanced by Lynn Hasher and Rose Zacks. This theory assumes a general deficit in old age in the ability to inhibit irrelevant, or no-longer relevant, information. Therefore, working memory tends to be cluttered with irrelevant contents which reduce the effective capacity for relevant content. The assumption of an inhibition deficit in old age has received much empirical support but, so far, it is not clear whether the decline in inhibitory ability fully explains the decline of working-memory capacity.

An explanation on the neural level of the decline of working memory and other cognitive functions in old age was been proposed by Robert West. He argued that working memory depends to a large degree on the pre-frontal cortex, which deteriorates more than other brain regions as we grow old.[2] Age related decline in working memory can be briefly reversed using low intensity transcranial stimulation, synchronizing rhythms in bilateral frontal and left temporal lobe areas.

1. Salthouse, TA (1996). The processing-speed theory of adult age differences in cognition. Psychology Review. Retrieved from https://www.ncbi.nlm.nih.gov/pubmed/8759042.
2. West, Robert (1996). An application of prefrontal cortex function theory to cognitive aging. Psychological Bulletin. Retrieved from https://www.ncbi.nlm.nih.gov/pubmed/8831298.

The Long-Term Memory

Long-term memory involves the storage of information for long periods of time. Retrieving such information depends on how well it was learned in the first place rather than how long it has been stored. If information is stored effectively, an older person may remember facts, events, names and other types of information stored in long-term memory throughout life. The memory of adults of all ages seems to be similar when they are asked to recall names of teachers or classmates. And older adults remember more about their early adulthood and adolescence than about middle adulthood (Berk, 2007). Older adults retain semantic memory or the ability to remember vocabulary.

Younger adults rely more on mental rehearsal strategies to store and retrieve information. Older adults focus rely more on external cues such as familiarity and context to recall information (Berk, 2007). And they are more likely to report the main idea of a story rather than all of the details (Jepson & Labouvie-Vief, in Berk, 2007).

A positive attitude about being able to learn and remember plays an important role in memory. When people are under stress (perhaps feeling stressed about memory loss), they have a more difficult time taking in information because they are preoccupied with anxieties. Many of the laboratory memory tests require comparing the performance of older and younger adults on timed memory tests in which older adults do not perform as well. However, few real life situations require speedy responses to memory tasks. Older adults rely on more meaningful cues to remember facts and events without any impairment to everyday living.

New Research on Aging and Cognition

Can the brain be trained in order to build cognitive reserve to reduce the effects of normal aging? ACTIVE (Advanced Cognitive Training for Independent and Vital Elderly), a study conducted between 1999 and 2001 in which 2,802 individuals age 65 to 94, suggests that the answer is "yes." These participants received 10 group training sessions and 4 follow up sessions to work on tasks of memory, reasoning, and speed of processing. These mental workouts improved cognitive functioning even 5 years later. Many of the participants believed that this improvement could be seen in everyday tasks as well (Tennstedt, Morris, et al, 2006). Learning new things, engaging in activities that are considered challenging, and being physically active at any age may build a reserve to minimize the effects of primary aging of the brain.

WATCH IT

Watch this video from SciShow Psych to learn about ways to keep the mind young and active.

- https://youtu.be/5DH9IAqNTG0

Wisdom

Wisdom is the ability to use common sense and good judgment in making decisions. A wise person is insightful and has knowledge that can be used to overcome obstacles they encounter in their daily lives. Does aging bring wisdom? While living longer brings experience, it does not always bring wisdom. Those who have had experience helping others resolve problems in living and those who have served in leadership positions seem to have more wisdom. So it is age combined with a certain type of experience that brings wisdom. However, older adults generally have greater emotional wisdom or the ability to empathize with and understand others.

Changes in Attention in Late Adulthood

Divided attention has usually been associated with significant age-related declines in performing complex tasks. For example, older adults show significant impairments on attentional tasks such as looking at a visual cue at the same time as listening to an auditory cue because it requires dividing or switching of attention among multiple inputs. Deficits found in many tasks, such as the Stroop task which measures selective attention, can be largely attributed to a general slowing of information processing in older adults rather than to selective attention deficits per se. They also are able to maintain concentration for an extended period of time. In general, older adults are *not* impaired on tasks that test sustained attention, such as watching a screen for an infrequent beep or symbol.

The tasks on which older adults show impairments tend to be those that require flexible control of attention, a cognitive function associated with the frontal lobes. Importantly, these types of tasks appear to improve with training and can be strengthened.[3]

An important conclusion from research on changes in cognitive function as we age is that attentional deficits can have a significant impact on an older person's ability to function adequately and independently in everyday life. One important aspect of daily functioning impacted by attentional problems is driving. This is an activity that, for many older people, is essential to independence. Driving requires a constant switching of attention in response to environmental contingencies. Attention must be divided between driving, monitoring the environment, and sorting out relevant from irrelevant stimuli in a cluttered visual array. Research has shown that divided attention impairments are significantly associated with increased automobile accidents in older adults[4] Therefore, practice and extended training on driving simulators under divided attention conditions may be an important remedial activity for older people.[5]

Problem Solving

Problem solving tasks that require processing non-meaningful information quickly (a kind of task which might be part of a laboratory experiment on mental processes) declines with age. However, real life challenges facing older adults do not rely on speed of processing or making choices on one's own. Older adults are able to resolve everyday problems by relying on input from others such as family and friends. They are also less likely than younger adults to delay making decisions on important matters such as medical care (Strough et al., 2003; Meegan & Berg, 2002).

Cognitive Function in Late Adulthood

Abnormal Loss of Cognitive Functioning During Late Adulthood

Dementia is the umbrella category use to describe the general long-term and often gradual decrease in the ability to think and remember that affects a person's daily functioning. Common symptoms also include emotional problems, difficulties with language, and a decrease in motivation. A person's consciousness is usually not affected. Globally, dementia affected about 46 million people in 2015. About 10% of people develop the disorder at some point in their lives, and it becomes more common with age. About 3% of people between the ages of 65–74 have dementia, 19% between 75 and 84, and nearly half of those over 85 years of age. In 2015, dementia resulted in about 1.9 million deaths, up from 0.8 million in 1990. As more people are living longer, dementia is becoming more common in the population as a whole.

3. Glisky EL. Changes in Cognitive Function in Human Aging. In: Riddle DR, editor. Brain Aging: Models, Methods, and Mechanisms. Boca Raton (FL): CRC Press/Taylor & Francis; 2007. Chapter 1. Available from: https://www.ncbi.nlm.nih.gov/books/NBK3885/
4. McDowd JM, Shaw RJ. Attention and aging: a functional perspective. In: Craik FIM, Salthouse TA, editors. The Handbook of Aging and Cognition. 2.
5. Erlbaum; Mahwah, NJ: 2000. p. 221., FN Park DC, Gutchess AH. Cognitive aging and everyday life. In: Park D, Schwarz N, editors. Cognitive Aging: A Primer. Psychology Press; Philadelphia, PA: 2000. p. 217.

Dementia generally refers to severely impaired judgment, memory or problem-solving ability. It can occur before old age and is not an inevitable development even among the very old. Dementia can be caused by numerous diseases and circumstances, all of which result in similar general symptoms of impaired judgment, etc. Alzheimer's disease is the most common form of dementia and is incurable, but there are also nonorganic causes of dementia which can be prevented. Malnutrition, alcoholism, depression, and mixing medications can also result in symptoms of dementia. If these causes are properly identified, they can be treated. Cerebral vascular disease can also reduce cognitive functioning.

Delirium, also known as acute confusional state, is an organically caused decline from a previous baseline level of mental function that develops over a short period of time, typically hours to days. It is more common in older adults, but can easily be confused with a number of psychiatric disorders or chronic organic brain syndromes because of many overlapping signs and symptoms in common with dementia, depression, psychosis, etc. Delirium may manifest from a baseline of existing mental illness, baseline intellectual disability, or dementia, without being due to any of these problems.

Delirium is a syndrome encompassing disturbances in attention, consciousness, and cognition. It may also involve other neurological deficits, such as psychomotor disturbances (e.g. hyperactive, hypoactive, or mixed), impaired sleep-wake cycle, emotional disturbances, and perceptual disturbances (e.g. hallucinations and delusions), although these features are not required for diagnosis. Among older adults, delirium occurs in 15-53% of post-surgical patients, 70-87% of those in the ICU, and up to 60% of those in nursing homes or post-acute care settings. Among those requiring critical care, delirium is a risk for death within the next year.

Alzheimer's Disease

Alzheimer's disease (AD), also referred to simply as Alzheimer's, is the most common cause of dementia, accounting for 60-70% of its cases. Alzheimer's is a progressive disease causing problems with memory, thinking and behavior. Symptoms usually develop slowly and get worse over time, becoming severe enough to interfere with daily tasks.[6]

The most common early symptom is difficulty in remembering recent events. As the disease advances, symptoms can include problems with language, disorientation (including easily getting lost), mood swings, loss of motivation, not managing self care, and behavioral issues. In the early stages, memory loss is mild, but with late-stage Alzheimer's, individuals lose the ability to carry on a conversation and respond to their environment.

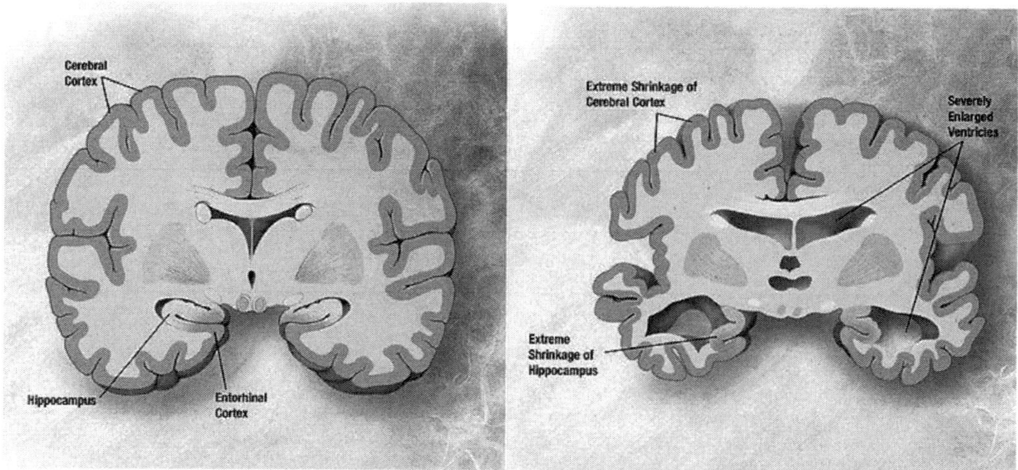

Figure 2. Alzheimer's disease is not simply part of the aging process. It is a disease with physiological symptoms and decay in the brain.

6. What is Alzheimer's? *Alzheimer's Association*. Retrieved from https://www.alz.org/alzheimers-dementia/what-is-alzheimers

Alzheimer's is the sixth leading cause of death in the United States. On average, a person with Alzheimer's lives four to eight years after diagnosis, but can live as long as 20 years, depending on other factors. Alzheimer's is not a normal part of aging. The greatest known risk factor is increasing age, and the majority of people with Alzheimer's are 65 and older. But Alzheimer's is not just a disease of old age. Approximately 200,000 Americans under the age of 65 have younger-onset Alzheimer's disease (also known as early-onset Alzheimer's).[7]

The cause of Alzheimer's disease is poorly understood. About 70% of the risk is believed to be inherited from a person's parents with many genes usually involved. Other risk factors include a history of head injuries, depression, and hypertension. The disease process is associated with plaques and neurofibrillary tangles in the brain. A probable diagnosis is based on the history of the illness and cognitive testing with medical imaging and blood tests to rule out other possible causes. Initial symptoms are often mistaken for normal aging, but examination of brain tissue, specifically of structures called plaques and tangles, is needed for a definite diagnosis. Though qualified physicians can be up to 90% certain of a correct diagnosis of Alzheimer's, currently, the only way to make a 100% definitive diagnosis is by performing and autopsy of the person and examining the brain tissue. In 2015, there were approximately 29.8 million people worldwide with AD. In developed countries, AD is one of the most financially costly diseases.

WATCH IT

This Ted-Ed video explains some of the history and biological diagnosis of Alzheimer's.

- https://youtu.be/yJXTXN4xrI8

LINK TO LEARNING

Samuel Cohen researches Alzheimer's disease and other neurodegenerative disorders. Listen to Cohen's TED Talk on Alzheimer's disease to learn more.

GLOSSARY

Alzheimer's disease:
an irreversible, progressive brain disorder that slowly destroys memory and thinking skills, and eventually the ability to carry out the simplest tasks

delirium:
an abrupt change in the brain that causes mental confusion and emotional disruption. It makes it difficult to think, remember, sleep, pay attention, and more

7. What is Alzheimer's? Alzheimer's Association. Retrieved from https://www.alz.org/alzheimers-dementia/what-is-alzheimers.

dementia:
a cause of neurocognitive disorder, characterized by progressive and gradual cognitive deficits due to severe cerebral atrophy

long-term memory:
the storage of information over an extended period

working memory:
a cognitive system with a limited capacity that is responsible for temporarily holding information available for processing

Psychosocial Development in Late Adulthood

What you'll learn to do: describe psychosocial development in in late adulthood

Our ideas about aging, and what it means to be over 50, over 60, or even over 90, seem to be stuck somewhere back in the middle of the 20th century. We still consider 65 as standard retirement age, and we expect everyone to start slowing down and moving aside for the next generation as their age passes the half-century mark. In this section we explore psychosocial developmental theories, including Erik Erikson's theory on psychosocial development in late adulthood, and we look at aging as it relates to work, retirement, and leisure activities for older adult. We'll also examine ways in which people are productive in late adulthood.

LEARNING OUTCOMES

- Describe theories related to late adulthood, including Erikson's psychosocial stage of integrity vs. despair
- Describe examples of productivity in late adulthood
- Describe attitudes about aging
- Examine family relationships during late adulthood (grandparenting, marriage, divorce, widowhood, traditional and non-traditional roles; co-habitation, LGBTQ+)

Psychosocial Development in Late Adulthood

Erikson: Integrity vs. Despair

As a person grows older and enters into the retirement years, the pace of life and productivity tend to slow down, granting a person time for reflection upon their life. They may ask the existential question, "It is okay to have been me?" If someone sees themselves as having lived a successful life, they may see it as one filled with productivity, or according to Erik Erikson, integrity.

Here integrity is said to consist of the ability to look back on one's life with a feeling of satisfaction, peace and gratitude for all that has been given and received. Erikson (1959/1980) notes in this regard:

> "The possessor of integrity is ready to defend the dignity of his own lifestyle against all physical and economic treats. For he knows that an individual life is the accidental coincidence of but one life cycle within but one segment of history; and that for him all human integrity stands and falls with the one style of integrity of which he partakes." (Erikson, 1959/1980, p. 104)

Thus, persons derive a sense of meaning (i.e., integrity) through careful review of how their lives have been lived (Krause, 2012). Ideally, however, integrity does not stop here, but rather continues to evolve into the virtue of wisdom. According to Erikson, this is the goal during this stage of life.

If a person see's their life as unproductive, or feel that they did not accomplish their life goals, they may become dissatisfied with life and develop what Erikson calls despair, often leading to depression and hopelessness. This stage can occur out of the sequence when an individual feels they are near the end of their life (such as when receiving a terminal disease diagnosis).

Erikson's Ninth Stage

Erikson collaborate with his wife, Joan, through much of his work on psychosocial development. In the Erikson's older years, they re-examined the eight stages and created additional thoughts about how development evolves during a person's 80s and 90s. After Erik Erikson passed away in 1994, Joan published a chapter on the ninth stage of development, in which she proposed (from her own experiences and Erik's notes) that older adults revisit the previous eight stages and deal with the previous conflicts in new ways, as they cope with the physical and social changes of growing old. In the first eight stages, all of the conflicts are presented in a syntonic-dystonic matter, meaning that the first term listed in the conflict is the positive, sought-after achievement and the second term is the less-desirable goal (ie. trust is more desirable than mistrust and integrity is more desirable than despair).[1] During the ninth stage, Erikson argues that the dystonic, or less desirable outcome, comes to take precedence again. For example, an older adult may become mistrustful (trust vs. mistrust), feel more guilt about not having the abilities to do what they once did (initiative vs. guilt), feel less competent compared with others (industry vs. inferiority) lose a sense of identity as they become dependent on others (identity vs. role confusion), become increasingly isolated (intimacy vs. isolation), feel that they have less to offer society (generativity vs. stagnation), or[2] The Erikson's found that

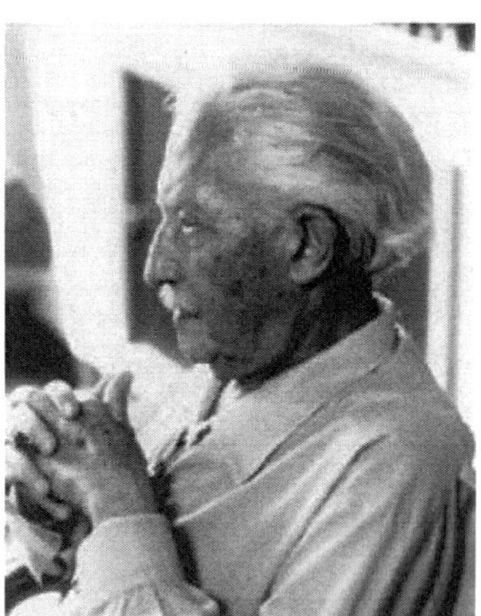

Figure 1. Erikson emphasized the importance of integrity, and feeling a sense of accomplishment as an older person looks back on their life.

1. Perry, T. E., Ruggiano, N., Shtompel, N., & Hassevoort, L. (2015). Applying Erikson's wisdom to self-management practices of older adults: findings from two field studies. Research on aging, 37(3), 253–274. doi:10.1177/0164027514527974
2. Gusky, Judith (2012). Why aren't they screaming? A counselor's reflection on aging. Counseling Today. Retrieved from https://ct.counseling.org/2012/04/why-arent-they-screaming-a-counselors-reflection-on-aging/

those who successfully come to terms with these changes and adjustments in later life make headway towards gerotrancendence, a term coined by gerontologist Lars Tornstam to represent a greater awareness of one's own life and connection to the universe, increased ties to the past, and a positive, transcendent, perspective about life.

Activity Theory

Developed by Havighurst and Albrecht in 1953, activity theory addresses the issue of how persons can best adjust to the changing circumstances of old age–e.g., retirement, illness, loss of friends and loved ones through death, etc. In addressing this issue they recommend that older adults involve themselves in voluntary and leisure organizations, child care and other forms of social interaction. **Activity theory** thus strongly supports the avoidance of a sedentary lifestyle and considers it essential to health and happiness that the older person remains active physically and socially. In other words, the more active older adults are the more stable and positive their self-concept will be, which will then lead to greater life satisfaction and higher morale (Havighurst & Albrecht, 1953). Activity theory suggests that many people are barred from meaningful experiences as they age, but older adults who continue to want to remain active can work toward replacing opportunities lost with new ones.[3]

Disengagement Theory

Disengagement theory, developed by Cumming and Henry in the 1950s, in contrast to activity theory, emphasizes that older adults should not be discouraged from following their inclination towards solitude and greater inactivity. While not completely discounting the importance of exercise and social activity for the upkeep of physical health and personal well being, disengagement theory is opposed to artificially keeping the older person so busy with external activities that they have no time for contemplation and reflection (Cumming & Henry, 1961). In other words, disengagement theory posits that older adults in all societies undergo a process of adjustment which involves leaving former public and professional roles and narrowing their social horizon to the smaller circle of family and friends. This process enables the older person to die more peacefully, without the stress and distractions that come with a more socially involved life. The theory suggests that during late adulthood, the individual and society mutually withdraw. Older people become more isolated from others and less concerned or involved with life in general. This once popular theory is now criticized as being ageist and used in order to justify treating older adults as second class citizens.[4]

Continuity Theory

Continuity theory suggests as people age, they continue to view the self in much the same way as they did when they were younger. An older person's approach to problems, goals, and situations is much the same as it was when they were younger. They are the same individuals, but simply in older bodies. Consequently, older adults continue to maintain their identity even as they give up previous roles. For example, a retired Coast Guard commander attends reunions with shipmates, stays interested in new technology for home use, is meticulous in the jobs he does for friends or at church, and displays mementos from his experiences on the ship. He is able to maintain a sense of self as a result. People do not give up who they are as they age. Hopefully, they are able to share these aspects of their identity with others throughout life. Focusing on what a person can do and pursuing those interests and activities is one way to optimize and maintain self-identity.

3. Håkan Nilsson, Pia H. Bülowac, Ali Kazemib (2015). Europe's Journal of Psychology, 2015, Vol. 11(3), doi:10.5964/ejop.v11i3.949. Retrieved from https://ejop.psychopen.eu/article/view/949/html.
4. Håkan Nilsson, Pia H. Bülowac, Ali Kazemib (2015). Europe's Journal of Psychology, 2015, Vol. 11(3), doi:10.5964/ejop.v11i3.949. Retrieved from https://ejop.psychopen.eu/article/view/949/html.

Generativity in Late Adulthood

People in late adulthood continue to be productive in many ways. These include work, education, volunteering, family life, and intimate relationships. Older adults also experience generativity (recall Erikson's previous stage of generativity vs. stagnation) through voting, forming and helping social institutions like community centers, churches and schools. Psychoanalyst Erik Erikson wrote "I am what survives me."[5]

Productivity in Work

Figure 2. Many choose to retire at age 65, but some enjoy a productive work life well beyond their 60s.

Some continue to be productive in work. Mandatory retirement is now illegal in the United States. However, many do choose retirement by age 65 and most leave work by choice. Those who do leave by choice adjust to retirement more easily. Chances are, they have prepared for a smoother transition by gradually giving more attention to an avocation or interest as they approach retirement. And they are more likely to be financially ready to retire. Those who must leave abruptly for health reasons or because of layoffs or downsizing have a more difficult time adjusting to their new circumstances. Men, especially, can find unexpected retirement difficult. Women may feel less of an identify loss after retirement because much of their identity may have come from family roles as well. But women tend to have poorer retirement funds accumulated from work and if they take their retirement funds in a lump sum (be that from their own or from a deceased husband's funds), are more at risk of outliving those funds. Women need better financial retirement planning.

Sixteen percent of adults over 65 were in the labor force in 2008 (U. S. Census Bureau 2011). Globally, 6.2 percent are in the labor force and this number is expected to reach 10.1 million by 2016. Many adults 65 and older continue to work either full-time or part-time either for income or pleasure or both. In 2003, 39 percent of full-time workers over 55 were women over the age of 70; 53 percent were men over 70. This increase in numbers of older adults is likely to mean that more will continue to part of the workforce in years to come. (He et al., article, U. S. Census, 2005).

Volunteering: Face-to-face and Virtually

About 40 percent of older adults are involved in some type of structured, face-to-face, volunteer work. But many older adults, about 60 percent, engage in a sort of informal type of volunteerism helping out neighbors or friends rather than working in an organization (Berger, 2005). They may help a friend by taking them somewhere or shopping for them, etc. Some do participate in organized volunteer programs but interestingly enough, those who do tend to work part-time as well. Those who retire and do not work are less likely to feel that they have a contribution to make. (It's as if when one gets used to staying at home, their confidence to go out into the world diminishes.) And those who have recently retired are more likely to volunteer than those over 75 years of age.

5. Havey, Elizabeth A. (2015). "What's Generativity and Why It's Good for You." Huffington Post. Retrieved from https://www.huffpost.com/entry/whats-generativity-and-why-its-good-for-you_b_7629174?guccounter=1&guce_referrer=aHR0cHM6Ly93d3cuZ29vZ2xlLmNvbS8&guce_referrer_sig=AQAAAISJrz_B9ylovtOxRuUNpAiqtA6GZvMM8nUxuyG0eL1AwbMX0F2fElL6QyV_FFiZfAf4oNBhRfajbOpAJu1L8tGsPe1My9RCv7X-hFjvhxNcr11Z5VRkfmmim1nxpi2cA-cF4SYXbn9OyhdIzXtdHB-UwJqn73I0rFzpLKpv35gT.

New opportunities exist for older adults to serve as virtual volunteers by dialoguing online with others from around their world and sharing their support, interests, and expertise. According to an article from AARP (American Association of Retired Persons), virtual volunteerism has increased from 3,000 in 1998 to over 40,000 participants in 2005. These volunteer opportunities range from helping teens with their writing to communicating with 'neighbors' in villages of developing countries. Virtual volunteering is available to those who cannot engage in face-to-face interactions and opens up a new world of possibilities and ways to connect, maintain identity, and be productive (Uscher, 2006).

Education

Twenty percent of people over 65 have a bachelors or higher degree. And over 7 million people over 65 take adult education courses (U. S. Census Bureau, 2011). Lifelong learning through continuing education programs on college campuses or programs known as "Elderhostels" which allow older adults to travel abroad, live on campus and study provide enriching experiences. Academic courses as well as practical skills such as computer classes, foreign languages, budgeting, and holistic medicines are among the courses offered. Older adults who have higher levels of education are more likely to take continuing education. But offering more educational experiences to a diverse group of older adults, including those who are institutionalized in nursing homes, can enhance the quality of life.

Religious Activities

People tend to become more involved in prayer and religious activities as they age. This provides a social network as well as a belief system which can combats the fear of death. Religious activities provide a focus for volunteerism and other activities as well. For example, one elderly woman prides herself on knitting prayer shawls that are given to those who are sick. Another serves on the alter guild and is responsible for keeping robes and linens clean and ready for communion.

Political Activism

The elderly are very politically active. They have high rates of voting and engage in letter writing to congress on issues that not only affect them, but on a wide range of domestic and foreign concerns. In the past three presidential elections, over 70 percent of people 65 and older showed up at the polls to vote (U. S. Census Bureau).

Attitudes about Aging

Attitudes about Aging

Stereotypes about people of in late adulthood lead many to assume that aging automatically brings poor health and mental decline. These stereotypes are reflected in everyday conversations, the media and even in greeting cards (Overstreet, 2006). The following examples serve to illustrate.

> 1) Grandpa, fishing pole in one hand, pipe in the other, sits on the ground and completes a story being told to his grandson with ". . . and that, Jimmy, is the tale of my very first colonoscopy." The message inside the card reads, "Welcome to the gross personal story years." (Shoebox, A Division of Hallmark Cards.)
>
> 2) An older woman in a barber shop cuts the hair of an older, dozing man. "So, what do you say today, Earl?" she asks. The inside message reads, "Welcome to the age where pretty much anyplace is a good place for a nap." (Shoebox, A Division of Hallmark Cards.)
>
> 3) A crotchety old man with wire glasses, a crumpled hat, and a bow tie grimaces and the card reads, "Another year older? You're at the age where you should start eatin' right, exercisin', and takin' vitamins . . ." The inside reads, "Of course you're also at the age where you can ignore advice by actin like you can't hear it." (Hallmark Cards, Inc.)

Figure 3. Word used to describe the elderly are often negative and biased. Research by the Australain Human Rights Commusion polled people on the following question: "Thinking about everything you see and hear in the media (including on TV, online, on the radio and in newspapers and magazines), how does the media portray older people?" Their responses are listed here, with the larger words being listed more often. Retrieved from the https://www.humanrights.gov.au/our-work/chapter-4-role-and-influence-media.

Of course, these cards are made because they are popular. Age is not revered in the United States, and so laughing about getting older is one way to get relief. The attitudes above are examples of ageism, prejudice based on age. **Ageism** is prejudice and discrimination that is directed at older people. This view suggests that older people are less in command of their mental faculties. Older people are viewed more negatively than younger people on a variety of traits, particularly those relating to general competence and attractiveness. Stereotypes such as these can lead to a self-fulfilling prophecy in which beliefs about one's ability results in actions that make it come true.

Ageism is a modern and predominately western cultural phenomenon—in the American colonial period, long life was an indication of virtue, and Asian and Native American societies view older people as wise, storehouses of information about the past, and deserving of respect. Many preindustrial societies observed **gerontocracy**, a type of social structure wherein the power is held by a society's oldest members. In some countries today, the elderly still have influence and power and their vast knowledge is respected, but this reverence has decreased in many places due to social factors. A positive, optimistic outlook about aging and the impact one can have on improving health is essential to health and longevity. Removing societal stereotypes about aging and helping older adults reject those notions of aging is another way to promote health in older populations.

Figure 4.What comes to mind when you think about an elderly person? Do you view this picture of an older gentleman as positive or negative, capable and independent or frail and needing assistance?

In addition to ageism, racism is yet another concern for minority populations as they age. The number of blacks above the age if 65 is projected to grow from around 4 million now to 12 million by 2060. Racism towards blacks and other minorities throughout the lifetime results in many older minorities having fewer resources, more chronic health conditions, and significant health disparities when compared ~~against~~ to older white Americans. Racism towards older adults from diverse backgrounds has resulted in them having limited access to community resources such as grocery stores, housing, health care providers, and transportation.[6]

6. African American Older Adults and Race-Related Stress How Aging and Health-Care Providers Can Help. American Psychological Association. Retrieved from https://www.apa.org/pi/aging/resources/african-american-stress.pdf.

Elderly Abuse

Nursing homes have been publicized as places where older adults are at risk of abuse. Abuse and neglect of nursing home residents is more often found in facilities that are run down and understaffed. However, older adults are more frequently abused by family members. The most commonly reported types of abuse are financial abuse and neglect. Victims are usually very frail and impaired and perpetrators are usually dependent on the victims for support. Prosecuting a family member who has financially abused a parent is very difficult. The victim may be reluctant to press charges and the court dockets are often very full resulting in long waits before a case is heard. "Granny dumping" or the practice of family members abandoning older family members with severe disabilities in emergency rooms is a growing problem; an estimated 100,000 and 200,000 are dumped each year (Tanne in Berk, 2007).

WATCH IT

This clip from the Big Think examines some of the negative prejudices about the elderly.

- https://youtu.be/oX3Lw5JMRi4

You can watch another video from Ashton Applewhite in this TED talk "Let's End Ageism."

Relationships in Late Adulthood

During late adulthood, many people find that their relationships with their adult children, siblings, spouses, or life partners change. Roles may also change, as many are grandparents or great-grandparents, caregivers to even older parents or spouses, or receivers of care in a nursing home or other care facility.

Grandparenting

Figure 5. Grandparenting styes can vary depending on a variety of factors such as relationships, personality, and proximity.

It has become increasingly common for grandparents to live with and raise their grandchildren, or also to move back in with adult children in their later years. According to the U.S. Census Bureau, there were 2.7 million grandparents raising their grandchildren in 2009. The dramatic increase in grandparent-headed households has been attributed to many factors including parental substance abuse.

Grandparenting typically begins in midlife rather than late adulthood, but because people are living longer, they can anticipate being grandparents for longer periods of time. Cherlin and Furstenberg (1986) describe three styles of grandparents:

1. Remote: These grandparents rarely see their grandchildren. Usually they live far away from the grandchildren, but may also have a distant relationship. Contact is typically made on special occasions such as holidays or birthdays. Thirty percent of the grandparents studied by Cherlin and Furstenberg were remote.

2. Companionate Grandparents: Fifty-five percent of grandparents studied were described as companionate. These grandparents do things with the grandchild but have little authority or control over them. They prefer to spend time with them without interfering in parenting. They are more like friends to their grandchildren.

3. Involved Grandparents: Fifteen percent of grandparents were described as involved. These grandparents take a very active role in their grandchild's life. The grandchildren might even live with the grandparent. The involved grandparent is one who has frequent contact with and authority over the grandchild.

An increasing number of grandparents are raising grandchildren today. Issues such as custody, visitation, and continued contact between grandparents and grandchildren after parental divorce are contemporary concerns.

Marriage and Divorce

Most males and females aged 65 and older had been married at some point in their lives. According to the U.S. Census Bureau, 2016 American Community Survey, among the population 65 and older, males were significantly more likely to be married (70 percent) compared with females (44 percent) in the same age group. Even at the oldest age group, 85 and older, 54 percent of males were still married compared with 15 percent of females.[7]

Figure 6. Both divorce and remarriage are on the rise for older Americans.

Twelve percent of older men and 15% percent of older women have been divorced and about 6 percent of older adults have never married.[8] Many married couples feel their marriage has improved with time and the emotional intensity and level of conflict that might have been experienced earlier, has declined. This is not to say that bad marriages become good ones over the years, but that those marriages that were very conflict-ridden may no longer be together, and that many of the disagreements couples might have had earlier in their marriages may no longer be concerns. Children have grown and the division of labor in the home has probably been established. Men tend to report being satisfied with marriage more than do women. Women are more likely to complain about caring for a spouse who is ill or accommodating a retired husband and planning activities. Older couples continue to engage in sexual activity, but with less focus on Intercourse and more on cuddling, caressing, and oral sex (Carroll, 2007).

Divorce after long-term marriage does occur, but is not as common as earlier divorces, despite rising divorce rates for those above age 65. Older adults who have been divorced since midlife tend to have settled into comfortable lives and, if they have raised children, to be proud of their accomplishments as single parents. Remarriage is also on the rise for older adults; in 2014, 50% of adults ages 65 and older had remarried, up from 34% in 1960. Men are also more likely to remarry than women.[9]

Widowhood

With increasing age, women were less likely to be married or divorced but more likely to be widowed, reflecting a longer life expectancy relative to men. About 2 out of 10 women aged 65 to 74 were widowed compared with 4 out of 10 women aged 75 to 84 and 7 out of 10 women 85 and older. More than twice as many women 85 and older were widowed (72 percent) compared to men of the same age (35 percent).[10] The death of a spouse is one of life's most disruptive experiences. It is

7. Roberts, Andrew and Stella U. Ogunwo (2016). The Population 65 Years and Older in the United States: 2016 American Community Survey Reports. Retrieved from https://www.census.gov/content/dam/Census/library/publications/2018/acs/ACS-38.pdf
8. Roberts, Andrew and Stella U. Ogunwo (2016). The Population 65 Years and Older in the United States: 2016 American Community Survey Reports. Retrieved from https://www.census.gov/content/dam/Census/library/publications/2018/acs/ACS-38.pdf
9. Livingston, Gretchen (2014). *Chapter 2: The Demographics of Remarriage.* Pew Research Center. Retrieved from https://www.pewsocialtrends.org/2014/11/14/chapter-2-the-demographics-of-remarriage/.
10. Roberts, Andrew and Stella U. Ogunwo (2016). The Population 65 Years and Older in the United States: 2016 American Community Survey Reports. Retrieved from https://www.census.gov/content/dam/Census/library/publications/2018/acs/ACS-38.pdf

especially hard on men who lose their wives. Often widowers do not have a network of friends or family members to fall back on and may have difficulty expressing their emotions to facilitate grief. Also, they may have been very dependent on their mates for routine tasks such as cooking, cleaning, etc.

Widows may have less difficulty because they do have a social network and can take care of their own daily needs. They may have more difficulty financially if their husband's have handled all the finances in the past. They are much less likely to remarry because many do not wish to and because there are fewer men available. At 65, there are 73 men to every 100 women. The sex ratio becomes even further imbalanced at 85 with 48 men to every 100 women (U. S. Census Bureau, 2011).

Loneliness or solitude?

Loneliness is a discrepancy between the social contact a person has and the contacts a person wants (Brehm et al., 2002). It can result from social or emotional isolation. Women tend to experience loneliness as a result of social isolation; men from emotional isolation. Loneliness can be accompanied by a lack of self-worth, impatience, desperation, and depression. This can lead to suicide, particularly in older, white men who have the highest suicide rates of any age group; higher than Blacks, and higher than for females. Rates of suicide continue to climb and peaks in males after age 85 (National Center for Health Statistics, CDC, 2002).

Being alone does not always result in loneliness. For some, it means solitude. Solitude involves gaining self-awareness, taking care of the self, being comfortable alone, and pursuing one's interests (Brehm et al., 2002).

Couples who remarry after midlife, tend to be happier in their marriages than in first marriage. These partners are likely to be more financially independent, have children who are grown, and enjoy a greater emotional wisdom that comes with experience.

Single, Cohabiting, and Remarried Older Adults

About 6 percent of adults never marry. Many have long-term relationships, however. The never married tend to be very involved in family and care giving and do not appear to be particularly unhappy during late adulthood, especially if they have a healthy network of friends. Friendships tend to be an important influence in life satisfaction during late adulthood. Friends may be more influential than family members for many older adults. According to **socioemotional selectivity theory**, older adults become more selective in their friendships than when they were younger (Carstensen, Fung, & Charles, 2003). Friendships are not formed in order to enhance status or careers, and may be based purely on a sense of connection or the enjoyment of being together. Most elderly people have at least one close friend. These friends may provide emotional as well as physical support. Being able to talk with friends and rely on others is very important during this stage of life.

About 4 percent of older couples chose cohabitation over marriage (Chevan, 1996). The Pew Research Center reported in 2017 that the number of cohabiters over age 50 rose to 4 million from 2.3 million over the decade, and found the number over age 65 doubled to about 900,000.[11] As discussed in our lesson on early adulthood, these couples may prefer cohabitation for financial reasons, may be same-sex couples who cannot legally marry, or couples who do not want to marry because of previous dissatisfaction with marital relationships.

Elderly and LBGTQ+

There has been a growth of interest in lesbian, gay, bisexual, transgender, and queer (LGBTQ+) aging in recent years. Many retirement issues for lesbian, gay, bisexual, transgender (LGBT) and intersex people are unique from their non-LGBTI counterparts and these populations often have to take extra steps addressing their employment, health, legal and

11. Stepler, Reneee. Number of U.S. adults cohabiting with a partner continues to rise, especially among those 50 and older. Pew Research Center. Retrieved from https://www.pewresearch.org/fact-tank/2017/04/06/number-of-u-s-adults-cohabiting-with-a-partner-continues-to-rise-especially-among-those-50-and-older/

housing concerns to ensure their needs are met. Throughout the United States, there are 1.5 million adults over the age of 65 who identify as lesbian, gay, or bisexual, and two million people above the age of 50 who identify as such. That number is expected to double by 2030, as estimated in a study done by the Institute for Multigenerational Health at the University of Washington. While LGBTQ+ people have increasingly become more visible and accepted into mainstream cultures, LGBTQ+ elders and retirees are still considered a newer phenomenon, which creates both challenges and opportunities as they redefine some commonly held beliefs about aging.

LGBTQ+ individuals are less likely to have strong family support systems in place to have relatives to care for them during aging. They are twice as likely to enter old age living as a single person; and two and a half times more likely to live alone. Because institutionalized homophobia as well as cultural discrimination and harassment still exist, they are less likely to access health care, housing, or social services or when they do, find the experience stressful or demeaning. Joel Ginsberg, executive director of the Gay Lesbian Medical Association, asserts "only by pursuing both strategies, encouraging institutional change and encouraging...and empowering individuals to ask for what they want will we end up with quality care for LGBT people."[12]

These older adults have concerns over health insurance, being able to share living quarters in nursing homes and assisted living residences where staff members tend not to be accepting of homosexuality and bisexuality. SAGE (Senior Action in a Gay Environment) is an advocacy group working on remedying these concerns. Same-sex couples who have endured prejudice and discrimination through the years and can rely upon one another continue to have support through late adulthood.

LGBTQ+ Aging Centers have opened in several major metropolitan areas with the goal of training long-term care providers about LGBT-specific issues, an area of frequent discrimination. Legislative solutions are available as well: "California is the only state with a law saying the gay elderly have special needs, like other members of minority groups. A new law encourages training for employees and contractors who work with the elderly and permits state financing of projects like gay senior centers."[13] Twenty states prohibit discrimination in housing and public accommodation on the basis of sexual orientation.

Older Adults, Caregiving, and Long-Term Care

Older adults do not typically relocate far from their previous places of residence during late adulthood. A minority lives in planned retirement communities that require residents to be of a certain age. However, many older adults live in age-segregated neighborhoods that have become segregated as original inhabitants have aged and children have moved on. A major concern in future city planning and development will be whether older adults wish to live in age-integrated or age-segregated communities.

Over 60 million Americans, or 19% of the population, lived in multigenerational households, or homes with at least two adult generations. It has become an ongoing trend for elderly generations to move in and live with their children, as they can give them support and help with everyday living.[14]

Population rising in different types of multigenerational households

In millions

	2012	2016
Two adult generations	27.4	32.3
Three or more generations	26.5	28.4
Skipped generations	2.9	3.2

Note: Skipped generation households include grandparents and grandchildren younger than 25.
Source: Pew Research Center analysis of 2012 and 2016 American Community Survey (IPUMS).

PEW RESEARCH CENTER

Figure 7. More elderly are living in homes with their children or grandchildren.

Most (70 percent) of older adults who require care receive that care in the home. Most are cared for by their spouse, or by a daughter or daughter-in-law. However, those who are not cared for at home are

12. Cassell, Heather (18 October 2007). "LGBT Health Care Movement Gains Momentum". Bay Area Reporter. Retrieved 2007-10-20.
13. Gross, Jane (October 9, 2007). "Aging and Gay, and Facing Prejudice in Twilight". The New York Times. Retrieved May 7, 2010.
14. Passel, Jeffrey and Cohn, D'Vera. A record 64 million Americans live in multigenerational households. Pew Research Center. Retrieved from https://www.pewresearch.org/fact-tank/2018/04/05/a-record-64-million-americans-live-in-multigenerational-households/.

institutionalized. In 2008, 1.6 million out of the total 38.9 million Americans age 65 and older were nursing home residents (U. S. Census Bureau, 2011). Among 65-74, 11 per 1,000 adults aged 65 and older were in nursing homes. That number increases to 182 per 1,000 after age 85. More residents are women than men, and more are Black than white. As the population of those over age 85 continues to increase, more will require nursing home care. Meeting the psychological and social as well as physical needs of nursing home residents is a growing concern. Rather than focusing primarily on food, hygiene, and medication, quality of life for the seniors within these facilities is important. Residents of nursing homes are sometimes stripped of their identity as their personal possessions and reminders of their life are taken away. A rigid routine in which the residents have little voice can be alienating to anyone, but more so for an older adult. Routines that encourage passivity and dependence can be damaging to self-esteem and lead to further deterioration of health. Greater attention needs to be given to promoting successful aging within institutions.

GLOSSARY

ageism:
discrimination based on age

activity theory:
suggests that people are barred from meaningful experiences as they age and that physical and social activities are important

continuity theory:
suggests that as people age, they continue to view the self in much of the same way as they did when they were younger

disengagement theory:
suggests that during late adulthood, the individual and society mutually withdraw

gerontocracy:
a type of social structure wherein the power is held by a society's oldest members

integrity:
Erikson refers to this as reflecting on one's life and experiencing a sense of satisfaction and accomplishment

socioemotional selectivity theory:
theory that as time horizons shrink, people become increasingly selective, investing greater resources in emotionally meaningful goals, activities, and relationships

Putting It Together: Late Adulthood

The period of late adulthood, which starts around age 65, is characterized by great changes and ongoing personal development. Older adults face profound physical, cognitive, and social changes, and many figure out strategies for adjusting to them and successfully cope with old age. In late adulthood people begin the decline that will be part of their lives until death. The declines in the senses—vision, hearing, taste, and smell—can have major psychological consequences. Most illnesses and diseases of late adulthood are not particular to old age, but the incidences of cancer and heart disease rise with age. People in late adulthood are also more prone to develop arthritis, hypertension, major neurocognitive disorders, and Alzheimer's disease. Proper diet, exercise, and avoidance of health risks can all lead to overall well-being during old age, and sexuality can continue throughout the lifespan in healthy adults. Thus, many older adults can maintain physical and mental strength until the they die, and their social worlds can also remain as vital and active as they want.

Cognitively, we find that older people adjust quite well to the challenges of aging by adopting new strategies for solving problems and compensating for loss abilities. Although some intellectual abilities gradually decline throughout adulthood, starting at around the age 25, others stay relatively steady. For example, research shows that while fluid intelligence declines with age, crystallized intelligence remains steady, and may even improve, in late adulthood. Many cognitive abilities can be maintained with stimulation, practice, and motivation. Declines in memory affect mainly episodic memory and short-term memory, or working memory. Explanations of memory changes in old age focus upon environmental factors, information processing declines, and biological factors. Due to this perceived loss of abilities by others, older people are often subject to ageism, or prejudice and discrimination against people based on their age.

Socially, many of older adults become adept at coping with the changes in their lives, such as death of a spouse and retirement from work. Erikson calls older adulthood the integrity vs. despair stage. According to Erikson, individuals in late adulthood engage in looking back over their lives, evaluating their experiences and coming to terms with decisions. Other theorists focus on the tasks that define late adulthood and suggest that older people can experience liberation and self-regard. Marriages in older adulthood are generally happy, but the many changes in late adulthood can cause stress which may result in divorce. The death of a spouse has major psychological, social, and material effects on the surviving widow and makes the formation and continuation of friendships highly important. Family relationships are a continuing part of most older people's lives, especially relationships with siblings, children and grandchildren. Friendships, an important source of social support, are not only valued, but needed in late adulthood.

Whether death is caused by genetic programming or by general physical wear-and-tear is an unresolved question. Life expectancy, which has risen for centuries, varies with gender, race, and ethnicity and new approaches to increasing life expectancy is a growing topic of research.

Discussion: Late Adulthood

DISCUSSION: In this discussion, reflect upon and discuss BOTH of the following questions:

- Q1: What do you think helps make a successful transition into old age?
- Q2: Write a letter to your 65-year-old self. Where do you think you will be and what do you hope to accomplish by that time?

STEP 1: First, write a response with at least EIGHT substantial sentences, integrating concepts you learned from the reading and other materials (include links when necessary). Show that you can think critically on the topic by integrating your own thoughts, analysis, or experiences.

STEP 2: Then return to the discussion to comment on at least TWO classmates' posts (in at least FIVE sentences). Expand on a classmate's comments in a value-adding, topic-related way. Promote a collaborative, supportive community, and advance the dialogue through follow-up questions. Reply posts cannot be one-liners, off-topic posts, vague statements, unsupported opinions, inadequate explanations or simply say, "I agree" or "good job."

MODULE 11: DEATH AND DYING

Why It Matters: Death and Dying

Why learn about experiences and emotions related to death and dying?

Figure 1. Some form of marker is used in cemeteries to identify who is buried there. Headstones such as this one may vary by religion with prayers and symbols, as well as the deceased's name, years of birth and death, and family relationships. More elaborate stones and statues often reflect family prominence or wealth. Photo Courtesy Robert Paul Young

> *"Everything has to die," he told her during a telephone conversation.*
>
> *"I want you to know how much I have enjoyed being with you, having you as my friend, and confidant and what a good father you have been to me. Thank you so much." she told him.*
>
> *"You are entirely welcome." he replied.*
>
> *He had known for years that smoking will eventually kill him. But he never expected that lung cancer would take his life so quickly or be so painful. A diagnosis in late summer was followed with radiation and chemotherapy during which time there were moments of hope interspersed with discussions about where his wife might want to live after his death and whether or not he would have a blood count adequate to let him precede with his next treatment. Hope and despair exist side by side. After a few months, depression and quiet sadness preoccupied him although he was always willing to relieve others by reporting that he 'felt a little better' if they asked. He returned home in January after one of his many hospital stays and soon grew worse. Back in the hospital, he was told of possible treatment options to delay his death. He asked his family members what they wanted him to do and then announced that he wanted to go home. He was ready to die. He returned home. Sitting in his favorite chair and being fed his favorite food gave way to lying in the hospital bed in his room and rejecting all food. Eyes closed and no longer talking, he surprised everyone by joining in and singing "Happy birthday" to his wife, son, and daughter-in-law who all had birthdays close together. A pearl necklace he had purchased 2 months earlier in case he died before his wife's birthday was retrieved and she told him how proud she would be as she wore it. He kissed her once and then again as she said goodbye. He died a few days later.*[1]

1. *Overstreet, Laura. Personal Notes. Psyc 200 Lifespan Psychology.*

A dying process that allows an individual to make choices about treatment, to say goodbyes and to take care of final arrangements is what many people hope for. Such a death might be considered a "good death." But of course, many deaths do not occur in this way. Not all deaths include such a dialogue with family members or being able to die in familiar surroundings; people may die suddenly and alone, or people may leave home and never return. Children sometimes precede parents in death; wives precede husbands, and the homeless are bereaved by strangers.

In this module, we will look at death and dying, grief and bereavement, palliative care, and hospice to better understand these last stages of life.

Understanding Death

What you'll learn to do: describe the leading causes and types of deaths

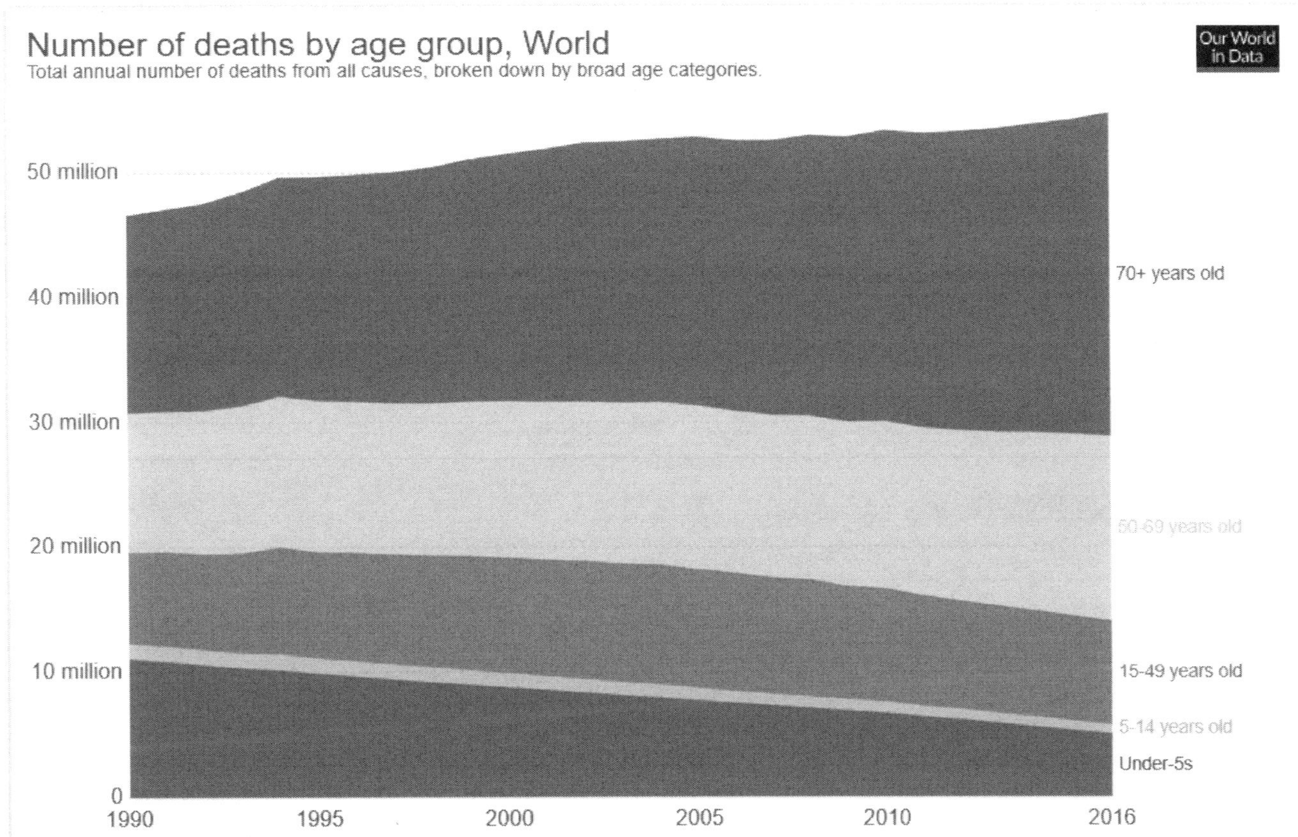

Figure 1. With advances in health care, nutrition, and technology, fewer young people are dying. With an aging population, this means that the death rate for those above the age of 70 is steadily growing throughout the world.

While death has always been a universal component in the human experience, its prevalence and circumstances have changed over the years. Today, we associate death with the elderly, but looking back even one hundred years ago, death was more common among children and in various age ranges. At that time, it was not uncommon for American families to lose a child during childbirth or infancy. Today less than 10% of all deaths worldwide occur to children under the age of 5, but as recently as 1990, that number was nearly 25%.[1]

The graph above shows data from 2016, which reveal that nearly half of the 55 million global deaths occurred to those aged 70 years or older. There is still a great amount of disparity in death statistics based on location and access to medical care. In the United States, for example, deaths in that same age group of 70 years old or older accounted for 65% of total deaths. In this section, we'll look more closely at the leading causes of deaths in the United States and throughout the globe.

1. Ritchie, H. and Roser, M. (2019) "Causes of Death" Published online at OurWorldInData.org. Retrieved from: 'https://ourworldindata.org/causes-of-death' [Online Resource]

LEARNING OUTCOMES

- Examine the leading causes of death in the United States and worldwide
- Explain physiological death
- Describe social and psychological death

Most Common Causes of Death

The United States

In 1900, the most common causes of death were infectious diseases, which brought death quickly. Due to advances in healthcare and medicine over the years, this has changed, alongside an increase in average life expectancy. According to national data, chronic diseases, or those in which a slow and steady decline causes health deterioration, were the most common causes of death in the United States in 2016[2] In addition, accidents were more common than in previous years, often resulting in quick or unexpected death. How might this impact the way we think of death, the way we grieve, and the amount of control a person has over his or her own dying process, in comparison to the infectious diseases that were prevalent in 1900?

The 15 leading causes of death and number of deaths per category in 2016 in the United States are listed below.[3]

Table 1. Leading Causes of Death in the United States

Rank (2016)	Cause of Death	Percentage of total deaths 2016	Percentage of total deaths 2015
1	Heart disease	23.1	23.4
2	Cancer	21.8	22.0
3	Accidents	5.9	5.4
4	Chronic lower respiratory diseases	5.6	5.7
5	Strokes	5.2	5.2
6	Alzheimer's Disease	4.2	4.1
7	Diabetes	2.9	2.9
8	Influenza and Pneumonia	1.9	2.1
9	Kidney Disease	1.8	1.8
10	Suicide	1.6	1.6

2. Xu, J., Murphy, S. L., Kochanek, K. D., Bastian, B., & Arias, E. (2018). Deaths: Final data for 2016. National Vital Statistics Reports 67(5), 1-76.
3. Heron M. Deaths: Leading causes for 2016. National Vital Statistics Reports; vol 67 no 6. Hyattsville, MD: National Center for Health Statistics. 2018.

These data reflect both similarities and differences when compared with data from 2004. All of these top causes of death, with the exception of two—accidents and suicides—continue to be related to physical illnesses. Many are linked at least in part to lifestyle choices, including diet, exercise, and substance abuse. Similarly, many are preventable, to some extent, and some are avoidable if the proper actions are taken. Although these causes of death remain the same as they were in 2004, the order has changed for several of them by 2016. For example, accidents and unintentional injuries shifted from #5 in 2004 to #3 in 2016. Alzheimer's disease became slightly more common, moving from #7 to #6, as did suicide, moving from #11 to #10. In contrast, strokes became slightly less common, moving from #3 to #5, along with diabetes, which moved from #6 to #7. Septicemia (blood disease) followed a similar trend, shifting from #10 to #11. These changes are likely attributable to a variety of factors, including lifestyle choices, social pressures and norms, and changes in responsibilities and obligations.

Deadliest Diseases Worldwide

The top 10 deadliest diseases in the world from 2015 are listed below, along with the percentage of deaths for which they were accountable. These reflect disease-related deaths only, and do not reflect deaths due to violence or suicide.[4] Notice there are several similarities between these and the top 15 causes of death in the United States described above.

1. Heart disease – 15.5%
2. Stroke – 11.1%
3. Lower respiratory infections – 5.7%
4. Chronic obstructive pulmonary disease – 5.6%
5. Trachea, bronchus, and lung cancers – 3%
6. Diabetes – 2.8%
7. Alzheimer's disease and other dementia – 2.7%
8. Dehydration due to diarrheal diseases – 2.5%
9. Tuberculosis – 2.4%
10. Cirrhosis – 2.1%

Similar to the top 15 general causes of death listed above, these remained fairly consistent over the years, despite increases and decreases in each. Deaths caused by heart disease, for example, increased from 2000 by 2.8 million, and deaths caused by stroke increased by .5 million.[5] Lung disorders and cancers also rose by .5 million deaths, while diabetes rose by .6 million. Alzheimer's disease and other forms of dementia also accounted for an additional .3 million deaths. Decreases were seen in lower respiratory infections, which decreased by .2 million, as well as dehydration due to diarrheal diseases, which decreased by .8 million. Furthermore, tuberculosis deaths decreased by 1 million, and cirrhosis deaths decreased by .2 million.

While the top 15 causes of death presented previously were only for the United States, these top 10 deadliest diseases are for the entire world, including both developed and undeveloped nations. Differences in various factors including but not limited to economic status, access to medical care, belief systems, and natural resources play a major role in many of these causes of death, and tend to vary substantially between countries. This presents challenges for the interpretation of this list, making it difficult to determine the true prevalence of each in specific locations.

4. World Health Organization. (2018). The top 10 causes of death. Retrieved from https://www.who.int/en/news-room/fact-sheets/detail/the-top-10-causes-of-death.
5. World Health Organization. (2018). The top 10 causes of death. Retrieved from https://www.who.int/en/news-room/fact-sheets/detail/the-top-10-causes-of-death.

WATCH IT

Watch this video to learn about another way to measure and compare life expectancies, known as years of life lost, which measures how many years short of the life expectancy people die. Looking at ~~this~~ these data reveals some of the leading causes of death across the globe.

- https://youtu.be/aQO_oexCm5s

A Comparison of Death by Age in the United States

The major causes of death vary significantly among age groups. As you can see in Figure 1, congenital diseases and accidents are major causes of death among children, then accidents and suicides are the leading causes of death between ages 10 and 24. This changes again in~~to~~ middle and late-adulthood, as heart disease and cancer combined cause over 50% of deaths for those aged between 45 and 65.

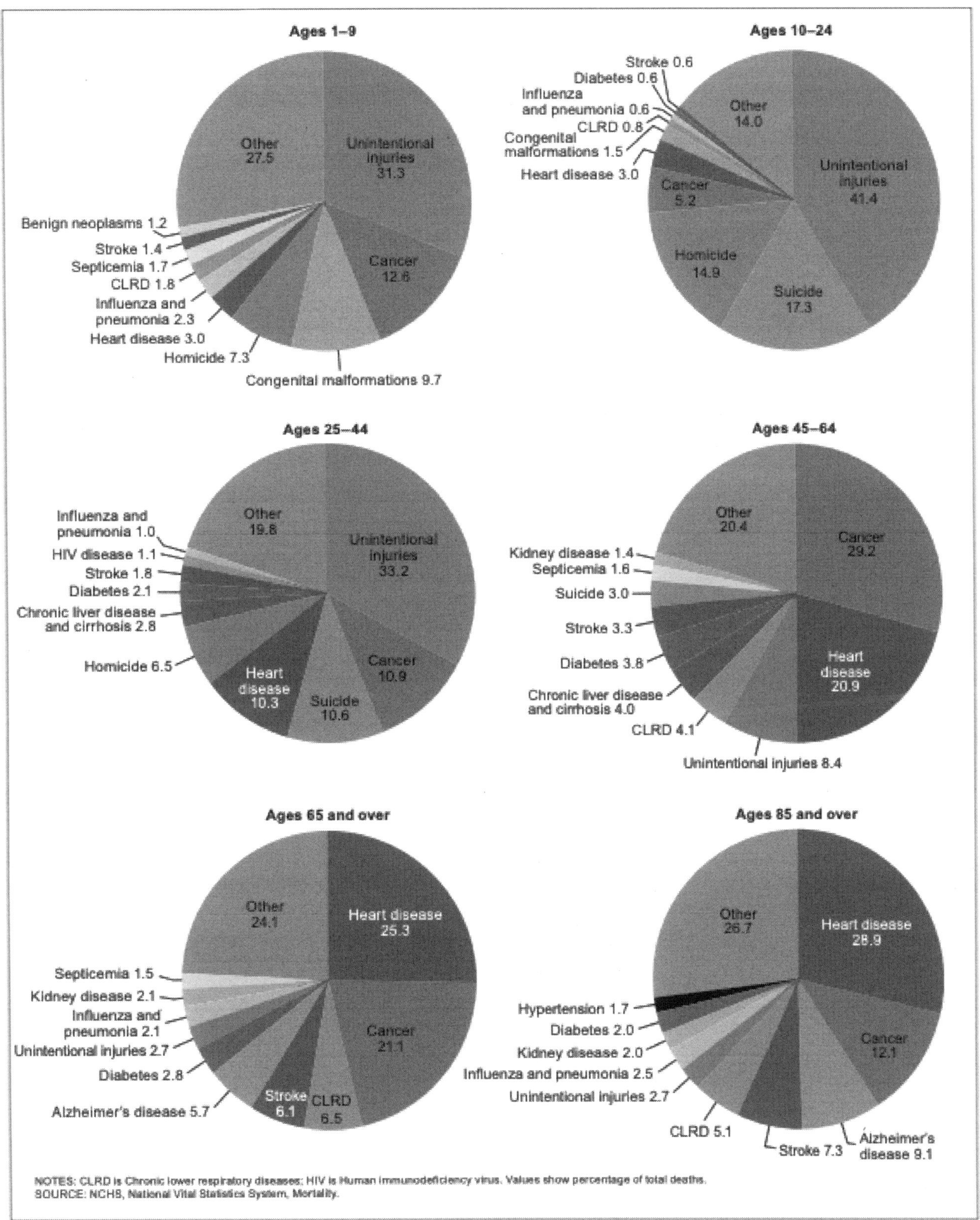

Figure 2. Percent distribution of the 10 leading causes of death, by age group: United States, 2016.

Notice that unintentional injuries are the leading cause of death for the widest variety of ages, and recall from the previous section above that accidents were also found to have become increasingly common as causes of death within the United States population between 2000 and 2016.[6][/footnote] These were the top causes of death for various age groups in the United States in the year 2016:

- < 1 year – Congenital anomalies
- 1 – 4 years – Unintentional Injury
- 5 – 9 years – Unintentional Injury
- 10 – 14 years – Unintentional Injury
- 15 – 24 years – Unintentional Injury
- 25 – 34 years – Unintentional Injury
- 35 – 44 years – Unintentional Injury
- 45 – 54 years – Malignant Neoplasms (cancer)
- 55 – 64 years – Malignant Neoplasms (cancer)
- 65 + – Heart Disease

The causes of death on this list resemble the causes presented in the previous sections, but the breakdown of these causes by age group highlights the true prevalence of each. Unintentional injury (accidents), for example, was found to be the third most common cause of death within the United States population, but it becomes apparent from this list that it is the most common for the widest range of age groups or developmental stages.[7] Heart disease was found to the be the most common cause of death overall, but this list shows that it is more restricted to one age group (65+) than other causes. Similarly, cancer was found to be the second most common cause of death within the United States population, but this list reveals that it is most prevalent for individuals in middle to late adulthood.

6. [footnote]Centers for Disease Control and Prevention. (2018). Diseases and Conditions. Retrieved from http://www.cdc.gov.
7. Xu, J., Murphy, S. L., Kochanek, K. D., Bastian, B., & Arias, E. (2018). Deaths: Final data for 2016. National Vital Statistics Reports 67(5), 1-76.

DEATH AND THE MEDIA

Causes of death in the US

What Americans die from, what they search on Google, and what the media reports on

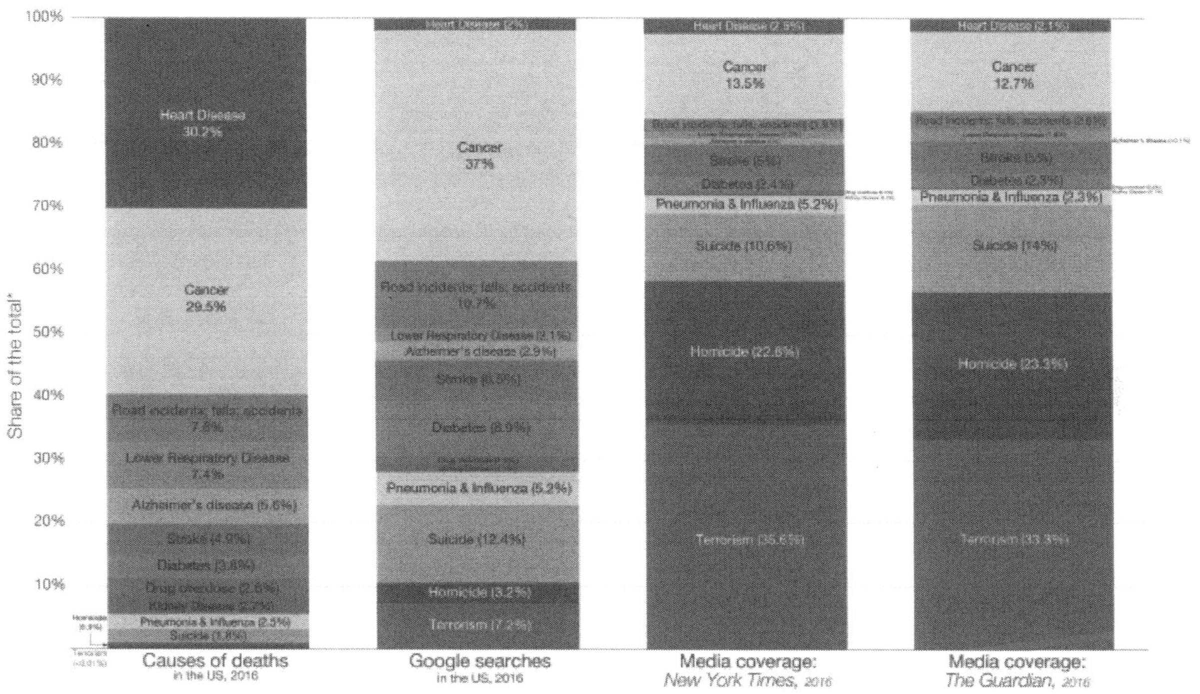

*This represents each causes's share of the top ten causes of death in the US plus homicides, drug overdoses and terrorism. Collectively these 13 causes accounted for approximately 88% of deaths in the US in 2016. Full breakdown of causes of death can be found at the CDC's WONDER public health database: https://wonder.cdc.gov/

Based on data from Shen et al (2018) – Death: reality vs. reported. All data available at: https://owenshen24.github.io/charting-death
All data refers to 2016.
Not all causes of death are shown: Shown is the data on the ten leading causes of death in the United States plus drug overdoses, homicides and terrorism.
All values are normalized to 100% so they represent their relative share of the top causes, rather than absolute counts (e.g. 'deaths' represents each causes' share of deaths within the 13 categories shown rather than total deaths). The causes of death shown here account for approximately 88% of total deaths in the United States in 2016.
This is a visualization from OurWorldinData.org, where you find data and research on how the world is changing.

Figure 3. Actual causes of death compared with media coverage of death.

Interestingly, the things that actually result in death are not often the things we hear about on the news. Because of the availability heuristic—a cognitive shortcut in which people rely heavily on information that is most readily available in their mind, people may erroneously be more afraid of sensational deaths than death by more normal causes, such as heart disease.[8]

8. Ritchie, Hannah (2019). Does the news reflect what we die from? Our World in Data. Retrieved from https://ourworldindata.org/does-the-news-reflect-what-we-die-from?linkId=68864855

The Process of Dying

Aspects of Death

One way to understand death and dying is to look more closely at physiological death, social death, and psychological death. These deaths do not occur simultaneously, nor do they always occur in a set order. Rather, a person's physiological, social, and psychological deaths can occur at different times.[9]

Physiological death occurs when the vital organs no longer function. The digestive and respiratory systems begin to shut down during the gradual process of dying. A dying person no longer wants to eat as digestion slows, the digestive track loses moisture, and chewing, swallowing, and elimination become painful processes. Circulation slows and mottling, or the pooling of blood, may be noticeable on the underside of the body, appearing much like bruising. Breathing becomes more sporadic and shallow and may make a rattling sound as air travels through mucus- filled passageways. **Agonal breathing** refers to gasping, labored breaths caused by an abnormal pattern of brainstem reflex. The person often sleeps more and more and may talk less, although they may continue to hear. The kinds of symptoms noted prior to death in patients under hospice care (care focused on helping patients die as comfortably as possible) are noted below.

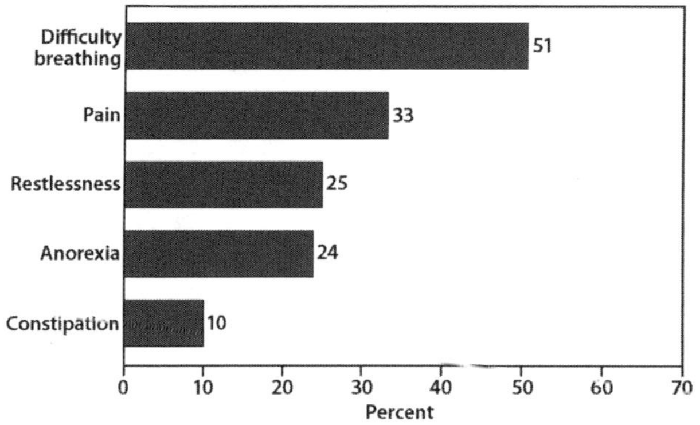

Figure 4. These are common symptoms reported prior, but close to, death.

When a person is **brain dead**, or no longer has brain activity, they are clinically dead. Physiological death may take 72 or fewer hours. This is different than a **vegetative state**, which occurs when the cerebral cortex no longer registers electrical activity but the brain stems continues to be active. Individuals who are kept alive through life support may be classified this way.

WATCH IT

This video explains the difference between a vegetative state, a coma, and being brain dead.

- https://youtu.be/cFVL4AQO2hM

9. Butow, P. (2017). Psychology and end of life. Australian Psychologist, 52(5), 331-334.

Social death begins much earlier than physiological death. Social death occurs when others begin to withdraw from someone who is terminally ill or has been diagnosed with a terminal illness. Those diagnosed with conditions such as AIDS or cancer may find that friends, family members, and even health care professionals begin to say less and visit less frequently. Meaningful discussions may be replaced with comments about the weather or other topics of light conversation. Doctors may spend less time with patients after their prognosis becomes poor. Why do others begin to withdraw? Friends and family members may feel that they do not know what to say or that they can offer no solutions to relieve suffering. They withdraw to protect themselves against feeling inadequate or from having to face the reality of death. Health professionals, trained to heal, may also feel inadequate and uncomfortable facing decline and death. A patient who is dying may be referred to as "circling the drain," meaning that they are approaching death. People in nursing homes may live as socially dead for years with no one visiting or calling. Social support is important for quality of life and those who experience social death are deprived from the benefits that come from loving interaction with others.

Psychological death occurs when the dying person begins to accept death and to withdraw from others and regress into the self. This can take place long before physiological death (or even social death if others are still supporting and visiting the dying person) and can even bring physiological death closer. People have some control over the timing of their death and can hold on until after important occasions or die quickly after having lost someone important to them. In some cases, individuals can give up their will to live. This is often at least partially attributable to a lost sense of identity.[10] The individual feels consumed by the reality of making final decisions, planning for loved ones—especially children, and coping with the process of his or her own physical death.

Interventions based on the idea of self-empowerment enable patients and families to identify and ultimately achieve their own goals of care, thus producing a sense of empowerment. Self-empowerment for terminally ill individuals has been associated with a perceived ability to manage and control things such as medical actions, changing life roles, and psychological impacts of the illness.[11]

Treatment plans that are able to incorporate a sense of control and autonomy into the dying individual's daily life have been found to be particularly effective in regards to general attitude as well as depression level. For example, it has been found that when dying individuals are encouraged to recall situations from their lives in which they were active decision makers, explored various options, and took action, they tend to have better mental health than those who focus on themselves as victims. Similarly, there are several theories of coping that suggest **active coping** (seeking information, working to solve problems) produces more positive outcomes than **passive coping** (characterized by avoidance and distraction). Although each situation is unique and depends at least partially on the individual's developmental stage, the general consensus is that it is important for caregivers to foster a supportive environment and partnership with the dying individual, which promotes a sense of independence, control, and self-respect.

GLOSSARY

active coping:

seeking information, working to solve problems; tends to produce more positive outcomes than passive coping

agonal breathing:

gasping, labored breaths caused by an abnormal pattern of brainstem reflex

10. Butow, P. (2017). Psychology and end of life. Australian Psychologist, 52(5), 331-334.
11. Butow, P. (2017). Psychology and end of life. Australian Psychologist, 52(5), 331-334.

brain dead:
when all brain function ceases to occur

clinical death:
when the individual is brain dead

passive coping:
characterized by avoidance and distraction; outcomes tend to not be as positive as with active coping

physiological death:
when vital organs no longer function

psychological death:
when a dying person begins to accept death and to withdraw from others and regress into the self

social death:
when others begin to withdraw from someone who is terminally ill or has been diagnosed with a terminal illness

vegetative state:
the cerebral cortex no longer registers electrical activity but the brain stem continues to be active

Emotions Related to Death

What you'll learn to do: examine emotions related to death and dying

While death is inevitable, our emotional responses and reactions to it vary dramatically. In this section, we'll take a closer look at the emotions that are involved in death, both for the individual who is dying as well as their family and friends. We'll also learn more about the stages of grief and how to cope with death.

LEARNING OUTCOMES

- Explain common perceptions and attitudes toward death
- Explain bereavement and types of grief
- Explain Kübler-Ross' stages of loss
- List and describe the stages of grief based on various models

Attitudes about Death

Bereavement refers to outward expressions of grief. Mourning and funeral rites are expressions of loss that reflect personal and cultural beliefs about the meaning of death and the afterlife. When asked what type of funeral they would like to have, students responded in a variety of ways; each expressing both their personal beliefs and values and those of their culture.

> *I would like the service to be at a Baptist church, preferably my Uncle Ike's small church. The service should be a celebration of life . . .I would like there to be hymns sung by my family members, including my favorite one, "It is Well With my Soul". . .At the end, I would like the message of salvation to be given to the attendees and an alter call for anyone who would like to give their life to Christ. . .*

> *I want a very inexpensive funeral-the bare minimum, only one vase of flowers, no viewing of the remains and no long period of mourning from my remaining family . . . funeral expenses are extremely overpriced and out of hand. . .*

> *When I die, I would want my family members, friends, and other relatives to dress my body as it is usually done in my country, Ghana. Lay my dressed body in an open space in my house at the night prior to the funeral ceremony for my loved ones to walk around my body and mourn for me. . .*

I would like to be buried right away after I die because I don't want my family and friends to see my dead body and to be scared.

In my family we have always had the traditional ceremony-coffin, grave, tombstone, etc. But I have considered cremation and still ponder which method is more favorable. Unlike cremation, when you are 'buried' somewhere and family members have to make a special trip to visit, cremation is a little more personal because you can still be in the home with your loved ones . . .

I would like to have some of my favorite songs played . . .I will have a list made ahead of time. I want a peaceful and joyful ceremony and I want my family and close friends to gather to support one another. At the end of the celebration, I want everyone to go to the Thirsty Whale for a beer and Spang's for pizza!

When I die, I want to be cremated . . . I want it the way we do it in our culture. I want to have a three day funeral and on the 4th day, it would be my burial/cremation day . . .I want everyone to wear white instead of black, which means they already let go of me. I also want to have a mass on my cremation day.

When I die, I would like to have a befitting burial ceremony as it is done in my Igbo customs. I chose this kind of funeral ceremony because that is what every average person wishes to have.

I want to be cremated . . . I want all attendees wearing their favorite color and I would like the song "Riders on the Storm" to be played . . .I truly hope all the attendees will appreciate the bass. At the end of this simple, short service, attendees will be given multi-colored helium filled balloons . . . released to signify my release from this earth. . .They will be invited back to the house for ice cream cones, cheese popcorn and a wide variety of other treats and much, much, much rock music . . .

I want to be cremated when I die. To me, it's not just my culture to do so but it's more peaceful to put my remains or ashes to the world. Let it free and not stuck in a casket.

These statements reflect a wide variety of conceptions and attitudes toward death. Culture plays a key role in the development of these conceptions and attitudes, and it also provides a framework within which they are expressed. However, it is important to note that culture does not provide set rules for how death is viewed and experienced, and there tends to be as much variation within cultures as well as between.

WATCH IT

What happens after death? This question has plagued humans since the beginning, and there are countless numbers of philosophies and religions that attempt to explain the next life (if there is one). Some, like Buddhism, Jainism, Hinduism, and Sikhism, support the idea of reincarnation, or the idea that a living being starts a new life in a different physical body or form after each biological death. Some belief systems, such as those in the Abrahamic tradition (Christians, Jews, and Muslims), hold that the dead go to a specific plane of existence after death, as determined by God, or other divine judgment, based on their actions or beliefs during life.

The following video presents philosophical views of death from well-known figures throughout history, including Socrates and Epicurus.

- https://youtu.be/mjQwedC1WzI

You can watch this video, "Social Attitudes Toward Death" to learn more about various perspectives on death.

Another important consideration related to conceptions and attitudes toward death involves social attitudes. Death, in many cases, can be the "elephant in the room," a concept that remains ever present but continues to be taboo for most individuals. Talking openly about death tends to be viewed negatively, or even as socially inappropriate. Specific social norms and standards regarding death vary between groups, but on a larger societal level, death is usually a topic reserved only for when it becomes absolutely necessary to bring up.

Figure 1. Ceremonies, such as this burial service, are customary in nearly every culture to celebrate or honor those who have passed.

Regardless of variations in conceptions and attitudes toward death, ceremonies provide survivors a sense of closure after a loss. These rites and ceremonies send the message that the death is real and allow friends and loved ones to express their love and duty to those who die. Under circumstances in which a person has been lost and presumed dead or when family members were unable to attend a funeral, there can continue to be a lack of closure that makes it difficult to grieve and to learn to live with loss. And although many people are still in shock when they attend funerals, the ceremony still provides a marker of the beginning of a new period of one's life as a survivor.

THE BODY AFTER DEATH

In most cultures, after the last offices have been performed and before the onset of significant decay, relations or friends arrange for ritual disposition of the body, either by destruction, or by preservation, or in a secondary use. In the U.S., this frequently means either cremation or interment in a tomb.

There are various methods of destroying human remains, depending on religious or spiritual beliefs, and upon practical necessity. Cremation is a very old and quite common custom. For some people, the act of cremation exemplifies the belief of the Christian concept of "ashes to ashes". On the other hand, in India, cremation and disposal of the bones in the sacred river Ganges is common. Another method is sky burial, which involves placing the body of the deceased on high ground (a mountain) and leaving it for birds of prey to dispose of, as in Tibet. In some religious views, birds of prey are carriers of the soul to the heavens. Such practice may also have originated from pragmatic environmental issues, such as conditions in which the terrain (as in Tibet) is too stony or hard to dig, or in which there are few trees around to burn. As the local religion of Buddhism, in the case of Tibet, believes that the body after death is only an empty shell, there are more practical ways than burial of disposing of a body, such as leaving it for animals to consume. In some fishing or marine communities, mourners may put the body into the water, in what is known as burial at sea. Several mountain villages have a tradition of hanging the coffin in woods.

Since ancient times, in some cultures efforts have been made to slow, or largely stop the body's decay processes before burial, as in mummification or embalming. This process may be done before, during or after a funeral a ceremony. The Toraja people of Indonesia are known to mummify their deceased loved ones and keep them in their homes for weeks, months, and sometimes even years, before holding a funeral service. Read more about that in this Post Magazine article "Living with Corpses: How Indonesian's Toraja People Deal with Their Dead."

Watch this TED talk, "The Corpses that Changed my Life" by Caitlin Doughty, a mortician and activist, who strives to encourage Americans to overcome their phobia of death and to be more open and involved in dealing with their deceased loved ones.

Developmental Perspectives on Death

Another key factor in individuals' attitudes towards death and dying is where they are in their own lifespan development. First of all, individuals' attitudes are linked to their cognitive ability to understand death and dying. Infants and toddlers cannot understand death. They function in the present and are aware of loss and separation, as well as disruptions in their routines. They are also attuned to the emotions and behaviors of significant adults in their lives, so a death of a loved one may cause a young child to become anxious and irritable, cry, or change their sleeping and eating habits.

A preschooler may approach death by asking when a deceased person is coming back and might search for them, thinking that death is temporary and reversible. They may experience brief but intense reactions, such as tantrums, or other behaviors like frightening dreams and disrupted sleep, bedwetting, clinging, and thumbsucking. Similarly, those in early childhood (age 4-7), might also ask where the deceased person is and search for them, as well as regress to younger behaviors. They might also think that the person's death is their own fault, as per their belief in the power of their own thoughts and "magical thinking." Their grief might be expressed through play, rather than verbally.[1]

Those in middle childhood (ages 7-10) begin to see death as final, not reversible, and universal. Developing Piaget's concrete operational thinking, they may engage in personification, seeing death as a human figure who carried their loved one away. They may not really believe that death could happen to them or their family, maybe only to the very old or sick—they may also view death as a punishment. They might act out in school or they might try to keep a bond with the deceased by taking on that person's role or behaviors.[2]

Preadolescents (ages 10-12) try to understand both biological and emotional processes of death. But they try to hide their feelings and not seem different from their peers; they may seem indifferent, or they may have outbursts.[3] As Amsler (2015) noted, children's and teens' experiences with death and what adults tell them about death will also influence their comprehension. As teens develop formal operational thinking (ages 12-18), they can apply logic to abstractions; they spend more time pondering the meaning of life and death and what comes after death. Their understanding of death becomes more complex as they move from a binary logical concept (alive or dead) to a fuzzy logical concept with potential life after death, for instance. Adolescents are also tasked with integrating these beliefs into their own identity development.[4]

What about attitudes toward death in adulthood? We've learned about adults becoming more concerned with their own mortality during middle adulthood, particularly as they experience the deaths of their own parents. Recently, (Sinoff, 2017) research on thanatophobia, or death anxiety, found differences in death anxiety between elderly patients and their adult children. Death anxiety may entail two different parts—being anxious about death and being anxious about the process of dying. The elderly were only anxious about the process of dying (i.e., suffering), but their adult children were very anxious about death itself and mistakenly believed that their parents were also anxious about death itself. This is an important distinction and can make a significant difference in how medical information and end-of-life decisions are communicated within families.[5] Consistent with

1. Amsler, K. (2015). Conceptualizations of death in middle childhood and adolescence. Childlife Resources. Retrieved from www.childlifersources.com/conceptualizations-of-death-in-middle-childhood-and-adolescence/
2. Amsler, K. (2015). Conceptualizations of death in middle childhood and adolescence. Childlife Resources. Retrieved from www.childlifersources.com/conceptualizations-of-death-in-middle-childhood-and-adolescence/
3. Children's Developmental Stages Concepts of Death and Responses. Vitas Healthcare. Retrieved from https://www.vitas.com/family-and-caregiver-support/grief-and-bereavement/children-and-grief/childrens-developmental-stages-concepts-of-death-and-responses/
4. Amsler, K. (2015). Conceptualizations of death in middle childhood and adolescence. Childlife Resources. Retrieved from www.childlifersources.com/conceptualizations-of-death-in-middle-childhood-and-adolescence/
5. Sinoff, G. (2017). Thanatophobia (death anxiety) in the elderly: The problem of the children's inability to assess their parents' death anxiety state. Frontiers in Medicine, 4:11. doi:10.3389/fmed.2017.00011

this, if elders resolve Erikson's final psychosocial crisis, ego integrity versus despair, in a positive way, they may not fear death, but gain the virtue of wisdom. If they are not feeling desperate ("despair" with time running out), then they may not be anxious or fearful about death.

Bereavement and Grief

Grief is the psychological, physical, and emotional experience and reaction to loss. People may experience grief in various ways, but several theories, such as Kübler-Ross' stages of loss theory, attempt to explain and understand the way people deal with grief. Kübler-Ross' famous theory, which we'll examine in more detail soon, describes five stages of grief: denial, anger, bargaining, depression, and acceptance.

Grief reactions vary depending on whether a loss was anticipated or unexpected, (parents do not expect to lose their children, for example), and whether or not it occurred suddenly or after a long illness, and whether or not the survivor feels responsible for the death. Struggling with the question of responsibility is particularly felt by those who lose a loved one to suicide.[6] These survivors may torment themselves with endless "what ifs" in order to make sense of the loss and reduce feelings of guilt. And family members may also hold one another responsible for the loss. The same may be true for any sudden or unexpected death, making conflict an added dimension to grief. Much of this laying of responsibility is an effort to think that we have some control over these losses; the assumption being that if we do not repeat the same mistakes, we can control what happens in our life. While grief describes the response to loss, **bereavement** describes the state of being following the death of someone.

As we've already learned in terms of attitudes toward death, individuals' own lifespan developmental stage and cognitive level can influence their emotional and behavioral reactions to the death of someone they know. But what about the impact of the type of death or age of the deceased or relationship to the deceased upon bereavement?

Death of a child

Death of a child can take the form of a loss in infancy such as miscarriage or stillbirth or neonatal death, SIDS, or the death of an older child. In most cases, parents find the grief almost unbearably devastating, and it tends to hold greater risk factors than any other loss. This loss also bears a lifelong process: one does not get 'over' the death but instead must assimilate and live with it. Intervention and comforting support can make all the difference to the survival of a parent in this type of grief but the risk factors are great and may include family breakup or suicide. Feelings of guilt, whether legitimate or not, are pervasive, and the dependent nature of the relationship disposes parents to a variety of problems as they seek to cope with this great loss. Parents who suffer miscarriage or a regretful or coerced abortion may experience resentment towards others who experience successful pregnancies.

Suicide

Suicide rates are growing worldwide and over the last thirty years there has been international research trying to curb this phenomenon and gather knowledge about who is "at-risk". When a parent loses their child through suicide it is traumatic, sudden, and affects all loved ones impacted by this child. Suicide leaves many unanswered questions and leaves most parents feeling hurt, angry and deeply saddened by such a loss. Parents may feel they can't openly discuss their grief and feel their emotions because of how their child died and how the people around them may perceive the situation. Parents, family members and service providers have all confirmed the unique nature of suicide-related bereavement following the loss of a child. They report a wall of silence that goes up around them and how people interact towards them. One of the best ways to grieve and move on from this type of loss is to find ways to keep that child as an active part of their lives. It might be privately at first but as parents move away from the silence they can move into a more proactive healing time.

6. Gibbons, J. A., Lee, S. A., Fehr, A. M., Wilson, K. J., & Marshall, T. R. (2018). Grief and avoidant death attitudes combine to predict the fading affect bias. International Journal of Environmental Research and Public Health, 15(1736), 1-19.

Death of a spouse

The death of a spouse is usually a particularly powerful loss. A spouse often becomes part of the other in a unique way: many widows and widowers describe losing 'half' of themselves. The days, months and years after the loss of a spouse will never be the same and learning to live without them may be harder than one would expect. The grief experience is unique to each person. Sharing and building a life with another human being, then learning to live singularly, can be an adjustment that is more complex than a person could ever expect. Depression and loneliness are very common. Feeling bitter and resentful are normal feelings for the spouse who is "left behind". Oftentimes, the widow/widower may feel it necessary to seek professional help in dealing with their new life.

After a long marriage, at older ages, the elderly may find it a very difficult assimilation to begin anew; but at younger ages as well, a marriage relationship was often a profound one for the survivor.

Furthermore, most couples have a division of 'tasks' or 'labor', e.g., the husband mows the yard, the wife pays the bills, etc. which, in addition to dealing with great grief and life changes, means added responsibilities for the bereaved. Immediately after the death of a spouse, there are tasks that must be completed. Planning and financing a funeral can be very difficult if pre-planning was not completed. Changes in insurance, bank accounts, claiming of life insurance, securing childcare are just some of the issues that can be intimidating to someone who is grieving. Social isolation may also become imminent, as many groups composed of couples find it difficult to adjust to the new identity of the bereaved, and the bereaved themselves have great challenges in reconnecting with others. Widows of many cultures, for instance, wear black for the rest of their lives to signify the loss of their spouse and their grief. Only in more recent decades has this tradition been reduced to shorter periods of time.

Death of a parent

For a child, the death of a parent, without support to manage the effects of the grief, may result in long-term psychological harm. This is more likely if the adult carers are struggling with their own grief and are psychologically unavailable to the child. There is a critical role of the surviving parent or caregiver in helping the children adapt to a parent's death. Studies have shown that losing a parent at a young age did not just lead to negative outcomes; there are some positive effects. Some children had an increased maturity, better coping skills and improved communication. Adolescents valued other people more than those who have not experienced such a close loss.[7]

When an adult child loses a parent in later adulthood, it is considered to be "timely" and to be a normative life course event. This allows the adult children to feel a permitted level of grief. However, research shows that the death of a parent in an adult's midlife is not a normative event by any measure, but is a major life transition causing an evaluation of one's own life or mortality. Others may shut out friends and family in processing the loss of someone with whom they have had the longest relationship.[8]

Death of a sibling

The loss of a sibling can be a devastating life event. Despite this, sibling grief is often the most disenfranchised or overlooked of the four main forms of grief, especially with regard to adult siblings. Grieving siblings are often referred to as the 'forgotten mourners' who are made to feel as if their grief is not as severe as their parents grief (N.a., 2015). However, the sibling relationship tends to be the longest significant relationship of the lifespan and siblings who have been part of each other's lives since birth, such as twins, help form and sustain each other's identities; with the death of one sibling comes the loss of that part of the survivor's identity because "your identity is based on having them there."

7. Ellis, J; Lloyd-Williams, M (July 2008). "Perspectives on the impact of early parent loss in adulthood in the UK: narratives provide the way forward". European Journal of Cancer Care. 17 (4): 317–318. doi:10.1111/j.1365-2354.2008.00963.x. PMID 18638179.
8. Marshall, H (2004). "Midlife loss of parents: The Transition from Adult Child to Orphan". Ageing International. 29 (4): 351–367. doi:10.1007/s12126-004-1004-5.

The sibling relationship is a unique one, as they share a special bond and a common history from birth, have a certain role and place in the family, often complement each other, and share genetic traits. Siblings who enjoy a close relationship participate in each other's daily lives and special events, confide in each other, share joys, spend leisure time together (whether they are children or adults), and have a relationship that not only exists in the present but often looks toward a future together (even into retirement). Surviving siblings lose this "companionship and a future" with their deceased siblings.[9]

Loss during childhood

When a parent or caregiver dies or leaves, children may have symptoms of psychopathology, but they are less severe than in children with major depression. The loss of a parent, grandparent or sibling can be very troubling in childhood, but even in childhood there are age differences in relation to the loss. A very young child, under one or two, may be found to have no reaction if a carer dies, but other children may be affected by the loss.

At a time when trust and dependency are formed, a break even of no more than separation can cause problems in well-being; this is especially true if the loss is around critical periods such as 8–12 months, when attachment and separation are at their height information, and even a brief separation from a parent or other person who cares for the child can cause distress.

Even as a child grows older, death is still difficult to fathom and this affects how a child responds. For example, younger children see death more as a separation, and may believe death is curable or temporary. Reactions can manifest themselves in "acting out" behaviors: a return to earlier behaviors such as sucking thumbs, clinging to a toy or angry behavior; though they do not have the maturity to mourn as an adult, they feel the same intensity. As children enter pre-teen and teen years, there is a more mature understanding.

Children can experience grief as a result of losses due to causes other than death. For example, children who have been physically, psychologically or sexually abused often grieve over the damage to or the loss of their ability to trust. Since such children usually have no support or acknowledgement from any source outside the family unit, this is likely to be experienced as disenfranchised grief.

Relocations can also cause children significant grief particularly if they are combined with other difficult circumstances such as neglectful or abusive parental behaviors, other significant losses, etc.

Loss of a friend or classmate

Children may experience the death of a friend or a classmate through illness, accidents, suicide, or violence. Initial support involves reassuring children that their emotional and physical feelings are normal. Schools are advised to plan for these possibilities in advance.

Survivor guilt (or survivor's guilt; also called survivor syndrome or survivor's syndrome) is a mental condition that occurs when a person perceives themselves to have done wrong by surviving a traumatic event when others did not. It may be found among survivors of combat, natural disasters, epidemics, among the friends and family of those who have died by suicide, and in non-mortal situations such as among those whose colleagues are laid off.

Anticipatory grief occurs when a death is expected and survivors have time to prepare to some extent before the loss. Anticipatory grief can include the same denial, anger, bargaining, depression, and acceptance experienced in loss one might experience after a death; this can make adjustment after a loss somewhat easier, although a person may then go through the stages of loss again after the death. A death after a long-term, painful illness may bring family members a sense of relief that the suffering is over or the exhausting process of caring for someone who is ill is over.

9. P. Gill White, Sibling Grief: Healing After the Death of a Sister or Brother (iUniverse, 2006), 47.

Complicated grief involves a distinct set of maladaptive or self-defeating thoughts, emotions, and behaviors that occur as a negative response to a loss.[10] From a cognitive and emotional perspective, these individuals tend to experience extreme bitterness over the loss, intense preoccupation with the deceased, and a need to feel connected to the deceased. These feelings often lead the grieving individual to engage in problematic behaviors that further prevent positive coping and delay the return to normalcy. He or she may spend excessive amounts of time visiting the deceased person's grave, talking to the deceased person, or trying to connect with the deceased person on a spiritual level, often forgoing other responsibilities or tasks to do so. The extreme nature of these thoughts, emotions, and behaviors separate this type of grief from the normal grieving process.

Disenfranchised grief may be experienced by those who have to hide the circumstances of their loss or whose grief goes unrecognized by others. Loss of an ex-spouse, lover, or pet may be examples of disenfranchised grief.

It has been said that intense grief lasts about two years or less, but grief is felt throughout life. One loss triggers the feelings that surround another. People grieve with varied intensity throughout the remainder of their lives. It does not end. But it eventually becomes something that a person has learned to live with. As long as we experience loss, we experience grief.

There are layers of grief. Initial denial, marked by shock and disbelief in the weeks following a loss may become an expectation that the loved one will walk in the door. And anger directed toward those who could not save our loved one's life, may become anger that life did not turn out as we expected. There is no right way to grieve. A bereavement counselor expressed it well by saying that grief touches us on the shoulder from time to time throughout life.

Grief and mixed emotions go hand in hand. A sense of relief is accompanied by regrets and periods of reminiscing about our loved ones are interspersed with feeling haunted by them in death. Our outward expressions of loss are also sometimes contradictory. We want to move on but at the same time are saddened by going through a loved one's possessions and giving them away. We may no longer feel sexual arousal or we may want sex to feel connected and alive. We need others to befriend us but may get angry at their attempts to console us. These contradictions are normal and we need to allow ourselves and others to grieve in their own time and in their own ways.

The "death-denying, grief-dismissing world" is often the approach to grief in our modern world. We are asked to grieve privately, quickly, and to medicate our suffering. Employers grant us 3 to 5 days for bereavement, if our loss is that of an immediate family member. And such leaves are sometimes limited to no more than one per year. Yet grief takes much longer and the bereaved are seldom ready to perform well on the job. It becomes a clash between life having to continue, and the individual being ready for it to do so. One coping mechanism that can help smooth out this conflict is called the **fading affect bias**. Based on a collection of similar findings, the fading affect bias suggests that negative events, such as the death of a loved one, tend to lose their emotional intensity at a faster rate than pleasant events.[11] This is believed to help enhance pleasant experiences and avoid the negative emotions associated with unpleasant ones, thus helping the individual return to his or her normal daily routines following a loss.

10. Boelen, P. A., & Prigerson, H. G. The influence of symptoms of prolonged grief disorder, depression, and anxiety on quality of life among bereaved adults. Eur. Arch. Psychiatry Clin. Neurosci. 2007, 257, 444–452
11. Walker, W. R.; Skowronski, J. J.; Gibbons, J. A.; Vogl, R. J.; Thompson, C. P. On the emotions that accompany autobiographical memories: dysphoria disrupts the fading affect bias. Cogn. Emot. 2003, 17, 703–723.

LINK TO LEARNING

Sociologist Nancy Berns explains that in the United States and other western societies, people are encouraged to deal with grief or loss through closure. She contradicts this advice and explains that people do not necessarily need closure in order to "move on." Watch Nancy Berns' TED talk "Beyond Closure" to learn more.

Stages of Loss

The complex construct of death is associated with a variety of thoughts, emotions, and behaviors, that vary between individuals and groups. To some, death is the final end, when the body ceases to function, with nothing occurring next. To others, death is the start of a new journey, and is its own beginning. These varying viewpoints are shaped by numerous factors related to culture, religion, social norms, personal experiences, and more. It is no surprise then that multiple theories have been created to understand the occurrence of death on cognitive, emotional, and behavioral levels; each offering different explanations for what individuals go through during death.

Kübler-Ross' Stages of Loss

Kübler-Ross (1965) described five stages of loss experienced by someone who faces the news of their impending death (based on her work and interviews with terminally ill patients). These "stages" are not really stages that a person goes through in order or only once; nor are they stages that occur with the same intensity. Indeed, the process of death is influenced by a person's life experiences, the timing of their death in relation to life events, the predictability of their death based on health or illness, their belief system, and their assessment of the quality of their own life. Nevertheless, these stages provide a framework to help us to understand and recognize some of what a dying person experiences psychologically. And by understanding, we are more equipped to support that person as they die.[12]

> **Denial** is often the first reaction to overwhelming, unimaginable news. Denial, or disbelief or shock, protects us by allowing such news to enter slowly and to give us time to come to grips with what is taking place. The person who receives positive test results for life-threatening conditions may question the results, seek second opinions, or may simply feel a sense of disbelief psychologically even though they know that the results are true.
>
> **Anger** also provides us with protection in that being angry energizes us to fight against something and gives structure to a situation that may be thrusting us into the unknown. It is much easier to be angry than to be sad or in pain or depressed. It helps us to temporarily believe that we have a sense of control over our future and to feel that we have at least expressed our rage about how unfair life can be. Anger can be focused on a person, a health care provider, at God, or at the world in general. And it can be expressed over issues that have nothing to do with our death; consequently, being in this stage of loss is not always obvious.
>
> **Bargaining** involves trying to think of what could be done to turn the situation around. Living better, devoting self to a cause, being a better friend, parent, or spouse, are all agreements one might willingly commit to if doing so would lengthen life. Asking to just live long enough to witness a family event or finish a task are examples of bargaining.

12. Kübler-Ross, E. (1975). Death: The final stage of growth. Englewood Cliffs, N.J.: Prentice-Hall.

Depression is sadness and sadness is appropriate for such an event. Feeling the full weight of loss, crying, and losing interest in the outside world is an important part of the process of dying. This depression makes others feel very uncomfortable and family members may try to console their loved one. Sometimes hospice care may include the use of antidepressants to reduce depression during this stage.

Acceptance involves learning how to carry on and to incorporate this aspect of the life span into daily existence. Reaching acceptance does not in any way imply that people who are dying are happy about it or content with it. It means that they are facing it and continuing to make arrangements and to say what they wish to say to others. Some terminally ill people find that they live life more fully than ever before after they come to this stage.

In some ways, these five stages serve as cognitive defense mechanisms, allowing the individual to make sense of the situation while coming to terms with what is happening. They are, in other words, the mind's way of gradually recognizing the implications of one's impending death and giving him or her the chance to process it. These stages provide a type of framework in which dying is experienced, although it is not exactly the same for every individual in every case.

Since Kübler-Ross presented these stages of loss, several other models have been developed. These subsequent models, in many ways, build on that of Kübler-Ross, offering expanded views of how individuals process loss and grief. While Kübler-Ross' model was restricted to dying individuals, subsequent theories tended to focus on loss as a more general construct. This ultimately suggests that facing one's own death is just one example of the grief and loss that human beings can experience, and that other loss or grief-related situations tend to be processed in a similar way.

WATCH IT

Watch the first six minutes of this video to learn more about how the Kübler-Ross model evolved since its inception. The latter half of the video focuses on several other models that focus on how people can deal with the loss of loved one, or with grief in general. While the Kübler-Ross model remains important and useful today, it is does not fit everyone's experience with grief, and research continues today to understand how people cope with grief.

- https://youtu.be/9LudhIlbeXs

Other Models on Grief

One such model was presented by Worden (1991), which explained the process of grief through a set of four different tasks that the individual must complete in order to resolve the grief. These tasks included: (a) accepting that the loss has occurred, (b) working through and experiencing the pain associated with grief, (c) adjusting the the changes that the loss created in the environment, and (d) moving past the loss on an emotional level.[13]

Another model is that of Parkes (1998), which broke down grief into four stages, including: (a) shock, (b) yearning, (c) despair, and (d) recovery. Although comprised of somewhat different stages than those of Kübler-Ross' model, Parkes' stages still reflected an ongoing process that the individual goes through, each of which was characterized by different thoughts, emotions, and behaviors. Throughout this process, the individual gradually moves closer to accepting the situation, and being able to continue with his or her daily life to the greatest extent possible.[14]

13. Buglass, E. (2010). Grief and bereavement theories. Nursing Standard, 24(41), 44-47.
14. Buglass, E. (2010). Grief and bereavement theories. Nursing Standard, 24(41), 44-47.

A different approach was proposed by Strobe and Shut (1999), which suggested that individuals cope with grief through an ongoing set of processes related to both loss and restoration. The loss-oriented processes included: (a) grief work, (b) intrusion on grief, (c) denying or avoiding changes toward restoration, and (d) the breaking of bonds or ties. The restoration-oriented processes included: (a) attending to life changes, (b) distracting oneself from grief, (c) doing new things, and (d) establishing new roles, identities, and relationships. Since each individual experiences grief and loss differently, in light of personal, cultural, and environmental factors, these processes often occur simultaneously, and not in a set order.[15]

LINK TO LEARNING

Visit "Grief Reactions Over the Life Span" from the American Counseling Association to consider how various age groups deal with the death of a loved one.

We no longer think that there is a "right way" to experience grief and loss. People move through a variety of stages with different frequency and in different ways. The theories that have been developed to help explain and understand this complex process have shifted over time to encompass a wider variety of situations, as well as to present implications for helping and supporting the individual(s) who are going through it. The following strategies have been identified as effective in the support of healthy grieving:[16].

- **Talk about the death.** This will help the surviving individuals understand what happened and remember the deceased in a positive way. When coping with death, it can be easy to get wrapped up in denial, which can lead to isolation and lack of a solid support system.
- **Accept the multitude of feelings.** The death of a loved one can, and almost always does, trigger numerous emotions. It is normal for sadness, frustration, and in some cases exhaustion to be experienced.
- **Take care of yourself and your family.** Remembering to keep one's own health and the health of their family a priority can help with moving through each day effectively. Making an conscious effort to eat well, exercise regularly, and obtain adequate rest is important.
- **Reach out and help others dealing with the loss.** It has long been recognized that helping others can enhance one's own mood and general mental state. Helping others as they cope with the loss can have this effect, as can sharing stories of the deceased.
- **Remember and celebrate the lives of your loved ones.** This can be a great way to honor the relationship that was once had with the deceased. Possibilities can include donating to a charity that the deceased supported, framing photos of fun experiences with the deceased, planting a tree or garden in memory of the deceased, or anything else that feels right for the particular situation.

GLOSSARY

bereavement:
the period of mourning following the death of someone

15. Buglass, E. (2010). Grief and bereavement theories. Nursing Standard, 24(41), 44-47.
16. American Psychological Association. (2019). Grief: Coping with the loss of your loved one. Retrieved from https://www.apa.org/helpcenter/grief.

complicated grief:
when feelings of grief are persistent and incapacitating

disenfranchised grief:
grief that is not acknowledged by others

fading affect bias:
idea that negative events, such as the death of a loved one, tend to lose their emotional intensity at a faster rate than pleasant events

grief:
the psychological, physical, and emotional experience and reaction to loss

survivor guilt:
mental condition that occurs when a person perceives themselves to have done wrong by surviving a traumatic event when others did not

Facing Death

What you'll learn to do: examine care and practices related to death

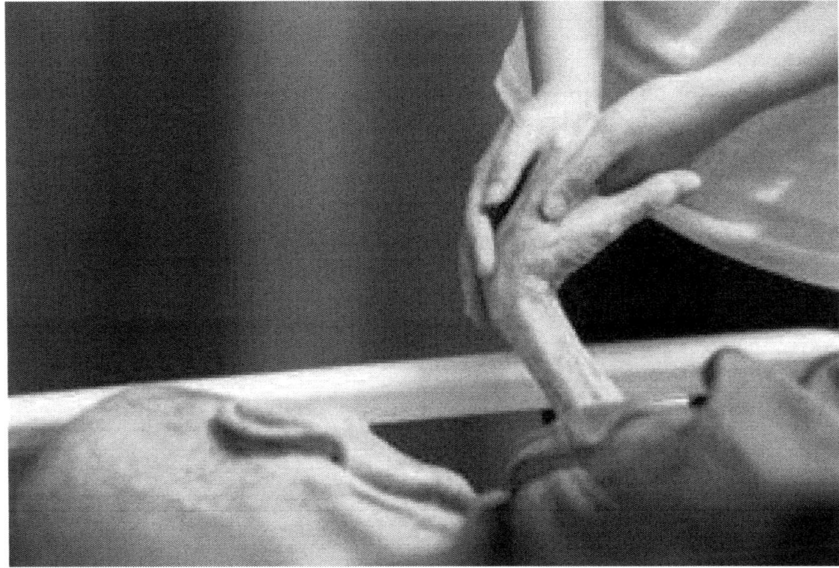

In this section, we'll turn our attention from the process of dying to the actual death of the individual. We'll examine various ways in which in which deliberate death can occur, along with the supportive practices that are available for those who are dying. We will also take a closer look at cultural and legal implications of end-of-life practices.

LEARNING OUTCOMES

- Explain the philosophy and practice of palliative care
- Describe hospice care
- Summarize Dame Cicely Saunders' writings about total pain of the dying
- Differentiate attitudes toward hospice care based on race and ethnicity
- Describe and contrast types of euthanasia and physician-assisted suicide

Palliative Care and Hospice

Palliative Care

Palliative care is an interdisciplinary approach to specialized medical and nursing care for people with life-limiting illnesses. It focuses on providing relief from the symptoms, pain, physical stress, and mental stress at any stage of illness, with a goal of improving the quality of life for both the person and their family. Doctors who specialize in palliative care have had training tailored to helping patients and their family members cope with the reality of the impending death and make plans for what will happen after.[1]

Palliative care is provided by a team of physicians, nurses, physiotherapists, occupational therapists, speech-language pathologists, and other health professionals who work together with the primary care physician and referred specialists or other hospital or hospice staff to provide additional support to the patient. It is appropriate at any age and at any stage in a serious illness and can be provided as the main goal of care or along with curative treatment. Although it is an important part of end-of-life care, it is not limited to that stage. Palliative care can be provided across multiple settings including in hospitals, at home, as part of community palliative care programs, and in skilled nursing facilities. Interdisciplinary palliative care teams work with people and their families to clarify goals of care and provide symptom management, psychosocial, and spiritual support.

Hospice

In many other countries, no distinction is made between palliative care and hospice, but in the United States, the terms have different meanings and usages. They both share similar goals of providing symptom relief and pain management, but **hospice care** is a type of care involving palliation without curative intent. Usually, it is used for people with no further options for curing their disease or in people who have decided not to pursue further options that are arduous, likely to cause more symptoms, and not likely to succeed.The biggest difference between hospice and palliative care is the type of illness people have, where they are in their illness especially related to prognosis, and their goals/wishes regarding curative treatment. Hospice care under the Medicare Hospice Benefit requires that two physicians certify that a person has less than six months to live if the disease follows its usual course. This does not mean, though, that if a person is still living after six months in hospice he or she will be discharged from the service.

WATCH IT

Watch this video to better understand the setting, circumstances, and services associated with hospice care.

- https://youtu.be/lFjLGYsOIfU

Hospice care involves caring for dying patients by helping them be as free from pain as possible, providing them with assistance to complete wills and other arrangements for their survivors, giving them social support through the psychological stages of loss, and helping family members cope with the dying process, grief, and bereavement. It focuses on five topics: communication, collaboration, compassionate caring, comfort, and cultural (spiritual) care. Most hospice care does not include medical treatment of disease or resuscitation although some programs administer curative care as well. The patient is allowed to go through the dying process without invasive treatments. Family members who have agreed to put their loved one on hospice may become anxious when the patient begins to experience death. They may believe that feeding or breathing tubes will sustain life and want to change their decision. Hospice workers try to inform the family of what to expect and reassure them that much of what they see is a normal part of the dying process.

1. National Institute on Aging. (2019). What are palliative care and hospice care? Retrieved from http://www.nia.nih.gov/health/what-are-palliative-care-and-hospice-care

WATCH IT

One aspect of palliative and hospice care is helping dying individuals and their families understand what is happening, and what it may imply for their lives. The following video provides an example of palliative care in a hospital setting.

- https://www.youtube.com/embed/jaB9M8B_Tuw

The History of Hospice

Dame Cicely Saunders was a British registered nurse whose chronic health problems had forced her to pursue a career in medical social work. The relationship she developed with a dying Polish refugee helped solidify her ideas that terminally ill patients needed compassionate care to help address their fears and concerns as well as palliative comfort for physical symptoms. After the refugee's death, Saunders began volunteering at St Luke's Home for the Dying Poor, where a physician told her that she could best influence the treatment of the terminally ill as a physician. Saunders entered medical school while continuing her volunteer work at St. Joseph's. When she achieved her degree in 1957, she took a position there.

Saunders emphasized focusing on the patient rather than the disease and introduced the notion of 'total pain', which included psychological, spiritual, emotional, intellectual, and interpersonal aspects of pain, the physical aspects, and even financial and bureaucratic aspects. This focus on the broad effects of death on dying individuals and their families has provided the foundation for modern day practices related to hospice care services.[2] Saunders experimented with a wide range of opioids for controlling physical pain but also considered the needs of the patient's family.

Saunders disseminated her philosophy internationally in a series of tours of the United States that began in 1963. In 1967, Saunders opened St. Christopher's Hospice. Florence Wald, the Dean of Yale School of Nursing who had heard Saunders speak in America, spent a month working with Saunders there in 1969 before bringing the principles of modern hospice care back to the United States, establishing Hospice, Inc. in 1971. Another early hospice program in the United States, Alive Hospice, was founded in Nashville, Tennessee on November 14, 1975. By 1977 the National Hospice Organization had been formed.

Hospice Care in Practice

The early established hospices were independently operated and dedicated to giving patients as much control over their own death process as possible. Today, it is estimated that over 40 million individuals require palliative care, with over 78% of them being of low-income status or living in low-income countries.[3] It is also estimated, however, that less than 14% of these individuals receive it. This gap is created by restrictive regulatory laws regarding controlled substance medications for pain management, as well as a general lack of adequate training in regards to palliative care within the health professional community. Although hospice care has become more widespread, these new programs are subjected to more rigorous insurance guidelines that dictate the types and amounts of medications used, length of stay, and types of patients who are eligible to receive hospice care. Thus, more patients are being served, but providers have less control over the services they provide, and lengths of stay are more limited. Patients receive palliative care in hospitals and in their homes.

2. Richmond, C. (2005). Dame Cicely Saunders. Retrieved from https://www.ncbi.nlm.nih.gov/pmc/articles/PMC1179787/.
3. World Health Organization. (2019). Palliative care. Retrieved from http://www.who.int/new-room/fact-sheets/detail/palliative-care.

The majority of patients on hospice are cancer patients and they typically do not enter hospice until the last few weeks prior to death. The average length of stay is less than 30 days and many patients are on hospice for less than a week.[4] Medications are rubbed into the skin or given in drop form under the tongue to relieve the discomfort of swallowing pills or receiving injections. A hospice care team includes a chaplain as well as nurses and grief counselors to assist spiritual needs in addition to physical ones. When hospice is administered at home, family members may also be part, and sometimes the biggest part, of the care team. Certainly, being in familiar surroundings is preferable to dying in an unfamiliar place. But about 60 to 70 percent of people die in hospitals and another 16 percent die in institutions such as nursing homes. Most hospice programs serve people over 65; few programs are available for terminally ill children.[5]

Hospice care focuses on alleviating physical pain and providing spiritual guidance. Those suffering from Alzheimer's also experience intellectual pain and frustration as they lose their ability to remember and recognize others. Depression, anger, and frustration are elements of emotional pain, and family members can have tensions that a social worker or clergy member may be able to help resolve. Many patients are concerned with the financial burden their care will create for family members. And bureaucratic pain is also suffered while trying to submit bills and get information about health care benefits or to complete requirements for other legal matters. All of these concerns can be addressed by hospice care teams.

The Hospice Foundation of America notes that not all racial and ethnic groups feel the same way about hospice care.[6] Certain groups may believe that medical treatment should be pursued on behalf of an ill relative as long as possible and that only God can decide when a person dies. Others may feel very uncomfortable discussing issues of death or being near the deceased family member's body. The view that hospice care should always be used is not held by everyone and health care providers need to be sensitive to the wishes and beliefs of those they serve. Similarly, the population of individuals using hospice services is not divided evenly by race. Approximately 81% of hospice patients are White, while 8.7% are African American, 8.7% are multiracial, 1.9% are Pacific Islander, and only 0.2% are Native American.[7]

WATCH IT

The following video from the National Hospice and Palliative Care Organization discusses some of its goals regarding the increase in hospice care availability.

- https://youtu.be/WUNV6Lbvyn8

Euthanasia and Physician-Assisted Suicide

Euthanasia, or helping a person fulfill their wish to die, can happen in two ways: voluntary euthanasia and physician-assisted suicide. **Voluntary euthanasia** refers to helping someone fulfill their wish to die by acting in such a way to help that person's life end. This can be **passive euthanasia** such as no longer feeding someone or giving them food. Or it can be **active euthanasia** such as administering a lethal dose of medication to someone who wishes to die. In some cases, a dying individual

4. World Health Organization. (2019). Palliative care: Cancer. Retrieved from http://www.who.int/palliative/en/
5. World Health Organization. (2019). Access to palliative care. Retrieved from http://www.who.int/news-room/fact-sheets/detail/palliative-care.
6. Hopsice Foundation of America. (2019). Aging America. Retrieved from https://hospicefoundation.org/.
7. Campbell, C., Baernholdt, M., Yan, G., Hinton, I. D., & Lewis, E. (2014). Racial/ethnic perspectives on the quality of hospice care. American Journal of Palliative Care, 30(4), 347-353.

who is in pain or constant discomfort will ask this of a friend or family member, as a way to speed up what he or she has already accepted as being inevitable. This can have lasting effects on the individual or individuals asked to help, including but not limited to prolonged guilt. [8]

Physician-Assisted Suicide: Physician-assisted suicide occurs when a physician prescribes the means by which a person can end his or her own life. [9] This differs from euthanasia, in that it is mandated by a set of laws and is backed by legal authority. Physician-assisted suicide is legal in the District of Columbia and several states, including Oregon, Hawaii, Vermont, and Washington. It is also legal in the Netherlands, Switzerland, and Belgium.

LINK TO LEARNING

Dr. Jack Kevorkian is the individual most commonly associated with physician-assisted suicide. He was a pioneer in this practice, sparking ethical, moral, and legal debates that continue to this day. This video from the New York Times "Jack Kevorkian and the Right to Die" provides an overview of his work, and his role in the beginning of physician-assisted suicide.

The specific laws that govern the practice of physician-assisted suicide vary between states. Oregon, Vermont, and Washington, for example, require the prescription to come from either a Doctor of Medicine (M.D.) or a Doctor of Osteopathy (D.O.). [10] These state laws also include a clause about the designated medical practitioner being willing to participate in this act. In Colorado, terminally ill individuals have the option to request and self-administer life-ending medication if their medical prognosis gives them six months or less to live. In the District of Columbia and Hawaii, the individual is required to make two requests within predefined periods of time and also complete a waiting period, and in some cases undergo additional evaluations before the medication can be provided.

A growing number of the population support physician-assisted suicide. In 2000, a ruling of the U.S. Supreme Court upheld the right of states to determine their laws on physician-assisted suicide despite efforts to limit physicians' ability to prescribe barbiturates and opiates for their patients requesting the means to end their lives. [11] The position of the Supreme Court is that the debate concerning the morals and ethics surrounding the right to die is one that should be continued. As an increasing number of the population enters late adulthood, the emphasis on giving patients an active voice in determining certain aspects of their own death is likely.

PHYSICIAN-ASSISTED SUICIDE

In a recent example of physician-assisted death, David Goodall, a 104 year old professor, ended his life by choice in a Swiss clinic in May 2018. Having spent his life in Australia, Goodall traveled to Switzerland to do this, as the laws in his

8. Meier, D. E., Emmons, C. A., Wallenstein, S., Quill, T., Morrison, R. S., & Cassell, C. K. (2009). A national survey of physician-assisted suicide and euthanasia in the united states. New England Journal of Medicine, 338(17), 1193-1201.
9. Collier, R. (2017). Assisted death gaining acceptance in the US. Retrieved from https://www.ncbi.nlm.nih.gov/pmc/articles/PMC5250524/
10. Theil-Reiter, S., Wetterauer, C., & Frei, I. A. (2018). Taking one's own life in hospital? Patients and health care professionals vis-a-vis the tension between assisted suicide and suicide prevention in Switzerland. International Journal of Environmental Research and Public Health, 15(6).
11. Collier, R. (2017). Assisted death gaining acceptance in the U.S. Retrieved from https://www.ncbi.nlm.nih.gov/pmc/articles/PMC5250524/

country do not allow for it. Swiss legislation does not openly permit physician-assisted suicide, but it does not forbid an individual with "commendable motives" from assisting another person in taking his or her own life.[12] Watch this video of a news conference with Goodall "104-year-old Australian Promotes Right to Assisted Suicide" that took place the day before he ended his life with physician-assisted suicide.

Another public advocate for physician-assisted suicide and death with dignity was 29-year old Brittany Maynard, who after being diagnosed with terminal brain cancer, decided to move to Oregon so that she could end her life with physician-assisted suicide. You can watch this video "The Brittany Maynard Story" to learn more about Brittany's story.

GLOSSARY

active euthanasia:
a type of voluntary euthanasia that is active, such as administering a lethal dose of medication to someone who wishes to die

euthanasia:
helping a person fulfill their wish to die

hospice:
a type of care involving palliation without curative intent. Usually, it is used for people with no further options for curing their disease or people who have decided not to pursue further options that are arduous, likely to cause more symptoms, and not likely to succeed

palliative care:
an interdisciplinary approach to specialized medical and nursing care for people with life-limiting illnesses. It focuses on providing relief from the symptoms, pain, physical stress, and mental stress at any stage of illness, with a goal of improving the quality of life for both the person and their family

passive euthanasia:
a type of voluntary euthanasia that is passive, such as no longer feeding someone or giving them food

physician-assisted suicide:
occurs when a physician prescribes the means by which a person can end his or her own life. This differs from euthanasia, in that it is mandated by a set of laws and is backed by legal authority. Physician-assisted suicide is legal in the District of Columbia and several states, including Oregon, Hawaii, Vermont, and Washington. It is also legal in the Netherlands, Switzerland, and Belgium

voluntary euthanasia:
helping someone fulfill their wish to die by acting in such a way to help that person's life end

12. Bever, L. (2018). David Goodall, 104 just took his own life, after making a powerful statement about assisted death. Retrieved from https://www.washingtonpost.com/news/to-your-health/wp/2018/05/09/this-104-year-old-plans-to-die-tomorrow-and-hopes-to-change-views-on-assisted-suicide/?utm_term=.236176920e3c

Putting It Together: Death and Dying

Death is something we all must face at some point. It occurs on physiological, psychological, and social levels, each of which have unique implications for the dying individuals and those close to them. Physiological death occurs as the body ceases to function, eventually rendering the individual unable to engage in basic necessary processes, such as breathing and eating. Psychological death occurs when the individual begins to face his or her impending death and consequently regresses into the self. Societal death occurs when others withdraw from the individual, perhaps unable to effectively cope with the impending loss and its implications. In some cases, palliative care or hospice services are utilized to assist both the dying individual and his or her family throughout the dying process. These services include care for the dying individual, as well as support for the family. In addition, several states allow terminally ill or dying individuals to utilize physician-assisted suicide, in which a medical practitioner prescribes and/or administers life-ending medication at the individual's request. The utilization of palliative or hospice care services, as well as physician assisted suicide, vary between individuals, cultures, and racial groups, ultimately reflecting the legal, ethical, and moral complexity of both types of practices.

The way in which we view death, talk about it, prepare for it, and what we do when it happens, vary both within and between cultures. Coping with the grief that is associated with death and loss is a complex but necessary process, with a number of strategies for working through the situation in a healthy and positive way. Several theories have been created to explain how grieving happens, some including stages of grief that the individual experiences, others including tasks that the individual must complete. These stages and tasks on their own are neutral, with the potential to facilitate positive coping, but can also become maladaptive if the individual does not work through them in a healthy way. Death is ultimately the end of lifespan development, an occurrence that takes place for everyone at some time. It is the culmination of the other stages of development, many of which play a role in shaping how the individual handles death when the time comes, both for the self and for loved ones.

Discussion: Death and Dying

DISCUSSION: In this discussion, reflect upon and discuss TWO of the following questions:

- Q1: Physician-assisted suicide is legal in a few states and in a few countries. Do you believe that more states should make this legal? Why or why not?
- Q2: How would you define a "good death?" Why?
- Q3: Imagine that you are training others to work with people who are terminally ill or in grief. Advise your group about how to work most effectively with those populations.

STEP 1: First, write a response with at least EIGHT substantial sentences, integrating concepts you learned from the reading and other materials (include links with necessary). Show that you can think critically on the topic by integrating your own thoughts, analysis, or experiences.

STEP 2: Return to the discussion to comment on at least TWO classmates' posts (in at least FIVE sentences). Expand on a classmate's comments in a value-adding, topic-related way. Promote a collaborative, supportive community, and advance the dialogue through follow-up questions. Reply posts cannot be one-liners, off-topic posts, vague statements, unsupported opinions, inadequate explanations or simply say, "I agree" or "good job."

Late Adulthood

LEARNING OUTCOMES

- Describe age categories of late adulthood

Defining Late Adulthood: Age or Quality of Life?

Photo Courtesy Overstreet

We are considered in late adulthood from the time we reach our mid-sixties until death. Because we are living longer, late adulthood is getting longer. Whether we start counting at 65, as demographers may suggest, there is a greater proportion of people alive in late adulthood than anytime in world history. In this module, we will learn how many people are in late adulthood, how that number is expected to change, and how life changes and continues to be the same as before in late adulthood. About 13 percent of the U. S. population or 38.9 million Americans are 65 and older (U. S. Census Bureau, 2011). This number is expected to grow to 88.5 million by the year 2050 at which time people over 65 will make up 20 percent of the population. This group varies considerably and is divided into categories of 65 plus, 85 plus, and centenarians for comparison by the census. Developmentalists, however, divide this population in to categories based on health and social well-being. Optimal aging refers to those who enjoy better health and social well-being than average. Normal aging refers to those who seem to have the same health and social concerns as most of those in the population. However, there is still much being done to understand exactly what normal aging means. Impaired aging refers to those who experience poor health and dependence to a greater extent than would be considered normal. Aging successfully involves making adjustments as needed in order to continue living as independently and actively as possible. This is referred to as selective optimization with compensation and means, for example, that a person who can no longer drive, is able to find alternative transportation. Or a person who is compensating for having less energy, learns how to reorganize the daily routine to avoid over-exertion. Perhaps nurses and other allied health professionals working with this population will begin to focus more on helping patients remain independent than on simply treating illnesses. Promoting health and independence are important for successful aging.

Age Categories: *The young old* 65 to 74

These 18.3 million Americans tend to report greater health and social well-being than older adults. Having good or excellent health is reported by 41 percent of this age group (Center for Disease Control, 2004). Their lives are more similar to those of midlife adults than those who are 85 and older. This group is less likely to require long-term care, to be dependent or to be poor, and more likely to be married, working for pleasure rather than income, and living independently. About 65 percent of men and 50 percent of women between the ages of 65-69 continue to work full-time (He et al., 2005). Physical activity tends to decrease with age, despite the dramatic health benefits enjoyed by those who exercise. People with more education and income are more likely to continue being physically active. And males are more likely to engage in physical activity than are females. The majority of the young-old continue to live independently. Only about 3 percent of those 65-74 need help with daily living skills as compared with about 22.9 percent of people over 85. (Another way to consider think of this is that 97 percent of people between 65-74 and 77 percent of people over 85 do not require assistance!) This age group is less likely to experience heart disease, cancer, or stroke than the old, but nearly as likely to experience depression (U. S. Census, 2005).

The old old 75 to 84

This age group is more likely to experience limitations on physical activity due to chronic disease such as arthritis, heart conditions, hypertension (especially for women), and hearing or visual impairments. Rates of death due to heart disease, cancer, and cerebral vascular disease are double that experienced by people 65-74. Poverty rates are 3 percent higher (12 percent) than for those between 65 and 74. However, the majority of these 12.9 million Americans live independently or with relatives. Widowhood is more common in this group-especially among women.

The oldest old 85 plus

The number of people 85 and older is 34 times greater than in 1900 and now includes 5.7 million Americans. This group is more likely to require long-term care and to be in nursing homes. However, of the 38.9 million American over 65, only 1.6 million require nursing home care. Sixty-eight percent live with relatives and 27 percent live alone (He et al., 2005; U. S. Census Bureau, 2011).

The Centenarians

There are 104,754 people over 100 years of aging living in the United States. This number is expected to increase to 601,000 by the year 2050 (U. S. Census Bureau, 2011). The majority is between ages 100 and 104 and eighty percent are women. Out of almost 7 billion people on the planet, about 25 are over 110. Most live in Japan, a few live the in United States and three live in France (National Institutes of Health, 2006). These "super-Centenarians" have led varied lives and probably do not give us any single answers about living longer. Jeanne Clement smoked until she was 117. She lived to be 122. She also ate a diet rich in olive oil and rode a bicycle until she was 100. Her family had a history of longevity. Pitskhelauri (in Berger, 2005) suggests that moderate diet, continued work and activity, inclusion in family and community life, and exercise and relaxation are important ingredients for long life.

The "Graying" of America and the globe:

This trend toward an increasingly aged population has been referred to as the "graying of America." However, populations are aging in most other countries of the world. (One exception to this is in sub-Saharan Africa where mortality rates are high due to HIV/AIDS) (He et al., 2005). There are 520 million people over 65 worldwide. This number is expected to increase to 1.53 billion by 2050 (from 8 percent to 17 percent of the global population.) Currently, four countries, Germany, Italy, Japan, and Monaco, have 20 percent of their population over 65. China has the highest number of people over 65 at 112 million (U. S. Census Bureau, 2011).

As the population ages, concerns grow about who will provide for those requiring long-term care. In 2000, there were about 10 people 85 and older for every 100 persons between ages 50 and 64. These midlife adults are the most likely care providers for their aging parents. The number of old requiring support from their children is expected to more than double by the year 2040 (He et al., 2005). These families will certainly need external physical, emotional, and financial support in meeting this challenge.